ENCYCLOPEDIA OF COMPLEMENTARY HEALTH

Commissioning Editors: Sian Facer, Jane McIntosh
Art Director: Keith Martin
Art Editor: Les Needham
Project Manager: Mary Lambert
Editors/writers: Clare Hill, Diana Vowles, Diana Craig and Nance Fyson
Assistant Editor: Humaira Husain
Proofreader: Anne Crane
Consultant Editor: Nikki Bradford
Illustrators: Jo Agis, Birgit Eggers, Steve Rawlings, Philip Wilson
Picture Research: Liz Fowler
Production Controller: Nick Thompson

First published in Great Britain in 1996 by Hamlyn
an imprint of Octopus Publishing Group Limited

This 2001 edition published by Chancellor Press,
an imprint of Bounty Books,
a division of Octopus Publishing Group Limited
2-4 Heron Quays, London E14 4JP

ISBN 0 7537 0472 2

A CIP catalogue record for this book is available from the British Library

Produced by Toppan Printing Co Ltd

Printed in China

Note

This book is not intended as an alternative to personal medical advice. The reader should consult a physician in all matters relating to health and particularly in respect of any symptoms which may require diagnosis or medical attention. While the advice and information are believed to be accurate and true at the time of going to press, neither the authors nor the publisher can accept any legal responsibility or liability for any errors or omissions that may be made.

ENCYCLOPEDIA OF

COMPLEMENTARY

HEALTH

CONSULTANT EDITOR: NIKKI BRADFORD
WRITERS: SHEILA LAVERY KAREN SULLIVAN
WITH CLARE HILL, DIANA VOWLES AND NANCE FYSON
CLINICAL RESEARCH: FARA BEGUM-BAIG

CHANCELLOR
PRESS

CONTENTS

Introduction

In the fast pace of today's world where everybody is under constant pressure, people are now taking more interest in maintaining good health and well-being. There is general concern about disease and the environment: in particular how pollutants are affecting our health, and the way in which pesticides or contaminated animal feeds are affecting the vegetables and meat that we eat in our daily diet. Adults and children also seem to be developing more allergic reactions to food and general pollutants in the environment, and diseases such as asthma are now particularly affecting children. One theory is that childhood asthma is on the increase because of increased traffic fumes, and also dust mites that are present in everybody's homes.

People are also developing an increasing resistance to antibiotics given to treat different infections and are investigating alternative healthcare treatments that will help to build up their immune systems. There are also new diseases, such as Myalgic Encephalomyelitis (ME), which can start after a viral infection, that have arisen over the last 10–15 years. There is no cure at present for ME, however, alternative healthcare treatments such as aromatherapy, Western herbalism and nutritional therapy have been found to help sufferers by improving and balancing their general diet and boosting their immune systems, which are often at a very low ebb.

There has also been an overall rejection of the materialistic values of the hedonistic Eighties. In the more caring Nineties, people are having to work harder, often juggling work and children, and are suffering more stress because of it. But today they are more willing to undertake holistic therapies such as yoga, tai chi and massage to help them cope with tension and overwork by relaxing both their bodies and minds.

Alternative therapies are definitely becoming more popular. In fact, in recent research it was discovered that eight out of ten people had tried a treatment and three-quarters of them reported that it had either helped or cured them. Doctors are also becoming more aware of the benefits of alternative health therapies when orthodox treatment alone does not seem to work. In fact, they will now often refer a patient to an osteopath or chiropractor, for example, for manipulation of a back problem that is proving difficult to resolve. Some doctors are also trained in an alternative therapy, such as homeopathy, and this treatment is now becoming more widely available.

Alternative health treatments can do so much to improve a person's mental attitude and to help or cure various ailments, but in cases of serious or terminal illness only certain therapies will be suitable and should never be undertaken instead of orthodox treatment, but rather alongside it. Acupuncture, for example, can greatly boost the immune systems of cancer or HIV patients while also improving their overall mental attitude and their general perspective of their disease.

HOW TO USE THIS BOOK

The One Spirit Encyclopedia of Complementary Health is a comprehensive reference book which is divided into two major sections: the first section discusses in detail 30 major and minor therapies; the second section covers the illnesses that can affect everyone, what is the orthodox medical treatment, and which alternative treatments can help relieve or cure the condition. An Index of Symptoms and a useful Directory of resources is also included.

THE THERAPIES

The first section of the book contains 30 major and minor therapies. Each one is clearly explained under headings such as how it works, what happens in a consultation, what problems can it treat and is it safe for everyone. All the therapies are addressed in the same way, whether it is a well-known treatment such as Aromatherapy or a lesser known one such as Cymatics.

To make it easier to find specific therapies, helpful colored symbol icons are used to identify them so that you can easily locate where they are in this section and elsewhere in the book.

Therapists tailor their treatments very much to the individual: the precise nature of the treatment that people receive will vary, depending on their medical history, symptoms, lifestyle and other relevant details. The information contained in this book indicates the type of things a therapist is most likely to do or recommend. Do not be surprised if because of your symptoms they feel you need something slightly different. The information on alternative healthcare is meant purely as an indication of likely treatments; it is not meant as a self-help guide to the medical uses of the different therapies.

The results from clinical studies that have been carried out in recent years have been included at the end of the therapies, where they have been available. The bibliographical references for these studies can be found in the acknowledgments section on page 378.

Some of the clinical studies in the book have been termed:
Single-blind trial – this means that the patient is unaware of the type of treatment they are being given.
Double-blind trial – this means that the patient and observer are unaware of the type of treatment being given.
Controlled trial – This means that the groups of people involved in the trial either have specific treatment in connection with the therapy or do not receive any medical treatment at all.

The term **placebo** has also been used. This is when the patients in the trial are given a treatment that in acupuncture, for example, uses dummy points, or a medication is given that has no active ingredients.

THE AILMENTS

The second section of the book contains the ailments which appear in either two-page, one-page or half-page entries. These sections are color-coded according to body system. There are 13 body systems in all and two further sections on Infants and Children and Home and Emergency First Aid. If you were looking for an entry on Anemia, for example, you would find it under the Circulatory system, which is color coded dark red. If you then wanted to find Angina, which is in the same section, you could use the index or contents or just look through the dark-red section until you found the right entry.

The orthodox medical treatment that is recommended to a patient is covered first in each ailment entry followed by the most suitable alternative treatments, which are again highlighted by colored icons to make them instantly recognizable and simple to find.

INDEX OF SYMPTOMS

This section has been compiled as a ready reference section so that people can look up a person's symptoms and be referred to the possible ailment (one or more) and the relevant page number.

THE DIRECTORY

The Directory of resources includes an overview of the alternative therapy; general information, when practical, about treatment and costs; and information about how to find a qualified practitioner.

NOTE

This book is not intended as an alternative to personal, professional medical advice. The reader should always consult a physician in all matters relating to health, particularly with respect to any symptoms that may require diagnosis or medical attention. While the advice and information are believed to be accurate and true at the time of publication, neither the authors nor the publisher can accept any legal responsibility or liability for any errors or omissions that may be made.

ACUPUNCTURE is now enjoying renewed popularity as a highly sophisticated and effective form of alternative treatment. Indeed, many of us tend to think of stimulating the body's healing energy as a peculiarly 1990s phenomenon, but acupuncture as a holistic treatment appears to have existed long before anyone chose to record it. Stone acupuncture needles dating from the Neolithic period (2500 BC) have been found in tombs in inner Mongolia. The earliest written account of acupuncture appears in the *Nei Jing* (*The*

ACUPUNCTURE

ACUPUNCTURE is a traditional Chinese health treatment, which involves the use of needles to stimulate energy points in the body. It can help many conditions including stress, back pain, menstrual problems and addictions.

Yellow Emperor's Classic of Internal Medicine), which dates from around 200 BC and is the oldest comprehensive medical text book. Pien Chueh, a famous physician of his time, used stone acupuncture needles, moxibustion and herbs to bring a prince out of a coma. So important was his work that even though the incident took place in the fourth century BC, the Chinese still celebrate his birthday every year on April 28th.

In China, acupuncture has been a major part of primary healthcare for the last 5,000 years. Its uses range from preventing and treating disease, to relieving pain and even anesthetizing patients for surgery. However, the emphasis has always been on prevention. In traditional Chinese medicine, the highest form of acupuncture was given to enable you to live a long, healthy life. To the Chinese, a sick man visiting an acupuncturist is comparable to a thirsty man starting to dig a well.

What is acupuncture?

Acupuncture literally means "needle piercing," a rather painful-sounding term for the practice of inserting very fine needles into the skin to stimulate specific points called acupoints. The acupoints are stimulated to balance the movement of energy in the body and the process can cause slight discomfort rather than the pain that its name suggests. Acupuncture is a major part of traditional Chinese medicine (TCM), a sophisticated and complex system of healthcare that also includes the use of moxibustion, herbalism (see Chinese herbalism pages 24–29), massage (see pages 54–59), dietary therapy and also exercise such as tai chi (see pages 130–131).

Acupuncture has become very popular in recent years among conventional doctors in the West, some of whom now use it to treat symptoms of disease as if it were just another part of Western medicine. But it has been shown to work best when it is kept within the context of the Chinese tradition in which it is so firmly entrenched.

To really understand how acupuncture works, you need to make yourself familiar with the basics of Chinese philosophy. The philosophies of the Dao or Tao, yin and yang, the eight principles, the three treasures and the five elements are all fundamental to traditional Chinese acupuncture and its specific role in helping to maintain good health and a person's wellbeing.

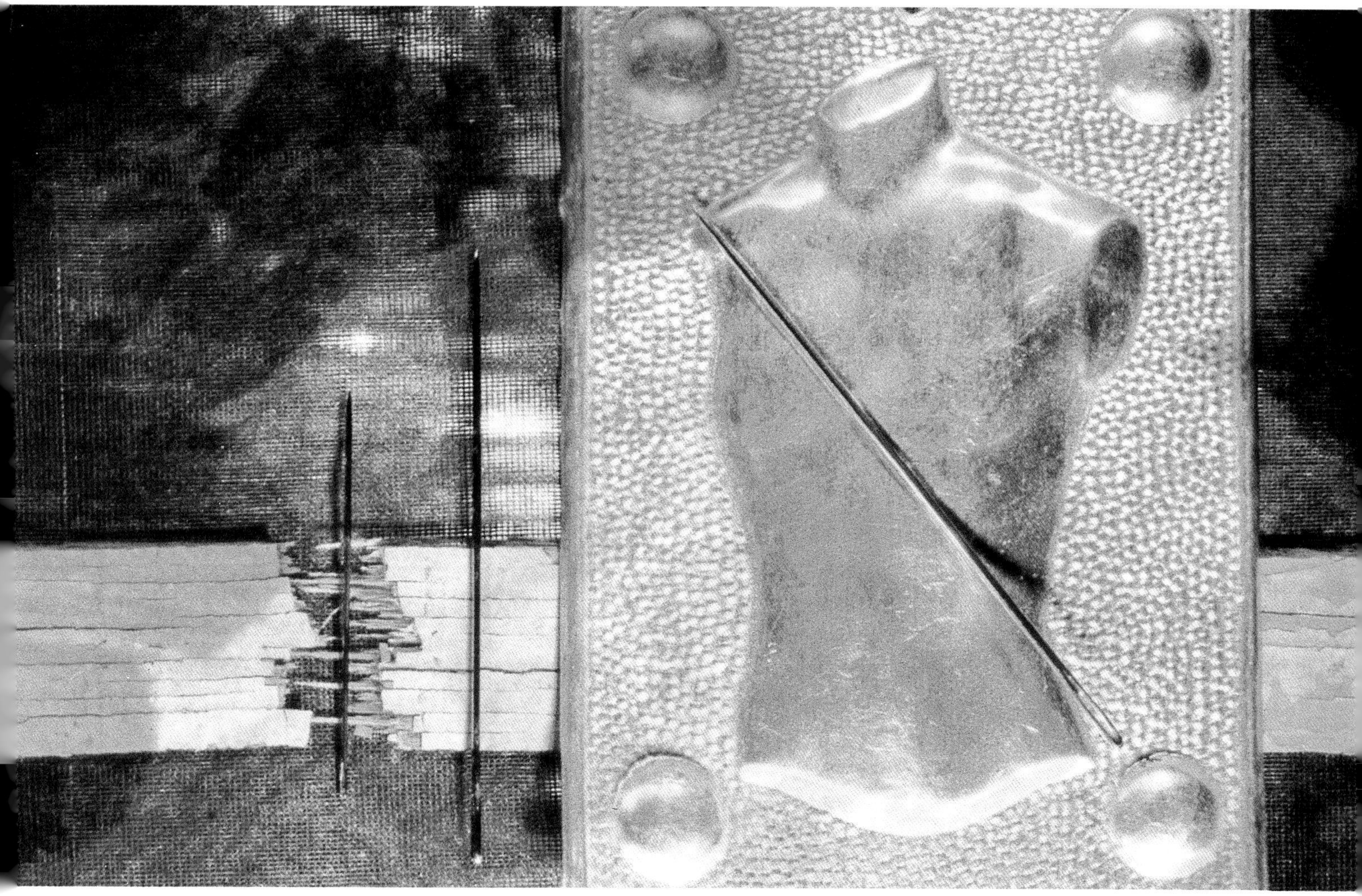

The philosophy of the Dao

There is no accurate translation of the Dao, but it can be described as "the path" or "the way of life." The laws of the Dao advocate moderation, living in harmony with nature and striving for balance. Moderation applies to all areas of life, and the ancient Chinese believed that it was essential to a long and fruitful life. Their reasoning was perfectly logical. They claimed we are "fueled" by three treasures: Qi or Chi (pronounced chee), Shen, and Jing. Chi is energy and will be discussed in detail later on. Shen is the spirit, the treasure that gives brightness to life and is responsible for consciousness and mental abilities, and Jing is

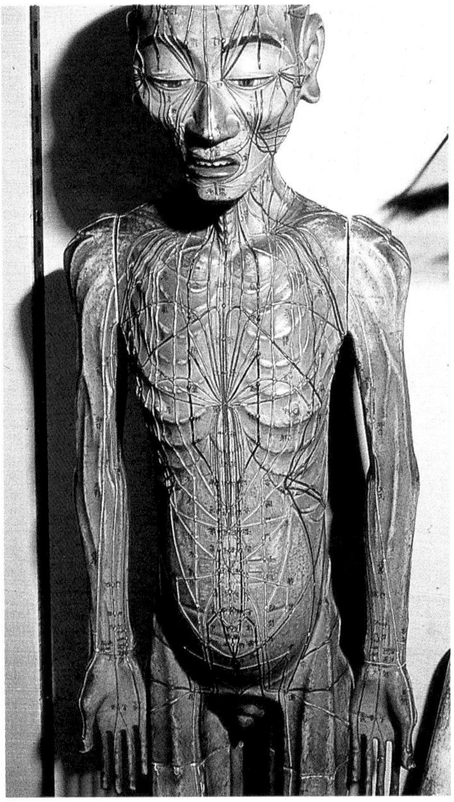

ABOVE: This ancient acupuncture study figure was used for reference by the Chinese therapists of the Ming Dynasty in the 17th century.

our essence. Jing is responsible for growth, development and reproduction. We are born with our full quota of Jing and it is lost little by little as we go through life. The important thing to remember about Jing is that once you lose it, you cannot get it back. It is depleted by wrong or careless living, but preserved by moderation, and its loss can be slowed down to some degree by acupuncture. The role of the acupuncturist therefore is to restore your health and enable you to live a little closer to the Dao. By doing so, you can preserve your Jing and consequently live to a ripe old age. By overdoing it and living a life of excess you squander your Jing and get burned out. Drinking too much depletes your Jing, as does excessive emotional reactions. Working too hard also depletes it as does inappropriate sexual behavior. The ancient Chinese had some very balanced views about sex. In the West we worry about not getting enough sex, but the Chinese have always been concerned about getting too much. Too many ejaculations, they claimed could deplete a man's Jing because he loses his essence and, not surprisingly, giving birth too many times could deplete a woman's. So seriously did the Chinese take this subject that they laid down guidelines for the minimum and

ABOVE: Here in this ancient Sung Dynasty painting a country doctor is burning the herb moxa on a man's back to stimulate the relevant acupuncture point.

maximum number of ejaculations a man should have at any given age. *The Classic of the Simple Girl* (Sui Dynasty AD581–681) contains the guidelines which cover the age groups 15–70. For example, a 20-year-old man in good health should not ejaculate more than twice a day; if he is in average health it should be no more than once a day. On the other hand, a healthy 60-year-old man should leave a space of ten days between each performance and 20 days if he is only moderately healthy. The guidelines seem strict, but the message of the Dao was intended to be more moderate. The emphasis was not on cooling sexual relations, but on sharing intimacy. By shifting the emphasis from the male orgasm, the man could concentrate on giving pleasure to his partner in other ways, so that there was a balance of sexual power and balance in all things was considered the key to good health and long life.

In order to increase their understanding of the Dao, the Chinese developed two concepts that together form the basis of Chinese thought: yin and yang and the more detailed system of the five elements.

Yin and Yang

ABOVE: The tai chi symbol shows how yin and yang are opposites, but inseparable.

The idea of harmony and balance are also the basis of yin and yang. The belief that each person is governed by the opposing, but complementary forces of yin and yang, is central to all Chinese thought because it is believed to affect everything in the universe, including ourselves.

Traditionally, yin is dark, passive, feminine, cold and negative; yang is light, active, male, warm and positive. Modern therapists would simply say that there are two sides to everything – happy and sad, tired and energetic, cold and hot.

Yin and yang are the opposites that make the whole, they cannot exist without each other and nothing is ever completely one or the other; there are varying degrees of each within everything and everybody. The tai chi symbol illustrates how they flow into each other with a little yin always within yang and a little yang always within yin. The same happens within the body as after exercise (yang) the body wants to rest (yin), after a fever breaks (yang), you get chills (yin) and within the head (yang) the mind is yin. The body, mind and emotions are all subject to the influences of yin and yang. When the two opposing forces are in balance we feel good, but if one force dominates the other, it brings about an imbalance that can result in ill health.

One of the main aims of the acupuncturist is to maintain a balance of yin and yang within the whole person to prevent illness occurring and to restore existing health.

Yin and yang are also part of the eight principles of traditional Chinese medicine. The other six are: cold and heat, internal and external, deficiency and excess. These principles allow the practitioner to use yin and yang more precisely in order to bring more detail into his diagnosis.

The five elements

The yin and yang philosophy was further refined into the system of the five elements to gain a deeper understanding of how the body, mind and spirit work.

The five elements have numerous associations. Among other things each one is related to a season, an organ, a taste, a color, a smell, an emotion, a body part and even a grain. The system is a complex one, based on the belief that life is an ever-changing process. It is probably most simply explained in terms of seasonal change and the smooth cyclical process of nature. The five elements of wood, fire, earth, metal and water relate to the seasons in the following way: wood to spring, fire to summer, earth to late summer, metal to autumn and water to winter, and each element then flows into the next in the same way that one season slowly gives way to another.

THE QUALITIES OF THE FIVE ELEMENTS:

	Wood	Fire	Earth	Metal	Water
Color	green	red	yellow	white	blue/black
Emotion	anger	joy	sympathy	grief/sadness	fear
Voice	shouts	laughs	sings	weeps	groans
Smell	rancid	scorched	fragrant	rotten	putrid
Taste	sour	bitter	sweet	pungent	salty
Season	spring	summer	late summer	autumn	winter
Climate	windy	hot	humid/damp	dry	cold
Body part	soft tissue	heart/blood	flesh	skin/hair	bones/marrow
Officials	liver gall bladder	heart small intestine pericardium three heater*	spleen stomach	lungs large intestine	bladder kidneys

In the same way, a seed planted in spring blooms in summer, seeds itself in late summer to autumn, dies in winter, and a new seed grows again in spring. It is part of a never-ending cycle and each phase has its role to play in maintaining the balance of nature. The same process of change occurs within the body. Cells grow and die to make way for new cells, and body systems depend upon each other in a similar way to the seasons, working together to ensure the balanced functioning of the body, mind and spirit and the healthy flow of life through the whole person.

Within the person, the five phases relate to organs and the emotions associated with those organs. For example, summer is connected to the fire element which contains the heart, the small intestines, the heart protector (pericardium) and the three heater* (the body's physical and emotional thermostat). The pericardium is often associated with physical heart problems such as palpitations or angina, while the heart itself is related to more spiritual, mental and emotional concerns. Most importantly, the heart is the home of Shen. Shen is the spirit, the driving force of the mind and the personality, and ruler of all the organs. It is forever changing and developing and is as vital to the mind and emotions as the heart is to the body.

It is worth mentioning that the Chinese compared the body to their own kingdom and gave the organs names to signify their position and function within the kingdom. Not surprisingly, the heart is the emperor presiding over his kingdom, in charge of various ministers who have specific functions within the body, mind and spirit. The gall bladder minister is responsible for making decisions, the liver is likened to a general who uses his planning, judgment and organizational abilities to keep the kingdom running smoothly. The small intestine has the job of separating the good from the bad, both physically and mentally. The spleen is the transport minister, responsible for the smooth conveyance of thought, energy, blood and so on. There are 12 officials within the kingdom, which lie within the five elements and keep the body, mind and emotions running smoothly.

The aim of the treatment is not only to cure health problems but to balance the body and prevent illness occurring.

Like the kingdom, each one of us possesses all five elements. When we are functioning well, all the elements are in balance. But ill health arises from a weakness or excess of one of the elements, which throws the rest of the body out of balance. The imbalance is demonstrated by a specific color, tone of voice, smell, taste, season, inappropriate emotional behavior and ultimately physical illness. For example, someone with an imbalance in their earth element may love the color yellow, can have a yellow tinge to the skin on their face, has a sing-song voice and loves to sing, has a fragrant smell, craves sweet things, loves or hates late summer, needs lots of sympathy or is sympathetic by nature, worries too much and may have digestive problems, eating disorders, menstrual problems, or a bad memory.

The thrust of five element diagnosis is to isolate and treat the imbalanced element, because an imbalanced element is like a weak link in your energetic chain that can undermine the strength of your mind, body and spirit.

How does it work?

There are a variety of scientific theories about how acupuncture works. These range from the belief that acupuncture works on the nervous system to the fact that it helps release endorphins – the body's natural pain relievers. But, although scientific theories can in part explain the immediate pain-relieving effects of acupuncture, they cannot explain acupuncture's ability to relieve chronic health problems, conditions which are not pain-related and the effect of the therapy on the whole person.

The Chinese explanation is more philosophical than scientific, but it does explain the holistic benefits of acupuncture. The Chinese believe that disease affects us on every level – a physical illness upsets the mind and emotions and mental anxiety registers in a related organ. So a worrier could have a stomach ulcer, because excessive mental activity affects the functioning of the stomach, while an imbalance in the liver can express itself as inappropriate anger. For this reason illness is never treated as a set of isolated symptoms or diseased organs, but as an expression of disharmony within the mind, body and spirit. To arrive at a diagnosis, the acupuncturist usually aims to do two things: identify a weak link in your energetic chain through the system of the five elements and weave all the symptoms of your disease together to make up "a pattern of disharmony."

The concept of Chi

Inner harmony relies on a healthy, balanced and unobstructed flow of Chi. Chi could be described as the vital energy or life force which drives every cell of the body. It supports, nourishes and defends the whole person against mental, physical and emotional disease. It is an invisible, intangible flow of energy which modern researchers have described in terms of electromagnetic energy. Chi flows around the body in invisible channels known as meridians. There are 12 main meridians, six of which are yin and six are yang and numerous minor ones, which form a network of energy channels throughout the body.

Each meridian is related to, and named after, an organ or function, the main ones are: the lung, kidney, gallbladder, stomach, spleen, heart, small intestine, large intestine, gall bladder, urinary bladder, san jiao (three heater) and pericardium (heart protector/ or circulation sex meridian).

Dotted along these meridians are 365 main acupuncture points. These are listed by name, number and the meridian to which they belong. The names are very descriptive and often beautiful, but the numbers are possibly more useful. For example, "Leg three miles" is the name for stomach 36 (St 36), "Happy calm" is Liver 3 (Liv 3) and "Bright and Clear" is gall bladder 37 (GB37). One point has 17 different names.

When Chi flows freely through the meridians, the body is balanced and healthy, but if the energy becomes blocked, stagnated or weakened, it can result in physical, mental or emotional ill health. An imbalance in a person's body can result from inappropriate emotional responses such as: excess anger, over-excitement, self-pity, deep grief and fear.

Other factors, which are what the Chinese call the "pernicious external influences" are: cold, damp/humidity, wind, dryness, and heat. Any one or more of the internal and external factors can upset the balance of Chi by making it too hot, too cold, excessive, deficient, too fast, stagnant or causing it to become blocked. Other causes are wrong diet, too much sex, overwork and too much exercise.

To restore the balance, the acupuncturist stimulates the acupuncture points that will counteract that imbalance. So, if you have stagnant Chi, he will choose specific points to stimulate it. If the Chi is too cold, he will choose points to warm it. If it is too weak, he will strengthen it. If it is blocked, he will unblock it, and so on. In this way, acupuncture can effectively rebalance the energy system and restore health or prevent the development of disease. The points that the practitioner chooses to stimulate will not necessarily be at the site of the symptoms. For example, headaches can often come from a liver or gall bladder imbalance. The gall bladder meridian runs from the top of the head by the side of your eye to the toe next to the little toe. Consequently, depending on the type of headache, the acupuncturist could stimulate any point on that meridian from the toe to the top of the head, although the main points lie below the knee.

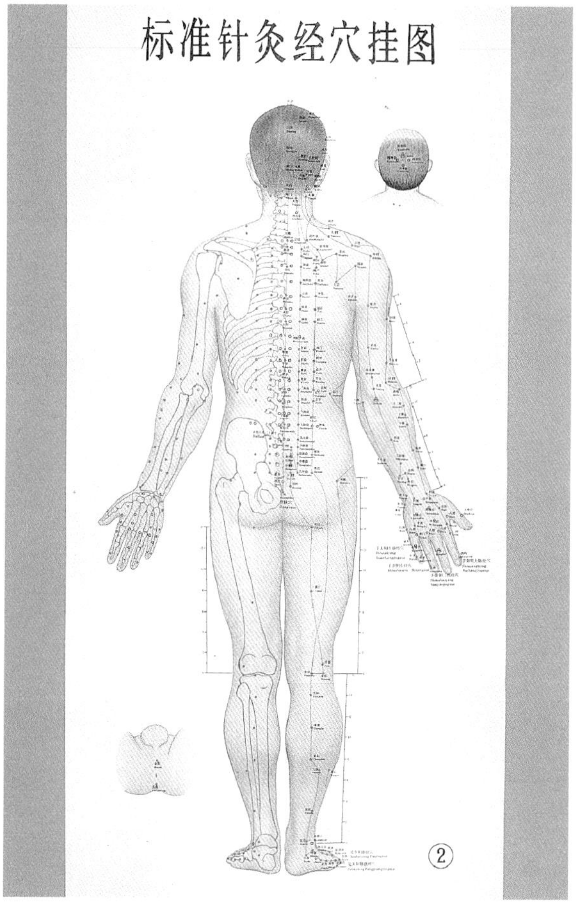

ABOVE: In acupuncture there are 12 main meridians situated throughout the body. These form energy channels in the body that can be stimulated if there is a blockage.

What happens in a consultation?

Much of the consultation will be devoted to a detailed system of diagnosis. Successful acupuncture treatment depends on an accurate diagnosis, so every first consultation begins with the four types of examinations, that is, looking, asking, listening, smelling and touching.

Asking: Like all holistic therapists, the acupuncturist will ask you questions about yourself and your health. He will listen to why you have come to see him and ask you a series of questions about yourself. Typically, he will want to know about:

- *Your complete medical history*
- *The symptoms you are experiencing*
- *Any pain you have had or are suffering*
- *What your sleep patterns are*
- *Any sensations of hot and cold*
- *Whether you feel dizzy*
- *What your eating habits are*
- *Bowel movements and urination*

He will ask details about your lifestyle, exercise routine, family, work and hobbies. He will also want details of your parents' health and past illnesses, including any illnesses that run in your family. He will also ask about your childhood experiences and relationships. Details such as how often you moved house, your relationship with your parents, siblings, friends and partner are all important. After he has listened and taken notes, he will continue with the looking diagnosis.

Looking: The practitioner notes your general appearance and your posture. He looks for one of the predominant colors on your face. Facial color is significant:

- *A white face is linked to disharmony or cold*
- *A yellow complexion is related to dampness*
- *A red face is a sign of excess heat*

He will look at your eyes to ascertain the state of Shen. If they are bright and shiny, Shen is in harmony, but a blank expression, with lusterless eyes is a sign of disharmony. Often your tongue will be looked at as part of the diagnosis. The acupuncturist will look at its color, coating and condition. A healthy tongue should be light red in color with a moist, thin whitish coating called "moss." A purplish tongue is a sign of stagnant Chi and blood, a thin coating points to deficiency, while a thick one indicates excess. The different areas of your tongue also correspond to body organs: the tip relates to the heart, the middle to the spleen, the root to the kidneys and the sides to the liver and gall bladder. The acupuncturist may make a sketch of your tongue to be kept in your notes for future reference.

Listening and smelling: The acupuncturist will listen to your breathing patterns, your speech and your cough, if you have one. The tone of your voice is important. There are five different tones which relate to the five elements. So, for example, if you have an imbalance in your wood elements, you will tend to have a shouting voice. Your choice of words and the expressions that you use are also significant. Smell also forms part of the listening examination. Each element has a smell and the odor that you give off will point to an imbalance in one of the five elements:

- *A sour or rancid smell like butter that has gone off indicates the wood element*
- *A scorched smell that resembles freshly ironed clothes is a sign of a fire imbalance*

Touching: This is the last and most important of the four examinations. It involves:

- *Touching or palpating the patient's skin*
- *Taking accurate pulse readings on each wrist*

The pulse reading is much more detailed than a Western pulse reading. It is important that you are relaxed for this part of the diagnosis, so if you rushed to make your appointment, you may have to lie still for a few minutes to get your pulse rate back to normal. There are six basic Chinese pulses, which lie on the radial artery on the wrist – three on each wrist. From these the acupuncturist can test for up to 28 pulse qualities. Some acupuncturists will take 12 pulses, each of which corresponds to an organ or function. He will test the pulses for the volume of the blood and energy passing through that spot on the wrist as well as the quality of the energy.

On the left wrist are: the heart, the small intestine, the liver, the gall bladder, the kidney and the bladder. On the right are the lungs, colon, stomach, spleen, circulation, sex (pericardium) and three heater. The acupuncturist will spend a lot of time taking the pulses, which he will test with three fingers, the index, middle and ring finger. He may take them two or three times during the initial consultation and, while he is doing it, a good acupuncturist will concentrate entirely on the task, because it is so important.

There are 28 pulse qualities which the ancient Chinese texts described in such terms as "a cork bobbing on the water," "a pearl spinning in a dish" or "a tight lute string." They can also be described as empty, deep, slow or choppy, full, fast, slippery or superficial. After the pulse taking, the acupuncturist may also press or palpate certain areas of your abdomen to see if you experience any discomfort. This is known as Japanese abdominal diagnosis. It enables the practitioner to test the area for sensitive points, which relate to certain organs. He will also feel three areas for heat balance, below the navel, above the navel and in the chest area. This is the area governed by the three heater which is the body's thermostat. Irregularities in temperature can indicate that the three heater itself is out of balance or there may be an imbalance in one or more of the individual organs which it governs. He may also feel the umbilical pulse in the navel, to check that it is centered as it is important for balance.

Some practitioners use the Akabane test. They pass a lighted taper across the tips of the fingers and toes to test how long it takes for the heat to come to a point. This is to to see if the meridians are balanced on both sides of the body. The practitioner counts how many times it crosses before the heat comes to the points, if it takes say five times on the left and ten on the right, there is an obvious imbalance in energy. Finally, he may run his hands along your limbs to test for cold or hot spots.

Ultimately, the four examinations should all point to the same conclusion. So if you have a slight green tinge around your mouth, you are easily angered, if you have a rancid odor and a

BELOW: An acupuncturist will look at a patient's tongue to diagnose any body deficiencies. She may take a sketch of the tongue to keep for reference.

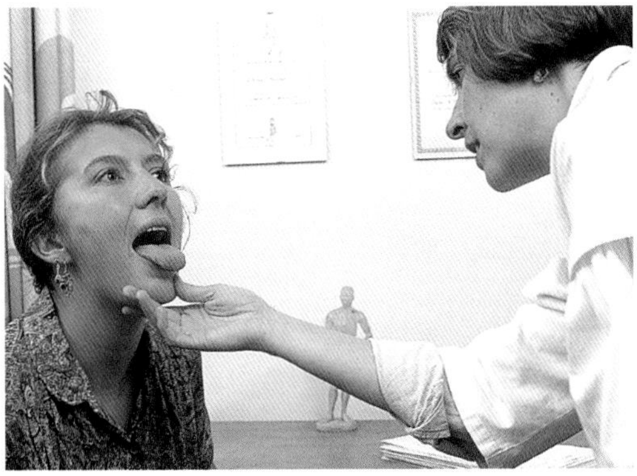

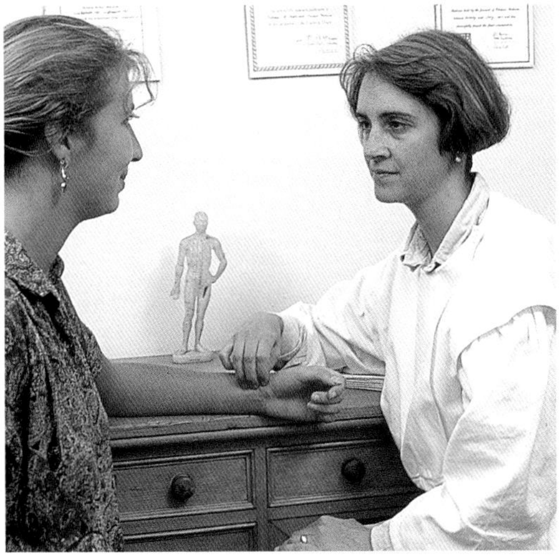

ABOVE: Pulse taking is very important in acupuncture. There are six pulses, three on each wrist, but as many as 28 pulse qualities are taken to aid diagnosis.

SPECIFIC USES OF ACUPUNCTURE

Pain relief *Pain in muscles and joints is the most common problem that acupuncturists are asked to treat. This may be for two reasons. Acupuncture has a strong analgesic effect, which has been scientifically explained by theories such as the endorphin theory and "the gate" theory. The endorphin theory states that stimulating points releases pain-relieving endorphins. The "gate theory" is more complicated, but it simply means that the spine is made up of "gates" which can open to let pain in or close to shut it out. The gates open or shut in response to messages from the nervous system.*

Supporters of this theory believe that acupuncture works on the nervous system to instruct the gates of the spine to shut out pain. But acupuncture's high success rate with pain relief in particular may simply be because many types of pain, especially back pain are so unresponsive to conventional treatment so more cases get referred or people seek out acupuncture.

Addictions *Ear acupuncture in particular (see Auricular therapy pages 20–21) has proved very successful with drug addictions, because it lessens the withdrawal symptoms. Studies have shown it to be beneficial in weaning people off hard drugs such as cocaine and heroin as well as more common addictive substances such as cigarettes and alcohol. Successful withdrawal usually involves intensive specialized treatment.*

Childbirth *Acupuncture is proving effective for pain relief in labor and the associated back pain before and after giving birth. It is particularly beneficial because it does not harm the baby and eliminates the need for drugs which could affect the child. Acupuncture can calm an anxious mother-to-be and is believed to reduce labor pain by up to a third. A well-known point on the little toe can help turn the fetus if it is in breech position.*

Surgery *Acupuncture has been used as a form of anesthetic in China and is suitable for some patients, especially those at risk of anemia, but it is not widely used in the West. One of the main problems is that not everyone responds to the treatment and it is more time consuming than giving a conventional anesthetic. Acupuncture can also be used in dentistry.*

Lack of energy *Acupuncture can have a dramatic impact on those people who feel generally unwell or constantly tired. This may be due to acupuncture's ability to restore harmony to the body and normalize body systems. Acupuncture also has a psychological effect. Studies conducted on patients who received acupuncture show changes in brain activity, which can result in a relaxing or "energizing effect."*

Acupuncture for animals *The remarkable success of acupuncture in treating animals appears to disprove that acupuncture works simply because you believe in it.*

shouting voice it points to an imbalance in your gall bladder or liver. Some of the diagnostic signs are more important then others. The practitioner's skill lies in extracting the most important aspects of the examinations to arrive at an accurate diagnosis.

He will then decide on a course of treatment to work on restoring your energy and aim to get your body back in balance. For the treatment you will have to lie on a couch and undress sufficiently to allow the practitioner to get to the relevant points on your body. You do not have to remove all your clothes, you may simply have to remove your top, roll up your trouser leg, or strip to your underwear. The parts of your body not being worked on can be covered by a sheet or blanket. The treatment can involve any of the methods mentioned below, but needling and moxibustion are the most common.

When the needles go in they may cause a pinprick sensation followed by tingling or numbness, some people feel a slight ache. It depends on the point being treated and the depth to which the needle is inserted, but it is not a big ordeal. The acupuncturist can use just one or two needles, but usually between four and eight and will manipulate them to stimulate or calm the point. The needles can either be in and out of the body in a second or left in for up to half an hour.

You may feel no different after treatment, but some people feel, sleepy, revitalized or sometimes a little "spaced out." You can feel an immediate improvement after acupuncture, especially if you have gone specifically for pain relief, but it usually takes a couple of days to feel any other benefits. It is common to feel a little worse before you feel better as acupuncture brings physical, mental and emotional problems to the surface. However, this is a positive sign, so do not worry about it. As with any treatment, complete recovery takes time and patience.

How many sessions do I need?

The length of treatment depends on the type of illness that is involved, its duration, your age, and your individual healing abilities. But normally you should see some noticeable improvement after three or four treatments.

Which problems can it help?

The acupuncturist would not make a distinction between you and your illness and would aim to improve your whole health. However, in the context of Western medicine, acupuncture has been shown to benefit all types of aches and pains from arthritis to back pain and sports injuries, stress, depression, fatigue, circulation and digestive problems. It can also help menstrual, gynecological and sexual problems, hay fever, asthma and unspecified ailments such as Myalgic Encephalomyelitis and fatigue.

In general, it works best as a preventative treatment, helps acute (short-term) conditions or relieves the early stages of an illness. As with any other form of medicine, acupuncture cannot reverse any tissue damage, so although it can reduce pain, stiffness and swelling and improve mobility in rheumatoid arthritis, for example, it cannot reverse any muscle wasting or bone deformities that have already occurred in the body.

Treatment

Needling *is the most common form of acupuncture. Very fine, sterile stainless steel needles are inserted into the skin at the site of the relevant points. The needles are so fine that they do not cause any bleeding and are usually 12mm–24mm (½ in–1 in) long. They are usually inserted to a depth of 8mm–1.25cm (¼ in–½ in), although some can be a little deeper than 2.5cm (1 in). The depth depends on the patient, their problem and the points being treated. A qualified therapist will always use sterile needles. He will use disposable needles if you ask him to.*

Moxibustion *can also be used on most acupuncture points and is used to warm and stimulate energy in a patient with cold, damp conditions or generally to reinforce the treatment. It comes from the Japanese word,* mokusa, *which means burning herb, and it works by bringing an impulse of heat to the point. There are three ways to use moxa, which is made from the dried herb, mugwort: on the head of a needle, in the shape of a small cone or in a stick or roll. In the first, a plug of moxa or a piece of moxa wool is burnt on the end of a needle that is inserted into an acupuncture point. The burning herb warms the needle and stimulates the point without harming the skin.*

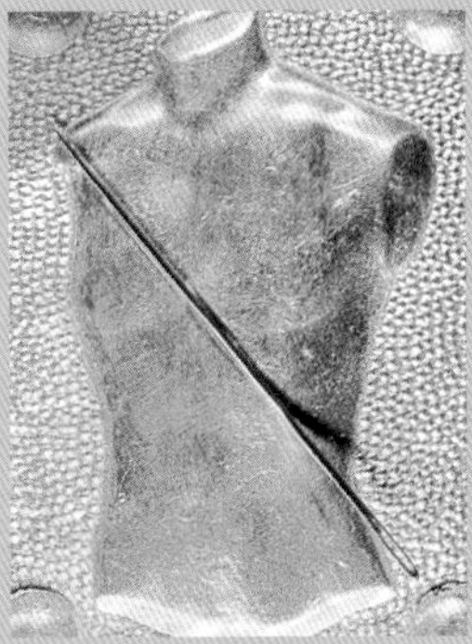

In the second method, a small cone of moxa is burnt on the skin over an acupuncture point and is removed as soon as you feel the heat. Moxa sticks are cigar-shaped sticks of the dried herb which are lit and held over the point or waved over a larger area until you feel it is too hot. The stick has a glowing tip which warms, but does not touch the skin. Moxa has a wonderful smell and is a very pleasant form of treatment.

Cupping *is sometimes used for cold, wind and damp problems. It is the treatment acupuncturists will consider for problems such as bronchitis, colds, and arthritis. Glass, metal, wood or bamboo cups of different sizes are warmed and placed top-side down on a specific point or area. The warmed cup creates a vacuum which sucks the skin into it, bringing blood and energy to the point and the surrounding area. Cups need to be placed on flat areas, often the back, abdomen or legs.*

Electroacupuncture *is used mostly by modern acupuncturists (see Auricular therapy pages 20–21), although some traditional practitioners also use it. As the name suggests, a small electrical current is used to stimulate points. It is based on the modern belief that acupuncture points are in fact areas of low electrical resistance. The theory is that an organ affected by injury or illness, affects the electrical resistance of the corresponding points on the skin. By stimulating the points with a small electrical current through needles or a pen-like conductor, the balance, and health, of the organ can be restored. In electro-acupuncture needles tend to be left in for less time than in normal acupuncture. The frequency of the electrical current can be varied according to the treatment and the required effects. This type of acupuncture is sometimes used for pain relief in labor.*

Laser acupuncture *is especially effective for treating babies, young children and people who are afraid of needles. Small, pen-like tools, which produce an infrared low-power laser beam, can be used on specific points or waved along the meridians to stimulate the energy flow. The lasers are designed to deliver just the right concentration of energy for the patient and do not hurt or burn the skin.*

Ultrasound and light therapy *Ultrasound, sound waves and light waves can also be used on acupuncture points with significant success, although they are not very common. The practice is based on the belief that acupuncture points seem to respond to energy from any source, be it heat, sound, light, pressure, or electricity.*

Herbs *Some traditional acupuncturists are also trained in prescribing herbs, which they may use to support acupuncture treatment (see Chinese herbalism pages 24–29). The type of acupuncture used will depend on your problem and the acupuncturist's skills. All the methods are effective and the key to successful treatment depends more on accurate diagnosis and choice of points, than the stimulation method.*

Is it safe?

When it is practiced by a qualified practitioner, acupuncture is perfectly safe for everyone. In fact young children often respond very well because their imbalances can be treated before they become a health problem. If you think acupuncture could help your baby or child, it is advisable to see an experienced practitioner and preferably one who specializes in child acupuncture. Acupuncture can be used during pregnancy, and it can also give pain relief and stimulate contractions during labor. However, as with all responsible forms of healthcare, acupuncturists avoid unnecessary intervention during pregnancy.

of Substance Abuse at Lincoln Hospital, New York. By the start of the acupuncture study in 1994, he had treated over 10,000 crack/cocaine addicts. One hundred and fifty addicts were treated over a period of one month with either acupuncture or dummy treatments.

Although the final treatment retention was similar for both groups, after two weeks the acupuncture patients had significantly lower cocaine levels in their urine. Both groups also reported that they used less cocaine during the trial. (**2**)

BELOW: Electroacupuncture is mainly used by modern acupuncturists. Electrodes are placed on the skin and a small electrical current is passed through them to stimulate the points.

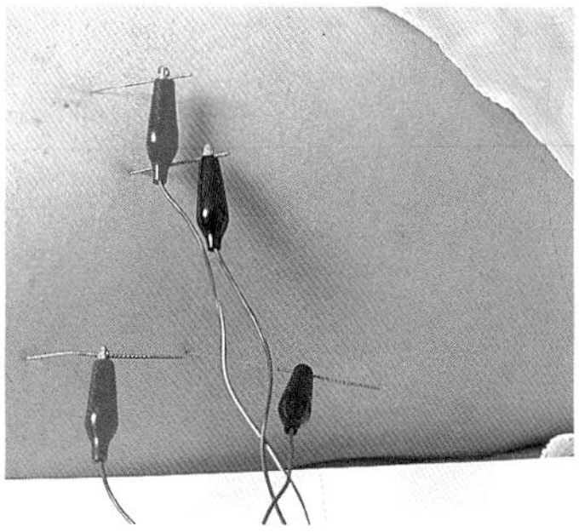

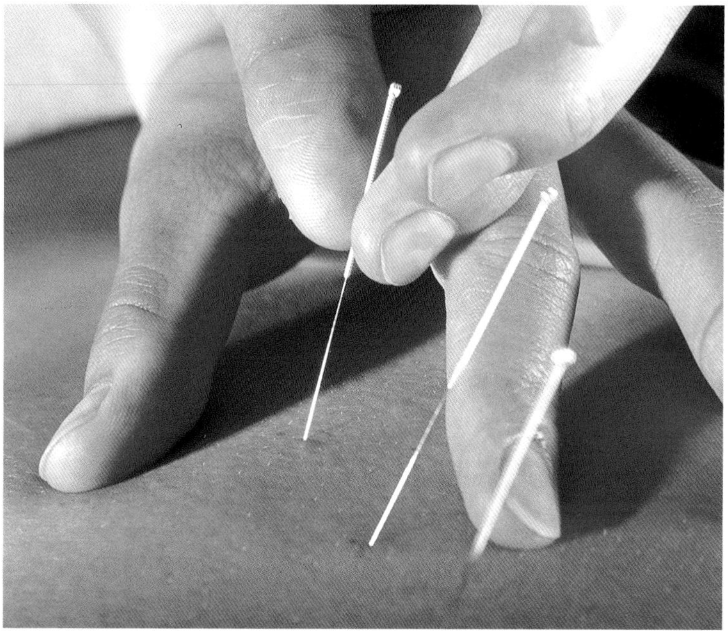

LEFT: Needling is the most popular acupuncture treatment. Fine, sterile needles are inserted in the skin at the relevant points. They can be left in just briefly, or can be inserted for about half an hour depending on the condition.

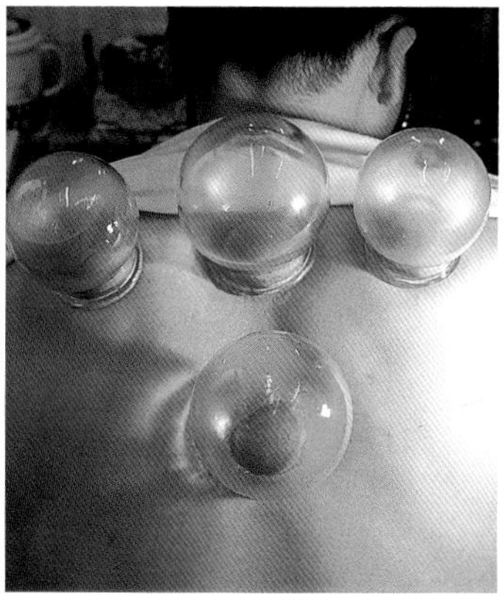

ABOVE: Cupping involves placing warmed cups on specific acupuncture points to bring blood and energy to the surface.

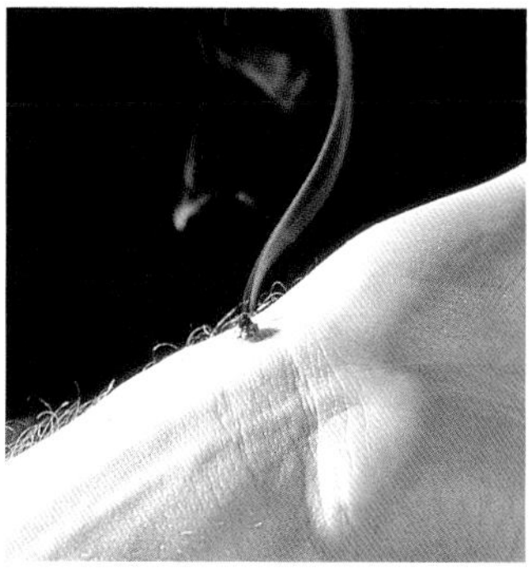

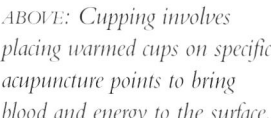

RIGHT: In moxibustion, burning moxa cones are placed on the skin to heat up points.

Clinical studies

The benefits of acupuncture have been proven in several clinical studies where it is used to help different addictions and ailments.

In 1989, 137 male chronic alcoholics who had not responded well to previous orthodox treatments were treated at Hennepin County Detoxification Center with acupuncture at detoxification points or placebo points. Those treated at the detoxification points reported half the drinking bouts of the control group and also had lower admission to detox programs. (**1**)

Acupuncture has also been used to treat drug addicts as long ago as the 1970s. It was pioneered by Dr. Mike Smith, Director

In connection with helping people to stop smoking, a control study was set up in 1985 of 651 smokers who compared acupuncture with nicotine gum to help them kick the habit. Both the acupuncture and gum were equally effective and both were still making an impact at one and 13 month follow-ups, unlike the control group who had minimum intervention. The number of people who started smoking again was high at one month – only 19 percent of acupuncture patients and 22 percent of nicotine gum were still not smoking – and this decreased to eight percent and 12 percent after 13 months. (**3**)

On the ailment front, in a four-week Swedish study, 21 patients suffering from angina were treated three times weekly with either acupuncture or a placebo tablet treatment. Results showed that the acupuncture patients had four fewer angina attacks per week compared to the placebo group. In exercise tests it showed that although the patients' performance seemed unaffected by acupuncture, the chest pain they experienced only appeared when they had to work harder and was less intense. Other benefits were that all the patients reported improved feelings of wellbeing. (**4**) (*For clinical references see How to use this book*).

FOR INFORMATION ON HOW TO CHOOSE AN ACUPUNCTURIST SEE THE DIRECTORY.

AURICULAR THERAPY

AURICULAR THERAPY is a specific branch of acupuncture that focuses on the ear. It appears to have been the poor relation of traditional Chinese medicine (TCM) acupuncture until it was revived and updated by the French acupuncturist Dr. Paul Nogier in the 1960s.

However, its origins are a matter of some dispute. Nogier's followers, known as Modern acupuncturists because they use high-tech equipment and modern forms of diagnosis, see it very much as Nogier's therapy. But Chinese practitioners claim to have ancient texts that show auricular therapy to be Eastern in origin. Not surprisingly, there are two distinct schools of auricular therapy which use the treatment very differently. The extent to which it is used also differs: auricular therapy forms one of the cornerstones of modern acupuncture, while it still only remains on the fringes of TCM acupuncture. In TCM it tends to be used as an additional tool for treatment only by specially trained therapists.

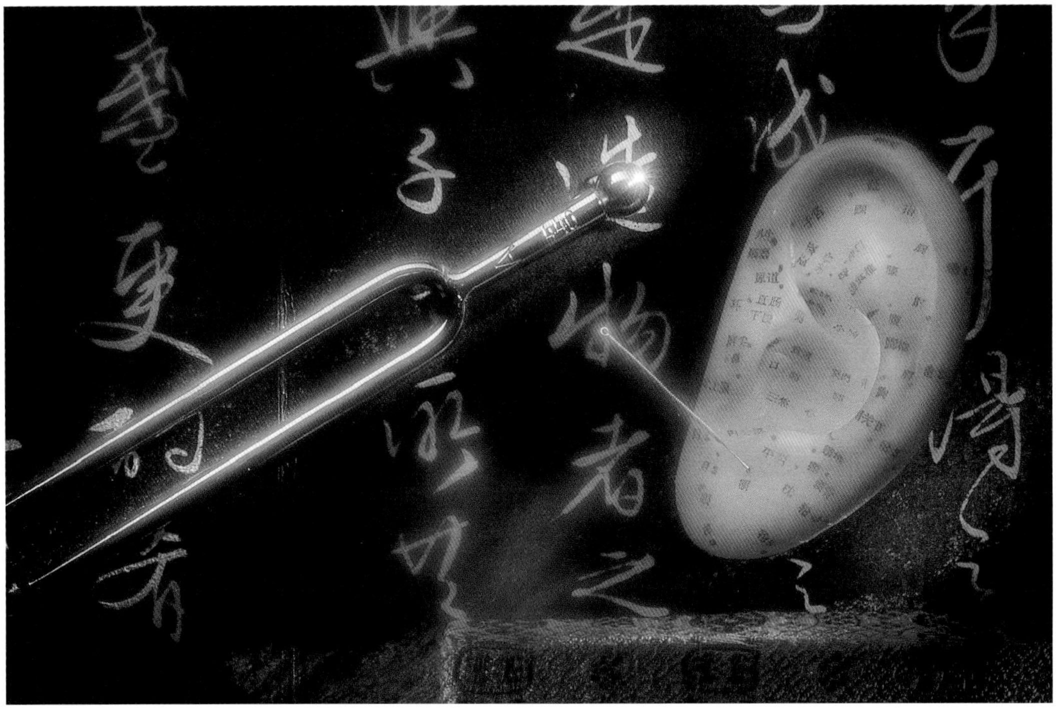

ABOVE: Ear acupuncture points are stimulated using small, fine needles, light therapy, electro-therapy or magnetically-charged ball bearings.

AURICULAR THERAPY is a type of acupuncture that focuses on the ear. Either needles or a more modern electrical impulse is used for treatment. It can be used for pain control, to help headaches or migraines, arthritis and gastric problems.

What is auricular therapy?

Auricular therapy is literally acupuncture treatment on the ear. Paul Nogier was inspired to try it when some of his patients reported that their sciatica had been relieved by a therapist who had cauterized part of their earlobes. Nogier searched historical medical texts and found references to auricular treatment that dated right back to ancient Egyptian times. When he examined his patients who were suffering from painful conditions, he found that many of them had tender points on their ears. When he applied needles to these areas, they seemed to alleviate the pain they felt in other parts of the body.

Nogier then drew up charts to show which points related to which parts of the body. He went on to develop the Punctoscope, a specially designed electrical instrument to use on the ear instead of needles. His belief that acupuncture points were areas of altered electrical resistance and his electrical testing and treating equipment have been embraced by modern acupuncturists. Thanks to Nogier, auricular therapy remains popular in France, where it is known as auricular medicine and is regularly used by the French medical profession.

According to auricular therapists the main benefits of the treatment are:

- *It provides quick access to diagnostic information.*
- *You do not have to be treated with needles. Therapists can use very fine, small needles that just go into the skin, but they can also use light therapy, electrotherapy or very small magnetically charged ball bearings, which press down onto the relevant points.*
- *You can have semi-permanent treatment. Small needles can be embedded in the ear, or small ball bearings can be taped over the necessary points, for up to a week at a time. This way you can press on the point when you feel the need.*
- *It is less invasive than body acupuncture, so is better for those patients who are feeling anxious about their problem or the treatment, or who are just rather reluctant to get undressed for the therapy.*
- *It is an effective form of pain control with an immediate calming effect.*

How does it work?

The ear is believed to mirror the shape of the fetus in the womb: the lobe represents the head, and points relating to the tongue, eyes, tonsils, teeth and ears, are all found on the lobe. The rest of the points are positioned on the ear where they would match exactly the organs to which they correspond if a miniature fetus were superimposed over the ear. Opinions vary as to how many points there are on the ear; some say there are 200, others say it is over 300, but each one relates to a specific organ or area of the body. Inserting the needles, or otherwise stimulating a point on the ear, affects the corresponding organ or meridian in exactly the same way that stimulating an acupuncture point on a person's body would.

Auricular therapy is an example of holographic therapy – the belief that small bits of the body can reflect the whole person. Therapists use the analogy of a mirror to explain the concept. If you look in a mirror it reflects your image, but if you smashed the mirror into hundreds of pieces each small piece would still reflect your whole image. The Chinese consider the ear to be perfect for holographic therapy because it is a reflection of the kidneys. To the Chinese the kidneys are the root of everything and can affect every diagnosis and treatment.

What happens in a consultation?

Before treating you, a therapist will go through the usual diagnostic process using the four methods of diagnosis:

- *Looking*
- *Asking*
- *Listening and smelling (see Acupuncture pages 10–19)*
- *Touching*

The diagnostic approach may differ, however, between modern and traditional therapists. For example, modern acupuncturists do not use the traditional pulse diagnosis, instead they take electrical readings of acupuncture points. To do this they use machinery that measures the electrical energy of each point in millivolts. Readings that are too high or too low indicate inflammation or degeneration in that area. This method of diagnosis is based on the belief, which has been backed by German research, that acupuncture points have measurable electrical properties. Practitioners will then follow the diagnosis with an ear examination to find out about your present and past health.

Modern acupuncturists also use different terminology from the traditionalists. Where a TCM acupuncturist might say you have a "wind-related problem" a modern acupuncturist might say that there is a problem with the gall bladder duct.

The Modern treatment employs electromagnetic, electrical or light methods of point stimulus. These appear to have no advantage over traditional needling techniques except that some patients do not like needles. However, even needles are unlikely to hurt. A consultation lasts for about an hour and if needles are used, they can be kept in for up to 40 minutes. Electrical stimulus can be applied for a few minutes using one or both ears.

How many sessions do I need?

The number of treatments you will need depends on your illness, how long you have had it, and how you react to the sessions. Generally, modern acupuncturists say you should feel some benefit after one treatment.

Which problems can it help?

TCM auricular therapists use it mainly for treating addictions, some respiratory disorders, for relieving labor pains and for pain control in terminal illness. Modern acupuncturists believe it is more comprehensive and can be used on three levels:

- *For local injury such as musculoskeletal problems.*
- *For an energy-system problem, such as those caused by scar tissue after an operation, headaches, migraines and sinus problems.*
- *To control an overall energy dysfunction as in cases of arthritis, gastrointestinal and urino-genital conditions.*

Is it safe?

When practiced by a qualified practitioner auricular therapy in the same way as traditional acupuncture is perfectly safe for both adults and children.

FOR INFORMATION ON HOW TO CHOOSE AN AURICULAR THERAPIST SEE THE DIRECTORY.

SHIATSU & ACUPRESSURE

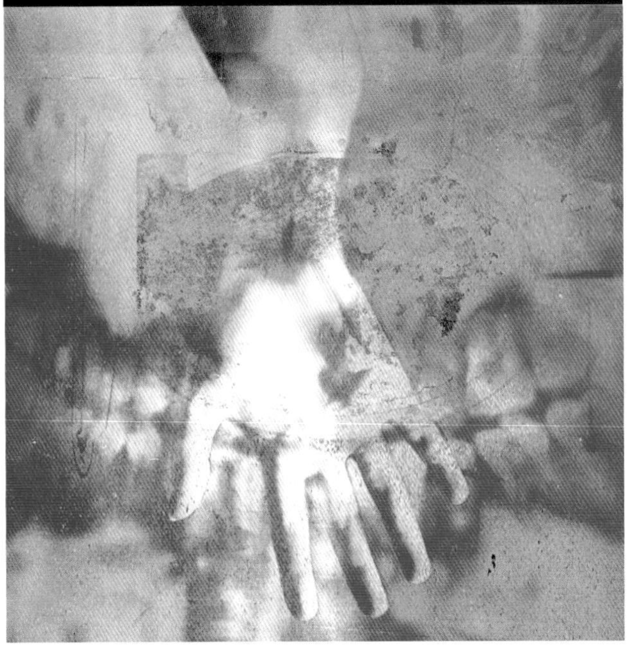

SHIATSU originated in Japan as a holistic therapy for treating the mind, body and spirit. It is very much a 20th century therapy, but one which is closely related to its oriental ancestor called "amma." This ancient massage therapy involved rubbing and pressing on the body to treat common ailments. It evolved alongside acupuncture and Chinese herbalism, but became much more established in Japan around the 16th century. Early this century, practitioners of amma started borrowing knowledge and techniques from osteopathy and chiropractic and combined these with the traditional oriental body work system to develop shiatsu.

What is shiatsu?

Shiatsu is a Japanese word which means "finger pressure." The term is slightly misleading as practitioners use their fingers, palms, elbows, arms, knees and feet to apply pressure to points called "*tsubo*," which are dotted along the body's 12 main energy channels called meridians. The treatment has been described as acupuncture without needles. This is reasonably accurate as both therapies share similar philosophy, principles, diagnostic methods and treatment points. Shiatsu practitioners, however, might argue that shiatsu is more nurturing as it uses therapeutic touch.

How does it work?

Shiatsu works on the body's energy system. Practitioners apply pressure to points or *tsubo* on the meridians to stimulate "*ki*," the Japanese word for Chi or energy. Diagnosis is similar to the Chinese method. There are several strands in the diagnostic process: looking (*Bo-shin*), touching (*Setsu-shin*), asking (*Mon-shin*) and sense diagnosis (*Bun-shin*), which also involves intuition.

Treatment involves different techniques to relieve pain and release the energy blockages causing your particular problem. The therapist treats your whole body using various methods for different areas. For example, he may rotate and manipulate your leg to relieve associated back pain, or use his elbow to stimulate points on the spine that relate to the chest, digestion or circulation problems. He will often rub and apply finger pressure to specific points to open up a blocked meridian and may even walk on the soles of your feet to stimulate the kidney meridian.

What happens in a consultation?

You do not have to undress for treatment, although some parts of your body may be briefly exposed during examination, so wear loose, comfortable clothes. For your treatment practitioners recommend that you refrain from alcohol and do not eat for two hours beforehand. If you have a particular medical condition, bring any medication details. The session usually lasts an hour, with at least 40 minutes being devoted to treatment. The first

SHIATSU AND ACUPRESSURE are treatments similar to acupuncture where pressure points in the body are stimulated, but fingers, palms, elbows, arms, knees and feet are used instead of needles. Different techniques are used to relieve tension, insomnia or back or joint pain.

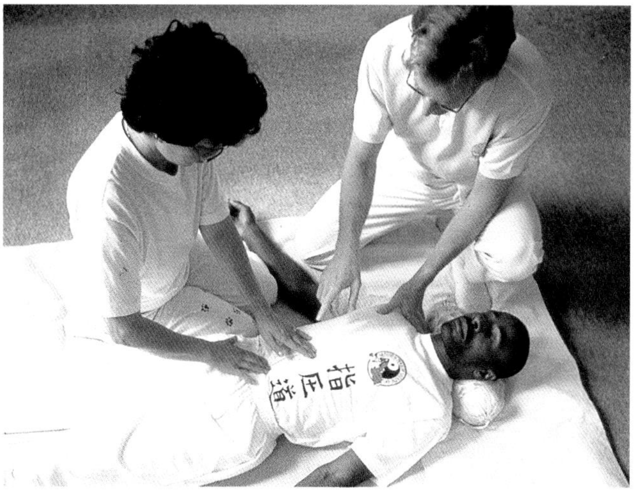

ABOVE: *For shiatsu treatment you lie on a mat on a floor and finger pressure is put on points on your body to produce a relaxing effect.*

appointment starts with the practitioner taking a case history. Practitioners ask questions about:

- *Your current health and medical history.*
- *What type of work you do.*
- *What sort of diet you eat.*
- *Your relationships with friends and family and your lifestyle.*

These facts are needed to discover what is causing your problem. The look and feel of certain parts of the body can also give an indication of underlying problems. A red face, for example, points to problems with circulation and the shoulders give information about the digestive system, the chest and upper back reflect heart and lung energy and your emotional health. In fact, the back and the abdomen are the most important of all. The abdomen or "*hara*" is called "the ocean of *ki*," and is used to diagnose and treat problems in all 12 meridians. Touching the *hara* and other parts of the body gives the practitioner the most detailed information.

Some therapists take readings from the same pulse points on the wrist used by acupuncturists (see Acupuncture pages 10–19) and all feel the muscle and skin tone, for signs of excess or deficient *ki*. They also listen to your breathing and voice.

To arrive at a final diagnosis the practitioner will piece together these different diagnostic strands and then back them up with his basic gut feeling about what he believes to be your health problem.

Most treatment takes place with you lying on a mat. The therapist will work on your body at superficial and deep levels, producing a relaxing sensation often described as "pleasurable pain." Some people feel good after a treatment, others can feel unwell for about 24 hours. This is because shiatsu can trigger a sort of "healing crisis" as toxins are released and *ki* is unblocked. Common symptoms include fatigue, headaches, flu-like symptoms or bowel changes. Try to relax until the symptoms pass, but call your therapist if they persist.

How many sessions do I need?

On average it takes four to eight treatments to clear common problems. But this varies depending on the problem. Chronic (long-term) conditions can require extensive treatment.

Which problems can it help?

Shiatsu improves health generally by relieving stress, calming the nervous system and stimulating the circulatory and immune systems. It is particularly effective for stress-related tension and illnesses, insomnia, back pain, headaches and digestive upsets.

Is it safe?

Shiatsu given by a qualified therapist is safe for everyone and particularly beneficial for pregnant women. Some therapists also treat small children and the elderly. It is not suitable, however, for people with cancer of the blood or lymphatic systems.

Clinical studies (Acupressure)

The use of acupressure has been found in various medical studies to be beneficial in relieving pain and sickness.

In 1986, car factory workers were screened in a study to exclude any with organic disease or infection, and 142 workers with chronic lumbar pain were treated with acupressure daily for 21 days on points along the spine, back and front of legs. A marked improvement was found in 29 percent of patients, 68 percent were cured, while 3.5 percent had no noticeable change. Additional benefits reported were improved sleep. **(5)**

Acupressure was used to treat morning sickness on 350 women attending the Royal Maternity Hospital in Belfast in 1988. They were randomly allocated to three groups, and the severity of morning sickness was recorded daily for four days. The treatment group pressed a wrist acupuncture point, whereas the second group used a pretend acupressure point, and the control group had no treatment. There was much less sickness in the genuine and dummy pressure groups compared with the control group. No adverse side effects were reported in the patients' pregnancies. **(6)** *(For clinical references see How to use this book).*

WHAT IS ACUPRESSURE?

Acupressure is similar to shiatsu in that it involves using finger pressure on acupuncture points throughout the body to stimulate the flow of Chi through the body's energy channels (see Acupuncture pages 10–19). Unlike shiatsu, acupressure involves mostly thumb and fingertip pressure, although it can also incorporate massage along the meridians. In the West the use of acupressure has been largely overshadowed by shiatsu. It is usually incorporated into other therapies such as shiatsu or Chinese massage, or used simply for self-help. There is no central body of acupressure practitioners in Britain.

FOR INFORMATION ON HOW TO CHOOSE A SHIATSU PRACTITIONER SEE THE DIRECTORY.

CHINESE HERBALISM

CHINESE HERBALISM is an ancient traditional medicine that uses different herbs to treat and also prevent physical, mental and emotional ill health in everyone. It can help conditions such as eczema, hay fever and infertility.

CHINESE HERBAL MEDICINE is part of the ancient system of traditional Chinese medicine (TCM), which after 5,000 years of practice in its homeland, has taken the West by storm. Many people, disillusioned with quick-fix Western medicine, are taking advantage of this more sympathetic system. Western medicine is also turning to the East for inspiration. American scientists have shown that the root of the Chinese herb kudzu vine, which is a traditional Chinese treatment for alcoholism, contains chemicals that suppress the desire for alcohol. Western medicine's enthusiasm for herbalism is viewed by the profession as both encouraging but also disappointing. It is encouraging that Chinese medicine is gaining acceptance, but disappointing that the herbs are just being seen as substitute pills.

Scientists are extracting the active ingredients and using them to suppress the symptoms of disease – whereas the Chinese use a combination of whole herbs or whole parts of several herbs to treat the person, not their disease. Consequently, we hear that Chinese herbal medicine is good for particular conditions, skin diseases being one of the most common.

What is Chinese herbalism?

Chinese herbalism involves using herbs to treat and prevent mental, physical and emotional ill health. Together with acupuncture, it forms the bulk of Chinese medical treatment. Although in the West acupuncture is often seen as being more important than herbalism, the number of Chinese doctors who use herbs exclusively is greater than those who use only acupuncture. However, most practitioners combine both therapies to complement each other in the treatment and prevention of illness.

In the Chinese philosophy of the complementary opposites yin and yang, acupuncture is considered yang, because it moves from the outside in, while herbalism is yin because it works from the inside out. Herbalism can support acupuncture treatment, or be used on its own for conditions such as viral infections and blood disorders like anemia or menstrual problems, which can sometimes be better suited to herbal treatment than acupuncture.

Herbs also strengthen those people who are too weak for acupuncture. Acupuncture works with the body's own energy, but very weak patients have little energy with which to work, so the response may not be very good. Herbal treatment, however, adds nourishment to the body. For those who want Chinese treatment but hate needles, herbs also prove invaluable. Traditional Chinese diagnostic techniques determine the cause of ill health and "patterns of disharmony" in the body, and herbs are prescribed to restore harmony to the mind, body, and emotions.

Chinese herbs are imported mostly from mainland China and Taiwan. They are stored in cool, dry places although small amounts are displayed in Chinese pharmacies in glass jars or wooden drawers. Although herbs are dispensed in these pharmacies, the herbalists who work in them are not necessarily qualified to prescribe. The terminology used for Chinese practitioners is often confusing, so you need to distinguish between a Chinese herbal doctor or practitioner and a pharmacist.

A practitioner of Chinese herbal medicine is someone who is trained to diagnose and treat people using herbal remedies, while a herbal pharmacist is someone who dispenses herbs and is not registered to practice herbal medicine.

How does it work?

To understand Chinese medicine you need a basic understanding of the concepts of yin and yang, the eight principles, Chi or energy, and the five elements and their role in maintaining health.

The Chinese believe that each one of us is governed by the opposing, but complementary forces of yin and yang. Yin and yang are the opposites that make the whole, they cannot exist without each other and nothing is ever solely one or the other, there are elements of each within everybody.

RIGHT: At a roadside "pharmacy" this eastern doctor and his wife prepare a herbal remedy.

BELOW: Ginseng is used in Chinese herbal remedies for its stimulating properties.

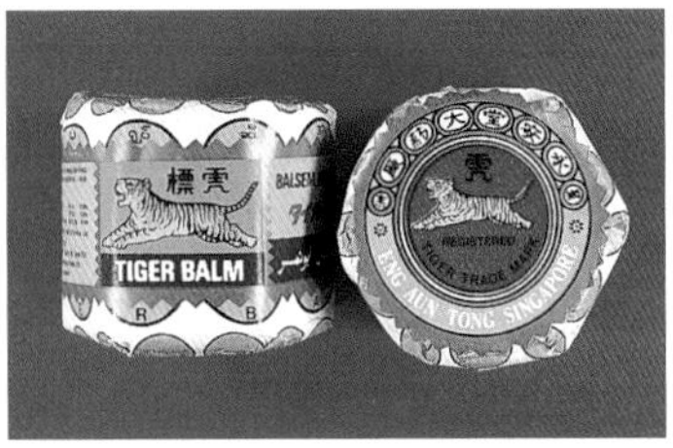

LEFT: Tiger balm is used to relieve headaches and backache.

LEFT: Sun Sze-Miao was the ancient lord of medicinal plants who was revered by the Chinese people.

The tai chi symbol illustrates how yin and yang move into each other with a little yin always within yang and a little yang always within yin. When the two opposing forces are in balance you feel good, but if one force dominates the other, the resulting imbalance can lead to ill health.

This concept of balance affects us through the eight principles, which include yin and yang and more detailed subdivisions of these two, namely cold and heat, internal and external, deficiency and excess. As aspects of yin and yang, the principles apply to every part of us. While they work in harmony you stay healthy, but any imbalance can cause illness. For example, too much heat in the body indicates an excess of yang and can lead to symptoms such as constipation or hot, swollen and painful joints.

Chi is also important to health because it is the energy that binds yin and yang. Together with blood and moisture it flows around the body keeping us healthy. When Chi flows freely, yin, yang and the whole person are in balance. But when it is blocked, stagnant or unbalanced it can lead to illness. Chi flows through meridians. There are 12 major meridians, and numerous other meridians including tiny ones called collaterals which intersect these. Six of the 12 major channels are yin and six are yang. They all relate to and are named after major organs. These are the Lungs, Large intestine, Stomach, Spleen, Heart, Small intestine, Bladder, Kidney, Pericardium (heart protector), San jiao (triple warmer), Gall bladder and Liver. If there is disharmony in a meridian it can affect the corresponding organs. Likewise disharmony in the organ can also disrupt the meridian. For example, toothache in the upper gums can come from some disharmony in the stomach meridian as this meridian runs through the upper gums. Like acupuncture, herbalism works directly on the meridians and their associated organs to rebalance yin and yang by helping Chi flow smoothly along the meridian pathways, thereby restoring harmony to the whole person.

The concepts of yin, yang and Chi are further refined into the theory of the five elements. The Chinese believe that individuals, like nature, are governed by the five elements of metal, water, wood, fire and earth. Each element is associated with a particular season and each has its role to play in the body, in the same way that each of the seasons has a role in nature. All the organs and emotions are related to the five elements (see Acupuncture page 13). When Chi flows smoothly between the elements they stay balanced, but if one becomes imbalanced this flow is disrupted and may result in physical, mental or emotional ill health.

Through detailed diagnosis the Chinese herbalist can identify energy imbalances. For example, a diagnosis such as "kidney yang deficiency with exterior heat in the stomach meridian" involves details about yang, deficiency, heat and exterior, which are four of the eight principles; kidney and stomach, which refer to organs and meridians and also to the five elements, where kidney is water and the stomach is earth. A combination of herbs would be prescribed to rectify these disharmonies.

The causes of disharmony include internal, external and miscellaneous influences such as emotional problems, stress, eating habits, poor diet, environmental factors. The environmental factors are what the Chinese call the six pernicious influences: wind, dryness, cold, heat or fire, dampness, and summer heat.

How herbs can restore balance

Herbs are prescribed to exert a specific effect on the meridian responsible for the imbalance thereby rebalancing Chi and the associated element. The effect of a herb on the meridian depends on its properties. The various causes of disharmony result in conditions such as deficient or stagnant Chi or blood, excess of cold or heat or dampness and so on. Herbs have specific properties such as warming, damp dispelling, wind dispelling, blood regulating and Chi regulating, which means they can restore warmth to cold Chi, move stagnant Chi, or slow raging Chi, and restore the body to balance.

They are usually defined by their properties and how they work in the body. For example, zhi mu or Anemarrhena rhizome, is a cold herb or antipyrectic (anti-heat) which would be prescribed for someone with a high temperature in a dosage to reduce the temperature without making the patient too cold.

Herbs also have their own particular tastes, each of which affects a different organ and element, as illustrated in the five elements table (see Acupuncture page 13). For example, sweet flavors are believed to tonify the spleen because sweet is the taste associated with the earth element which governs the spleen. Sour flavors, on the other hand, are often prescribed to soothe the liver because this taste relates to the liver and both are governed by the wood element. The herbs are never prescribed alone but in combinations. Sometimes they are mixed together to counteract any side effects from a particularly strong herb.

Prescribing, however, is a minor part of Chinese herbalism; diagnosis is the real herbalist's skill. He must know what individual signs and symptoms to look for and how much emphasis to place on them to diagnose what the Chinese call "a pattern of disharmony." Each symptom is useless by itself, it is the pattern that they make together that is significant. This system of looking at the symptoms in the context of the whole is why herbs are prescribed for the person, not the illness. Attention to detail, however, is imperative so the Chinese herbalists use the four examinations of looking, listening and smelling, asking, and touching to diagnose patterns of disharmony.

What happens in a consultation?

The consultation and diagnosis is similar to that given by a TCM acupuncturist except that you do not need to undress (see Acupuncture pages 10–19). Chinese herbalists' consulting rooms sometimes share clinic space with a herbal dispensary, which can look a bit like an old-fashioned pharmacy, and your herbal prescription is dispensed from here as you leave. Other practitioners, however, dispense the herbs themselves. The consulting room itself will probably be equipped for both acupuncture treatment and herbal prescribing. When you enter the consulting room the herbalist will immediately begin his looking examination, probably without you realizing it.

Looking: This examination is the first of the four procedures. The practitioner will note your general appearance, your size and shape and general demeanor. He will check the color of your face and examine your tongue – its color, coating and condition. Close examination of your face and posture are important in revealing the state of the Shen or spirit. Shen is the power behind your personality, it guides the emotions and rules over all the organs. The eyes reveal the state of Shen so the practitioner will take a look at your eyes. If they are bright and shiny it is a sign that the Shen is in harmony, but blank lusterless eyes show disharmony of spirit. The color of your face is also significant: a white face indicates a cold disharmony and is linked to an imbalance in the metal element, a yellowish complexion is related to dampness and the earth element; while a red face is a sign of too much heat and points to an imbalance in the fire element.

A patient's symptoms are useless in themselves, it is the pattern that they make together that is significant.

The practitioner will then look at your tongue. Tongue diagnosis and pulse taking form the most important part of the examination. Chinese herbalists treat the tongue and its coating as two separate elements in the diagnosis. A normal tongue should be pale red and moist, which is a sign that Chi and blood are flowing smoothly. If you are sick, a healthy-looking tongue is a sign that your illness has caused no long-term damage and that you should recover well. The tongue coating should always be white, moist and thin enough to be transparent. A coating that is too thin is a sign of deficiency in the body, while a thick coating is a sign of excess. Color is also very important as is the shape of the tongue and how it moves.

Listening and smelling: The herbalist will listen to your breathing patterns, your speech and your cough if you have one. Shortness of breath usually suggests deficiency and loss of voice would point to pernicious influences. Your voice can help the practitioner diagnose an element imbalance. For example, a shouting voice is a sign of a wood imbalance, which can point to liver or gall bladder problems and can also show itself emotionally as inappropriate anger, while a laughing voice indicates a fire imbalance, which can relate to heart or circulation problems and can show its emotional side as hysteria.

Asking: Like all therapists the Chinese herbalist will ask you questions about yourself, your lifestyle and your health. He will want to know about your home, work and relationships. He will also want to know your medical history, your symptoms, any pain you have had, sleep patterns, sensations of hot and cold, dizziness, eating habits, and toilet habits. Cold and heat relate to yin and yang respectively, perspiration indicates the state of Chi and the type of pain points to its cause. For example, chest pain is a sign of disharmony in the heart and lungs. The quality of pain is also important. If the pain is relieved by touch it suggests deficiency, whereas pain that is worse after eating suggests excess.

Touching: This is the last examination. The herbalist may palpate your body where there is pain such as your back or abdomen, and will touch your skin if you have a rash, but more importantly, he will take your pulses. He will test three pulse positions in each wrist with the index, middle and third finger of one hand. Using a combination of light, moderate and heavy pressure he will look for 28 different pulse qualities. Pulses are described as empty, full, choppy, sinking, large and so on, with each type relating to a particular problem. A large pulse, for example, can suggest excess heat in the stomach, while a sinking pulse can be a sign of internal disharmony.

This incredibly detailed diagnostic procedure will take about an hour and maybe longer. Some Chinese herbalists will prescribe herbs at the end of your first consultation, give you patent (ready-made) remedies as pills or they may prescribe a mixture of concentrated herbal powders. You may, however, leave your first consultation empty-handed and return a week later for a mini check-up and to receive your herbs. Your herbal prescription will be aimed at balancing your mind and body, although you may also be given something else to alleviate any particularly distressing symptoms that you are experiencing.

Your prescription will be tailored to your needs and its strength will be determined by your age and the severity and duration of your illness. One pack of herbs, containing a mixture of leaves, stems, seeds and bark, usually lasts for one day, but to reduce cost and the effort of boiling up the herbs, some practitioners will give a pack to last two or three days, rarely longer. From the one pack you will be able to make two doses of herbal tea. You will be told how much water to use and how to add the herbs. You make the tea in two boilings at the intervals advised by the herbalist. Some herbs need to be soaked first. They will make enough tea to fill two mugs and your herbalist will give your instructions about when to drink them. Generally speaking, you should not eat for an hour before or after drinking the tea. You will probably be asked to return a week later. Each time you return, the herbalist will carry out a mini check-up.

RIGHT: The time-consuming task of chopping up herbs is essential in the preparation of all the different types of herbal medicines.

FAR RIGHT: Here in a Chinese dispensary, a girl is precisely weighing out a special herbal preparation.

How many sessions do I need?

It is difficult to say. Serious or chronic (long-term) illnesses, especially those that have been suppressed by years of drug treatment will need several weeks of treatment to show any improvement, and maybe months for any significant change. However, it is possible to notice improvements after a week's treatment, especially with related symptoms such as insomnia.

Which problems can it help?

The World Health Organization (WHO) has published a list of ailments that can benefit from Chinese herbalism. Numerous health problems from arthritis to depression, eczema, hay fever,

PATENT CHINESE HERBAL REMEDIES FOR MINOR AILMENTS

These remedies are recommended for short-term use only. If you do not see an improvement within a week, stop using them and consult a practitioner.

Burns

Remedy: *Jing Wan Hung ointment*
Properties: *Stops pain, reduces inflammation, clears heat, promotes healing. Excellent for burns. Can also help bedsores.*

Colds and flu

Remedy: *Yin Qiao Jie Du Pian (Honeysuckle and forsythia febrifugal pills)*
Properties: *Expels wind-heat. Best for colds and flu in first few days when you feel hot, have a sore throat, sneezing and catarrh.*
Remedy: *Tong Xuan Li Fei Wan*
Properties: *Expels cold and wind. Best for colds and flu in first few days when you feel chilled and achy, sneezing, maybe watery catarrh.*

Coughs and bronchitis

Remedy: *Qing Qi Hua Tan Wan (clear breathing and transform phlegm pills)*
Properties: *Clears phlegm and heat from the lungs, stops coughing. Take the remedy for chest congestion, a cough and coughing up thick yellow phlegm. Symptoms may be acute (short-term) or chronic (long-term) and can be accompanied by fever. Stop taking if you become thirsty.*
Remedy: *Chuan Bei Pi Pa Lu (Fritillaria and loquat extract) (cough syrup)*
Properties: *Clears phlegm and heat from the lungs, stops coughing. Use for all coughs which produces thick phlegm.*

Digestive disturbances

Remedy: *Huo Xiang Zheng Qi Wan (Herba agastachis pills)*
Properties: *Regulates digestive system Chi, clears cold and damp. For acute (short-term) attacks of nausea, vomiting and diarrhea with abdominal pain, especially when there are chills. If no improvement within a day, seek professional advice.*

Menstrual problems

Remedies: *Dang Gui Pian (Angelica tea), Shi Chuan Da Bu Wan (Ten flavor tea), Wu Ji Rai Feng Wan (white phoenix pills)*
Properties: *Supplements Chi and blood. There may be many causes of menstrual problems. For persistent problems, consult a practitioner. Dang Gui Pian is good for menstrual cramps.*

infertility, sciatica, herpes, insomnia, PMS and vaginitis appear on that extensive list, with some surprising entries such as cerebral palsy, impotence, diabetes and strokes.

Is it safe?

Chinese herbs are available over the counter, but apart from patent remedies for minor ailments, you should not buy them without a prescription from a qualified practitioner who has made a full diagnosis. Some herbs are not safe for public use, or are safe only in specific doses. When prescribed by a qualified Chinese herbalist, the remedies are usually suitable for everyone.

However, there have been a few rare problems with Chinese herbs. Often these have been because the herbs have been prescribed by non-qualified practitioners, in non-traditional ways, or can be linked to poor quality control. These problems can be avoided by consulting a fully trained and qualified practitioner. Very rarely someone, perhaps one person in 10,000, experiences an allergic-type reaction to the herbs (particularly those used for skin diseases). If you feel unwell or have flu-like symptoms, nausea or diarrhea while taking the herbs, stop taking them immediately and contact your practitioner. Because this rare allergic-type reaction affects the liver, you should tell your practitioner if you have ever suffered from a liver disease such as jaundice or hepatitis. A good practitioner will always be available if you need to contact him.

A practitioner registered with the Register of Chinese Herbal Medicine will be fully informed and will follow detailed guidelines and a code of practice produced by the Register. Remember Chinese herbal remedies are prescribed for the individual. Do not ever assume that a remedy which has been prescribed for a friend or partner will be right for you.

Clinical studies

Chinese herbalism has been used in several studies to help with the treatment of various ailments and diseases.

A study at Long Hua Hospital in Shanghai in 1991, involved 76 women with endometriosis who took pills that were made mainly from rhubarb, a plant used in Chinese herbalism to clean the blood and improve circulation. In four out of five women the treatment worked. There was also about 67 percent reduction in pelvic pain and a 72 percent reduction in intercourse pain. (**7**)

When used to treat AIDS, traditional Chinese medicine aims to strengthen the immune system which has been debilitated by the HIV virus. Western medicine, on the other hand, aims to kill off the HIV virus itself. However, the use of various Chinese Herbal medicines in China and Tanzania with 158 AIDS patients over three years until 1995 proved effective in reducing symptoms in almost 40 percent of cases. They can also be used to reduce the side effects of Western anti-HIV treatments. A combination of the two approaches seems to prove most effective. (**8**) (*For clinical references see How to use this book*).

FOR INFORMATION ON HOW TO CHOOSE A CHINESE HERBALIST SEE THE DIRECTORY.

AYURVEDIC MEDICINE

Over 3,000 years ago the great sages or seers of ancient India discovered "Veda" the knowledge of how our world works. Contained within Veda were the secrets of sickness and health. These they organized into a system called Ayurveda, a Sanskrit word meaning: "the science of life." Ayurveda is a combination of science and philosophy, which details the physical, mental, emotional and spiritual components necessary for holistic health. The sophistication of this system is apparent in the famous, ancient

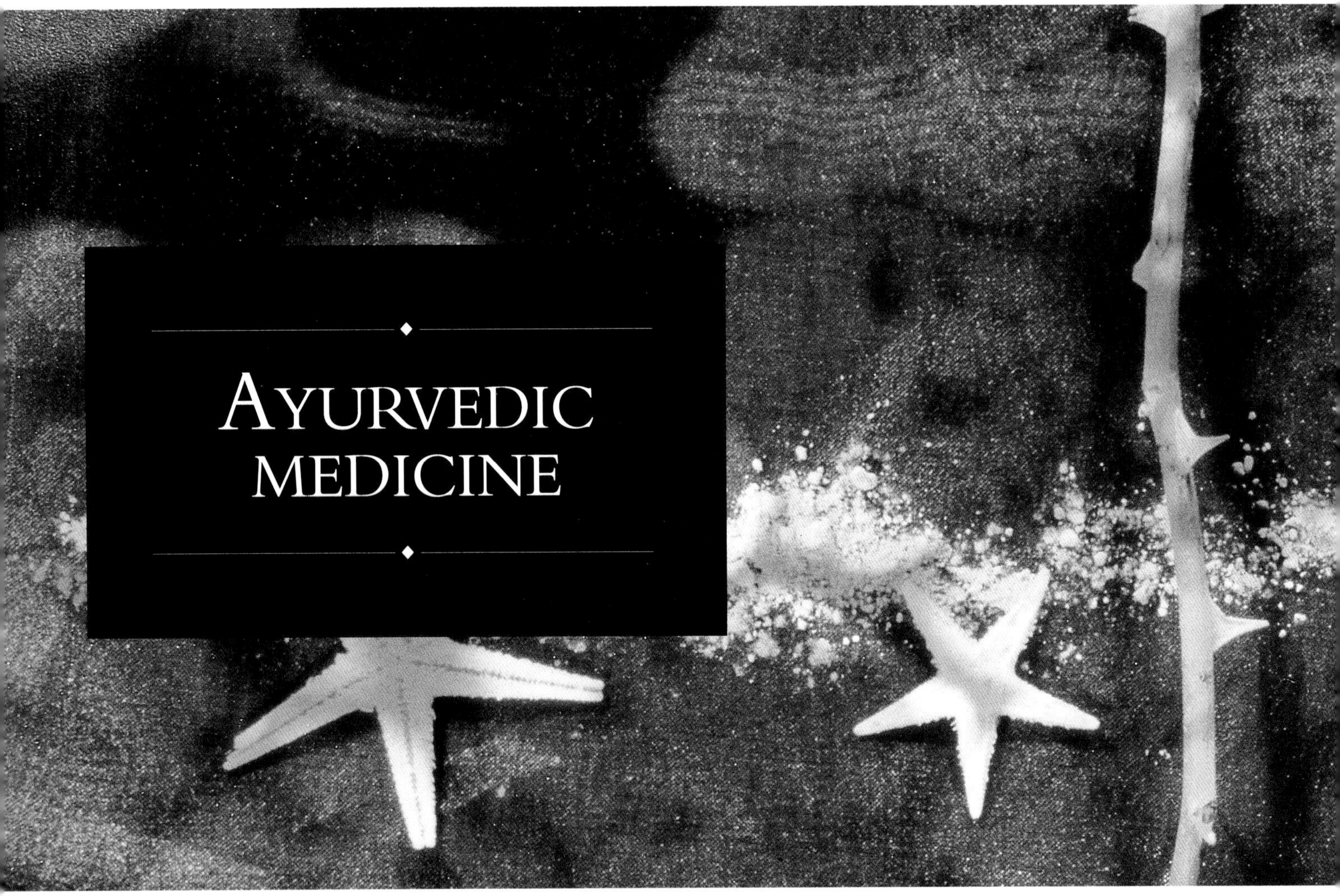

Ayurvedic medicine is a traditional Eastern medicine mainly practiced in India and Sri Lanka. It is a complete healthcare system and involves detoxification, diet, exercise, use of herbs and techniques to improve mental and emotional health.

Ayurvedic text, the *Charaka samhita*. This classic of internal medicine, written 2,000 years before the invention of the microscope, describes the body as being composed of cells. It lists 20 different microscopic organisms that can cause disease and describes how disease spreads.

Another of the texts, *Susrutha samhita*, offers guidance on surgery, surgical equipment, suturing (stitching) and the importance of hygiene during and after an operation. Detailed medical information is teamed with common sense advice on how to live a healthy and meaningful life. In Vedic philosophy our lives become meaningful when we strive to fulfill our potential, but that cannot be achieved without basic good health. Most modern Ayurvedic practitioners work with traditional beliefs and practices, although some practitioners in the West have adapted these to make them more acceptable to Western thinking.

What is Ayurvedic medicine?

Ayurvedic medicine is the traditional system of medicine practiced in India and Sri Lanka. Like traditional Chinese medicine, or Western medical practices, Ayurveda is a complete and complex system of healthcare. As such, its many components – detoxification, diet, exercise, herbs, and techniques to improve mental and emotional health – work together to contribute to a way of life rather than an occasional treatment.

The fundamental belief in Ayurveda is that everything within the universe, including ourselves, is composed of energy or "*prana.*" We may look like solid structures of bone, muscles and tissues, but this appearance belies the fact that we are simply bundles of vibrating energy. Consequently, we are forever changing in ways that are either positive or negative. To ensure that most of the changes are positive, we must live in a way that encourages energy balance. Energy controls every cell, thought, emotion and action, so every aspect of our lives affects the quality of energy and our health. Ayurvedic practitioners recognize that there is no one prescription for health that caters to everyone. The balance of energies that contribute to good health in your body may lead to sickness in someone else. In Ayurvedic medicine every person must be treated individually. The practitioner's skill lies in identifying each person's constitution, diagnosing the causes of imbalance and treating them accordingly.

How does it work?

Your individual constitution and how it relates to your energies is the key to understanding Ayurvedic medicine. A good constitution is your best defense against illness. If you are functioning well, disease cannot take hold, but when your constitution is weakened you can get ill. Ayurveda aims to prevent disease by working with your body rather than trying to change it.

Each of us has a unique constitution, determined by the balance of three vital energies in the body, known as the three doshas or "tridoshas." The three doshas are known by their Sanskrit names of *vátha*, *pitha* and *kapha*. Everyone's constitution is governed by these doshas in varying degrees, but each of us is also controlled by one or possibly two dominant doshas, so that you are classed as either a *vátha* type, *pitha* type or *kapha* type, or a *vátha/pitha*, *pitha/kapha* and so on.

Your dosha not only determines your constitution, and the illnesses to which you might succumb, but it also determines your temperament, the color of your hair, your tendency to put on weight, and which type of foods you should eat. In short, your dosha affects every aspect of your everyday life.

"*prakruthi*" state, which means that you are born with levels of the three doshas that are right for you. But, as we go through life, diet, environment, stress, trauma and injury cause the doshas to become imbalanced, a state known as the "*vikruthi*" state. When this imbalance becomes excessively high or low it can lead to ill health. Ayurvedic practitioners prescribe treatment to restore each individual to their "*prakruthi*" state.

Your constitution is not something that you can change, nor should you want to. The object is to learn to understand it and

ABOVE: A selection of herbal remedies on display at a roadside in Kathmandu, Nepal.

ABOVE RIGHT AND RIGHT: Herbs are an important part of the Ayurvedic therapy. They are normally used in the detoxification processes and may also be prescribed as a herbal remedy in liquid or dried herb form.

ABOVE: This Indian sadhu is collecting herbs for the local Ayurvedic doctor at Gangotri in the Himalayas.

live in a way that emphasizes its positive aspects and reduces it negative effects. This is not always easy as we tend to be attracted to foods or activities that lead to imbalance.

For example, *kapha* people who can be quite large and rounded often overindulge in *kapha* foods which include sugar, hard cheeses, dairy produce and fried foods. Consequently, their *kapha* dosha becomes imbalanced, they put on weight easily, and can suffer diseases related to a fatty diet. Working on the principle that "like increases like," *kapha* people should attempt to maintain balanced *kapha* levels by eating more *vátha* and *pitha* foods such as hot and spicy dishes.

In Ayurveda, all ill health is related to disturbances in the three doshas. The doshic imbalances affect other body factors, culminating in imbalances that cause disease. These other factors include the five elements (*panchabhuta*), the ten pairs of qualities (*gunas*), *agni*, the three *malas*, and the seven tissues (*sapha dhathu*).

You keep healthy when all three doshas work in balance. Each one has its role to play in the body. For example, *vátha* is the driving force; it relates mainly to the nervous system and the body's energy. *Pitha* is fire; it relates to the metabolism, digestion, enzymes, acid and bile. *Kapha* is linked to water in the mucous membranes, phlegm, moisture, fat, and lymphatics. The balance of the three doshas depends on many factors, principally good diet and exercise, maintaining good digestion, healthy elimination of body wastes and balanced emotional and spiritual health.

Your constitution is determined by your parents' doshas at the time of your conception and each individual is born in the

The five elements

The elements are ether (space), air, fire, water and earth and each one is created out of the other. All five elements exist in all things, including ourselves. Ether corresponds to the spaces in the body:

Palmer located the cause of the problem at the fourth thoracic vertebra of the spine and then set out to cure it through a precise system of spinal manipulation. Palmer achieved this objective, and succeeded not only in correcting Harvey Lillard's hearing but in founding a completely new branch of medicine. The medical establishment, however, was less than enthusiastic about Palmer's new therapy and Palmer then served time in prison for practicing medicine without a license. Those early days of trouble and ridicule served as a harsh apprenticeship for a budding profession, but chiropractic now ranks as the third largest primary healthcare profession in the world.

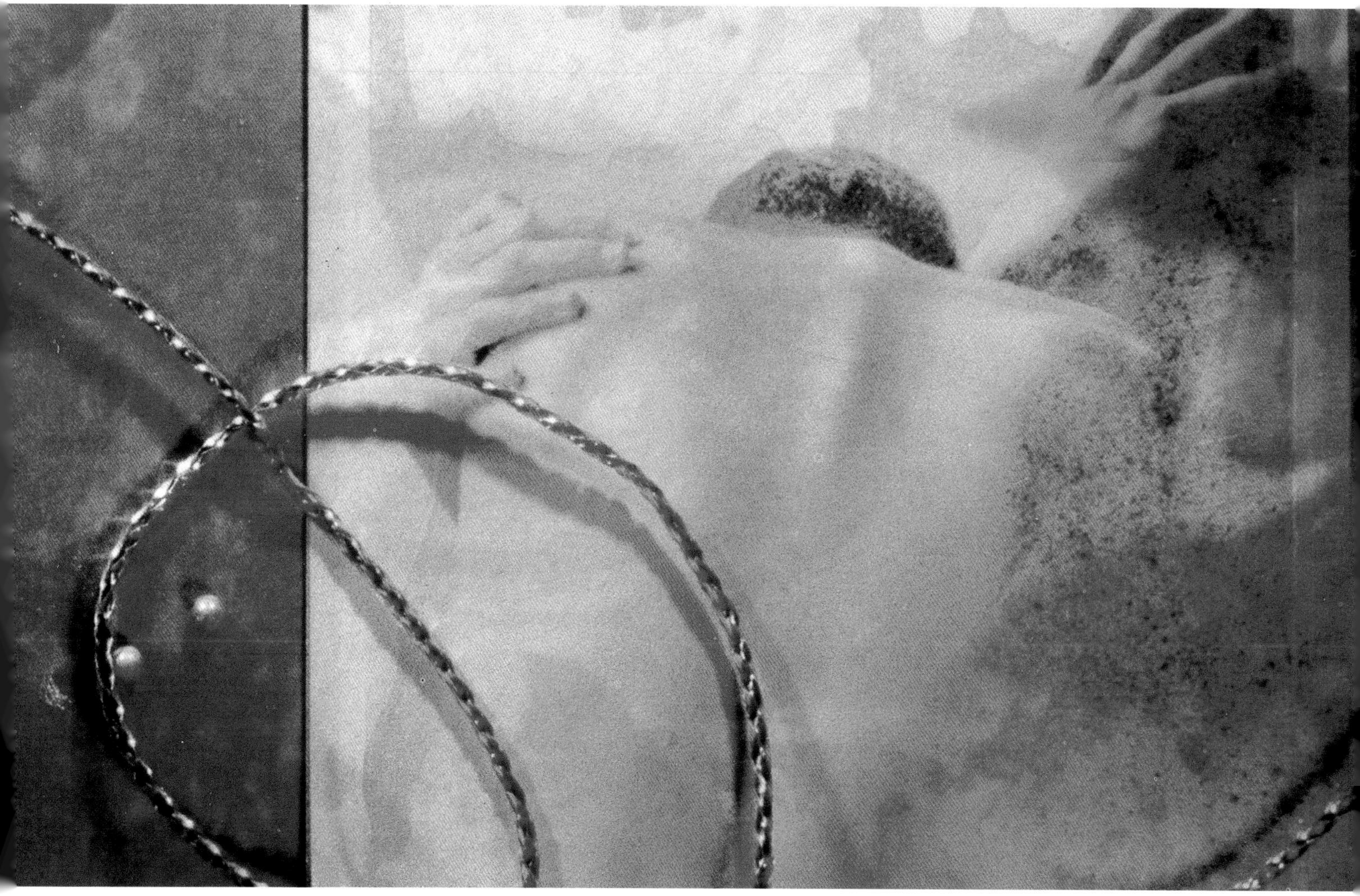

What is chiropractic?

Chiropractic is a therapy which works on the musculo-skeletal system of the body, focusing mainly on the spine and its effects on the nervous system. The term musculo-skeletal refers to the body's structure: the bones, joints, muscles, ligaments and tendons that give the body its form. Through a series of special examination and manipulative techniques, chiropractors can diagnose and treat numerous disorders associated with the musculo-skeletal system. The emphasis chiropractors put on the spine has led many people to believe that the therapy is useful only for treating back pain. This is a gross underestimation of the power and range of chiropractic. In fact, skilled therapists can treat every structural problem from headaches caused by misalignment through to ankle pain – they can even adjust the three small bones found in the inner ear!

The spine itself plays more than a purely structural role in the body. It is the bony structure that surrounds the spinal cord. The brain and spinal cord make up the central nervous system and give rise to nerves which spread to all parts of the body. Part of the central nervous system is called the autonomic nervous system, which controls involuntary body functions. The bony structures of the spine protect the central nervous system and the autonomic nervous system which, in turn, is linked to most body functions. Consequently any damage, disease or structural change of the spine can affect the health of the rest of the body. Through spine manipulation, chiropractors can improve bone structural problems such as sciatica or ones relating to sports injuries, but can also help with other conditions which you may not think of as being related to the body's structure. For example, asthma can be helped by easing tension in the chest muscles.

How does it work?

Chiropractic is a complicated and highly specialized therapy that may be best understood in terms of its principal aim, systems of analysis and techniques. It is similar in theory and practice to osteopathic treatment (see Osteopathy pages 38–45) and can help with similar problems. But it differs from osteopathic treatment in several ways: chiropractic concentrates on specific adjustment, manipulating one joint at a time, while osteopaths can stretch several joints at a time using "long lever" techniques. Chiropractors may also use X-rays as part of the diagnosis, while osteopaths rarely do. As already mentioned, spinal manipulation is fundamental to chiropractic treatment, but it is not central to osteopathic treatment.

BELOW: Chiropractic treatment concentrates on the musculo-skeletal system and focuses on the spine.

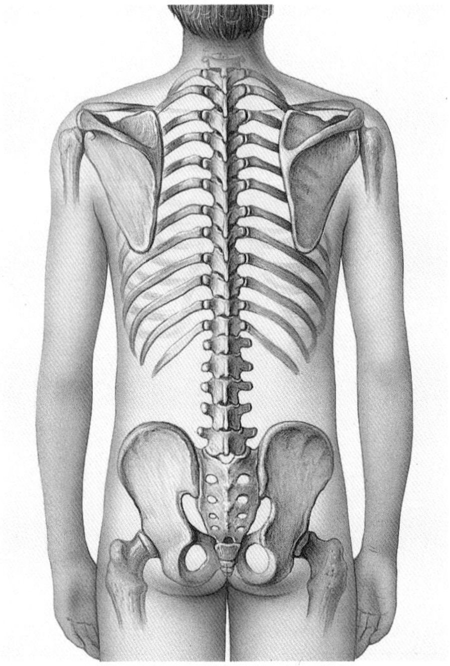

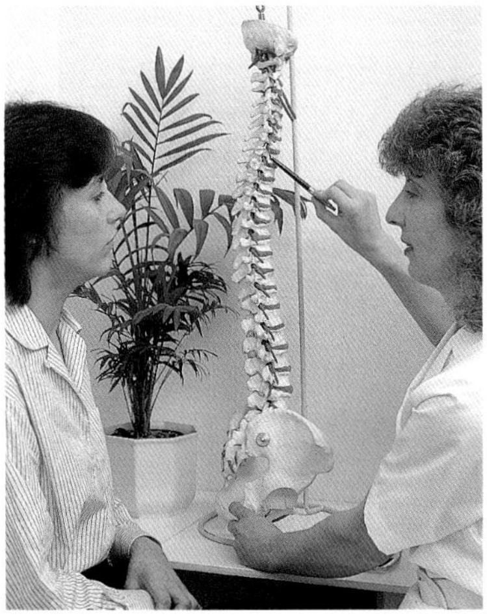

LEFT: When you first visit a chiropractor she will discuss your problem, often using a spinal skeleton to explain what she is going to do.

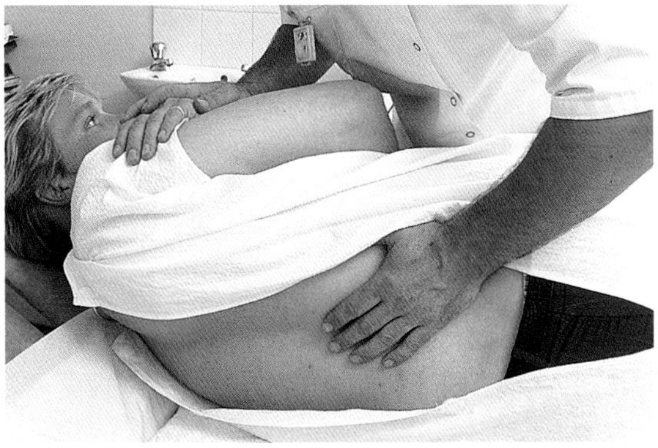

ABOVE: Direct thrust techniques are often used by chiropractors to make the necessary adjustments to the spine.

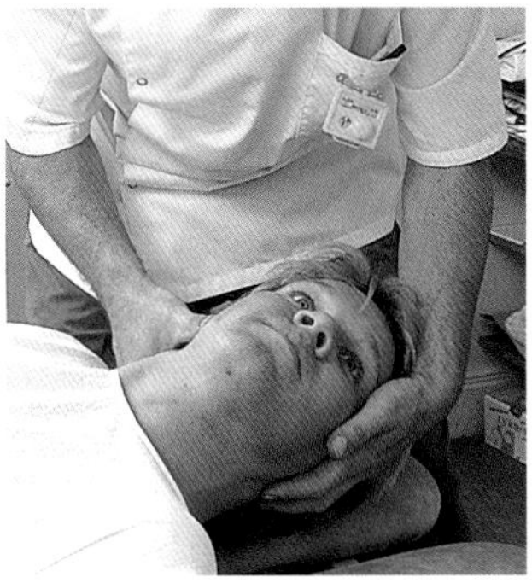

ABOVE: To make a correction to a patient's neck the chiropractor will use his fingers or his wrist bone to apply the pressure.

It is every chiropractor's aim to restore the spine to its natural, perfectly functioning state as appropriate to each individual. Chiropractic treatment can benefit both structural and non-structural illnesses because manipulating the spine and musculo-skeletal system not only restores mobility to the body structure but also takes the pressure off the nervous system which connects the spine with all the major organs of the body.

Chiropractors diagnose problems through observation and palpation (hands-on examination). X-rays are used to pinpoint the area of damage, assess the extent of the injury, and decide if chiropractic treatment is suitable. They aim to restore the spine and musculo-skeletal system to normal function by using a variety of special chiropractic manipulative techniques. Whereas mobilization involves moving a joint as far as it will comfortably go within its normal range of movement, manipulation involves shifting it even further with any one of a number of different techniques. Where manipulation is involved, the chiropractor will use the correct amount of force at the correct speed to thrust into the spinal joint to the correct depth. There are around 150 different chiropractic techniques, the most common of which can be classified as:

Direct thrust techniques: These are rapid, forceful movements, also known as high-velocity thrusts, which are central to chiropractic treatment. The chiropractor will make contact with different parts of the hand on the specific joint he wishes to adjust (or manipulate). The part of the hand used varies with the part of the spine being adjusted. For example, the chiropractor will use the middle or base of the index finger when adjusting the neck, or will use the bony area of the wrist bone when adjusting the thoracic area or lumbar spine. The chiropractor then takes the joint to its extreme range of movement and applies a direct high-velocity movement into the joint to make the right adjustment. This may be accompanied by a loud cracking noise when the joint moves; this is due to the gas bubbles in the fluid bursting between the joint surfaces.

Indirect thrust techniques: These are used where the previous method may be too uncomfortable. With this method it takes a few minutes to gently stretch the joint over a pad, towel or wedge-shaped block.

Soft tissue techniques: These manipulations are often used before an adjustment to reduce the muscle spasm and to relax the joints to allow easier adjustments. They are also commonly used to release "trigger points," which frequently become tender with musculo-skeletal conditions and can feel like having a trapped nerve. These trigger points are similar to acupuncture or reflex points and when the tension is released will help reduce the pain and discomfort as part of the overall treatment.

What happens in a consultation?

Your initial appointment will last on average 30–45 minutes. That time will be divided between discussion, examination, diagnosis and possibly treatment, although that may not begin until your second visit. Like any other form of holistic treatment, it is important for the chiropractor to know as much as possible about you and your particular problem, so that he can diagnose and treat you as effectively as possible. Consequently, the consultation will begin with the chiropractor taking a detailed case history. He will ask you why you have come to him, where you feel pain, when it started, how long you have had it and if you have had similar pain before. He will want to know the exact location of the pain and if it moves when you sit, stand, bend, walk, or lie down. Details of your sleeping pattern, your diet and exercise routine and history of illness or injury are also important. The nature of your work and whether it involves a lot of driving, lifting or sitting also forms a typical part of the case history. The practitioner will then pursue certain avenues of questioning, depending on your answers to these initial questions.

The chiropractor will then want to examine you. For this you will need to strip down to your underwear, although women can wear a back-opening treatment gown, which allows the practitioner to observe the spine for tension, curvatures, abnormalities or postural problems. When you have undressed the chiropractor will carry out a series of routine medical tests. These are similar to those your doctor would do. They involve taking your pulse, testing blood pressure, checking reflexes and possibly taking a blood or urine sample. Such tests can help the chiropractor with his diagnosis.

The aim of the treatment is to restore the individual's spine to normal function.

His next step will be to examine your spine while you sit, stand and lie on his treatment couch. While you are lying down, he may ask you to raise your leg, then ask you to stand up and bend your spine forward and backward as far as you comfortably can and then bend from left to right. You may also have to walk across the room so that he can note your posture. Chiropractors call these the "gross movements." Simply by carefully watching these movements a practitioner can spot irregularities in the way you use your spine.

To find out exactly where the spine is malfunctioning he will ask you to sit on a stool while he palpates or touches the spine, first using "motion palpation" to move each part of the spine through its normal range of movements until he can locate where the joints are either not moving freely enough or are moving more than they ought. Then while you are still sitting in a relaxed position, or lying on the couch, he will check the spine and surrounding muscles and tissues; this is called "static palpation." He may also motion palpate the joints, which involves applying slight pressure to the joints to assess how much they move while you remain still. This sort of spinal examination is essential in diagnosing your problem and in determining which treatment techniques would work best. The chiropractor may then complete the examination by taking X-rays. X-rays form a very

McTIMONEY CHIROPRACTIC

This particular branch of chiropractic follows the teachings of John McTimoney (1914–1980). McTimoney was a silversmith, engineer and illustrator, who was so delighted with the chiropractic treatment he received after he damaged his arm in a fall that he gave up his career to retrain in chiropractic. He trained originally in Palmer's method and then went on to develop the method to treat the joints of the whole body rather than just the spine. The McTimoney philosophy and method is similar in many ways to straight chiropractic. It works on the structure of the body with the emphasis on the spine and the nervous system, but it also takes into consideration all the other areas, such as arms, legs, hands and feet, thorax and skull, where joints can go out of alignment. Practitioners take a thorough case history, observe your posture and check your spine and the angle of your pelvis. In most of us the pelvis is out of alignment, often giving the appearance to the practitioner that one leg is longer than the other, although in fact it rarely is.

McTimoney chiropractic is a gentle form of chiropractic treatment, that involves manipulation by the practitioner's hands only. Practitioners tend not have X-ray facilities on the premises. If your practitioner thinks you need an X-ray he will refer you back to your doctor or to a hospital. The McTimoney chiropractor's specialism is a type of swift thrust known as the "toggle recoil" technique. This is a technique which was introduced by B.J. Palmer (D.D. Palmer's son) and which is used to some degree by most other chiropractors, but not to the extent to which McTimoney chiropractors use it. To perform the toggle recoil, the practitioner uses one hand as a "hammer" and the other as a "nail." He uses the "hammer" to push and twist the "nail" near the joint in the desired direction with one swift, painless movement. This effectively frees the joint and eases the tension in the surrounding muscle. A McTimoney chiropractor will also examine and adjust all the other joints in your body as well as your spine, if necessary, aiming for a balanced skeletal alignment.

When to see a McTimoney chiropractor

A McTimoney chiropractor can help with any of the problems with which you would normally consult a chiropractor. You would choose a McTimoney chiropractor if you preferred to be treated by a chiropractor who looked at your whole body at every treatment, rather than just your spine.

important part of the diagnostic process and most chiropractors have facilities on the premises.

Not everyone needs to have an X-ray, but it can help to pinpoint the problem and reveal the extent of damage. It also helps the practitioner to decide which techniques would work best or if he should treat you at all. If the X-ray revealed a tumor or fracture, for example, chiropractic treatment would not be suitable. X-rays are taken in a weight-bearing position, so that the practitioner can see what your spine looks like under normal,

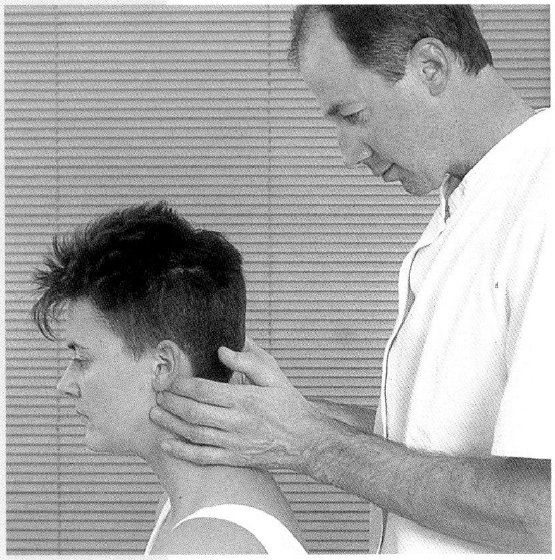

LEFT: McTimoney chiropractic is a gentle treatment that assesses the whole body. Here the practitioner looks at the position of the atlas bone supporting the skull.

RIGHT: A McTimoney practitioner looks at the alignment of a patient's sacrum before starting any corrective treatment.

working circumstances. If your problem is in your lower back you would probably stand for the X-ray, whereas it would be best to sit for a neck X-ray. If the examination reveals a "subluxation," then the chiropractor will treat you. "Subluxation" is the term used for defective joint movement and its effect on the nervous system and surrounding structures.

Treatment may involve soft tissue work and then manipulation, but the type of techniques used will be tailored to suit you. They can sometimes feel uncomfortable, but the type of treatment and the amount of pressure used is worked out to your individual needs. Often very little force is necessary. No chiropractor wants you to suffer unnecessarily, so he will treat you according to your problem, age, build, general health and pain levels, often using massage and "trigger points" to loosen knots and to warm up tense, painful muscles. Ice treatments may also be used to reduce pain and any swelling that is apparent.

For the manipulation and mobilization treatment you will be asked to sit, lie down or stand depending on the parts of the body that are being treated. For example, your neck can be treated while you are sitting down, and although the lower back area can also be treated while you are sitting, it is more common for you to lie down. Each adjustment takes only seconds to complete. For each maneuver you will be asked to breathe deeply and as it is completed you may hear a cracking noise as already mentioned. Hearing this is often the worst part of the treatment.

The type of treatment you receive and how often you need it will depend on whether your problem is acute (short-term) or chronic (long-term), or somewhere in between. Acute problems can vary a great deal. For example, a sports injury can be treated relatively quickly and easily. The practitioner may see you two or three times in one week and then do a check-up a week later. A prolapsed disc in the back may take much longer to sort out. You

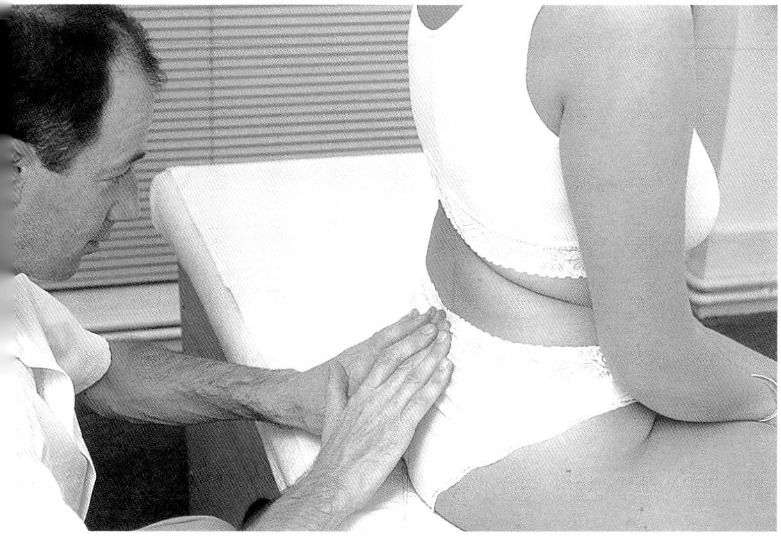

might find you need 10–12 treatments over a period of six to eight weeks. Chronic cases, where a patient may have been suffering for years with a problem such as sciatica or a frozen shoulder, will take much longer to treat. It is unlikely that chronic problems would be treated at your first visit, treatment would probably start on the second visit after the chiropractor has had a chance to study your X-rays. If your problem is somewhere between acute and chronic, the chiropractor may carry out some pain-relief treatment on your first visit and follow up with further treatment over the next few days.

In addition to the structural treatment, the chiropractor may also give you some helpful advice on posture, how to lift, sit and bend, as well as useful dietary information. You are also likely to be advised on the best sort of exercise to take up to suit your particular problem.

After the treatment, your body may need a couple of days to settle down. It is not unusual to feel sore during this period or even to feel slightly worse. Reactions can vary – some people find they are buzzing with energy, others just want to go home and sleep. The effectiveness of the treatment will depend on your age and general health: if you are young and fit with no other signs of illness you will recover much faster than an elderly person who has a variety of other health problems.

How many sessions do I need?

You can often feel an improvement after just one treatment, but the time it takes for a complete recovery depends on your type of problem, how long you've had it, and how old you are. You may need two or three visits in the first seven to ten days and then weekly, ten day or biweekly appointments until the condition clears. After that you may need a check-up every few months or twice a year. The average number of visits is about seven.

Which problems can it help?

Any kind of pain or disability relating to the musculo-skeletal system, and the associated nervous system. It can help neck, shoulder and lower back pain and give relief to indigestion, constipation, menstrual pain, headaches and asthma.

Is it safe?

Chiropractic is not suitable for damaged bones or for people with bone disease such as bone cancer. Otherwise, it is safe for all, from newborn colicky babies to elderly people with osteoporosis.

Pregnant women can also be treated. Chiropractors do not use X-rays in the diagnosis of pregnant women as this can pose a risk to the unborn child. The practitioner will adapt treatment to ensure it is safe and suitable for use in all stages of pregnancy; different techniques can particularly help back pain.

Clinical studies

Chiropractic treatment has been shown in several studies to be particularly effective in treating different back problems.

In 1995, a three year Medical Research Council study was carried out at 11 centers with 741 patients suffering from low back pain. They were randomly allocated to physiotherapy outpatient departments (357) or sent for chiropractic manipulation (384). They were then assessed using the Oswestry Disability Index questionnaire weekly for six weeks, at six months, and at one and two years.

Patients given chiropractic manipulation were more satisfied with their treatment after six weeks and could raise their legs higher with less pain. They also showed improvements in pain over the physiotherapy group at six, 12 and 24 months.

Five years later further analysis showed smaller benefits than previously reported but they were still 20 percent better for the chiropractic group, who also voiced greater long-term satisfaction with the treatment than the hospital patients. (**13**)

In 1985 a study was carried out with 155 patients at three Egyptian hospitals who had leg or low back pain. The results showed that chiropractic treatment was more effective for pain relief for chronic (long-term) patients or those under 40 than either of the two control treatments with pretend manipulation or drug treatment and bed rest. Details taken on eight visits showed that the chiropractic group had greater pain reduction. (**14**) (*For clinical references see How to use this book*).

FOR INFORMATION ON HOW TO CHOOSE A CHIROPRACTOR SEE THE DIRECTORY.

MASSAGE as a therapy has evolved out of one of our most instinctive desires – the desire to touch and be touched. We touch each other for many reasons: to show love, offer security, but also to make us feel better. As a species we can exist without many things, but physical contact is not one of them.

Over the years much evidence has been collected to prove the necessity of touch and the benefits of therapeutic massage. The University of Miami has conducted extensive research into this area. Some references from the early 1900s show that institutionalized orphans with a normally fatal wasting disease called marasmus did not die when they were regularly touched.

MASSAGE

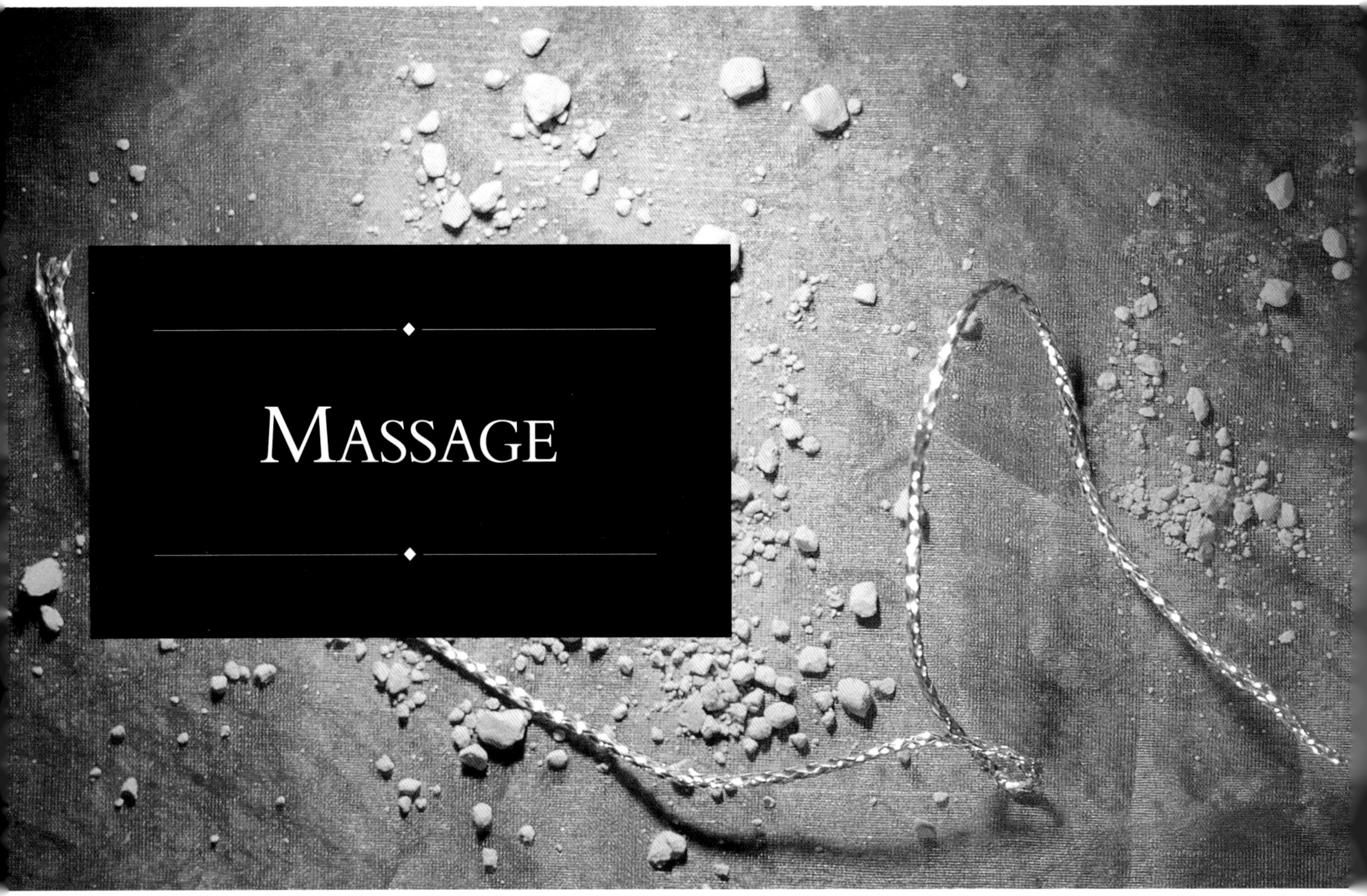

MASSAGE is a very pleasant therapy that uses stroking, kneading and other techniques to manipulate the soft tissues of the body. It is ideal for stress relief, relaxation and as a remedial treatment for physical and emotional problems.

Massage therapy has had something of a checkered history. It is one of the oldest therapies in the world, predating acupuncture and was popular with the Greeks and Romans. In fact, up until the Middle Ages, it played a vital part in healthcare. But the Catholic church consigned it to the realm of the sinful and left it with a rather seedy image that the more recent "massage parlors" only served to increase. It is an image that modern therapists have worked hard to dispel and it is now disappearing.

The father of therapeutic massage was Swedish gymnast turned therapist Professor Per Henrik Ling (1776–1839). Ling gave us an updated form of therapeutic massage, known as Swedish massage, which still forms the basis for modern massage.

Today, massage has found its way into therapy rooms, beauty salons, homes, sports clubs and hospitals. It complements conventional treatment in the care of the chronically ill and helps patients recovering from heart attacks or heart surgery. It is ideal for stress relief and can help in the care of the mentally ill.

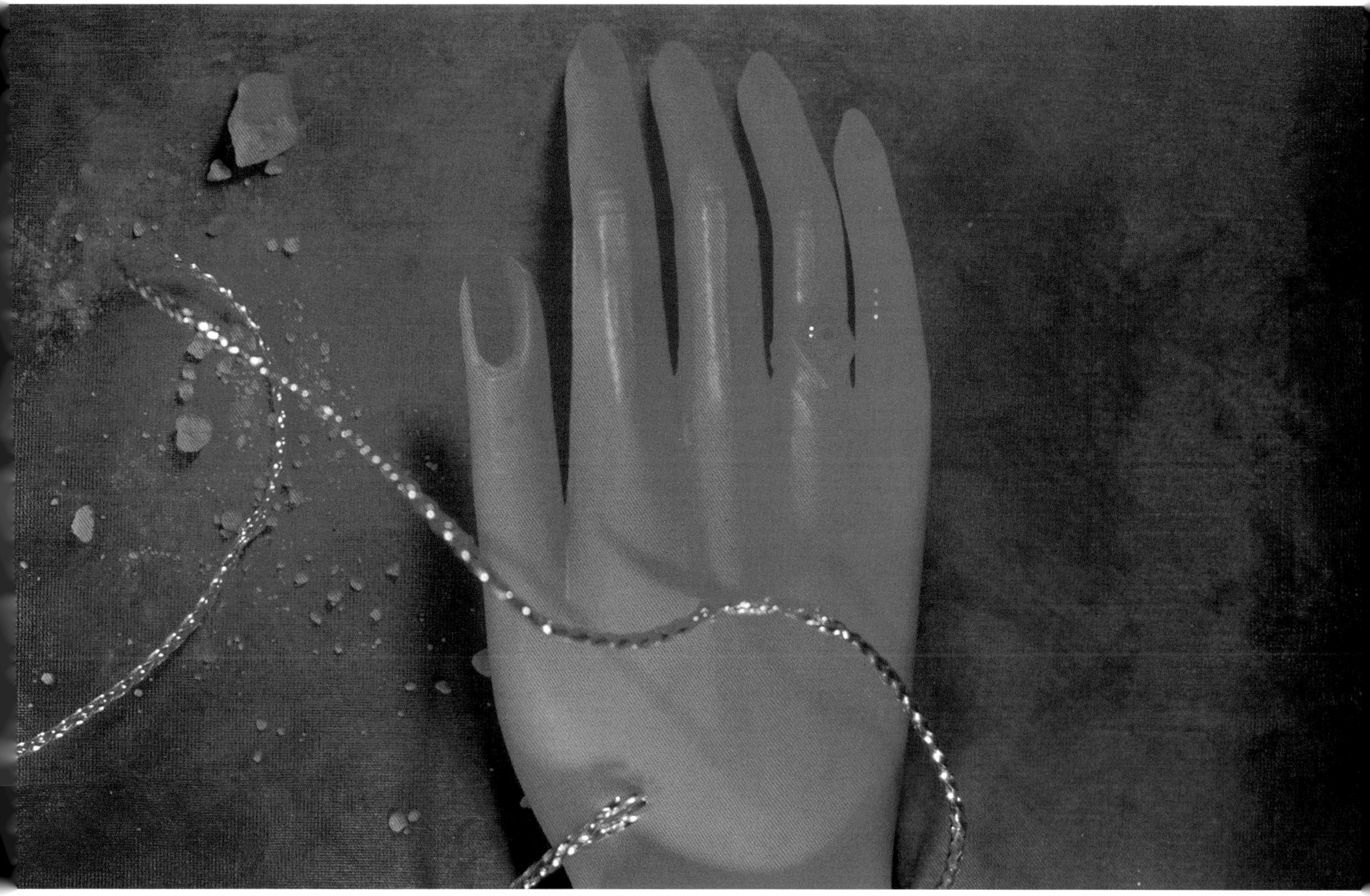

What is massage?

Massage is the manipulation of the body's soft tissues with specific techniques to promote or restore health. Massage therapists use their hands to detect and treat problems in the muscles, ligaments and tendons in the body's soft tissue.

Most therapists, and certainly those who work holistically, believe that regular body massage can release emotional tension and promote physical health, gradually restoring the whole person to balanced health. Massage also forms the basis of other therapies such as aromatherapy (see pages 68–73), shiatsu, and physiotherapy, and plays an important part in Chinese and Ayurvedic medicine (see pages 30–35). Massage is primarily about touch, and touch in itself has healing qualities for reasons that are beyond our understanding. It may best be explained by the following experiment. Researchers at Harvard Medical School in the United States studied the recovery rates of two groups of patients who were being prepared for an operation. The night before their operation half the group received the usual briefing from the anesthetist about the next day's procedure. The other half received the same information, but it was delivered in a warm and friendly way and the anesthetist held each patient's hand as he talked.

After their operation the patients in the latter group asked for less pain relief and were discharged from hospital three days earlier than the group who had not been comforted and held. Clearly human contact helps enormously in the healing process.

How does it work?

There are many different types of massage, some which work on pressure or reflex points such as shiatsu (see pages 22–23), reflexology (see pages 60–65) and Chinese massage, others concentrate on relieving specific conditions, for example, remedial massage is used to treat sports injuries and muscle strains, and manual lymphatic drainage (MLD) is used to stimulate the lymphatic system. But basic massage techniques such as stroking, kneading, wringing, pummeling and knuckling, have been shown to stimulate physical and emotional healing in two ways: by a mechanical and a reflex action.

The mechanical effects of massage: These are the physical results of pressing, squeezing and moving the soft tissues. Depending on the massage techniques used, this can be relaxing or stimulating. Tense muscles can cause sluggish circulation because they force the body's blood vessels to constrict. Massaging the muscles relaxes them and stimulates the circulation so that blood flows freely, carrying oxygen and nutrients to where they are needed. By working on the circulation regular massage can help to normalize blood pressure, easing the pressure on over-burdened arteries and veins. Massage also stimulates the lymphatic system, which is responsible for nourishing cells, carrying waste products out of the body and defending the body against infection.

The reflex action: This is the involuntary reaction of one part of your body to the stimulation of another part. Because the body, mind and emotions form one intricate organism, connected by energy channels and a complex nervous system with receptors in the skin, stimulus in one part of the body can effect several other parts. So a relaxing back massage can also ease leg pain.

Massage is a physical therapy, but one with a strong emotional content. Austrian psychoanalyst, Wilhelm Reich(1897–1957) was the first modern therapist to understand the effects of massage on emotions. He introduced the concept of "body armoring," the belief that unexpressed emotions, such as anger or grief, are held in the body. Tense, rigid muscles are not healthy for the body and suppressed emotions are not good for the mind. Reich's philosophy paved the way for massage as a holistic therapy. It was later developed by the Esalen Institute in California into a therapy for releasing and encouraging personal growth.

The latest research from the United States reinforces what Reich proposed so many years ago. Internationally recognized pharmacologist Dr. Candace Pert maintains that the mind and body are so interrelated that it is impossible to make a clear distinction between them. She says that old emotions are stored in the ganglion of the spinal cord and other parts of the autonomic nervous system. Massage can free them by inducing relaxation, releasing endorphins – the body's pain relievers, but also by triggering neuropeptides – molecules which act as intercellular messengers within the nervous system.

Massaging the skin releases the peptides affecting the mind, stimulating the immune system and improving overall body health. According to Dr. Pert the preventive benefits of massage are so great that, "we could replace 90 per cent of mainstream medicine with a weekly massage."

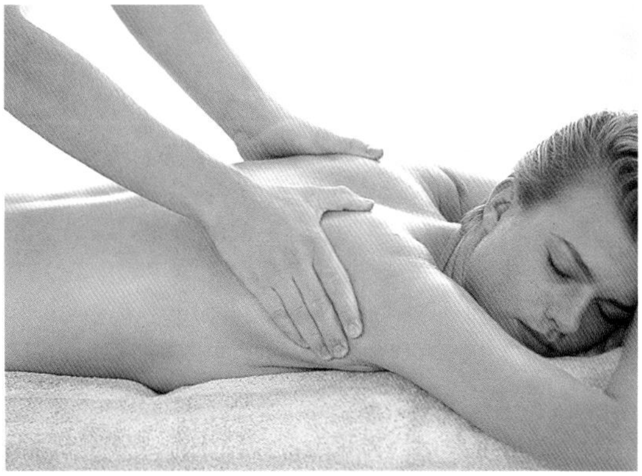

ABOVE: Having a massage is a very relaxing experience. It can help release muscle tension particularly in the neck, back and shoulders.

RIGHT: Sometimes a massage is given under a water spray. The pounding spray helps to relax and loosen up the body muscles.

The four stages of healing

When you accept that massage can heal the body it helps to understand how healing takes place. Massage can have immediate benefits but, if you are ill, recovery takes time. Massage therapists have identified four stages in the healing process:

Relief: The first few treatment sessions relieve pain, reduce tension and sedate stressed nerves. They do not necessarily solve the problem, but ease the symptoms so that you feel better.

Correction: When the pain has been relieved the therapist can work on the underlying cause to prevent the problems' return. Correctional work involves retuning muscles, decongesting a sluggish lymph system, or freeing knotted or scarred fibers.
Strengthening: This is important in a badly damaged area. Weaknesses at the injury site can mean recurring problems in the future. For example, sports injuries can cause problems long after they have healed if the tissues around them have been weakened by the injury and a long period of recuperation. Massage can strengthen the surrounding tissues enabling them to provide adequate support when the injury has healed.
Maintenance: This is both the final stage of healing and the first step in preventative care. Therapists recommend occasional massage treatments to keep problems at bay and prevent any annoying health problems from becoming major health issues.

With the aid of massage, a person can be restored to a balanced state of health.

MASSAGE GUIDELINES

Before you start to massage a partner at home, make sure you heed these tips:

- *Choose a firm massage surface. A bed is not suitable as it tends to "give" under pressure. Instead spread several thick towels on the floor. Put a duvet under the towels if it is too uncomfortable.*
- *Make sure your partner is warm and comfortable.*
- *Relax and concentrate on the massage. If you are unsure about what to do just start by stroking, then concentrate on tense areas.*
- *If you use aromatherapy oils, mix five drops to one teaspoon of a vegetable carrier oil, such as grapeseed or almond for adults. Use half the strength for children under seven and a quarter strength for children under three. Do not use essential oils to massage newborn babies.*
- *Never pour oil directly onto your partner's skin. Warm it in your hands. If you add oil during the massage, pour it over the back of your hand to warm it before rubbing it into your partner's skin.*
- *Vary the pressure and the length of the strokes you use – take your lead from the person you are massaging.*
- *Make your massage strokes flowing and rhythmic, keeping one hand in contact with the body at all times.*
- *Work in a comfortable way. But stroke toward the heart and finish by holding your partner's feet for a few seconds to "ground" him.*
- *Do not massage anyone who has an infectious skin disease, an inflammatory condition such as thrombosis, is pregnant, chronically ill, in severe pain, or who has just eaten.*

What happens in a consultation?

The type of treatment you receive will depend on your problem, your personal preferences and the therapist's skills. You should not eat or drink heavily before your appointment or attend with an inflamed or infectious skin condition. There are no hard and fast rules, but your appointment should normally begin with the obligatory interview about:

- *Why you have come*
- *Your current state of health*
- *Your medical history*
- *Details of any medication that you take*
- *General lifestyle inquiries*

The therapist will usually then not talk unless she needs to ask you something or you want to discuss something. She may play some relaxing music and dim the lights.

For the massage you will need to undress, normally in privacy, and lie on the massage table. You do not have to undress completely, you can keep on your underpants, if you wish. But even if you strip completely the therapist will cover you with a towel and only uncover the part of your body on which she needs to work. It is important that you like the massage and feel comfortable, warm and happy with the treatment.

The therapist may use some essential oils. She may choose a blend she thinks appropriate or ask you if there is anything that you like. She might massage your back, work down your body, then turn you over and work down the front, paying particular attention to knotty or tense areas. The massage should be relaxing, although you may feel pain in tense areas. You should not feel severe pain, however, so speak out if an area hurts badly.

A full body massage can last 90 minutes, but is usually an hour. Afterward you may be left alone for a few minutes. This is important as massage can leave you feeling a little spaced out, and although the therapist will "ground" you (hold your feet for about 20 seconds), you will benefit from time on your own.

Everybody reacts differently to a massage: you may feel relaxed, energized, slightly tired or ache a little the next day. You might cry – this is not unusual if you've been bottling up feelings.

How many sessions do I need?

You can enjoy a massage as often as you like. If you are receiving massage therapy for a specific condition, the number of appointments depends on how serious the problem is and your powers of recovery. Be prepared for extensive treatment.

Basic massage techniques

Effleurage

Effleurer means to touch lightly or stroke. This is the most useful massage stroke. You can massage the whole body using simple stroking techniques – just vary the speed and pressure. How to do it:

Fan stroking *Start with your hands side by side flat on the base of your partner's back. Slide them upward leading with your fingers. Lean into the palms and heels of your hands to add pressure. At the shoulders, fan your hands out to each side, reducing pressure as you do so and stroke smoothly over the area. Stroke lightly down the sides of the body, following the contours. Squeeze in slightly at the waist and pull your hands back up onto the back. Repeat, varying the stroke length, but apply the pressure in the upward movement.*

Circle stroking *Use this when you want a continuous flowing movement. Place both hands on your partner about 15cm (6in) apart and stroke in a wide circular action. Put the pressure into the upward stroke and then glide your hands back down again. As your arms will cross, simply lift one hand over the other and continue.*

Cat stroking *This soothing, sleep-inducing movement requires hardly any pressure. Stroke down the body with the flat of one hand, and follow with the other. Return the first hand to the top once you reach the bottom of the back and then repeat.*

Thumb stroking *On small areas, such as the arms and bottom of the legs, stroke with your thumbs. Stroke firmly upward and outward with one thumb pushing higher than the other with every stroke.*

Where to use it? *Almost any body area that is suitable for massage. It is especially good on the back and chest, but partners should take care if massaging breasts.*

What it does *Firm brisk massage strokes improve circulation and gentle rhythmic strokes stimulate the lymph glands and help eliminate body wastes. Slower strokes can ease tense muscles, reduce stress, lower blood pressure and generally relax someone.*

Problem areas *Do not massage over varicose veins, or repeatedly stroke people with very hairy skin as it can cause a rash.*

Petrissage

The two main types of petrissage are kneading and wringing. These similar techniques are useful for deeper massage, but only after you have warmed up the muscles with effleurage. Kneading can be used lightly or as a much deeper technique. Wringing is always a deep massage technique. How to do it:

Kneading *Place both hands on the body with your fingers pointing away from you. Press into the body with the palm of one hand, pick up the flesh between your thumb and fingers and press it toward the resting hand. Release and do the same with the other hand, rhythmically squeezing and releasing. Apply light or deep pressure.*

Wringing *This is similar to kneading but you add a twist to the method, so you work on the flesh as if you were wringing out a towel.*

Where to use it? *It is suitable for the shoulders and fleshy areas, such as the hips and thighs.*

What it does *It releases tension from stiff muscles, improves circulation and helps eliminate metabolic wastes, and breaks down fatty deposits, so they can be reabsorbed by the lymph system and eliminated more easily.*

Problem areas *Do not apply on a recent injury, or on scar tissue that is less than six months old, varicose veins, or an area of inflammation. Do not work on the abdomen of people with digestive or abdominal inflammatory disorders or on pregnant women.*

Pressures

These techniques apply a firm penetrating amount of pressure to specific areas. Use the two main types: static and circular pressure using pressure on tension areas. Do not use too much oil as your fingers will slide, and try not to dig your nails into your partner. How to do it:

Static pressure *Place the pads of your thumbs on the skin at the points where your partner is most tense. Experienced masseuses can detect tensions areas, but a beginner may have to rely on her partner to tell her where he has pain, stiffness or a knotted feeling. Gradually lean your weight into your thumbs and hold for a few seconds. Release and slide your thumbs along to the next tension point and repeat until you have worked over the whole knotted area.*

Circular pressure *Press as before and maintain the pressure as you move your thumbs in small circles, working into the muscle.*

Where to use it? *On the shoulders, either side of the spine (never massage over the spine itself), on other bony areas such as the base of the skull, or on specific tension spots.*

What it does *It releases muscular tension, loosens knots, and increases the blood flow to the area.*

Problem areas *Do not use over bruised, delicate or broken skin, recent scar tissue or varicose veins.*

Percussion

This is a pounding stroke, used to stimulate fleshy, muscular areas. There are different percussion techniques, of which hacking and pummeling are the most common. If you are giving a stimulating massage, use them as a wake-up technique at the end of the massage. Practice on yourself to test for the right amount pressure, rather than bruising your partner. How to do it:

Hacking *Using both hands with palms facing, strike the skin with the outside edge of your hand in a chopping motion, Flick it up as soon as you touch the skin and chop with the other hand. Use your hands alternately to keep the movement rhythmic. Keep your hands relaxed and your movements light and fast. Your hands should bounce, not thump, off your partner's skin.*

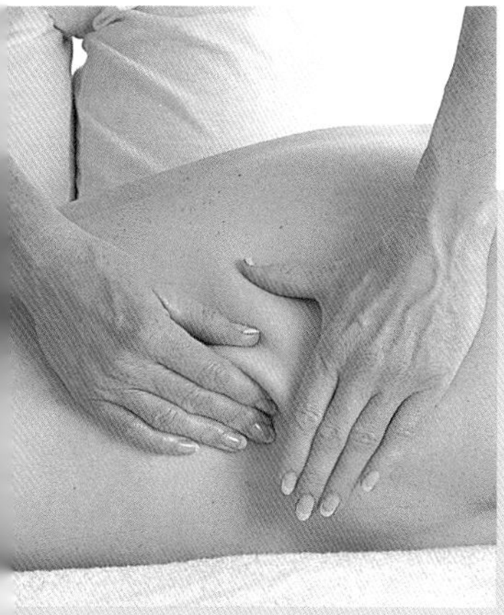
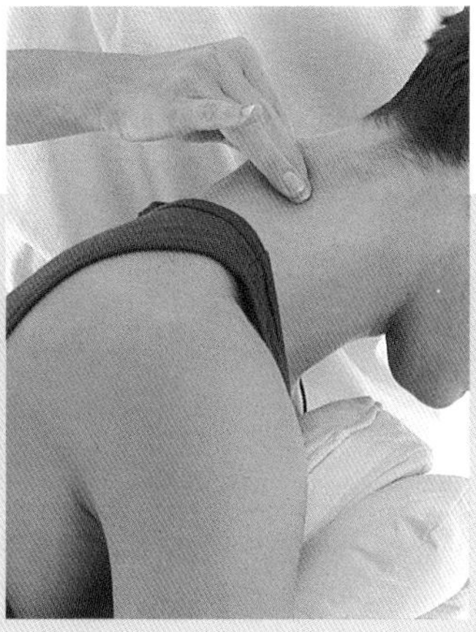

ABOVE: Kneading is a form of petrissage which can be used after effleurage.

ABOVE: Tension around the neck can be treated with the thumb-stroking technique.

BELOW: Effleurage is the basic massage technique and uses light massage strokes.

BELOW: Fan stroking is a form of effleurage where the hands massage the body side by side.

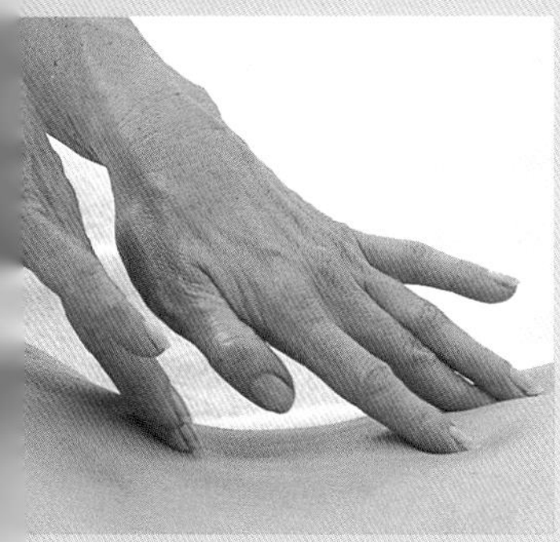
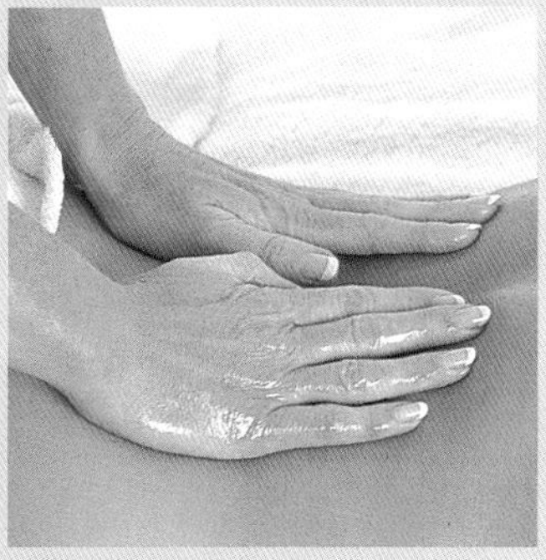

Pummeling *Using the same movement as before, make your hands into loose fists. Keep your wrists relaxed and gently bounce the edge of them off your partner's body.*
Where to use it? *On large muscular or fleshy areas, such as the buttocks or thighs.*
What it does *It stimulates the whole body, improving circulation. It improves muscle tone and can help to break up cellulite.*
Problem areas *Do not use on bony areas such as the shins where the nerve endings are near the surface or over bruises or broken veins.*

Knuckling

Use this movement with deep or light pressure. The sensation is wonderful for the person being massaged, especially when applied to the feet. How to do it:
The technique *Make a loose fist with your hands and uncurl your fingers so that the middle section rests on the skin. Move your fingers in a circular motion to give a rippling effect.*
Where to use it? *On the soles of the feet, palms of the hands, shoulders and chest*
What it does *Increases the blood flow to the specific body area, and releases muscular tension.*
Problem areas *Do not use on the abdomen, any inflamed area, over delicate or broken skin, recent scar tissue or varicose veins.*

Which problems can it help?

Massage can treat many complaints. But it is particularly good for stress and stress-related conditions, insomnia, depression and circulation problems. It is also good for helping aching and strained muscles, arthritis, rheumatism and sciatica. People with digestive disorders such as irritable bowel syndrome and constipation also benefit from the treatment as do women with PMT.

Is it safe?

Massage is a proven, gentle and effective therapy that is suitable for everyone from premature babies to pregnant women. It can also be given to the weak and terminally ill, but only when practiced by a qualified therapist. Basic relaxation massage for healthy adults can be performed by anyone with essential skills.

Clinical studies

The power of touch is well known and the benefits of massage to treat various conditions has been discovered in different studies.

In 1992 a hospital study was carried out on 52 children and adolescents suffering from depression or adjustment disorders. The results revealed that the group who were given a daily back massage for five days were less depressed and anxious than the control group who just watched relaxing videos. It was also found that they slept better after massage. (**15**)

A study was also done on 30 surgical patients at St. Mary's Hospital in London in 1990 in connection with pain relief and insomnia. The patients were massaged on the back, face or feet and were then monitored for any physical and psychological changes. Most of the people receiving treatment reported relief from pain, anxiety and muscle spasm. Other benefits were improved sleep and general wellbeing. The two nurses who performed the massage also had better rapport with the patients. (**16**)

In a study on breast cancer in 1986, six patients who were receiving radiotherapy were given slow stroke back massage. The effects of this treatment were examined by monitoring how each patient felt and their distress before and after treatment. The 13 distress symptoms measured were intensity and frequency of nausea and pain, physical appearance, breathing patterns, whether they had a cough, concentration levels, general outlook, fatigue, quality of appetite, bowel pattern and insomnia.

After massage treatment there was a general improvement in the symptom distress and the patients' general mood in comparison to the control group who had just rested. The women said they felt less tense, were not so tired and had more vitality. (**17**)

Young babies have also benefited from massage. In 1990, 40 premature babies were randomly assigned to massage or control groups with no treatment as soon as they were stable. Massage was given to some babies for 15 minutes hourly for three hours a day. After 10 days of massage the babies averaged a 21 percent daily weight gain and were discharged five days earlier than the control group. (**18**) *(For clinical references see How to use this book.)*

FOR INFORMATION ON HOW TO CHOOSE A MASSAGE THERAPIST SEE THE DIRECTORY.

Reflexology

REFLEXOLOGY is a therapy that involves applying pressure to points on the feet and sometimes the hands. Therapists believe that by working on a particular point they can stimulate energy by a reflex action to a related muscle or organ and encourage healing. The treatment is relaxing and can help stress and digestive problems.

PEOPLE OFTEN take some convincing to try reflexology for the first time and for many it is the last resort after many failed treatments. It is certainly difficult to understand how pressing a point on your foot could relieve toothache or the itch of eczema when you are brought up to believe that the problem is always at the point of pain. But results can be so impressive that many people are having regular treatments to overcome illness, to stay healthy or simply to relax. Studies in Britain have shown that pregnant women who had ten reflexology treatments were in labor for half the time that medical textbooks claim is the average. Many people who have tried reflexology claim relief from such diverse conditions as asthma and the depression and side effects associated with cancer treatment. Others find it a soothing form of stress relief.

Reflexology is usually practiced by qualified, non-medical therapists, working in clinics, treatment rooms or who visit offices for on-the spot stress relief. But demand for the therapy is so great, and its effects so impressive, that some medical staff have also taken up reflexology training. Like most alternative therapies reflexology is not a new therapy. It has its roots in the ancient civilizations of Egypt, India and China as well as among African tribes and native American Indians.

But the therapy did not make any real impact in the West until the early 20th century when Dr. William Fitzgerald, an ear, nose and throat specialist at Boston General Hospital, became interested in zone therapy, which provided the foundations for reflexology. In zone therapy the body is divided into ten vertical zones, running from the tips of the toes to the top of the head and back down to the finger tips and all the parts of the body within one zone are linked. By applying pressure to one part of the body, Fitzgerald was delighted to discover that it was possible to relieve pain in other areas within the same zone.

It is not clear where or how Fitzgerald found out about zone therapy, but it is assumed that it was while he was in Europe, because on his return to the United States he began to introduce his patients to zone therapy. He applied pressure to their feet and hands to relieve pain in other parts of the body. He shared his knowledge with a colleague Dr. Joe Riley.

Through Riley a physiotherapist named Eunice Ingham got to know about zone therapy. She was fascinated by the concept and began to use it on her patients. To her satisfaction, Ingham noticed a marked speeding up of her patients' healing abilities when they were treated with zone therapy.

It was Ingham who developed and renamed zone therapy as reflexology. She also mapped out the feet's reflex zones as charts that are used today. Ingham also made the important discovery that applying pressure to reflex points could have a much wider therapeutic effect than just pain relief. Reflexology was brought to Britain in 1966 by a pupil of Ingham's, Doreen Bayly.

What is reflexology?

Reflexology is the practice of applying pressure to points on the feet and hands, usually the feet, to stimulate the body's own healing system. The name "reflexology" may come from the fact that reflexologists believe parts of the body are reflected on the feet and hands, or it may come from the concept of a reflex action. A reflex action occurs in a muscle or organ when it is activated by energy from a point of stimulus on the body. In reflexology the point of stimulus is on the hand or foot.

Reflexologists believe that applying pressure to these reflex points can improve physical and mental health. Depending on the points chosen, therapists can use the therapy to ease tension, reduce inflammation, improve circulation and eliminate body toxins. Reflexology is a safe, effective form of treatment, which practitioners use to stimulate the body to heal itself.

They do this by working on the physical body to stimulate the healing at the physical, mental and emotional levels. And, although the therapy involves no conscious effort on the patient's part it encourages the body's healing system to search for its point of balance or "homeostasis."

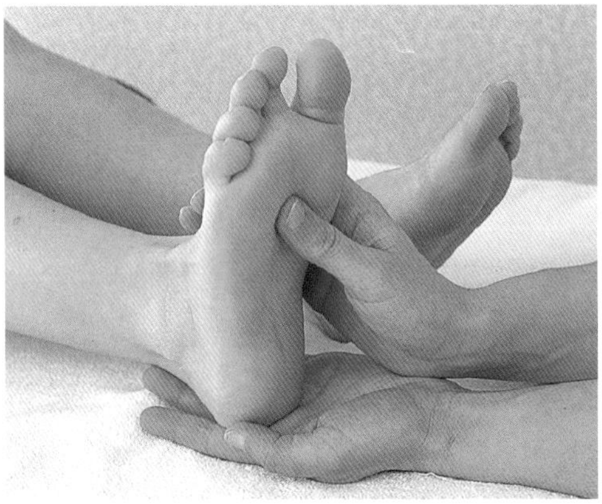

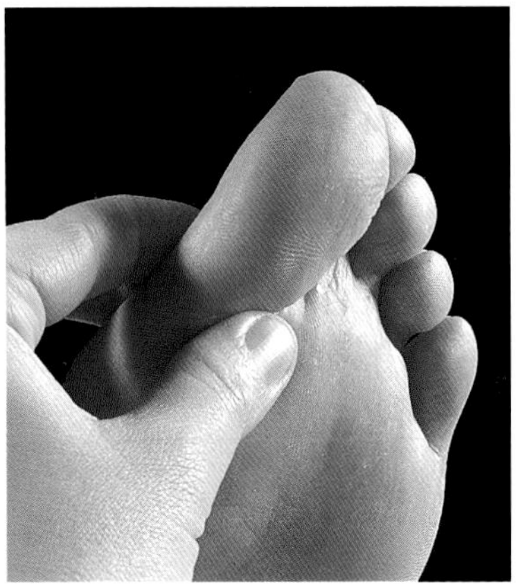

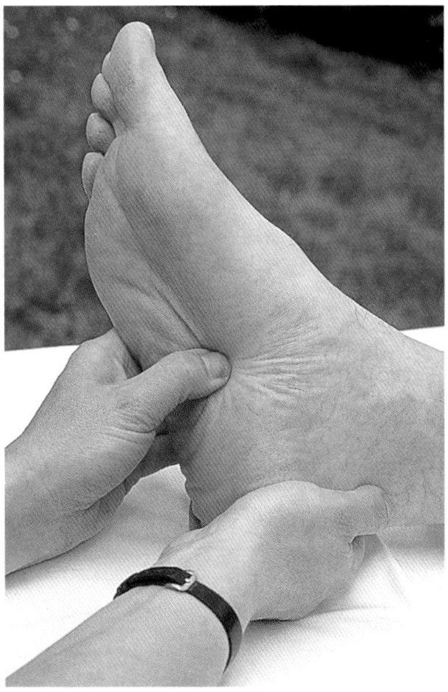

FAR LEFT, BOTTOM LEFT AND LEFT: To give a reflexology treatment a therapist mainly uses his thumb, or sometimes his finger, to apply pressure to different points to release any blockages. Where there is a blockage the reflex can feel taut and is often painful for the patient. The relexologist will gently work away at the point until the blockage is released.

How does it work?

No one knows exactly how reflexology or zone therapy works beyond the physical act of stimulating nerve endings in the foot. But it has been explained in terms of electrical or electro-chemical energy which operates along the pathways of an autonomic reflex system, working with the autonomic nervous system.

In a healthy body the brain is constantly sending out and receiving messages along the pathways of the nervous system. Good communication is necessary for good health. But sometimes the pathways get blocked and messages cannot get through. Reflexology may be able to operate by stimulating the autonomic reflex system to clear blockages, so that the communication lines stay open and the body, mind and emotions stay healthy.

We know that there are over 70,000 nerve endings on the sole of each foot which, when stimulated, can send messages along the pathways of the autonomic nervous system to all areas of the body and brain. Pressure applied to nerve endings can influence the body systems, including the circulation and lymphatic systems. Improvements in circulation and the lymphatic system result in improved body functioning because nutrients and oxygen are transported more efficiently round the body and toxins are eliminated more easily. Through this physical reflex action, reflexology can stimulate the body's energy to improve general wellbeing and effectively clear out congestion. Reflexologists access the energy through zones.

The body is divided into ten vertical zones or channels, five on the left and five on the right. Each zone runs from the head right down to the reflex areas on the hands and feet and from the front through to the back of the body. All body parts within any one zone are linked by the nerve pathways and are mirrored in the corresponding reflex zone on the hands and feet.

By applying pressure to a particular point, known as a reflex point or area, the therapist can stimulate or rebalance the energy in the related zone. For example, the left kidney, which is in zone two of the left-hand side of the body, is reflected at the same point in zone two of the left foot. If an energy blockage occurs in a zone, it can affect several body parts within that zone, causing more than one symptom of ill health. For example, someone with a problem in the left kidney can sometimes develop problems in the left eye because the eyes and kidneys are both linked by the energy in zone two.

The therapy involves no conscious effort on the part of the patient, but it encourages the body's healing system to balance itself.

Reflexologists also make use of the principle of cross reflexes. According to this principle, parts of the upper body correspond to parts of the lower body and can be used as substitutes for treatment. For example, the right arm cross-reflexes with the right leg; the right shoulder matches the right hip and the right hand corresponds to the right foot. Cross-reflexing is helpful for the reflexologist if the body part that needs treating is inaccessible. For example, a dislocated left shoulder can be too painful to work on so the pain can be relieved indirectly by working on its cross reflex, which is the left hip.

The feet as a mirror of the body

It is sometimes easier to envisage the reflex areas on the feet if you think of how the shape of the feet relates to the body's shape.

Reflexology, like auricular therapy (see pages 20–21), is a form of holography, the belief that small parts of the body can be used to treat the whole. The body is believed to be mirrored in the shape of the feet, so that if you were lying down with your feet together, heels resting on the floor and toes pointed toward the ceiling, the shape of your feet would match the outline of your body. The organs and body parts would appear in the reflex areas of the feet in the same position as they would appear in the body. Think of it in terms of a miniature body being superimposed on the soles of the feet, with each foot reflecting half the body. It should match up in the following way:

- *The toes correspond to zones in the head and neck, covering the head, brain, eyes, nose, teeth and so on.*
- *The soft fleshy balls of the feet reflect the lungs, chest and shoulders generally.*
- *The section from the ball of the feet to the middle of the arch*

Reflexology for Common Ailments

To give yourself a reflexology treatment sit with your bare right foot resting on your left leg. Hold your foot with your left hand and work on it with your right. Change position to work on your left foot. When you thumb walk (see How to give a treatment on page 64) repeat at least three times and when pressing a point, hold for about 30 seconds. Repeat the treatment until symptoms subside, but do not overdo it. Begin every treatment by working all over the foot (see chart on page 65), giving special emphasis to these reflex points:

Anxiety *Begin by stroking all over the foot. Then press the pad of your thumb into the solar plexus, the kidney and the adrenal gland reflexes. Rotate your thumb to work more deeply into the reflex area. If your anxiety is registering in your stomach, for example, pay particular attention to that area, too. Finish by stroking all over the foot.*

Backache *Begin by thumb walking across the shoulder area and then thumb walk down the spine to your heel. Do this four times on each foot, concentrating on the area of pain.*

Colds *Work the head area. Then work with your thumb on the affected areas such as the nose, throat and chest. If you also have a temperature, work on the pituitary gland reflex.*

Headache *Work on both feet, starting with the right. Thumb walk over the head and neck areas and then the small intestine and finish by thumb walking along the spine.*

Indigestion *Start under your toes and press your thumb into the stomach, intestine, diaphragm and solar plexus areas on both feet.*

Period problems *Work all over the feet, paying special attention to the endocrine glands (Pituitary, thyroid and adrenals) and finish by pressing the solar plexus reflex on both feet. Thumb walk over the ovaries, uterus and Fallopian tubes. The ovaries are on the outside of the foot between the ankle bone and the back of your heel. The uterus reflex is at the same point on the inside of your foot and the fallopian tube runs across the top of each foot from below the ankle bone.*

Note: *These recommendations are for acute (short-term) ailments only. If symptoms persist consult a qualified therapist and/or your doctor, or your dentist for teeth problems.*

covers the area from the diaphragm to the waist.

- *The area from the middle of the arch to the start of the heel relates to the waist and pelvic area.*
- *The heels themselves relate to the left and right pelvic area and the sciatic nerve.*
- *The inside curve of each foot mirrors the curves of the spine.*
- *The outsides of the feet, starting from the top and working down, relate to the arms, shoulders, hips, legs, knees and lower back.*
- *The ankles cover the pelvic area and reproductive organs.*

What happens in a consultation?

The reflexologist's therapy rooms should be warm and comfortable and may have pleasant music playing in the background. Treatment and length of appointments varies from one practitioner to another. Your first appointment will probably last for about 90 minutes to allow for consultation time, but subsequent appointments are 30–60 minutes. The reflexologist will ask you questions about yourself and why you have come to see her:

- *She will ask details about your medical history, including childhood illnesses, accidents or operations.*
- *You will need to tell her if you are under the care of a doctor at present or receiving drug treatment for an illness or any chronic (long-term) condition.*

The reflexologist will also want to know how you feel about yourself and your life. She will ask about your work and leisure activities, your diet, drinking and lifestyle habits.

To carry out the treatment the therapist will ask you to sit in a reclining chair or to lie on a treatment couch. She will ask you to remove your shoes and socks or tights and may wipe your feet with some cotton wool soaked in witch hazel. She may then apply some talcum powder or cream which makes it easier for her to carry out the treatment. Reflexologists often say that feet tell your body's history, so do not be surprised if your therapist picks up on past health problems.

The therapist usually begins and ends a treatment with some relaxation techniques to relax the diaphragm, free the ankle and loosen the joints. She will work over all the foot, before giving specific attention to any problem areas. If you feel pain or tenderness in a certain area, it is an indication of a blockage or imbalance in the corresponding organ or body part. The reflexologist will then pay extra attention to these tender areas.

The intention is not to cause you pain, but pain is a sign of blocked energy, and she will want to free the blockage to stimulate the healing process. Blocked energy is often indicated by crystalline deposits under the skin, which can feel like grains of sugar, or the reflexes can be taut or particularly spongy. The reflexologist will spend time working on these areas to eliminate these blockages.

For most people, the treatment is relaxing rather than painful, although you can experience various sensations. It is normal, for example, to feel a tingling sensation in your arms and hands. This is a good sign as it points to increased circulation.

The treatment itself can take between 30–60 minutes to complete. Afterward you may feel tired, or completely revitalized, it depends on you. The appointment usually ends with you making a follow-up appointment for a week later. Some people's symptoms seem to get worse before they get better. This can sometimes happen if your are fighting an infection or overcoming a painful condition.

How to give a treatment

Reflexologists talk of "working" the reflex areas of the feet to release blockages and stimulate healing. They use several techniques to do this, normally using the thumb and occasionally the index finger. The reflex points are small, so the movements must be small and controlled. Use different pressure, but place the emphasis on being "firm," not hard or painful. When using the thumb or finger, bend it slightly and work into the point with the flat pad of the finger so that your nails do not dig in. Always move your thumb or finger forward and support the foot with your other hand.
Here are some of the most common techniques:

Thumb walking *This is the most common Western method. It is done with the pad of the thumb. Bend the thumb and rest your other fingers around the foot on which you are about to work. Press your thumb into the reflex point you want to treat. Then, release some of the pressure, slide you thumb along like a caterpillar, stop and press again. Press on the precise area, keeping your movements slow and rhythmic. (This is good for all over the foot.)*
Finger walking *Similar to thumb walking except it is done with the side of the index finger, using your thumb and other three fingers for support. (This is good for bony areas such as the ankle and top of the foot.)*
Rotating *With your left hand supporting the foot, press your right thumb into the reflex point. Press and rotate your thumb into the reflex point, using your others fingers for support on the other side of the foot. (This is good for tender reflexes.)*
Flexing *Hold the toes with your left hand while you press into the desired point with your right thumb. Gently bend the foot backward and forward, so that your thumb presses and releases the point in a rhythmic fashion. (This is good for the solar plexus area.)*

How many sessions do I need?

The number of treatments you need depends on your problems, how long you have had them, and whether or not they have been suppressed by drugs. The effect is usually cumulative: you may feel more relaxed, in control, or sleep better after your first treatment and this can then give you the incentive to continue.

Which problems can it help?

Reflexology is a good all-round "whole system" therapy for people of all ages. However, it works well for any conditions that needs to be cleared or regulated, for example: digestive and menstrual irregularities, stress and fatigue, aches and pains and inflammatory skin conditions such as eczema. Studies have shown impressive results when reflexology has been used to aid pregnancy, and to help childhood problems, such as glue ear.

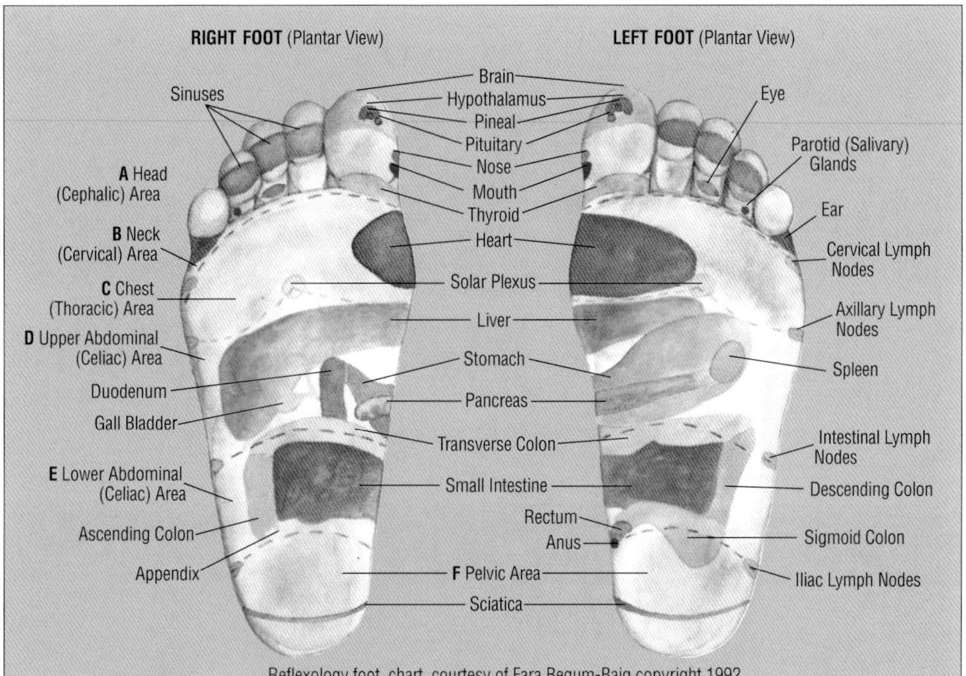

Reflexology foot chart courtesy of Fara Begum-Baig,copyright 1992.

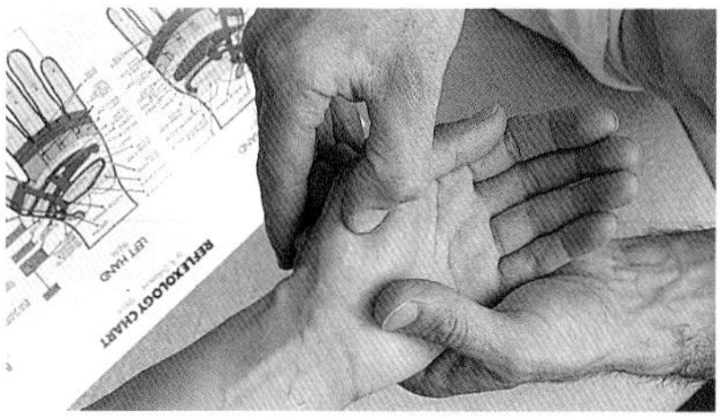

ABOVE: The hand can also be used for reflexology treatment, but is only used by the therapist occasionally.

ABOVE: In Bangkok, Thailand people can have a reflexology treatment on the street.

Is it safe?

Reflexology by a qualified therapist is safe for everyone. It can be a wonderfully relaxing treatment during pregnancy as it relieves back pain, nausea and heartburn. If you are in the early stages of pregnancy, you should tell the therapist so she can tailor the treatment to suit your needs. Children can also benefit from short reflexology sessions; infants' feet just need gentle stroking.

Self-treatment is safe for minor ailments, but is not recommended if you are pregnant, diabetic, epileptic or receiving medical treatment for a serious illness. If you are under a doctor's care let him and the reflexologist know before treatment begins.

Clinical studies

In several clinical trials reflexology has been proven as an effective treatment for work-related problems and other ailments.

Between 1990 and 1993, 235 of the 1,450 postal workers in Odense, Denmark were given reflexology. A typical course consisted of 8–10 half-hour treatments every week. The reflexologist treated symptoms of overwork such as neck and back strains, headaches, sinusitis, sciatica and gastrointestinal problems.

Of those treated, 73 percent reported a good result – 25 percent had some improvements and two percent felt it made no difference. A teacher of ergonomics was also employed to teach correct lifting. The two approaches together reduced the number of sick days per employee from 11.4 to 8.5 days per year. (**19**)

In a London study in 1995, 37 pregnant women completed a course of ten reflexology treatments to help with childbirth at least 20 weeks into pregnancy. For the group the average length of first stage labor was only five hours (compared to a more normal 16–24 hours); the second stage was 16 minutes (compared to a normal one to two hours). Only 2.5 percent of the women required an epidural (compared to an average 20 percent) and only 5.4 percent needed an emergency caesarean (compared to an average 13 percent). (**20**)

In a 1993 study, ear, hand or foot reflexology or a placebo treatment (treating inappropriate reflex zones, too roughly or too lightly) was given to 35 women suffering from PMS. Each woman kept a symptom diary for two months before, during and after eight, half-hour relexology treatments. Thirty-nine symptoms were assessed on a four-point scale. The women given reflexology treatment had an average 63 percent reduction in their PMS symptoms and discomfort; the placebo group had a 25 percent reduction. (**21**) (*For clinical references see How to use this book).*

FOR INFORMATION ON HOW TO CHOOSE A REFLEXOLOGIST SEE THE DIRECTORY.

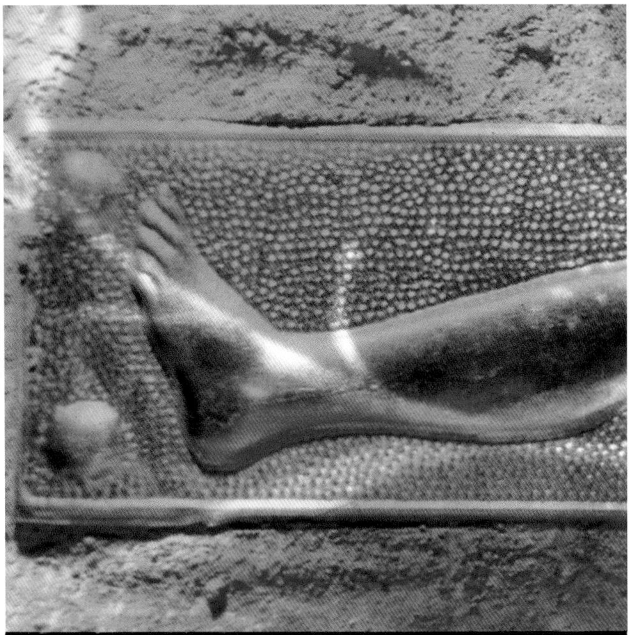

METAMORPHIC TECHNIQUE

METAMORPHIC TECHNIQUE is one of the lesser-known and more esoteric of the alternative therapies. Practitioners believe that our feet represent our whole being. They keep us in contact with the earth, bear our weight and, most importantly, they represent movement, which is the essential quality of humans. Movement is what enables change and development to take place. It is seen as the trigger to our evolution and is therefore more fundamental than intellect.

Metamorphic technique was originally called prenatal therapy by the British naturopath and reflexologist who developed it, Robert St. John. St. John used reflexology to treat mentally handicapped children, but found that it did not help as much as he had hoped. He discovered that many of the ailments that were helped by working on specific reflex points on the sole of the foot could also be relieved when he worked along the spinal reflex area only. (The spinal reflex follows the inside curve of the foot running from the big toe to the heel.) He also noticed psychological differences in the children when these reflexes were stimulated. St. John concluded that a psychological reflex map could be superimposed over the physical map to effect more fundamental changes than simply health improvements.

Furthermore, he believed his technique could change the patterns of our lives, our personality, behavior and health, which were formed while we developed in the womb. Support for his theory came when he used the technique on a baby with Down's syndrome and after a year the child became normal. Practitioners still report particular success with Down's syndrome and autistic children, but the effects tend to be more subtle.

What is metamorphic technique?

Metamorphic technique is about transformation. It is not a therapy or a treatment but a sort of trigger that sets our life force, or internal energy, in motion. The technique works on the basis that we each have a life force that can change us into something greater than we are. In the same way that a caterpillar metamorphoses into a butterfly, we too can change and grow. Granted, our development is restricted by our bodies, but this does not affect our potential for spiritual and emotional growth. The role of the metamorphic practitioner is to awaken this life force so that we can realize our full potential.

How does it work?

Practitioners believe that life does not begin at birth, but at conception. Over the nine months in the womb our physical, mental, emotional and behavioral patterns are established. Our parents thoughts, actions, diet and environment all contribute to these patterns. By working on the points that relate to these, therapists

METAMORPHIC TECHNIQUE is a form of foot manipulation, similar to reflexology, that stimulates our internal energy into motion to enable us to reach our full potential. It is a useful treatment for people with relationship problems, long-term illness or mental disability.

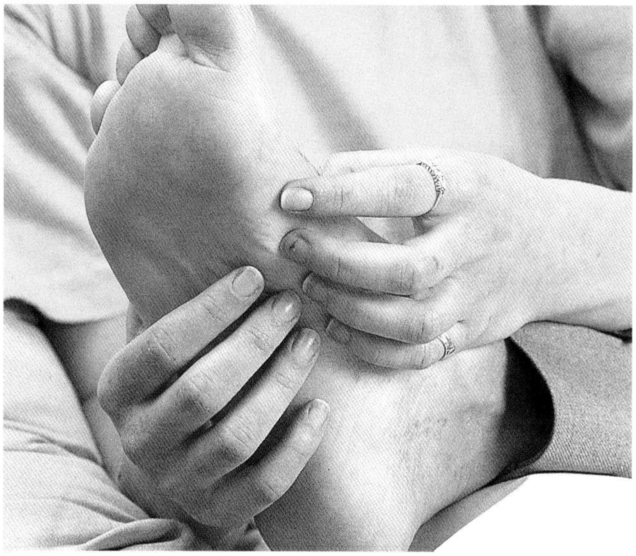

ABOVE: The metamorphic technique is like reflexology but only the spinal reflex is worked on to stimulate energy and aid emotional growth.

claim to be able to loosen their structure and allow changes. The technique is like reflexology as it works on reflex points on the feet, hands and head. The feet are most important as they express movement – the primary function. Working on the hands and head is secondary, but necessary because the hands express doing and the head, thinking; both help precipitate change.

Unlike a reflexologist, however, the practitioner will not concentrate on blocked or painful areas of the feet, she simply acknowledges that they exist.This is because it is not her role to decide what ought to be healed, only to stimulate the patient's own life force to do the healing where needed. For this reason practitioners prefer to be called catalysts rather than therapists.

The task of the practitioner is to awaken our life force to develop us spiritually or emotionally.

The main reflexes used are those on the spinal reflex area of the foot, the corresponding reflexes on the thumbs of both hands and along the center and base of the skull. Different points on these reflex areas relate to stages before birth, and the emotional, behavioral and physical patterns laid down at each stage affect how we are today. For example, on each foot there are what St. John called the mother and father principles. The mother point is at the heel. It relates to birth, the relationship between the patient and his mother, and to the mothering qualities within the patient. The point around the first joint of the big toe relates to the father principle and signifies conception. In psychological terms it relates to the father or other authority figure in the patient's life or to the inner authority or fathering qualities of the patient. Between the father and mother points are 38 other points; together they relate to 40 weeks in the womb.

To date there has been no scientific evidence to prove how working on these reflexes can or does change lives. Medical opinion is divided, many doctors and therapists find it too esoteric to be acceptable, others claim to be impressed with the results despite not knowing how the technique works.

What happens in a consultation?

Unlike other therapies, the practitioner does not take a case history. She will ask you to sit or lie down, take off your shoes and socks and place your foot in her lap. She will probably sit slightly to one side rather than opposite you as it is important for her to remain uninvolved, after all she is a catalyst, not a therapist. She will then work on each foot, using a light, rhythmic, circular and probing movement. She will work all over both feet, concentrating on the spinal reflex area along the inside of each foot.

After about 20 minutes, she will move onto your hands, working from the outside edge of the thumb down to the wrist for five to ten minutes. She will then finish off by touching your head, along the center of your skull, along the base and then up the sides toward your ears. This takes about ten minutes.

Some people claim that the treatment makes them recall scenes from their life or even prebirth experiences, but for many people it simply feels comforting, leaving them feeling rebalanced. The practitioner may suggest you come back in a week or wait to see if you want another appointment.

Good practitioners will not press you as the emphasis of the technique is that you become directed by your life force not by outside influences.

How many sessions do I need?

There is no set period of time for treatment. Most people have weekly sessions for as long as it takes them to feel they can cope alone, others have occasional treatments.

Which problems can it help?

The technique is not intended to cure anything, but aims to help people realize their potential and cope with chronic (long-term) physical illness or disability and long-term mental illness or mental handicap. It is also useful for people who find it difficult to move on from relationships or destructive circumstances. Practitioners claim that it is good for children with learning difficulties, Down's syndrome and autism.

Is it safe?

The technique is easy to learn and can be used on anyone in any state of health. A therapist would aim to teach it to you so that you could use it on other family members. It can be used on pregnant women, even when in labor, and even newborn babies are believed to benefit.

FOR INFORMATION ON HOW TO CHOOSE A METAMORPHIC PRACTITIONER SEE THE DIRECTORY.

AROMATHERAPY

AROMATHERAPY IS ONE OF THE FASTEST GROWING alternative therapies. It is used in homes, therapy rooms, clinics and beauty salons all over the country. Nurses trained in aromatherapy are using essential oils in hospitals as pain relief for women in labor. Many more are using them in hospices and hospitals for cancer patients suffering from the side effects of chemotherapy. The therapy is also used to rehabilitate cardiac patients, and in many more areas of patient care. Scientific investigation has begun to prove the effi-

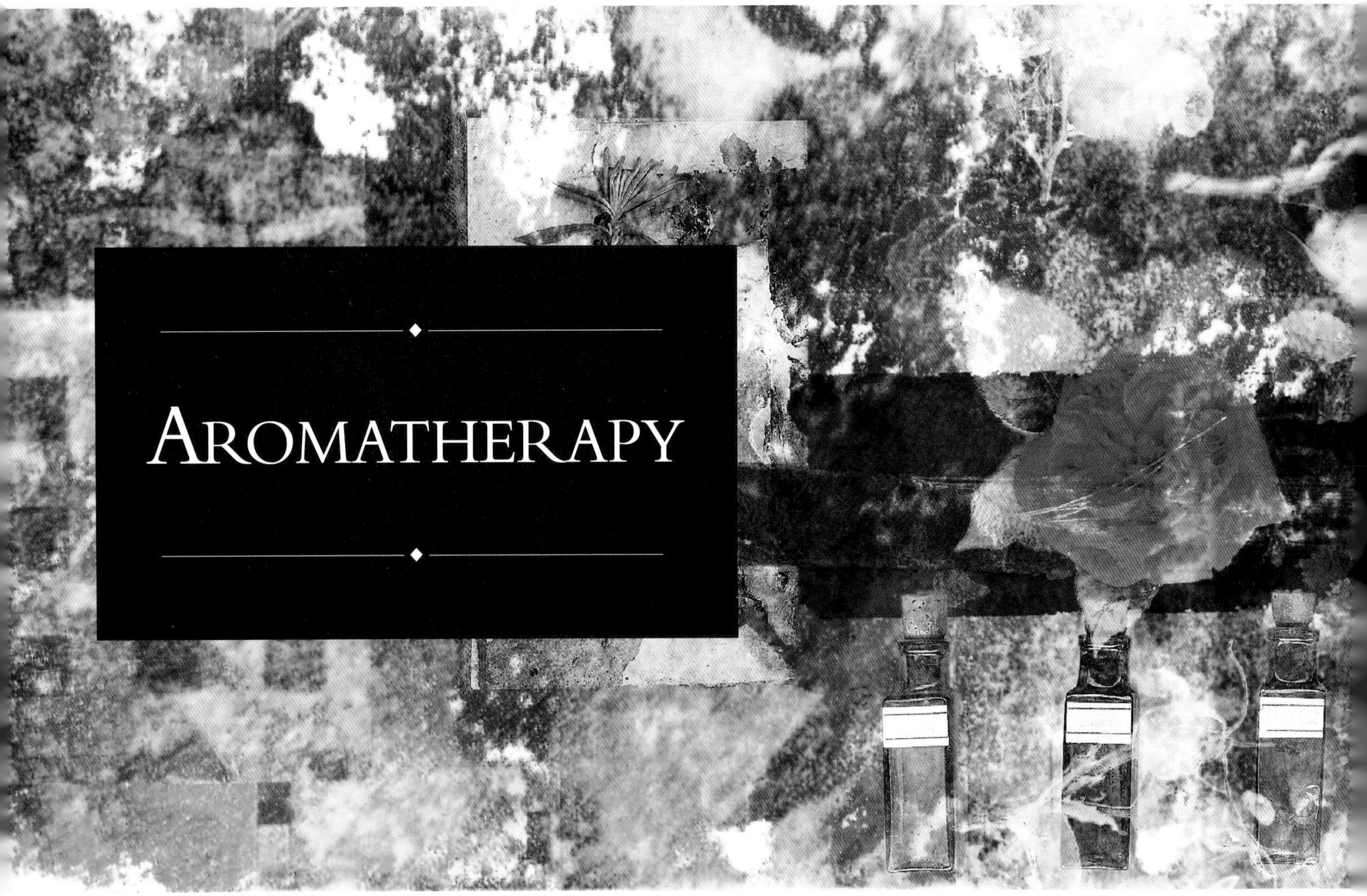

AROMATHERAPY uses pleasant-smelling essential oils to help relieve tension and improve a person's general health and well-being. They can be used as part of a relaxing massage, in steam inhalations, in baths, or in diffusers and vaporizers to release calming or invigorating smells into the atmosphere.

cacy of this centuries-old treatment and it is being embraced by the medical profession as a therapy that complements orthodox treatment. Industry too, is poised to reap the benefits of essential oils. In Japan engineers are incorporating aroma systems into new buildings. In one Japanese bank, for example, the essence of lavender and rosemary is wafted through the customer area in order to calm any waiting customers, while the stimulating fragrances of lemon and eucalyptus are pumped behind the counters to try to keep the staff alert.

However, science has a long way to go. The Greeks, Romans and ancient Egyptians all made use of aromatherapy oils. Nearly

6,000 years ago the Egyptian physician Imhotep, who became the god of medicine and healing, recommended fragrant oils for bathing and massage. Hippocrates, the Greek father of medicine, recommended regular aromatherapy baths and scented massage and placed such store by the power of scent that he used aromatic fumigations to rid Athens of the plague. In England, essential oils were used to ward off the plague long before drugs and synthetic perfumes took their place. However, it was not until the 1930s that French chemist René-Maurice Gattefossé developed the use of aromatherapy as we know it today. Gattefossé originated the term aromatherapy to define the therapeutic use of essential oils as a discipline in its own right.

His interest in the therapy stemmed from his personal experience of the benefits of lavender oil. Apparently, according to the story, he burned his hand in a laboratory experiment and plunged it into the nearest liquid, which happened to be a container of lavender oil. His hand healed remarkably quickly, without infection and with no trace of scarring. This remarkable discovery left Gattefossé eager to find out more about the benefits of aromatherapy. He saw his discovery as an "embryo" of truth that future generations could encourage to grow into a more complete therapy. He based his belief on his own experience with the oils, the testimonies of others, and his scientific investigations. As a chemist he understood the "powerful vitalizing action, the undeniable healing power and the extensive therapeutic properties" of the oils. He also noted that they possessed psychotherapeutic benefits.

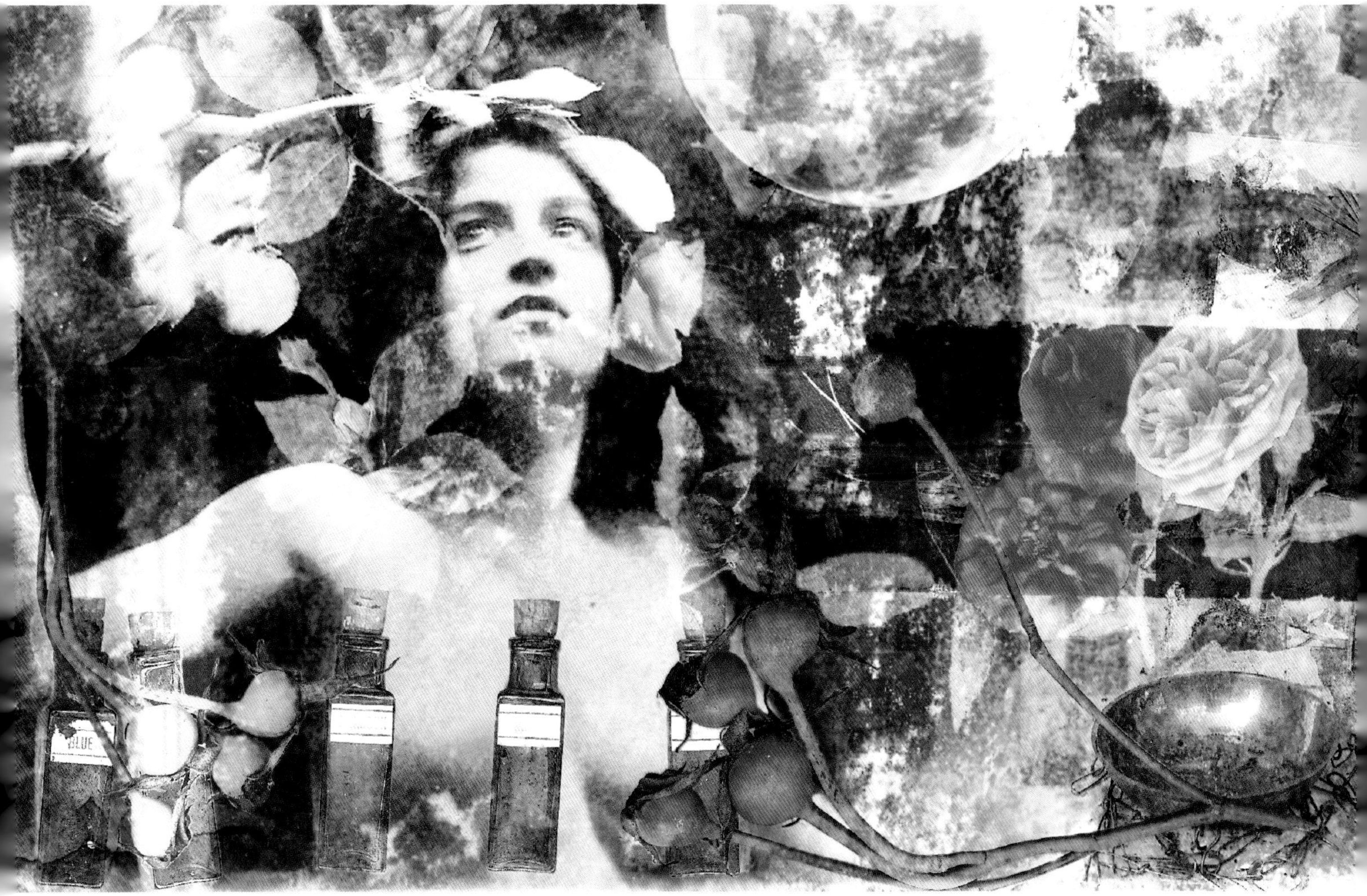

His work was expanded upon by French army surgeon Dr. Jean Valnet, who used essential oils as antiseptics during World War II. But it was Madame Marguerite Maury who developed the idea of aromatherapy as a holistic therapy. She introduced the concept of prescribing oils for the individual, and was the first to combine the effects of essential oils with massage.

Building on the information received from all of these pioneering aromatherapists, modern therapists agree that essential oils should be prescribed for the individual and that they are most effective when massaged into the skin.

Aromatherapists also believe that one of the therapy's greatest attributes is that it works on the mind and body simultaneously, making it a perfect, gentle, mind and body medicine.

ABOVE: Essential oils were used to make perfumes years ago. Here they are being made in a perfume factory in 1858 in St. Katherine's Dock, London.

RIGHT: An oil chest containing a selection of aromatherapy oils, including sweet almond and bergamot.

What is aromatherapy?

The word aromatherapy means "treatment using scents." It refers to the use of essential oils in holistic treatments to improve health and emotional well-being and restore balance to the body. Essential oils are aromatic essences extracted from plants, flowers, trees, fruit, bark, grasses and seeds with distinctive therapeutic, psychological and physiological properties, which improve and prevent illness. Around 150 essential oils have been extracted, each with its own unique scent and healing property. All essential oils have valuable antiseptic properties. Some have particular ones that make them antiviral, anti-inflammatory, pain-relieving, antidepressant, expectorating and antiseptic. Others are stimulating, relaxing, aid digestion or have diuretic properties.

In fact, all the properties, and none of the side effects, of tailor-made drugs occur naturally in plants and their benefits are extracted through essential oils. These pure oils are usually extracted by steam distillation, but other methods, such as solvent extraction, effleurage, and expression can be used. The sources of the oils can be commonplace or rare and exquisite and this is evident in the price. For example, it takes approximately 100kg (220 lbs.) of lavender to yield 3kg (6½ lbs.) of oil so lavender oil is fairly cheap, but it takes approximately eight million jasmine flowers hand-picked at dawn to yield just 1kg (2¼ lbs.) of oil. Not surprisingly, pure jasmine oil is very expensive. To get their optimum benefits, essential oils must be extracted from natural raw ingredients and remain as pure as possible. Synthetic copies simply do not work.

How does it work?

Leading aromatherapist Valerie Worwood describes essential oils as "the little keys that can unlock our physical and mental mechanisms." This seems to be what they do. Scientific research has identified numerous chemical components in essential oils that can exert specific effects on the mind and body. There are many more which have yet to be identified. Those we know of include aldehydes, which are calming, coumarins, which are good for bruising, phenols, which act as a tonic, and alcohols, which are stimulants. Each oil is in fact a combination of at least 100 chemical components. These work together to exert a healing effect on the whole person, yet every oil has a dominant characteristic, which makes it relaxing, stimulating, pain-relieving and so on. Some oils, such as lemon and lavender, are adaptogenic, meaning they adapt to what the body requires of them at the time. Nobody really understands how or why distilled plant essences can do this. It may have something to do with the fact that chemically we are much closer to plants than we care to think. Whichever way it happens, we do know that essential oils are absorbed into the body and exert an influence on it. They can also affect our mind and emotions, and are dispersed from the body leaving no toxic residue. They enter the body in two ways: by inhalation and through absorption.

ABOVE: A variety of essential oils can be used in massage to relieve different symptoms. Lavender helps to relax a stressed person, while lemon or basil can act as body stimulants.

Inhalation: Essential oils have a direct effect on our mind and emotions through our sense of smell. We have the capacity to distinguish 10,000 different smells, many of which can affect us without our knowing. Unlike those in other parts of the body, the smell detector nerve endings are constantly renewing themselves, which seems to indicate the importance of smell. No one knows exactly how smells affect the brain, but the theory is that a smell enters the nose and connects with cilia (the fine hairs lining the nose). The receptors in the cilia are linked to the olfactory bulb (the end of the smelling tract) which, in turn, is linked to the brain itself. Smells are converted by the cilia into electrical impulses which, through the olfactory system, are transmitted to the brain. The part of the brain that the impulses reach is the limbic system – associated with our moods, emotions, memory and learning. So a smell that reaches the limbic system can have a direct chemical effect on our moods and emotions, and as studies have shown, greatly improve our general mental alertness and overall concentration.

The limbic system is also a storehouse of millions of "remembered" smells. When a smell is remembered it can trigger the feeling associated with that memory. That's why the smell of hay can trigger happy memories of a childhood in the country or the smell of pipe tobacco can remind you of a loving grandfather. We also know that the scent of essential oils can exert specific therapeutic effects on our mind and emotions. Aromatherapists know this from clinical practice, but research also supports their claims. In Japan a fragrance company tested the effects of individual essential oil fragrances on the concentration levels of keyboard staff. When lavender essence (usually a relaxant) was pumped into the air, staff made 20 percent fewer keying mistakes; when jasmine (an uplifting fragrance) was used, they made 33 percent fewer, but when lemon (a sharp, refreshing stimulant) was released, mistakes fell by 54 percent. Despite all attempts at scientific explanation we still do not know exactly why this happens. Aromatherapists maintain that essential oils like homeopathic, herbal and flower remedies have a life force that vibrates within the body, each one exerting a unique benefit that is often too subtle to evaluate.

Absorption through the skin: Essential oil molecules are so small that they can be absorbed through the pores of the skin, affecting the skin itself, the bloodstream and the whole body including the brain. Absorption is considered to be more effective than inhalation, and massage is believed to be the best method. It can take anything from 20 minutes to several hours for oils to be absorbed into the body, but the average time is about 90 minutes. Studies detecting essential oils in the blood and body fluids of patients shortly after an aromatherapy massage, have proved that they do enter the body in this way. Heat also helps their absorption, so warm hands and a warm room are necessary for this type of massage. Hot water also helps them to be absorbed from bath water. Applying oils to the body is more powerful than inhalation because they begin to work on the fabric of the body as soon as they touch the skin. It also means that oils can be applied to specific areas such as a patch of eczema or an aching joint where they can get to work immediately.

Once they have done their work, the oils leave the body in various ways: some are exhaled or excreted in urine and feces, while others are sweated out of the system. The process can take up to six hours in a healthy person, but up to 14 hours in someone who is unhealthy or seriously overweight.

How the oils are used

Essential oils are used in a variety of ways, most of which you can do at home.

Inhalations: These can be direct inhalations or steam inhalations. One or two drops of your chosen oil on a handkerchief and you can inhale the oils while at work or traveling. A couple of drops of a relaxing oil on a tissue inside your pillow helps you sleep. Steam inhalations with three or four drops in a large bowl of hot water helps clear congestion or catarrh. Eucalyptus, pine, lavender, black pepper, lemon or peppermint oils are helpful for coughs, colds, bronchitis, sinus problems and headaches.

Diffusers and vaporizers: These release scent of essential oils into the air, providing natural fragrance, while distributing their therapeutic benefits. Diffusers can be electrical, burners that use candles, or a simple ceramic ring that is warmed by a light bulb. Choose a stimulating oil such as lemon or rosemary for the office; a relaxing oil such as lavender or camomile for the bedroom; and an antiseptic such as tea tree to disinfect a sickroom.

Essential oils have distinctive therapeutic, psychological and physiological properties that improve health and prevent illness.

Massage: This is the most common form of treatment used by aromatherapists, simply because it is so effective (see Massage pages 54–59). The combination of touch and the therapeutic benefits of the oils improves circulation and releases trapped energy from tense muscles. The fragrance also promotes a feeling of well-being. The essential oil is diluted in a vegetable carrier oil such as grapeseed or sweet almond oil. Aromatherapists recommend proportions of five drops of essential oil to 5ml (1tsp) of carrier oil for adults, half that strength for children under seven, and a quarter of the strength for children under three. For newborn babies it is best to avoid essential oils altogether.

Baths: Scent with your chosen oil(s). Any oil can be used in the bath. Add up to eight drops for adults, four for children over two, and stir though the water with your hand. Footbaths with two or three drops of lemon, cypress or lavender are good for chilblains, while bergamot and cypress deodorize sweaty feet. Five or six drops of grapefruit essential oil on a flannel or sponge gives an invigorating finish to your morning shower. Use eucalyptus and inhale deeply if you have a cough or cold.

Compresses: These help relieve bruising, skin problems, and muscle and period pain. Use 1–2 drops of an oil like lavender in a bowl of warm water. Soak a piece of cotton in the water and wring out so it does not drip. Put the cotton over the area to be treated and cover with a warm towel. Leave at least two hours.

YOUR AROMATHERAPY STARTER KIT

Clary Sage (SALVIA SCLAREA)
Properties: *Warming, soothing, aphrodisiacal*
Uses: *Menstrual problems, depression, anxiety and high blood pressure*

Eucalyptus (EUCALYPTUS GLOBULUS)
Properties: *Antiseptic, decongestant, antiviral*
Uses: *Colds, chest infections, aches and pains*

Geranium (PELARGONIUM GRAVEOLENS)
Properties: *Soothing, refreshing, relaxing, antidepressant, astringent*
Uses: *PMT, menopause, apathy, anxiety, and skin complaints*

Lavender (LAVENDULA VERA OFFICINALIS)
Properties: *Soothing, antiseptic, generally therapeutic*
Uses: *Skin problems, insomnia, stress, indigestion, cystitis, headache and burns*

Lemon (CITRUS LIMONEM)
Properties: *Refreshing, antiseptic, stimulating*
Uses: *Warts, depression, acne and indigestion*

Peppermint (MENTHA PIPERITA)
Properties: *Digestive, cooling, refreshing, mentally stimulating*
Uses: *Muscle fatigue, bad breath, toothache, bronchitis, indigestion and travel sickness*

Petitgrain (CITRUS AURANTIUM LEAVES)
Properties: *Soothing, calming, antidepressant*
Uses: *Skin problems, apathy, irritability and depression*

Rosemary (ROSMARINUS OFFICINALIS)
Properties: *Stimulating, refreshing*
Uses: *Muscle fatigue, colds, poor circulation, aches and pains and mental fatigue*

Tea tree (MELALEUCA ALTERNIFOLIA)
Properties: *Antifungal, antiseptic*
Uses: *Dandruff, mouthwash, cuts, insect bites and candida*

Ylang Ylang (CANANGA ODORATA)
Properties: *Euphoric, aphrodisiacal, relaxing*
Uses: *Depression, tension, high blood pressure and digestive upsets*

Neat: Lavender oil has an amazing healing effect when used undiluted on burns. It soothes pain, eases the shock, promotes healing and reduces scarring. Tea tree is also effective when used on cuts, grazes, spots, bites and stings. Most essential oils, however, should not be used neat as they can cause irritation.

Taken internally: In France patients are sometimes prescribed essential oils to take internally. This takes place only under the guidance of qualified medical doctors. In Britain, aromatherapists are more reluctant to follow this course, and with good cause. Essential oils may be gentle and fragrant, but they can have remarkable effects, sometimes undesirable ones. Taken internally, essential oils appear to work faster and more intensively. There have been very few cases of oils having serious adverse effects, but those that have been reported were the result of taking oils internally. You are advised never to take essential oils by mouth except under the guidance of a qualified doctor.

What happens in a consultation?

Your first appointment with the aromatherapist will last between one and one and-a-half hours. The smell of the aromatherapist's treatment room is likely to be your first and most lasting impression of your treatment. The room should be warm, comfortable and clean. There will, of course, be a massage table and a plentiful supply of towels, probably a sink and the therapist's stock of oils. Lighting is usually subtle and flattering and there may be soft, relaxing music playing in the background. As with all forms of holistic therapy, the therapist will begin by interviewing you:

- *She will want to know about you and your medical history and why you have come.*
- *She will need to know which oils would be best to use, but also which ones she should avoid. If you are pregnant, have sensitive skin, blood pressure problems, epilepsy, or have had a recent operation there some oils which are not safe to use.*
- *If you are pregnant you will avoid basil, rosemary, sage, thyme, clary sage, juniper oils, and others, because they are toxic, or may harm the fetus or even induce a miscarriage.*

The therapist will ask about your stress levels, as many people choose aromatherapy for stress relief. She will ask if you are taking any medicines or homeopathic remedies as strong smells can negate the effects of homeopathic remedies. She will also want to know how you feel, what mood you are in and what kind of day you have had. This consultation will take about 20 minutes and you may be asked to sign a consent form at the end of it.

You will be asked to undress and lie down on a massage table with a towel over you. You need not undress completely if it would make you uncomfortable. While you do this the therapist will turn away or she may leave the room to give you some privacy. If you lie on the table with a towel over you the therapist will leave the towel over you and move it as she works around your body. That way you can stay warm and also feel less exposed.

She will decide on a blend of oils that she thinks will suit you. She may ask if there are any oils of which you are fond. As a rule of thumb, those you like best are a good indication of what will work best for you. Then with a blend of oils, mixed in a carrier oil, the therapist will begin your massage using traditional Swedish massage techniques, perhaps incorporating shiatsu, a type of massage that works on pressure points of the body (see Shiatsu and acupressure, pages 22–23). Most aromatherapy massage tends to be straightforward and gentle. During the massage itself the therapist will talk very little if at all, it will depend on whether or not you want to talk. Most people just prefer to relax. A full body massage lasts about 30–45 minutes. When the massage is over, you have a few minutes to relax before dressing.

ABOVE: A lot of lavender is needed to just make one small bottle of essential oil.

TOP RIGHT: Lemon essential oil is a good stimulant.

RIGHT: Sometimes an aromatherapist will hold a plumbline over a patient then a chart to choose the right oil.

There may be shower facilities, but for maximum benefit you may be advised not to bathe or shower for a few hours after massage so that the oils are absorbed and the pleasant smell reminds you of the wonderful treatment. The therapist may conclude by giving you oils to use in the bath at home.

How many sessions do I need?

As a relaxation or anti-stress treatment you can have a treatment when you like. But for a specific health problem you will need several visits depending on the problem, the length of time you have had it, and your body's healing abilities. A condition, like PMT, may need three or four treatments before improvement is noticed, and up to ten weekly treatments for symptomatic relief.

Which problems can it help?

Like all forms of holistic medicine aromatherapy works on the whole body to make you feel better generally. It is particularly effective for stress and anxiety-related problems, muscular and rheumatic pains, digestive disorders and women's problems, such as PMS, menopausal complaints and postnatal depression.

Is it safe?

Essential oils are safe for all, but can be strong. Always follow instructions carefully and do not exceed dosages. Be careful if you are pregnant, have an allergy or a medical condition such as eczema, high blood pressure or epilepsy. In such cases consult a qualified practitioner for treatment. Take care when using essential oils on babies or young children. Use undiluted oils on the skin or internally only when advised by a practitioner. If neat oils splash on your skin, or in your eyes wash them off with water. If you, or a child, swallow an essential oil by accident, drink plenty of milk, eat soft bread and consult your doctor immediately.

Clinical studies

Aromatherapy has been found in clinical research to aid recovery from ailments and from surgery.

In 1989 in the Rhone-Alp region of France 94 chronic bronchitis patients received aromatherapy treatment and another group of 88 were treated with a plain oil placebo. Supervised by 27 doctors the aromatherapy patients took 20 drops of "Gouttes aux Essences" (a decongestant oil) orally three times a day for five months (this treatment is not allowed in Britain). There was a drop of infections in those taking aromatherapy, but the overall number of infections and need for antibiotics were unaffected. (**22**)

In Paris in 1985 at The Faculty of Medicine de Bobigny, Dr. Paul Belaiche treated 28 women with Oil of Melaleuca alternifolia, a powerful antifungal and antiseptic oil, for thrush. After 90 days, biological and clinical examinations revealed that 21 women were cured, four had to continue treatment, and only one woman had to stop treatment because of vaginal intolerance. (**23**)

In 1994, a randomized controlled trial was carried out using aromatherapy massage on 100 patients who had received heart surgery. The results showed there were increased psychological benefits with both groups who received massage with plain oil or neroli (from the bark of orange blossom) compared to the control group who had no massage. The main physiological difference was a reduced breathing rate immediately after massage. Five days after treatment, questionnaires revealed that those massaged with neroli oil had more longer lasting psychological benefits than those massaged with the plain oil. (**24**)

In 1993, the emotional and behavioral stress level of 28 patients who were given heart bypasses were monitored before and after treatment on two consecutive days with the support of the Bristol cardiac team. *The Lavender burnatii* oil was twice as effective as naturally occurring *Lavender augustifolia* in reducing their anxiety. However, 20 out of 24 patients said that both oils helped their breathing. This study also showed that the therapeutic effects of aromatherapy are not only due to massage or touch. (**25**) (*For clinical references see How to use this book*)

FOR INFORMATION ON HOW TO CHOOSE AN AROMATHERAPIST SEE THE DIRECTORY.

HOMEOPATHY

Millions of people in Britain, Europe and America use a safe, reliable, natural form of medicine which is known as homeopathy. Homeopathy, which uses neither drugs nor surgery, is based on the belief that everyone is an individual and should be treated accordingly. It first gained prominence in the 19th century after extensive pioneering work by the German physician and chemist Samuel Hahnemann (1755–1843). But its origins date from the 5th century BC, when the Greek physician

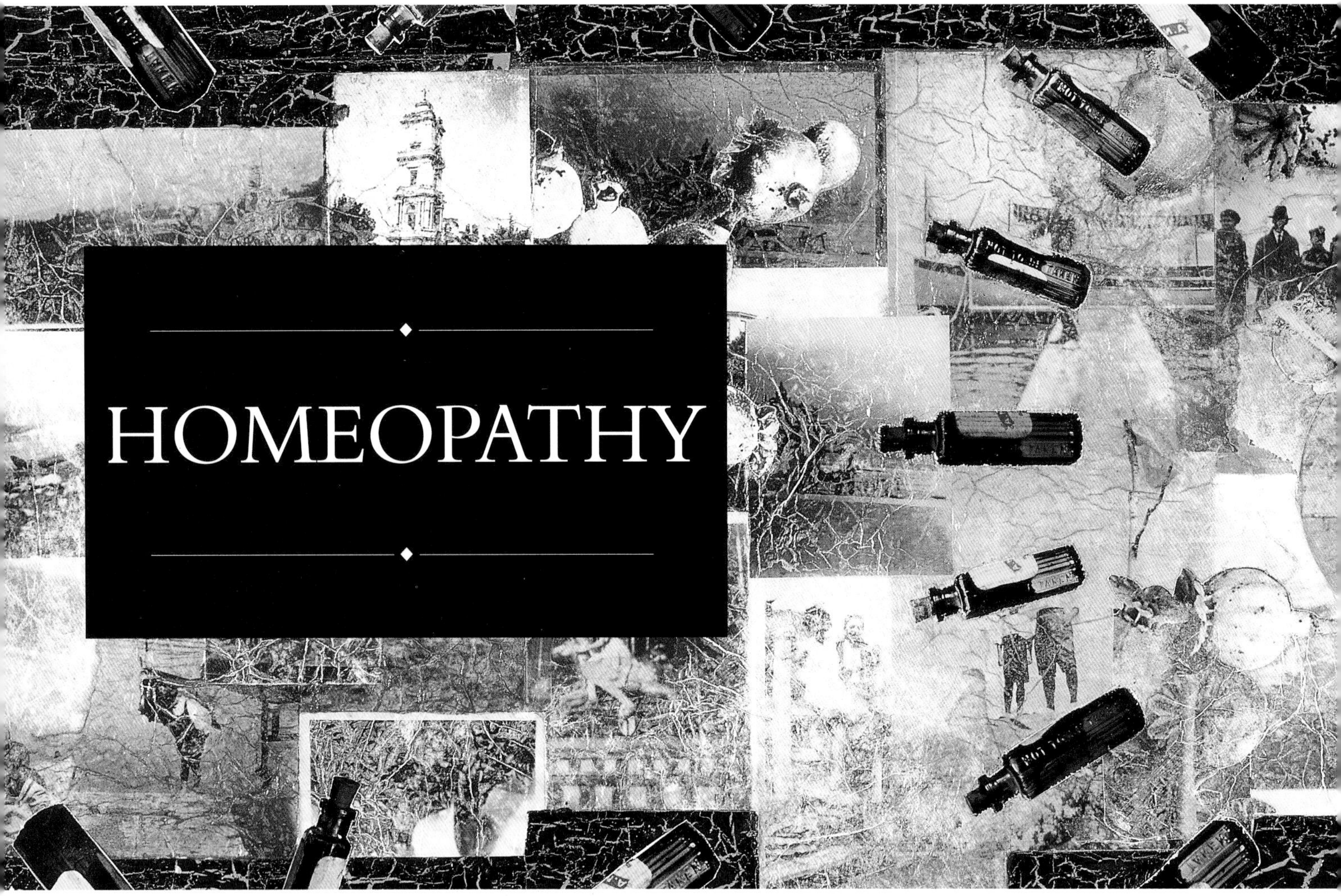

Homeopathy is a holistic medicine which uses animal, vegetable and mineral preparations to cure a person's illness. Its philosophy is to treat "like" with "like" to heal a person. It can help simple ailments like colds and diarrhea and more serious conditions such as fibrositis and psoriasis.

Hippocrates – known as the "father of medicine" – introduced homeopathic remedies to his medicine chest.

However, it was Hippocrates' understanding of disease and how it affects our bodies, rather than his remedies, that made his discoveries homeopathic. He believed that understanding each individual's symptoms, how they reacted to disease, and their powers of healing were vital in diagnosing and treating illness. This understanding of the individual remains the cornerstone of homeopathy today.

After Hippocrates, homeopathy was largely neglected until Hahnemann reinvented it in the late 18th century. Medical treatments had become increasingly violent and invasive, yet disease was rampant, and Hahnemann found clinical medicine totally unacceptable. He wrote extensively on medicine and chemistry and protested against the poor hygiene that was accelerating the spread of disease. He argued against the brutal medical practices and the use of strong medications that caused terrible side-effects. His disillusionment finally led him to give up medicine to work as a translator. Some time later while translating *A Treatise on Materia Medica* by Scottish physician Dr. William Cullen, Hahnemann made the discovery that was to make him the true founder of homeopathy. Cullen stated that quinine was an effective treatment for malaria because of its astringent properties. Hahnemann knew quinine helped to fight malaria, but doubted that its astringent properties had much to do with it. He made investigations. For days he dosed himself with quinine and noted his reactions. He was amazed to find that, one by one, he developed the symptoms of malaria even though he did not have the disease. Each time he took another dose of quinine the symptoms recurred and when he didn't take it, they went away. He believed it was quinine's ability to cause the symptoms of malaria that made it such an effective treament. To illustrate his theory he conducted some tests that he called "provings" on several volunteers and noted each individual's reactions. He conducted the same sort of scientific tests using other popular medicines such as arsenic, which was at that time being prescribed in toxic doses. He noted, as Hippocrates had before him, that the severity of symptoms and healing responses depended on the individual. Some symptoms were common among most testers and these he called keynote or first-line symptoms. Second-line symptoms were those that were less common, and very rare symptoms he named third-line symptoms.

From this system of testing he built up a drug picture for each of the substances he tested. From his research into drug pictures, Hahnemann's next stage was to build a "symptoms picture" of each patient before he prescribed them treatment. He discovered that the more information he could glean from each patient about their symptoms, likes and dislikes, and what made them better or worse, the more accurately he could prescribe a suitable remedy. His drug pictures are still in use today to prescribe the best homeopathic treatment.

BELOW: Samuel Hahnemann, a physician and chemist in the 19th century, is regarded as the founder of homeopathy as we know it today.

ABOVE: A homeopathic dispensary will dispense a homeopath's prescriptions but other items can also be bought over the counter.

ABOVE: Only a small amount of each herbal and vegetable ingredient is used to make up all the different homeopathic remedies that are available.

What is homeopathy?

This is a form of medicine that treats the body as a whole and helps it to heal itself. The treatment works for acute (short-term) illnesses and chronic (long-term) ailments and the aim is to prevent illness as well as treat it. The name homeopathy comes from the Greek word "*homios*" meaning like and "*pathos*" meaning suffering. Homeopathy simply means treating like with like.

In practice, this means a substance that causes symptoms of illness in a well person can also cure similar symptoms when they result from illness. This view is the opposite of conventional or "allopathic" medicine which treats illness with an antidote rather than a similar substance. For example, an allopathic doctor would treat diarrhea with a substance that causes constipation, while a homeopath or homeopathic doctor would treat it with a minute dose of a substance that would actually cause diarrhea if given in a larger dose.

The minute substances used in treatment are called homeopathic remedies. These remedies are prescribed for the person and how they are reacting to the ailment, not just the disease. A remedy is not homeopathic because it is prescribed by a homeopath, but because it matches the patient's condition. There are over 2,000 homeopathic remedies that are usually referred to by their abbreviated name, for example, *Argentum nitricum* is known as Arg nit. In addition to homeopathic remedies, homeopaths (and other therapists such as medical herbalists), also prescribe tissue salts.

Biochemic tissue salts are homeopathically prepared ingredients which were introduced at the end of the 19th century by a German doctor, Wilhelm Schussler. He believed that many diseases were caused by a deficiency of one or more of 12 vital minerals, and that a deficiency in each salt would manifest itself as specific symptoms. Lack of *Calcerea phosphorica* (Calc phos), for example, would show up as teeth problems or an inability to absorb nutrients properly, while lack of magnesium phosphate (Mag phos) would affect nerve endings and muscles. He replaced the missing mineral with a minute dose of the tissue salt to correct the problem.

Tissue salts are prepared from mineral sources, but homeopathic remedies are made from animal, vegetable and mineral sources. These can be as exotic as snake's venom, or as common as onions, but they are all diluted to such an extent that there can be no possible side-effects from even the most toxic substances. Extracts of the natural ingredient are dissolved in a mix of alcohol and water and left to stand for two–four weeks. During this time they are shaken occasionally and then strained. The strained solution is known as the mother tincture. The mother tincture is then diluted to make the different potencies. Dilutions are measured according to either the decimal (x), centesimal (c) or millesimal (M) scale. On the decimal scale the remedies are diluted to the ratio 1:10, on the centesimal scale it is 1:100 and on the millesimal scale it is 1:1000.

Between every dilution the remedy is shaken vigorously. To produce a 1c (one hundredth) dilution, one drop of the mother tincture is added to 99 drops of an alcohol and water mix and then shaken. To produce a 6c (six hundredth) potency, this happens six times, each time the one drop is taken from the previously shaken solution. By the time it is diluted to the 12c (twelve hundredth) potency, it is unlikely that any of the original ingredient remains. This is often the reason why skeptics are so reluctant to believe that homeopathic remedies can really work. Finally, these drops are added to tiny lactose (milk sugar) tablets, pillules, granules or powder and stored in a dark colored bottle.

Symptoms of an illness are seen as the body's positive attempts to heal itself.

How does it work?

Conventional doctors treat the symptoms of disease because they see the symptoms as a manifestation of the illness. They prescribe pharmaceutical drugs that deliver a dose of painkilling antibiotic or anti-inflammatory ingredients in a dose great enough to dampen the symptoms of the condition or to kill the bacteria causing it.

Homeopaths, however, see symptoms as an expression of the body's attempts to heal itself. They see them as a positive sign that the body is fighting illness and so they should not be suppressed. Homeopathic remedies are aimed at stimulating and supporting the body's healing mechanism. For this reason they can sometimes provoke what homeopaths call an "aggravation," whereby symptoms may get worse before they improve.

Homeopathic remedies are prescribed for the whole person and are based on the principles established by Hahnemann: the law of similars, the principle of the minimum dose and prescribing for the individual.

The law of similars: This states that a substance, which in large doses can produce symptoms of illness in a well person, can, in minute doses, cure similar symptoms of disease in a sick person. According to Hahnemann, this is because nature does not allow two similar diseases to exist in the body at the same time. To rid the body of one disease, homeopaths introduce a similar artificial disease that pushes the original one out, but is too fleeting to cause any long-term suffering.

The minimum dose: This states that extreme dilution enhances the curative properties of a substance, while eliminating any possible side-effects. You need only use a minute dose of the active ingredient to stimulate an improvement in health.

Whole person prescribing: This is the third and vitally important principle, which has been mentioned in the introduction. A homeopath studies the whole person: their temperament, personality, emotional and physical responses when prescribing a remedy. Therefore a homeopath will not treat flu, he will treat a person who has flu-like symptoms. So, although a conventional doctor could see ten people with flu and prescribe the same treatment for all of them, a homeopath might well give each one a different remedy, depending on how they were responding as individuals to their illness.

In addition to the three principles, homeopaths believe that treatment works according to the Laws of Cure. There are three laws of cure which state simply that a remedy starts at the top of the body and works downward; it works from within the body outward, and from major to minor organs. It also states that symptoms clear in reverse order of appearance. So you will start to feel emotionally better before feeling physically better. Also if you had an illness which manifested itself first as a rash, followed by vomiting and then a fever, the fever would subside first, then the vomiting would stop and finally the rash would disappear.

Homeopaths often find that the effective way to prescribe treatment is according to constitutional type. They believe a person's constitution is made up of inherited and acquired physical, mental and emotional characteristics and these can be matched to a remedy to improve their health, no matter what the illness.

Most people have difficulty in understanding how homeopathic remedies work when they contain such minute traces of the original remedy.

Homeopaths believe it is the energy or "vibrational pattern" of the remedy, rather than its chemical content, that stimulates healing by activating what Hahnemann called the Vital Force. The vital force is simply the healing power or energy that exists within all of us. It is what the Chinese call "Chi" and the Indians call "Prana." It fuels the body, mind and emotions, keeping us healthy and balanced. But when the balance of the vital force is disturbed by factors such as stress, pollution, inadequate diet and lack of exercise, it becomes weakened and illness can result. The symptoms of illness are the body's way of attracting our attention to the fact that the vital force is struggling to fight off disease.

Hahnemann could not prove how minute doses of homeopathic remedies could restore health, but he could prove that they did. His own belief that they somehow strengthened the embattled vital force, enabling it to restore the body to health remains the predominant belief among homeopaths today, even though science has been unable to support this belief.

YOUR HOME FIRST AID KIT

Successful homeopathic treatment is best given by a skilled homeopath; however, a selection of remedies work for a variety of common ailments and so are suitable for using at home.

Note: c = one hundredth
Take the remedies in the 6c (for acute problems) or 30c potency (for less acute problems) every two hours for up to six doses, then three times a day between meals. Put a pill or tablet under your tongue and allow it to dissolve. For babies, crush the tablet on a spoon and put it in the baby's mouth. Take three times a day between meals until symptoms improve. If you have just eaten, rinse your mouth with water before you take the remedy.
Arnica *6c 30c for shock after injury and bruising, cramp, burns, stings, black eye, nose bleed, sprains, strained or torn muscles, eczema, boils, whooping cough and child bed wetting.*
Apis *30c for insect stings that are hot and swollen, cystitis, hives, edema, arthritis, allergic reactions in eyes, throat and mouth. (Avoid during pregnancy).*
Bryonia *30c for swollen painful joints, swollen painful breasts, heat exhaustion, bursting headache and nausea, screaming colicky babies, colds and flu.*
Cantharis *6c for burns, scalds and blisters, cystitis, burning diarrhea, any burning or stinging sensation.*
Euphrasia *6c for eye injuries, conjunctivitis, eye strain or foreign bodies in the eyes, bursting headaches, constipation and at the onset of measles.*
Glonoin *30c for heat exhaustion and bursting headaches.*
Hypericum *30c for wounds with shooting pains, for injuries where the nerves are affected: crushed fingers or toes, head wounds and cut lip, nausea, indigestion and diarrhea.*
Ledum *6c for insect stings and wounds that feel numb and cold and for a painful black eye, prevents infection.*
Nux vomica *6c for travel sickness and nausea with a headache, digestive problems, heavy periods, hangover, morning sickness or cystitis.*
Phospate *6c for nose bleeds caused by severe blowing.*
Rhus tox *6c for red, swollen, itchy blisters, diaper rash, painful stiff muscles, cramp, rheumatic or arthritic pain that is eased by moving.*
Ruta grav *6c for pain and stiffness in pulled muscles, eye strain, rheumatism and deep aching pain in bones and muscles.*
Silica *6c for splinters that could cause infection, migraine, recurrent colds and infections, spots and weak nails.*
Tabacum *6c for travel sickness, nausea, vomiting, faintness, dizziness and anxiety.*
Urtica *6c for stinging burns, scalds and allergic skin, insect stings, cystitis and hives.*

What happens in a consultation?

The consultation will begin with the homeopath "taking your case." This means he will ask numerous questions about yourself and your lifestyle and make copious notes. The purpose of taking your case is to build up a picture of you and your mental, physical and emotional health so that the practitioner can understand the type of person you are and prescribe the best remedy.

Typically, the questions asked focus on five different aspects of your life concerning the: physical, mental, emotional, spiritual and general aspects. The first four include such information as:

- *Details about your past illnesses and any inherited family health problems*
- *How you feel about taking on new challenges*
- *If you are afraid of the dark and any other relevant details*

General information includes such details as how you tend to react to hot and cold, whether you are at your best in the morning or evening, your favorite season, and whether you prefer to eat sweet, salty or spicy food.

Most homeopaths will not examine you, but if your homeopath is also medically qualified, he can carry out a physical examination, if it is needed. For this reason, if you consult a homeopath who is not a doctor, it is also advisable to remain under the care of your doctor as well.

When your homeopath is satisfied that he has all the information he needs he will prescribe a remedy. He will normally only prescribe one remedy at a time, although the prescription can change later as your symptoms change.

For example, you may need to take one remedy four times a day for three days and another remedy once a day for the next week. The remedy will be small pills, tablets, granules, powder or a tasteless, colorless liquid. You will be advised not to touch it but to take it on a spoon or tip a pill under your tongue, and to keep it away from any strong-smelling substances as these can negate the remedy. You may also be asked to abstain from eating peppermints and drinking coffee during your treatment. Your practitioner may also advise taking the remedy in a "clean mouth," that is not to eat, drink or smoke for half an hour beforehand. When you do take the remedy place it under your tongue and let it dissolve.

Your homeopath may not tell you what he prescribed until later on in your treatment. This is usually because most people rush to the nearest reference book to find out which type of person they are, only to be disappointed or offended. The homeopath may advise on diet and lifestyle changes if he thinks that these would help your condition.

Your first visit will probably end with you making a follow-up appointment, usually for a month later so that the practitioner can assess your progress.

How many sessions do I need?

Some people recover more quickly than others, depending on the ailment and their response to the remedy. Treatment may take only one or two visits, but it can take more. Sometimes a homeopath will change your remedy if the first one proved unsuitable

BELOW: When you first visit a homeopath he will ask you many questions about yourself so that he can prescribe a remedy that is right for you, not your illness.

ABOVE: Homeopathic remedies are also suitable for children, and are safe to use at home to treat minor ailments.

ABOVE: When a homeopathic remedy is prepared it is succussed (shaken vigorously).

and this can take some weeks. The length of treatment also depends on the severity of your illness and how long you have had it. However, if there is no improvement after four or five visits, see another homeopath or try an alternative therapy.

Which problems can it help?

It is probably fair to say that homeopathy works well for everything, but doesn't work for everyone. Minor ailments such as colds, constipation, vomiting and diarrhea respond well. With more serious conditions, it can help rheumatoid arthritis, fibrositis and psoriasis. Because a homeopathic remedy stimulates your body to heal itself it, will help rectify emotional, mental or physical complaints, but some people respond better than others.

Is it safe?

Homeopathic remedies are so diluted that they are safe for everyone to take, from babies, to pregnant women and the elderly. Even if a child were to swallow a bottle of pills, he would suffer nothing more than a little diarrhea from the effects of the lactose. However, as with all medicines, take the remedies only as long as you need to. You can happily take homeopathic medicine while receiving conventional treatment although some chemical drugs may affect their action.

Clinical studies

Homeopathy has been shown in several clinical studies to be effective in treating many types of ailments and illnesses and various skin complaints.

A study was carried out at the Glasgow Royal Infirmary in 1994 by a multidisciplinary team led by Dr. Reilly which assessed the effects of homeopathy or a placebo on 28 asthmatic patients allergic to dust mites. After one week's treatment, nine out of the 11 patients being given homeopathy improved, compared to only five of the 17 placebo patients. Severe asthmatic conditions responded best to the remedies that were given. The effects of one week's homeopathic treatment lasted up to eight weeks and improvements continued for all patients. (**26**)

In another trial, Dr. Schawb Alenavia used a sulphur homeopathic remedy plus a placebo to treat patients suffering from dermatological complaints.

In two trials 26 patients took the homeopathic remedy or a placebo. Around 50 percent of the subjects reacted to the homeopathic treatment and none to the placebo. Typical reactions were an aggravation of the skin conditions with some patients experiencing symptoms characteristic of sulphur – diarrhea, thirst, itching and heat sensitivity. The skin complaints then started to get better, with 58 percent of the patients experiencing permanent improvements. Those patients with the worst conditions showed the best recoveries. (**27**)

In a trial in Verona, Italy, in 1991 60 migraine sufferers were randomly divided into groups receiving treatment or just a placebo. The groups were compared to ensure that they had similar characteristics. Two different remedies were chosen for each patient from belladonna, ignatia, lachesis, silicea, gelsemium, cyclamen, *Natrium muriaticum* and sulphur according to the subject's individual reaction and needs.

The subjects were given a 30c potency dose four times over a two-week period. While the placebo group showed a slight drop in migraine attacks, the treatment group's average dropped from ten to three per month after two months, going down to 1.8 after four months. The length and intensity of attacks also improved. (**28**) (*For clinical references see How to use this book*)

FOR INFORMATION ON HOW TO CHOOSE A HOMEOPATH SEE THE DIRECTORY.

NUTRITIONAL THERAPY

FOR YEARS nutrition has formed the backbone of health-care. Hunting for and gathering food consumed most of the preagricultural societies' time and energy. Food and herbs were our first medicine, which were used to treat a large number of conditions ranging from wounds and insect bites, to infection and broken limbs.

From the earliest days of medicine, it became clear that food had a medicinal effect, and that a varied diet, rich in natural ingredients, was a prerequisite for good health. So, diet became a fundamental part of most early health therapies, and an integral element in almost all later medical systems.

NUTRITIONAL THERAPY is the use of a special diet to balance the body and to prevent illness. A macrobiotic diet is based on the Chinese philosophy of yin and yang. Yin and yang foods can be adjusted by the therapist to restore the body to health.

For example, in the 18th century English sailors were given lime or lemon juice in order to prevent scurvy, a disease caused by lack of Vitamin C, which occurred as a result of long periods of time away at sea without fresh fruits or vegetables.

In the late 19th century naturopaths (see Naturopathy pages 98–103) drew attention to the use of food and how nutritional elements could be used as medicine, a concept which was not new, but which had not been acknowledged as a therapy in its own right until that time. Naturopaths used a nutritional diet and fasting to cleanse the body, and to encourage its ability to heal itself. As knowledge about food, its make-up, and its effects on the body became greater as biochemistry developed, the first nutritional specialists undertook to treat specific ailments and symptoms with the food components.

By the middle of the 20th century, scientists had put together a profile of proteins, carbohydrates and fats, plus vitamins and minerals, which were essential to life and to health. More than 40 nutrients were discovered, including 13 vitamins. It was found that minerals were needed for healthy body functions, and a new understanding of the body and its biochemistry fed the growing interest in the subject.

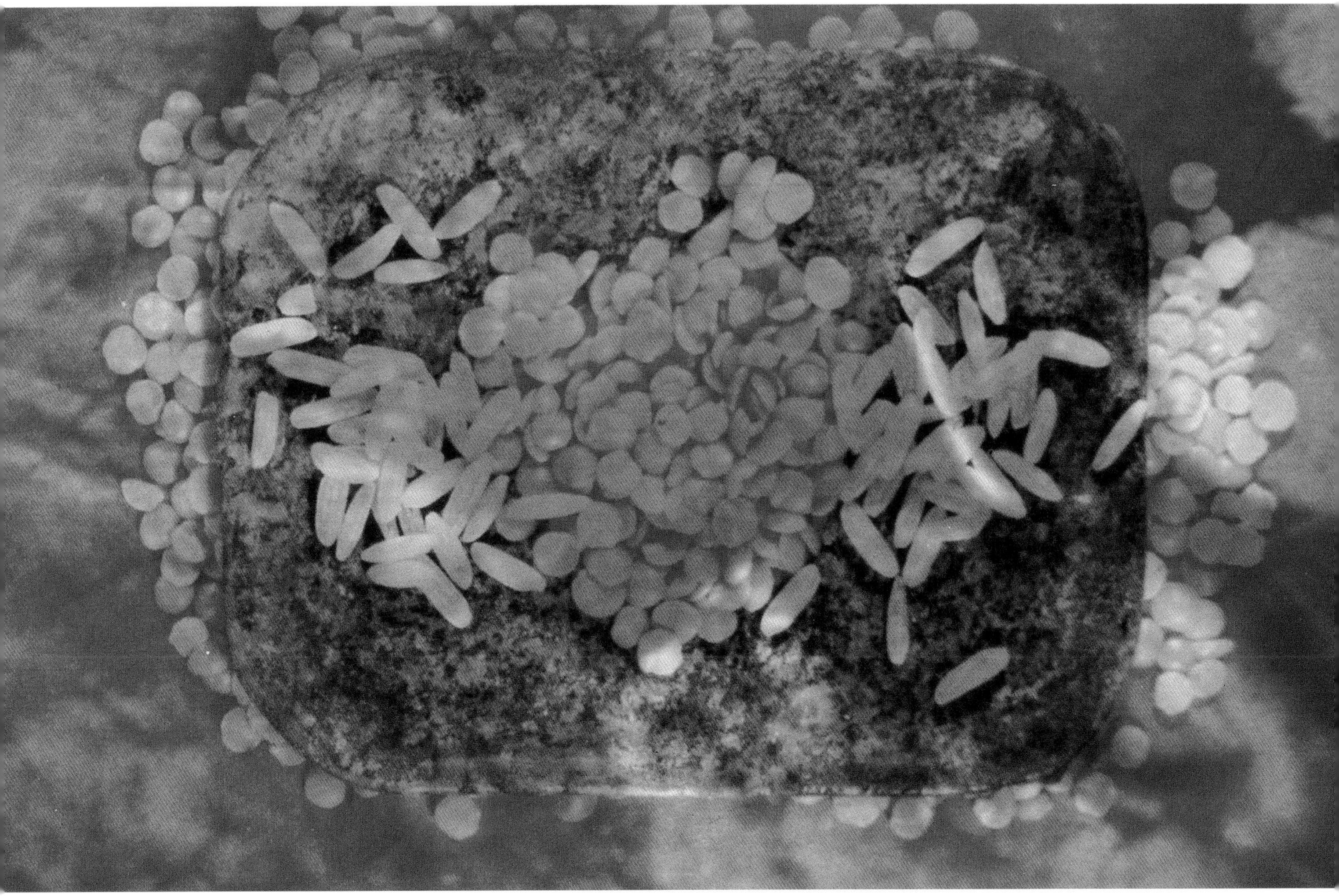

In the 1960s, Stanford chemistry professor Linus Pauling published a paper in the journal *Science*. He talked about creating the best molecular environment in the mind by supplying the right concentration of certain biochemicals such as vitamins. He named the term orthomolecular. The now controversial fields of orthomolecular psychiatry and orthomolecular medicine were then defined, and doctors began to treat patients with special diets and supplements, which were prescribed according to individual symptoms, health problems and special needs. While conventional medical doctors still discussed nutrition in terms of basic food groups (it is only studied briefly in medical school), orthomolecular nutritionists were regularly prescribing high levels of vitamin supplements. Doctors used biochemicals to correct nutritional deficiencies they saw as factors in a huge range of physical and mental diseases.

Nutrition then spread from being a mainly doctor-led dietary therapy, also called clinical nutrition, into a more profound theory of health control based on treating the patient as a whole (holistic health), and looking for specific deficiencies that could be causing illness in an individual.

The term "Macrobiotics" comes from the Greek words *makros* which means "large" and *biokos* which means "life," and macrobiotics is based on the fundamental belief that everyone should be healthy enough to enjoy life to the full.

Macrobiotics has a rich and lively heritage, which originated in early Tibet and China, where the early philosophy was largely inspired by three books – *The Nei Ching, The I Ching*, and *The Tao Te Ching*. The overwhelming emphasis of these books was diet, seasonally and individually adjusted. Remedies and first aid were drawn from Japanese folk medicine, and practical guidelines for a healthy lifestyle were drawn from *The Nei Ching*, – a comprehensive study of anatomy, physiology and diagnosis. This book also held a cosmological view of human beings, derived from the major world religions.

In the 1960s, Michio Kushi, one of Ohsawa's students, began teaching the philosophy in the United States and Europe, and he broadened the dietary guidelines and further developed Ohsawa's ideas. The result of his ideas and ideals is the modern-day macrobiotics, which has evolved from being a fairly strict regime to include all of the essential elements of basic nutrition. The idea is that you can live life to its full potential, assisted by a diet promoting physical, mental, emotional and spiritual health.

RIGHT: Many people have a sweet tooth and cannot resist cakes and cookies; however these should be eaten in moderation as too much sugar is bad for you.

ABOVE: Eggs are a good source of protein and french fries contain some useful vitamins, but frying them in oil greatly increases the fat content and should be avoided.

RIGHT: The recommended daily diet should contain only a small amount of fat, so snacks such as fatty hamburgers should be eaten only occasionally.

the idea that humanity is part of the environment and the cosmos, and that health and judgment is a reflection of our appreciation, connection and intake from the world around us.

In the 1880s, a Japanese doctor, Sagen Ishizuka, discovered that many health problems could be treated with dietary changes, which often involved whole grains and vegetables. Refined carbohydrates and white rice were removed from the diet. His work was published in two volumes, and was later used for reference by George Ohsawa, who, by 1945, had synthesized all the beliefs and adopted the term "Macrobiotics." Ohsawa wrote over 300 books, which dwelt on the importance of a healthy, balanced,

What is nutritional therapy?

Nutritional therapy is using diet to treat and prevent illness, and to restore the body to a natural, healthy equilibrium. It is believed that subclinical deficiencies are responsible for much of the disease and weakness in the body. These are in fact vitamin and mineral deficiencies which are too slight to produce obvious deficiency diseases, such as scurvy or anemia, but which are enough to reduce the body's ability to function efficiently. These minor deficiencies can often start with niggling and annoying symptoms which may not, on their own, be enough for most people to seek medical attention.

Indeed, we have today come to accept many of these symptoms as just part of our day-to-day stressful living. Problems like fatigue, susceptibility to colds and other viruses, skin ailments and lethargy are common symptoms of nutritional subclinical deficiency, experienced by most of us at some time.

One of the problems is that the diet of the modern Western world fails to provide adequate nutrition for people in general. In fact it can contribute not only to ill-health but to obesity, heart disease, cancer, digestive disorders, premature ageing, and in many cases death. The Western world is overfed but undernourished and, although food is plentiful, it is often food devoid of any nutritional value. Over the past few years research has indicated that many health conditions are caused by allergies or intolerance to various kinds of foods, but that certain foods have therapeutic properties. For example, some are known to aid digestion, reduce inflammation or mucous production, and many conditions such as asthma or eczema can be treated almost entirely by changing the diet. Similarly, rheumatism and arthritis sufferers can reduce the frequency of attacks or clear their conditions by changing the food that they eat.

A healthy diet is one in which the food you eat contains all the nutrients needed by the body to exist.

The modern world has also placed new stresses on our bodies, exposing them to environmental and psychological demands which did not exist even two decades ago. This means that our bodies are often depleted of protective and important nutrients, which results in ill-health plus a variety of other common ailments.

In an ideal world it should be possible to get all of the nutritional elements that we need from a balanced diet, but with intensive farming methods, pesticides, preservatives, additives and hormones, our diets are often far less nutritious than they appear. The soil is no longer as rich with minerals as it used to be, and vegetables and fruit grown in it are therefore correspondingly less nutritious. Cattle grazing on the land reap much less nutritional goodness from the grass because it too was grown from the depleted soil. Also alcohol, tobacco, drugs, stress, environmental pollution and various additives all help to rob the body of the nutrients it needs, so even a healthy individual can suffer from day-to-day living in the modern world. Today as manufacturers and food producers strive to make food last longer they now contain a mixture of:

- *Colorants, preservatives, flavorings, emulsifiers and polyphosphates*
- *Contaminants from agriculture, antibiotics and growth promoters, industrial contaminants and also radioactive contamination*

Nutritional therapy is a sophisticated system of healthcare, which depends on an increasingly broad-based knowledge of biochemistry, physiology and nutrition to address the health needs of the individual. There are three basic diagnoses which are made by the nutritional therapist, and these are: allergy (or intolerance) to food, nutritional deficiencies (often subclinical) and finally toxic overload.

Food allergies

Many practitioners believe that about 20 percent of people have some kind of allergy, although this is controversial. A food allergy can be caused by almost any kind of food, and common symptoms include nausea, vomiting and diarrhea. The most common allergens are dairy produce, nuts, eggs, yeast, shellfish, wheat, flour, citrus fruit and artificial colorings. Many children are affected by food additives, especially tartrazine and benzoate, which cause hyperactivity and other behavioral problems.

If you suspect an allergy, your therapist might suggest an elimination diet, which will allow her to pinpoint which foods are causing your symptoms. Elimination programs should never be undertaken without professional supervision. There are other means of identifying allergies including kinesiology, kirlian photography, (see Diagnostic therapies pages 153–155) biofeedback, and blood tests, although their reliability may be disputed.

Some of the common foods you can be allergic to are:

- *Gluten (wheat), tea, seafood, tomatoes, coffee, bananas, dairy produce and animal fats*
- *Yeast, oranges, peppers, eggs, rye, cheese and potatoes*
- *Alcohol, onions, strawberries, pineapple, tap water, condiments and garlic*
- *Corn, wine, nuts, oats, chocolate and mushrooms*
- *Rice, pork and soya*

Nutritional deficiencies

Few people show signs of a serious vitamin or mineral deficiency, such as scurvy, but it is now known that many people suffer slight shortages in the body. These can be tested for by symptom analysis, hair mineral analysis, "Touch for Health" muscle testing, and perhaps blood or sweat analysis.

Toxic overload

Toxic overload is identified by the nutritionist analyzing the combination of the symptoms experienced and the normal lifestyle of the sufferer. Toxins are effectively poisons which can be in our food, or are created within our bodies by intestinal bacteria or as ordinary waste products of metabolism.

VITAMINS AND MINERALS

It is important that the nutritional therapist finds out if any deficiencies exist for the following vitamins and minerals:

Vitamins

- *Vitamin A (retinol, carotene), B1 thiamine, B2 riboflavin, B3 niacin, B5 pantothenic acid and B6 pyridoxine*
- *B12 cobalamin, cynocobalamin, folic acid and biotin*
- *Vitamin C (ascorbic acid) and vitamin D (calciferol, viosterol)*
- *Vitamin E (tocopherol) and vitamin F (fatty acids), Vitamin H (biotin) and vitamin K (menadione)*
- *Vitamin M (folic acid), vitamin P (bioflavonoids) and vitamins T and U*

Minerals

- *Calcium, chlorine, chromium and copper*
- *Iodine, iron, magnesium and molybdenum*
- *Potassium, selenium, sodium, sulphur, vanadium and zinc*

How does it work?

Nutritional therapy is based on the knowledge that each part of the body is made up of elements that were once the nutritional elements of food. The idea is that functions deteriorate when some of these elements are in short supply for too long, or the body is being mildly poisoned. The nutritional therapist will decide how to improve these functions, using a good nutritional diet and body knowledge.

Dozens of laboratory tests measuring everything in a patient's body from sugar intolerance and blood levels of vitamins and minerals, to thyroid function and levels of insulin, can help the nutritional therapist to find out what may be causing or aggravating an illness. Hair analysis can be used to evaluate levels of trace minerals.

A healthy body is strong and resistant to illness, so while the nutritional therapist will treat the symptoms of one illness by meeting the body's needs, very often other unrelated conditions can also be cured.

A nutritional therapist believes that many of the ailments common to Western people are provoked by a toxic overload, food allergies or nutritional deficiencies in their diet. She may recommend the use of vitamin and mineral supplements and other substances to restore the body's natural balance, along with a diet that includes plenty of vegetables, fruit and whole grains. Nutritional therapists believe that the recommended level of intake of vitamins, minerals, and other elements of nutrition, do not take into account the very wide range of individual requirements. Certainly any difficulty in absorbing one particular vitamin, or even a slight deficiency in another can set the whole system awry, because they are all necessary to complete the chain of nutrition. After a full consultation, and perhaps some tests, a nutritional therapist will diagnose possible nutritional deficiencies and ensure that your diet is better balanced to incorporate these elements. She might also prescribe supplements or some herbs to speed up the healing process. Possible food allergies and intolerance may be identified, and some extra foods suggested to give a therapeutic effect.

Some controlled use of supplements may be recommended as research suggests they can treat certain conditions. For example, there is increasing evidence that some PMT sufferers are deficient in gamma-linolenic acid (GLA), found in evening primrose oil, and a course of this supplement may be recommended. Some types of neuralgia or carpal tunnel syndrome may indicate a deficiency of B-vitamins; tyrosine, an amino acid, has been very successfully used to treat depression and anxiety. A deficiency in Vitamin A may aggravate a number of different skin conditions.

These are only some of the treatments offered by a nutritional therapist, and treatment will always be tailored to the individual. The consistent use of supplements or mega-doses (which is not usually recommended) should, however, always be supervised by a registered therapist because many supplements can be toxic in high doses.

A healthy diet

The Western diet is generally high in cholesterol and fats, especially saturated fats, low in fiber, and high in refined sugars and animal products. Diets which are low in fat and cholesterol, but high in dietary fiber, fruits and vegetables, are healthier and provide much more energy. Ailments such as odd aches and pains, headaches, some types of diabetes, immune deficiencies, skin problems and digestive disorders all disappeared when the right diet is followed.

A healthy diet is one in which the food you eat contains all the nutrients needed by the body for it to grow, heal and to function normally on a day-to-day basis. A balanced diet provides energy, and allows you to function at your optimum level, free from disease and malaise.

There are three essential nutrient food groups: proteins, carbohydrates, fats plus minerals and vitamins. You also need water, which is found in most foods and which makes up a large proportion of our body. Roughly speaking, proteins should make up about 15 percent of the diet, carbohydrates 60 percent or more, and fats a maximum of 25 to 30 percent. Vitamins and minerals are found within each of these groups, and a balanced diet should have all or most represented in adequate levels. Dietary fiber is also important for your health.

Choosing fresh and wholesome foods

Fresh fruits, vegetables and salads should form part of your daily diet, and ideally fresh meat and fish should be used instead of packaged or frozen foods. Many of the processes used to preserve food, such as freezing and canning, can result in a loss of nutrients. Wherever possible, try to choose local and fresh produce, since long storage or periods of traveling can cause beans, peas or lentils, one serving of milk, cheese or another dairy product; four servings of complex carbohydrates such as bread, brown rice, pasta, potatoes or muesli and finally five servings of fresh fruit, vegetables or salads, and as little fat as possible. Children, pregnant women and breastfeeding mothers may need more dairy products and occasionally they may need more fat than other groups.

Ideally, organically produced foods should be eaten whenever possible as they are more healthy and nutritious. However, they are usually more expensive to buy than their non-organic equivalents and fruit and vegetables can appear more pitted and less attractive because pesticides have not been used.

There are a number of diets which are based around special needs: for example, sufferers of heart disease should eat a low-fat and low-salt diet. There are also a wide range of diets to treat different illnesses, for example, fasting or eating raw food diets to cleanse the system. Unless strictly short-term, all diets should be varied, with as few restrictions as possible.

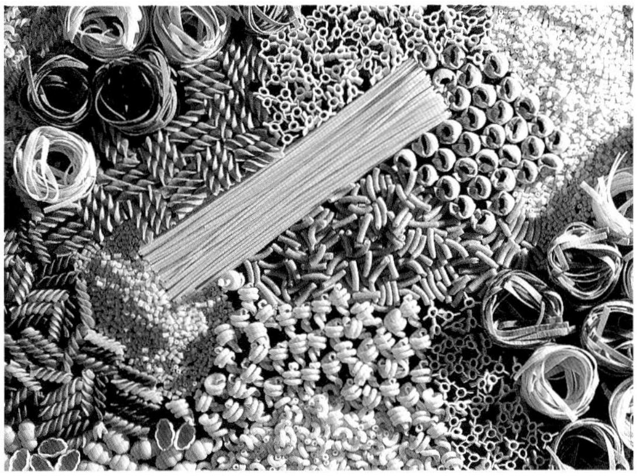

TOP AND ABOVE: Both bread and pasta are an important source of carbohydrates and should be regularly included in the daily diet. The whole meal varieties also contain good quantities of fiber.

LEFT: Fish should be a regular part of a healthy diet as it contains protein. Oily fish, such as mackerel, contain oils which can help prevent the onset of heart disease.

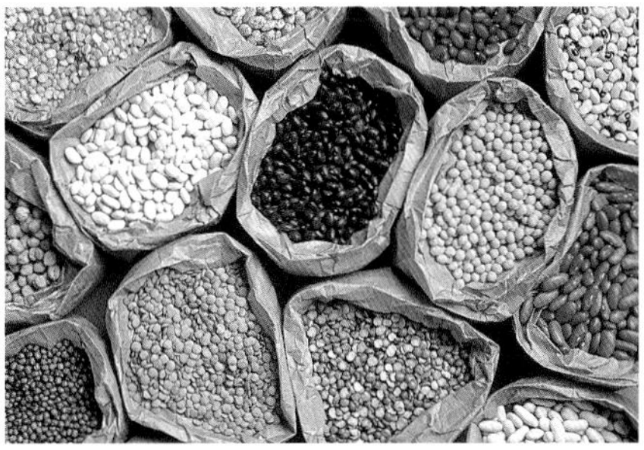

LEFT: Beans and pulses also contain protein and high levels of natural fiber, which is essential for a balanced diet.

nutrients to be lost. It is essential that you read the labels of foods carefully. Products which contain flavorings, preservatives and colorings have been linked with health problems.

A balanced diet is based on eating whole foods, which means unrefined foods. With refined foods, certain parts are removed during the refining process and in this way vital nutrients and natural fiber are lost. The result is a product with a reduced nutritional value, and one which is less easily digested, since natural fiber aids the process of elimination and digestion.

Generally speaking whatever your age, you should have two servings a day of protein, preferably meat, fish, poultry, nuts,

The benefits of fiber

Doctors increasingly believe that fiber-rich diets make a positive contribution to good health. Fiber swells the bulk of the food residue in the intestine, and then helps to soften it by increasing the amount of water retained within it. This lessens the strain on the bowel, since feces pass through more easily, and decreases the amount of time that toxins being eliminated in the feces remain in the body. Many practitioners believe that this reduces, for instance, the likelihood of cancer, since cancer-causing substances are eliminated from the body before they can do any damage.

Fiber also reduces the number of calories that are absorbed from food, while ensuring that the remaining calories are absorbed into the body more slowly. It also helps to increase the content of friendly bacteria which work to protect the body against infection and yeast conditions such as thrush. Rich

BELOW: Water is an important part of the daily diet as it can help to flush out the toxins in our bodies.

BELOW: Milk and milky drinks are good sources of protein and contain calcium which is necessary for healthy bones.

ABOVE: Fruit is an essential part of our daily diet as it is contains many of the vitamins and minerals needed to keep our bodies functioning well.

ABOVE: Vegetables are full of minerals, vitamins and dietary fiber and should form a large part of the daily diet.

sources of fiber include whole meal bread, brown rice and other cereals, vegetables (both leafy and root), fruits (both fresh and dried), salads, beans, peas and other pulses.

What happens in a consultation?

Nutritional therapists are sometimes medical doctors, who have become particularly interested in nutrition. The practitioners of other alternative therapies, such as Naturopathy (see pages 98–103), homeopathy (see pages 74–79) and Chinese and Western herbalism (see pages 24–29 and 92–97) may also offer healthy eating advice as part of their treatment.

A consultation normally takes up to an hour, during which time the therapist will take a full case history:

- *She will look at your current diet and habits, including how much you drink or smoke.*
- *She will discuss your exercise patterns and your emotional and physical history.*
- *She will ask whether you take any medication or drugs, such as the Pill, and note any physical symptoms that you are currently experiencing.*

Many practitioners suggest testing hair, urine, sweat and muscles and use a questionnaire to pinpoint specific deficiencies. Therapy will also be based on your physical symptoms. The practitioner will take into account any nutritional deficiencies, food intolerances and also the possibility of a toxic overload. From this information a special diet plan will be produced for you, tailored to your needs, and any vitamin or mineral supplements will be prescribed. An exercise program and some herbal treatments may also be incorporated into the treatment. You may also be referred to another alternative therapist. Nutritional therapists will always advise you to consult a doctor as well if you have not already done so.

How many sessions do I need?

The number of sessions required depends on how quickly you respond to treatment, how long you have suffered from your symptoms or illness, and how carefully you incorporate the lifestyle and dietary changes suggested.

Which problems can it help?

Nutritional therapy can help with almost anything, since food is the basis and the fuel of all the chemical processes which take place in the body. Therefore, almost all types of ill-health can stem from missing or insufficient nutritional elements within the diet.

Nutritional therapists have had great success treating conditions such as rheumatism and arthritis, high blood pressure, fatigue, constipation and other digestive disorders, the healing and recuperation processes following injury or surgery, skin problems and many psychological and behavioral problems. Neuralgia, osteoporosis, PMT, post-natal illness, pregnancy problems, reduced immunity, stress and viruses may also respond to dietary treatment. In effect, however, all the body systems will be improved by a healthy diet. In a fit state you are much more likely to fight off infection and deal efficiently with any health problems or injury.

The benefits of incorporating a healthy, balanced diet into your lifestyle are profound. A large proportion of today's ailments are caused by food allergies, and these can be pinpointed by your therapist. If the relevant foods are avoided many illnesses can be prevented.

Is it safe?

In the hands of a trained practitioner, nutritional therapy treatment is one of the safest alternative therapies available. Reputable practitioners will always be wary of promoting extreme or highly restrictive diets administered for lengthy periods of time. Nutritional therapy should always be undertaken on the advice of a registered practitioner and he or she should always be informed of every other aspect of your current physical and mental condition.

There are many ailments which contraindicate the use of certain supplements, as they would be dangerous, and it is essential that your therapist is always aware of everything which may affect your health.

People of any age can benefit from the prudent use of nutritional therapy, and there are always different regimes for babies, pregnant women, young children, the elderly, and those suffering from chronic (long-term) health conditions.

Elements of Nutrition and Supplementation

These are the main ingredients of good nutrition and supplementation:

- *Vitamins and minerals*
- *Amino acids*
- *Lipids and derivatives*
- *Herbs*
- *Others, including: acidophilus, bioflavonoids, yeast, co-enzyme Q10, enzymes, gandulars, charcoal, bee and flower pollen, royal jelly, seaweeds and derivatives, spirulina and chlorella*

Macrobiotics

What is macrobiotics?

Macrobiotics is based on the Chinese philosophy of yin and yang, which are two qualities that balance one another, and which exist in every natural object and cycle. Yin is the flexible, fluid and cool side of nature, while yang is the strong, dynamic and hot side. There are yin and yang elements in everything, including people, and macrobiotics is a philosophy aimed at balancing them to promote good health.

Yin qualities are peacefulness, calm, creativity, sociability and a relaxed attitude and behavior. Yang qualities include activity, alertness, energy and precision. Most people have both these qualities, however, when one becomes stronger than the other, a state of imbalance can occur, which can result in illness. Too much yin can lead to depression, fatigue and sleeping problems; too much yang can cause tension, irritability, hyperactivity and also insomnia.

The macrobiotic therapist would attempt to right that balance by suggesting an increased intake of yin foods for someone suffering from too much yang, and the opposite for someone with too much yin. There are many other factors involved in this theory, including exercise, which is broken into yin and yang (yoga is yin; aerobics is yang), temperature and climate.

The macrobiotic diet

The macrobiotic diet is similar to that of the traditional Japanese peasant, which consists of:

- *Fifty percent cooked whole cereal grains, pasta, bread, porridge, stir-fried rice or noodles*
- *Twenty-five percent of local seasonal vegetables, cooked in a variety of ways (for example, raw, pickled, steamed, sautéed, or boiled)*
- *Ten percent protein, to be drawn from local fish, beans and*

soybean products such as tofu or tempeh

- *Five percent sea vegetables, used in soups or stews*
- *Five percent soups, including miso soup, fish soup, bean soup and vegetable soup, among others*
- *Five percent desserts and teas, including simple teas and grain coffees, and desserts using fruits and fermented rice (amaskae), agar agar (sea vegetable), seeds and nuts*

In fact, surveys show that most macrobiotic practitioners use the diet as a basis for healthy living but also enjoy a five to ten percent intake of other foods either socially, or to give a dietary balance. Emphasis is placed on the art of cooking, and on the variety of cooking styles and ingredients.

LEFT: Nuts and other foods should make up about five percent of the macrobiotic diet, while pulses and other proteins form about ten percent.

BELOW: Seasonal vegetables are a major part of the macrobiotic diet and can be cooked in different ways.

RIGHT: Rice, particularly brown, and other grains should form about 50 percent of the macrobiotic diet.

Foods which are excluded from the diet include sugar, spices and alcohol (which are said to be too much yin), and meat, eggs and cheese (which are said to be too much yang). These foods are generally believed to be too strong for human consumption, unbalancing the system and causing illness. The best balanced foods containing yin or yang are:

- *Yin – fruit, leafy green vegetables, nuts and seeds, tofu and tempeh, fruit and vegetable juices, jams (made without refined sugar), barley malt.*
- *Yang – whole grain cereals, such as brown rice, bread, flour, whole oats, root vegetables such as potatoes, parsnips and turnips, fish and shellfish, cottage cheese, beans, peas and lentils, salt, miso and shoyu soya sauce.*

The macrobiotic lifestyle

Macrobiotics is believed to be the natural cycle of life, an example of the universal rhythms of yin and yang which occur everywhere and in everything. During your more difficult periods, it is suggested that you read case histories and accounts of others whose lives have been radically improved by macrobiotics.

Macrobiotic practitioners urge you to live each day happily, without being preoccupied with your condition, or dwelling on negative thoughts, ideas or emotions.

It is a fundamental belief that nature is essential to life, and that regular contact with nature is necessary to enjoy optimum health and well-being. There are five daily practices which are helpful in creating a more stable and harmonious lifestyle:

- *Greet everyone happily and with appreciation.*
- *Initiate and maintain a regular correspondence with all family members, expressing thanks for their part in your life.*
- *Enlarge your circle of friends and acquaintances, including people from different lifestyles.*
- *Share your food more often by having people around; food prepared in larger quantities is more satisfying and the act of sharing food is a universal gesture of human kindness and brotherhood.*
- *Put aside some time each day for peace and quiet, and thank your forebears and teachers for their help. Repeat your dedication to aid and support those who look to you for guidance.*

Macrobiotic Guidelines for a Healthy Lifestyle

In order to establish a firm foundation of natural health, physiological stability, and adaptability, it is vital that the following factors in our daily lives that have led to symptoms of suffering or sickness are recognized, so that we may seek to correct them.

1 *Live each day happily without being constantly preoccupied about your state of health.*
2 *Include some regular physical exercise in your daily life – even rather mundane activities such as scrubbing floors and cleaning windows are beneficial. Some form of systemic exercise may be very helpful, such as yoga, tai chi or other martial arts and long walks. Regular deep breathing may be of benefit in strengthening the body's ability to discharge accumulated toxins as well as calming the mind and establishing a more even energy flow.*
3 *For a deep and restful sleep, get to bed before midnight and rise early in the morning. Try to avoid eating for three hours before going to sleep.*
4 *Get plenty of fresh air, and when you can, walk barefoot on the soil, grass or beach. Keep large green plants in your home to increase the circulation of fresh oxygen, and open windows wherever possible. It is best to use central heating and air conditioning only to the extent necessary for reasonable comfort. Allow yourself to experience the natural seasonal changes of temperature appropriate to the climate where you live.*
5 *Bathe as needed, but try to avoid lengthy hot baths or showers, as they can deplete the body of minerals and have a weakening effect. Preferably take brief baths or showers with a moderate temperature If you feel fatigued after bathing you may drink a small cup of shoyu-bancha, or miso soup to replenish your energy.*
6 *To revitalize the blood and stimulate lymph circulation, scrub and massage the whole body with a hot, damp cotton towel or flannel until your skin becomes flushed, each morning or night. At least scrub the arms, legs, hands and feet, including each finger and toe.*
7 *All fabrics used for daily living should ideally be as natural as possible, as synthetic materials can disrupt the body's energies. Wear cotton clothing next to your skin. Use cotton sheets and towels and wool blankets. Incandescent (non-fluorescent) lighting, natural wood furnishings and wool or cotton carpeting all contribute to a more natural environment.*
8 *Try to avoid or minimize the use of electric appliances close to the body, including hair dryers and electric blankets. A gas or wood stove is recommended for cooking. It is preferable to use earthenware, glass, cast iron or stainless steel cookware rather than aluminum, coated or electric cooking pots.*
9 *Television can exert a draining influence, as do all radiation emitting devices, such as computer terminals, video games and X-ray machines. If you watch television, do so in moderation and at a reasonable distance.*
10 *To maintain healthy skin function, which plays a vital part in the excretory system's regular discharging of toxins, avoid using chemically produced cosmetics and body care products. Try to use natural cosmetics from vegetable sources only. Try to care for your teeth with toothpaste made from natural substances such as sea salt, dentie or clay.*

Macrobiotic philosophy

The macrobiotic philosophy is essentially one of being responsible for your health, your aspirations and your actions. This comes through clearly in the works of Ohsawa, and he and the early Chinese doctors made it clear that their job was to prevent illness rather than "fixing things" later, when they were not working properly.

As the Yellow Emperor said thousands of years ago in the book: *Nei Ching*: "it is hardest to treat someone who has become rebellious [sick] – a wise doctor helps those who are well and have not become rebellious."

How does it work?

Macrobiotic practitioners believe that macrobiotics changes the condition of your blood, which is made of three main components – plasma, red blood cells and white blood cells. Plasma amounts to about 50 percent of the cells, and this changes every ten days. Therefore, the changes to your health will be noticeable in ten-day cycles.

When you begin a macrobiotic program, you will notice some large changes during the first ten days, mainly as a reaction or a "discharge process." Tiredness, irritability, sweating, insomnia and cravings are common. After about 10–30 days, reports vary, but generally people tend to feel brighter, and more alert, with an increased appetite, and a calmer, more focused and flexible outlook.

When people continue for six to eight months on a macrobiotic program, their blood will show a great improvement and have perfectly balanced yin and yang. If regular physical activity is kept up, and there is plenty of variety in the diet and lifestyle, then chronic (long-term) ailments should normally start to show noticeable improvement.

Changing your diet is a very big step to take; approaching it in the right way and getting support and feedback are essential to minimize mistakes. It takes commitment and patience to practice, but macrobiotic practitioners say that when it becomes effortless and you are genuinely enjoying all the food you eat, then you have become macrobiotic.

RICH SOURCES OF VITAMINS & MINERALS IN HERBS & FOOD

VITAMINS, MINERALS AND THEIR ROLES	HERBS	FOOD
Calcium: *protects and builds bones and teeth, aids blood clotting and buffers acid in the stomach*	*Comfrey, marestail, oatstraw, licorice*	*Sesame seeds, seaweeds, kale, turnips, almonds, soybeans, dandelion leaves, hazelnuts, horseradish, honey, salmon*
Chromium: *breaks down sugar for use in the body, it deters diabetes, and helps maintain the correct blood pressure*		*Whole meal bread, potatoes, spinach, spaghetti, bananas, haddock*
Copper: *converts iron to hemoglobin, staves off anemia*	*Ephaedra*	*Peaches, turnips*
Iron: *aids growth, promotes immune system, prevents fatigue, essential for metabolism of reproduction of hemoglobin*	*Red raspberries, yellow dock, kelp, nettle*	*Wheat and rice (bran and germ,) Brazil nuts, greens, apples, grapes, walnuts, dill, dandelion leaves, pumpkin, squash, plums*
Manganese: *needed for normal bone structure, important for thyroid gland's hormone production and important for digestion*	*Comfrey, cramp bark, uva ursi, gravel root*	*Apples, peaches, rye, turnips, tea, whole meal, bread, avocados*
Magnesium: *essential for nerve and muscle functioning, known as anti-stress mineral, improves cardiovascular system*	*Valerian, kelp, dandelion*	*Wheat (bran & germ), whole oats, walnuts, almonds, rice, sorrel, rye, cashews, cabbage, okra, oats, dill, aubergine, oranges*
Phosphorus: *needed for formation of bones, teeth and nerve impulse transfer, assimilates niacin present in every body cell*	*Yeast*	*Rice, wheat (bran and germ), squash seeds, sesame seeds, Brazil nuts, fish, kale, mustard, radishes, aubergine, leek, seafood*
Potassium: *regulates body's water balance, aids muscle function, helps dispose of body waste, supports allergy treatment*	*Kelp, dulse, Irish moss*	*Soybeans, bananas, cayenne pepper, artichokes, asparagus, cauliflower, kale, grapefruit, radishes, sorrel, tomatoes*
Selenium: *anti-oxidant, preventing or slowing down ageing, important for prostate glands in males, prevents skin conditions*		*Wheat germ, bran, onions, broccoli, tomatoes, shellfish, tuna*
Sodium: *essential for normal growth, aids in preventing sun-stroke, helps nerves and muscles function, excessive in most diets*	*Kelp, seaweed, marigold, bladderwrack*	*Olives, dulse, apricots, currants, figs, dates, eggs, horseradish, lentils, oats, red cabbage, strawberries, turnips, celery, cayenne pepper*
Sulphur: *tones up skin and hair, helps fight bacterial infection, aids liver, part of tissue-building amino acids*	*Garlic, kelp, dandelion*	*Onion, sprouts, coconut, cucumber, garlic, figs, egg yolk, greens, kale, okra, parsnips, potatoes, strawberries,turnips, carrots*
Zinc: *accelerates healing, prevents infertility, helps prevent prostrate problems, promotes growth and mental alertness*	*Red raspberries, alfalfa, uva ursi, slippery elm*	*Apricots, peaches, nectarines, oysters, wheat germ, cocoa, mustard seeds, brewer's yeast, eggs, pumpkin seeds*
Vitamin A: *counteracts night blindness, builds resistance to respiratory infections, promotes growth of teeth, bones and hair*	*Alfalfa, oatstraw, dock*	*Carrots, asparagus, cayenne pepper, sorrel, carrots, kale, spinach, cress, sweet potatoes, parsley, apples, garlic, ginger, papaya, rye*
Vitamin B1 (Thiamine): *promotes growth, aids digestion, improves mental attitude, helps nervous system and prevents stress*	*Oatstraw, red clover, alfalfa*	*Rice, bran, wheat germ, sunflower seeds, apples, garlic, papaya, turnips, rye, peanuts, oatmeal, sesame seeds*
Vitamin B2 (Riboflavin): *aids growth and reproduction, promotes hair, skin and nail growth, helps eyesight*	*Alfalfa, oatstraw, red clover*	*Hot red chilis, wheat germ, millet, apples, garlic, ginger, rye, leafy green vegetables, fish, eggs, yeast, cheese, liver, kidney, almonds*
Vitamin B3 (Niacin): *essential for sex hormones, increases energy, aids nervous system, helps digestion and prevents migraines*	*Alfalfa, red clover*	*Apples, garlic, ginger, onions, papaya, rye, turnips, wheat, parsley, watercress*
Vitamin B5 (Panthothenic acid): *aids in healing wounds, fights infection, strengthens immune system, builds cells*	*Barberry*	*Rye, turnips, garlic, papayas, parsley*
Vitamin B12 (Cobalamin): *forms and regenerates red blood cells, increases energy, improves concentration, maintains nervous system*	*Alfalfa, comfrey, red clover*	*Rye, sprouted seeds, legumes, eggs, kidney, liver, milk*
Vitamin B17 (Amygdalin): *purported to control cancer*		*Apricots, peach seeds, apples, cherries, plums, nectarines*
Vitamin C (Ascorbic acid): *helps body to absorb calcium, helps form collagen, heals wounds, aids immune system*	*Alfalfa, barberry, hawthorn, rosehip*	*Oranges, apples, watercress, garlic, onions, turnips, cayenne, sweet red pepper, parsley, walnuts, lemons, green leafy vegetables*
Vitamin D: *prevents rickets, essential for calcium and phosphorus utilization and necessary for strong teeth and bones*	*Alfalfa, fenugreek*	*Apples, watercress, fish liver oils, tuna, milk, salmon, herring*
Vitamin E: *antioxidant, anticoagulant and anti-ageing*	*Alfalfa, flaxseed*	*Apples, parsley, rye, wheat germ, whole wheat, broccoli, eggs*

What happens in a consultation?

Practitioners are skilled in Oriental diagnosis, with the same background as an acupuncturist or Chinese herbalist. There are four methods of diagnosis:

- *Seeing – visual diagnosis of the face, tongue, fingers and nails.*
- *Listening – studying your voice during the interview to ascertain whether the condition is yin or yang.*
- *Touching – feeling the pulses on the inside of the wrist.*
- *Questioning – about lifestyle, habits, diet, symptoms and medical history.*

The practitioners will then give advice, generally aimed at the three branches of macrobiotics:

Dietary advice suggests which foods to avoid for 30 days, and which foods to incorporate. It will possibly include other extras such as special herbal teas. This advice is based on Michio Kushi's Standard Macrobiotic Diet, with any necessary adjustments, deletions, or extra dishes.

Lifestyle and exercise suggestions to improve your health and well-being will also be made. There may also be suggested referrals to other practitioners working within the Chinese medical field.

On the philosophy side, suggestions for a more harmonious life will be offered.

How many sessions do I need?

Normally two sessions, 30 days apart, are needed with the macrobiotic therapist to sort out your diet. Each session will take about an hour.

Which problems can it help?

Macrobiotics helps to strengthen the immune system and enables you to maintain good health. It is also good for preventing or reducing digestive complaints, obesity, fatigue, poor concentration, physical inflexibility or lack of stamina. Some practitioners claim to have had success in treating and curing arthritis and some forms of cancer.

The macrobiotic diet is considered to be excellent for healthy individuals as it can help prevent disease forming.

Is it safe?

In the 1970s and 1980s there was a dangerous version of macrobiotics being practiced. This system involved eating little other than brown rice. Many men, women and children developed severe malnutrition, which instantly gave the therapy a bad reputation. Since that time, the diets have been modified to reflect current thinking on balanced nutrition within the diet. Under the supervision of a registered practitioner, macrobiotics is normally very safe.

Many children adopt a liberal macrobiotic diet without any problems, however, it should only be undertaken under the guidance of a doctor. Similarly, breastfeeding mothers, pregnant women, and those wishing to conceive should discuss the possibility of adopting macrobiotics with their doctor before attempting to start the diet. Most registered practitioners will be quite happy to modify the diet to suit your individual needs.

Clinical studies – Nutritional therapy

Various medical studies have found that the use of nutritional therapy or vitamin supplements has been very beneficial in the treatment of ailments.

Between 1990 and 1993 Dr. Begg referred 298 NHS patients to a nutritional therapist. All were attending a doctor's surgery with chronic (long-term) minor health problems for which conventional treatments could not cure satisfactorily. Of the third of the patients who attended follow-up appointments after consulting a nutritional therapist a high percentage reported "definite lasting improvement." Eighty-five percent reported improvement for headaches and migraines, 82 percent for digestive problems, 70 percent for hormone-related problems, 55 percent for chronic fatigue and 54 percent for skin problems.

As a result of the success with the migraine patients alone – 30 percent had no symptoms over a ten-week period and most cases were controlled just by diet – it was suggested that nutritional therapy could be a viable, cheap and effective alternative to drug treatment. **(29)**

In 1990 a study was conducted at Baragwanath Hospital in South Africa involving nine patients with severe clinical esophagitis/pellagra (a skin disorder). They were treated with vitamin therapy compared with 31 control patients who had no treatment but were matched for sex and age. Patients were assessed by pathological tests of the esophagus. After a week's treatment there was improvement in the esophagitis of five of the treatment group. **(30)**

In an American study of 87,245 female nurses between the ages of 34 and 59 in 1993, it was found that the use of vitamin E supplements could have a significant effect in reducing the risk of coronary heart disease. The eight year study showed that, after taking into account age and smoking, those women who had a high vitamin E intake reduced their risk of heart disease to 66 percent compared to those with a low intake. In addition, those taking vitamin E supplements for more than two years reduced their risk to 59 percent. **(31)**

In studies back in 1973 magnesium supplements have been found to reduce the symptoms of PMS. Although the studies did not include a control and could only record subjective measures of symptomatic relief, a significant effect was reported. A double blind trial reported reductions in pain and emotional distress plus other menstrual symptoms in the patients.

In another study of 192 women, a noticeable reduction in breast pain was reported in 96 percent of subjects, reduced weight gain in 95 percent, less nervous tension in 89 percent and fewer headaches in 43 percent. **(32)** (*For clinical references see How to use this book*)

FOR INFORMATION ON HOW TO CHOOSE A NUTRITIONAL OR MACROBIOTIC THERAPIST SEE THE DIRECTORY.

The tradition of using herbs for healing dates from ancient times. Their appeal is universal and no one person, country or culture can lay claim to first discovering the therapy. Herbalism forms part of our Western heritage, but it has proved equally important in Africa, India and China (see Chinese herbalism pages 24–29). But, although herbalism's origins are lost in the distant past, its appeal has proved timeless. Herbs and their derivatives have formed the basis of many modern medicines. Steroids and amphetamines

WESTERN HERBALISM

WESTERN HERBALISM uses the curative aspects of numerous plants to keep people healthy and their bodies balanced. It is an ancient healing art and can ease eczema, cystitis and irritable bowel syndrome.

both originate from herbs, but willow bark and foxglove are probably the most famous that have been reproduced for pharmaceutical use.

Willow bark, one of the best known anti-inflammatory plants, has been chemically reproduced as aspirin, and foxglove's active ingredient digitalis is a heartbeat regulator used in conventional medicine as the drugs dixogin and digitoxin. In fact, for the first half of the 20th century most orthodox drugs were derived from herbal origins. But using herbs as the natural equivalent of "a pill for every ill" underestimates their power and deprives us of an effective healing system.

Science has begun to prove what herbalists always knew: that herbs are made up of mutually dependent complex chemicals and they work best when the active parts are used whole and in their natural state. Herbs are also more effective when they are prescribed specifically for the person rather than the illness. Consequently, in keeping with the general movement toward the natural and holistic, many people are turning away from drugs in favor of herbalists who prescribe whole herbs in order to stimulate healing in the whole person.

What is medical herbalism?

Medical herbalism is the use of plants as medicines to restore and maintain health by keeping the body balanced. It relies on the curative qualities of plants, flowers, trees and herbs to stimulate our own healing system when the body is ill. Like most holistic practitioners, herbalists believe that we all possess healing energy within us, which they call the "vital force" (see Homeopathy pages 74–79). This vital force works constantly to maintain our whole health, physically, mentally and emotionally. Sometimes, however, the vital force is weakened by factors such as stress, poor diet and pollution, and we get ill. Herbalists see the symptoms of disease as the result of the vital force's attempts to maintain harmony in the body when it is under threat from illness. The symptoms are an indication that the body is trying to beat the illness on its own.

Herbal remedies are prescribed to support the affected body systems in their fight against disease. Herbs are used, therefore, not just to alleviate disease, but prevent it recurring, to detoxify the system, and also to support the immune system and maintain homeostasis – the state of being in perfect balance.

Medical herbalists combine traditional knowledge of herbs and healing with modern scientific developments. They are trained in the same examination techniques as your doctor and have a thorough medical knowledge of the body. In the same way herbs from ancient times have found a new role in our high-tech world. Aloe vera, for example, which can be traced back to the fourth century BC, and is reputed to have played a part in Cleopatra's beauty routine, has been found by American researchers to be the best treatment for radiation burns. What we know now is that it is herbs' properties, and how they work together, that makes them effective in bolstering our healing systems.

BELOW: In this 15th-century painting a man is teaching a student about the different herbs in Edward IV's herb garden in Bruges, Belgium.

Herbalists have always believed that a herb is greater than the sum of its parts. They understand that the dominant ingredient will work more effectively, without side effects and for the whole body, if it is backed up by the many secondary ingredients that the plant contains. This is known as synergism.

A simple example of the benefits of synergism over prescribed drugs is to compare garlic with antibiotics. Antibiotics can kill infection, but they also kill the body's good bacteria and upset the balance of flora (microorganisms) in the gut. Because of this they can cause or exacerbate yeast infections, such as thrush. Garlic, on the other hand, is a natural antibiotic with properties that stimulate the gut flora to work more efficiently, thereby eliminating the risk of yeast infection.

LEFT: A herbal pharmacy dispenses herbs in a dried form for use in infusions or as capsules to be taken internally.

ABOVE: Many different types of herbs, roots, barks nuts and seeds are used to make up the complex herbal prescriptions used by Western herbalists.

How does it work?

Despite extensive research and analysis, scientists are still unable to identify every chemical component of which herbs are composed and so far have not been able to reproduce them synthetically. They have discovered, however, that herbs contain vitamins, minerals, carbohydrates and trace elements and healing agents such as tannins, bitters, volatile oils, mucilage, glycosides, saponins and alkaloids. These as well as other properties enable herbs to aid the body's fight against infection, to sedate overactive organs, relax tense muscles and nerves, improve circulation, and reduce any inflammation.

Herbs are classified in a similar way to drugs, but are often prescribed to support body systems rather than relieve symptoms of disease. For example, laxatives such as dandelion root and yellow dock are prescribed to aid the digestive system and diuretics such as dandelion leaf are prescribed to aid the urinary system, if the complaint is fluid retention. The skill of the herbalist lies in prescribing the most suitable herb for an individual. The main difference between a herbal prescription and a prescription from a doctor is that the herbs are chosen for you, not your illness.

For example, if you have difficulty sleeping, the herbalist might prescribe one or more of the numerous hypnotic, sedative or soporific herbs to relieve the problem. Based on your other symptoms, and your lifestyle, the herbalist must choose the herbs that she feels will best fulfill your needs. Valerian, passionflower and Jamaican dogwood all help to relieve insomnia. But apart from their sedative effects they also have other properties: Jamaican dogwood is a pain reliever, passionflower, too, relieves pain but is also antispasmodic and valerian relaxes the digestive system. So, if you were an insomniac, but also suffered from breathing spasms with asthma, you may be prescribed passionflower, but if you were kept awake by digestive upsets, valerian would be a better choice.

The chemical complexity of herbs means they can often achieve what a synthetic drug cannot. For example, some herbs are adaptogenic. Traditionally, this has meant that they help the body cope with stress, mainly by supporting the adrenal glands which are designed to do just that. All forms of ginseng are adaptogens. Today the term adaptogen is sometimes used in a wider sense to apply not only to stress but also to body systems. For example, camomile is considered an adaptogen because it helps to regulate the digestive system, activating enzymes in a sluggish system but also relaxing spasms in an overactive condition such as irritable bowel system (IBS).

Herbs are used to help fight disease in the body and also to prevent it recurring again

The remedies

Herbal remedies are prescribed to be taken internally or applied to the skin. They come as tinctures, creams, compresses, poultices, infusions, decoctions, oils to use in the bath or as tablets and capsules. You may even be given fresh herbs to incorporate into your diet.

Tinctures: These are the most common type of internal remedy prescribed. They are made by soaking the flowers, leaves or roots of the chosen herbs in alcohol to extract and preserve their useful properties. Tinctures keep well, are easy to store and you only need take a small amount at a time.

Infusions: Always less concentrated these are an easy way to take herbs at home. The herbalist prescribes fresh or dried flowers, leaves or green stems of the herbs that you make into a "tea," a rather misleading word as it suggests a pleasant drink, which is rarely the case with prescription herbs. To make an infusion use one teaspoon of dried herbs to one cup of boiling water, leave to infuse for 10–15 minutes, strain and drink hot. Sweeten with honey if preferred. The properties of some herbs such as comfrey, marshmallow and valerian root are destroyed by heat so they should be infused or "macerated" in cold water for up to 12 hours.

Decoctions: are similar to infusions but these are made from materials such as roots, barks, nuts and seeds. Using the same proportions as for an infusion, place the herb mixture and water in a saucepan and bring to the boil, simmer for ten minutes. Strain and drink hot.

Tablets and capsules: All are taken in the same way as a prescription drug (often with water after food) and are useful for people who would rather not taste the remedy.

Creams and ointments: These are applied externally to soothe irritated or inflamed skin conditions or to ease sprains or bruises. A cream moistens the dry or cracked skin and massaging an ointment into bruises and sprains helps to ease the pain. In both cases the herb's active ingredients pass through the pores of the skin into the bloodstream to encourage healing.

Hot or cold compresses: Both can help with aches, pains and swollen joints. Begin by folding a clean piece of cotton into an infusion of the prescribed herb and apply to the painful area. Repeat as the hot compress cools or, with the cold compress, hold there until the pain eases.

Poultices: These are made from bruised fresh herbs or dried herbs moistened into a paste with hot water. They are good for painful joints or drawing out infection from boils, spots or wounds. Place the herb paste on a clean piece of cotton and position it on the affected area with a bandage. Leave for a couple of hours or until symptoms ease.

Suppositories and douches: Sometimes prescribed for rectal problems such as piles or vaginal infections respectively. The suppositories will come ready made for you to insert. Douches are made from an infusion or decoction that has cooled.

Herbal baths: These are the ultimate in pleasant herbal treatments, and are a useful supplement to other treatments. Lemon balm, lavender or elderflowers make a fragrant, relaxing bath, but herbs can also help promote sleep, boost circulation or calm your nerves. Tie a handful of herbs in a muslin bag and hang from the bath tap so that the water runs through it or use essential oils (see Aromatherapy, pages 68–73). The heat of the water activates the properties of the volatile oils so that they are absorbed through the pores of the skin and inhaled through the nose. In both cases they pass into the bloodstream and when inhaled they pass through the nervous system, to the brain, healing both the mind and the body.

What happens in a consultation?

Visiting a medical herbalist is rather different from seeing your doctor. Your first consultation will last for about an hour, so book as soon as you can as it is not possible to simply turn up. On-the-spot prescribing has no place in the holistic philosophy of medical herbalism and herbalists are forbidden by law to prescribe a treatment for someone whom they have not seen.

Your consultation will begin with the information-gathering process that happens with every form of alternative medicine. The herbalist will begin by taking down details such as:

YOUR HOME HERBAL MEDICINE CHEST

Bergamot *essential oil is nature's antidepressant, add five or six drops in the bath.*
Calendula *cream is a wonderful antiseptic for cuts, scrapes and minor skin irritations.*
Camomile *tea soothes digestive upsets, and helps teething and colicky babies.*
Comfrey *ointment is a useful remedy for bruises and sprains.*
Echinacea *tablets are wonderful for fighting infection and warding off colds, flu and sore throats.*
Elderflower *tea is excellent for coughs, colds, flu, fevers and hay fever symptoms. Combine with peppermint for relief of catarrhal problems.*
Garlic *raw or in a capsule, is best used as a preventive for coughs, colds and to reduce blood cholesterol. Its antiseptic and antifungal properties make it invaluable for chest infections and fungal infections such as thrush.*
Ginger *is good for indigestion and wind, circulation, arthritis, morning sickness and travel sickness. Chew on the fresh root, make it into a tea, or take in capsule form.*
Lavender *essential oil relieves stress and promotes relaxation. Add five or six drops in the bath.*
Lime blossom *tea is a relaxant, good for tension headaches or tension-related insomnia*
Lemon balm *is wonderful for relieving stress and stress-related digestive problems. Use the fresh leaves in a hot infusion (see page 95).*
Meadow sweet *tea is a gentle pain reliever and is also good for acid indigestion.*
Peppermint *tea is good for indigestion, flatulence, headaches and also for colds.*

- *Your name, address, age and current occupation.*
- *She will want to find out about your personality and what things are important to you.*
- *Whether you worry about the state of your children's health, for example.*
- *If you get concerned about the state of the environment.*
- *She will also ask if you are you a perfectionist, a rebel, money-conscious, or fashion-conscious.*
- *She will ask about your childhood, your appetite and sleeping patterns, family, job, previous illnesses and any medicines you have been prescribed in the past.*

As well as what you tell her, she will also want to know how you feel and will note the condition of your hair and skin, your facial expression, posture and how you move. These all provide important clues that will help with the diagnosis.

While you explain why you have come and your main symptoms, the herbalist will write down your case details in her notes. The interview is an opportunity for you to assess the therapist while being assessed yourself. Remember, if you do not feel comfortable with the questions or person you can always leave.

When the herbalist has collated all this information, she will aim to establish how your problem started, what conditions caused it or are making it worse, how it relates to previous illnesses and how you feel at this moment. Her intention is to find the cause of the problem and prescribe a remedy that will help you to overcome it, not necessarily to put a label on it.

For example, if you have a skin problem, she will note this and refer to it by how it looks and feels, she does not need to name it as eczema or acne, both of which can just be symptoms of a greater problem. Eczema can be a symptom of stress and acne a symptom of hormonal imbalance. In both cases the herbalist is not interested in prescribing a remedy to ameliorate the eczema or acne, but to help your body to handle the stress or correct the hormonal imbalance. However, if the skin condition is particularly distressing, she may also prescribe something else to ease the discomfort and alleviate any embarrassment it causes.

During the consultation the herbalist will also ask you about the health of your body's systems – the respiratory, circulatory, digestive, reproductive and so on. In herbalism, healthy systems contribute to a healthy person so many of the remedies are aimed at supporting and maintaining these systems. Your home and work environment will also be taken into account as the environment can have a toxic influence on the body.

Medical herbalists are qualified to carry out a physical examination. This will be similar to a check-up from your doctor. The herbalist may check your pulse, take your blood pressure, test your reflexes, listen to your heart and chest, examine your eyes, ears, and throat and skin. If necessary she may feel your abdomen for inflammation and bowel tone and possibly carry out a gynecological examination. If an extensive examination is necessary, you will need to undress, in which case the procedure is much the same as in your doctor's surgery, you would either undress behind a screen or the herbalist will leave the room to let you undress in privacy.

Only after a full consultation and examination will the herbalist be able to make a diagnosis. She will explain to you what she believes to be the problem and how she can help to correct it. She will also advise on how you can help your healing by improving your diet and exercise regime and relaxing more. She may give you a diet sheet to take away with you recommending what you should eat, but also what you should avoid.

By the end of your appointment the herbalist should have decided on a suitable remedy (it can be more than one). These can be prescribed in any of the forms listed above, but most are usually given as creams or ointments for skin conditions and tinctures to be taken internally. The herbalist may mix several tinctures in one bottle to make your remedy and you will be told how and when to take the medicine. This will usually be by mouth two or three times a day.

The remedies you receive are prescribed for you, not for your ulcer, hay fever or eczema. This is why over-the-counter herbal remedies can never achieve what a herbalist's prescription can. As with many forms of alternative treatment, herbal remedies can occasionally make you feel worse before you feel better. This is because they are not prescribed to alleviate your symptoms, but to eliminate the problem from your system.

Your appointment may end with you being asked to return for a follow-up appointment in a few days, a week or even two weeks' time. The timing of the follow-up session will depend on the nature and severity of your problem.

LEFT: Here a herbalist is decanting a tincture into a bottle. It can be made from the flowers, leaves or roots of a herb.

ABOVE: Garlic has useful antiseptic properties for treating chest infections.

ABOVE: Herbal infusions "teas" can be prescribed as a treatment, but will often need sweetening.

How many sessions do I need?

Acute (short-term) conditions can be resolved within a few days and you may need one or two appointments. Chronic (long-term) conditions, such as arthritis or eczema, need several appointments, especially if you have had them for a while or suppressed by drugs. Repeated appointments may be necessary so that the herbalist can check on your progress and possibly change your prescription as your condition improves.

Which problems can it help?

Herbalism can help with most illness and disorders, but it does seem particularly effective with skin conditions such as eczema, urinary problems such as cystitis and digestive problems such as irritable bowel syndrome.

But, herbalism does not have all the answers. If you had a condition that required surgery the herbalist would refer you to your doctor. For muscular, bone or joint problems, she would recommend an osteopath or chiropractor. A herbalist cannot reverse damage caused by serious or life-threatening diseases such as cancer, diabetes or Aids, but she can relieve the symptoms, support your immune system and improve your well-being.

Is it safe?

Herbal medicines have proved their efficacy over centuries of use and have a much better safety record for everyone from babies to pregnant women and the elderly than that of pharmaceutical drugs. But it is a mistake to think that natural means harmless as any substance can be abused. All medicines should be treated with respect – do not take herbal remedies unnecessarily, in greater doses or for longer than you need.

Some herbs are toxic when taken in large doses. A herbalist will not usually prescribe these herbs even in small doses and the dosage of certain herbs is controlled by law. Safe herbal preparations for minor or acute ailments are also available over the counter, but if unsure ask your herbalist for guidance, especially if you are taking the herbs during pregnancy or giving them to babies or children. If you are going to take herbal medicines in conjunction with conventional medicine, consult your doctor as well as the herbalist.

Clinical studies

Several trials have shown that Western herbal remedies can help treat different medical conditions.

In 1994, a German pilot study was carried out that involved 14 elderly insomniacs. Eight were given daily doses of valerian extract, while a placebo (an inactive plant extract) was given to six control patients. The trial lasted one week and the subjects sleep pattern was studied before the trial and on the first and last night. The effects were measured using a sleep polygraph. The authors concluded that valerian increases short-wave sleep in subjects with insomnia. (**33**)

Another study was carried out in 1993 where garlic powder tablets were assessed for their effect on serum lipids and lipoproteins, glucose and blood pressure in patients with high cholesterol levels. Forty-two subjects with high serum total cholesterol levels were treated with 300mg tablets, or a placebo, three times a day in a trial lasting 12 weeks. The authors concluded that the garlic treatment significantly reduced the levels of serum total cholesterol compared to the placebo. There were no odor problems. (**34**) (*For clinical references see How to use this book*).

FOR INFORMATION ON HOW TO CHOOSE A HERBALIST SEE THE DIRECTORY.

ONLY NATURE HEALS is the philosophy of naturopathy, a system of holistic medicine, which has been around since ancient times. Hippocrates, the Greek father of medicine, could more specifically be called the father of naturopathic medicine since, like modern naturopaths, he incorporated diet, fasting, hydrotherapy, exercise and manipulative techniques into his healthcare system. Naturopathy does not rely on one treatment, but is multidisciplinary, embracing many natural ingredients.

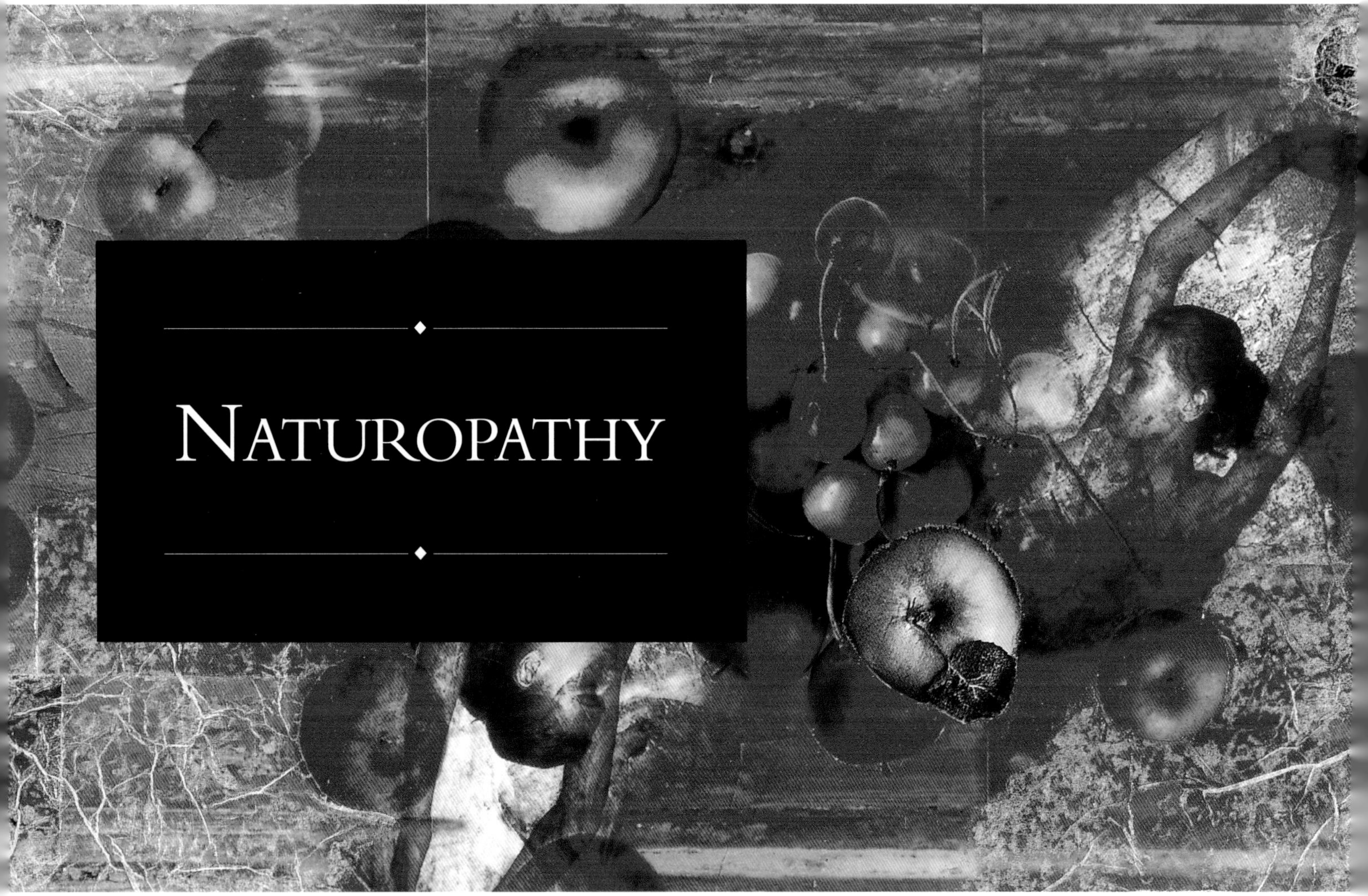

NATUROPATHY

NATUROPATHY is a healthcare system that features only natural ingredients and disciplines. Treatment might include a healthy diet, fasting, hydrotherapy exercise and relaxation techniques.

Healthy eating, clean water, exercise and relaxation, what any doctor, healthcare professional or enlightened individual would recognize as essential ingredients for a healthy lifestyle, are also the foundations on which naturopathic medicine is built.

Naturopathy as a scientific discipline did not make an impact until the 19th century, when drugs and surgery were becoming established as the accepted tools for health. While orthodox medicine was striving to prove how disease was becoming increasingly complex, naturopaths, on the other hand, emerged to prove its simplicity. The secret of good health, they claimed, lay in using the healing power of nature, not drugs.

Naturopathy remained a fringe therapy, however, outlawed for a time in America and swamped by the political power of the orthodox profession, until recent years. The 1970s and 1980s saw a shift in health consciousness from the pharmaceutical to the natural and holistic, and the message of early 20th-century naturopaths such as Dr. Henry Lindlahr, Stanley Lief and Alfred Vogel started to receive wider recognition. They maintained that living in harmony with nature was the only way to achieve lasting good health.

Since then naturopathy has grown in popularity as research confirms that its components are indeed those required for good health.

What is naturopathy?

Naturopathy is a treatment system that uses natural resources to help the body heal itself. It is founded on these basic principles:

The vital force: The body can fight disease and recover from illness because it possesses a "vital curative force" that enables the body systems to return to a state of harmony known as homeostasis. This state tends toward perfect health, and the naturopath's aim is to restore and preserve it. In naturopathy, health is not simply the absence of disease, but a state in which each person feels physically, mentally and emotionally well.

Naturopaths see disease as a natural phenomenon: Disease occurs in plants, animals and people when any part of the whole organism is not working well. Bad diet, poor elimination of body wastes, injury, hereditary factors, destructive emotions, suppressive drugs or lack of exercise and environmental pollutants can all affect the healthy functioning of cells so that the body is thrown out of balance. The aim of the naturopath is to identify the cause of the illness, help the vital force eliminate it, and restore the body to a state of balance.

The symptoms of disease: These are often evidence of the healing process in action. They are the signs that the vital force is striving to balance the body and they ought not to be suppressed in healthy individuals. Going through acute (short-term) illnesses such as measles or flu is seen as normal in a healthy body.

Naturopaths also see childhood illnesses such as mumps and chickenpox as necessary to develop a strong adult immune system. The object therefore is not to vaccinate against them, but to ensure that the child's diet is one that will strengthen his immune system and when he succumbs to illness to nurse him through using natural treatments. This procedure is seen as a way of ensuring that there are fewer complications and greater possibility of having a stronger, healthier child. Likewise, the odd cold or flu and occasional bout of diarrhea at any age is seen as a healthy way for the body to eliminate toxins. For example, naturopaths know from experience that colds and flu which are allowed to work their way out of the system reduce the risk of bronchitis or degenerative diseases such as arthritis later in life.

ABOVE: The naturopathic diet should be virtually vegetarian and include as many raw foods as possible. Some proteins and unrefined carbohydrates will also be necessary.

RIGHT: Yoga might well be recommended as part of your treatment as it will help to relax your body.

Treatment should be holistic and natural: This is prescribed to activate and strengthen the body's innate healing ability and to bring the diseased organ or body part into balance with the rest of the body. The components of the treatment are based on naturally occurring substances such as water, whole foods, sunlight, relaxation, fresh air and exercise and the emphasis is not only on natural treatment, but on maintaining a natural lifestyle.

The whole person approach of naturopathy means that practitioners are less concerned with naming diseases, than understanding the nature of health and disease and achieving and maintaining good body health.

Naturopaths believe in the triad of health: This in simple terms, means that good health depends on maintaining a balance between three things: the body's structure, its biochemistry and the emotions. The health of the body's structure, good posture, the bones, muscles, tendons and ligaments are vital to the body as a whole as any structural problems can have a damaging effect on the nervous system and internal organs. Biochemical health refers to the effects of food and drink on the body. Good nutrition is essential for growth and repair and immunity to disease.

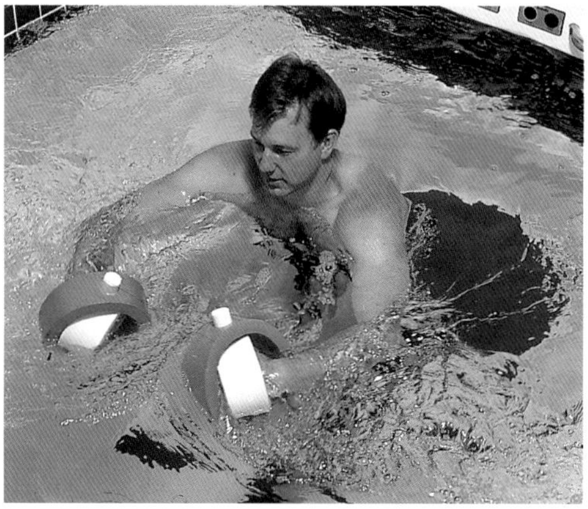

ABOVE: Hydrotherapy treatment is regularly recommended as part of naturopathy to improve a patient's circulation and general vitality.

Poor nutrition not only fails to give the healing system the support it needs, but can be physically damaging due to chemical and toxic content. Emotions have a strong influence on a person's health, affecting mental stability and physical well-being. Feelings such as fear, hate or resentment can upset the digestion, hormone balance, blood flow and the body's biochemistry.

Like many other natural therapists, especially homeopaths, naturopaths also believe in the law of cure. This states that in healing all disease moves from within out, from the top to the bottom and symptoms disappear in reverse order of their appearance. In simple terms, this means that chronic diseases can appear worse before they get better as symptoms come to the surface and in a respiratory disease such as asthma that may have started with eczema, the rash is often the last to go.

How does it work?

Naturopathy is a philosophy for life rather than a set of inflexible principles. Naturopaths aim to prevent and treat disease by detailed diagnosis and a wide range of treatments, many of which must be integrated into a person's lifestyle for lasting health.

Diagnosis

The main purpose of diagnosis is to find out how well the vital force is working. Practitioners carry out normal medical investigations such as taking the pulse and blood pressure, listening to heart and lungs, and assessing breathing capacity, if necessary. Naturopaths are usually trained osteopaths, so observing and palpating the body structure also provides information about vitality and how well the body's systems and organs are functioning. For example, a saggy abdomen can indicate poor lymphatic and blood circulation.

Practitioners also make use of biotypology. This is not so much a part of diagnosis as a way of assessing health trends in the individual. Everyone is classified according to biotype or constitution. This can be either endomorphy: soft and round, mesomorphy: quite muscular and stocky or ectomorphy: long and lean. Each type has numerous characteristics, which can point toward certain illnesses that are common to that type. Endomorphs, for example, tend to have gall bladder problems, ectomorphs are prone to rheumatoid arthritis and mesomorphs are inclined to suffer degenerative arthritis. Each type also has particular dietary needs.

Iridology: Iris diagnosis (see Iridology pages 153–154) also gives insights into a patient's general constitution and has been shown to be effective in pinpointing areas of weakness.

Mineral analysis: Hair and sweat can be tested for mineral levels, trace elements and also for any heavy metal poisoning. A spectroscope can measure the energy frequencies of minerals in a hair shaft.

Bioelectronic diagnosis: This form of dowsing is also used to take a reading from a hair sample, toe nail clipping, drop of blood or saliva. The hair or other body material is used as a "witness," from which the naturopath can read the patient's energy using special equipment.

Treatment

Treatment is diverse and flexible. Different practitioners incorporate or emphasize different aspects of treatment. Below are the most widely used:

Diet: This is the most important factor in naturopathy. It can be broken down into good diet and the more specific form of nutritional medicine. Whole foods form the core of the naturopathic diet. Food should be close to its original state. The diet should tend towards vegetarianism and be organic where possible. It should include many raw foods as the nutritional benefits are greatly reduced by cooking, although this is not essential for everyone. Some protein (preferably plant) and unrefined carbohydrates and grains should be included.

Nutritional medicine involves prescribing special diets to alleviate specific ailments. Food allergies or intolerances may contribute to ill health. Elimination diets which avoid certain suspect substances, often wheat and dairy products, can be important in naturopathic treatment. But here the naturopath must determine the underlying imbalance which leads to intolerance. In other words, the intolerance can be a symptom of a greater problem such as a digestive disease or irritated mucous membranes caused by poor diet generally. Depending on the illness, diets can range from a basic whole food diet through to a raw juice diet and often a complete fast.

Fasting: This means abstaining from food for a specified time. One, three, five and seven-day fasts are advocated. Fasts are sometimes carried out for longer, but only under supervision and in severe cases. Fasting serves several purposes, it gives the digestive system a rest, it detoxifies the system and it stimulates the metabolism so that healing and renewal can take place.

Naturopaths recommend that most of us should fast one day a month, even when healthy, just to keep well. There are various types of fast, some moderate, some extreme. The Guelpa fast, for example, is a saline fast that lasts for three days and is often prescribed for rheumatic problems. There is also the grape fast, which has become quite well-known. Grapes are valued for their detoxifying properties. A patient can eat up to 2.7kg (6 lbs.) of grapes a day with just water or grape juice for several days. Most common, however, are short fasts on juice or water.

Hydrotherapy: This therapy can be used to improve circulation and increase vitality so that the vital force can work more efficiently. It can also ease pain. Hot, cold and alternate hot and cold water is used to achieve specific effects. Hot water is initially stimulating but has a secondary relaxing effect; cold water has an invigorating and tonic effect. Alternate hot and cold baths or showers stimulate the blood and lymph circulation, help to remove congestion and revive the body tissues.

To live in balance with all things natural is the only way to achieve lasting good health.

Naturopaths use many forms of water therapy. These include cold compresses to boost the elimination of toxins, cold baths, hot baths, saunas, and sitz baths. Sitz baths are hip baths where you sit in alternate hot and cold water. They can help pelvic disorders such as fibroids and constipation.

Osteopathy: Most naturopaths will work on posture, joints and muscles, not just to correct any structural problems, but because structural integrity also affects the internal organs and body tissue. Structural disorders can also be affected by unhealthy emotional problems, especially in the case of recurring structural problems. Naturopaths work on the body's soft tissues using neuro-muscular techniques (NMT). This particularly gentle technique that is suitable for the elderly, for freeing adhesions that occur after an operation and for relieving abdominal pain.

Psychotherapy: The mind and emotions are regarded as an integral and vitally important part of total health. Naturopaths approach mental health from the perspective of removing destructive emotions. They are not equipped to deal with serious mental illness such as schizophrenia, but can pinpoint and

JUICE FASTING FOR BEGINNERS

Why fast? *Naturopaths recommend fasting on pure fruit and vegetable juices for one day a week, or one day a fortnight, if this is too difficult. Fresh fruit and vegetable juices are packed with vitamins and minerals in an easily absorbable form which means they nourish as they cleanse. You may find the fast difficult to stick to, but persevere and you will be rewarded with increased good health, improved vitality and you might also lose some unwanted body fat.*

Preparation *A one-day fast means fasting for 24 hours, not 12. It can run from dinner time the previous evening to dinner time on your fast day or from first thing in the morning to the same time the following morning; it is up to you. Choose a day when there are few demands on your time and energy. It is hard to fast when you have to work or have children or visitors to attend to.*

Start preparing for your fast the day before by eating plain whole foods: cooked and raw vegetables, salads, fruit and brown rice are all allowed. But try to avoid animal products and sweetened foods. Drink fruit juice, water and herb teas in place of coffee, tea and alcohol.

What to drink and how much? *On your fast you can drink fruit and vegetable juices, but do not mix them in the same glass as they tend to cause wind (mixed apple and carrot juice is the exception). You can, of course, also drink spring, filtered or non-carbonated mineral water. Drink fresh juice only, preferably squeezed from organic produce. For this it helps to have a special juicer, otherwise it can work out very expensive. One to two liters (two to four pints) of fluid (juice and water) a day is an acceptable volume for first-time fasters.*

Your choice of juices *Most fruits and vegetables can be juiced and it is a good idea to include different types for flavor and the particular nutrients and properties they possess. For example, watermelon is a wonderful diuretic, while apples contain numerous vitamins and a substance called pectin which helps to remove toxins. Vegetable juices such as carrot, spinach, beetroot, celery and tomato can combine to make tasty cocktails. Season vegetable juices with herbs, if you like, but do not add salt as this can cause water retention.*

Symptoms during fasting *Fasting can cause various symptomatic reactions in the body: headaches, fatigue, increased body odor and bad breath. They are encouraging signs that elimination is taking place. These unpleasant symptoms are one reason why it is best not to socialize or work while fasting.*

Breaking your fast *Coming off your fast correctly is as important as the preparation. Fueled by hunger pangs you may be tempted to gorge yourself on your favorite foods. To do so would render the whole fasting process a waste of time. So, wean yourself gradually onto solid foods, starting with small amounts of vegetables, fruit and salads and vegetable soups. You can then introduce whole grains and other food in a balanced diet.*

When not to fast? *Only reasonably fit and healthy people should fast. Those who should definitely not fast are people with diabetes, epilepsy, anemia or wasting diseases such as cancer, leukemia or TB. People who become light-headed or develop headaches when they miss a meal could have a blood sugar problem, so they should not fast, neither should people who tire easily. Both groups should consult a practitioner for diagnosis and advice.*

eliminate the origins of psychosomatic illnesses, mostly through counseling and relaxation techniques.

Naturopaths are often trained in other disciplines, like herbalism or homeopathy, which they can include in the treatment, but they are extra, not necessary parts of the therapy.

What happens in a consultation?

As with most holistic therapies the consultation will take about an hour. The naturopath will ask you questions and takes notes about you, your lifestyle, problems and medical history. The questions asked range from:

- *Enquiries about what and how much you eat and drink*
- *Questions about your bowel movements*
- *How you sleep*
- *Details of your job*
- *Your relationships with family, friends and colleagues*

He will then give you a routine medical check-up, and use some or all of the diagnostic techniques described.

For the osteopathic examination you will be asked to undress to your underwear. If further medical tests such as blood or urine analysis or scans are needed, the naturopath will arrange for these to be carried out at your nearest hospital. If he discovers a problem for which immediate medical attention or surgery are necessary, he will also recommend that you see your doctor. Neither the examination nor treatment is painful, although the program will require some dedication on your part.

The naturopath will start a treatment program based on what he has gleaned from you during the consultation. The treatment is gradual and can be adapted as your health improves. But early recommendations often include dietary changes, perhaps a detoxifying fast, or a diet to build up strength and immunity and perhaps some relaxation exercises.

A good practitioner will talk through the treatment process with you, explaining each aspect of it and why he believes it is necessary. He will want to know how you feel about the treatment plan and if there are any problems. If you object to any treatment you are not obliged to have it, so do not feel that you must do everything that is recommended. Naturopathy is not about dispensing cures for ills, it requires commitment and often major lifestyle changes by the patient. It is also a joint responsibility between you and your practitioner.

Forms of hydrotherapy can either be carried out in the clinic or you will be advised on how to use them at home. Any diet and exercise changes need to be implemented at home. You will probably leave your first appointment with a diet sheet and possibly fasting information. It is normal to make a follow-up appointment as you leave. This can be for a week or two later, depending on how acute your condition is and the treatments you are receiving. If any problems occur at home during your treatment, ring your practitioner immediately.

ABOVE: *Many naturopaths are trained osteopaths and will often work on the body tissues and structure to balance the body.*

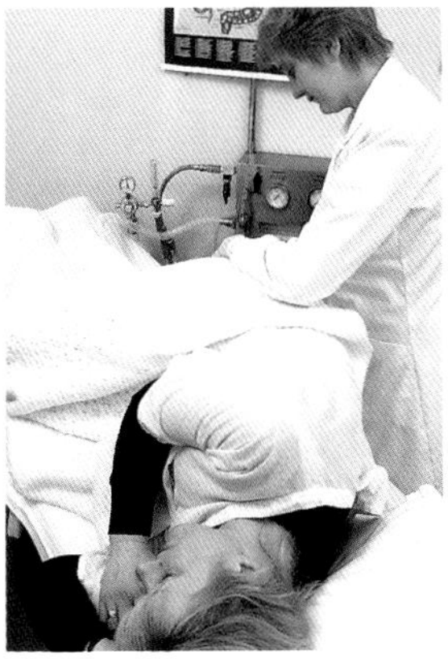

ABOVE: *Occasionally colonic irrigation will be recommended by the practitioner as part of your naturopathic treatment.*

How many sessions do I need?

The length of treatment depends on your illness, how long you have had it, how long it has been suppressed, your age and how healthy you are. For example, in the case of irritable bowel syndrome in an otherwise fit and healthy young adult, two to four weeks of dietary changes can bring relief. But it takes longer to learn how to handle stress using relaxation techniques.

More established disorders could take six months or more of advice and treatment for self-sufficiency. Bringing out long-suppressed symptoms or restoring health in the case of chronic disease can cause healing crises, where your symptoms appear to get worse before better. This is a good sign, but can be difficult to bear if you are already ill or in pain. For this reason treatment often needs to be prolonged so progress can be slow and steady. In all cases, the aim is to educate you to look after yourself.

Which problems can it help?

Naturopathy can help with many acute (short-term) and chronic (long-term) problems, such as anemia, allergies, arthritis, bronchitis, candida, circulation disorders, constipation, cystitis, eczema and other skin diseases, hangovers, irritable bowel syndrome, migraine, premenstrual syndrome, sinusitis and ulcers. In the case of life-threatening disease, it can improve your resistance to infection so there is less risk of complications.

Is it safe?

As with all medicine, naturopathy is safe for everyone when practiced by a qualified practitioner. Not all treatment will suit everyone, but a skilled naturopath can decide on which form to concentrate and which to avoid.

Responsibly practiced, naturopathy, however, is good for young children because their vital force is more easily brought into balance. It can also be used with most elderly patients who can benefit from nutritional and dietary improvements.

Pregnant women with morning sickness can also safely benefit from naturopathy.

Clinical studies

In special medical trials, a naturopathic diet treatment has been shown to be helpful in treating diseases of the joints.

In 1991 a year-long trial was held with people suffering from rheumatoid arthritis. One control group of 26 people stayed at a convalescent home for four weeks and ate an ordinary diet for the study; the other group of 27 patients stayed at a health farm where they were put on a week's fast. They were then given special diets for the year. After four weeks, the special diet group showed improvement in their gripping strength, the pain suffered, and in tender, swollen joints. They all also had improvements in blood levels in relation to joint inflammation. After one year the control group felt less pain, while the special diet patients still experienced all the previous improvements. (**35**)

In connection with rheumatic disease, a questionnaire survey was carried out in 1991 involving the diets of 742 rheumatic patients. Of the people questioned, about 42 percent of those with juvenile rheumatoid arthritis and primary fibromyalgia reported worsening of their disease after eating certain foods. Fewer, only a third of those with ankylosing spondylitis, rheumatoid arthritis, and psoriatic arthopathy reported the same.

All the groups tried controlled diets to help their symptoms and similar benefits were reported by all. Forty-six percent of patients had reduced pain and stiffness, but only 36 percent had less joint swelling. All these symptoms were improved by 20 percent for ankylosing spondylitis and rheumatoid arthritis patients with fasting. (**36**) (*For clinical references see How to use this book*)

FOR INFORMATION ON HOW TO CHOOSE A NATUROPATH SEE THE DIRECTORY.

THERE ARE FEW THERAPIES as simple and gentle as the Bach Flower Remedies. These 38 little bottles of tincture are on sale in most chemists and health food stores and are being used by everyone from students to company executives. Rescue Remedy, in particular, has become as popular as the filofax, establishing itself as an indispensable ingredient of modern living. No doubt the creator, Dr. Edward Bach (pronounced Batch) would have been delighted to see his simple natural remedies embraced with such fervor.

BACH FLOWER REMEDIES

BACH FLOWER REMEDIES were developed by Dr. Bach to heal and balance negative thoughts that everybody has as these can lead to physical disease. They can help all types of personalities and different emotional trauma.

Dr. Edward Bach trained as a physician, bacteriologist and then a homeopath, but was dissatisfied with the scientific approach to medicine and believed that healing lay not in the laboratory, but in nature. In 1930 at the age of 43 he shocked his medical colleagues by giving up his thriving Harley Street practice to pursue natural remedies. He moved to Mount Vernon, in Oxfordshire to a house that is now known as the Bach Centre.

Dr. Bach was unusual among doctors of his time because he believed in treating people, not their illnesses. He believed that a person's nature had a direct impact on their physical health. He talked to his patients, comforted them, and watched them for signs of how their nature affected their disease. After considerable study, he concluded that disease is simply a manifestation of negative thoughts such as fear, anxiety, grief, frustration and despair. The way to heal people, he believed, was to cure the negative thoughts that made them ill.

Bach's training in homeopathy introduced him to the concept of vibrational healing. He discovered that homeopathic substances, once diluted so that none of their original material remained, could heal on a vibrational level within the body.

While working at the London Homeopathic Hospital, Dr. Bach developed the seven Bach Nosodes that are still used today. Nosodes are homeopathic preparations made from the discharges of disease which, in minute quantities, can be used to treat the after-effects of the related disease.

He discovered that all patients with the same emotional difficulties could be cured with the same nosode, irrespective of their physical symptoms. His initial investigations into the emotional origins of disease gave him the impetus to look for other natural remedies which could address the emotional and mental causes of disease before they turned into physical symptoms.

What are Bach Flower Remedies?

There are 38 Bach Flower Remedies developed to support every conceivable personality, attitude and negative state of mind. They were developed as a complete system and, before his death, Bach gave instructions that no more remedies were to be added. His aim was to keep the system simple, and although some therapists may find the system restrictive, the remedies were devised for self-help and most users value their simplicity. Bach classified all emotional problems into seven major groups: fear, uncertainty and indecision, insufficient interest in present circumstances, loneliness, oversensitivity, despondency or despair, and overcare for the welfare of others. Through their subtle vibrational energy the remedies work to heal every negative aspect of all seven types of emotional illness, thereby restoring mental harmony and preventing any physical illness from taking hold. Flower remedies can complement other therapies such as herbalism, homeopathy or aromatherapy or be used alone.

The remedies were produced by Bach when he was looking for pure natural remedies that could work in a similar way to his homeopathic nosodes. Every morning he went out walking and noticed the dew on flowers. He thought that while dew rested on the plant it must absorb some of the plant's properties. He collected and tested the dew from certain flowers and noticed that it could have a positive effect on the mind. He tested several flowers and plants, apparently by instinct, and arrived at 38 remedies.

Bach tested the remedies on himself. For several days before he found each flower, he would experience a particular negative state of mind and the resulting physical symptoms which needed a remedy. Then he would go in search of the flower that would restore his peace of mind and body. He tested each flower by placing a petal on his tongue or in his hand and immediately felt the benefits of the one that worked. He would first feel the mental benefits and then the physical symptoms would disappear.

People have emotional or physical reactions when using the remedies. This is positive as destructive emotion is being released.

BELOW: In the sun method of extraction, flowers are left for several hours in a bowl of spring water. The energized water is then added to bottles half filled with brandy. This then becomes the mother tincture.

BELOW: The boiling method is a stronger process. Flowers, buds or cones are simmered in spring water for about 30 minutes. The water is then cooled, filtered and brandy is added before bottling.

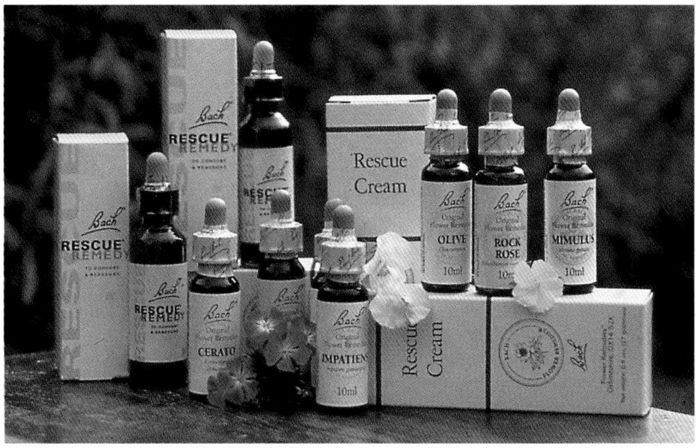

ABOVE: There are 38 Bach Flower Remedies to choose from to suit your mood or emotion.

LEFT: You can take a remedy by adding four drops to water, or placing them on your tongue.

He discovered that the dew from the flowers exposed to sunlight was more potent and the plant's energy was most concentrated when the flower was in full bloom. Having satisfied himself that the flowers could yield their energy to sun-warmed dew, he decided to devise a more practical method of extraction. In fact, he developed two methods: the sun method and the boiling method. Both of which are still used.

The sun method: The best flowers are picked and put in a glass bowl of spring water. The bowl is left in strong sunlight for several hours to allow the plant to energize the water. The blooms are removed with a twig or part of the parent plant to avoid human contact with the essence, and it is poured into bottles half filled with brandy. The brandy preserves the essence which becomes known as the mother tincture. This is further diluted in brandy to make the stock remedies, sold in small brown bottles.

The boiling method: This is reserved for essences which qualify for a stronger extraction process. In this process the buds, cones or flowers of the plant are simmered for 30 minutes in a pan of spring water. When cooled, the liquid is filtered, mixed with brandy and bottled.

How do the remedies work?

Bach Flower Remedies are so simple that they are often dismissed as placebos. The do not work in any biochemical way and because no physical part of the plant remains in the remedy, its properties and actions cannot be detected or analyzed like a drug or herbal preparation. Therapists believe the remedies contain the energy or imprint of the plant from which it was made and work in a similar way to homeopathic remedies – that it provides the stimulus needed to kick-start your own healing mechanism. Some of the remedies are known as "type remedies." Your type remedy is effectively the remedy that is most compatible to your personality or basic character, and you take it when the negative side of your character threatens the positive.

The difficulty with the type remedy lies in analyzing your character and deciding which remedy matches it best. You may not be the best person to decide on this as it is easy to read through the list of remedies and think that most of them could apply to you to a degree, or be appropriate at a different times in your life. However, usually only one truly complements your basic nature, although some people do seem to be a mixture of two types. To find your type remedy, sift through the events in your life and make a note of how you reacted to them:

- *Think of how you were as a child*
- *What you felt like when you started school*
- *How easy or difficult it was to make new friends*
- *Think of how you are in your present relationships*
- *How you respond to criticism*
- *How you cope with crises, illness or pain*

These are all tests to find out about your true nature. This memory dredging may suggest several similar remedies. For example, if you think that you are an outspoken extrovert and natural leader, remedies such as Vine, Impatiens, and Vervain, are possibilities. But, by a process of elimination you must try to narrow it down to one that is most like you. Alternatively, ask a friend to tell you, or consult a therapist who uses the remedies.

You should also consult a therapist if you have serious or long-term emotional problems that need resolving. You can use any number of remedies for mental and emotional balancing, but most people take only one or two at a time, keeping Rescue Remedy on hand for emergencies.

There are no rules about taking the remedies. Four drops at least four times a day is suggested, but not the rule. Let your instinct guide you. All the remedies are available in ready-to-use preparations that you drop on your tongue or mix in water.

What happens in a consultation?

Bach remedies were created to be so simple to use that people could treat themselves. However, many practitioners of other disciplines such as herbalism, homeopathy and aromatherapy use Bach remedies to complement their own remedies. A few Bach Flower therapists use the remedies exclusively.

Most therapists have their own ways of working. But every consultation should begin with an interview between you and the therapist. This can last about 15 minutes or go on for over an hour. The therapist will explain the Bach system to you if you do not already know how it works. She will ask why you have come to see her and will listen while you talk about yourself and your worries. She will observe your posture and appearance and will listen to the tone of your voice and the way you say things as these can be as revealing as what you actually say.

While you talk, she may take notes and ask questions to work out, by a process of elimination, which remedies would be best for you. She might ask questions about your fears, how you feel about your children, or how easily you give up when something you attempt does not work out. It is not enough for her to know that you have a problem at home or at work. She needs to know how you feel about it and how you react to it.

For example, if your boss does not appreciate how hard you work, you could respond in any number of ways. You might hate him, or it may make you even more desperate to please him, or you could pretend you simply do not care. Each reaction points to a different remedy. At the end of the consultation the therapist will prescribe the remedies. The number of remedies prescribed depends on the individual, but it is unlikely to be more than six, usually fewer. Most people feel better at the end of the consultation because they have been able to talk through their problems.

How many sessions do I need?

The number of sessions you need depends on the individual. If you have quite complex problems you may want to visit a therapist several times. When self-prescribing, you can take the remedies as and when needed. The length of time it takes to notice an improvement also depends on the person and the problem. Many people notice an immediate benefit, but it can take some time to get back in balance. It is possible to have an emotional or physical reaction while taking the remedies. Therapists would say "you cannot stir a muddy pool without bringing silt to the surface."

Which problems can it help?

The Bach remedies help with mental problems and emotions rather than physical ailments. Problems such as fear, anxiety, loneliness and depression can all be relieved with the right remedy.

Is it safe?

The remedies are not addictive, dangerous, nor do they interfere with any other treatment. They are suitable for all ages. They are safe for pregnant women, babies and children and can also be given to animals and plants.

USING THE REMEDIES

Successful treatment with the remedies depends on an accurate diagnosis. Get to know the Bach system and then aim to match the remedies to yourself, your family and animals. Start with Rescue Remedy as it is the easiest choice. From there you can get to know the remedies as you need to use them.

For yourself *If you find it hard to decide on a remedy, make a note of the one you think you need and then ask yourself the same questions you would ask someone else for whom you were prescribing – How do you feel? Why do you feel that way? How does it affect you? What could have caused it?*

For children *Notice the nature of the child in their behavior and play. Try to match their behavior to the remedy. Is he always active like Vervain? Timid and shy like Mimulus? Gentle and obedient like Centaury? Bossy like Vine? Or sulky like willow?*

For animals *You need to know the animal's nature and note how differently he behaves when ill. For example, a dog who looks sorry for himself needs Willow; an aggressive one needs Holly or Vine; and cats often need Water Violet for their pride and independence. It is good to start with Rescue Remedy, because many animal problems are caused by shock or terror. Add four drops to a small animal's drinking water and ten drops for large animals such as horses and cows and give at least four times a day.*

The Bach flower remedies

Agrimony ⋆
For those who always hide their feelings behind a cheerful face. They claim that all is well even when it is not. ***The remedy*** *helps them to talk through their problem and put it into perspective.*

Aspen
This "trembling tree" remedy is for fear of unknown things. ***The remedy*** *encourages the person who takes it to feel safe and relaxed.*

Beech ⋆
For the perfectionist who finds it hard to tolerate or understand the shortcomings of those they believe to be foolish or ignorant. ***The remedy*** *can help them to become more understanding.*

Centaury ⋆
For those who are kind, gentle and eager to please, but are so unwilling to let anyone down that they can't say no. ***The remedy*** *will help them remain gentle but firm, so that others respect and appreciate them.*

Cerato ⋆
For those who seek the reassurance of others because they do not trust their own judgment or intuition. Dithering means they often miss out on opportunities. ***The remedy*** *gives them the ability to trust their own judgment.*

Cherry Plum
For irrational thoughts and for people who fear losing their sanity. They often feel anxious and depressed. ***The remedy*** *helps them to handle their inner turmoil.*

Chestnut Bud ⋆
For those who keep making the same mistakes, never seeming to learn from past experiences. ***The remedy*** *encourages them to focus on the present and to learn from every experience.*

Chicory ⋆
For the mothering type who is loving, but overprotective and possessive. She always demands the love, sympathy and appreciation of others. ***The remedy*** *will help her to let go without feeling rejected. It also helps "clingy" children.*

Clematis ⋆
For the artistic dreamer, who may become absent-minded, inattentive and easily bored. ***The remedy*** *can recall them from their dream world and focus their attention on everyday life.*

Crab Apple ⋆ *(illustrated)*
For those who feel infected or unclean, who are revolted by eating, sex or have a hygiene fixation. ***The remedy*** *helps them to put everything in perspective. It can be useful during puberty.*

Elm ⋆
For those who are overwhelmed and made to feel inadequate by pressure from work, family and other commitments. ***The remedy*** *helps to calm them and make them think clearly, restoring confidence.*

Gentian
For the eternal pessimist, who is easily discouraged, even when they are doing well. ***The remedy*** *encourages perseverance and gives them the will to succeed. It is also good for loss of faith after failure.*

Gorse
For those who believe that they were born to suffer and they are pessimistic about everything. ***The remedy*** *helps them to realize that all is not lost.*

Heather ⋆
For those who always talk about themselves, so nobody else can get a word in edgeways. They do not like being alone, but leave other people so exhausted that they tend to be avoided. ***The remedy*** *makes them feel secure so that they become more relaxed and less self-obsessed.*

Holly
For those who develop the victim mentality, overcome with hatred, jealousy, envy or suspicion. They may keep their feelings to themselves, but burn with resentment for others. ***The remedy*** *enables them to feel happy for others, even if they are having problems themselves.*

Honeysuckle
For those who dwell in the past to the extent that they lose interest in the present. ***The remedy*** *puts the past in perspective and helps them focus on today. It also helps with bereavement.*

Hornbeam
For those who are mentally exhausted at the thought of work, so that what used to a pleasure becomes a chore. The thought of what lies ahead makes them tired. ***The remedy*** *gives them the emotional strength to face the day ahead.*

Impatiens ⋆
For those who do everything in a hurry. They are brusque, finish sentences for people, fidget, and edge toward the door when others are still talking. ***The remedy*** *encourages a calmer outlook, more tolerance and patience.*

Larch ⋆
For those with ability but no confidence. They need to believe in themselves and not miss opportunities because of self-doubt and feelings of inferiority. ***The remedy*** *makes them bold enough to take the plunge. Encourages determination, even when they have experienced some setbacks.*

Mimulus ⋆
For those who are shy, nervous and blush easily. They feel uneasy with people they do not know, dislike parties and always feel self-conscious. This is also the remedy for fear of known things. ***The remedy*** *helps to give them courage.*

Mustard
For those who are gloomy for no reason. The mood can sometimes stay for months. ***The remedy*** *helps them find a way out of their despair.*

Oak ⋆
For the fighter who never gives in. He is solid like the tree itself and others come to him for guidance. But sometimes he overdoes it and suddenly he finds he has no strength left. ***The remedy*** *rebuilds strength and gives patience.*

Olive
For those who are exhausted due to overwork or over-exertion. When they have no energy or strength left and life is no longer fun. ***The remedy*** *replaces lost energy. Also good for when people are being mentally stretched or after illness.*

Pine ⋆
For those who feel guilty, even when it was not their fault. They blame themselves for others' mistakes and are always apologizing. ***The remedy*** *eases their conscience and stops feelings of self-reproach*

Red Chestnut ⋆
For those who are over-anxious for family and friends and afraid of impending disaster. They do not worry about themselves, but are distressed by reports of disasters. ***The remedy*** *helps put their fears in perspective.*

Rock Rose
For terror or panic, which may not be rational but is still real. It is also the remedy for accidents or sudden illness and for when there seems little hope. ***The remedy*** *helps to give courage and strength.*

Rock Water ⋆
For those who are strict with themselves, and demand perfection. They are inflexible and self-righteous. They do not criticize others but do play the victim. ***The remedy*** *helps them to be more lenient with themselves.*

Scleranthus ⋆
For emotional distress due to indecision. Making the smallest choice throws them into a dilemma. They do not usually discuss their difficulties with others. ***The remedy*** *makes them more focused, so they have clearer options and know their own mind.*

Star of Bethlehem
For the inconsolable after shock, bereavement, bad news or trauma. ***The remedy*** *eases emotional pain and lightens the feeling of sorrow.*

Sweet Chestnut
For those in utter despair. When they can see no way out of the darkness and wish they could die, but do not believe that death could release them from their pain. ***The remedy*** *gives them hope and restores their faith in life.*

Vervain ⋆
For the enthusiastic, talkative, principled perfectionist who is incensed by injustice and fights for the underdog. ***The remedy*** *encourages them to spend more of their time resting and relaxing.*

Vine ⋆
For the leader – the strong, dominant, ambitious and determined, but sometimes tyrannical. ***The remedy*** *encourages understanding without taking away their leadership qualities.*

Walnut
This is the remedy for change. It settles people into new environments and helps them cope with life changes such as marriage, divorce, birth, puberty and the menopause. ***The remedy*** *helps with fresh starts and keeps them on their chosen path.*

Water Violet ⋆
For reserved, self-contained and dignified people. They like peace and quiet, but at times can seem aloof and this encourages isolation. ***The remedy*** *makes them appear more friendly while also helping to retain some calmness and serenity.*

White Chestnut
For those who are tormented with persistent worries and unwanted thoughts. Their mind is so full of arguments that they find it difficult to concentrate. ***The remedy*** *restores peace of mind.*

Wild Oat ⋆
For those who are dithering at a crossroads in life. They are discontented with their career or their lifestyle and may want something more fulfilling, but do not know where to look. ***The remedy*** *clears the confusion and helps to make them decisive and clear-headed.*

Wild Rose
For those who drift along and have not the enthusiasm or ambition to change their lives. They let illness and misfortune triumph over them and are willing to accept whatever fate delivers. ***The remedy*** *helps to revive their zest for life.*

Willow ⋆
For the irritable, introspective pessimist, who dwells on misfortune and tends to wallow in self-pity. ***The remedy*** *lifts the gloom and self-pity from their shoulders and helps to encourage some positive thinking for the future.*

Rescue Remedy
This is the most frequently used remedy. It is a "composite" remedy, made up of Star or Bethlehem, Rock rose, Impatiens, Cherry Plum and Clematis. As the name suggests, it helps in emergencies – when you feel panic, shock, loss of control and mental numbness. It is often the remedy that triggers the body's healing response during illness. Rescue Remedy can calm exam nerves, and relieves the anxiety of flying. You can also dab it on stings and bruises. Always keep a bottle close at hand.

⋆ *indicates a type remedy*

FOR INFORMATION ON HOW TO CHOOSE A BACH FLOWER THERAPIST SEE THE DIRECTORY.

RELAXATION & VISUALIZATION

RELAXATION & VISUALIZATION are two separate stress-relieving techniques that are often practiced together. The relaxation techniques help to calm tense muscles and the visualization methods use positive and appealing images to overcome mental and emotional problems.

SCIENCE HAS ONLY recently discovered that the mind and body function as a complete working unit. It is a belief long held by Eastern philosophers and holistic medical practitioners, but it took the new science of psychoneuroimmunology to convince the medical establishment that mental activity has a direct effect on the body and vice versa. This is particularly important with regard to stress and relaxation.

Research has shown that feelings are linked to posture; if your body is relaxed your mind will follow suit and a relaxed mind produces significant physical benefits. It has been found, for example, that relaxation can slow down the heart rate, lower blood pressure and regulate breathing and the metabolic rate. It also reduces adrenaline levels and allows the immune system to function more efficiently. This is because the body's two defense systems – the alarm and immune – work well together to ensure our survival.

The alarm system is the body's fight-or-flight system which is mobilized by stress. It reacts quickly to stressors, increasing adrenaline levels to make us run from a threat or stand and fight. When the threat is passed, our adrenaline levels should return to normal, but under constant stress, they rarely get the chance. Consequently, the body feels as if it is under constant attack. This feeling of continued pressure has a cumulative effect on the immune system, which protects us from disease and relies on good nutrition and positive mental attitude for strength. An alarm system, on constant alert, overstimulates the immune system so it cannot distinguish between real and presumed threats and so disease can take hold. Scientists are researching the belief that one of the most powerful influences on the immune system may be our view of how well we cope with stress. Stress is a normal and necessary part of life, but it must be kept under control. The key to controlling it is relaxation. For many of us this involves lying on the couch watching television at the end of a long day. This form of passive relaxation has no real therapeutic benefits for the body. The stresses of the day, the criticisms, disappointments and anger stay locked inside causing anxiety, frustration, depression and muscle tension.

True relaxation is a healing process that focuses on calming mind and body. It involves turning your attention inward to control and resolve the effects of stress rather than suppressing them with short-term measures such as drugs, cigarettes or alcohol. Relaxation is an acquired skill. Practiced correctly it helps prevent disease and increases feelings of well-being.

What is relaxation and visualization?

Relaxation and visualization are two separate disciplines, often combined to form a single therapy. Simplistically, relaxation could be thought of as a technique to combat stress. But as a therapeutic exercise it is more accurately a state of physical and mental relief, where tension, fear and anxiety are released and replaced with calm and peaceful feelings. It is a state of being rather than an activity or form of inactivity. You do not need to be lying down with your eyes closed to relax, although this is how most people learn the skill. Once learned, you can bring about relaxation wherever you are and whatever you are doing.

Not everyone finds it easy to relax; it can take some effort to learn the techniques. This is especially true if you are a naturally tense, nervous or frightened person, or a dynamic go-getter. One of the most useful ways to increase the benefits of relaxation is to use your imagination.

Visualization is the conscious use of your imagination in order to create attractive and positive images that can be used to heal or change aspects of your life. You need to be relaxed to be able to visualize, but used well, it can help to deepen the relaxation process and overcome many of the mental and emotional problems that can lead to ill health. It is often goal-directed, which means you set yourself a mental goal such as "I feel calm and in control" and your mind learns to accept this. It is a technique that is used by people in all walks of life: An athlete can be

RIGHT, BELOW AND BOTTOM RIGHT: A remembered image of a beautiful beach, a glorious sunset or a tranquil lake can help to induce a calm and relaxed state during the visualization process.

ABOVE: A favorite scene from a good holiday could be used as part of your visualization therapy to help counteract negative thinking.

motivated to win a race by picturing himself way ahead of his competitors. Relaxation therapists encourage you to use the skill to picture yourself overcoming a problem or an illness and to replace negative and destructive emotions with positive, life-enhancing alternatives.

Some relaxation therapists, in particular Americans Dr. Carl and Stephanie Simonton, encourage people to destroy their cancers and relieve other serious health problems by imagining their medication destroying the disease and visualizing the body using its healing powers to get well. This is a valid and useful way of working with these techniques, but one which therapists must obviously use with caution.

How does it work?

Relaxation works by rebalancing the sympathetic and parasympathetic parts of the autonomic nervous system. The sympathetic system deals with how the involuntary systems of the body, such as heartbeat, circulation, breathing and glands such as the adrenals, respond to stress. It is the system involved in the "fight-or-flight" syndrome.

Basic techniques

The following five categories introduce the basic techniques and how they work. The categories are broad, not mutually exclusive. For example, visualization plays a part in most techniques.

Tense release *Tensing and releasing muscles forms the basis of many relaxation techniques. It has been used for years in general medicine, midwifery and yoga classes and remains one of the most common methods practiced and taught by therapists. The object is to tense your muscles, then relax them, to feel the physical and mental release that accompanies each movement. The practitioner first demonstrates the technique and then asks you to lie on the couch while she talks you through the action on each major muscle group, while you breathe deeply and calmly. Then she will instruct you to work around your body, possibly starting with an arm or leg and focusing on every detail. She will guide your attention to your abdomen, chest, shoulders and head. For each muscle group, she commands you to tense on a single word such as "tense" or "now," hold it for about ten seconds and release it when she says to. After 20–30 minutes she will tell you to open your eyes, stretch and see how relaxed and refreshed you feel.*

Passive muscular relaxation *requires knowledge of tense-release so you "know" your muscles, but has some advantages. One advantage is that it is a quicker process, and can be practiced anywhere. It is also good for those with physical disabilities (like multiple sclerosis or rheumatoid arthritis) who are unable to tense their muscles. The basic technique is similar to tense-release, but instead of tensing a muscle group you focus attention on it, acknowledge the tension there and release it. You may be asked to imagine a slow, warm wave of relaxation washing through the muscles, lengthening and expanding them and freeing constrictions held by tension.*

Visualization *often involves using a special imaginary place. When you are relaxed and lying with your eyes closed, the therapist will tell you to retreat in your mind to a special place, such as a secret garden or a tropical island. She will encourage you to use all your senses to explore the place: feel the temperature, smell the flowers, see the rainbow, hear the birds and so on. The therapist will lead you in the exercise, she will give you ideas, but you can put what you like into your special place as this is your imagination. The idea is to choose what works for you. When your special place is established in your mind, you can put yourself into the image to achieve your goals. A relaxed mind is receptive to anything you want to give it. For example, you can go into your special place to resolve a conflict and your mind will be willing to accept your decision. You can use it to make positive statements about yourself, such as, "I am successful" or "I feel healthy and strong."*

Deep techniques *These methods are long and complicated and should only be attempted with a well-trained practitioner as they can lower blood pressure considerably. Techniques involved in this sort of work include hypnotherapy (see pages 122–127), autogenic training (see pages 132–133), biofeedback and meditation. With biofeedback you are attached by electrodes to machinery which measures your body's and brain's responses to stress. The object is to recognize how your brain, temperature, pulse, respiration and blood pressure, are affected by stress, and learn to control them. As you relax these physiological changes register on screen and over time you recognize the effects of relaxation without using machinery. The system is effective in bringing about deep relaxation. Meditation, however needs no apparatus. It is a state of deep relaxation where the mind is emptied of thoughts. It differs from other forms of relaxation because you do not set yourself goals and rather than become sleepy you feel heightened awareness. The object is to achieve inner harmony and a quiet mind. During the 1970s, physiologist Herbert Benson of Harvard University recorded how transcendental meditation (TM) could reduce blood pressure and counteract the effects of stress. TM is a special meditation, but Benson found it worked well as long as the practitioner adhered to four basic rules: choose a quiet environment with no distractions, adopt a comfortable position, focus on a word or object that will hold your attention, and develop an attitude of passive acceptance. Passive acceptance is vital to meditation. It is based on the fact that it is very difficult to stop thoughts entering your head, so rather than fight them, you should acknowledge each thought and let it drift away. This takes practice, but initial attempts at meditation can still leave you feeling relaxed. When using any deep technique, you or the therapist should bring it to a gradual end. The therapist may count you out or tell you that she is bringing the session to an end and that when you open your eyes you will feel relaxed and refreshed. Do not get up immediately as the drop in blood pressure may make you giddy.*

Applied relaxation *This term is used for shortened versions of relaxation techniques, which can be used for on-the-spot stress reduction. These techniques are usually taught on a one-to-one basis. The aim is to relax in seconds rather than 15 minutes or more. The technique can only be learned after mastering the longer methods. The idea is to learn a tense-release technique, which may take 20 minutes to induce, then learn a release-only technique, which you might induce in half that time and gradually work your way through some shortened versions until you can relax in seconds. This quick-relaxation technique is useful for those prone to anxiety or panic attacks, but can take several weeks to learn as you must learn the longer methods first.*

By focusing your attention on what is happening inside your body and mind and away from outside concerns, relaxation frees the mind from stress, allows the muscles to relax and switches the autonomic nervous system over to the parasympathetic, which is responsible for rest and repair. This results in reduced adrenaline production, slowed heart rate, relaxed breathing and general rest. The sympathetic and parasympathetic systems need to be balanced to maintain good health; continual stress works against that balance, relaxation helps to restore it.

Therapists use and teach different techniques to bring about physical and mental relaxation. Physical relaxation is the term used for techniques which distress the body's muscles and induce a calm mind and body. Techniques such as the Alexander Technique (see pages 116–121) and the basic-tense release technique described opposite, fit into this category.

Mental relaxation techniques such as visualization, use the power of the mind to enhance physical relaxation. The brain is divided into two hemispheres: the left is concerned with logic and reason and the right relates to creativity, imagination and emotions. Most of the time we use the left side to work, study and carry out our daily tasks. The right side we use much less, but any images that we create in it are believed to be directly linked to physical body responses. So that memories of being chased by a mad dog, for example, can produce the physical stress symptoms caused by the original event. Likewise soothing or positive images can give a sense of calm or well-being in the body.

Therapists use and teach different calming techniques to achieve the right physical and mental relaxation for individuals.

Visualization encourages right-brain activity and uses the images it provides to override destructive effects wrought by the left side. If you give your mind a strong, positive image it will accept it, providing it is one in which you are involved, and your goal is both attainable and one in which you believe.

Deep relaxation involves techniques such as hypnosis, meditation, autogenic training and biofeedback, which induce a trance-like state. The effects of deep relaxation are more long-lasting than those of brief relaxation techniques, which are used for coping with everyday stresses.

What happens in a consultation?

Relaxation sessions can take place on a one-to-one basis or in groups and can vary from one practitioner to another. The average session, including consultation, is anything between 45 and 90 minutes. It begins with a chat between you and the therapist. Usually the therapist will take a medical history and details about your life and the factors that may be causing you anxiety:

- *She will ask about your medication and if you are using any other therapies or have used any in the past. (You can use these techniques with any other therapies, but if you are having a treatment such as hypnotherapy, it can become rather confusing.)*
- *The therapist may take your blood pressure, if she is trained to do so.*

Depending on your physical condition and the type of relaxation you are going to learn, you may be asked to lie on a couch, or on the floor, or sit on a chair. The room should be quiet, warm and clean. The therapist may sometimes use other relaxation aides. She will explain how the therapy works and what you can hope to gain from the session.

You will probably begin with a basic tense-release exercise. You may be asked to take off your shoes, glasses, watch and jewelery and loosen any tight clothing. The therapist will then take you through the chosen relaxation technique. In all relaxation methods, you remain in control of your own mind and are not under the therapist's control. The depth and quality of relaxation achieved depends on your willingness to participate in the process. This exercise itself should last 20–30 minutes.

The tone of voice is important in relaxation. The therapist may start the session with a friendly tone, but it will get quieter, slower and more monotonous as you relax. She may tape the session for you to use at home or may offer you some specially recorded tapes to take home. Some therapist dislike either practice as they prefer you to learn the technique independently right from the start. That way you can relax as and when you need to, not just when you are lying down with your tape recorder placed by your side.

Relaxation sessions often prove cathartic, provoking emotions such as sadness, anger, elation or confusion. The practitioner should be experienced enough to deal with what happens and should advise you at the outset about possible emotional upset. Her knowledge of your medical history may enable her to preempt distressing outbursts by steering the visualization exercise away from any images associated with anxiety. The session should end with a rest of up to 20 minutes to enable your body to return to normal. The therapist may suggest you practice an exercise for 10–20 minutes twice a day.

How many sessions do I need?

Providing you do your homework, it is usual to learn any of the techniques, even deep techniques in five to ten sessions.

Which problems can it help?

Numerous mental and physical problems associated with stress. It can also help insomnia, nausea, vomiting (including chemotherapy induced), loss of appetite, pain, anxiety, panic attacks, asthma, constipation, blood pressure, heart disease, arthritis, stress management. It is most commonly used for pain control, anxiety and insomnia.

BELOW: A basic relaxation exercise that your therapist may teach you involves lying on a mat on the floor with your knees bent and your head supported. You tense your stomach muscles as you lift your head off the floor.

ABOVE: You need to hold the tense position for several seconds and then relax back on the floor. Do the exercise several times to feel really calm and relaxed.

Is it safe?

Relaxation and visualization techniques are safe for anyone, even small children. Anyone can use the various methods provided the session is tailored to their abilities and certain medical and mental conditions are considered. For example, people with low blood pressure, joint or limb problems including arthritis, or those with muscular damage such as that caused by a stroke or accident or diseases such as MS may need an experienced therapist who understands their disease or disability. This is because the standard techniques, which often include lying on the floor, or sitting still for long periods of time are not always suitable. Patients who are mentally ill and suffer from hallucinations (schizophrenia) need to find a therapist trained in mental health.

Visualizations involving grass and flowers can trigger an attack in patients with allergies. Patients with breathing difficulties may have problems initially, if they are asked to concentrate on their breathing (and most methods do this). Some techniques can cause added fatigue for patients with chronic fatigue syndrome (ME), those having chemo- or radiotherapy or are in terminal care. Patients with cardiac disease may become more aware of their heart beat and an increase in regularity at first. Provided enough support is given for the spine, relaxation techniques are safe and beneficial for pregnant women.

Clinical studies

Relaxation techniques have been shown in several medical studies to be helpful in treating different ailments.

In 1986, 80 inflammatory bowel disease (IBD) patients were randomly allocated to either a control group taking medication or an intervention group which was given six stress management classes. All the patients were interviewed at the start and at four monthly intervals for a year. At all the assessment points, noticeable physical and mental improvements were noted in the patients having stress management training. The control group, however, showed no significant change and as medication was closely monitored between the groups, it was not responsible for the marked differences. (**37**)

In 1991, a study was undertaken into treating 55 patients suffering from tension headaches with autogenic training and hypnosis using visualization. The study also looked at the subjects' ability to respond to imagery and relaxation techniques along with how depressed and anxious they felt. The group was divided in two and each group had four treatment and two assessment sessions, with one of the two therapists.

While no significant differences were noted after the patients had either autogenic training or sessions with future-oriented hypnotic imagery therapists, they had pain relief from headaches. Also the subjects' ability to use relaxation techniques and visualization effectively at home helped reduced the effects of stress. (**38**)

In 1980 a study was undertaken on 23 patients suffering from the circulatory ailment Raynaud's disease. The patients were given training in progressive muscle relaxation, autogenic training and a combination of autogenic training and biofeedback techniques (a way of learning how to control autonomic body responses) to teach them to raise their skin temperature.

Laboratory tests measured the effectiveness of the training and records of the frequency of circulatory attacks were kept to assess the treatment. Over the nine weeks of training and assessment, no significant difference between the three techniques was measured. There was, however, a good improvement in how the patients maintained their skin temperature and their symptoms improved. (**39**) *(For clinical references see How to use this book)*

FOR INFORMATION ON HOW TO CHOOSE A RELAXATION & VISUALIZATION THERAPIST SEE THE DIRECTORY.

ALEXANDER TECHNIQUE

THE ALEXANDER TECHNIQUE was developed by Frederick Matthias Alexander who believed that, "Every man, woman and child holds the possibility of physical perfection; it rests with each of us to attain it by personal understanding and effort."

Alexander, an Australian actor, was born prematurely in 1869 and led a rather sickly childhood, which left him with a slight build, but a strong character. In the early days of his acting career Alexander was giving recitals of "dramatic and humorous

THE ALEXANDER TECHNIQUE is a special method that is taught in lessons to reeducate us to regain our natural posture and use our bodies more efficiently. It can help relieve stress-related conditions, breathing disorders and neck and joint pain.

pieces" when he started to lose his voice for no apparent reason. His doctor diagnosed inflamed vocal cords and prescribed various treatments and rest, but his condition worsened. When faced with an operation or giving up his career, Alexander resolved to find the cause of the problem himself.

He noted that his voice was all right when he was not working, so he began to analyze what he did differently when he spoke on stage. He arranged mirrors all around the room to watch himself and noticed that as he recited he sucked in air and pulled his head down, depressing his larynx. This reaction shortened his spine and narrowed his back, affecting his breathing. He noticed that when he spoke normally, he adopted a similar stance but in a less exaggerated way. He realized that this posture represented a pattern of misuse that affected his voice, and that this, in turn, was related to a general pattern of tension in his body.

Over the years he tried many new ways of using his body to prevent his old habits affecting his voice. He finally discovered that the relationship between his head and neck and how the head and neck related to the rest of his body were crucial to correct body use. He called this "The Primary Control" because this relationship determines the poise and quality of the whole body. He believed that when the head, neck and back worked in harmony it contributed to balance in the whole person. Through using The Primary Control, Alexander prevented further problems with his voice and his general health and well-being improved dramatically. He noticed that fellow actors and friends were guilty of similar patterns of contraction and, through wider observation, concluded that such patterns of misuse were common among many people. He taught his technique to his colleagues, who benefitted from it, and then to anyone who sought his advice. As he taught it he developed and refined it into the

combination of verbal instructions and manual guidance that became the Alexander Technique.

What is the Alexander Technique?

The Alexander Technique is not a therapy as such, but a process of reeducation, which aims to teach us to rediscover our natural poise, grace and freedom, and use our bodies more efficiently. It is often referred to as posture training, which is not strictly correct, although improved postural balance is often an obvious benefit. It is taught in lessons where the practitioner is referred to as a teacher, not a therapist, and the individual taking the lessons is known as a pupil, not a patient or client.

The Alexander Technique works on the principle that mind and body form a complex and integrated whole. Today, with advances in psychosomatic medicine and the development of body-oriented therapies, this principle does not seem so radical. Most of us now accept that mental, emotional and physical health are linked. But when Alexander was writing at the turn of the century, his holistic theories were considered revolutionary. As a holistic system, the Technique is not taught in order to alleviate specific ailments, such as a stiff neck or aching back, but to address the source of such problems. However, it has been found that in the process of restoring harmony to the whole person, specific problems often disappear.

Most of us upset the balance of our bodies through poor use. We slump instead of standing upright, slouch instead of sitting poised and move in a way that puts unnecessary strain on joints.

The Alexander Technique does not emphasize correcting poor posture but aims to get people to move with the ease and grace of a child and walk with increased balance and poise. Alexander believed that a combination of evolution and environment made us lose our instinctive ability to use our bodies well. He claimed that we began to misuse ourselves when, as a species, we became more involved in occupations that restricted our natural movements. First agriculture, then industry and now technology have forced our movements to become less spontaneous and more repetitive.

BELOW: Office life today is very sedentary with many people spending most of their day hunched over a computer, which causes postural imbalances.

ABOVE: Slouching in a chair might make you feel relaxed and comfortable, but in fact you are not supporting your back, and should be sitting upright with your spine straight.

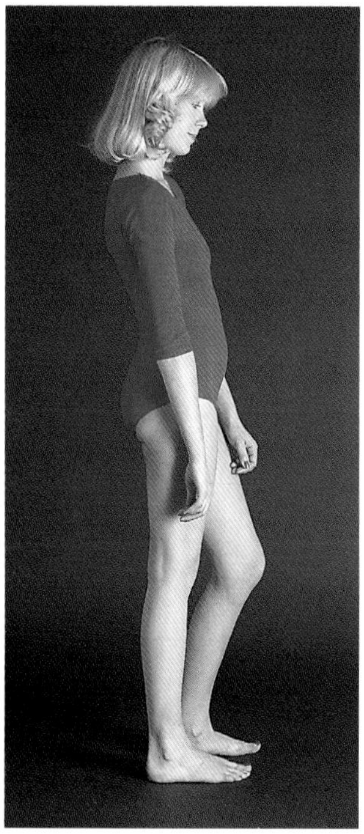

ABOVE: Standing with hunched shoulders is bad for your spine as it creates unnecessary tensions.

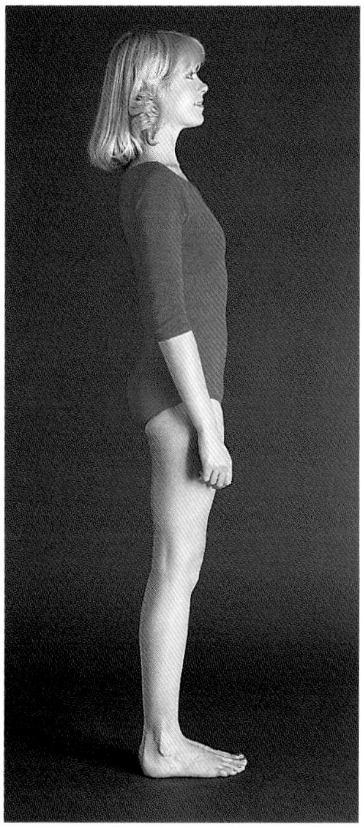

ABOVE: The correct standing posture is with your back upright, shoulders back and stomach in.

Along with restricted activity, we have become more involved in mental activities so that we devote more time to using our brain and less to using our body. Consequently, according to Alexander, our lives have changed beyond recognition over a few thousand years while evolution, which takes place over millions of years, has not equipped us to cope with this rapid change. One of the casualties of change has been our sensory apparatus. It served as an accurate guide in our ancient and more natural environment, but has become unreliable over time.

Alexander also believed that our stressful modern lifestyle takes its toll on our, mental, physical and emotional health and that we develop poor postural habits. In childhood we often suffer distress, trauma and physical and emotional abuse. This leaves its scars on our mind and body and sets up patterns of tension which affect our muscles, mobility and coordination.

Today we also lead sedentary lifestyles, first bent as children over school desks, then over office desks, computers, counters, and production lines. We force our body into postures that it was never designed to hold for long periods, and not surprisingly, it retaliates with aches and pains. Also, our lives are full of stress with demanding tasks, deadline pressures and fears of unemployment, so that at the end of a day we collapse in front of the television, holding all our tensions inside. Alexander believed that his technique could help us to undo and prevent the bad habits which so often lead to aches and pains and poor functioning. Today teachers agree that through the Alexander Technique we can recover our poise and rediscover our freedom and health.

The technique works on the principle that mind and body form a complex and integrated whole.

How does it work?

The Alexander Technique has to be experienced to be properly understood. It is difficult to understand the principles when reading them from a book and as a result most people who read about the technique have vague and confused ideas about how it works, while those who have taken lessons are amazed at how simple it all seems in practice.

It may best be understood in terms of The Primary Control. This refers to the dynamic relationship between the head, neck and back. The aim is to direct the head away from the spine without tensing and narrowing the back. It is possible to think of The Primary Control as a barometer for our general state of psychophysical health. When the head, neck and back are working well, we tend to feel good in every respect. But when the neck is unnecessarily tense, it pulls the head back and down toward the spine. This causes the spine to shorten and the back to narrow, a sign of misuse that corresponds to the "startle pattern," which we instinctively adopt when we brace ourselves for a shock. This pattern was originally a precursor to action but, for most of us, it is activated and reinforced in everyday activity because of the numerous stresses in modern life. Through education, the Alexander Technique aims to change this startle pattern so that it is only happens in appropriate situations.

This system of changing the startle pattern can be achieved through the Alexander practice of inhibition. Inhibition refers to the potential not to react immediately to stimulus. Alexander claimed that success with the Technique could only be achieved if we stopped being dominated by unconscious impulses and made reasoned choices about every movement that we made. In his opinion, the way to lasting health was to develop conscious use of ourselves in our daily activities. Through inhibition we gradually sustain good primary control of our head, neck and back and achieve a postural homeostasis (balance) that corresponds to mental balance.

It is difficult to explain exactly how this can be achieved. But it can be allied to the osteopathic concept of spinal health and postural alignment, to emotional health in psychotherapy, to the enhancement of skills of the performing artist and to improved self-management. Ultimately, the Technique can only be understood through practice.

What happens in a lesson?

Lessons take place on a one-to-one basis. The lesson will begin with a discussion between you and your teacher about why you have come and what you hope to get from the course. If you have a particular problem that needs resolving, ask her if she thinks Alexander can help and how many lessons she thinks you might need. The discussion gives the teacher the opportunity to explain to you the principles of the Alexander Technique and talk you through the stages she aims to cover in the lesson. You should wear loose comfortable, casual clothes for the lesson. You do not need to remove any clothes, although some therapists may suggest that you take off your shoes so that you can feel more "centered" by keeping contact with the floor.

Each teacher will have her own system, but every lesson will involve guidance and verbal instructions to help pinpoint and unravel patterns of misuse and restore your natural reflexes.

For example, the teacher may ask you to get up from a chair or sit down on a chair, while she guides and instructs you in this movement. You may have to carry out several movements such as walking, bending, sitting, talking and lifting. Sometimes you may be asked to bring into class something that you use habitually such as a musical instrument or lap-top computer to illustrate how you use yourself in routine activities. If you are a singer, you may be asked to show the teacher how you use your body when you perform. The teacher will guide and direct you in all of these activities so that you can feel how effortless and smooth the movements can be compared to your usual patterns of misuse.

Throughout the lesson, the teacher will talk to you about what she is doing, pointing out your bad habits and teaching you to replace them with good ones. This is when your inhibiting skills come into play; you must make a conscious decision to refuse to contract into each movement and think about new ways

Principles of the Alexander Technique

False sensory awareness *Alexander believed that we had to reeducate our sensory awareness to achieve success with the Technique. Early on in his experiments he discovered that what he felt he was doing was not what he was doing in reality. For example, when he was reciting he felt that his head was away from his spine, but when he looked in the mirror he saw that he was actually pulling his head down into his spine. This made him realize that you cannot rely on your senses to tell you what is right or wrong when you have misused your body for a long time. Alexander abandoned all attempts to change his body use with sensory awareness and relied on mirrors to reflect the true picture. Today, pupils have the benefit of teachers to guide them through the movements long enough to reeducate their sensory awareness to become again a reliable barometer.*

Integration of mind and body *Many people think of the Alexander Technique as a purely physical activity, when in fact it is based on the principle that mind and body form a complete working unit. Some teachers tend to interpret this as improved mental health being the result of improved postural balance, others subscribe to the more radical approach that the body reveals the mind. So, the Alexander Technique can be seen as the process of becoming aware of how we manage or mismanage our total selves, and not just our bodies, in any given situation.*

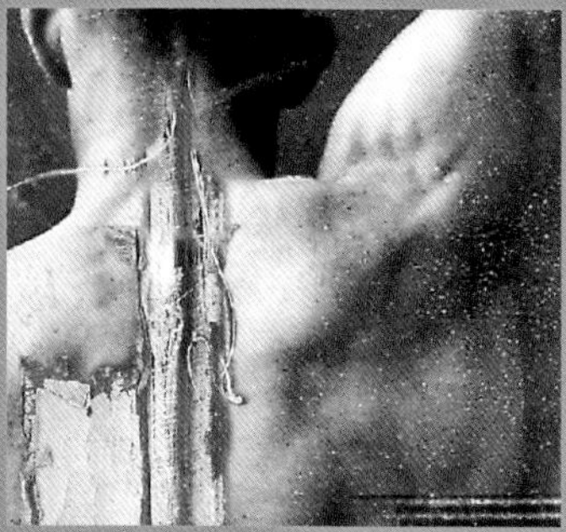

The force of habit *Everyone has patterns of misuse which show themselves in repetitive activity. Together the Alexander teacher and pupil investigate these patterns. For example, a student may come to the teacher complaining of back pain, a stiff neck or the inability to be assertive at work. The teacher will then observe how the pupil uses himself in situations: when sitting at his desk, typing or taking a telephone call. It soon becomes apparent that certain patterns of use dominate the pupil's life. The habitual slumper makes himself look small when presented with difficulty; the cringer twists and turns in the face of a challenge; and the dominant individual puffs up his chest to meet difficulties. These are all postural patterns which are strongly integrated with personality and mental attitude. Any changes to habitual patterns must be gradual, with respect for the individual.*

Inhibition and giving directions *To bring about the changes needed for good body, use the Alexander Technique uses the tools of inhibition and giving directions. Inhibition in Alexandrian terminology means withholding an automatic nervous reaction to stimuli, because change is only possible if you stop reacting impulsively and act consciously. For example, you can learn not to stiffen your neck and tense your body when confronted with a deadline, even though that may be your instinctive reaction to pressure. Inhibition is a much underused skill and one which requires training and practice to master. When we can inhibit our instinctive response, we can start to replace them with more appropriate mind body responses. The Alexander pupil uses "directions" to ask his mind and body to react in the way that he wants. For example, in order to let the head release forward and away from the spine and to allow the spine to lengthen and the back to widen, he reminds himself to, "Let the neck be free," to "Let the head go forward and up," and to "Let the back lengthen and widen."*

End gaining and the means whereby *Inhibition allows us time to consider the means to a particular end. Alexander termed our desire to do everything too quickly and want results immediately as end gaining. He believed that this hastiness to see results without any regard to how we achieved them was the greatest obstacle to success of the Alexander Technique. This end-gaining approach to life can have damaging effects on postural balance and psychological equilibrium, as it creates muscle tension and causes contractions throughout the body. We overstrain ourselves while performing simple everyday tasks. By teaching us to pay attention to how we use ourselves when achieving a goal, rather than going straight for the goal itself, the Alexander Technique aims to promote optimum mind and body health.*

of using your body so you keep your spine free of tension. The lesson may involve some table work. The teacher will ask you to lie on your back on a therapy couch with your knees bent and a small stack of books under your head so that your neck is roughly parallel with the table top. This is what is known as the semi-supine position and it is believed to be the most restful posture for the spine. The teacher will gently coax you to let go of muscle tension, release your joints and lengthen your spine.

At the end of a lesson most people say they feel taller and lighter, as if walking on air. You may also feel any number of other sensations: rejuvenated, energized, relaxed and "centered" are just some of the words used to describe the effects of a lesson. After several lessons you will start to react and move without tension and eventually without the guidance of the teacher.

Before you leave each lesson the teacher may give you some homework to practice regularly. This may be a suggestion to observe how you hold your breath when you are tense, how you brace yourself before performing a simple activity, or how you stiffen your neck when concentrating. You may also be asked to adopt the semi-supine position for ten to 15 minutes every day to reinforce the techniques you have learned in the lessons and to relax and lengthen your spine.

BELOW: When you start your Alexander lessons, you will often be asked to lie on the floor with your knees bent and your head supported in a semi-supine position. The practitioner will then encourage you to let go of tension, relax your joints, and to lengthen your spine.

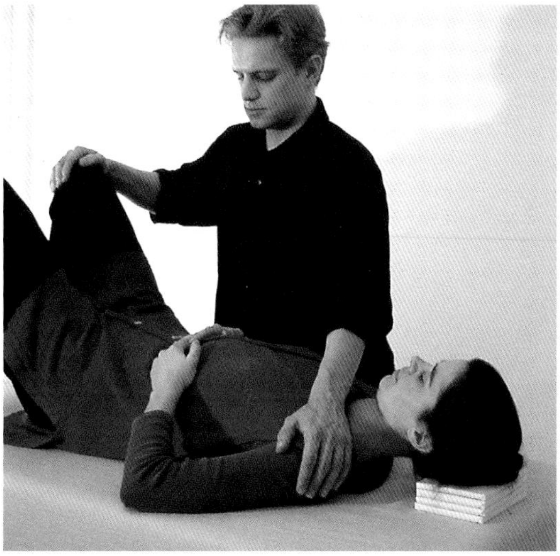

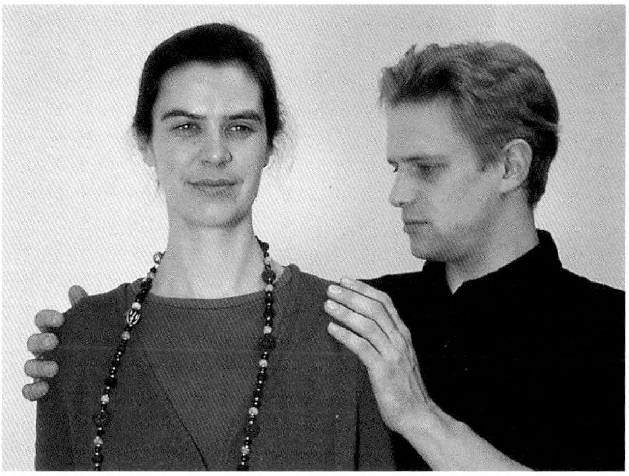

ABOVE: Your postural habits, such as how you normally stand or sit, at home and work, will be closely studied by your Alexander teacher to see what patterns of misuse you have built up in your body over the years.

How many sessions do I need?

Alexander recommended a minimum of 30 lessons, but most teachers believe there are no hard-and-fast rules, and the number of lessons needed depends on the individual. However, a course of 25 to 40 lessons is about the minimum. Lessons usually last between 30–45 minutes and it is best to begin with two or three a week.

Which problems can it help?

The Alexander Technique is not a cure for any condition or illness, although many symptoms appear to improve during practice. To date there is not much scientific evidence for the benefits of the Technique, but students and teachers report an improvement with numerous problems. Stress-related conditions, general fatigue and lethargy, anxiety, breathing disorders, back, neck and joint pain are all believed to benefit from the technique. It has been shown to help in the recovery from illness or injury, is believed to increase self-awareness and also improve both personal and professional relationships.

Actors, singers and dancers claim it enhances their performance and sportspeople believe it improves their coordination and helps them to use their energy more efficiently.

Is it safe?

When taught by a qualified teacher, the Alexander Technique is safe for everyone. Young children do not usually need the Technique as they have natural poise and balance, but they can be taught it as a preventative technique. Children with physical, handicaps such as polio and scoliosis of the spine can also benefit. The technique is safe to learn at any stage in pregnancy. Pregnant women may find that it helps them to cope with their changing shape and the pressure it puts on their spine and many women who learned it during pregnancy believe it enabled them to have an easier labor.

Clinical studies

The Alexander Technique has been shown in many clinical studies to help breathing control, stress relief and improve posture.

Dr. Wilfred Barlow studied the posture and performance of 40 Royal College of Music students and found an average of 11 postural faults in men and nine in women which were reduced to five and four respectively after the group were given Alexander lessons. A control group of 44 students from the Central School of Speech and Drama were just given posture improving exercises instead of the Alexander Technique and they in fact showed a slight deterioration in overall faults from 10.6 to 11.7 for men and 7.5 to 7.9 for women.

At the same time, tutors reported a surprising improvement in the Alexander students' singing and acting abilities as well as other good psychological effects.

As a comparison, Dr. Barlow also studied 112 female physical education teaching students and found an overall average of 8.5 postural defects even in these fit young people. **(40)**

A more objective study was made by Dr. Elizabeth Valentine, Senior Lecturer in Psychology at Royal Holloway College, University of London on performance stress reduction. Twenty-seven music students were given Alexander Technique lessons or were in a control group who were just assessed. Blind trials showed there was less variability in heart rates in high-stress situations and improved performance with the Alexander subjects compared to the control group. They also reported improved posture awareness and the ability to cope better with stressful situations. **(41)** *(For clinical references see How to use this book)*

FOR INFORMATION ON HOW TO CHOOSE AN ALEXANDER TECHNIQUE TEACHER SEE THE DIRECTORY.

FEW THERAPIES ARE as misunderstood or as misrepresented as hypnotherapy. In both Britain and the United States it has been used to improve physical and mental health at all levels for many years. Patients with terminal illness can find relief from pain and anxiety, and it is used with cancer patients to alleviate nausea caused by chemotherapy. Dentists use the technique to switch off patients' pain response during treatment, and hypnotherapists are helping people to find relief from the discomfort of irritable bowel syndrome and the

HYPNOTHERAPY

HYPNOTHERAPY is a form of psychotherapy that puts patients in a trance-like state to facilitate healing or change. It can be very effective for treating addictions, phobias, traumas and stress-related conditions.

pain of migraine. On an everyday level, many people use self-hypnosis techniques for stress management or pain relief.

The therapeutic use of hypnosis dates from primitive times when healers used trances to plant suggestions that could stimulate self-cure in the minds of the sick. However, most people's overriding impression of hypnotism is of the stage variety, designed to baffle and amuse audiences. Both uses of the technique owe much to the famous hypnotist: Anton Mesmer. Despite his flamboyance and controversial techniques, Mesmer successfully treated many people with his form of "mesmerism," before he was discredited by the French government who believed his cures were the result of patients' imagination. Mesmer's reputation and hypnosis generally, never quite recovered, despite the fact that this therapy has been used successfully for generations and is now one of the most scientifically validated of all alternative therapies.

What is hypnotherapy?

There is no single accepted definition of hypnotherapy. But it can be described as a form of psychotherapy which works on the subconscious to change thought and behavior patterns. The word "hypnosis" refers to the trance-like state, somewhere between waking and sleeping, which you enter when you are hypnotized, and "hypnotherapy" is the practice of bringing about healing or facilitating change while under hypnosis. Originally, hypnotists believed hypnosis to be a form of sleep and relied on inducing a deep trance in their patients, using authoritarian techniques, where the therapist "commands" you to make the change.

Modern therapists build up a rapport with their clients which enables them to "suggest" changes. It is now also believed that the depth of trance has no bearing on the treatment. Modern hypnotherapists use simple techniques to induce a light trance, which can have the most amazing results. While in a trance you are much more suggestible and compliant than you would be normally and your mind is more willing to accept new information, but only what you want to hear.

Consequently, the therapist can make suggestions which you will store in your mind, effectively reprogramming it to accept or reject certain beliefs or patterns of behavior. If you have a fear of spiders, for example, she can suggest that you are no longer

afraid of spiders. If you are willing to overcome your phobia, your eager mind will absorb the suggestion and replace the old fear with the new lack of fear. The same can happen with pain. Pain may be a physical sensation, but it is one which registers in the brain. If, under hypnosis, your mind accepts that you do not feel pain, then you will not feel it.

The mind is incredibly powerful and is inextricably linked to the body. This is demonstrated during a hypnotic trance when breathing, heart-rate and metabolism can be slowed, allergic reactions stopped and pain reduced. Every thought or sensation experienced in the mind shows itself as some physical change in the body and every physical change will have mental and emotional associations. So an emotional problem, such as prolonged and unexplored grief, can cause physical illness and an injured limb can leave mental scars. Hypnotherapists believe that the mind has the power to create any disease and the power to cure it by activating the healing and repair mechanism, which is controlled by the subconscious.

Hypnotherapy can be used alongside other therapies such as osteopathy or acupuncture to reinforce their benefits. Its success depends on the subject cooperating with the therapist, but most people who go for hypnotherapy are ready and willing to change.

BELOW: A hypnotherapist will often put you into a trance by speaking in a relaxing, soothing voice and getting you to focus on an object while breathing deeply.

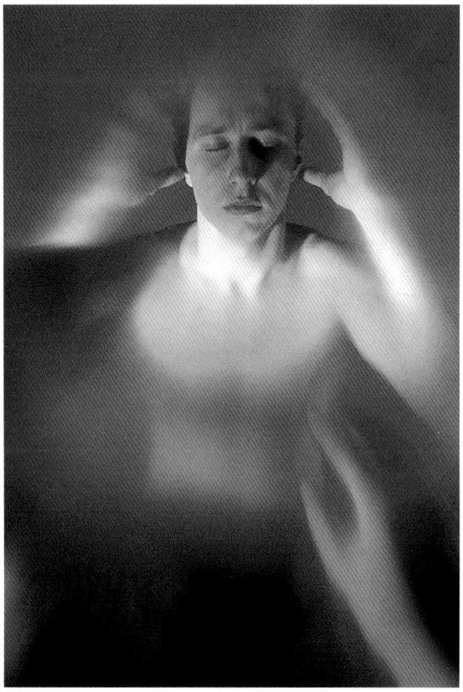

BELOW: When you are hypnotized your brain patterns will resemble those of a sleeping person.

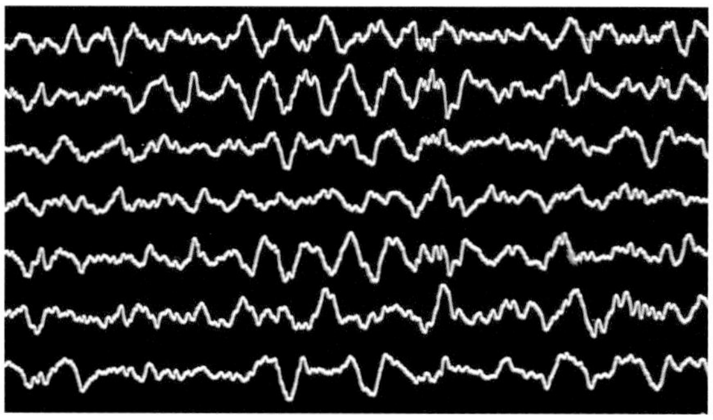

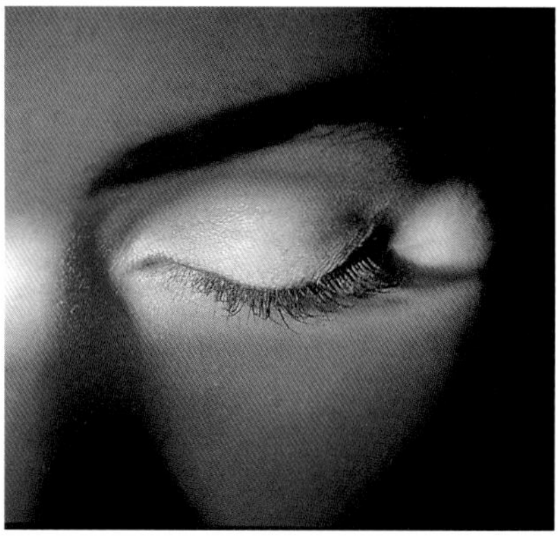

ABOVE: When you go into a trance, your eyes will close and you will appear to be asleep.

How does it work?

There is not complete agreement about how hypnosis works, but the commonly accepted theory is that the mind has two parts: the conscious and the subconscious. We are aware of the conscious mind because we use it to make everyday decisions. But the conscious mind is ruled by the desires of the much larger subconscious, as are all mental and physical functions from regulating blood pressure to storing memories. A subconscious desire is so strong that it will always triumph over a conscious desire. For example, you might make a conscious decision to stop smoking, but if your subconscious does not want to, then you will not stop.

Hypnotherapists believe the subconscious mind is the source of human energy and power and the home of the real you. If you do not learn to understand your subconscious, you will never understand yourself and, if you do not learn to use your subconscious, you will never realize your true potential. One other important point about the subconscious is that it will believe anything you tell it. Hypnotism exploits this mental submission by putting the conscious mind to sleep temporarily to reach the subconscious where you can replace negative beliefs with positive ones and introduce constructive emotions in place of those which are destructive. This reprogramming is done by suggestion which means that the therapist suggests to you targets or beliefs aimed at counteracting your problem. For example, if you want to give up smoking she may tell you that you will never want to smoke again. This plants the seed of a belief in your subconscious, which, if regularly reinforced, it will eventually accept. Every time you want a cigarette your subconscious will remind you to act according to your new belief. Hypnotherapists reach the subconscious by inducing a trance in the subject. The trance can be light, medium or deep, depending on your needs and your suitability. Deep trances are rarely induced, partly because as few as ten percent of people are believed to be susceptible to them, and partly because they are often unnecessary.

Therapists begin hypnosis by encouraging you to relax. There are several way of doing this, the most common is through the use of your imagination. Alternative methods include the heavy arms and semaphore techniques.

Imagination: The therapist talks to you in a relaxing, controlled way, which encourages you to concentrate on her voice. She asks you to focus on a point such as a real or imagined spot on the ceiling or an object in front of you. This serves to hold your visual

Hypnotherapists believe that the mind has the power to create disease and the power to cure it by activating healing.

concentration. She may ask you to take several deep breaths, suggesting that with every breath exhaled you feel more relaxed and sleepy. On the final breath you are told to close your eyes. The therapist then asks you to imagine a particular scene such as a beautiful sunlit garden and talks you through what you will see and encounter there, encouraging you to use all of your senses to make sure that you hear the birds, smell the flowers and see the beautiful colors around you.

She may count you down imaginary steps, counting them back from ten to one. At this point, she might test the depth of your trance by instructing you to perform a simple action such as raising your right arm. Throughout, the therapist encourages you to let go of the conscious world by enticing you into this imaginary one. In unaccustomed subjects it can take up to 20 minutes, sometimes more, to get to a level where you are open to suggestions. After several sessions, a trance can be induced in seconds, often by just a wave of the therapist's hand.

Heavy arms: While sitting in a chair, you will be asked to relax your arms and let them hang loose. You will be told to concentrate on your hands and notice how they become heavier and heavier until the therapist suggests that they are so heavy that you cannot lift them. If you are unable to lift them it indicates that your subconscious is open to suggestions. The therapist may then ask you to lift your arms and relax before continuing with a deepening technique.

The semaphore method: This works by the therapist asking you to close your eyes and visualize that a balloon is tied to your right wrist, pulling it upward while your left arm is being dragged down by a huge weight. The therapist will guide you back and forth between the two arms, one floating up and the other being dragged down before asking you to open your eyes and relax. If your right arm is slightly higher than your left you will be at a suggestible stage.

When you are relaxed the therapist can use any number of therapeutic techniques, such as the following:

Direct/auto suggestion therapy When you are in a trance, the therapist gives you direct suggestions, which are always specific, positive and in the present tense. Your mind accepts these suggestions because the trance state causes the critical factor of your mind to shut down. Being in a trance makes you keen to go along with the therapist's suggestions, providing they do not conflict with your own principles. This therapy is excellent for calming exam nerves and stopping nervous habits such as nail biting. It can help you to stop smoking, as you readily believe the therapist who tells you that you never want to smoke another cigarette.

The first session is usually the most difficult. Some therapists record the session and give you a tape to play at home to reinforce the treatment. Several sessions of autosuggestion may be needed, during which the therapist will change the suggestions as changes start to take place in you.

Age regression The therapist uses this technique to take you back to discover how your present problems may result from past incidents. She enables you to see childhood events from an adult perspective. This helps you to put the event in context and lets the therapist see how certain ideas fixed themselves in your mind. In most cases the event itself was meaningless, but as a child, you may have attached some significance to it. Interpretation of events is what retains such a hold on the mind and exerts control over our behavior. Many people are afraid to be regressed; a good therapist will explain that returning to review a painful situation does not mean going through it again.

Parts therapy This therapy is aimed at holism. Many of our problems are caused by factors which are not immediately obvious and those problems which appear at first glance to be unconnected can actually stem from the same source. For example, being overweight, aggressive and unfriendly can all come from the need to protect yourself against being hurt. Through regression, the therapist aims to discover the relationship between all the affected parts in order to try to bring them together and deal with the real root of the problem.

Hypnohealing is aimed at healing pathological disease. The therapist helps you uncover the cause of your illness and through visualization encourages you to release it. The therapy is based on the belief that every thought has a physical response in the body and that nothing is more positive than thought. The therapist shows you how to think, imagine and feel diseases such as asthma, angina, cancer and kidney stones being eradicated from your body. She encourages you to see your healthy cells as the most powerful force in your body, regenerating and growing in strength to defeat the diseased cells and clearing the way for new, healthy cells.

Seven steps to self-hypnosis

Read the following exercise onto a tape in a slow, relaxed voice and play it back when you want to go into hypnosis.

1 *Choose a time and a place where you will not be disturbed, take the phone of the hook and remove any distractions. Later, when more practiced, you can go into hypnosis anywhere, even in crowds, without anyone knowing, but to begin with you need to find somewhere where you can concentrate. Sit or lie down with your feet apart and your hands separated.*

2 *Roll back your eyes as if you were looking for your eyebrows and feel them straining. This will give you a rush of alpha brain waves, which bring about a more relaxed state of awareness. Fix your gaze on a real or imagined spot on the ceiling and keep your eyes glued to that spot.*

3 *Take three deep, exaggerated breaths:*
(a) Inhale and hold for ten seconds, exhale slowly and as you do say mentally, "sleep now."
(b) Inhale and hold for longer, exhale slowly and as you do say mentally, "sleep now."
(c) Inhale and hold for as long as possible, exhale slowly and as you do say mentally, "sleep now."

4 *Keeping your eyes glued to the spot on the ceiling, inhale once more and as you release the breath close your eyes.*

5 *Allow a drifting, floating feeling to happen in your body. Do not force it to happen, just imagine it. Let a wave of relaxation wash over you. Now imagine there are ten steps in front of you. Start to walk down the steps counting backward from ten to one with each step. Use all your senses to see yourself or just your feet walking down the steps. Feel the steps under your feet, hear the sound your feet make and smell the material from which the steps are made. It helps to get the sensation of looking over the banister or looking down the sweep of a staircase.*

6 *When you have descended the stairs, give yourself the appropriate suggestions using positive words, phrases or images. Forget the part of yourself that you want to change and focus on the positive, changed you. Make your suggestion personal and specific. Be as clear as possible about what you want and focus on it at length, retaining the image and repeating the suggestion over and over: "See it, smell it, touch it, hear it, enjoy it." For example, if you want to be relaxed say "I am calm, comfortable and relaxed" and picture yourself as such. Keep your suggestions in the present tense as the subconscious only responds to the present tense. Use words which have an impact, such as dynamic, magnetic, ecstatic and powerful.*

7 *After five to 15 minutes of repeating your suggestions and dwelling on positive images, count yourself out from one to three, telling yourself that on three you will open your eyes feeling relaxed, refreshed and ready to get on with your day.*

What happens in a consultation?

The initial consultation can last for 60–90 minutes, although subsequent sessions rarely last for longer than one hour. The first session is principally an assessment session. Much of the time will be spent in conversation with the therapist:

- *She will ask you why you have come to see her, explain how hypnosis works and advise you on what you can hope to get out of the treatment.*
- *She will hopefully put your mind at rest about the safety of the therapy and encourage you to voice any fears that you may have and win your trust.*

Trust is important in any therapy, but especially in hypnosis, as your cooperation is essential if it is to work. Different therapists can use different techniques, so it is best to know what will happen from the outset.

If there is time, the therapist may induce hypnosis in the first session, but often it will not begin until the second session.

The treatment itself is often much less dramatic than many people expect. You lie on a couch or sit in a comfortable chair while the therapist induces a trance-like state. This can be done in many ways depending on what the therapist prefers to use and believes to be best for you. She then uses suggestions to deepen the relaxation into a trance. When in the trance you may look like you are asleep but it will not feel like it. Most people feel relaxed, others claim to feel dreamy, or feel as if they are floating or watching themselves sleep. You will, however, be aware of what is happening throughout.

It is important to remember that while in a trance you are in complete control and the therapist cannot make you do or say something that you do not want to or that goes against your principles. If there is any part of the treatment with which you feel uncomfortable, you can always get up and leave.

While you are in the trance, the therapist will address the problem with which you consulted her, possibly in one of the ways mentioned above.

At the end of the session, she will encourage you to work your way back to consciousness. She will gently talk you through the process by telling you what she is about to do and how you will feel afterward. For example, she may say, "You will awake on the count of three, and when you do, you will be feeling relaxed and refreshed."

Over the course of the treatment, the therapist will probably encourage you to learn self-hypnosis, which you can use at home to back up the work you have done with the therapist and to equip you to overcome any future problems.

How many sessions do I need?

It is difficult to say. It depends on the person, the problem, and the treatment method. For a straightforward problem such as stopping smoking or losing weight, you may need about four or five weekly sessions, sometimes less. For chronic health problems or deep mental or emotional problems, it is more likely to take about 12–15 weekly sessions. Some people can be taught self-hypnosis in one or two sessions.

BELOW: If you are determined to give up smoking, hypnotherapy sessions can give you the willpower.

BELOW: If you find you are working under a lot of stress, you might find a course of hypnotherapy will help.

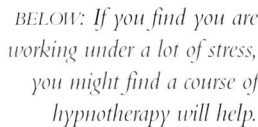

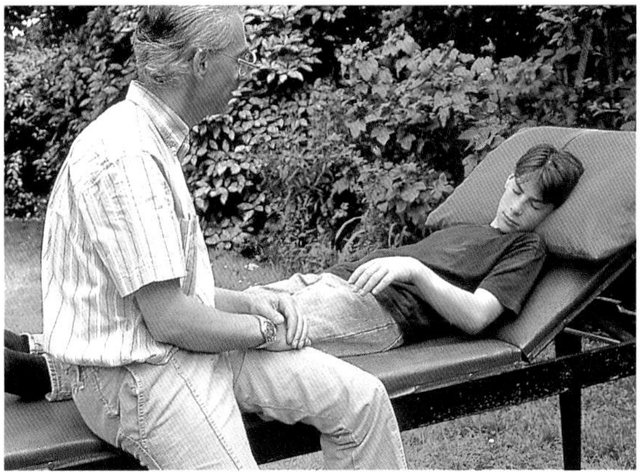

ABOVE: During a hypnotherapy session, the therapist will get you to lie on a couch and then relax you prior to inducing a trance-like state.

Which problems can it help?

Hypnosis can help with many physical, psychosomatic and mental problems. It has been successful with habit problems and addictions such as smoking and overeating; problems which originate from past traumas; phobias, and stress-related problems such as irritable bowel syndrome, eczema, anxiety and insomnia.

Is it safe?

There is understandably concern about the safety of hypnotherapy. Horror stories abound about people not being counted out properly or of women being taken advantage of. You are safe in the hands of a qualified practitioner, so check their qualifications and telephone the association of which they claim membership for verification. It also pays to see someone that you like. Hypnotherapists maintain that there is no such thing as not coming out properly – you are either under hypnosis or you are not. Children under the age of four cannot be hypnotized as they are too young to cooperate with the therapist.

Clinical studies

In several studies, hypnotherapy was found to be helpful in treating different types of ailments and addictions.

In one medical study in 1978, two Americans studied the effect of hypnotherapy to control burns. Two groups of patients were studied. The first group had 24 patients with 0–30 percent of surface burns, the second group of 18 had 31–60 percent. The control group, who were just looked after, were matched with the other group who were hypnotized. The results showed that there was a noticeable decrease in pain treatment of those patients who were receiving hypnotherapy. (**42**)

Research that was held in an ENT department at the Royal Berkshire Hospital, Reading, in 1985 investigated the effects of hypnosis in a trial on 14 patients suffering from tinnitus. All patients had previously been resistant to all other forms of therapy and were hypnotized in random order, and either tinnitus suppression or ego-boosting suggestions were given to the patients in the trance state. Five patients reported benefits from the technique in making their tinnitus easier to bear, but only one of the patients had a significant reduction in the loudness and quality of the problem. (**43**)

A study was held in Australia at the University of Tasmania in 1978 where one session of hypnosis was used to modify 75 patients' smoking habits. The session included favorable hypnotic suggestions including ego-boosting, stopping smoking and other positive visualizations. Results showed that 45 patients had stopped smoking straight after the hypnosis and of these, 34 were still nonsmokers six months later. (**44**)

In another trial in 1985, dental patients were studied to see the effectiveness of combined hypnotic suggestion and relaxation to control headaches which stemmed from neck tension as they had not responded to conventional treatment. Of the 23 patients, 12 reported complete relief and ten had mild improvement. Only one patient did not have any relief. These effects were sustained over a three-month and ten-month follow-up period. (**45**)

A trial in 1992 in the United States showed that direct suggestion in hypnotherapy was successful in removing warts (*Verruca vulgaris*) in 80 percent of patients. All prepuberty children responded well to the hypnosis treatment. Some adults were resistant, but they did respond to hypnotherapy and psychotherapy. Out of 41 patients, 33 were completely cured, six did not respond to treatment and two patients were lost in follow-up. (**46**) *(For clinical references see How to use this book)*

FOR INFORMATION ON HOW TO CHOOSE A HYPNOTHERAPIST SEE THE DIRECTORY.

YOGA

YOGA IS OFTEN portrayed as a mystical Eastern relaxation system that involves intricate postures that only the most supple and double-jointed people would dare to attempt. But, the movements can be so simple that even the very stiff, elderly, ill and disabled can benefit from yoga. Certainly, the discipline appears to be Eastern in origin. Ancient Indian statues illustrate that it practiced in northern India at least 4,000 years ago, but the details of its origins are indistinct. We do know, however, that it was originally practiced by Indian philosophers or yogis who lived hermetic lives of meditation. But, today the benefits of yoga have spread internationally and it is now practiced in nonreligious, noncultural-based classes all over the Western world.

What is yoga?

Yoga is a gentle exercise system that benefits both body and spirit. The word yoga comes from the Sanskrit word for union. Practicing the discipline is believed to encourage union of mind, body and spirit and restore the whole person to balance. Yoga benefits the body by relaxing muscles and improving suppleness, fitness and physical function. It also relaxes the mind, and teaches us how to control stress, destructive emotions and unhealthy habits. A relaxed mind encourages the concentration and serenity that and allows spiritual development.

There are many different forms of yoga, but most Western forms are based on hatha yoga. The principles of hatha yoga were laid down by the eighth century Indian sage, Patanjali. Patanjali's yoga code advocates developing healthy attitudes and values such as honesty, nonacquisitiveness and moderation in preparation for the more serious business of spiritual enlightenment. The three aspects of the code on which yoga concentrates most are: *Pranayama* (breathing), *Asanas* (postures), and *Dhyana* (meditation). Through rigorous practice of these principles, the practitioner aims to achieve the ultimate goal of self-enlightenment.

How does it work?

Harmony between body, mind and spirit is achieved through correct breathing, postural exercises and meditation. To yoga practitioners, breathing correctly is a way of controlling all mental and bodily functions and is essential for relaxation and meditation. Most of us tend to breathe incorrectly: anxiety and tension cause us to take short breaths that are centered in the upper chest, while lack of energy can cause weak breathing lower down in the diaphragm. Yoga breathing, on the other hand, encourages us to make full use of our lungs, so we strengthen them, increase our energy and vitality, and improve our circulation. The yoga postures exercise the body muscles and encourage relaxation and meditation. They are easier to demonstrate than describe and

YOGA is an ancient exercise system that uses stretching movements and meditation techniques to relax both body, mind and spirit. With regular practice it can help relieve such conditions as anxiety, backache, arthritis and depression.

ABOVE: *Meditation in yoga is normally done in the famous Lotus position.*

must be practiced regularly to be appreciated. The famous Lotus position represents self-awareness and is the pose most often adopted by experienced meditators. Other postures with names such as Cheetah, Cobra, Ostrich, Butterfly and Praying mantis are based on the naturally relaxed and graceful movements of animals. These movements stretch the muscles to release pent-up

Yoga breathing encourages us to make full use of our lungs, increasing energy, vitality and improving circulation.

tension and encourage strength and flexibility in the limbs and spine. *Asanas* are performed in a particular sequence, designed to exercise all the major muscle groups in the correct order, to encourage good circulation and to flush toxins out of the body. Meditation is a form of deep relaxation used to calm or focus the mind. It is an important, but not essential part of yoga, particularly with beginners. Yoga practitioners often see meditation as a natural progression from becoming competent at performing the postures and breathing exercises.

What happens in a class?

Yoga is taught in classes of about 15–20 people lasting from one to two hours. You do not have to complete a questionnaire or be interviewed before the class, but you ought to tell the teacher if you suffer from any physical disabilities or illness so that she can advise you on which movements to avoid or adapt. Some specially trained practitioners give one-to-one session or teach small groups of people with specific medical problems. To carry out the postures with ease and comfort, you should go barefoot and wear clothes which allow movement – a leotard or track suit is best. You will also need a rubber mat on which to work. The teacher often provides these, but many people buy their own. Classes vary in structure, but in a 90-minute class you would usually begin by focusing on breath control for about ten minutes, followed by 15–20 minutes of gentle warm-up exercises. It takes time to master the postures, so be realistic about what you can achieve and do not push yourself too hard. Perform them slowly and smoothly and hold each one only for as long as is comfortable, concentrating on your breathing throughout. Postures are usually performed for about 25 minutes, followed by 20 minutes of relaxation exercises. The class may end with five to ten minutes of reflection and the advice to practice at home in a warm, quiet, well-ventilated room. Early morning sessions are recommended, but you can practice yoga at any time of the day, providing you do so at least two hours after eating.

How many sessions do I need?

Like any other exercise or relaxation system, yoga needs to be practiced regularly to have lasting effect. It should be part of your everyday lifestyle. However, even after one session most people feel more relaxed and many will start to sleep better immediately.

Which problems can it help?

Any type of stress-related problems such as anxiety, high blood pressure, circulation and heart problems, backache, asthma, digestive problems such as irritable bowel syndrome (IBS), fatigue, arthritis, rheumatism and depression.

Is it safe?

Yoga is safe for everyone. It is suitable for people of all ages and levels of fitness. Children, pregnant women, the elderly and people with chronic health problems can all practice yoga under the guidance of a qualified instructor. You may also want to discuss your intentions with your doctor. In the case of illness it is important to remember that yoga is complementary rather than an alternative to conventional treatment.

Clinical studies

In several medical studies the use of yoga techniques has given relief to people with various ailments.

In 1994 a random selection of patients with osteoarthritis in the hands were given yoga practice once a week for eight weeks. Other patients in a control group were given a similar exercise regime but no therapy. Those who practiced yoga had a significant improvement in finger mobility and also had reduced pain. (**47**)

In 1985, 53 patients with bronchial asthma were matched with a control group of similar age, sex and severity of illness. The control group just took drugs, while the yoga group had two weeks exercise training, meditation and devotional sessions. They were asked to do yoga for 65 minutes daily. The yoga group had fewer asthma attacks and needed less drugs than the control group. (**48**) *(For clinical references see How to use this book)*

FOR INFORMATION ON HOW TO CHOOSE A YOGA CLASS SEE THE DIRECTORY.

TAI CHI

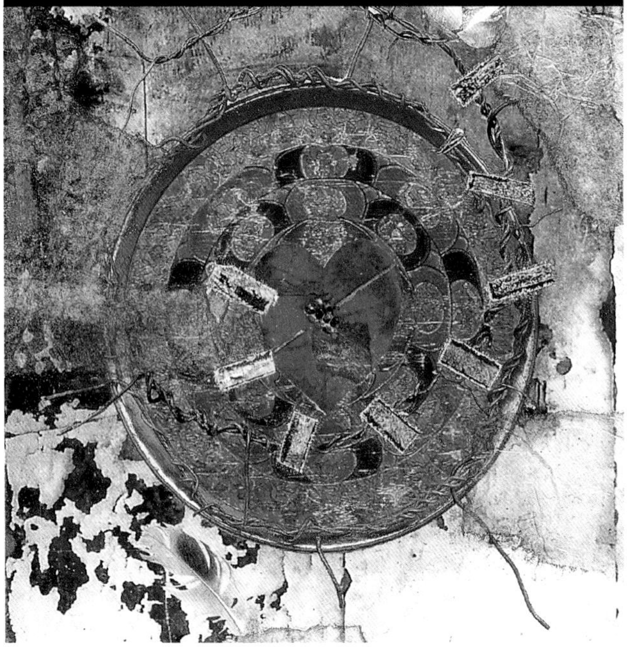

LIKE MANY ANCIENT SKILLS, there are numerous theories about the origins of tai chi. One of the most popular is that it was founded by Taoist monk and martial arts expert, Chang San Feng, who lived in the Sung dynasty (AD 960–1279). Legend has it that Chang San Feng watched a battle between a crane and a snake, in which the snake outwitted the much bigger, stronger bird by dodging and weaving each attack and retaliating with lightening speed. The monk is believed to have been so impressed by the flexibility and natural grace of the snake's movements that he decided to integrate them into his own special system of martial arts.

The new postures were combined with ancient Taoist breathing exercises, which were used to stimulate chi, and this formed the basis of tai chi. From this beginning, the present exercises are believed to have been developed.

Research has shown that regular practice of tai chi relaxes and de-stresses the muscles and the nervous system. Through the nervous system, the benefits filter through to the glandular system, improving metabolism and enhancing the immune system. The body also benefits from improved posture and joint flexibility, and circulation and breathing also get a boost.

If you combine these benefits with the mental and spiritual aspects of a system steeped in meditation, it is easy to see why so many people today are including tai chi in their program of preventative healthcare.

What is tai chi?

Tai chi is more accurately known as tai chi chuan, which means "the supreme way of the fist." It is a noncombative martial art system that includes meditation and exercises to promote and enhance total health. Tai chi is part of the complex system of Oriental medicine which also includes acupuncture, acupressure, herbal medicine and massage. Together with these other areas, tai chi is used to promote longevity and aid spiritual awareness.

The system itself has in time developed and divided into many different styles such as the Yang style, Chen style, Lee style and Wu style. The Yang style, for example, is slow, strong, rhythmic and flowing, while the Chen style is varied, and constantly changes pace from slow to fast. These various styles illustrate that there is no one correct way to perform tai chi. Ultimately, it is a very personal endeavor. And, although an instructor can show you a style and the different movements, it is basically up to you to make tai chi your own.

How does it work?

The basis of every style of tai chi is the practice of "the form." A form is a set of slow-moving, graceful exercises performed in a definite pattern. There are short forms and long forms, which

TAI CHI is a gentle martial art that involves a combination of meditation and flowing exercises to help improve the health of the body and mind. With regular practice it can relieve stress and improve the metabolism and the immune system.

ABOVE: In China the gentle and relaxing movements of tai chi are regularly practiced outside by all age groups

vary from one style to another. Traditionally, a long form involves 108 movements and can take anything from 20 minutes up to one hour to perform. A short form can involve 48 or sometimes only 37 movements, and rarely takes more than five to ten minutes to perform.

The movements of the form are essentially self-defense movements, they have names such as, "Kick with right heel" and "Punch with concealed fist." They are practiced in a slow, flowing sequence in order to encourage general relaxation and harmony between the mind, body and spirit. The movements achieve this harmony because they are designed to rebalance the flow of chi or energy that flows through channels in the body called meridians (see Acupuncture, pages 10–19) and by regulating the circulation of body fluids, such as blood and lymph.

The movements are practiced in a slow, flowing sequence to encourage harmony between the mind, body and spirit.

Ideally, tai chi should be practiced outdoors. In China it is traditional to practice the form near trees so that the performers can absorb the energy given off by the trees.

Wherever you practice tai chi, it is important to relax and focus your mind and concentrate on how you breathe, so that you can coordinate breathing with all the movements of your body. This special attention to breathing has earned tai chi the special title of "meditation in motion."

What happens in a class?

Tai chi can be learned on a one-to one basis from a tai chi master, but is usually taught in a class of 15–30 people. When deciding on a class, it is important to feel happy with the instructor's qualifications and experience. The class usually lasts for about 90 minutes and although no special clothes are necessary, it is customary to wear loose comfortable clothes and socks or soft flat-soled shoes. Tai chi classes in the West usually take place indoors in a well-ventilated, quiet space. There is no consultation, nor does the instructor take a case history, but you should tell him if you have any health problems that might affect your ability to do the movements or render some of them unsuitable. The instructor may explain the purpose of tai chi and advise you to take the exercises at your own pace.

The class will usually begin with 10–30 minutes of basic warm-up exercises before you move on to learning the components of a form. Learning a form is not as easy as it sounds. It can take up to year to learn a short form and possibly two years to learn the long form, as continual practice is needed in order to perfect each movement.

The tai chi exercises are meant to encourage you to feel more balanced and relaxed. So early lessons may focus on encouraging you simply to feel rooted or "centered." You are taught to stand and move in ways that allow your "awareness" to move down into your abdomen and legs, making you strong and balanced and relieving tension. A tai chi class should not make you feel sore or tired as you are advised from the outset not to overstretch yourself. At the end of the class you will be advised to practice the movements you have learned at home.

How many sessions do I need?

You need to practice tai chi regularly to gain any noticeable benefits. A weekly class is believed to be the minimum to consider, especially for beginners.

Which problems can it help?

Tai chi can help stress-related problems. Anxiety, tension, blood pressure and circulation are all problems which have been alleviated by the exercises. Tai chi has been shown to benefit people suffering from arthritis, to aid recovery from injury, and even to assist in the rehabilitation of heart attack patients. Those people who practice the art long-term have been shown to be more flexible and less susceptible to spinal problems and some bone conditions such as osteoporosis. It is also used by the Chinese for the treatment of chronic disease.

Is it safe?

As with any therapy when taught by an experienced and knowledgeable instructor and practiced correctly, tai chi is a gentle art and a perfectly safe system of exercise for people of any age and all levels of fitness.

FOR INFORMATION ON HOW TO CHOOSE A TAI CHI CLASS SEE THE DIRECTORY.

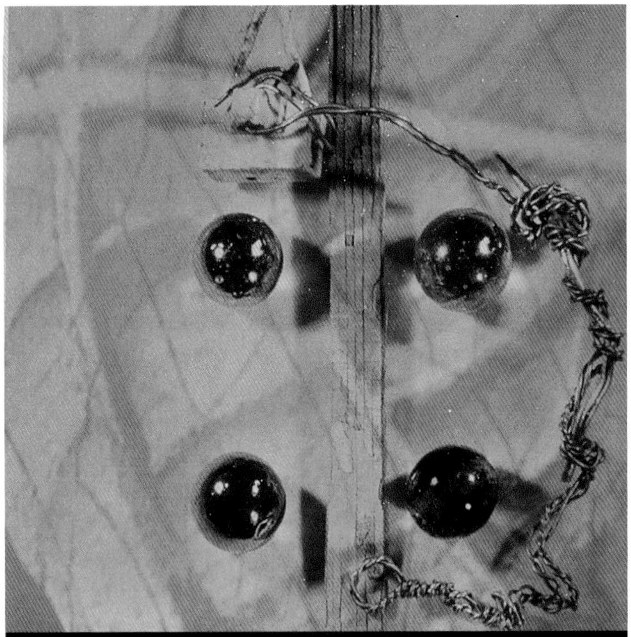

AUTOGENIC TRAINING

FOR THOUSANDS OF YEARS Indian yogis have known that the mind can be trained to influence our body systems. Breathing, blood circulation and the autonomic nervous system, which controls muscle and gland responses to stress, can all be regulated by a well-trained mind. Mental training, however, was neglected in Western medicine until Autogenic Training took the principles of Eastern meditation and made them more acceptable for Westerners.

Autogenic Training was originated in Berlin in the 1920s by a German psychiatrist and neurologist, Dr. Johannes H. Schultz. He had been a student of neuropathologist Oskar Vogt, who was involved in research into sleep and hypnosis. From Vogt he learned that people who had been hypnotized quickly learned how to hypnotize themselves and while in a hypnotic state were deeply relaxed and free from the psychosomatic disorders that plagued them in everyday life. Schultz pinpointed two effects of this type of self-hypnosis: a heavy sensation in the body brought about by deeply relaxed muscles, and a feeling of warmth associated with the increased dilation of the blood vessels. He believed that we could all be taught to bring about these sensations by suggesting to ourselves that they were happening in our bodies. By doing so we could go into a state of "passive concentration" and effectively switch off the body's alarm system long enough to rest our body and mind after a stressful day.

The technique was introduced into Britain in the 1970s by Dr. Malcolm Carruthers. It has since become one of the most consistently researched stress-relief methods available.

What is autogenic training?

Autogenic training (AT) is a form of deep relaxation, using mental exercises to relieve the effects of stress and illness on the mind and body. It has been compared to self-hypnosis, but is closer to meditation. The term "autogenic" means "produced by the self" or "generated from within." And this is the key to how AT differs from hypnosis. In hypnosis you or the therapist plant suggestions into your subconscious. In AT you focus your attention on certain words or phrases that trigger your relaxation response.

Mastering the technique consists of learning a series of easy mental exercises that switch off the body's stress response. Research has shown that over 80 physiological changes take place in the body during a single autogenic exercise.

How does it work?

Autogenic training works by achieving a shift in consciousness that enables you to control your autonomic nervous system, switching it from the sympathetic (which reacts to stress) to the parasympathetic (which instills rest and relaxation) at will. Research shows that it helps to rebalance the left and right hemi-

AUTOGENIC TRAINING involves teaching people a series of special mental exercises to help them relax mentally and physically from day-to-day stress. This calming process can help relieve conditions such as asthma, high blood pressure and colitis.

LEFT: *In an autogenic session you will be asked to sit or lie comfortably as you are talked through the relaxing mental exercises.*

spheres of the brain, to enable a person to move toward a balanced state in which the conditions are right for self-healing.

Learning the techniques involves mastering two groups of exercises which are introduced progressively. The first group consists of six standard autogenic exercises which use key phrases such as, "My arms are warm and heavy" to focus your attention on the physiological changes occurring when you start to relax. These changes are: heaviness and warmth in limbs; a calm and regular heartbeat; regular breathing; warmth in the abdomen and a feeling of coolness on the forehead. The second group are called "intentional exercises." These are taught with the autogenic exercises and should be practiced at home. They focus on releasing emotional and physical tension in direct ways such as crying, shouting and punching pillows. Over the weeks you build up several techniques to equip you to deal with stress.

With AT, attention is focused on certain words or phrases to trigger a relaxation response.

What happens in a consultation?

Training is taught individually or in small groups. You will need to complete a form about your health and medical history and attend a preliminary session for an assessment. Then begins the first in a series of about eight weekly sessions during which you will be taught the simple exercises. There is no need to wear special clothes, remove them or get into unusual positions. The exercises are mental ones. You just sit or lie comfortably and relax. All sessions last an hour. You must also practice the exercises for no more than 15 minutes, three times a day, every day. Early on in the training it is not uncommon to experience "autogenic discharges." These are temporary symptoms which may mimic past illnesses or emotional problems, and their coming out is part of the healing process. About six weeks after your last session you will have a follow-up session to assess your progress.

How many sessions do I need?

A course is eight to ten weeks, except in exceptional circumstances such as in the case of chronic depression. You must practice the techniques regularly to reap the benefits.

Which problems can it help?

As a holistic therapy, autogenic training focuses on the physical, mental and emotional health of the whole person rather than on individual ailments. However, numerous conditions seem to respond well. These include: irritable bowel syndrome, asthma, tension headaches, high blood pressure, anxiety, insomnia, PMT, bladder problems, epilepsy, arthritis, colitis and infertility.

Is it safe?

People of all ages can safely practice autogenic training provided they are taught by a qualified teacher. Pregnant women in particular can benefit from the calmness induced by the exercises. Sometimes, it is necessary to inform your doctor of any plans to have training, especially if you have a medical condition such as diabetes, as the exercises can affect blood sugar levels and your medication may need to be adjusted. If you experience persistent "autogenic reactions" during the course, see your doctor.

Certain people are not suitable for autogenic training. These include those with personality disorders or acute psychoses.

Clinical studies

Autogenic training has been used in several clinical experiments and has helped relieve many stress-related ailments.

In 1988, a five-year study was conducted of 90 patients with hypertension (high blood pressure). It involved 44 patients who were given autogenic training and 46 control patients who were not. The results showed a significant difference between the two groups. The ones who had autogenic training experienced reduced blood pressure. Psychological benefits were also reported for the treated group, who also had less sick leave. The results were comparable to patients given regular medication, and the mild hypertensive patients seemed to respond more effectively to the autogenic training than those with moderate hypertension. (**49**)

In a study in 1994, German researchers recruited 27 anxiety and panic disorder patients and gave them short-term outpatient treatment with autogenic training or hypnosis. The patients were psychologically examined before and after each six weekly group sessions and again after three months. Both groups showed a significant decrease in psychosomatic complaints and feeling anxious after treatment and these effects were still present after three months. (**50**) (*For clinical references see How to use this book*)

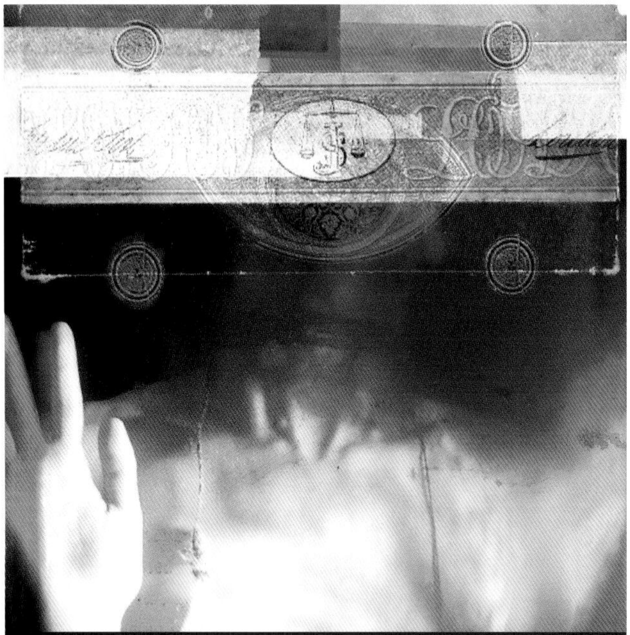

SPIRITUAL HEALING

MANY PEOPLE ARE benefiting today from spiritual healing, which is now an established therapy in its own right. Many doctors are now training to develop their own healing powers.

What is spiritual healing?

The channeling of healing energy from its spiritual source to someone who needs it is called spiritual healing. The channel is usually a person, whom we call a healer, and the healing energy is usually transferred to the patient through the healer's hands. The healing does not come from the healer, but through him.

The word "spiritual" refers to the divine nature of the energy, which healers agree comes from one external, invisible intelligent source. The healing energy from this source is available to all.

Healers see the body mind and spirit as one interdependent unit and believe all three must work in harmony to maintain positive health. Any problem – be it a broken leg or depression – needs the power of healing to restore the balance of the whole person. It is felt that sickness often starts in the mind, or at the deeper level of the spirit, and it is often here that healing begins.

How does it work?

The theory is that everyone has a healing mechanism that flows as an energy force around the body, mind and spirit to keep them in perfect order. Unfortunately, stress, an inadequate diet, a negative attitude and other adverse factors can block our healing mechanism so that it cannot function correctly and we get ill. Spiritual healing provides the energy needed to crank our own healing mechanism back into action. When a healer lays his hand on you, he acts as a conductor or channel for the healing energy which he believes has the "intelligence" to go where it is needed.

Healers say that all of us have the power to heal, if we choose to develop it. However, some do seem to have a healing gift.

Healing does not always work at a physical level; the illness may remain but the ability to cope with it improves. Sometimes it does not work at all. This may be because the sick person "blocks" the healing forces – some people subconsciously prefer to be ill. It may also be because we "need" to remain ill.
Healing is not just about living well, but also dying well. People healed when they are dying may die more peacefully.

What happens in a consultation?

Healing sessions can take place in groups or individually. They are generally held in informal, warm and comfortable rooms. Often there will be soft music playing in the background in order

SPIRITUAL HEALING is when energy is transmitted through a healer's hands to the person who needs it. The treatment works on the body, mind and spirit, which are seen as one unit that must harmonize for good health. This healing can help mental and emotional problems and physical conditions such as a frozen shoulder.

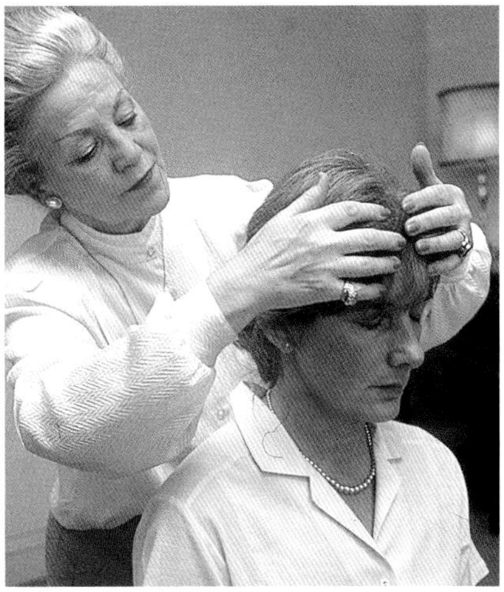

RIGHT: In a treatment a spiritual healer may ask you to sit down and will then place her hands for a few minutes on the area that needs treatment.

to create a relaxed atmosphere. You do not have to undress, you just take off your shoes and coat. You will then be invited to sit on a chair while the healer sits opposite and asks you some details about yourself:

- *The problems you are experiencing, and previous treatments.*
- *He will want to know about any emotional or spiritual problems.*
- *He will also want to be told about any physical complaints.*

This discussion usually takes about 20 minutes and the healer may take confidential notes. He will then stand up to begin the healing. He may ask you to remain seated or to lie down on a treatment couch. He will put his hands on or over the part of your body that needs healing and hold them there for a few minutes. If the healing is to be concentrated on the breasts or genitals, his hands will not touch you.

To begin the treatment the healer will attune with the healing energy. Then he may scan your body, with his hands hovering just above you. This scanning is to take a reading of your body's energy levels and to locate areas of low or blocked energy where healing is needed. How long the healer spends on each area is determined by your body's needs. Generally, the session lasts about an hour. All healers work in this way, but some employ additional healing tools such as visualization, past lives therapy, aura healing or they may concentrate on using the "chakras" – the seven main energy centers of the body.

If they decide to use these methods, they will discuss them further with you. During the treatment you may feel heat coming from the healer's hands, although some people feel a draught, a tingling sensation, pins and needles, or a feeling of light-headedness.

Afterwards, most people say they feel relaxed and peaceful, although you might feel thirsty or sleepy. You will be advised by the healer to leave a few days or a week between sessions to give the healing time to work.

How many sessions do I need?

According to most spiritual healers, you should feel an improvement in your condition after six healing sessions.

Which problems can it help?

Healing can help with any problem, mental, physical or emotional, although it seems to be especially effective for musculo-skeletal problems, such as frozen shoulders, stiff necks and bad knees.

Is it safe?

Healing cannot harm anyone. A respectable healer will not promise to cure you or ask you to give up any conventional treatment that you are receiving. Healers are not allowed to attend women in childbirth or for ten days afterward and are not to give healing to children under 18 years old, unless the child's parents or guardian has sought medical help and have given their permission for healing.

Clinical studies

Several medical studies were undertaken showing how spiritual healing has helped minor ailments and disease.

In 1990 a study was done on 46 healthy volunteers who had incisions made on their arms. Twenty-three of them unknowingly had noncontact spiritual and therapeutic touch and standard wound dressing. Others in a control group were placed daily in an isolated room but were not sent healing treatment to their arm. Both the physician who performed the incisions and the technician who measured the wounds were unaware of the true nature of the study. By day eight the size of the wounds of the treated group was ten times smaller than for those in the control

When a healer lays his hand on you, he acts as a conductor for the healing energy to go to your pain.

group. After 16 days the wounds had healed in 13 of those who received healing while none in the control group had healed. (**51**)

Another study was carried out in 1986 on 60 patients suffering from tension headaches. Half were given spiritual, therapeutic touch, the rest had a placebo treatment. Results indicated that patients given the therapeutic treatment had greater, longer pain relief from the headaches than the control group. (**52**)

In 1988, a study was undertaken in connection with healing treatment and heart disease. Heart care patients were divided into two groups, 192 were given absent spiritual healing, while 201 in a control group had no healing. No significant differences were found between the groups with such conditions as heart enlargement, pulmonary edema, hypertension or congestive heart failure. However, compared to the control group, patients sent healing treatment had less cardiopulmonary arrests, intubation/ventilation, or congestive heart failure, and they also needed less drug treatments. (**53**) *(For clinical references see How to use this book)*

COLOR THERAPY

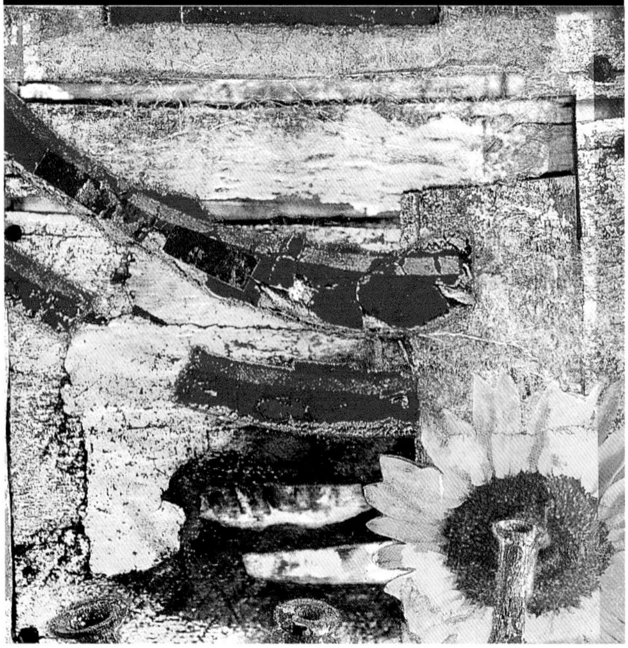

COLOR HAS SUCH A subtle effect on our lives that we rarely give it a second thought, so it is often a surprise to learn that color can heal. Color comes from daylight, which contains all eight colors of the spectrum: red, orange, yellow, green, turquoise, blue, violet and magenta. It is also a form of radiation and while we accept that other forms such as X-rays and ultraviolet light have their part to play in healthcare, we are often reluctant to accept that color can also maintain and restore health.

But, research has begun to validate the importance of color in treating disease. For example, looking at blue light has been shown to lower blood pressure by calming the autonomic nervous system, while red light causes it to rise.

What is color therapy?

Color therapy uses color to treat mental, emotional and physical problems and restore the whole person to health and harmony. Color can be used in many different ways. Some therapists combine it with reflexology, aromatherapy and acupuncture.

How does it work?

Each color vibrates at its own frequency. Everything in the world, including human body cells also vibrate at their own frequency. When we are healthy and balanced, the frequency of our cells remains constant, but ill health disturbs this frequency, causing disharmony throughout the person. Choosing a color which vibrates at a frequency needed to restore the cells to balance is believed to initiate healing.

Therapists must not only choose the correct color, but administer it in the right amount and ensure that you receive the right balance. This is because each color has both negative and positive attributes. For example, magenta is the color of "letting go." It can liberate you from destructive emotions, but too much can be mentally disturbing. Each color also has a complementary color. Many therapists like to use a color with its complementary color to get the right balance.

One way of working with color is for the therapist to show you eight colored cards and ask you to choose the three that are most appealing. This is based on the Lüscher color test. The three colors chosen can reveal your emotional, mental and physical state and may point to weak areas that need to be balanced by a complementary color. Many therapists also work with your "aura" and "chakras."

Your aura is your energy field, which some gifted individuals claim to see as a haze of colored light surrounding your body. The colors in the aura have their own significance and are affected by your health and energy quality. The chakras are the seven main energy centers of the body. They are situated in the sacral region,

Color therapy uses different colors to help treat mental, emotional and physical illness and restore the body to full health and harmony. It is sometimes used with other therapies and can help to relieve insomnia, depression and stress-related problems.

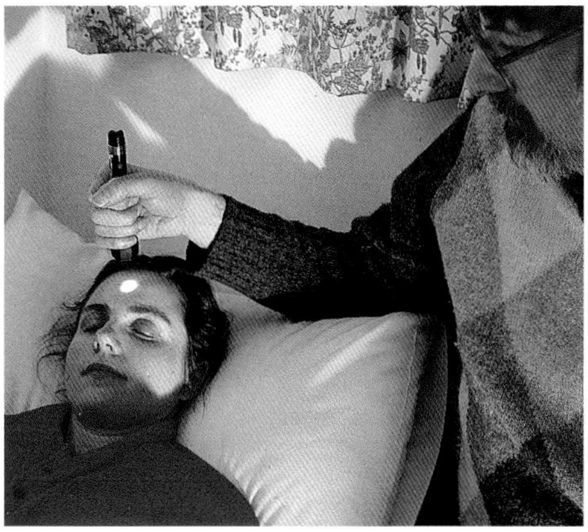

RIGHT: Color therapists sometimes use a color crystal torch to transmit the chosen color onto the patient's body.

abdomen, solar plexus, heart, throat, brow and crown of the head and roughly correspond to the plexuses of the autonomic nervous system. Each one has its own color and its own physical, mental and spiritual keynotes.

What happens in a consultation?

A first session usually lasts up to two hours and subsequent ones last an hour. You will complete a questionnaire about:

- *Your medical history and your present health problems*
- *Details of your emotional or personality profile*
- *You will also need to give details of best times of the day and your favorite colors*

The therapist may make a color diagnostic chart based on the 32 vertebrae of the spine. These are divided into four sections each relating to the eight colors in the spectrum. The first eight relate to mental health, the second to emotional health, the third to metabolism and the fourth to physical health.

Therapists who use this system ask you to sign the back of the chart along the spine. Your signature contains your vibration and acts as a witness (your energy representative) which the therapist "dowses" to find which vertebrae need treatment. Dowsing is a diagnostic system using a pendulum, which the practitioner holds over the witness to assess vibrations in the vertebrae.

Choosing a color which vibrates at a frequency needed to restore cells to balance is believed to initiate healing.

Therapists who work with the aura and chakras may see or sense which colors are lacking. The therapist may also touch your body to visualize which colors those areas need.

Many therapists treat people with colored light. For this treatment you will be given a white robe to wear and be asked to sit or lie under a light machine. Light is shone through stained glass filters and focused on the body parts that require treating. The therapist will set the machine so that it delivers the colors and complementary colors in the correct amounts. These are beamed onto your body for precisely 19¾ minutes. Some practitioners use a color crystal torch, an instrument which transmits colored light through a quartz crystal tip. Alternatively, therapists drape colored silks around your body or they are used with a lamp to flood the room with your required color for 20 minutes. Afterward, you will be left to bask for several minutes in the complementary color.

At the end you are given homework. This is essential and involves wearing particular colors, eating foods of those colors, and visualizing with the color two or three times a day.

How many sessions do I need?

People who practice their homework can improve considerably after three weekly sessions. Some seriously ill people need two years of treatment to improve.

Which problems can it help?

Practitioners believe that color therapy can help people with mental, emotional and physical problems including insomnia, asthma, depression, pain, anxiety, stress-related disorders and behavioral problems. It can also speed recovery from disease or after an operation. Some therapists treat people with Aids and cancer, but only alongside conventional medical treatment.

Is it safe?

Color therapy is safe for everyone providing you receive treatment from a qualified practitioner. Too much of one color can adversely affect your health. Red, in particular should be used with caution. It can lower your resistance to pain and raise blood pressure causing changes in heart and brain function. It is also important to be careful during pregnancy as color can affect the embryonic cell structure. Most therapists will use silks rather than lights during this time.

Clinical studies

Various medical trials have shown color therapy to be helpful in treating different ailments.

In 1982 a controlled study was held at San Diego State University School of Nursing involving 60 middle-aged women suffering from rheumatoid arthritis. They were exposed to blue light. The patients placed their hands into a box with a blue light and were exposed for only 15 minutes. This resulted in significant pain relief which improved with further exposure. (**54**)

In a study in 1990, flashing red lights were shone in the eyes of migraine sufferers at the start of an attack using special goggles. The light intensity and the frequency of flashing could be altered. Ninety-three percent of patients had some relief from the treatment with 72 percent reporting that severe migraines could be stopped within one hour. Lights of a higher intensity and greater flashing frequency were found to be the most effective. (**55**) *(For clinical references see How to use this book).*

FOR INFORMATION ON HOW TO CHOOSE A COLOR THERAPIST SEE THE DIRECTORY.

CRYSTAL & GEMSTONE THERAPY

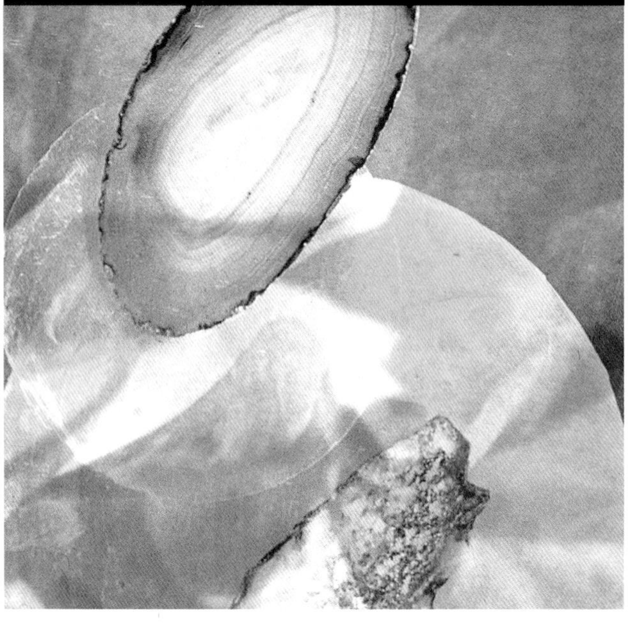

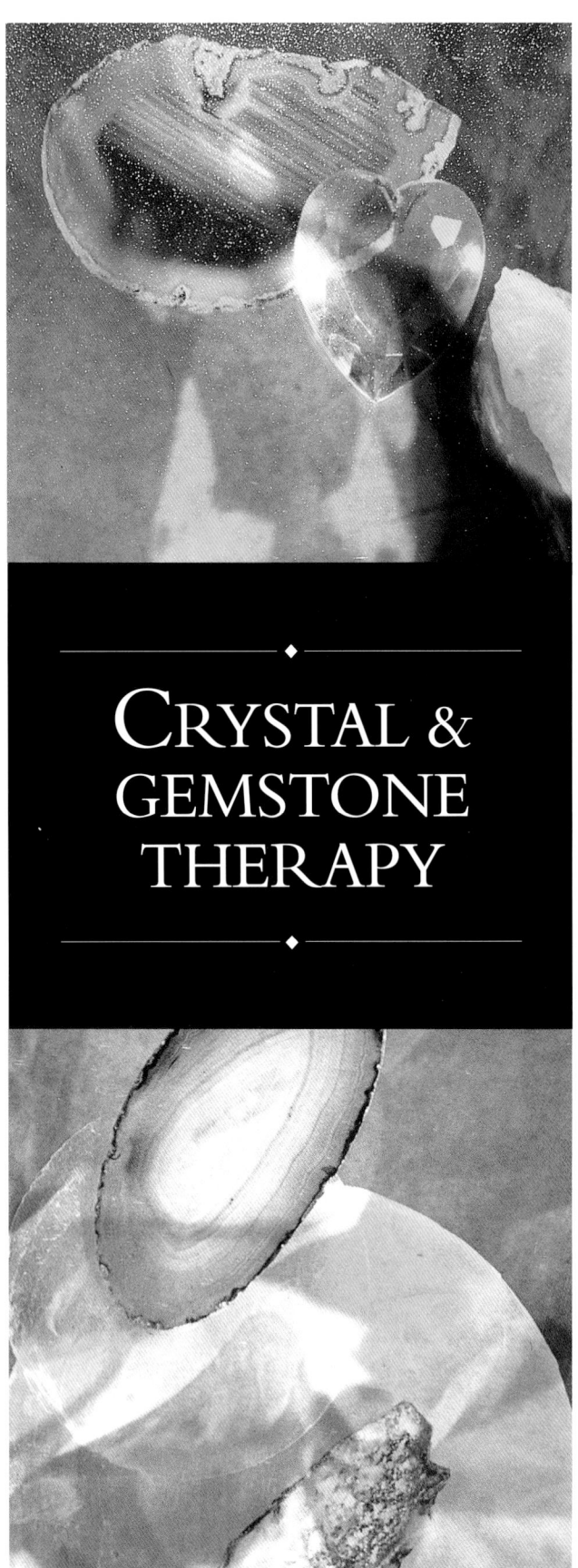

"FROZEN WATER FROM HEAVEN" or "solidified light" is how our ancestors described crystals. The word crystal comes from the Greek word for ice, but although some crystals such as quartz resemble ice, others such as aventurine and petrified wood have a more earthy appearance.

For centuries crystals have been credited with mystical and healing powers. They were used by ancient astrologers, diviners and priests, and have long been revered for their beauty and power. Buddhist monks carved crystal balls out of quartz which they claimed to be the "gem of enlightenment." Contemplation of the crystal's clarity started the tradition of crystal ball gazing.

For modern crystal and gem enthusiasts, however, the emphasis is on the healing power of crystals. Increasing numbers of crystal converts like to wear or hold their special crystal to benefit from its healing energy. They like to put it by their television or VDU screen to counteract negative vibrations, or even sleep with it under their pillow to ward off nightmares.

What is crystal and gemstone therapy?

Crystals and gems (semiprecious and precious stones) are used in crystal and gemstone therapy to bring about mental, spiritual and physical healing. A crystal is defined as a mineral that has a definite atomic structure, with smooth flat faces arranged into a geometric pattern. This may be a cube, a prism or a multifaceted shape, each one is individual and believed to be a perfect example of organized matter. If you are tuning into the perfection of the crystal, it is meant to bring you closer to perfection. Crystals are used to heal people, animals, buildings and the planet.

Specially trained crystal therapists and other alternative practitioners such as spiritual healers, aromatherapists, reflexologists and kinesiologists, use them for healing. There are about 3,000 minerals, at present, which have the potential to become crystals.

How does it work?

Like many other therapies, crystals work at an energy level. Energy is the spark that brings everything to life and the force that changes and renews every cell of living beings. Therapists believe our bodies house channels of energy called meridians and each of us is surrounded by an energy field known as an aura. This energy can be depleted or become unbalanced by external or internal influences: from thinking negatively to eating the wrong foods or absorbing radiation from computer screens.

Crystals and gemstones are believed to exert positive healing energies to rebalance our bodies as they match the energy of the human aura. It is logical to wonder how rocks could influence our lives. Crystal therapists say that all things have a consciousness, even rocks, and the consciousness inherent in crystals can help us get attuned with our "higher self" – our soul or spirit.

CRYSTAL AND GEMSTONE THERAPY uses the healing forces in semiprecious and precious stones to correct imbalances in our energy fields. It is believed to be effective for reducing stress and helping ailments such as back pain and arthritis.

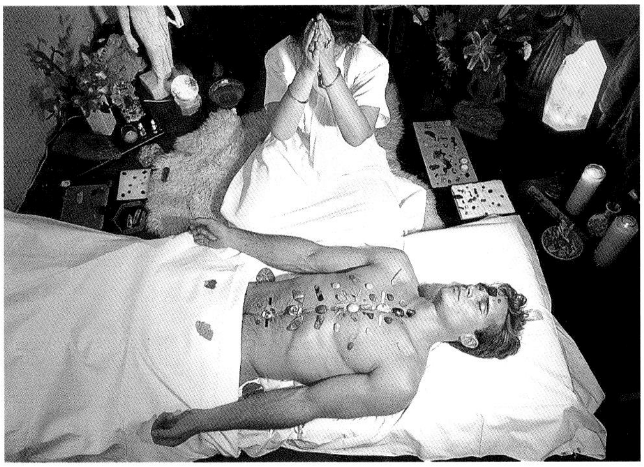

ABOVE: Depending on the treatment necessary, the crystal and gemstone therapist may place one or several stones on your body.

Crystals can generate, store and give off electromagnetic energy. Each crystal has its own particular energy which vibrates at a level that can have specific healing effects on mind, body and spirit. Quartz, for example, is known to generate small amounts of electricity called piezoelectricity, which is used in industry to power computers among other items. Therapists use crystals to stimulate healing in the whole person, not to treat specific diseases, but certain qualities have also been attributed to individual stones. The electrical qualities of quartz are believed to help you think more clearly and speed up healing, amber has a calming energy that may help ward off depression and moonstone may help maintain emotional and hormonal balance.

A crystal needs to be dedicated by visualizing or saying aloud that it is there to help and heal you

Gemstones, such as emeralds, garnet and jade, also vibrate with energy. They are used like other crystals, but also used to create gem essences. These work similarly to flower essences (see Bach Flower Remedies pages 104–109). The stones are immersed in purified water and left in the sun, so the sun's rays transmit the energy from gem to water. The same effect can be achieved using a pyramid, pendulum or a healer's energy. The energized water is poured into bottles, which you can use either by holding for some minutes or by placing drops under your tongue. Not all gems are suitable for essences as some, such as turquoise and malachite, contain copper and are poisonous to drink.

What happens in a consultation?

Like all other alternative therapists, a qualified crystal healer will usually begin your consultation with a discussion about you and your problems. Some practitioners combine crystals with other therapies, so there is no set formula for consultation and treatment can involve using crystals in several ways:

- *The therapist may place crystals around your chair or couch, if you are lying down, to surround you with healing energy.*
- *She may give you a crystal to hold.*
- *Some therapists will place crystals on the body's seven energy centers, known as chakras.*

If you have physical pain, the therapist may place a crystal over the site of the pain. Energy from the crystal then passes through the body to the point of pain or imbalance. The crystals can be left in place for a few seconds or for several minutes. The choice of the crystal or crystals depends on what the therapist believes to be right for you. Therapists believe crystals choose you rather than the other way round. She may ask you if there is one or more crystal to which you feel drawn. She may use one crystal, or combinations of stones arranged in complex patterns.

How the session affects you depends very much on the individual, but most people claim they feel more relaxed and have a more heightened sense of awareness. The session may end with you buying a crystal or crystals to take home and use.

If you acquire a crystal the therapist may advise you to:

- *Wash your crystal in cool water or place it in sun or moonlight to cleanse it. If it is a salt crystal that would dissolve in water, you will be told to visualize washing it or to pass it through the smoke of a burning herb.*
- *Dedicate your crystal by visualizing or saying aloud that it is to be used to help you, heal you or work in the name of love.*
- *Care for your crystal. Put it in a special place, preferably wrapped in silk or velvet. Do not leave it in the bottom of your handbag or your desk drawer.*

How many sessions do I need?

You should review the situation with your therapist after three sessions, by which time you should start to feel some benefits.

Which problems can it help?

Healers believe that crystals can help with all healing from strengthening your spirit to reducing stress levels and even helping to heal wounds. There has been considerable success with back pain and arthritis.

Is it safe?

Potentially, energy in crystals and gemstones can be used to heal or harm, so crystal therapists recommend that you dedicate your crystal to be used only for good. Crystal healing can be used for everyone, irrespective of age or health. However, the healer should note health problems such as high blood pressure or epilepsy and structure treatment accordingly. It is important that you tell the healer of any problems. No condition would make you unsuitable for crystal healing, but qualified therapists do take special care with babies and pregnant women.

CYMATICS

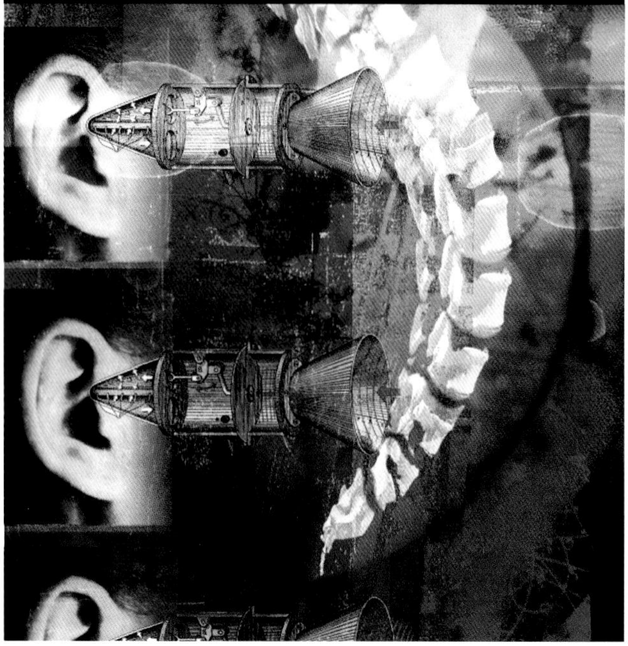

CYMATICS WAS DEVELOPED in the 1960s by a British medical doctor and osteopath, Dr. Peter Manners. The therapy grew out of early research into electromagnetic energy and the concept that every living thing – person, animal, plant or organism is surrounded by an energy field that resonates at its own particular frequency. Professor Gauvou of the Sorbonne in Paris, Dr. Brauna from Germany, Dr. Harold S. Burr from Yale University and Swiss scientist Dr. Hans Jenny, were all individually involved in research into the phenomenon in the 1950s.

The results of their work was collated by Dr. Manners and developed into the therapy of cymatics. Unlike many other types of alternative therapy, cymatics exploits the scientific possibilities of 20th century medicine and according to Dr. Peter Manners, is "founded on a true knowledge of man." Consequently, the medical profession is mostly appreciative of what it has to offer. In fact, the treatment has proved to be so successful, painless and easy to perform, that it is rapidly growing in popularity. There are now cymatic clinics in Britain, Europe, America, Canada, Japan, Australia, and others are soon to open in Brazil and Mexico.

What is cymatics?

Cymatics comes from the Greek word "*kyma*" meaning "a great wave." Cymatic therapy is a form of sound therapy, based on the principle that every cell in the body, of which there are believed to be millions, is controlled by an electromagnetic field which resonates at its own particular sound frequency. When we are well, this frequency is steady and constant, but any dysfunction or disease upsets the harmony of the body and the area affected then generates an increased resonance.

The practitioner uses the cymatic machinery to generate a frequency identical to that of healthy cells. His aim is to support what the cells are trying to do naturally, therefore aiding the healing process and restoring the body to good health and harmony.

How does it work?

Cymatics practitioners use special equipment to generate the required frequencies of harmonics to stimulate the affected cells in all areas of the body. Originally, the equipment was very large, cumbersome and expensive, but today it is much smaller, in fact about the size of a small briefcase. Treatment is applied either by means of a large hand-held applicator; directed through electroids, which attach onto the body; or via cymatic probes, which are small pencil-like applicators used to treat small areas. The practitioner chooses the treatment from around 850 frequencies, all of which have been calculated over a period of years. The treatment is then directed at the area of the body causing the

CYMATICS is a therapy that uses sound waves that operate on the same level as healthy cells to heal an unbalanced or diseased body. The treatment is painless and can relieve rheumatism, arthritis and back pain.

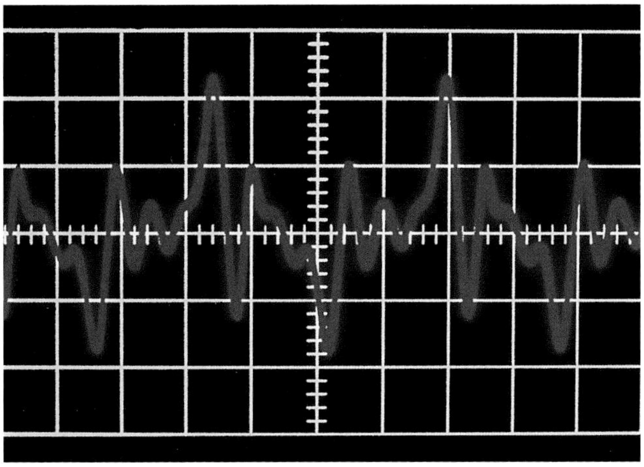

ABOVE: *Cymatic treatment works by generating corrective sound waves to the part of the body that is injured and rebalancing its energy.*

problem. This may be the point of pain, but often it is not.

Treatment works in the same way for all problems. If you have muscular pain, for example, the energy of that muscle and the frequency of its field will have been changed by the injury or condition affecting it. Transmitting a corrective frequency into the muscle, can rebalance its energy and almost immediately relieve the pain experienced.

In an asthmatic condition, for example, the asthmatic tension is released so that the patient is able to breathe more easily. Viral conditions on the other hand, can be cured because the sound waves set up a condition in the body which makes it intolerable for the virus to remain.

What happens in a consultation?

The first treatment lasts for an hour or more and begins with a normal medical check-up. If necessary, the practitioner will take your pulse, blood pressure, listen to your chest and carry out any other relevant conventional medical diagnostic tests. But, in the case of injury where the nature of the condition is obvious, this is not usually required. The practitioner will go on to ask you for details about:

- *Your general health and any conditions that you might be suffering from.*
- *What sort of food you eat in your normal diet.*
- *He will also require details of your occupation and will want to know about any aspects of your lifestyle that may also contribute to your condition.*

Practitioners trained in other forms of alternative therapy such as acupuncture or osteopathy may also use elements of those systems in the diagnosis. When he has arrived at his diagnosis, the practitioner will take you into a treatment room. Depending on the treatment required you may be asked to lie on a couch or sit in a specially designed structure in which you can rest your head, neck and shoulders, so that you are relaxed and ready for treatment.

Treatment can sometimes take the form of "aquasonics," in which case it takes place in a heated pool in an air-conditioned building. The molecular structure of water can be altered by certain sound frequencies, making it an easier medium in which people with mobility problems can move. People with arthritis, rheumatoid problems and physical disability are often treated in this way. Even patients with paralysis can experience some sense of movement because of their own dilation in the water.

The nature and length of treatment depends on your condition. For example, a difficult viral condition may need to be treated with several different frequencies for 45–60 minutes, but something as straightforward as arthritis could benefit from just 30 minutes of treatment. Treatment in the pool may last as little as 20 minutes, because it can be so relaxing that you want to fall asleep. In all cases the sensation is pleasant, relaxing and slightly stimulating as the sound frequencies are transmitted through your body.

How many sessions do I need?

It is impossible to say. It depends on the nature of your condition, how long you have had it and your body's individual healing ability. Treatment is believed to speed up a person's healing rate by 50 percent. You are recommended to have treatment twice a week to begin with and then once a week until the problem is cleared. You should start to see some positive benefits by about the third treatment.

By transmitting a corrective frequency into a muscle, energy can be rebalanced and pain relieved.

Which problems can it help?

The therapy reduces pain and inflammation and helps improve mobility. It has been noted as a successful treatment for conditions such as arthritis, rheumatism, back pain, post-operative healing, sports injuries, bone fractures and muscular injury. But Dr. Manners states that every condition, illness or psychological state can be treated or improved by the technique because it releases tension in the system and allows the mind and body to return to a normal level.

Is it safe?

Cymatic therapy, administered by a qualified therapist, is perfectly safe for everyone, irrespective of age or level of fitness. Pregnant women, very young babies, and the very frail and elderly can all be treated with cymatics. In over 30 years of practice, there have been no recorded side effects or adverse effects arising from the treatment.

RADIONICS

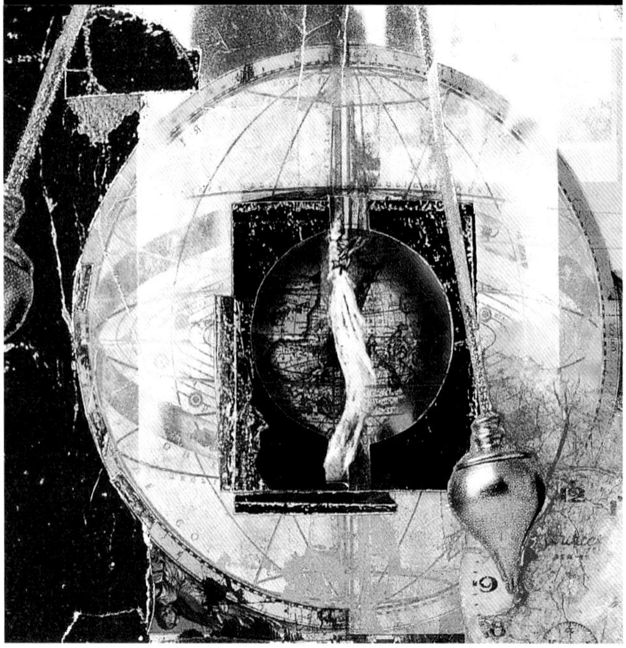

In the 1920s an American neurologist called Albert Abrams devised the system of alternative healthcare known as radionics. While percussing (tapping) a cancer patient's abdomen, Abrams detected a dull note, instead of the usual hollow sound, above the navel and could find no tumor or abnormality to account for it. When he examined other cancer patients, Abrams found the same phenomenon repeated in every one of them. He tried the test on patients with other illnesses and found that different illnesses gave rise to a dull sounding note in different areas of the abdomen. He also found that when a healthy person held a piece of diseased tissue, the same dull note could be detected.

From his investigations he deduced that disease was not so much a problem of cell degeneration but was a form of radiating energy, caused by an imbalance of electrons in the body. Problems started to arise with his simple system of diagnosis when the areas relating to each disease started to overlap.

For example, patients suffering from syphillis had a dull note in the same area as cancer patients. In order to distinguish between diseases which registered in the same area, he developed a variable resistance meter, called a biodynamometer, which would measure each patient's energy. This meter became known as Abrams' black box.

To analyze a patient's health, Abrams discovered he did not even need the patient present. He could simply put a sample of their blood in a container called the dynamizer, attach it to the biodynamometer and palpate the abdomen of a healthy "subject." Abrams taught his system to interested colleagues, but most of the medical establishment was horrified by his activities.

After his death, Abrams' work was developed by an American chiropractor called Ruth Drown. It was Drown who discovered that healing, as well as analysis, could be carried out at a distance. Unfortunately, Drown was imprisoned for fraud and medical quackery. In Britain, the cause was furthered by engineer George De La Warr, who conducted extensive research into the subject. In 1924 the Royal Society of Medicine commissioned a year-long enquiry into the efficacy of radionics. It concluded that Abram's theory appeared to work. Nevertheless, many people remain skeptical about an analysis system and treatment which, even today, remains so difficult to understand.

What is radionics?

Radionics is a form of health analysis and treatment which uses specially designed instruments to analyze and treat illness or the energy imbalances that can cause illness. The analysis and treatment is carried out at a distance by means of some complicated machinery, or computer, and a "witness." This is the term used for a drop of blood, a nail clipping, or more often, a lock of hair

RADIONICS is a type of healthcare that uses special analyzing equipment to work out a program to treat illness and energy imbalance. Often other alternative therapies will be prescribed. The treatment can help hay fever and asthma.

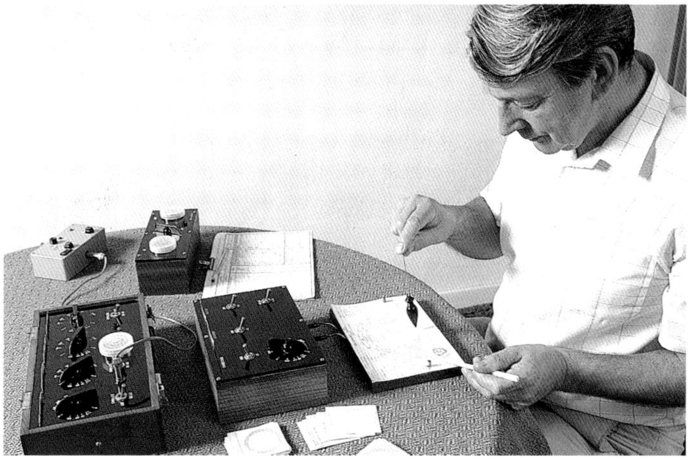

ABOVE: A radionics practitioner will use a witness, often a lock of hair, to get a reading of your energy levels and suggest corrective treatment.

that can be used for analysis and treatment. The hair itself is not analyzed, but is used as an energy link that allows the practitioner to tune into your energy field. The purpose of the analysis is to detect the quality of your mental, physical and emotional health.

How does it work?

Radionics practitioners believe each one of us is surrounded by an energy field. They aim to enhance our own healing ability by working with that energy field to rebalance our physical, emotional and mental states. How they do this in practice is detailed below. The theory of how the therapy works is more difficult to grasp. It relates to quantum physics, which theorizes that everything in the universe, including ourselves is composed of atoms, which are constantly moving and are linked by energy. The radionics practitioner claims that even if you and your snippet of hair are miles apart or the hair was cut some time ago, he can still read your energy levels, because the hair retains a link with its energy source and changes as the source changes.

The aim of radionic treatment is to improve your general health and well-being.

Likewise, in treatment, the practitioner tunes into you through your witness and energy flows from him to you through that link, causing the atoms of which you are made to vibrate. These vibrations change the state of your energy field and hopefully enable it to destroy any diseased particles in your body.

What happens in a consultation?

The practitioner will send you a case history form to complete, along with information about treatment cost. The questions tend to focus on your medical history and that of your parents and grandparents. You will be asked to name any drugs you have taken or are currently taking and to list your present health problems and symptoms. There will also be some questions about your lifestyle, interests, emotions and personality. You will be asked to return the completed form with a "witness." This will most likely be a lock of your hair.

When he receives your details your practitioner will use them and the witness to tune into your vibration. He will prepare an analysis sheet and label your witness for identification purposes. Using the witness to link his instrument with you, the practitioner takes readings of your body structure and systems, your emotional and mental state, your energy flow, any tendencies toward or progression of major diseases, and the causes of your overall problems. He will write back to you to tell you what he has found, what treatment he intends to give you and when you should let him know how you are feeling and progressing.

The practitioner uses a variety of treatment instruments, including a new automatic computerized treatment system (ACTS), which contains 260,000 treatments including homeopathy, acupuncture, herbalism, flower and gem remedies, color, sound and light therapy and energies of vitamins and minerals. The ACTS is connected to you through your witness and delivers the treatment, which it "knows" you need, at the right time and in the right quantities from its sophisticated database. The practitioner may suggest that you see your doctor or other health professional, such as a herbalist, homeopath, chiropractor or osteopath, if he feels it is appropriate.

How many sessions do I need?

There is no set time for a course of treatment. Some people consult a practitioner only when they are ill, others use the therapy long-term as a sort of health maintenance system. Acute (short-term) conditions improve quickly, while chronic (long-term) conditions can take several sessions of treatment.

Which problems can it help?

The aim of radionic treatment is to improve your general health and well-being. In doing so, practitioners claim that many problems including allergic conditions such as hay fever and asthma have been cleared. It has also been shown to alleviate pain in conditions such as arthritis and help people who are suffering from post-operative discomfort.

Is it safe?

Most doctors, even those who do not believe in radionics, admit that the therapy cannot do any harm and is therefore perfectly safe to use for people of all ages. It is compatible with other alternative therapies and there are no side effects. It can also be used on animals and even plants. In the case of young children or those who are very sick, it would be sensible to back up your diagnosis or treatment with a visit to your doctor.

BODYWORK

BODYWORK IS A TERM NORMALLY USED for manipulative techniques that include psycho-emotional work. Practitioners work on muscles or go deep into the connective tissues to rebalance the mind, body and emotions. Here we discuss: rolfing®, hellerwork and biodynamics.

ROLFING

What is rolfing?

Rolfing originated in the United States in the 1930s when biochemist Dr. Ida Rolf discovered that the network of connective tissue which encases every muscle could be manipulated to reshape a body that has been pulled out of alignment. She also recognized that gravity has a bearing on our shape. When we are well aligned and move in harmony with gravity, it can flow naturally through us, allowing us to move easily. But a poorly aligned body is pulled down by gravity and must struggle to keep its balance, compensating for misalignment in one area by making changes in another, until the entire structure is weakened.

The aim of the rolfer is to realign the body's structure, to restore it to balance, improve the general posture and consequently the person's all-round physical and emotional health. According to Ida Rolf's "gospel of rolfing," a body that is functioning well with the force of gravity flowing evenly through it is a body that can spontaneously heal itself.

How does it work?

Ida Rolf compared a misaligned body to a tower of children's bricks that are precariously balanced on top of one another. The slightest movement of one brick can undermine its whole structure and cause it to collapse. A similar arrangement in the body puts unnecessary stress on the supporting muscles so that they lose their elasticity and knots and adhesions develop in the connective tissue. The body uses up enormous energy trying to cope with and compensate for this state of unbalance and the force of gravity reinforces this poor structure.

Rolfers aim to reverse this unhealthy condition by manipulating the connective tissue to allow the body to move more appropriately so that it returns to a state of balance. When the body structure is balanced, the mind, nervous system, and all the organs and tissues to which it relates, function more efficiently and our innate healing system can then work at its best.

BODYWORK is a term that can be applied to massage and other structural body therapies such as chiropractic and osteopathy, but is usually reserved for those therapies, such as rolfing, hellerwork and biodynamic therapy which combine manipulative techniques with psycho-emotional or counseling work.

What happens in a consultation?

If you embark on a course of rolfing, be prepared for several sessions of treatment. It is usual, but not obligatory, to undress to your underwear for the consultation. You may have your photograph taken at the beginning, during and at the end of the course, but not all practitioners do this. The first session begins with the rolfer taking details about you and your medical history:

- *She will want to know whether you have had any injuries or structural weaknesses.*
- *She may ask you about your own aims, as rolfing can be used to support your personal development. For the treatment, you will be asked to lie down on a massage couch, where the rolfer will use her fingertips, hands, knuckles and sometimes elbows to work with the connective tissue. The first session usually involves the practitioner working on freeing restrictions around the rib cage and the upper half of the body to help you to breathe more deeply and expansively. In subsequent treatments, the practitioner will gradually work her way over your entire body.*

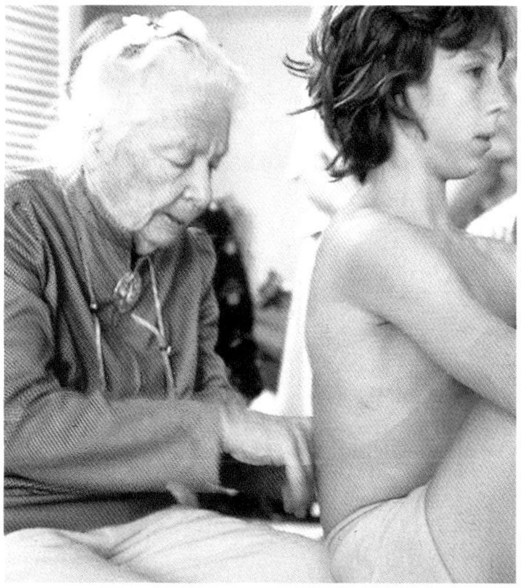

RIGHT: With rolfing the practitioner helps to balance a poor body structure by carefully manipulating the body tissues with fingertips, hands and knuckles to release any knots and lesions present.

Rolfing is often described as uncomfortable and you may find some areas of your body are particularly sensitive to the treatment. But the system has evolved since it was first practiced and the range and depth of touch varies with each practitioner. It is no longer considered painful and any slight discomfort normally preludes a wonderful sense of relief.

Movement and psychology have also become more integrated into the training, and practitioners do not simply use deep manual pressure to stimulate changes. Emotional and physical problems may surface during the course of treatment, causing you to feel slightly uncomfortable before you feel better. If you have experienced traumatic injuries in the past, you may also experience flashbacks. Well-trained practitioners are equipped to deal empathetically with any such occurrences.

How many sessions do I need?

A full course of rolfing involves ten treatments, lasting between 60 and 90 minutes, often a week or more apart. These sessions have been designed to work gradually from the outer surface structures (sessions one to three) to the deeper ones (four to seven), ending with an integration of the two (eight to ten). You may start to feel an improvement after one or two sessions, but it is best to complete the series to reap the long-term benefits. These can range from being more supple and strong to feeling more confident, positive and energetic. You can also continue to have treatments as and when you feel you need them.

Which problems can it help?

Rolfing is not aimed at alleviating specific conditions, but many people find they gain relief from aggravating back pain, neck, shoulder and joint pain as well as asthma and digestive problems. Any problems resulting from bad posture can also benefit as can emotional problems. Rolfing does more than simply sort out structural problems. It was part of the human potential movement which evolved in the 1960s and continues to take a serious mind/body approach to personal development.

Is it safe?

Rolfing is safe for adults and children who are not suffering from organic or inflammatory diseases such as cancer or rheumatoid arthritis. A modified version of rolfing is safe for women who are more than three months pregnant and babies and children suffering from structural problems such as scoliosis of the spine.

HELLERWORK

What is Hellerwork?

Hellerwork is a derivative of rolfing and as such it is aimed at re-aligning the body and rebalancing the connection between the mind and body. It was developed in the United States in 1978 by a former US aerospace engineer called Joseph Heller. He applied the principles he had learned from engineering to the human body to help prevent illness and improve vitality.

How does it work?

Hellerworkers believe that every movement is stressful to a body that is structurally misaligned. Misalignment can occur as a result of bad postural habits or in response to emotional stress. Physical and emotional stress affect the fascial tissue (connective tissue) which holds together all the body muscles and which also thickens to form ligaments and tendons.

In a balanced body this tissue should be loose and moist; under stress it becomes rigid and "knotty." Any one area of stressed tissue sets up tension in the rest of the body, leading to a state of general imbalance. The object of the Hellerworker is to realign the body and release the rigid physical, mental and emotional patterns that caused the misalignment in the first place. To achieve this they use a combination of manipulation, movement reeducation and discussion.

Manipulation concentrates on stretching tightened and shortened fascia back to its normal shape. Movement reeducation involves learning to move effortlessly, allowing your body to maintain perfect alignment. Through discussion, the practitioner aims to make you aware of you how your emotions and attitudes can cause structural tension.

The aim of bodywork techniques is to balance both the body and the mind.

What happens in a consultation?

The complete Hellerwork program consists of several sessions. You are advised not to eat for a couple of hours before each consultation and you will be asked to undress to your underwear for each treatment. At the start of the first session the therapist will talk to you about:

- *Your medical history and illnesses you have had in the past*
- *Your specific needs and how Hellerwork may help you*

The practitioner will take a photograph at the beginning and end of the program to show how your posture and appearance changes over the course of 11 weeks. The work itself takes place on three different levels: the superficial, the core and the integrative. Some of the deeper work can hurt slightly, but it is never unbearable and most people feel relaxed and energized at the end of each session.

Practitioners begin by working on the superficial layers of connective tissue and the first three sessions of treatment focus on realigning and freeing tension in the chest area, feet and arms. They believe that by working on these areas you deal with the fundamental childhood issues of breathing, standing up and reaching out.

Sessions four to seven are known as the core sessions because they work more deeply into the body's core. We tend not to use our core muscles enough which means they are usually tight, inflexible and primed for problems. The practitioner manipulates these muscles to allow your body to move more freely and harmoniously.

For example, session four concentrates on the muscles of the inside leg and the pelvic floor. Sessions five and six focus on the pelvis and spine respectively, while session seven is aimed at relieving any tension that is concentrated in the muscles of the head and neck area. Work on the core also aims to resolve central emotional issues which may have first arisen during your adolescence. The third group of sessions is known as the integrative sessions. The aim of this part of the treatment is to integrate the work of the superficial and core sessions by improving the body's overall movement and balance.

The final session is like a review session. Then by the end of the entire program you will be recommended not to have any further sessions for several months. This is so that you have enough time to get to use what you have learned by integrating it into your normal daily lifestyle.

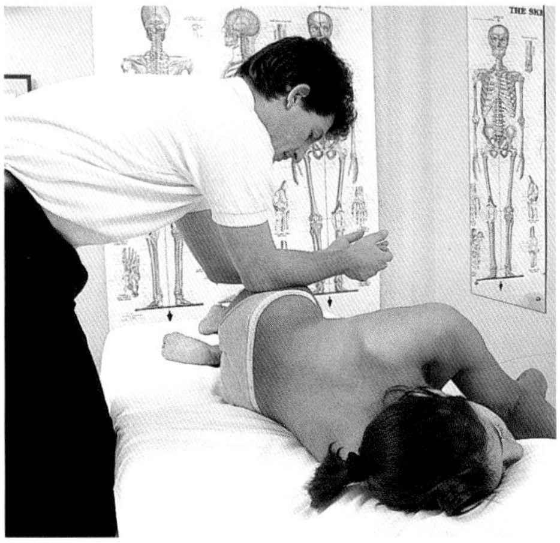

ABOVE: Hellerwork treatment involves sessions over an 11-week period where the practitioner attempts to realign the body, mainly through manipulation, to correct body problems.

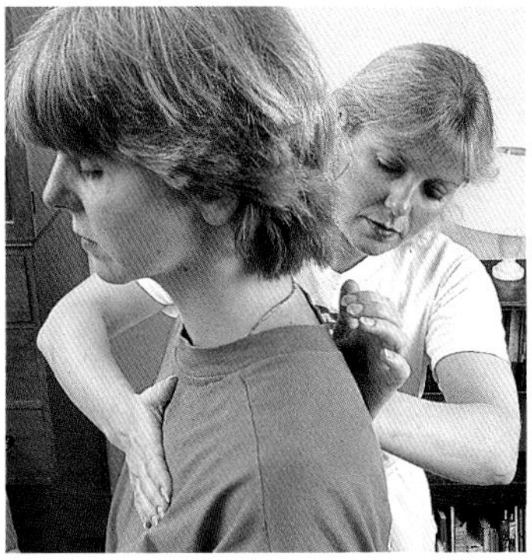

ABOVE: Biodynamic therapy uses massage and counseling techniques to help physical and emotional tension.

How many sessions do I need?

A full course of treatment consists of eleven 90-minute sessions. Some people choose to return for advanced sessions. Such people tend to have chronic problems such as scoliosis, a curvature of the spine. Many people claim to feel the benefits after just one treatment and use subsequent sessions to make any improvements permanent.

Which problems can it help?

Hellerwork is about disease prevention rather than just treatment. The aim of the practitioner is to try to keep mind and body in perfect balance, in order to prevent any health problems occurring. However, it has been shown to help with all sorts of aches and pains, as well as neckache, headaches and back pain.

Is it safe?

Hellerwork can be adapted to safely accommodate the needs of most people. Pregnant women can benefit from the treatment, as can children, although they rarely need this sort of work. Hellerwork is not a treatment for disease, although it can be used to complement medical treatment in certain cases. It is not suitable in some types of cancer where manipulation of the tissues might speed up the spread of the disease.

BIODYNAMIC THERAPY

What is biodynamic therapy?

Biodynamic therapy combines specialized massage techniques with advanced psychotherapy to bring about emotional and physical healing. It was developed by Norwegian psychologist and physiotherapist Gerda Boyesen who discovered that emotional and psychological problems registered in the muscles and organs of the body, especially in the intestines, which she saw as having a dual function: to digest food and digest stress.

In psychotherapy sessions she noted that many patients would produce loud intestinal gurglings, particularly when releasing emotions. She also noted that massage could cause patients to be sick or have diarrhea and that such patients improved more quickly than those who had no physical release.

Boyesen devised the word "Biodynamic" to describe the life force or energy which constantly flows through us, linking body, mind and emotions into one organic unit. She believes that energy in the body is a liquid, flowing force, which can become blocked by emotional or physical disturbances, such as severe shock, trauma or injury.

How does it work?

Through massage and counseling, biodynamic therapy works to release physical and emotional tension. For example, you may hold grief from a bereavement inside you until it becomes part of your structure and you no longer feel the emotion. In such a case, the biodynamic therapist would work on your body to release the unexpressed grief so that you could again experience a healthy emotional cycle. The emotional cycle is of central importance to biodynamic therapy.

Therapists believe that as every emotion rises it causes a physical reaction in every cell of the body. As it subsides, emotional residue is eliminated through the intestines and the breath level enabling body functioning in a healthy individual should then return to normal.

However, if your life is dogged by stress or tension, this cleansing process becomes impaired. The energy flow becomes sluggish and blocked and the muscles of the intestines will no longer function correctly. Consequently, much of the residue stays in your system to wreak physical and mental havoc. Therapists use massage to wring the residue out of the tissues, and to stimulate the flow of healing energy.

What happens in a consultation?

There is no predetermined course of treatment; it depends on you, the therapist and the interaction between you. A session usually lasts for an hour and the first one begins with a detailed interview with a consultant who will ask you:

- *For full details of your medical history, any problems that are bothering you.*
- *She will discuss areas of vulnerability that you have and whether you have tried previous therapies.*

The consultant will then decide on what approach would benefit you most and choose a suitable therapist to treat you. The therapeutic session might involve massage only, discussion only, or a combination of both.

Because the intestinal health is so important, therapists often listen to the intestines with a stethoscope and direct the treatment according to what they hear. A healthy relaxed abdomen may sound like a gurgling stream, a blocked one may make no sound at all, while one that is beginning to relax after being blocked for a long time may sound like a creaking door.

Therapists use a range of massage techniques to free emotions from clogged muscles and encourage energy flow. The treatment may unlock old memories or provoke emotional outbursts, which you will be encouraged to express by talk or action with the therapist. Biodynamic therapists claim to see results early on in the treatment, sometimes even after the first session.

How many sessions do I need?

On average, people tend to need about a year of weekly sessions, but this varies depending on the nature of the problem. Problems from the recent past can be resolved in a shorter time, whereas problems that can be traced back to childhood can take more than a year to resolve.

Which problems can it help?

The therapy is beneficial in all stress-related illnesses. This includes lower back pain, migraine, angina, MS, Parkinson's disease and rheumatoid arthritis. Therapists also claim success in helping clients to overcome deep-seated negative attitudes and feelings of hopelessness, fear and despair.

Is it safe?

Biodynamics is safe for most people except those who are in the advanced stages of disease. Most people who choose biodynamic therapy are adults with problems to work out, but children with psychological problems can also benefit from adapted techniques. Milder forms of the therapy can suit pregnant women.

FOR INFORMATION ON HOW TO CHOOSE A BODYWORK THERAPIST SEE THE DIRECTORY.

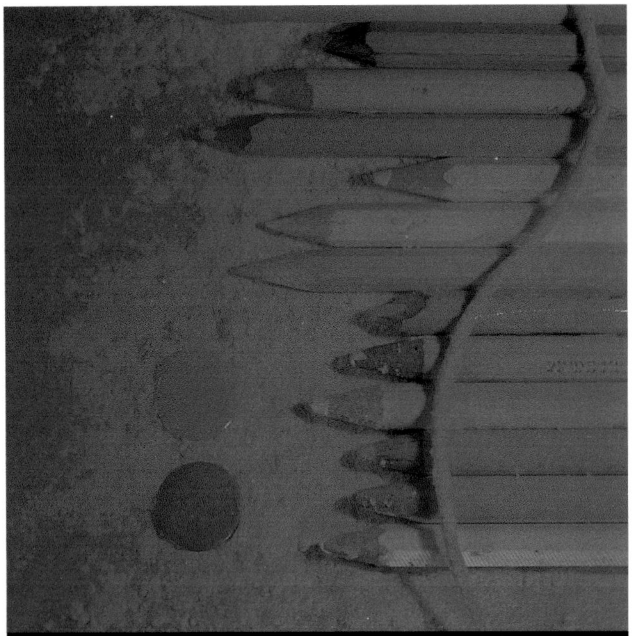

ARTS THERAPIES

PAINTING AND DRAWING, singing and playing musical instruments, dancing and acting are all powerful and exciting forms of self expression. It is no small wonder therefore that the arts have become a valuable therapeutic tool, especially in the rehabilitation of the mentally and emotionally disturbed. In the 1940s, some artists working in psychiatric hospitals began to realize that exploring, discussing and sharing the creation of a painting or other artwork could form the basis of a therapeutic relationship. Consequently, art as therapy evolved into art therapy, or art psychotherapy.

Similarly, other media also began to be used therapeutically and the arts therapies gradually became accepted and integrated into the healthcare system. Arts therapists are now valued and respected health professionals. And although the therapies have established themselves within the conventional medical system, arts therapists work to a holistic philosophy, which is in keeping with alternative medicine.

What are the arts therapies?

Arts therapies is the term used to encompass four different and distinct therapies – art therapy, music therapy, dramatherapy and dance movement therapy. Each can be used to help people with psychological problems to explore how they feel about themselves and their relationships with others. The aim of all four therapies is to develop deeper self-awareness, allowing people to either change or accept aspects of themselves that are preventing them from leading fulfilling and independent lives.

The choice of therapy is usually a personal preference, but professional assessment might indicate that one of the therapies is particularly appropriate. Talent is not important, and can sometimes be counterproductive, as a musician may concentrate on producing a piece of music that is aesthetically pleasing rather than one that is emotionally cathartic, and skilled artists, musicians, dancers or actors can use their skills to conceal what they need to explore. The only criterion required is a willingness to take part in what can be an unfamiliar and daunting experience.

How do they work?

Arts therapies are concerned with finding a language to demonstrate what cannot be expressed verbally. All four therapies work on the principle that art is cathartic. They can be used to access the unconscious mind in a way that is similar to how psychoanalysis uses the recalling of dreams. Emotional problems can arise from painful experiences that have been repressed, but survive as unconscious memories which subtly influence our lives. Because the arts therapies involve much nonverbal work, they

ARTS THERAPIES are made up of four different therapies – art therapy, music therapy, dramatherapy and dance movement therapy. Each one can help people suffering from psychological problems to explore their own feelings and to develop their relationships with others.

can explore even those painful experiences which occurred before we learned to talk. Through the chosen medium and discussion with you and your therapist, it is possible to bring these past issues to the conscious level to resolve them .

The feelings you experience as you paint, improvise some music, move or act a part, reflect what is happening in your unconscious. In each session the therapist aims to create an environment in which you can feel confident about exploring, experimenting and liberating your thoughts. This sort of "play" can help you develop a stronger sense of identity without needing conventional counseling. However, therapy can also involve some discussion to explore thoughts and feelings that emerge as your therapy progresses. Discussing your work with the therapist also gives you a chance to benefit from a relationship with someone who witnesses your work and accepts it without criticism.

ABOVE: Painting can be a very therapeutic experience, and can bring forth hidden emotions that are buried in the subconscious.

What happens in a consultation?

The therapy sessions can take place on a one-to-one basis or in a group, usually of no more than eight people. Adult therapy sessions last for about 60–90 minutes, children's sessions last about 30 minutes, but times tend to vary as does the basic structure of each session.

Before therapy begins the therapist will want to meet you for an individual assessment. This meeting gives you both the chance to decide if you could work together.

- *The therapist will ask you to describe your emotional problems and will want to know what it is that you expect to gain from the therapy.*
- *She will probably ask for details about your life and relationships, past and present.*

This is also a good time to ask any relevant questions you may have. Assessments sometimes include the use of the arts medium concerned so you can discuss how you feel about it. Some people need a second assessment before they can finally decide whether or not to go ahead with the therapy, or indeed which therapy to choose.

If you both decide to proceed you will agree on when it will begin, times of sessions and, if you are seeing the therapist privately, the treatment cost. It is important to understand that you are agreeing a contract with the therapist. You will also be expected to operate within the boundaries set by the therapist. The session will take place in the same place at the same time every time you attend. During the therapy session no one outside the group is allowed to enter the room and everything that is said or done within the group is treated as completely confidential.

The choice of therapy is normally personal preference, but one therapy might prove particularly appropriate.

There may sometimes be a delay between your assessment and when your therapy begins as it can take a little time to get a group of suitably sized people together. This situation is not ideal, so some therapists may decide to offer to see you once or twice on your own, if this delay becomes too protracted.

There is no set arts therapy session, different therapists take different approaches to their work and the course of the therapy will be determined by the needs of the individual or group members. Sessions usually include periods of reflection and discussion as well as creative activity. The amount of time allocated to each may change as the sessions progress. Often part of the therapeutic process can be for the group to negotiate how they want to work within each session.

Art therapy: This therapy helps people communicates through the creative use of paint, pastels, clay or other art materials. Your choice of medium can be as relevant as the work you create. For example, colored pencils make only a faint mark on paper and the person who chooses them is conveying a different message from someone who splashes paint everywhere. The former may be afraid to make their mark, while the latter may feel it is safe to let go or is simply not able to be more controlled.

You and the therapist will explore any problems you may have in approaching the work as well as the content of what you create. The therapist may invite you to share your feelings about your painting, but will not attempt to interpret or analyze it for you. Your work is confidential and is not displayed or shown outside the group. Group members can sometimes work on a single project or on a theme. Members of the group may also work individually, coming together to talk about the experience near the end of the session.

ABOVE: In dance movement therapy, movement holds the key to individual emotional disturbance. The therapist then works with you to resolve problems.

ABOVE: In music therapy people can, by their singing or playing style, interact with others to express their emotions or social problems.

LEFT: In dramatherapy, groups act out different ways of expressing themselves. This type of therapy can help improve communication in the relationships of each member.

Dance movement therapy: This uses movement techniques and dance to explore how a patient's emotional disturbance is linked to their bodily experiences. Everyone has an individual way of moving. The therapist observes and analyzes how you express yourself through the use of your body, she assesses your strengths and identifies areas in which you might benefit from therapy. The therapist may also work with you on an individual basis, using movements to help you build a stronger sense of your own identity. Movement can also be used to help resolve issues that may have occurred before you learned to speak, when movement was your natural means of expression. The benefits of movement are not to be underestimated in developing the often neglected qualities of playfulness and creativity.

In group work the therapist notes how members share emotional expression, assesses how the group works together, and judges when to intervene. For example, introducing the concept of leading and following may help to draw someone out of their self-preoccupied isolation.

As the session develops, the therapist may notice a particular theme emerging and may encourage the group to develop it. This could be something such as trust or assertiveness, which may have emerged from group discussion or some of the group's experiences. The therapist will have various pieces of equipment such as balls, bean bags and stretch cloths in the room, which can be used by the group to explore particular themes. For example, members of the group can pull and release cloths while exploring the theme of trust.

Music therapy: Group members use their voices or sounds produced by musical instruments as a means of expression. The way people sing, play and communicate musically with others can reflect their emotional or social problems. Music can form a link between people. It can also be used to symbolize feelings, for example, you may learn to control otherwise unmanageable feelings in an acceptable way – perhaps by challenging someone musically or by contradicting their musical style.

The therapist's role is to offer support, either through the music or through discussion. She can respond to you in several ways, perhaps by engaging in a playful musical "fight" or by meeting the energy of your play and playing along with you. By meeting you on a level where you feel you can communicate safely, the therapist can help you work through your feelings with the music so you emerge feeling calmer, safer or more confident.

If there is tension in the group, the therapist can also work toward understanding why it is there and attempt to dissipate it through the music.

Music is usually improvised by the group although composed pieces are sometimes used. Group members can choose from simple, usually percussion, instruments. With these they are not expected to give a performance, although the music produced can be a source of satisfaction.

Dramatherapy: This therapy uses various forms of drama to develop creativity, imagination, learning, insight and growth. The different forms used in practice can involve awareness, exploration and reflection of feelings and relationships. The group can act out different ways of thinking, feeling and behaving. Role play can be used to explore social situations where group members feel inadequate. Sessions can also involve exploring group feelings and areas of personal growth through the use of myth or metaphor. By acting out your story in a metaphorical, as opposed to an autobiographical way, you can explore the issues involved from a distance and benefit from taking a different perspective. Sessions may also simply focus on creating drama, working as part of a team, building self-confidence and self awareness, having fun and enjoying the company of the other people involved.

The therapist can introduce one or all of these forms of exploration into a session, depending on the individual or group needs as a whole. Central to all activity is the belief that dramatherapy provides a safe place for you to examine your "inner drama," in other words your beliefs, feelings and attitudes and to experiment with new ways of acting or being in the world.

Throughout the session the therapist encourages you to release your memories and anxieties, express your emotions and develop a better understanding of yourself and others. The therapist may become involved in activities such as role play, and this may be followed by group discussion. In other sessions all the work is contained in the metaphor or symbolism.

How many sessions do I need?

It is impossible to say how many sessions are needed, but be prepared to commit yourself to at least six months treatment and possibly much longer. Sessions are usually weekly, but it may be more appropriate for some people to attend more frequently.

Which problems can they help?

The arts therapies can benefit people with many types of psychological and emotional problems. In private practice, therapists may see patients who feel they are not fulfilling their potential, perhaps because they are hindered by anxiety or poor self-esteem. It can also benefit people with physical illnesses which are exacerbated by stress. Therapists who work in hospitals, day centers or institutions focus more on people who have been isolated by learning disorders, dementia or by severe psychiatric disorders such as schizophrenia. Patients with speech or hearing impairment can also communicate through their nonverbal aspects. All the therapies are effective with children.

Certain individual aspects of the therapies makes each one suitable in specific cases:

Art therapy: This is particularly valuable for people who feel threatened by close relationships as it gives them the space to express their feelings.

Music therapy: This is a traditional form of adolescent expression. It can also be appropriate for hyperactive children, or people who are suffering from Alzheimer's disease.

Dramatherapy: This can be used to improve relationships between couples, family or individuals within a group. Role play is a useful tool in teaching social skills such as assertiveness.

Dance movement therapy: This is effective with young children and can benefit the mother/baby relationship if both are seen in therapy together. Elderly patients in the advanced stages of dementia may still be reached through movement therapy.

Are they safe?

It is more appropriate to talk in terms of the suitability of the therapies rather than their safety. However, you should see a qualified therapist, who can deal with all psychological disturbance.

Clinical studies – Music therapy

Several studies have been undertaken to prove the benefits of music therapy in helping different conditions.

In 1995 in an American study at Bryan Memorial Hospital, Lincoln, 96 heart bypass patients were randomly assigned to three groups. The control group just rested while the two intervention groups had either music therapy or music-video therapy on days two and three after operations. Results showed that although all groups displayed reduced anxiety and improved mood, only the intervention groups showed general physiological relaxation with significant changes in blood pressure and heart rate prior to and during the intervention. (**56**)

In 1975, a study was undertaken of 108 anxious female students to see how they responded to three sessions of either music or muscle relaxation training. Both treatments significantly reduced their anxious state as measured by psychological questionnaires but neither reduced trait anxiety. (**57**)

In 1994, Stanford University School of Medicine studied 30 individuals aged over 80 who had been diagnosed with a depressive disorder. After being randomly assigned to three groups the participants learned stress-reducing techniques with music. These were either with weekly visits by a music therapist, or by themselves with a therapist making a weekly telephone call.

Both groups performed significantly better on normal depression tests on distress, mood and self-esteem compared with the control group on the waiting list who had no treatment. These improvements were maintained over the nine month follow-up period. (**58**) *(For clinical references see How to use this book).*

FOR INFORMATION ON HOW TO CHOOSE AN ARTS THERAPIST SEE THE DIRECTORY.

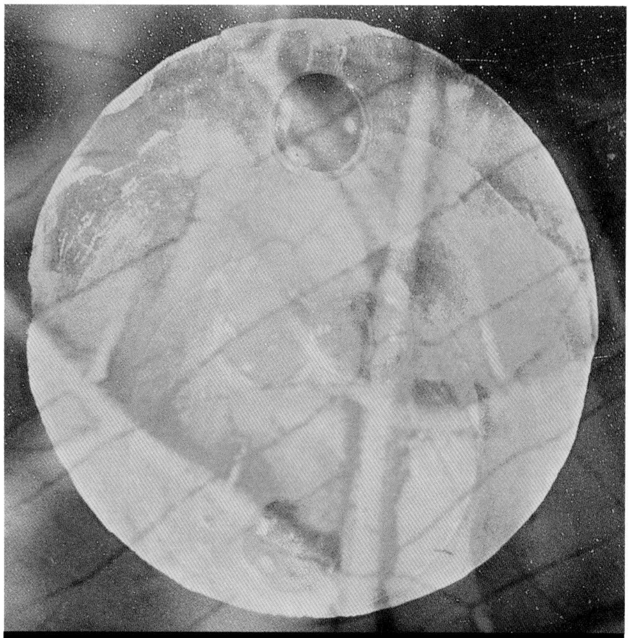

DIAGNOSTIC THERAPIES

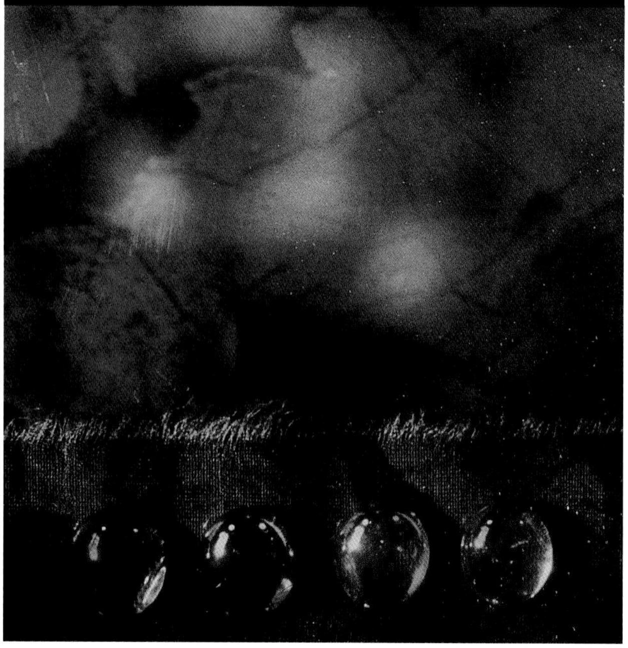

DIAGNOSTIC THERAPIES, which include kinesiology, iridology and Kirlian photography, are used mainly to find out what is causing an illness rather than to name a disease. They can help with digestive problems, predispositions to disease and identity problems.

DIAGNOSTIC THERAPIES are those which are principally used to analyze the causes of illness rather than diagnose and name specific diseases. All the therapies involve elements of diagnosis or analysis, but some are aimed specifically at reading your state of health from particular parts of your body such as the eyes, your muscles and even the the quality of your energy. Kinesiology, iridology and Kirlian photography are three such therapies, and are discussed in detail below.

KINESIOLOGY

What is kinesiology?

Kinesiology (pronounced kin-easy-ology) comes from the Greek word "*kinesis*" meaning motion, and is known as the study of movement. Certain aspects of the system have been used for years by conventional doctors and physiotherapists to test the range of movement, strength and ability of muscle-damaged patients. But it has only been used as a diagnostic tool since 1964, when Dr. George J. Goodheart, an American chiropractor, discovered that he could determine more about a patient's health by testing their muscles than by any other type of diagnosis.

He developed some muscle tests that enabled him to learn about the health of the whole body. This system, more accurately known as applied kinesiology, is used to detect and rectify functional imbalances before they develop into disease. The system is used by kinesiologists and practitioners of other therapies such as chiropractic (see pages 48–53).

How does it work?

Kinesiology is a combination of Western technology and the oriental principles of energy flow. Each of the major organs and systems of the body is fueled by an invisible channel of energy called a meridian (see Acupuncture pages 10–19). These channels work together to form an energy network that powers the mind, all the major functions, organs and muscles of the body.

When we are healthy, energy flows freely through these channels, but blocked energy can lead to weakness in the corresponding organ and will register in the muscle that relates to that organ. For example, the quadriceps in the front of the thigh are linked by energy to the small intestine and the hamstrings are similarly linked to the large intestine. So if you were sensitive to wheat and you ate a piece of bread, the intolerance would register first in the intestines and then in the corresponding muscles in your legs. A kinesiologist would test the strength of the relevant muscle and work backward to find the cause of the problem. This system works for physical, mental and emotional problems.

What happens in a consultation?

A first appointment usually lasts about an hour, although subsequent visits are shorter. The session begins with a detailed consultation. The kinesiologist asks questions about your health and

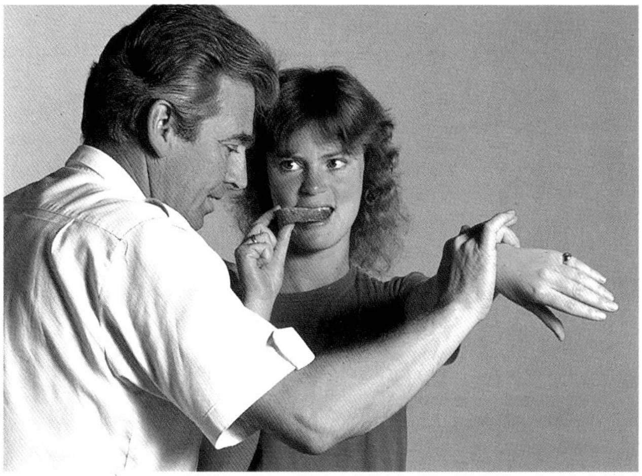

ABOVE: A kinesiologist will use several techniques to test muscle strength. Here a piece of toast is used to test for wheat sensitivity.

lifestyle. This background information enables him to build a picture of you and possible causes of your problem. He will then ask if you wish to proceed as it is believed that you must be a willing participant in your own treatment, if it is to work.

The diagnosis and treatment will vary depending on the practitioner. However, typically you will be asked to sit or lie on the treatment couch either fully clothed or undressed to your underwear. The tests are painless, a common one would involve the practitioner holding your arm or leg to isolate the muscle that he wants to test. He would then touch a point on your body, which is linked by a meridian to that particular muscle, while quickly and gently pressing down on the limb. You would have to try to resist this pressure. If you can it is a sign that the corresponding body part is healthy, but if your limb weakens under the pressure, it shows an energy imbalance in the related body part.

Another test, which is used especially for food sensitivities is to place a small piece of a suspect food under your tongue while testing the corresponding muscle in the same way.

The kinesiologist will note all weaknesses and imbalances revealed by the tests in order of priority. To bring about a lasting improvement he must correct the most important problem first and subsequent problems in descending order of importance. When your specific problems has been diagnosed, then the kinesiologist should also check for imbalances of the immune, endocrine, urinary and digestive systems and assess your nutritional status. When the diagnosis is complete, he will either give or recommend treatment. What this involves will depend greatly on your needs and the kinesiologist's additional training. Practitioners are usually trained in some other therapies such as massage, osteopathy, chiropractic, nutritional therapy, colonic hydrotherapy, acupuncture and Bach Flower Remedies.

How many sessions do I need?

Many people feel better after the first session, but most people tend to need several treatments. However, if you are feeling no improvement after three to six visits, it is unlikely that this therapy is working for you.

Which problems can it help?

Kinesiology is not a "cure" for any problem. It is concerned with finding and correcting minor problems before they become a major illness – what doctors call "subclinical" problems. It addresses many niggling little health problems that cannot be diagnosed or named because they are only precursors to illnesses. Food sensitivities, digestive problems, any joint stiffness, most aches and pains, headaches, backache and phobias can all be relieved by kinesiology.

Is it safe?

Kinesiology is a gentle, noninvasive therapy, with no side-effects. It is perfectly safe for people of all ages and states of health, even babies and pregnant women.

IRIDOLOGY

What is a iridology?

Iridology is the examination of the iris of the eye to ascertain the state of an individual's health and their tendency to develop a particular disease. Health practitioners have long believed that our eyes reveal much about our health. But it was only in the last century that a Hungarian doctor, Ignatz von Peczeley, discovered how detailed that information could be. As a child, von Peczeley was playing with an owl when he accidently broke the bird's leg. As he did so, he noticed a black mark appear in the owl's eye. Years later, when working as a homeopath, von Peczeley noticed a similar mark in the eye of a patient with a broken leg. Further investigations revealed to him that many signs of ill health registered in the iris of the eye.

However, iridology is not about diagnosing disease. It is concerned with detecting tendencies to ill health and taking measures to prevent those tendencies developing into disease.

How does it work?

Practitioners examine the color, texture and markings of the eye. The left iris relates to the left-hand side of the body and the right iris to the right-hand side. Color can give a general indication about constitution. For example, blue-eyed people have a tendency to develop acid conditions such as arthritis and ulcers, while brown-eyed people may have problems metabolizing fats, which could lead to arteriosclerosis or gallbladder problems. Mixed irises such as green or grey are known as "biliary" and indicate a tendency to digestive disorders. Spots of color, the fibers of the iris and the positioning of marks are all significant.

Iridologists use a detailed eye chart, which maps out how each part of the eye relates to a part of the body. The stomach, for example, is plotted immediately around the pupil in both irises and the skin is located in the outer rim. Using the map the practitioner detects potential physical and psychological problems.

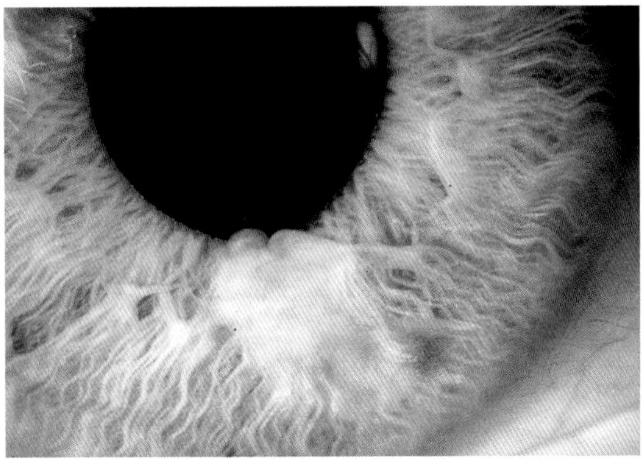

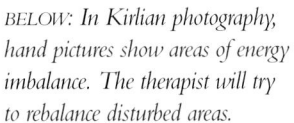

LEFT: In iridology, the eye's color and markings are studied in detail as they can indicate problems elsewhere in the body.

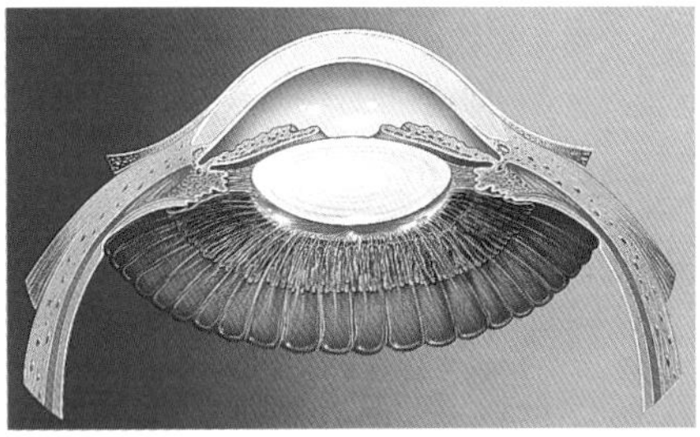

RIGHT: A detailed eye chart is used by iridologists to show how each part of the eye relates to other areas of the body.

BELOW: In Kirlian photography, hand pictures show areas of energy imbalance. The therapist will try to rebalance disturbed areas.

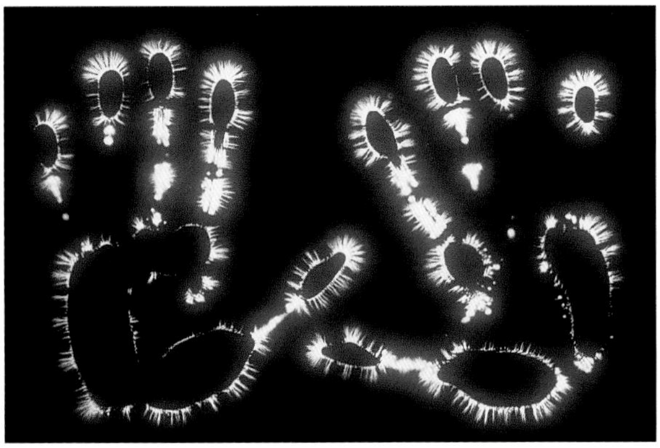

What happens in a consultation?

Some practitioners such as homeopaths and naturopaths use iridology in their diagnosis, but they may not be as detailed as an iridologist. A first visit with an iridologist usually lasts an hour. A good practitioner will rely only on the information he reads from your eyes:

- *He will look at your eyes with a small torch and a magnifying glass.*
- *He may then video the eye or take a photographic slide of it using a special camera and project the slide onto a big screen so that he can view the iris in detail.*

None of this procedure hurts or damages your eyes. The practitioner will talk through any obvious signs he has spotted with you there and then and may later compile a detailed analysis for you to keep. Before you leave you will be asked to complete a questionnaire about your health, medical history, lifestyle and diet, to be used as back-up information in prescribing treatment. The session will conclude with the practitioner recommending lifestyle changes or giving you some nutritional advice. If he is qualified to do so, he may also prescribe treatment. Otherwise, he may recommend that you see a suitable alternative practitioner or visit your doctor.

How many sessions do I need?

You may need only one appointment, although some people like to have a check-up every few months or once a year.

Which problems can it help?

Iridology is not used to diagnose illnesses, but to detect problems that can lead to illness. For example, an iridologist may be able to tell if your kidneys are having to work too hard or if your digestion is sluggish. He may also pick up on inherited predispositions to diseases such as heart problems or arthritis.

Is it safe?

Iridology is perfectly safe for people of all ages and levels of fitness. It is not intended as a substitute for conventional diagnostic tests. Iridologists frequently practice other therapies. Check that yours is qualified in the therapy with which he intends to treat you.

KIRLIAN PHOTOGRAPHY

What is a Kirlian photography?

Kirlian photography was developed in 1939 by a Russian electrician called Semyon Kirlian and his wife Valentina. The technique is a way of photographing the quality of the energy of the person or object. It is based on the belief that we are electrical beings and that human electrical energy can be photographed and analyzed. When it is used with people, the feet and hands are the parts most commonly photographed.

How does it work?

You place your fingertips, toes or hands on photographic plates on a machine that emits a high-frequency electrical signal. The image produced indicates the quality of your energy by showing your capacity to resonate with the frequency that is emitted through the plate. The image varies depending on how you feel. Sometimes it does not register at all, for example, if you are in shock or exhausted. If you are very worked up, on the other hand, you could produce an image which would have erratic "splines," the name for the white "hairy" fuzz around the outline of the prints. The therapist looks at the splines, and at the continuity of the "corona" or outline of the image, for information about the quality of your energy.

What happens in a consultation?

Kirlian photography is used in many ways. The most common method is the two-plate technique, which takes two photographs, one of the fingertips, the other of the toes. This technique is sometimes used by acupuncturists to back up their initial diagnosis. The pictures reveal imbalances of yin and yang between the left and right sides of the body, and each finger or toe relates to an acupuncture meridian (see Acupuncture pages 10–19).

A single-plate technique is used more to photograph objects or as a tool for personal growth. The therapist takes one photograph of both hands or feet and the image indicates your current state of energy. "Body logic counselors" use this technique to show you where you are holding tension and whether that tension is causing physical problems. It is not diagnostic in the sense that the therapist would use the image to detect stomach problems, for example, but if you have stomach problems she could relate them to how you are handling your energy. The session usually lasts an hour.

You may be asked to complete a questionnaire about yourself, but the therapist will not look at it before she explains your photograph. To take the photograph she will ask you to lay your hands as flat as is comfortable on the photographic pad. It takes about seven seconds to take the photograph, during which time you can feel a mildly "fizzy" sensation in your hands. She will then discuss your picture and the areas of imbalance, and use a simple balancing technique to enable you to feel more "centered." To understand yourself better is the goal of body logic. The therapist will want you to understand what throws your body off center and will use the balancing technique to illustrate how you can use your awareness to control your reactions to stress and begin to resolve some of the problems it triggers. She may take a second photograph to compare with the first, so you can see the change that occurs in your energy when you begin to understand yourself.

How many sessions do I need?

Usually just one, with perhaps a follow-up session six months or a year later.

Which problems can it help?

It can help people who have lost their identity after divorce, job loss or when their children leave home. It has been used in research to monitor the effects of medication in controlling chronic (long-term) conditions, to pinpoint the most fertile period in the menstrual cycle of sub-fertile women and to show the stage of development of a cancer so that the most appropriate treatment can be given.

Is it safe?

Kirlian photography is safe for everyone providing you do not have any metal present in your body. Metal objects such as pacemakers, pins or plates interfere with the imaging as do wheelchairs, occasionally.

This therapy is not suitable for babies, but can be beneficial for children. It has been used with pregnant women with no known side-effects.

Clinical studies – Iridology

There have been two interesting medical studies done in the past few years on the Arcus senilis/cholesterol ring (eye markings), which appear in the eye. Both studies confirmed the relationship between these features and the incidence of cardiovascular diseases.

In 1987, the Los Angeles Herald Examiner reported the findings of an eight-year study conducted by the National Heart, Lung and Blood Institute. The study revealed that men under 50 who had an Arcus senilis in their eyes had over double the risk of having a heart attack. The risk was also further increased by four times in the men who were found to have excess blood cholesterol levels. (**59**)

In another study in January 1990, reported in the Journal of the American Optometric Association, researchers found that there was a direct correlation – regardless of age – between the appearance of an Arcus senilis and high-serum cholesterol levels in patients. The researchers discovered that people who had an Arcus senilis/cholesterol ring in their eyes had significantly higher serum cholesterol levels in their blood than people who did not. (**60**) (*For clinical references see How to use this book*).

FOR INFORMATION ON HOW TO CHOOSE A DIAGNOSTIC THERAPIST SEE THE DIRECTORY.

INDEX OF SYMPTOMS

CIRCULATORY SYSTEM

What is it?

The circulatory system consists of the heart, blood vessels and blood. The heart is a small fist-shaped muscular pump, situated in the thorax. It has four chambers: the upper chambers or atria, and the lower chambers or ventricles. The right of the heart is separated from the left by a central wall (the septum).

The heart is used as a "double pump." Blood is sent to the lungs by the right ventricle. Here it collects breathed-in oxygen and releases carbon dioxide picked up from the peripheral tissues. This oxygenated blood then re-enters the heart, on the left, to be pumped round by the left ventricle.

Arteries and their branches, arterioles, carry blood from the heart. Their walls need to be strong to withstand the pressure that the blood experiences at this point in circulation. The arterioles divide into tiny capillaries through whose walls the blood supplies oxygen, nutrients and hormones, and also collects waste products and carbon dioxide for removal.

The capillaries eventually merge into venules and veins. By now the blood pressure is relatively low, so these vessels have thin walls with valves. The veins carry blood back to the right atrium.

A 155 lb adult male will have between 1–1 ¼ gal of blood circulating around his body, and have 5,000,000 red blood cells per cubic millimeter of blood. There are only 8,000 white blood cells per cubic millimeter; they help fight disease and maintain immunity. Platelets are crucial in blood clotting as they form a "plug" at leaking blood vessels.

What can go wrong?

The most serious problem to affect the circulatory system is if the pump is damaged, that is, a heart attack. The patient may have a severe indigestion-like pain in the chest or may collapse and die suddenly. This is the most common cause of death in the West, and is usually due to clogged arteries or *atherosclerosis*. Mild *atherosclerosis*, where not enough blood reaches the heart muscle, causes *angina*. A low-fat, low-cholesterol diet can help prevent heart disease. *High blood pressure* is probably the most common circulatory disease and can cause organ damage and lead to a stroke or heart attack. Blood disorders include *anemia* (inadequate red cells) and *leukemia*, a cancer of the bone marrow.

The heart pumps blood to carry oxygen via the arteries and capillaries (red). Blood returns to the heart carrying carbon dioxide via the veins (blue).

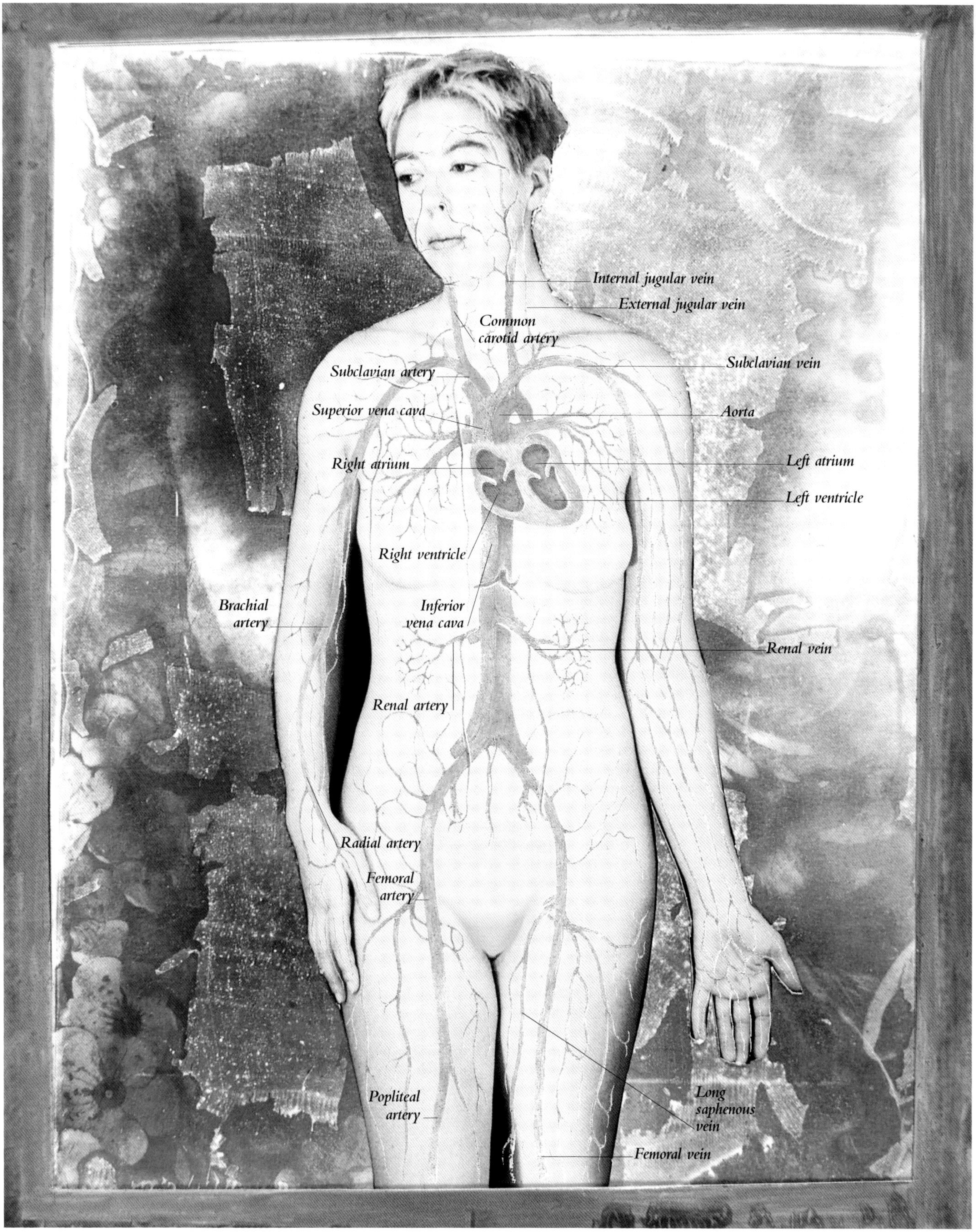
Internal jugular vein
External jugular vein
Common carotid artery
Subclavian vein
Subclavian artery
Superior vena cava
Aorta
Right atrium
Left atrium
Left ventricle
Right ventricle
Brachial artery
Inferior vena cava
Renal vein
Renal artery
Radial artery
Femoral artery
Long saphenous vein
Popliteal artery
Femoral vein

ANEMIA

What is it?

Anemia is a deficiency of the hemoglobin (the oxygen-carrying chemical of the red blood cells) in the blood. Under normal circumstances, hemoglobin is maintained in the correct concentrations by an exact balance between the production of red blood cells in the bone marrow and the destruction of red blood cells in the spleen. There are several different types of anemia.

Anemia has widespread effects, including weakness, headaches, dizziness, fatigue and breathlessness. Elderly patients, or those with very low hemoglobin, may develop heart failure with shortness of breath and swelling of the legs (edema) or worsening of angina. The skin, lips and lining of the eyes may appear pale and there may be other symptoms such as a sore tongue in iron or B12 deficiency. Jaundice may result from hemolytic anemias where red cells are broken down prematurely in the body.

Causes

Iron is an essential constituent of hemoglobin, and iron deficiency is the commonest cause of anemia. It may result from:

- *Poor diet*
- *Failure to absorb iron from food (malabsorption syndrome)*
- *Excessive blood loss from heavy menstrual bleeding, peptic ulcers, piles or bowel cancer)*

Other causes of anemia include:

- *Vitamin B12 deficiency (pernicious anemia)*
- *In inherited anemias (for example sickle cell anemia and thalassemia) the hemoglobin is abnormal in structure or not produced in sufficient amounts and the red cells are rapidly destroyed.*
- *Chronic diseases such as tuberculosis, rheumatoid arthritis, chronic renal failure and cancers.*
- *Pregnancy, when the level of hemoglobin falls to make the blood flow more easily through the uterus and placenta; pregnancy represents a drain of a small amount of iron.*
- *Bone marrow disorders such as leukemia* *(see page 171).*

As iron deficiency is the most common cause it is usually considered first, but it is important to confirm the diagnosis and to establish the cause of the iron deficiency by taking a dietary history, enquiring about bleeding and arranging appropriate investigations. Iron deficiency in men and post-menopausal women should always be investigated.

Vegetarians and vegans are more likely to suffer from iron-deficiency anemia because high-fiber foods such as pulses and whole grains bind iron, which makes absorption more difficult. Iron intake in vegetarians and vegans also tends to be less than in those eating a diet containing animal products.

Orthodox treatment

Depending on the type of anemia, treatment would consist of one or more of the following:

- *Iron supplements, usually by tablet but occasionally by injection*
- *For pernicious anemia, injections of vitamin B12 (usually given throughout life)*
- *For severe anemias, a blood transfusion is given*

ALTERNATIVE TREATMENT

Homeopathy

Remedies will be prescribed according to the patient's constitution. A homeopath may also recommend a varied diet, rich in iron and vitamin B12.

Chinese herbalism

A Chinese herbalist will diagnose the exact cause of the anemia based on the overall condition and using pulse and tongue diagnosis. He will prescribe a decoction which is tailor-made for each sufferer. Chinese herbalism is particularly good for iron-deficiency anemia, as many herbs act as a blood tonic. Only an extremely skilled practitioner could diagnose and successfully treat pernicious anemia.

Western herbalism

Treatment will be based upon individual diagnosis, but herbs which are rich in iron will almost always be prescribed (for example, nettles). Herbs which improve absorption and the functioning of the digestive system may also be useful.

Nutritional therapy

Anemia is usually caused by nutritional deficiencies, mostly iron, but also vitamin B6, B12, folic acid or zinc. Any such deficiencies can be treated according to individual diagnosis. In women, heavy menstrual periods may lead to excessive loss of iron, and the underlying cause of these may also be addressed by the therapist.

Other therapies

Spiritual healing can improve the body's ability to cure itself, and problems like poor absorption of iron or improper production of hemoglobin may be successfully treated. An **acupuncturist** may suggest moxibustion, which will address underlying weakness or energy blockages. **Kinesiology** can be used to determine iron deficiency and to check various supplements to find the most suitable. Raw spinach, capsicum capsules, vitamin A and kinesiology balancing may be suggested. If the anemia is due to nutritional deficiency, the standard **macrobiotic** diet may help. **Tai chi** and **shiatsu** are often recommended.

High Blood Pressure (Hypertension)

What is it?

Blood pressure varies constantly within the cardiac cycle of contraction and relaxation of the heart and is also affected by the level of physical exertion, anxiety, stress, emotion and other factors. It is determined by the force and volume of the heart output with each beat and on the resistance offered by the larger blood vessels. High blood pressure (hypertension) is a sustained rise in blood pressure above the normal and is associated with an increased risk of stroke and premature death.

Causes

Ninety percent of cases are of what is known as essential hypertension, meaning that there is no obvious underlying cause, although lifestyle factors such as obesity and alcohol and sugar intake play a role. There may also be genetic and ethnic factors (there is a higher incidence of hypertension in people of African origin). In societies with a Western-type diet and lifestyle, blood pressure rises with age.

The other 10 percent of cases have an underlying cause, which may be:

- *Diabetes (see page 200) or other endocrine disorders.*
- *Kidney disease (see page 238).*
- *Pregnancy (see pages 220–221).*
- *Medication such as the contraceptive pill or steroids.*

Contrary to popular belief, raised blood pressure seldom causes symptoms and is often found on routine screening.

SUSTAINED HIGH BLOOD PRESSURE IS VERY DAMAGING TO THE ARTERIES, CAUSING ACCELERATED ATHEROMA. IT LEADS TO PREMATURE HEART DISEASE AND STROKES AND AGGRAVATES KIDNEY DISEASE.

Orthodox treatment

The treatment of hypertension involves a change in lifestyle and, if necessary, the prescription of drugs. Four main classes are used:

- *Diuretics act on the kidneys to lose salt and also act directly on the blood vessels to reduce their resistance.*
- *Beta-blockers lower blood pressure by slowing the heart and reducing the force of contraction of the heart muscle.*
- *Vasodilators act on the arteries to widen them.*
- *ACE inhibitors act both as vasodilators and diuretics by inhibiting the synthesis of angiotensin, a powerful vasoconstrictor which also acts on the adrenal glands to retain sodium.*

Alternative Treatment

Naturopathy

A naturopath will probably suggest a diet low in animal fats, salt, sugar and stimulants such as caffeine and nicotine. An individual dietetic program would be tailored to the sufferer's needs. Hydrotherapy – in particular the contrast bathing of feet – may prove useful to the patient. Applied nutrition may include mineral therapy (for example magnesium and potassium), and relaxation and meditation instruction will be supplied.

Autogenic training

Autogenic training is very effective for borderline high blood pressure on the upper limits of normal, when no medication has been used. Very high blood pressure controlled by medication needs a considerable period of time before benefit is evident, but it can have an excellent result.

Alexander Technique

Blood pressure has been shown to drop markedly as a result of Alexander Technique reeducation. It seems likely that since most blood vessels pass through muscles, any over-contraction of the muscles will make it difficult for the heart to pump blood through the constricted vessels. Reduction in muscle tension can lead to less pressure on the heart and therefore lowered blood pressure.

Acupuncture

Acupuncture has proved very good in the treatment of high blood pressure, addressing underlying weaknesses and blockages in the energy system. The acupuncturist will look closely at lifestyle, eating habits and hereditary aspects. An auricular therapist may also provide successful treatment.

Nutritional therapy

A nutritional therapist will look at the cause of the high blood pressure. A good whole food diet rich in fruit and vegetables, regular consumption of oily fish and strict rationing of fatty or sugary foods will be suggested for those who are predisposed to develop it.

Other therapies

Control of blood pressure is helped by **osteopathy** because of the relationship between the joints, muscles, diaphragm and nerves controlling the blood pressure. A **Western herbalist** may suggest herbs to dilate blood vessels and reduce blood pressure, work on the heart muscle and relieve stress. **Relaxation and visualization**, **radionics** and **reflexology** may be useful. A **macrobiotic** diet may help if the cause of high blood pressure is excess weight. An **Ayurvedic** practitioner may recommend a selection of preparations that can be taken orally, along with *Panchakarma* to assist long-term recovery.

ATHEROSCLEROSIS

What is it?

Atherosclerosis is a degenerative disorder of large and medium-sized arteries characterized by the formation of atheromatous plaques on the inner lining. The plaques are localized and contain a central core of fats, mainly cholesterol, surrounded by smooth muscle cells and fibrous tissue. The plaques affect blood flow by causing narrowing and also weaken the vessel wall, which may balloon out, causing aneurysms (abnormal dilation) which may rupture. The surface of the plaque may act as a focus for blood clots and cause acute blockages, or plaques may split and bleed, or send off showers of fragments which cause blockages further down the arterial tree.

Half of all deaths are caused by circulatory disease and 40 percent of middle-aged men have evidence of atheroma. Although the changes are widespread, the arteries supplying the heart (coronary arteries), the brain (carotid arteries) and the legs (femoral arteries) bear most of the burden, causing heart attacks and angina, strokes and pain in the legs on walking respectively. By the time the patient experiences symptoms the disease is well advanced.

Causes

Risk factors that are known to contribute to the development of atherosclerosis include:

- *Cigarette smoking, which doubles the risk of heart disease and accelerates arterial disease in the legs.*
- *High blood pressure (see page 163), which accelerates the development of atheroma.*
- *Age – atherosclerosis is primarily a disorder of middle and later life.*
- *High blood cholesterol in the form of low-density lipoproteins.*
- *Gender – men are more affected than women, though after the menopause the rates in men and women are equal.*
- *A history of close relatives developing arterial disease under the age of 55.*
- *Diabetes (see page 200) – diabetics have twice the risk of strokes, three times the risk of heart attacks and are 50 times more likely to have amputation of a foot for gangrene.*

IT IS IMPORTANT TO ENSURE THAT THE DIET IS RICH IN ANTIOXIDANTS (VITAMINS A, C AND E AND THE MINERAL SELENIUM), WHICH HAVE BEEN PROVEN TO PREVENT THE BUILD-UP OF CHOLESTEROL DEPOSITS IN THE BLOODSTREAM.

Orthodox treatment

Orthodox medical practitioners view atherosclerosis in much the same way as do alternative therapists. The following will be suggested:

- *Reducing risk factors by making changes in lifestyle such as giving up smoking (the most important), losing weight, taking regular exercise, drinking alcohol only in moderation, reducing saturated fats in the diet and increasing the amount of fresh fruit and vegetables and complex carbohydrates.*
- *Drug treatment for high blood pressure and high blood cholesterol where dietary treatment has failed.*
- *Low-dose aspirin to discourage blood clots and reduce acute events like strokes and heart attacks.*
- *Where drug treatments fail, surgery such as balloon angioplasty (where a tube is passed down an artery under X-ray guidance and a balloon is blown up to widen a narrowed area) or bypass grafting may be suggested.*

ALTERNATIVE TREATMENT

Western herbalism

Some herbal remedies have a beneficial action on the arteries, reducing build-up of plaque and perhaps helping to remove existing deposits. Herbs will be prescribed according to individual diagnosis and the symptom pattern.

Naturopathy

A naturopath may recommend a diet low in animal fat, salt and sugar. Individual dietetic treatment will be tailored to the levels of blood fats which may need to be determined by a laboratory test. General guidelines on lifestyle will be offered.

Yoga

For atherosclerosis a yoga therapist may suggest gentle *asanas*, *pranayama*, relaxation, meditation, *shat kriyas* and advice on diet and counseling.

Other therapies

Macrobiotics provides excellent advice on the prevention of atherosclerosis, including the standard macrobiotic diet with emphasis on the intake of shiitake mushrooms in soups, stews or teas three times a week. In **Ayurvedic medicine** a practitioner will prescribe formulas for cleansing the circulatory system and *panchakarma* therapy for the management of the condition. A **Chinese herbalist** may achieve beneficial effects by using herbs to reduce clogging, cool excess heat and regulate the circulation of the blood.

Reflexologists always work holistically before paying special attention to problem areas, so a practitioner of this therapy will undertake complete treatment; this will include some relaxation techniques and will place particular emphasis upon the liver, circulatory system and the lymph glands. Both **tai chi** and **shiatsu** are also often recommended as helpful therapies for the treatment of this condition.

Angina

What is it?

Angina, properly called angina pectoris, is a tight, constricting pain which occurs in the middle of the chest, often spreading to the neck and left side of the jaw and down the left arm. It may also be felt between the shoulder blades. It is caused by narrowing of the arteries and consequent lack of oxygen to the muscle of the heart. Because it occurs when the heart is required to work harder, common causes include exercise, cold weather, large meals and strong emotion. Characteristically, the pain comes on with exertion, is relieved by rest and only lasts a few minutes, although it may be severe and frightening.

ATTACKS OF ANGINA OCCURRING MORE FREQUENTLY, LASTING LONGER, PRECIPITATED BY SLIGHT EXERTION OR COMING WHEN AT REST, CAN PRECEDE A HEART ATTACK AND SHOULD BE REPORTED TO YOUR DOCTOR.

Causes

Angina is more common in men than in women, although women are more often affected following the menopause. Causes of the condition include:

- *Coronary heart disease (narrowing of the arteries supplying the heart muscle, see opposite).*
- *Cigarette smoking.*
- *Diabetes (see page 200) – sufferers are three to five times as likely to develop angina as nondiabetics.*
- *High blood pressure (see page 163).*
- *High cholesterol.*
- *Excess weight and obesity (see page 252).*
- *Anemia (see page 162).*
- *Aortic stenosis (the narrowing of the aortic valve in the heart).*
- *Arrhythmias (abnormal heart rhythms).*

BY LIMITING EXERTION, GIVING UP SMOKING AND SEEKING MEDICAL TREATMENT, SUFFERERS CAN LIVE QUITE SAFELY WITH THE CONDITION FOR MANY YEARS.

Orthodox treatment

Giving up smoking, control of blood pressure and treatment of underlying causes are important. Drugs used include nitrates and other vasodilators which reduce the work of the heart by lowering the blood pressure. Beta-blockers lower blood pressure by reducing heart rate and force of contraction. Low-dose aspirin is thought to prevent heart attacks. If the coronary arteries are dangerously narrowed they may be widened by balloon angioplasty (see opposite). Bypass surgery is another option.

Alternative Treatment

Homeopathy

Treatment will be dependent on the cause of the angina, and recurrent angina will be treated constitutionally. Specific remedies may be used during mild or infrequent attacks, these include:

• Cactus when the chest is constricted, there is difficulty breathing, a cold sweat, pain down the left arm and low blood pressure in the sufferer.

• Spigelia where there is difficulty breathing, which is relieved by lying on the right-hand side with the head raised, palpitations, thirst for drinks of hot water.

• Latrodectus where there is violent pain in the chest and numbness in the fingers.

• Naja when the pulse is irregular, stimulants make the condition worse, and there is a feeling of weight on the heart. The sufferer may be afraid of death and be extremely anxious.

• Glonoinum when there is a sensation of blood flooding into the heart, difficulty in breathing, faintness, throbbing sensation all over the body, and heat making the symptoms worse.

Rolfing

In several of the sessions, rolfing works around the diaphragm, mid and upper spine and pectorals. Releasing these areas specifically can allow more space around the heart (which is held in place by the tascia called the pericardium), easing constriction. The relaxation and slower breathing that follows also helps to normalize the circulation.

Reflexology

Reflexologists always work holistically before paying special attention to problem areas. Therefore, complete treatment including relaxation techniques will be undertaken, with particular emphasis on the heart, adrenal glands, lymphatic glands and solar plexus.

Color therapy

Anginal pains due to tension may be improved by the use of color by a qualified color practitioner.

Other therapies

Angina may respond to **macrobiotics**, depending on the cause. A **naturopath** may recommend dietary changes, applied nutrition (for example, magnesium, potassium, vitamins E and C), relaxation instruction and graded exercise. Symptoms may subside as anxiety is reduced through **autogenic training**. A **yoga** therapist may recommend gentle *asanas*, *pranayama*, relaxation, meditation, *shat kriyas* and advice on diet, and counseling. **Tai chi** and **shiatsu** are often recommended.

Palpitations

What are they?

Palpitation is an unpleasant awareness of the heartbeat and may be experienced as a thumping sensation in the chest, consciousness of missed or extra beats or a racing of the heart. There may be awareness of the heart's pumping when lying on the left side, and anxious patients may be distressed by the rapid heart rate associated with emotion. Palpitations may be an important symptom of heart disease, especially if they are frequent and prolonged or associated with chest pain, dizzy spells or fainting, shortness of breath or worsening cardiac failure.

Causes

There are numerous causes for this condition, some of which may be serious. These include:

- *Tachycardia, when the heart suddenly beats very quickly.*
- *Extreme fright, strenuous exercise, fever or hyperthyroidism.*
- *Any cause of heart disease, for example, valvular heart disease, high blood pressure or coronary artery disease.*
- *Ectopic heartbeats, experienced as premature beats followed by an extended pause, usually caused by alcohol, caffeine, amphetamines and tobacco. They are common and can often be abolished by exercise. However, they may occur when the heart has been damaged by coronary artery disease.*

Orthodox treatment

Brief palpitations require no special treatment but if they are frequent, prolonged or are accompanied by symptoms such as dizzy spells or shortness of breath, then treatment is important. Drugs such as beta-blockers may be used and occasionally a pacemaker may be fitted.

Alternative Treatment

Homeopathy

The underlying cause will be treated constitutionally, but the following specific remedies may be useful:

- Nux when palpitations occur after overindulgence in food or alcohol, or after a bout of nervous energy.
- Cactus when palpitations are violent, made worse by lying on the left side, and worse before the menstrual period. They will be accompanied by dizziness, shortness of breath and flatulence.
- Lachesis when there is fainting, a constricted sensation across the chest, anxiety and menopausal symptoms.
- Spigelia when the breath is smelly, and there is great thirst for hot drinks, which seem to help.
- Moschus when palpitations occur after hysteria or exposure to cold; there is a trembling heart, weak pulse and possibly fainting.
- Pulsatilla when the palpitations are brought on by rich or fatty foods, or heat.
- Digitalis when palpitations begin with the sensation that the heart has stopped.
- Aconite when the symptoms occur suddenly, especially following a shock, and there is a fear of dying.

Ayurvedic medicine

An Ayurvedic practitioner would undertake *samana* treatment using special herbs, chosen according to the specific characteristics of the patient. The *panchakarma* method would be used for detoxification.

Kinesiology

Every patient would be treated individually, but the following action would probably be undertaken:

- A check for any imbalances in the endocrine, immune and urinary systems.
- A spinal examination.
- A nutritional analysis, looking for any deficiencies.
- An analysis of the digestive system, looking for any sensitivities.
- Dietary and lifestyle counseling, including advice about pure water consumption, bowel movements and cleansing, stress levels, anxiety, fear and phobias, rest, sleep, relaxation and exercise.
- Adrenal support and nutrition for stress.

Alexander Technique

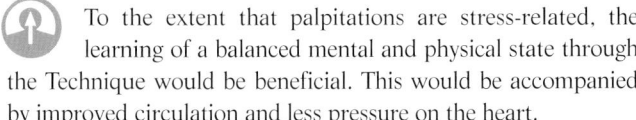

To the extent that palpitations are stress-related, the learning of a balanced mental and physical state through the Technique would be beneficial. This would be accompanied by improved circulation and less pressure on the heart.

Naturopathy

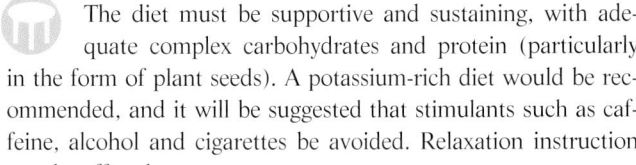

The diet must be supportive and sustaining, with adequate complex carbohydrates and protein (particularly in the form of plant seeds). A potassium-rich diet would be recommended, and it will be suggested that stimulants such as caffeine, alcohol and cigarettes be avoided. Relaxation instruction may be offered.

Other therapies

Depending on the cause, a **Western herbalist** may suggest herbs to relax the system; others may slow heart rate directly. An **acupuncturist** may address the underlying weakness or blockage in the energy system as well as looking at lifestyle and diet. A **nutritional therapist** will recommend reducing stimulants such as coffee: deficiencies of B vitamins or magnesium may also be to blame. **Rolfing** may help. **Massage** may be useful if the condition is stress-related. With **Autogenic training**, palpitations may be eliminated by learning to switch off the "fight-and-flight" impulse.

HEART FAILURE

What is it?

In spite of the name, heart failure does not mean that the heart has stopped altogether; it is in fact a condition in which the heart loses its ability to pump blood efficiently throughout the body and can no longer fulfill its function adequately. It is not an immediately life-threatening disease, and, depending on the underlying cause, may be treated and controlled.

Heart failure sometimes affects just one side of the heart, in which case it is known as left-sided or right-sided failure; if it affects both sides, it is called congestive heart failure. In left-sided heart failure, the veins that carry blood from the lungs become engorged and back pressure from the blood causes the lungs to become swollen and congested. The main symptom is therefore breathlessness, at first after exercise, but as the disease progresses even when at rest. In right-sided failure, back pressure in the blood circulation from the heart into veins in other parts of the body causes accumulation of fluid in the tissues (edema), particularly in the ankles and legs. Enlargement of the liver and congestion of the intestines are common, causing indigestion. In congestive heart failure, there will probably be symptoms of both right-sided and left-sided failure.

Causes

Left-sided heart failure is often caused by these problems:

- *Coronary artery disease (see page 164).*
- *High blood pressure (see page 163).*
- *A valve defect or congenital heart defect such as aortic stenosis.*
- *Anemia, overactive thyroid gland and arrhythmias (irregular heartbeat), which may also cause congestive heart failure.*

Right-sided heart failure is normally caused by:

- *Most commonly, left-sided heart failure.*
- *Chronic chest diseases such as chronic bronchitis or emphysema (see page 177).*
- *Coronary artery disease, valve defects or congenital heart defect.*

THE MOST COMMON CAUSE OF HEART FAILURE IN ADULTS IN THE WEST IS CORONARY ARTERY DISEASE.

Orthodox treatment

The traditional bed rest is no longer advised, but patients should refrain from exertion. By reducing excess fluid, diuretics relieve symptoms of breathlessness and edema. The ACE-inhibitor drugs help the heart by lowering blood pressure and acting as diuretics. Treatment will also include drugs to control arrhythmias (irregular heartbeat) and vasodilators, which reduce the work of the heart. While surgery is life-saving if there is an underlying anatomical problem such as a valvular or congenital heart disease, the symptoms of most heart failure patients can be successfully controlled by the use of drugs alone.

ALTERNATIVE TREATMENT

Naturopathy

A naturopath may suggest a supportive nutritional program, with a dietetic program to encourage the regulation of fluid and diuresis. Applied nutrition, perhaps in the form of vitamin E, magnesium and potassium, may be offered. Herbal and homeopathic remedies may be prescribed.

Homeopathy

In the case of heart failure constitutional treatment is recommended, but it is essential that you place yourself only in the care of a registered professional. The following specific remedies may also be advised, as well as individual treatment for edema, atherosclerosis or high blood pressure, where appropriate:

• Arsenicum when there is advanced heart disease and fluid in the lungs.

• Carbo veg when symptoms are accompanied by chilliness and blue extremities.

• Cactus when the symptoms are accompanied by those of angina, with pain in the left arm.

• Digitalis when palpitations occur at slight exertion, and when there are swollen ankles, blue lips, a feeling that the heart has stopped, and also an irregular pulse.

• Naja when symptoms are accompanied by angina, an irregular pulse, anxiety, and fear of dying.

• Spigelia when the symptoms are alleviated when the head is raised and by lying on the left side.

Yoga

For heart failure a yoga therapist may recommend gentle *asanas*, *pranayama*, relaxation, meditation, *shat kriyas*, advice on diet and counseling.

Other therapies

In **Ayurvedic medicine**, special heart tonifiers and stimulating preparations will be prescribed. A **Western herbalist** may use herbs with cardio-active properties and/or diuretics to remove excess fluid from the system, alongside general treatment. A **Chinese herbal** practitioner may suggest aromatic stimulants, herbal sedatives, herbs to decongest the system and tonic herbs for the blood or for increasing the yang energy of the heart and kidneys. **Acupuncture** may be useful. Although **autogenic training** does not cure it, regular practice can contribute to the prevention of heart disease.

CHILBLAINS

What are they?

Chilblains are an abnormal reaction to cold of the blood vessels under the skin. Under normal circumstances the vessels constrict to conserve heat, causing pallor of the skin. In a case of chilblains the area becomes extremely pale and possibly numb, with red or blue itchy, swollen areas of skin on the fingers and toes. They may be very painful and the skin may eventually break, which may in turn lead to infection.

Chilblains are more commonly found in people who suffer from poor circulation, and particularly elderly people, who may often develop chilblains on the backs of their legs as well; in general, women are more susceptible to them than men. Children may often get chilblains on their feet during the winter months.

Although chilblains are a nuisance, they are not likely to cause any lasting ill effects.

Causes

Chilblains are caused by the severe constriction of the blood vessels in the skin in response to cold. Local warming of cold skin by radiant heat leads to skin damage as the tissues' metabolism speeds up before the local blood supply increases to keep pace.

Orthodox treatment

Chilblains will usually heal on their own, without specific treatment. Protection from cold is very important; keeping the body core warm encourages blood vessels in the hands and feet to stay open. Keeping the hands and feet warm at all times in cold weather will help; always change damp gloves, socks and shoes as soon as possible. For severely affected people there are heated gloves available. If there is infection, antibiotic ointments may be applied. In the case of chilblains causing severe discomfort, a doctor may prescribe a vasodilator drug.

ALTERNATIVE TREATMENT

Homeopathy

There are a number of remedies which may be helpful, and not necessarily on a constitutional basis. If the following do not work within a couple of weeks, see your homeopath:

- Agaricus when the chilblains burn and itch, and when the skin is red and swollen and not relieved by applications of cold.
- Pulsatilla when the condition is worse when the limbs hang downward, and when the veins are swollen.
- Petroleum when the chilblains itch and burn, the skin is weepy and damp weather makes the condition worse.
- Calcarea when the conditions becomes worse in cold weather, the sufferer feels chilly, is prone to head sweats and puts on weight easily.

Western herbalism

Strong circulatory stimulants, used both locally as well as internally to improve the peripheral blood flow, are the most likely treatments to be offered for chilblains by a Western herbalist.

Kinesiology

A kinesiologist would provide treatment based on individual diagnosis. Tests for nutritional deficiencies would be undertaken; the spine would be checked and also the digestive system, in order to pinpoint any food sensitivities. There would be counseling on dietary matters, pure water consumption, bowel movements and cleansing, stress levels, rest, sleep, relaxation and exercise. In addition, the following treatment may be recommended:

- Capsicum (herbal remedy).
- Vitamin E supplementation.
- Evening primrose oil.
- Butcher's broom (herbal remedy).
- Regular kinesiology balancing.

Rolfing

Rolfing addresses the feet and leg areas, particularly in the second session, but also in later sessions. As a result of the muscles in these areas being able to slide and move more easily, circulation is improved.

Nutritional therapy

A nutritional therapist may suggest that although specific nutritional factors in chilblains are unclear, they are much more likely to occur when the diet is poor. Suggestions would therefore be made as to how to improve the diet.

Aromatherapy

Treatment may consist of foot and hand massage, with a blend of warming, circulation-enhancing oils, such as juniper, ginger or black pepper.

Other therapies

A **macrobiotic** diet with additional use of ginger in soups may be useful. **Shiatsu** massage and towel rubs can also help. In **Ayurvedic medicine,** *samana* therapy will be suggested for tridosha balance. **Acupuncture** may help to improve circulation. Chilblains often improve with **Autogenic training**, especially from the use of the warmth exercise. A **reflexologist** would offer complete treatment to improve overall circulation to the hands and feet, with particular emphasis on the heart.

VARICOSE VEINS

What are they?

Varicose veins are veins which are twisted and enlarged in both diameter and length. They are common in the legs but may also occur in the esophagus, scrotum, rectum, anus (see hemorrhoids, page 244) and vulva. In women, they are particularly troublesome in the legs and as hemorrhoids during pregnancy. Varicose veins may be a purely cosmetic problem with prominent unsightly grape-like veins or flare veins. However, if there is weakness of the valves in the deep veins or guarding the entrance to the deep system, back flow into the superficial vein system occurs. Symptoms of venous insufficiency, such as prominent distended veins, aching in the calves, swelling of the leg, pigmentation and purple discoloration, dry, flaky, thin and irritable skin (varicose eczema) and a tendency to ulcers which can be extensive and persistent, then result. Occasionally a varicose vein may rupture and bleed heavily.

Causes

Varicose veins are common and tend to run in families where there is an inherited weakness in the vessel walls or in the valves. The changes start where the superficial veins drain into the deep system at the knee or groin and the distension and varicosities spread throughout the system. The condition is aggravated by:

- *Obesity (see page 252).*
- *Pregnancy (see pages 220–221).*
- *Prolonged standing.*
- *Constipation (see page 243).*

Deep vein thrombosis causes varicose veins and venous insufficiency by blocking the deep veins and damaging the valves. Reflux of blood occurs from the deep to superficial system and varicose veins and venous insufficiency follow.

Orthodox treatment

Support of the surface veins by specially designed hosiery will prevent the blood from pooling and becoming stagnant in the veins, thus avoiding the build-up of toxins. Support hosiery will also divert the flow of blood from the surface to the deeper veins where the pumping action is stronger. Elastic bandages fulfill the same functions, but need to be applied correctly. Surgical treatment includes removing the varicosed veins (vein strip) or tying off the veins where the superficial system joins the deep system at the groin or where there are leaking perforating veins. Results are usually quite successful. There are also injections which can cause the affected veins to clot, so closing them off. This method is less reliably successful than stripping and so is less popular.

ALTERNATIVE TREATMENT

Homeopathy

Treatment will be constitutional, but your homeopath may recommend the following specific remedies. You should see your doctor if there is no marked improvement within two or three weeks, or if the condition deteriorates.

- Hamamelis when the veins feel sore and bruised. There may be hemorrhoids present.
- Carbo veg when the skin is mottled or discolored.
- Ferrum when the legs look pale, but become red easily; walking helps symptoms.
- Pulsatilla when warmth and swinging the legs make the condition worse, and the sufferer feels cold.

Western herbalism

A Western herbalist may recommend remedies to improve the venous blood flow, backed up by exercises, local applications and also dietary advice. With effort and patience a definite improvement is possible.

Rolfing

Rolfing addresses the feet and leg areas, particularly in the second session, but also in later sessions. As a result of the muscles in these areas being able to slide and move more easily, blood flow to the veins is improved.

Alexander Technique

The onset of varicose veins may have a postural component. The learning of an improved use of the body and of a more harmonious way of moving can help to alleviate such symptoms of misuse.

Other therapies

A **macrobiotics** practitioner will not be able to change or repair damaged veins, but further deterioration and relief from symptoms can be attained through the standard macrobiotic diet, by cutting out smoking and by adopting the recommended circulatory exercises. Herbal formulas, taken orally, with some *panchakarma* therapy for long-term management would be recommended by an **Ayurvedic** medical practitioner. **Acupuncture** may improve circulation. If the cause is associated with constipation, a **nutritional therapist** may recommend that the best prevention is a good diet with adequate fiber. A **naturopath** may recommend applied nutrition (for example, vitamin E and mineral therapy), attention to sluggish abdominal function and constipation, hydrotherapy, postural drainage and herbal tonics and astringents. **Reflexology** treatment will be individual, but with special emphasis on the endocrine glands, colon and circulatory system, avoiding working directly on the varicosities. **Tai chi** and **shiatsu** are often recommended.

Raynaud's Phenomenon

What is it?

Raynaud's phenomenon is a condition affecting the small arteries of the fingers and toes. In response to cold the arteries go into spasm and the fingers and toes become pale, cold and numb. They then become blue as a result of sluggish circulation; on warming up they turn red and the patient experiences a burning pain. The condition may be short-lived and affect the sufferer only sporadically in the early days, with the affected fingers and toes returning to normal. In severe cases these attacks last longer and occur more often, with damage to the vessel wall reducing blood flow and causing tissue damage with painful digital ulcers or, in fewer than one percent of cases, small patches of gangrene.

When the symptoms are present with no known cause, the condition is known as Raynaud's disease.

Causes

The condition affects five percent of the population and is most prevalent in women (90 percent of cases). It usually affects the fingers more than the toes. There is often a family history of Raynaud's phenomenon. Other causes include:

- *Sensitivity to certain drugs, including beta-blockers.*
- *Buerger's disease (inflammation of the arteries, nerves and veins, chiefly found in men below the age of 45 who are heavy smokers).*
- *Atherosclerosis (see page 164).*
- *Compression of the main artery in the arm.*
- *Occupational causes, especially the use of pneumatic drills.*
- *Scleroderma, a disease of unknown cause where the skin becomes bound down to underlying tissues and there is limitation of joint movement and involvement of internal organs.*

If you suffer from Raynaud's phenomenon, cold should be avoided, as should cigarette smoking, since nicotine causes the blood vessels to constrict.

Orthodox treatment

The treatment is the same for both Raynaud's phenomenon and Raynaud's disease, except that in the former the underlying cause will also be addressed. Keeping warm by means of appropriate heating and clothing, including hats, gloves, thick socks and boots, helps by reducing the arterial spasm. Electrically heated gloves are also available to keep the hands warm. Various drugs are used to relax the muscles in the artery walls, including calcium antagonists, for example, nifedipine. These drugs are vasodilators and are effective in preventing constriction of the arteries. Occasionally there may also be surgical disconnection of the nerve supply to the affected area.

Alternative Treatment

Homeopathy

Treatment will be constitutional, but the following specific remedies may be useful:

- Secale where there is a burning sensation in the fingers and toes which is made worse by heat, with the remainder of the body feeling cold.
- Carbo Veg where the skin is cold and mottled, and when natural color returns upon fanning.
- Cactus when the hands and feet are cold and swollen and the legs are restless.
- Arsenicum when there is itching, burning and swelling, made worse by cold.
- Pulsatilla when heat makes symptoms worse.
- Lachesis when the skin is blue or purple, particularly following a period of sleep.

Autogenic training

Autogenic training's warmth exercise encourages increased vascularity (blood flow) to the extremities that are affected by Raynaud's.

Reflexology

Reflexologists always work holistically before paying special attention to problem areas, so complete treatment including relaxation techniques will be undertaken, aimed at improving circulation to the hands and feet. Special emphasis will be paid to the adenoids and spleen.

Yoga

A yoga therapist may recommend gentle *asanas*, *pranayama*, relaxation, meditation, plus some advice on diet and counseling.

Others

A standard **macrobiotic** diet, along with a ginger compress twice each week to the lower back and a ginger towel rub to hands and feet in the mornings may be useful. In **Ayurvedic medicine** a practitioner will recommend balancing the tridoshas with Ayurvedic preparations, along with *Panchakarma* therapy. A **Western herbalist** would recommend internal use of herbs which improve peripheral blood flow and herbal foot or hand baths. A **Chinese herbalist** may suggest a blood tonic, along with aromatic herbs. **Acupuncture** may right any underlying imbalances or blockages in the energy system which may be causing the illness. A **nutritionist** may have some success through the use of essential fatty acid supplements. A **naturopath** may recommend applied nutrition and contrast bathing, alongside herbal medicine. **Polarity therapy** and **radionics** are often successful.

LEUKEMIA

What is it?

Leukemia is an umbrella term for cancer of the white blood cells, which protect the body from infection. In leukemia, a cancerous white blood cell reproduces in an uncontrolled way so that numerous cancerous cells replace the normal blood cells in the liver, spleen, lymph nodes, kidneys, ovaries and central nervous system. Untreated, leukemia will usually cause a fatal shortage of red blood cells (serious anemia) and/or bleeding and infection.

There are two main kinds of leukemia: acute and chronic. They are further classified into two main types according to which type of white cell the cancerous cells originate from: lymphoid (lymphoblastic or lymphocytic leukemia, meaning acute or chronic respectively) or myeloid (myeloblastic or myeloid leukemia, again acute or chronic respectively).

Acute lymphoblastic leukemia is most common in children (see page 334), and effects such as tiredness and pallor can become evident within a few weeks of the onset of the disease. Other symptoms include mouth ulcers, a lowering of resistance to infections, pains in the limbs and severe headaches. In chronic lymphocytic leukemia it may take five years from onset before symptoms such as anemia, recurring infections, persistent raised temperatures and enlarged lymph glands appear. The progress of this form of the disease is very slow, and patients may survive for 5–10 years from the time that diagnosis is made.

The symptoms of acute myeloblastic leukemia are similar, with tiredness, anemia, shortness of breath, a tendency to bleed or bruise easily and heart palpitations. In the chronic form, myeloid leukemia (which is mainly found among middle-aged and elderly people), tiredness, anemia, fever, night sweats, weight loss and a dragging sensation or pain in the left upper abdomen caused by damage to the spleen are the main symptoms. Visual disturbances and, with men, persistent, painful erection of the penis may also occur.

Causes

The causes of most individual cases of chronic lymphocytic and myeloid leukemia cannot as yet be identified. However, there are a number of known risk factors for acute leukemia. These include:

- *Drugs used in the treatment of other cancers.*
- *In cases of acute lymphoblastic leukemia, a possible delay in the immune system response in infancy.*
- *Exposure to some industrial chemicals.*
- *Exposure to radiation.*
- *Genetic disorders.*
- *Chromosomal disorders.*
- *Other blood disorders, including chronic myeloid leukemia.*

Orthodox treatment

The most common form of treatment for acute leukemia is anti-cancer drugs (chemotherapy), steroids and radiotherapy, the latter being more common in cases of acute lymphoblastic leukemia. The anti-cancer drugs that are intended to kill the cancerous cells will also lower the patient's resistance to infection, so powerful antibiotics may also be administered. The drugs are usually inserted via a catheter into a vein close to the heart. Blood transfusions may be necessary, as may white cell transfusions. Bone marrow transplants, originally used in the case of a relapse after a remission, are increasingly being used before relapse occurs as a preventative measure. Bone marrow may be treated with powerful drugs or removed in order to destroy the malignant cells, after which healthy marrow is replaced in the bones.

In a mild case of chronic lymphocytic leukemia, no treatment may be required at all. In severe cases of both types of chronic leukemia the treatment is similar to that in acute leukemia, with the use of anti-cancer drugs, transfusions of blood and radiotherapy.

ALTERNATIVE TREATMENT

Acupuncture

Practitioners will address the underlying weakness or blockage in the energy system, looking closely at lifestyle and eating habits to ensure holistic treatment of the condition. Hereditary aspects may be examined.

Nutritional therapy

Nutritional therapists aim to use individual dietary programs to improve the body's efficiency in combating illness in general. Many illnesses such as leukemia can benefit from this improved efficiency, but much depends upon how advanced the illness is, the person's constitution and other factors such as stress.

Reflexology

Reflexologists always work holistically before paying special attention to problem areas. Therefore, complete treatment including relaxation techniques will be undertaken, with gentle work on all reflexes to support the individual.

Other therapies

In **Chinese herbalism** depending upon the severity of the case, and also the practitioner's experience, herbs which act as blood tonics may have beneficial effects. A **yoga** therapist may recommend gentle *asanas*, *pranayama*, relaxation, meditation, *shat kriyas* and advice on diet and counseling. **Tai chi** and **shiatsu** are often recommended to give support to sufferers from leukemia.

RESPIRATORY SYSTEM

What is it?

The respiratory system allows us to breathe in oxygen – the essential ingredient for all bodily processes. With the breathing action carbon dioxide, the waste product from metabolism, is also removed. The intercostal muscles in the thorax link the ribs together and are arranged in three layers. As they contract they pull the ribs up and out. The other main muscle for breathing is the diaphragm and it pulls the chest cavity down. These two breathing processes expand the lungs, after cold air has been drawn in through the nose, warmed, and then taken down into the body. At the end of this process (inspiration) the muscles relax, the lungs compress and air is forced out (expiration).

The lower air passages are composed of the trachea (windpipe) and the bronchi. These bronchi infiltrate each lung, branching into ever smaller airways (bronchioles), which eventually terminate as microscopic air sacs called alveoli. Blood capillaries are linked to the alveoli allowing for the rapid exchange of oxygen and carbon dioxide. An average respiratory rate is 16 breaths per minute. The breathing rhythm is controlled by the body; if there is too much carbon dioxide and too little oxygen, for example, during vigorous exercise, or if a person is asthmatic, the rate of respiration increases and large "gulps" of air are taken in. Once gas levels are satisfactory breathing returns to normal.

What can go wrong?

The most common problems with the respiratory system are caused by viral infections, often the *common cold* or *influenza (flu)*. The patient gets a runny nose, temperature, sore throat and coughs, but it is normally short-lived. However, the virus can sometimes spread or cause a secondary infection resulting in *tonsillitis* or even *pneumonia*. Smoking destroys the "cilia," the tiny hairs in the respiratory tract that help to trap and remove foreign particles. Smokers can suffer particularly with their chests and can sustain damage to the lungs resulting in *catarrh*, *chronic bronchitis* and *emphysema*. Smoking is also one of the main causes of *lung cancer*, which is often diagnosed too late. *Asthma* can be an allergic reaction or is caused by environmental factors. It may come with eczema, particularly in children.

The respiratory system allows us to breathe in oxygen, which is essential for normal body fucntion. Air is inhaled, and the lungs expand. When we breathe out, the lungs are compressed and waste carbon dioxide is forced out.

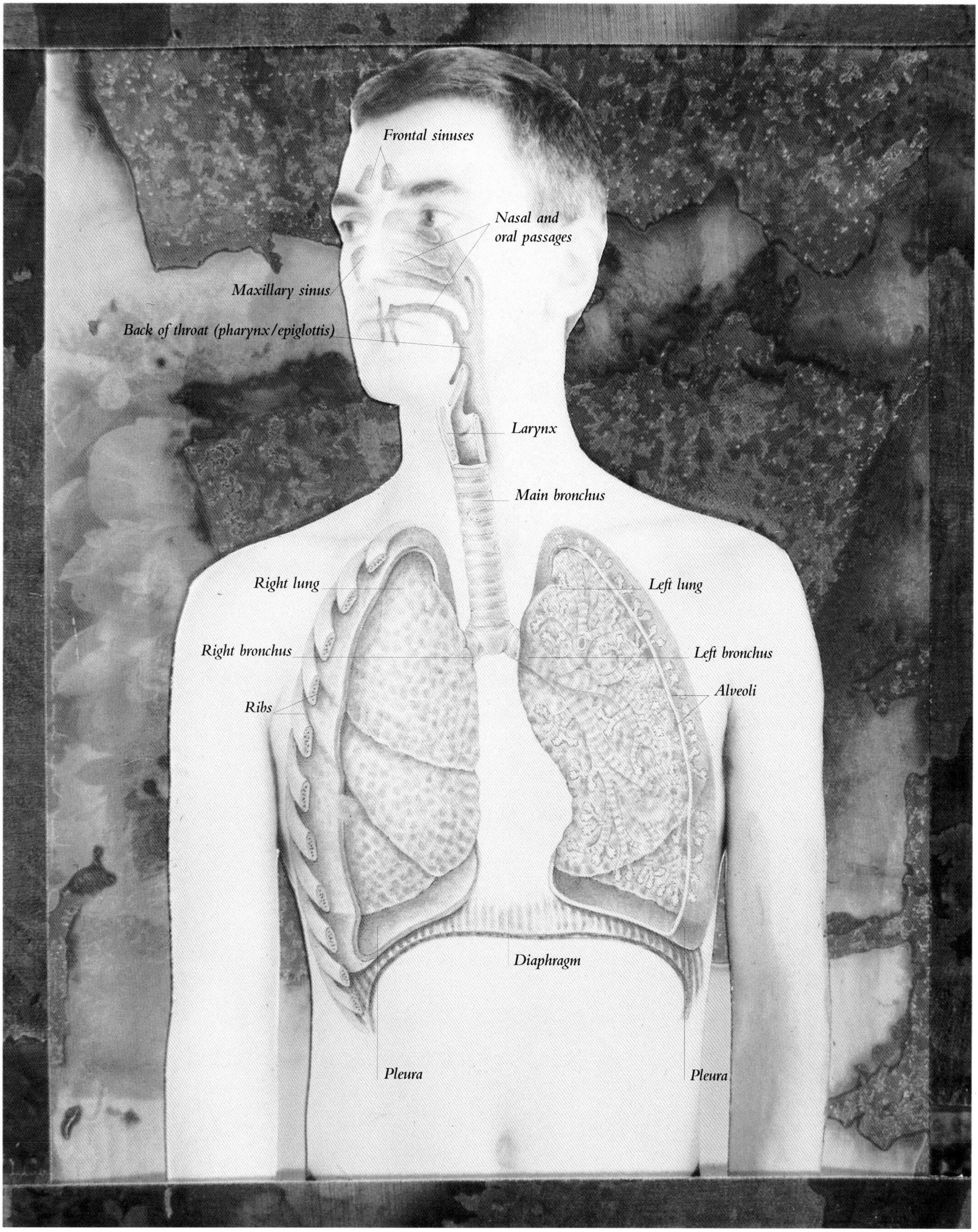
Frontal sinuses
Nasal and
oral passages
Maxillary sinus
Back of throat (pharynx/epiglottis)
Larynx
Main bronchus
Right lung
Left lung
Right bronchus
Left bronchus
Alveoli
Ribs
Diaphragm
Pleura
Pleura

COMMON COLD

What is it?

The common cold is an infection of the upper respiratory tract. Each time you catch a cold you build up an immunity to the strain you have at present, but every new strain requires a different set of immunities to be produced. Symptoms of a cold include mild fever, running nose, headache, sneezing, catarrh and occasionally a sore throat or laryngitis. The average cold lasts from five to ten days, with or without treatment, and after the first few days the symptoms gradually reduce in severity.

Colds are not dangerous, although in some cases complications may develop which can lead to sinusitis (see page 285), pneumonia (see page 180) and bronchitis (see page 177). However, babies, the very young or old and those with chronic illnesses such as diabetes, heart disease or lung conditions, or those whose immune systems are weakened by medical treatment, such as chemotherapy, should take particular care and seek medical attention if complications develop.

Causes

Colds are caused by a group of highly contagious viruses, of which there are over 100 different strains. The virus is transmitted either by inhaling infected droplets in the air, for example after someone has sneezed or coughed. The virus attaches itself to the cells lining the nose and sinuses, causing the characteristic runny nose with mucus production. Someone with a cold is most infectious in the first few days, so avoid coming into contact with anyone in the early stages of their cold to avoid contracting it. Being over-tired and under stress can compromise people's immune systems and make them more vulnerable to catching a virus such as a cold.

Orthodox treatment

Doctors will prescribe rest, extra fluids and warmth. Paracetamol may be suggested to bring down fever and relieve the discomfort. Decongestants or nasal sprays may be prescribed, but their long-term use is not recommended.

There are numerous over-the-counter treatments available aimed at relieving cold symptoms, but none of them can provide a cure; indeed, most doctors dispute their value, believing them to contain little of any benefit other than aspirin, paracetamol and caffeine.

As colds are viral, they cannot be treated with antibiotics, but secondary infections such as sinusitis or bronchitis may make a course of antibiotics necessary.

ALTERNATIVE TREATMENT

Acupuncture

The lung Chi may need attention. Daily treatment would help the body to fight off the cold. Regular treatment would encourage the immune system to fight off infections.

Naturopathy

Dietetic treatment, including fasting and a raw food diet, can promote detoxification and reduce mucus. A diet low in mucus-forming foods (such as dairy products) will be recommended. Applied nutrition, to support the immune system, will be suggested, with herbal and homeopathic remedies.

Nutritional therapy

At the first sign of a cold, take a level teaspoon of pure vitamin C powder dissolved in cold or lukewarm water or juice. Repeat every two hours until symptoms subside. Reduce the dosage and increase the time interval over two days. If any bowel discomfort occurs, reduce the dosage. Continue to take one gram of vitamin C and a cod liver oil capsule daily as a preventative measure.

Western herbalism

Hot drinks and sweating are believed to help get rid of a cold. Herbal teas and infusions may also be recommended, for example, boneset for fever and coltsfoot for coughs.

Homeopathy

Homeopaths may offer the following, depending on the type of cold and its particular symptoms:

- Ferrum phos. for a cold that comes on slowly with a red, swollen throat and possibly mild fever and nosebleeds.
- Nux vomica for colds with irritability and where there is chilliness, watery eyes, headaches and a sore throat.
- Natrum mur. for the early stages of a cold where there is a thin catarrhal discharge and sneezing and a desire to be left alone.
- Pulsatilla for a cold with yellow mucus and where there is a lack of thirst and a loss of smell.

Other therapies

Shiatsu, applied to the wrist joint, strengthens the defenses and may provide relief from symptoms. In **Ayurvedic medicine**, *samana* therapy for imbalanced *kapha* may be suggested, along with *panchakarma* for sinus cleansing. **Aromatherapy** may help ease the cold symptoms; tea tree, ravensara or thyme, rubbed on the palms of the hands, sides of the neck and the glands on the groin, will help. **Chinese herbalists** may suggest diaphoretic herbs for standard cases. For complications, antitussives, expectorants, antipyretics or febrifuge herbs may be used. **Color therapists** may use blues and greens for the heart and throat. **Autogenic training** makes one less prone to colds as the immune system becomes more efficient at fighting them off.

INFLUENZA (FLU)

What is it?

Influenza, or flu, is a severe, highly contagious viral infection. While its overwhelming characteristics are those of high fever, muscular aches, general weakness, stiffness and sometimes depression, symptoms may also, but not always, include those of a very bad cold. Real flu often goes undiagnosed because of the lack of cold symptoms.

Causes

There are three main viruses which cause influenza – A, B and C. Once the C virus has been caught an immunity develops and it cannot be contracted again. However, A and B are constantly mutating so our bodies are unable to develop immunity against them. Type A virus is highly unstable and new strains of it regularly develop throughout the world.

The virus is transmitted from inhaling the active virus from someone who has coughed, sneezed or breathed out while suffering from the virus. It takes approximately 18 hours to three days to incubate the virus and it is contagious for one or two days before the symptoms develop, making it impossible to stop it from spreading.

Orthodox treatment

Bed rest, fluids and paracetamol to bring down the fever are usually suggested. It is essential to stay away from work if you have flu so that you do not pass it to others.

Antibiotics do not work on viral infections, but they may be prescribed to prevent a secondary infection if this is likely to cause health complications. Severe influenza may have to be monitored in hospital.

Every year a vaccine is produced to combat the virus expected in the winter (influenza almost always strikes in the cold weather). It is approximately 70 percent effective if taken from September to October. High-risk groups whose health may be seriously compromised are advised to have a flu shot each year. Such groups include:

- *Those over 65 years of age.*
- *Those who smoke.*
- *Those with a chronic chest condition such as bronchitis or asthma or a heart problem.*
- *Diabetics.*
- *Those suffering illness due to a compromised immune system, for example AIDS sufferers.*

ALTERNATIVE TREATMENT

Homeopathy

Homeopaths will advise rest, fluids, fresh fruit and vegetables, and vitamins A, C with zinc and combination Q tissue salts. In addition they may offer the following, depending on the type of flu and its individual symptoms:

- Belladonna for flu that comes on quickly with throbbing pains and a red, dry, hot skin.
- Arsenicum album for flu accompanied by exhaustion and anxious feelings.
- Gelsemium for normal flu symptoms of shivering, aching and general fatigue.
- Pulsatilla for flu with stubborn catarrahal symptoms with yellow mucus and where there is a lack of thirst and a loss of smell.

Naturopathy

Dietetic treatment, including fasting and a raw food diet, can promote detoxification and reduce mucus. At the feverish stage elderflower tea and fruit juices will help. Herbal and homeopathic remedies, like garlic tablets, which are natural antiseptics as well as being anticatarrhal, will be given.

Nutritional therapy

At the first sign of flu, take a level teaspoon of pure vitamin C powder dissolved in cold or lukewarm water or juice. Repeat every two hours until symptoms subside, then tail off slowly, reducing the dosage and increasing the time interval over two days. If any bowel discomfort occurs, reduce the dosage. Continue to take one gram of vitamin C and a cod liver oil capsule daily as a preventative measure.

Western herbalism

Herbal remedies can reduce the length and severity of the infection, and are excellent for aftercare, with the use of tonics to strengthen the entire system. Hot ginger and cinnamon teas will help increase the circulation and provide warmth. Infusions of elderflower, yarrow and peppermint will help regulate temperature. Yarrow and lemon balm tea will help increase the appetite.

Other therapies

Aromatherapy may help alleviate the cold symptoms; tea tree, ravensara or thyme, rubbed on the palms of the hands, the sides of the neck and the glands on the groin, will also help. In **Ayurvedic medicine** a practitioner may suggest Ayurvedic oral preparations and also immune-enhancing preparations. **Hydrotherapy**, with wet packs or compresses to promote elimination, may be suitable. A **Chinese herbalist** may recommend diaphoretic herbs for standard cases. For complications they may prescribe antitussives, expectorants, antipyretics or febrifuge herbs. A standard **macrobiotic** diet, minus all fruit and fruit juices, may be advised. Bed rest and hot fluids will be prescribed. The **Alexander Technique** may help.

CATARRH

What is it?

Catarrh is the overproduction of mucus in the nose and respiratory tract, often caused by inflammation of the mucous membranes. This can cause a blocked nose, coughs and earache.

Causes

Catarrh is usually the result of inflammation, caused by colds or influenza. Other causes of catarrh include:

- *Inhaling irritant particles, such as dust or smoke.*
- *Chronic sinusitis, an infection in the lining of the sinuses.*
- *Infection of the upper respiratory tract.*
- *Allergy, such as hay fever, caused by inhaling dust or pollen.*
- *Nasal polyps swelling in the nasal membrane.*
- *Vasomotor rhinitis, triggered by hormone changes or drugs.*

Orthodox treatment

Catarrh does not usually require medical attention. However, if it is caused by an allergy or infection, these will be investigated and antihistamines or antibiotics may be prescribed. Nasal polyps may require surgical treatment.

ALTERNATIVE TREATMENT

Nutritional therapy

Nutritional therapists will investigate any allergies and advise against mucus-producing foods. Macrobiotic practitioners may suggest eliminating fruit for 30 days.

Homeopathy

Homeopaths may suggest iron, vitamins C and B complex, zinc and combination Q tissue salts.

Other therapies

Western herbalists may suggest cleansing herbs and immune stimulants. **Chinese herbalists** may prescribe herbal antitussives and expectorants. **Autogenic training** can help if the catarrh is linked to emotional upset. **Osteopathic** treatment will aim to improve sinus drainage. In **Ayurvedic medicine** treatment may be effective by balancing the tridoshas by Ayurvedic formulas. *Nasya* (inhalation) with herbal preparations may be appropriate.

PLEURISY

What is it?

Pleurisy is the inflammation of the membranes surrounding the lungs. The lubricated membrane allows the lungs to move against the chest wall when breathing, but when pleurisy develops, the surface becomes inflamed and roughened, and a characteristic crackling sound is heard when breathing.

Causes

Pleurisy is a viral, or rarely, a bacterial infection of the membrane surrounding the lung, causing a sharp, stabbing pain when inhaling or coughing. It is usually a complication of another illness such as tuberculosis, pneumonia (see page 180) and bronchitis (see page 177), or sometimes lung cancer (see page 181) or advanced rheumatoid arthritis (see pages 304–305).

Orthodox treatment

Pleurisy without complications is easily treated, but its underlying cause may be more serious and this will be investigated. Meanwhile, painkillers to ease the chest pain and antibiotics to combat any bacterial infection will be prescribed. X-rays may be taken as part of the investigation and, if an underlying cause is found, this will be treated, as appropriate.

ALTERNATIVE TREATMENT

Homeopathy

Always see a registered homeopath to ensure proper treatment for individual symptoms. Bryonia may be prescribed if there is a severe, stabbing chest pain near the rib cage.

Chinese herbalism

An experienced Chinese herbalist is likely to prescribe treatment consisting of: herbal carminatives, aromatic stimulants or herbal anodynes.

Other therapies

Western herbalists may give internal treatment backed up by herbal hot compresses and poultices to reduce inflammation. **Ayurvedic medicine** practitioners may balance the tridoshas. **Naturopaths** will back up orthodox treatment with hydrotherapy and applications of back and chest compresses to help reduce internal inflammation; high doses of vitamin C will be recommended to boost the immune system. **Crystal and gemstone therapy**, **spiritual healing**, **hypnotherapy** and **shiatsu** may help.

EMPHYSEMA

What is it?

Emphysema is a progressive respiratory disease in which the air sacs of the lungs become damaged, making them less efficient and reducing their flow of blood. In trying to get the blood to the lungs the heart is put under severe strain. Wheezing, breathlessness, coughing, swollen legs and blue-tinged skin are common.

Causes

The vast majority of emphysema cases are caused by smoking. Sometimes air pollution may be a contributory factor, as are hereditary influences. Tobacco damages the cells in the lung's air sacs, causing the release of enzymes which destroy the lung tissue. The walls of the air sacs swell and burst, resulting in a reduced surface area and elasticity. This causes serious oxygen deficiency and breathing is very difficult. Once damaged, lung tissue cannot be repaired. Emphysema is potentially fatal.

Orthodox treatment

Patients will be strongly advised to give up smoking. X-rays may be taken to determine the extent of the damage. Drugs may be given and oxygen may have to be administered for severe breathlessness. For some cases lung transplants may be suitable.

ALTERNATIVE TREATMENT

Western herbalism

With early symptoms gentle exercise, such as walking, will be advised to promote lung activity. Licorice root and comfrey will help relieve phlegm.

Naturopathy

Vitamin A is said to strengthen lung tissue and vitamin E may help with breathing difficulties. Dairy products should be avoided as they promote mucus formation.

Other therapies

Acupuncture can be effective during the early stages of emphysema. **Aromatherapists** would recommend inhaling the fumes of eucalyptus, hyssop or thyme to make breathing easier. **Chinese herbalists** may use carminative herbs and other herbs to clear retention of body fluid (dampness) and a mixture of antitussives and expectorant herbs. **Homeopaths** may suggest combination Q tissue salts. **Chiropractors** believe that certain breathing conditions are linked to the spine and will treat them accordingly.

CHRONIC BRONCHITIS

What is it?

Chronic bronchitis is a long-term condition in which the large air passages carrying air to the lungs become inflamed. Symptoms include a persistent cough that produces a thick mucus, wheezing, chest pains and breathing difficulties.

Causes

The main cause of chronic bronchitis is smoking. Other causes may be the result of air pollution, inhaling irritant substances such as coal or brick dust, or viruses or bacteria.

Orthodox treatment

Giving up smoking will be strongly recommended. Chest X-rays, lung function tests, blood tests and sputum analysis may all be necessary to determine the extent of the damage caused by chronic bronchitis. Broncholdialator drugs to widen the airways in the lungs may be given and antibiotic drugs may be prescribed if there is an underlying infection present. Oxygen may be necessary if breathing is severely impaired. Anti-flu shots may be recommended to avoid any complications involving the lungs. If blood is coughed up, tests for lung cancer may be carried out.

ALTERNATIVE TREATMENT

Aromatherapy

Inhaling a steam of cypress, eucalyptus and tea tree oils will help free mucus and clear the airways. Using the same oils as chest rubs three times a day may also be advised.

Western herbalism

Anti-infective remedies may be used alongside those with an expectorant and/or anti-inflammatory effect.

Other treatments

There are various **Ayurvedic** decongestant formulas to be taken orally. *Panchakarma* therapy may be appropriate. **Chinese herbalists** may use carminative herbs and herbs to clear retention of body fluid (dampness) and a mixture of antitussives, expectorants and anti-asthmatic herbs. **Naturopaths** will advise avoiding dairy products to reduce catarrh. **Osteopathy** may improve respiratory mechanisms and mucus drainage.

ASTHMA

What is it?

Asthma is a chronic disease of the respiratory system which makes breathing very difficult. It is characterized by the spasm of the major and minor airways in the lungs, due to inflammation and contraction of the muscles in the fabric of the lungs. Symptoms include difficulty in breathing, wheezing, a persistent cough and a sensation of tightness around the chest. During attacks the sufferer has to struggle for air.

Causes

Asthma has become very common. The reasons are unclear, but it is thought that pollution, allergies and fumes may be to blame. Asthma is divided into two categories: intrinsic, for which there is no identifiable cause for attacks, and extrinsic, which is caused by something, usually inhaled, that triggers an attack. Factors that play a part in developing or experiencing an attack include:

- *Heredity.*
- *Drugs, for example NSAIDs (nonsteroidal anti-inflammatory drugs) taken for other conditions.*
- *Allergies, including dust and dander allergies.*
- *Exercise. Attacks may be brought on by vigorous activity.*
- *High pollen count.*
- *Changes in the weather.*
- *Food allergies.*
- *Smoking.*

During an asthma attack the muscles of the small airways in the lung (bronchioles) tighten and narrow. This causes mucus to collect, making the obstruction worse. The characteristic dry cough of a sufferer occurs as the body attempts to clear the airway.

AN ASTHMA ATTACK THAT DOES NOT ABATE, DESPITE USING AN INHALER, IS A MEDICAL EMERGENCY.

Orthodox treatment

Treatment includes inhaling salbutamol or terbutaline, which relax the muscles around the airways, through an inhaler. For children, these relaxants also come in the form of a syrup. Steroids can be used preventatively and are also taken with an inhaler. The drug sodium cromoglycate can also prevent attacks. Emergency treatment may consist of strong doses of steroids, taken orally or by injection. Admission to hospital for nebulizer treatment and intravenous drugs may be required. With severe attacks medical treatment is essential, as asthma can be fatal.

ALTERNATIVE TREATMENT

Western herbalism

As well as reducing the sensitivity and irritability of the airways, herbal medicines can dilate the bronchial tubes and remove excess mucus, if needed. An overall, individual approach is always taken in herbal medicine, and asthma is no exception. Complete relief is possible for some people.

Ayurvedic medicine

Treatment might consist of balancing the tridoshas, according to the individual's condition. *Panchakarma* therapy may also be useful.

Autogenic training

Many sufferers report a significant reduction in the use of inhalers and medication after a short time of using autogenic training. Studies have shown the value of AT in the psychological control of asthma, especially by making the sufferer feel more in control of the condition.

Alexander Technique

Sufferers from asthma and other breathing conditions can benefit greatly from the breathing reeducation and relaxation of the Alexander Technique. It encourages a release of undue tension in the chest and a gradual increase of the intrathoracic capacity. It also improves stress management.

Naturopathy

Naturopathy may offer supportive therapy in the chronic adult, and therapeutic treatment in children. Dietary and physical management may be suitable, with applied nutrition for immune support.

Other therapies

Sufferers may respond to **yoga**, particularly through gentle *asanas*, relaxation, *pranayama*, meditation and *shat kriyas*. **Chinese herbal** treatment may include carminative herbs, herbs with fragrant odor to clear retention of body fluid (dampness) or herbal tonics and a mixture of antitussives, expectorants and anti-asthmatic herbs. In **nutritional therapy** deficiencies, food allergies, inhalant allergies and a toxic overload can all be important factors in the development of asthma and these would be addressed. For an attack, a **macrobiotic** practitioner might suggest a teaspoon of gomashio in a cup of bancha tea, or a cup of hot fresh apple juice. **Homeopaths** will treat chronic asthma constitutionally; their prescriptions and advice will be individual but compatible with orthodox treatment. **Aromatherapy** may use roman camomile to sooth and relieve spasms. **Bach flower remedies** may be helpful if attacks are stress or anxiety-related. Other therapies that may work for asthmatics include **acupuncture**, **auricular therapy**, **cymatics**, **hypnotherapy**, **osteopathy**, **cranial osteopathy**, **relaxation and visualization**, **shiatsu** and **rolfing.**

Hay Fever

What is it?

Hay fever, or allergic rhinitis, is an allergic reaction to an airborne substance such as pollens, which causes inflammation of the nasal mucous membrane. Symptoms include running nose, congestion, sneezing, reddened, itchy eyes, conjunctivitis and sore throat. If the lining of the bronchial tubes of the lungs is irritated, there may be wheezing and occasionally asthma may develop (see Asthma opposite).

ASTHMA SUFFERERS SHOULD BE ALERT TO THE POSSIBILITY OF ATTACK DURING THE POLLEN SEASON AND SHOULD *ALWAYS* CARRY THEIR INHALERS WITH THEM.

Causes

Sufferers are usually allergic to one of two kinds of pollen, which land on the lining of the nasal passages triggering a reaction that causes the nasal membrane to swell and excess mucus to be produced. It can also be provoked by allergies to:

- ◆ *Dust or dust mites*
- ◆ *Fur or animal dandruff*
- ◆ *Feathers*
- ◆ *Spores*
- ◆ *Molds*
- ◆ *Plants*
- ◆ *Chemicals*

For hay fever sufferers, all these substances can act as allergens, causing the body to produce antibodies which release a chemical substance, histamine, that in turn causes the allergic reaction. There is some suggestion that hay fever may be an auto-immune reaction. It may be linked to eczema (see pages 288–289) and it can be hereditary. Allergies tend to run in families and those who suffer are likely to have children who are affected by hay fever.

Orthodox treatment

Avoiding known allergens will help keep the symptoms at bay. Antihistamines will be suggested in order to control symptoms. Anti-inflammatory drugs may help itchy eyes and a running nose. Corticosteroid sprays, oral steroids and decongestants may also be used to alleviate symptoms. Your doctor may suggest removing carpets which might carry the dust mite (a common allergen) and avoiding family pets. For those with debilitating wheezing or asthma, a bronchodialator inhaler may be prescribed to help widen the airways. Allergy injections can be effective but they can have serious side effects and so are not often given.

Alternative Treatment

Acupuncture

An acupuncturist will look closely at the patient's lifestyle and eating habits, which, if changed, can dramatically affect health. Hereditary aspects will be taken into consideration and the underlying weakness or blockage in the energy systems will be addressed. In the case of hay fever, there is usually a weakness of the lung and kidney Chi, and the resulting disharmony can be addressed by stimulating points on the *ren*, the kidney and urinary bladder channels. Points on the urinary bladder and large intestine, combined with points on the lung and large intestine channels, could be stimulated to relieve sneezing and strengthen the lung Chi.

Homeopathy

Hay fever is a deep-seated condition which requires constitutional treatment. Hay fever may take two or three seasons to cure, but it is possible to do so. There are also preventative remedies, and the following may be recommended:

- Allium for hay fever with a burning nasal discharge brought on by allergy.
- Arsen. iod. where there is a constant desire to sneeze and it is brought on by allergy.
- Euphrasia for hay fever in which mainly the eyes are affected and which is brought on by allergy.
- Sabadilla for hay fever with a sore throat, brought on by allergy.

Shiatsu

A practitioner may suggest various channel exercises to improve the flow of *ki*. Exercises to promote vitality and to open up the nose and regulate breathing may also be suggested. Pressure points along the large intestine channel can help to release *ki*, expel wind and relieve sneezing and sore eyes.

Western herbalism

The symptoms can be relieved while also treating the individual weakness that contributes to the hypersensitivity. Complete relief is certainly possible.

Others

The **Alexander Technique** will help strengthen the immune system and free up breathing mechanisms. In **Ayurvedic medicine** a practitioner may increase the resistance of the respiratory mucous membranes and general body defenses using Ayurvedic preparations. For severe hay fever a **hypnotherapist** may provide instructions in breathing techniques and suggestions to help avert attacks. **Osteopathic** treatment may be useful, particularly cranial osteopathy to rectify imbalances which may be aggravating the condition. Soft tissue manipulations stimulate the flow of blood and lymph and clear the nerve channels. **Aromatherapists** may use melissa to sooth and calm the allergic reaction. **Color therapists** may use orange as it helps clear mucus.

PNEUMONIA

What is it?

Pneumonia, a collective term for a series of different types of lung infection. There are two main types of pneumonia: bronchopneumonia, which usually follows as a complication from another illness, such as bronchitis or influenza; and lobar pneumonia, which comes on abruptly and may occur in more than one lobe of the lung. When both lungs become infected, double pneumonia exists. Symptoms include a high fever, chills, sore throat and headache, and a cough which produces a thick mucus discharge. Sometimes there may be blood in the mucus. Chest pains are also common.

PNEUMONIA IS A SERIOUS CONDITION AND CAN CAUSE DEATH, PARTICULARLY IN THE VERY YOUNG OR ELDERLY AND IN THOSE WITH WEAKENED IMMUNE SYSTEMS. TREATMENT MUST BE SOUGHT IMMEDIATELY IF PNEUMONIA IS SUSPECTED.

Causes

Infection is always the cause of pneumonia, and it may be secondary to another illness. Infection is usually viral or bacterial, the most common bacterial infection being pneumococcal pneumonia. A rare form is Legionnaire's disease, caught by inhaling contaminated water droplets. There are numerous types of viral pneumonia, some caused by certain strains of influenza. Some cases of pneumonia may be caught through fungal or yeast infection. There is an increased risk in those who have a reduced immunity, and in those who smoke. Tuberculosis sufferers are also more prone to pneumonia.

Orthodox treatment

For bacterial pneumonia antibiotics will be prescribed, according to the particular organism causing the infection. Viral and fungal pneumonias can be serious, as they do not respond to antibiotics. Paracetamol may be suggested for fever and to alleviate some of the discomfort.

If the sufferer is taken to hospital, chest X-rays will be carried out to confirm pneumonia. Children and the elderly may require hospitalization, with antibiotics administered intravenously. Oxygen may be necessary to assist breathing. Physiotherapy may be necessary to loosen the phlegm. Pneumococcal and influenza vaccinations may be recommended as a preventative measure.

As pneumonia is often a complication of another illness, investigations will be carried out to identify and treat the underlying cause.

ALTERNATIVE TREATMENT

Chinese herbalism

Diaphoretics may be used if there is no sweating, along with astringents. These will be followed by antipyretics or febrifuges, and herbs for external pathogens.

Western herbalism

In conjunction with orthodox medical treatment, Western herbalists will aim to free mucus with lobelia or thyme, combined with other anti-infective herbs such as garlic and echinacea.

Naturopathy

In tandem with orthodox treatment, a diet of fresh fruit and vegetable juices may be recommended, later adding fruit, vegetables, grains and some protein. Dairy products and sweet foods should be limited or avoided as these promote mucus production. Supplements of vitamins C and A may be advised to boost the immune system.

Homeopathy

Treatment should only be undertaken for mild cases of viral pneumonia, and only following an orthodox consultation. Constitutional homeopathic treatment is recommended during and after recovery to boost resistance to further infection. Specific remedies might include:

- Aconite for coughs and sore throat.
- Phosphorus for respiratory problems where there is tightness in the chest.
- Bryonia for severe chest pain near the rib cage.

Acupuncture

An acupuncturist would look closely at the patient's lifestyle and eating habits, which, if changed, can dramatically affect health. Hereditary aspects will be taken into consideration, and the underlying weakness or blockage in the energy systems will be addressed.

Bach flower remedies

The Bach flower remedies will help the negative emotional outlook which is sometimes experienced by sufferers; in particular, gentian for discouragement, willow for self-pity, and olive or hornbeam for fatigue, etc.

Other therapies

In **Ayurvedic medicine** a practitioner might balance the tridoshas, and undertake *panchakarma* therapy. **Aromatherapists** may recommend inhaling ravensara, thyme and tea tree or linalol and myrtle to help ease symptoms. These can also be rubbed on the chest area. Osteopathy may improve respiratory mechanisms and contribute toward mucus drainage.

Lung Cancer

What is it?

Lung cancer causes the most deaths from cancer in the Western world. Lung cancer is effectively a slow-growing tumor and there are four different types:

- *Adenocarcinoma.*
- *Large cell carcinoma.*
- *Small (oat) cell carcinoma.*
- *Squamous cell carcinoma.*

Warning signs include a persistent cough and wheezing, chest pains and breathlessness. There may also be swollen lymph nodes and a general feeling of ill health, including unsubstantiated weight loss and coughing up blood. Recurrent chest infections and swellings on the neck and face are also indications of lung cancer.

COUGHING UP BLOOD IS ALWAYS A SIGNIFICANT AND SERIOUS SYMPTOM. SEE YOUR DOCTOR IMMEDIATELY.

Causes

The main cause of lung cancer is smoking cigarettes, although passive smoking can increase the risk in non-smokers. Other risk factors include inhaling dangerous irritants such as asbestos dust and air pollution. Lung cancer is caused when the inhaled substance damages the cells lining the large airways of the lungs (bronchi). The cells form a tumor which grows and spreads. These cancerous cells can be carried to other parts of the body via the blood, where they form other cancers (secondaries), for example liver, brain or bone cancer.

Secondary symptoms of lung cancer include headaches, dementia, pain in the bones, epilepsy or jaundice.

IT IS POSSIBLE TO CONSIDERABLY REDUCE THE RISK OF DEVELOPING LUNG CANCER BY GIVING UP SMOKING.

Orthodox treatment

Lung cancer is a very serious disease and is often fatal because by the time symptoms have developed, the condition is already quite advanced. However, early diagnosis offers the best outcome as the tumor may be small enough to remove successfully and there is less chance that the cancer has spread to other parts of the body. Abnormal breathing sounds may indicate an X-ray is necessary and this may reveal the cancer. A biopsy will be taken to confirm if it is cancerous. Radiotherapy and chemotherapy improve survival rates. Painkillers may also be offered.

Alternative Treatment

Autogenic training

This therapy does not claim to cure, but to help ease the distressing symptoms of this condition. The immune system will become more effective, which will certainly prevent the spread and the possibility of secondary cancers. In terminal illness, AT can give the patient a feeling of greater control and peace toward the end of life.

Nutritional therapy

Nutritional therapists aim to use individual dietary programs to improve the body's efficiency in combating illness in general. Many illnesses such as cancer can benefit from this improved efficiency, but much depends on how advanced the illness is, the person's constitution and other factors, like stress and anxiety levels.

Homeopathy

Homeopaths will try to support the body's defense systems and improve the body's ability to repair itself.

Naturopathy

Naturopaths believe diet and lifestyle changes can considerably improve the health of cancer sufferers. Depending on the individual, a personal diet plan will be recommended. This may place an emphasis on antioxidant foods such as raw fruit and vegetables and a high intake of beta-carotene found in foods such as carrots, oranges and broccoli. Different vitamin and mineral supplements may also be recommended by the practitioner.

Bach flower remedies

These remedies will play a role in helping to promote a more positive frame of mind in sufferers who are frightened, depressed or affected by other negative attitudes. Remedies should always be chosen on an individual basis, according to the personality and mood of the patient.

Other therapies

As with all forms of cancer, orthodox treatment tends to be geared toward the tumor. **Western herbal** treatment is more focused on the whole person, and a combined approach may be the most effective. Sufferers may also respond to the gentle *asanas*, relaxation, meditation, *pranayama* and *shat kriyas* of **yoga. Spiritual healing** has claimed many successes in treating cancer patients. **Cymatics, crystal and gemstone therapy, hypnotherapy, meditation, relaxation and visualization, Kirlian photography** and **shiatsu** may be useful. **Massage** may help promote a sense of well being and also tone up the immune system.

See also **Allergies** (Immune system pages 260–261)

MIND AND NERVOUS SYSTEM

What is it?

The nervous system is the body's control and communication center. The central nervous system consists of the brain and spinal cord. The "peripheral system" contains nerves which transmit messages to and from the central nervous system. The brain has two convoluted hemispheres called cerebrum, the cerebellum and the brain stem. It contains over 10 million nerve cells and weighs about 1.5kg (3¼lb). The meninges are a three-layered membrane covering the brain and spinal cord. The brain is encased by the skull, and is surrounded by a cerebrospinal fluid which acts as a shock absorber. This fluid extends right down to the spinal cord.

The central nervous system controls both conscious and unconscious bodily functions. Each cerebral hemisphere operates the motor functions of the opposite side of the body. In addition, the left side affects our speech, logic and analysis, while the right deals with thoughts, feelings and imagination. The cerebellum controls coordination and the brain stem maintains "automatic" functions such as breathing. The peripheral nerves are either sensory or motor. The sensory pathways which relay touch, pressure, pain or temperature can also warn of injury.

What can go wrong?

Different nervous system disorders can occur. Atherosclerosis in an artery supplying the cerebrum may cause a clot and possibly a *stroke*, which can paralyze the opposite side of the body. A severe *stroke* can be fatal. *Strokes* occur more often in patients with high blood pressure, so it should be regularly checked.

Migraines seem to be caused by constricting and dilating arteries which bring about the severe headaches. Infection of the meninges, the membranes surrounding the brain and spinal cord is called *meningitis*. It is a serious illness that particularly affects children and can be fatal. The patient has flu-like symptoms, and often neck stiffness and a rash. In suspected cases, hospital treatment is essential. *Shingles* is a painful infection caused by the chicken pox virus affecting the peripheral nerve. Psychological problems, such as *depression* and *anxiety* can be accompanied by *insomnia*, and are often caused by a chemical imbalance in the brain. Antidepressants can restore this balance.

The central nervous system controls both conscious and unconscious body movements. The peripheral nervous system relays touch or pain sensations, for example.

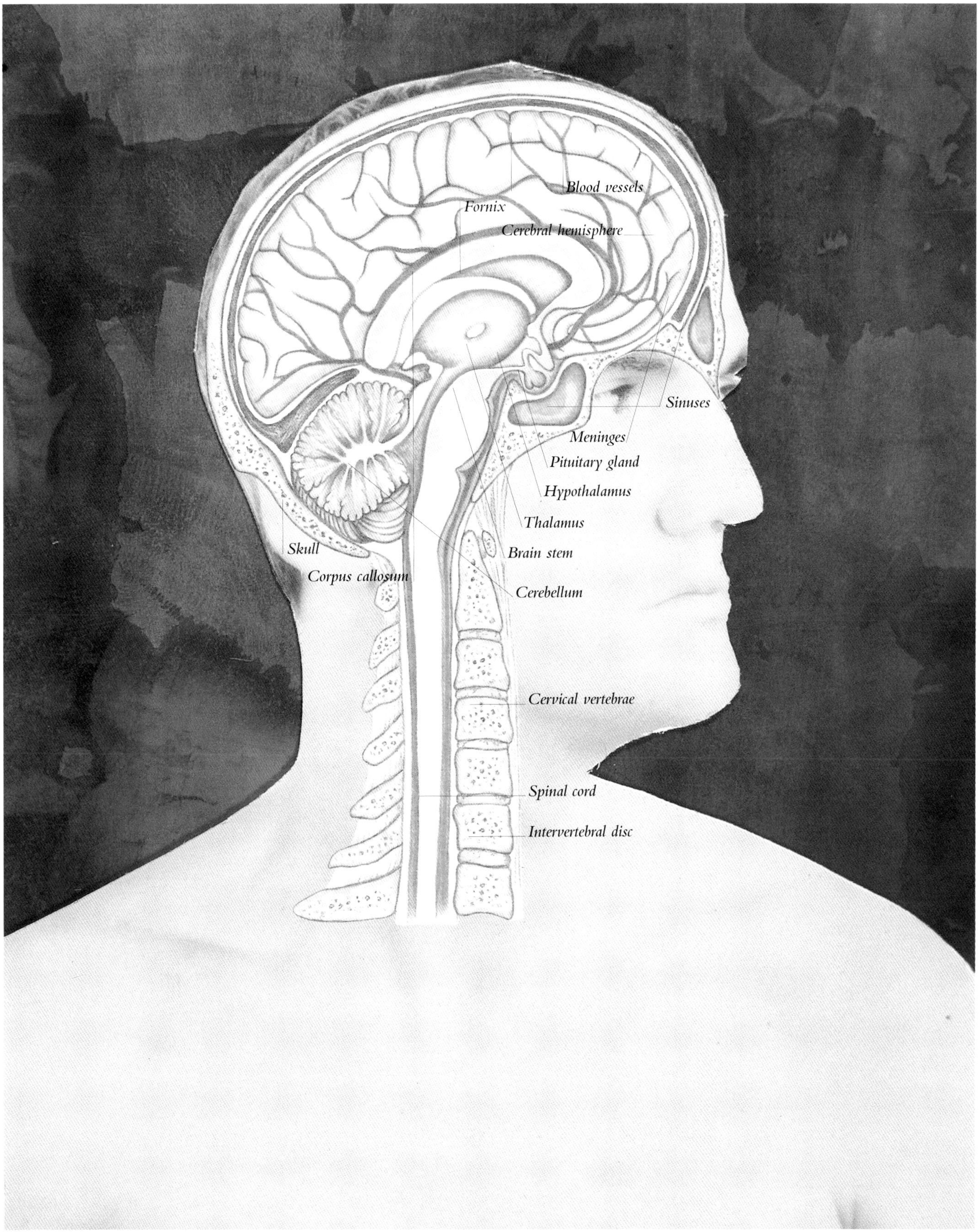
Blood vessels
Fornix
Cerebral hemisphere
Sinuses
Meninges
Pituitary gland
Hypothalamus
Thalamus
Brain stem
Skull
Corpus callosum
Cerebellum
Cervical vertebrae
Spinal cord
Intervertebral disc

Depression

What is it?

True depression is a mental illness that should not be confused with feeling depressed, which may simply be a normal response to events connected with work or personal life. Such depression will usually lift in a few weeks at most and is not a cause for alarm. In some cases, however, depression takes such a firm hold that the sufferer is unable to struggle out of its grip unaided and treatment becomes necessary. Symptoms include an overwhelming feeling of emptiness, low self-esteem, mood swings, insomnia, fatigue, despair, irritability, obsessional behavior, a concentration upon death and suicide and physical symptoms like backache, headache and palpitations. There may also be digestive disorders, anxiety attacks and loss of appetite and libido, and in severe cases the sufferer may experience hallucinations or delusions.

Causes

Depression may be caused by an overwhelming emotional trauma such as bereavement or a stressful event like moving home. Almost a quarter of women experience depression after childbirth (see pages 222–223), and there may be other physical origins. Often, however, there is no easily identifiable cause.

Orthodox treatment

Mild depression can be treated by talking things through with a doctor or a counselor. A depressive illness needs treatment with medication or psychotherapy, or both. The older antidepressant drugs, chiefly "tricyclics" such as amitriptyline, are considered safe and effective but may cause annoying side effects such as tremor, dry mouth and blunted reactions at the commencement of treatment. The newer antidepressants such as SRIs (Serotonin Re-uptake Inhibitors), among which fluoxetine (Prozac) has become famous, are popular with patients and doctors alike because they have fewer side effects; however, the ease with which they can be taken therefore brings its own drawbacks. ECT (Electro-Convulsive Therapy) is a controversial treatment which may be appropriate in severe depression, particularly if there is a risk of suicide.

Alternative Treatment

Homeopathy

Treatment will be constitutional, and there might be dietary advice as well as changes in lifestyle. Specific remedies which may be useful include:

- Arsenicum if the person is restless, chilly, exhausted, obsessively neat and tidy.
- Aurum if the person feels totally worthless, suicidal and disgusted with himself or herself.
- Ignatia if the depression follows deep grief or a failed love affair.
- Pulsatilla if the person bursts into tears at the slightest provocation, wanting a lot of reassurance and attention.

Alexander Technique

This works toward the reduction of dystonic use patterns. The connection between anxiety states and muscle tension is now generally accepted. In particular, chronically contracted muscles are associated with mental and emotional imbalances. The Alexander Technique enables a redistribution of muscle tension throughout the body, which seems to go hand in hand with an improvement in mental functioning. It may also teach a person how to react to life's challenges and stresses in a positive way, avoiding overreactions and distress.

Bach flower remedies

Depending on the cause and nature of the depression, individual remedies will be prescribed: among others, gorse may be chosen for a sense of hopelessness, sweet chestnut for bleak despair, mustard for depression with no identifiable cause, willow for depression caused by resentment, and honeysuckle for those whose thoughts dwell on happier times past.

Arts therapies

Art, dance, drama or music therapy can provide support as well as a chance for sufferers to discover aspects of themselves of which they were previously unaware.

Other therapies

Naturopathic treatment may be useful, since depression may be associated with metabolic imbalances or food intolerances. **Hellerwork** and **rolfing** may offer an opportunity to come out of the cycle of depression. **Acupressure** and **shiatsu** may be very useful; **auricular therapy** is particularly effective in calming the mind. Poor body image may be helped by **massage**. **Yoga** offers gentle *asanas*, relaxation, *pranayama*, meditation, *shat kriyas* and hand *mudras*. An **aromatherapist** will offer antidepressant essential oils. **Kinesiology** will check the need for vitamin B, phenylanaline, vitamins C and B5, and will offer support for all systems, where necessary. A **reflexologist** will address the endocrine glands, solar plexus and head. **Spiritual healing** helps to balance the mind/body/spirit relationship. **Hypnosis** can be used to change physiology, language and thought patterns, as well as belief systems and personal history. **Autogenic training** is excellent for short-term depression resulting from life events. **Chinese herbalism** takes all emotional disorders very seriously as each organ has an associated emotion. A **Western herbalist** will offer a remedies to tone and build up the nervous system.

Anxiety

What is it?

Anxiety and depression are often linked, and it is common to experience symptoms of both. Some anxiety is normal in everyday life, but persistent feelings of worry, fear or impending doom must be treated because they can lead to serious physical and psychological problems.

Physical symptoms of anxiety include digestive problems, headaches, high blood pressure, insomnia, muscular tension, panic attacks, skin problems, a rapid pulse, palpitations, breathlessness or hyperventilation, tightness in the chest, a feeling of faintness, sweating, fatigue, lightheadedness, weakness, nausea, diarrhea, abdominal pain and loss of appetite.

Causes

There are three main theories as to the cause of anxiety:

- ◆ *A physiological cause, where the individual has a raised level of arousal in the central nervous system which leads to heightened reactions and physical symptoms which contribute to the anxiety.*
- ◆ *A psychoanalytical cause, originating from repressed and unresolved childhood experiences or unconscious conflict.*
- ◆ *A behavioral cause, where the anxiety is a learned response to pain or stress which then becomes uncontrolled.*

Orthodox treatment

One of the talking therapies will be useful to understand the cause of the anxiety experienced, and learning to deal with the stresses of day-to-day life can help. Your doctor may teach you how to breathe in a panic attack to prevent some of the more frightening symptoms. Tranquilizers such as diazepam may be prescribed in an acute attack, although they are addictive if taken for long. Antidepressants and mild sedatives may help. Beta-blockers are sometimes given to reduce heart rate.

Alternative Treatment

Homeopathy

Constitutional treatment will be appropriate for chronic conditions, and there are a number of remedies which will be useful for acute attacks. These include:

- Arsenicum if a person is feeling restless, insecure, chilly, tired, and fending off anxiety by being meticulously tidy.
- Calcarea if someone is fearing for their sanity, forgets things, easily becomes overweight or feels the cold.
- Natrum mur. if a person is dwelling on morbid topics and hates fuss or sympathy.
- Tarentula if the nervous system is revving out of control due to overwork or if a person finds it difficult to relax, even in bed.

Alexander Technique

The connection between anxiety and tense, tight muscles is now well known. When muscles are severely constricted they can create mental and emotional imbalances. The Alexander Technique helps release all this muscle tension which then seems to bring about an improvement in the person's general mental health and well being.

Bach flower remedies

Remedies are prescribed according to the individual and the cause and nature of the anxiety. Anxiety for no apparent reason may be treated with aspen; anxiety over the welfare of loved ones may be red chestnut; anxiety about inability to cope would be elm or larch. There are many other good remedies.

Arts therapies

Some arts therapists would work toward identifying the root of the anxiety, and all would aim to develop a therapeutic relationship with the sufferer. General anxiety may be alleviated by exploring feelings in music-making. Dance movement therapy may allow a fresh light on problems and feelings.

Aromatherapy

A relaxing blend of essential oils of lavender, geranium and bergamot in sweet almond oil or peach kernel oil may be used in the bath at times of great stress and anxiety.

Other therapies

Naturopathy will include relaxation, applied nutrition and herbal and homeopathic support. **Hellerwork** may be useful, stabilizing the mind/body relationship. **Yoga** offers gentle *asanas*, relaxation, *pranayama*, meditation, *shat kriyas* and hand *mudras*. **Rolfing** will use different modes of touch and movement. **Auricular therapy** is very effective in calming the mind. There are specific **kinesiology** techniques for stress reduction and relief from anxieties, fears and phobias. A **reflexologist** will address the central nervous system, brain, solar plexus, neck and shoulder reflexes. **Spiritual healing** helps to balance the mind/body/spirit relationship. **Hypnotherapy** treatment may involve age regression, suggestion therapy, NLP, hypno-healing and self-hypnosis. **Autogenic training** helps to shift the "fight-and-flight" stress response to a recuperative calming of mind and body. **Chinese herbalism** can help with emotional disorders because all the organs have an associated emotion. **Western herbal** remedies act as relaxants and nervous restoratives. In **Ayurvedic medicine a** practitioner will balance the tridoshas and use *panchakarma* for balancing the *vatha*. **Massage** relaxes the mind, body and spirit. A **macrobiotic** practitioner may suggest a standard macrobiotic diet, with good warm and sweet foods.

STRESS

What is it?

Stress is not a dangerous condition in itself; in fact, it is actually healthy for us to have a certain amount of stress in our lives in order to provide us with challenge and stimulation. However, when the level of stress exceeds our ability to cope with it, or stretches us beyond healthy limitations, it becomes a problem. Unfortunately it is not always easy to tell when there is an overload of stress as the body will respond by working harder and harder, and it may seem that performance and efficiency are improved until the person finally succumbs, perhaps abruptly, to fatigue. Stress that is suffered on a long-term basis can be debilitating both physically and mentally. Under stress the body produces an increase in the hormones adrenaline, noradrenaline and corticosteroids, and in the short-term these hormones produce tense muscles, queasiness and an increase in breathing and heart rates. Long-term complaints that are stress-related include:

- *Allergies (see pages 260–261).*
- *Anxiety (see page 185) and depression (see page 184).*
- *Digestive disorders.*
- *Fatigue.*
- *Headaches and migraine (see page 192).*
- *Heart disease.*
- *High blood pressure (see page 163).*
- *Impotence and premature ejaculation in men.*
- *Insomnia (see page 189).*
- *Irritable bladder.*
- *Irritable bowel syndrome (see page 249).*
- *Menstrual problems in women.*
- *Mouth and peptic ulcers (see page 253).*
- *Muscular aches and pains.*
- *Palpitations (see page 166).*
- *Panic attacks.*
- *Skin complaints including eczema (see pages 288–289).*
- *Ulcerative colitis.*

A number of other diseases including multiple sclerosis, diabetes and genital herpes can also be aggravated by stress.

TOLERANCE OF STRESS LEVELS DIFFER FROM PERSON TO PERSON. MANY PEOPLE ARE ABLE TO SUSTAIN A HIGHLY STRESSFUL LIFESTYLE OR ADAPT THEMSELVES TO A SERIES OF STRESSFUL EVENTS EASILY, WHILE OTHERS SUCCUMB MORE READILY TO A VARIETY OF STRESS-RELATED ILLNESSES AND EVEN ACCIDENTAL INJURIES.

Causes

Stress is caused by a number of factors, some of which may be internal (such as problems connected with work, financial affairs or a relationship), or external (living by a noisy road, building work, rush-hour commuting). A significant change in lifestyle (such as divorce, a new job or moving house) can be extremely stressful, while the death of a spouse has been found to be the most stressful event that most people will experience in their lives.

Orthodox treatment

Most doctors will advise taking gentle exercise and perhaps working fewer hours. If the source of long-term stress is unidentifiable, you may be referred to a counselor to explore the problem further. Relaxation techniques and/or lifestyle changes are essential in order to avoid the problem persisting.

ALTERNATIVE TREATMENT

Homeopathy

In homeopathic medicine ailments such as food allergy, hypoglycemia, high blood pressure, asthma and digestive disorders are regarded as being manifestations of stress, so treatment is likely to be long-term and constitutional; however, in acute circumstances, one of the following remedies may be useful, according to a person's circumstances:

- Phosphoric ac. for stress due to grief or bad news.
- Picric ac. for stress due to overwork.
- Ignatia for stress following emotional upset such as a broken love affair.
- Nux for stress brought on by burning the candle at both ends, including smoking, eating or drinking too much, making the sufferer irritable.

Your homeopath may suggest you learn some form of relaxation or meditation and perhaps take supplements of vitamin B complex; taking exercise (although not pursuing it to the point of tiredness) may also be advised.

Color therapy

Color therapy helps to alleviate stress by utilizing the colors of the rainbow through visualization, colored oils, colored glass or colored silk in a therapeutic environment.

Aromatherapy

A relaxing blend of essential oils of lavender, geranium and bergamot in sweet almond oil or peach kernel oil may be used in the bath at times of great stress and anxiety.

Osteopathy

Osteopathy is a touch therapy, and, just like massage or aromatherapy, it uses a fine sense of touch and relaxation to achieve some of the required results with patients who are in pain or overstressed. The muscles at the back of the skull that connect the spine to the head can become very tense and tight as we become stressed. This can lead to headaches or neck pains, as well as pain in the shoulders and back.

Naturopathy

Naturopathy is excellent for treating stress, including psychotherapy, relaxation techniques, herbal and homeopathic support, and osteopathic soft tissue treatments where appropriate. Supplements of vitamins and minerals may be advised as these are used up more quickly when the body is under stress.

Massage

Massage helps to relax the mind, body and spirit, providing time and space for self, and a feeling of peace, calm and well being. It allows the nervous system to normalize itself, and may reduce many stress-related conditions, such as palpitations, negative emotional feelings and raised blood pressure.

Arts therapies

Dance movement therapy will allow sufferers to release their pent-up feelings in a manageable way, and to explore resources through the therapist. Art therapists will give the sufferer the opportunity to share and explore concerns through images. Through musical interactions, a music therapist will engage the sufferer in supportive and understanding relationships, which may help them to make more sense of their stressful situations.

Crystal and gemstone therapy

Under the guidance of a qualified practitioner, crystal healing may promote a feeling of relaxation and facilitate a release of stress. Crystals may be placed on or around the body or held in the hand during the session.

Bach flower remedies

Remedies will depend on the cause and the nature of the stresses. Stress due to frustration and a sense of injustice might respond to vervain. Stress due to impatience would be impatiens; stress due to responsibility, elm. Many others would be appropriate according to the personality and mood of the sufferer.

Kinesiology

There are specific techniques for stress reduction, emotional stress release and relief from anxieties, fears and phobias. Treatment offered may include:

- Vitamin B supplements.
- Checking the endocrine and immune systems for any nutritional deficiencies.
- Providing adrenal support and nutrition for stress.
- Checking the dural torque and the ileo-cecal valve.
- Checking the atlas and sacrum for lesions.
- Tests for food sensitivities and the monitoring of grain consumption.
- Regular kinesiology balancing.

Chiropractic

Anxiety and stress frequently attack the weak spots of the spine, and it is the spine that can cause general muscular tension, headaches, migraine, neck pain and back pain. This pain can then aggravate the stress and anxiety and so chiropractic treatment can be aimed at relieving any physical complaints which will in turn help with the mental conditions.

Yoga

Gentle *asanas*, relaxation, *pranayama* and meditation will keep stress levels low, maintain flexibility, and reduce back pain.

Alexander Technique

This works toward the reduction of dystonic use patterns. The connection between anxiety states and muscle tension is now generally accepted. In particular, chronically contracted muscles are associated with mental and emotional imbalances. The Alexander Technique enables a redistribution of muscle tension throughout the body, which seems to go hand in hand with an improvement in mental functioning. Patients may also learn to react to life's challenges and stresses in a positive way, avoiding overreactions and distress.

Western herbalism

Infusions of lime blossom, catmint, lemon balm or camomile have a calming effect. A herbalist may suggest taking skullcap, valerian or cowslip as stronger relaxants than the above, or the restoring herbs vervain and St. John's wort. Oats should be included in the diet.

Other therapies

Hellerwork may be useful by reducing symptoms and harmonizing the relationship to gravity. **Yoga** offers gentle *asanas*, relaxation, *pranayama*, meditation, *shat kriyas* and hand *mudras*. **Rolfing** may be very useful, since when the muscles are encouraged to move more appropriately, energy which has gone into unnecessary contraction is available for other purposes. **Auricular therapy** is particularly effective in calming the mind and inducing a feeling of relaxation. **Reflexology** will be very helpful. **Spiritual healing** helps to balance the mind/body/spirit relationship, bringing harmony to the whole being. **Autogenic training** teaches people to handle stress and its related symptoms more effectively. **Chinese herbalism** takes all emotional disorders very seriously because the organs have an associated emotion. A **macrobiotic** practitioner may suggest a standard macrobiotic diet to relax kidney energy, with no coffee or spices and a reduction in the intake of salt.

BEREAVEMENT

What is it?

The intensity and nature of emotions felt after the death of a loved friend or relative will depend upon the personality of the bereaved and the relationship he or she had with the deceased. The death may also bring practical problems that may add to the survivor's difficulties. While reaction to the loss is an individual one, there are recognized stages of bereavement. In the first, which may last from three days to three months, numbness and inability to accept the death are sometimes accompanied by hallucinations of seeing the deceased. Following this the bereaved person will suffer depression, often accompanied by anxiety, anger and despair. Generally, it takes about two years for the bereaved to regain emotional equilibrium. There can be physical symptoms accompanying each stage, including digestive problems, nausea, insomnia, overwhelming fatigue and apathy, muscular aches and pains, and also headaches.

Causes

Most bereavement is caused by a death, although other circumstances such as losing one's home, job, reputation, a marriage or long-term relationship can initiate symptoms which are consistent with bereavement, although to varying degrees.

Orthodox treatment

Treatment depends on the nature and severity of the condition. If grief, depression, anger and shock are extreme, medical intervention may be necessary, including sedatives and antidepressants. Some of the physical symptoms may be addressed separately.

ALTERNATIVE TREATMENT

Homeopathy

Treatment will be changed at different stages of grief, and there will be constitutional help if there is a failure to progress from one symptom to the next. In the early stages, the following are suggested:

- Arnica if the person wants to be left alone, insists he or she feels all right, does not want to be touched, or their reactions are those of someone in shock.
- Aconite if the person is fearful, on the verge of collapse.
- Opium if the person is very frightened by the death of loved one and is numb with grief.

Remedies for the later stages are:

- Nux if the person is extremely angry and critical of others.
- Phosphoric ac. if the person is very depressed and apathetic.
- Pulsatilla for sleeplessness, helpless weeping, catarrh.
- Natrum mur. if the person rejects consolation and sympathy because it makes him or her cry and prefers to hide feelings.
- Ignatia if the person finds emotions difficult to control, and laughs, sighs or cries at inappropriate moments.

The final stages are treated as for depression (see page 184).

Alexander Technique

Bereavement can often have a strong somatic element and the grief felt is retained in the body. The Alexander Technique can help to release such trapped emotion in a gentle self-righting process. The result is a deeper emotional and physical calmness and a release of stress.

Arts therapies

People who are experiencing difficulties in coming to terms with bereavement may benefit from having a period in one of the arts therapies, where they will be provided with support to work through the grieving process.

Naturopathy

Treatment will involve supportive nutrition, relaxation, applied nutrition and herbal support for resilience of the nervous system.

Aromatherapy

For sadness and depression, rose, geranium and bergamot are uplifting oils. Rose is a very warm, all-embracing oil which can be mixed in equal parts with rose geranium and rosewood for the sake of economy.

Bach flower remedies

Different people deal with grief in different ways, and the individual feelings therefore influence the choice of remedies. Remedies include: for the shock of bereavement and its sorrow, star of Bethlehem; for feelings of guilt, pine; for resentment, willow; for despair/bleak outlook, sweet chestnut; for loss of interest in the present, honeysuckle.

Other therapies

Hellerwork may be useful for expressing emotions that are trapped within the sufferer. **Acupressure** and **shiatsu** may be very useful. **Yoga** offers gentle *asanas*, relaxation, *pranayama*, meditation, *shat kriyas* and hand *mudras*. **Auricular therapy** is particularly effective in calming the mind and inducing a feeling of relaxation. **Western herbalism** will prescribe helpful herbs. The therapeutic use of **color** and light may bring an easement of grief. **Chinese herbalism** takes all emotional disorders very seriously because the organs have an associated emotion. **Autogenic training** can help to release grief. **Massage** may help the process of bereavement by conveying a sense of comfort and caring, and by offering the closeness of physical contact that the patient may have lost as a result of their bereavement.

INSOMNIA

What is it?

Insomnia is the inability to get to sleep or difficulty in remaining asleep. It is a common complaint; one in three adults suffer from insomnia at some point in their lives. Symptoms include daytime fatigue, irritability, tearfulness and headaches. The amount of sleep needed varies from person to person, and may be as little as three hours a night or as many as ten; most adults require seven or eight. Many people believe that they need more sleep than is strictly necessary and worry unnecessarily about insomnia. It is also the case the people with insomnia sleep more than they realize, but since they wake frequently the quality of sleep is poor.

Causes

The usual cause of insomnia is stress or worry. Waking in the middle of the night or very early in the morning and being unable to get back to sleep is a common characteristic of depression and of old age. Other causes of insomnia include:

- *Caffeine and alcohol.*
- *Environmental factors such as noise.*
- *Physical disorders such as any condition causing pain, sleep apnea (temporary cessation of breathing), restless legs (burning or pricking sensations in the legs) or prostate problems.*
- *Psychiatric illness such as depression, mania or schizophrenia.*
- *The use of some drugs, both prescribed and illicit.*

Orthodox treatment

Treatment would be aimed at the cause. Sleep-inducing drugs may be prescribed, although doctors are wary of this sort of medication as it can be addictive and does not in any way address the cause of the insomnia. Establishing a regular routine of activity during the day and set times for going to bed and getting up may solve the problem.

ALTERNATIVE TREATMENT

Homeopathy

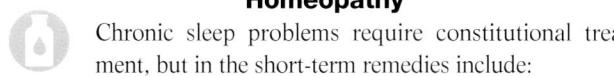

Chronic sleep problems require constitutional treatment, but in the short-term remedies include:

- Coffea if the mind is overactive as the result of good or bad news, or if it cannot be switched off.
- Nux if sleeplessness is due to great mental strain, overindulgence in food or alcohol, or withdrawal from alcohol or sleeping tablets, or if a person wakes around 3 or 4am then falls asleep again near getting up time, or is irritable during the day.
- Pulsatilla if a person is restless in first sleep, feels too hot and throws covers off, then feels too cold and lies with arms above head, not thirsty, or if the insomnia is worse after rich food.
- Opium if the person is feeling sleepy but unable to get to sleep, if the senses feel so sharp a fly can be heard walking on the wall, or if the bed is too hot, or else sleep comes but it is so heavy that the person snores and cannot be roused.

Chiropractic

Sufferers of neck and shoulder problems or chronic pain frequently experience insomnia. Treatment is aimed at relieving the physical condition to ease the tension.

Aromatherapy

A relaxing bath with essential oils of Roman camomile and geranium will help a person to unwind before sleep. A glass of camomile tea will complete the process.

Hypnotherapy

The hypnotherapist will uncover reasons for the insomnia, dealing with subconscious fears and anxieties, and then use suggestion in hypnosis for easy, normal sleep. Suggestions can be taped and played in bed. After several weeks of repetition the changes become part of the nervous system.

Bach flower remedies

Remedies will depend on the cause of the insomnia. Worrying thoughts and mental arguments may respond to white chestnut; indecision, scleranthus; stress, strain, frustration and inability to relax may be vervain, rock water, vine, elm, beech and impatiens.

Other therapies

Naturopathy may be very useful, including relaxation instruction, nutritional management and hydrotherapy prior to retiring. **Yoga** offers gentle *asanas*, relaxation, *pranayama*, meditation, *shat kriyas* and hand *mudras*. **Auricular therapy** is particularly effective in inducing a feeling of relaxation and calm. A **kinesiologist** will check the body for lesions, and also for deficiencies in magnesium, calcium and vitamin B, among others. A **reflexologist** will work all the reflexes to induce calm, ideally before bedtime. **Autogenic training** offers short- and long-term solutions. **Arts therapies** may help if the problem is stress-related. **Western herbalism** will offer herbal relaxants. **Chinese herbalism** is most effective combined with acupuncture. In **Ayurvedic medicine** a practitioner will balance the tridoshas. **Massage** just before retiring is an excellent way to help with insomnia. A **nutritional therapist** may examine some biological causes of insomnia, including coffee-drinking, magnesium and B-vitamin deficiency. A **macrobiotic** practitioner may suggest some treatment to relax the kidneys, a standard macrobiotic diet, hot fluids to be taken before going to bed, and lying on the back with feet in a basin of hot salty water for 30 minutes.

NEURALGIA

What is it?

Neuralgia is pain caused by damage or irritation to a peripheral nerve (a nerve not in the brain or spinal cord). The pain may be quite mild and only temporary, but is more often experienced as very sharp, sometimes shooting along the nerve, and attacking repeatedly in a short space of time.

Unspecific neuralgia may be the result of damage at any point along the route of a nerve, the pain being felt at the area the nerve serves. There are also specific types of neuralgia, including postherpetic neuralgia, a burning pain that may occur in the site of an attack of shingles; glossopharyngeal neuralgia, when an intense pain is experienced at the back of the tongue and in the throat and ear; and trigeminal neuralgia, a spasmodic pain in one side of the face. Sciatica (see page 314) is also a type of neuralgia.

Causes

Causes of neuralgia include injury to or abnormality in the nerve, or perhaps an infection which causes inflammation. Other causes include:

- *Stress and emotional problems.*
- *Migraine, which causes a form of neuralgia in which there are attacks of intense pain radiating around the eye.*
- *Shingles (see opposite), which may cause neuralgia for months or years after the attack of shingles is over.*
- *In trigeminal neuralgia, the trigeminal nerve in the face becomes inflamed; it is a condition most common in the elderly.*
- *Alcohol, drugs, excess glucose in the blood, vitamin deficiencies, lead, mercury and organo-phosphates (used in sheep dip and pesticides) can all cause damage to nerves.*

The causes of glossopharyngeal neuralgia are not known, but it can be brought on by eating, swallowing or talking. It may also occur spontaneously.

Orthodox treatment

The treatment offered will depend upon the site of the damaged or inflamed nerve and also the cause of the damage. Occasional mild attacks of neuralgia can be treated quite satisfactorily by analgesic drugs such as aspirin or paracetamol. There are drugs, for example, carbamazepine, which interrupt the passage of nerve impulses along nerves, which can help to ease the symptoms of postherpetic neuralgia, glossopharyngeal neuralgia and trigeminal neuralgia. Physiotherapy may be suggested. If the pain is severe and persistent, a nerve block may very occasionally be resorted to.

ALTERNATIVE TREATMENT

Homeopathy

Neuralgia should be treated by an experienced homeopath, and treatment should always be constitutional, although one of the following remedies may help while treatment is being sought:

• Aconite if the nerves flare up after exposure to cold, or if the affected part of the body feels congested as well as numb.
• Arsenicum if the attack is brought on by dry cold, or if the person feels chilly, exhausted or restless with burning pains.
• Colocynth, if the attack is brought on by cold or damp, pain that is violent and lacerating, and better for application of heat, particularly if person is suffering from facial neuralgia.
• Lachesis if the pain is worse after sleep.
• Magnesia phos. if the pain is alleviated by heat and pressure.
•Ranunculus if neuralgia is affecting the rib cage or is located above the right eye.
• Spigelia for pain above the left eye which worsens on movement.

Your practitioner may suggest extra vitamin E if neuralgia follows an attack of shingles; vitamins B1, B2 and biotin are good for nerves generally.

Acupuncture

Auricular therapy will give temporary relief of symptoms, and body acupuncture will be even more effective.

Reflexology

Treatment from a reflexologist will be aimed at the overall body, with special emphasis placed upon the reflexes relating to the cervical spine, adrenals, solar plexus and facial area.

Chiropractic

Facial neuralgia can be associated with neck disorders or a problem with one or both tempero-mandibular joints, which can all be treated using chiropractic manipulation. Other neuralgia in the body may respond as well.

Naturopathy

A naturopath may suggest hydrotherapy and contrast bathing to reduce the pain and inflammation of the nerves. Applied nutrition may consist of B-complex vitamins, calcium, magnesium and potassium.

Other therapies

Yoga offers gentle *asanas*, relaxation, *pranayama*, meditation, *shat kriyas* and hand *mudras*. **Aromatherapy** and **kinesiology** may be very helpful. **Color therapy** will offer oils or lights, specifically yellow. Pain control treatment is available through **hypnotherapy** and hypnohealing may be useful.

SHINGLES

What is it?

Shingles is a very painful and often debilitating condition caused by the herpes zoster virus, which is also responsible for chicken pox. After an episode of chicken pox the virus lies dormant at the root of a nerve, sometimes for years, and then reactivates itself, causing first sensitivity and then pain in the area served by the nerve, typically in the rib area but also on the lower part of the body, arm, neck or face. A rash appears within about five days, first as small red spots then blisters. Like the blisters of chicken pox, these fluid-filled sacs carry the herpes zoster virus. Within about two days the blisters become yellow and crusted, dropping off within about two weeks but occasionally leaving scarring. The pain may persist for months or even years.

Shingles on the face may affect only the forehead and eyelid. Opthalmic herpes zoster can damage the eye and must be treated by a hospital eye specialist.

Causes

Herpes zoster is common in people with a weakened immune system, such as AIDS patients or people taking anticancer or immunosuppressant drugs. Reactivation of the virus is also encouraged by these conditions; stress or contact with chicken pox may also cause an outbreak. Shingles is more common in the elderly, who tend to have less efficient immune systems.

Orthodox treatment

The most debilitating symptom of shingles is persistent pain, and this can be treated with anti-inflammatory drugs and very strong painkillers. As soon as the diagnosis of shingles is made, antiviral drugs such acyclovir may be prescribed in the hope of speeding recovery, though they do not effect a cure. The sooner the condition is treated the better the outlook, but the treatment may cause unpleasant side effects with very little benefit.

ALTERNATIVE TREATMENT

Homeopathy

While waiting for orthodox treatment, the following remedies may help:

- Rhus tox. if the skin is red, blistered, itchy and especially if the scalp is affected or the person is young, or if warmth and moving about make the symptoms more bearable.
- Arsenicum, if burning pains are worse between midnight and 2am, isolated skin eruptions become more numerous and merge together, a person is restless, anxious, exhausted and chilly, or symptoms are alleviated by warmth;
- Mezereum if there is severe pain, if the skin burns and itches and forms brown scabs, or if the person is middle-aged or elderly.
- Ranunculus, if there are nerve pains and itching, or the slightest touch, movement or eating makes the symptoms worse.
- Lachesis if the left side of the body is affected, plus some swelling, which is aggravated by warmth but is relieved by cold.
- Preventatively, variolinum can be given to anyone who has been in contact with chicken pox and shingles and should particularly be given to anyone elderly or infirm. The blisters can be sponged with hypericum and calendula solution (5 drops of each to 300ml (½pt) cooled boiled water). Hot and cold compresses will also relieve nerve pains.

Aromatherapy

An aromatherapist may recommend the application of neat tea tree oil, using a cotton bud. This will hurt but will stop the pain and itching and have a strong antiviral action.

Kinesiology

Treatment will consist of checking the endocrine and immune systems for nutritional deficiencies; providing adrenal and endocrine support, and nutrition for stress; checking for vitamin A deficiency; checking dural torque; offering counseling for stress reduction; checking the ileo-cecal valve; checking atlas and sacrum for lesions; checking for food sensitivities; checking grain and dairy consumption; suggesting bowel cleansing; and regular kinesiology balancing.

Chinese herbalism

Herbal detoxicants for external use might be offered, plus herbal tea detoxicants for internal use. Herbal anodynes might also be used in order to stimulate/subdue activity of the liver.

Western herbalism

Treatment is aimed primarily internally, to strengthen the nervous system and repair damage. A herbalist may also use analgesic and anti-inflammatory herbs and oils which will be applied to the affected area.

Other therapies

Naturopathic treatment may consist of applied nutrition, especially the B and C vitamins for promotion of healing and reduction of nerve sensitivity; herbal and homeopathic medicine can help to alleviate the symptoms. **Acupuncture, acupressure** and **shiatsu** may be very useful. **Yoga** offers gentle *asanas*, relaxation, *pranayama*, meditation, *shat kriyas* and hand *mudras*. **Color therapy** will offer colored oils or lights, specifically yellow. In **Ayurvedic medicine a** practitioner will improve general immunity by Ayurvedic preparations and *panchakarma*. A **nutritional therapist** may suggest vitamin C, B12 and E supplements for treating shingles.

Headaches and Migraines

What are they?

Headaches can range in severity from mere annoyance to debilitating pain and may be accompanied by nausea, vomiting and sensory or visual disturbances, as in migraine. They are the result of tension or stretching of the membranes around the brain and of the blood vessels and muscles of the scalp. However painful, they are not usually a sign of any serious underlying disorder.

HEADACHES WHICH ARE WORSE UPON WAKING, OR WHICH CAUSE A PERSON TO WAKEN IN THE NIGHT, COMING ON SUDDENLY AND SEVERELY, SHOULD BE CHECKED BY A DOCTOR.

Causes

The most common triggers for headaches include alcohol (hangover) and drugs, allergies, dental problems, eyestrain, head injuries, fever, neck and spine problems including poor posture, depression, anxiety, stress, sinusitis, weather conditions and a poor work environment. Some women experience headaches as a side effect of the contraceptive pill or hormone replacement therapy (HRT).Very occasionally, they may have a more serious cause such as hypertension (see page 163), brain tumor, temporal arteritis (inflammation of the arteries in the neck, face and scalp) or aneurysm (ballooning of a blood vessel) in the brain. Chronic headaches should always be reported to a doctor to establish their cause.

Orthodox treatment

The cause of the headache will be addressed first and foremost in order to prevent repeat attacks. If self-help remedies such as relaxation or taking mild analgesics do not help, a doctor will give the person a general physical examination and may suggest a visit to a neurologist for further tests.

Alternative Treatment

Homeopathy

Constitutional treatment is recommended for recurrent headaches caused by stress, anxiety or tension. However, a headache that is a symptom of another condition can be treated by specific remedies, which include:

- Aconite if a headache comes on suddenly, feels worse in the cold, or if a person is apprehensive, the headache feels like a tight band around head or it feels like the brains are being forced out.
- Arnica if the head feels bruised and aching, if the pain is occasionally sharp, or if it is made worse by stooping.
- Bryonia if the head feels bruised and there is a sharp, stabbing pain made worse by the slightest eye movement.
- Ruta for a pressing, bruising headache that is associated with fatigue, which is made worse by reading, and is alleviated by rest.

Chiropractic

Chiropractic treatment is very effective in dealing with headaches and migraines of a cervical origin (from the neck). Manipulation of the neck would need to be carried out, as appropriate, to the area concerned.

Color therapy

Headaches may be helped by a restful green color in the environment, or by visualizations, guided by a tape or whenever possible by a color therapist.

Macrobiotics

Treatment will relate to the cause. A frontal headache will be considered to have a yin cause, and be treated with hot bancha, with shoyu. A headache at the back of the head will have a yang cause, and will be treated with hot apple juice.

Hypnotherapy

Headaches may be caused by unexpressed anger and resentment. A hypnotherapist may use regression to uncover the source of the headaches and show the patient pain-control techniques. Suggestion therapy can also be used.

Alexander Technique

Headaches are often caused by overcontraction of the muscles in the back of the neck. The Technique teaches a release of the muscles and a reduction in over-reaction to stress.

Other therapies

Massage relaxes the muscular tension in the shoulder, neck and scalp which may be the cause of tension headaches. **Naturopathy** may be an excellent choice, since many headaches are multifactorial, and nutritional, structural and psychological factors can all be addressed. **Hellerwork** may help headaches by working with the tension of the neck, shoulders, scalp and jaw. **Acupressure** and **shiatsu** may be very useful. Yoga offers gentle *asanas*, relaxation, *pranayama*, meditation, *shat kriyas* and hand *mudras*. **Rolfing** helps by improving circulation and promoting relaxation. Depending on the cause, a **Western herbalist** may suggest different kinds of strategies, such as relaxation or reduction of stress or inflammation. A **reflexologist** will address the reflexes relating to the head, neck, solar plexus, spine, pituitary and digestive system. **Bach flower remedies** may be useful. **Chinese herbalism** will offer a number of treatments, depending on the cause. Headaches are often linked with poor liver function and food allergy, and a **nutritional therapist** may suggest special diets and herbs to improve liver function and also to help to identify problem foods.

Epilepsy

What is it?

There are many types of epilepsy, but all are the result of an abnormality in the electrical activity of the brain. The electrical impulses which govern intellectual and physical activity are normally regular and orderly, but in someone suffering from epilepsy a sudden burst of overactivity occurs, causing a seizure, or fit. This may be limited to one part of the brain (partial seizure) or spread over a wide area or even the whole of it (generalized seizure). Partial seizures are divided into simple or complex, while generalized seizures are described as grand mal or petit mal. In a grand mal attack the person will lose consciousness and the whole body will stiffen, then begin to twitch and jerk; the breathing is irregular or absent altogether. The muscles then relax and bladder and bowel control may be lost. The person returns to consciousness within 5–30 minutes but may be confused or disoriented at first, with no memory of the seizure. A headache is common, as is the desire to sleep.

In a petit mal attack there is again loss of consciousness, but this is experienced only as a short period of blankness lasting from a few seconds to up to half a minute. To an onlooker, it may seem a momentary lack of attention. Petit mal attacks are most commonly manifested in children.

Partial seizures typically begin with hallucinations of smell, vision or taste and abnormal twitching movements. In a simple partial seizure, consciousness is maintained, but in a complex partial seizure it is lost to the extent that the person has little or no memory of the seizure. However, to the onlooker the person merely seems dazed, though involuntary actions such as lip-smacking may occur.

A number of people have a single fit only. In children this is most often a febrile fit, which happens when the child has a high fever. In adults even a single fit should be investigated.

Causes

The cause of epilepsy is unknown, although brain damage increases the risk – whether it be by an injury to the head, a stroke, or birth problem. Brain tumors and brain infections like meningitis or encephalitis may cause seizures, as may diabetes, drug intoxication and drug and alcohol withdrawal.

Orthodox treatment

Anticonvulsant drugs will be prescribed for anyone suffering from recurrent seizures and these are usually successful in lessening frequency, though they may give rise to side effects such as drowsiness and impaired concentration. Medication may be lessened or stopped altogether if no seizure has occurred for two or three years. Surgery is very occasionally considered for brain damage when medication is not effective.

Alternative Treatment

Homeopathy

Most homeopaths acknowledge the need for orthodox control of this condition but constitutional treatment may be appropriate, though some orthodox drugs can work against the remedies. In the case of fits, remedies that may be given as soon as the fit wears off include:

- Aconite if the fit is brought on by fright or fever.
- Belladonna if the person is red-faced, feverish, with eyes that are wide and staring, plus symptoms made worse by jolting.
- Chamomilla if the fit is brought on by teething or an outburst of anger, especially if one cheek is red and the other white, there are greenish watery stools and thumbs clenched inside palms.
- Cuprum if the fit is very violent, the face and lips turn blue, and the thumbs are clenched inside fists.
- Glonoinum if the fit is brought on by intense heat, the head is hot and congested and the fingers and toes are spread wide
- Ignatia if the fit is brought on by emotional upset, the face is pale and twitching starts in the face.

Alexander Technique

The Alexander Technique promotes a balancing and calming of the nervous system and this may contribute to a reduction in attacks.

Western herbalism

Treatment from a herbalist may be helpful in reducing the severity and frequency of attacks, especially by relaxing the central nervous system.

Nutritional therapy

Epilepsy has been linked with poisoning by pesticides and other chemicals, food allergies and nutritional deficiencies, including magnesium, zinc, selenium and vitamin B6.

Spiritual healing

The frequency and duration of fits can be reduced with healing, which has a calming effect on the whole body.

Other therapies

Acupressure and **shiatsu** may be very useful. **Yoga** offers gentle *asanas*, relaxation, *pranayama*, meditation, *shat kriyas* and hand *mudras*. Depending on the pattern of fits, and whether they are controlled by mediating, **autogenic training** may improve the condition. **Acupuncture** is effective. **Chinese herbs** used include aromatic stimulants and sedatives, and treatment may be combined with acupuncture. **Ayurvedic medicine** offers *panchakarma* therapy for *vatha* balance, and medication.

Parkinson's Disease

What is it?

Parkinson's disease is a neurological disorder characterized by muscular tremor, stiffness and weakness. It affects about one in every 200 people and occurs mainly in the elderly, more commonly in men rather than women. The early symptoms are usually a slight tremor of one hand, arm or leg which virtually disappears when the hand or limb is in use, but as the disease progresses both sides of the body are affected. Walking is difficult and shuffling, with a tendency to break into tiny running steps, and there is involuntary movement of the hands and the head. The sufferer develops a permanent rigid stoop and an unblinking, rigid expression. Everyday activities become very difficult to perform, and depression and hallucinations are possible. Speech will become slower and more difficult, as the muscles controlling speech are affected. Many other symptoms can develop as the disease progresses, such as difficulty swallowing, constipation, sweating and dribbling. The mind continues to function at a normal level until the later stages of the disease, when there can be dementia.

Causes

Parkinson's disease is the result of damage to or degeneration of nerve cells in the brain and is not reversible. There is, however, a disorder called parkinsonism which mimics the symptoms of Parkinson's disease but is due to other causes including carbon monoxide poisoning and certain antipsychotic drugs and recreational designer drugs.

Orthodox treatment

In the early stages treatment will be limited to advice on exercise and special aids in the home. In later stages modern drug treatment can significantly improve quality of life. Levodopa, which the brain converts into dopamine, is usually the first drug to be tried, and may be used in conjunction with other medication such as anticholinergic drugs, which are designed to improve specific symptoms. Experimental transplants of dopamine-secreting tissues taken either from the patient's adrenal glands or from the brain tissues of aborted fetuses are taking place, with variable results.

Alternative Treatment

Homeopathy

Although homeopathy can offer a number of specific remedies for occasional use, the condition requires the ongoing care of an experienced homeopath. The recreational drug MTPP, which can produce the symptoms of parkinsonism, can be used to treat people genuinely afflicted when prepared in homeopathic potency. Specific remedies include:

- Mercurius if there is an overproduction of saliva, a sweet/metallic taste in the mouth, trembling hands, tremor accompanied by perspiration and made worse by it, equal sensitivity to heat and cold, patchy memory and concentration, or loss of willpower.
- Agaricus if the limbs tremble, twitch and jerk, there is stiffness and itchiness in affected limbs and the spine feels sensitive.
- Rhus tox. where the main complaint is stiffness or cramp, made worse by damp or immobility but is alleviated by moving, tremor which is not very marked.

Arts therapies

In the earlier stages of the disease, art therapy, dance movement therapy or music therapy may help people come to terms with the diagnosis. Music therapy is often used to improve motor function because rhythm helps us to organize movement. The arts therapies also provide an alternative means of communication for those who have difficulty with speech.

Nutritional therapy

Studies have shown nutritional approaches to be useful, including a low-protein diet, supplements of vitamins B1, B6 (this must only be administered to Parkinson's patients by a doctor), C, E, octacosanol and essential fatty acids. Nutritional therapists also aim to reduce any toxic overload.

Reflexology

Treatment will be aimed at reflexes associated with the central nervous system, brain and adrenal glands.

Autogenic training

A report on a group of 21 patients showed that regular practice of autogenic training reduced emotional excitement and fatigue, which in turn reduced tremors and rigidity.

Aromatherapy

Oils good for muscles, such as ginger or juniper, will improve circulation and aid muscle relaxation, which will relieve muscle stiffness in the later stages of the disease.

Other therapies

Acupressure and **shiatsu** may be very useful. **Yoga** offers gentle *asanas*, relaxation, *pranayama*, meditation, *shat kriyas* and hand *mudras*. **Bach flower remedies** can help to promote a more positive frame of mind in sufferers who are frightened, depressed or affected by other negative attitudes. In **Ayurvedic medicine** a therapist will balance the tridoshas, with *panchakarma* for *vatha* balance. **Massage** can enhance feelings of self-esteem and positive body image. A **macrobiotic** practitioner may suggest a liberal, relaxed standard macrobiotic diet, with plenty of variety.

STROKE

What is it?

A stroke (also called a CVA, or cerebro-vascular accident) results when the blood supply to part of the brain is interrupted or blood leaks through the walls of blood vessels. The function, sensation or movement which is controlled by that part of the brain may then be impaired. Even a very minor stroke is a warning signal of insufficiency in the blood supply to the brain. If a person suffers from suddenly slurred speech or sudden loss of consciousness, contact a doctor immediately.

Strokes are one of the biggest causes of death in the developed world. About a third are fatal, another third cause disability to some extent, and the final third cause no lasting effects at all. Complications of stroke include pneumonia and thrombosis (clotting in the veins) in the legs. This may travel to the lung and cause a potentially fatal pulmonary embolism.

Causes

The risk factors for a blockage to an artery or rupture of a blood vessel occurring in the brain include:

- ◆ *Atrial fibrillation (irregularity of heartbeat), damaged heart valve or recent myocardial infarction (heart attack).*
- ◆ *Atherosclerosis* *(see page 164)**.*
- ◆ *Diabetes* *(see page 200)**.*
- ◆ *Cigarette smoking.*
- ◆ *High blood pressure* *(see page 163)**.*
- ◆ *Hyperlipidemia (high levels of fats in the blood).*
- ◆ *The contraceptive pill increases the incidence of stroke in women under the age of 50.*

Orthodox treatment

Emergency treatment such as clearing airways will be given where necessary, followed by longer-term rehabilitative treatment. Anticoagulant drugs may be prescribed if the stroke was caused by a blood clot, or, less frequently, thrombolytic drugs. Long-term low-dose aspirin is often prescribed. Loss of movement is treated with physiotherapy, and speech therapy is given where there has been loss of speech. Some patients may require occupational therapy and aids in the home.

COMPLEMENTARY TREATMENT

Homeopathy

Constitutional treatment from an experienced homeopath can aid recovery. Changes in diet, exercise and lifestyle may be recommended. Specific remedies can be used during a stroke, while awaiting medical attention. These include:

- Belladonna for a hot, flushed face, headache and staring eyes.
- Aconite, if the person is panicky and afraid of dying once he or she realizes what is happening.
- In the two weeks following the stroke, arnica should be given.

During recovery, remedies include:

- Baryta, if person is elderly or physically and mentally weak.
- Gelsemium where the main after-effects are numbness and trembling, inability to speak and pain at back of the head.

Alexander Technique

This offers a more efficient motor coordination, which will prevent maladaptive and compensatory patterns of movement. Rehabilitation will be aided by modified reactions to stress and the learning of postural and emotional homeostasis.

Osteopathy

Osteopaths, like physiotherapists, work with post-stroke victims to stretch out contracted muscles and to help in the overall rehabilitation program.

Arts therapies

The arts therapies offer an alternative means of communication for people whose speech is impaired, and may help in the coming to terms with loss of faculties. Music therapy may be especially useful, since the ability to sing can be left unaffected; it may also help to develop motor function.

Nutritional therapy

Prevention is easier than cure, and a good intake of oily fish and vitamin E with a whole food diet is the best prevention against blood clots in the brain. Nutritional therapists use the herb *Ginkgo biloba* after a stroke to improve the circulation in the brain and help to prevent further strokes.

Other therapies

Bach flower remedies may help to promote a more positive frame of mind in patients who are frightened, depressed or affected by other negative attitudes. **Acupressure** and **shiatsu** may be very useful. **Yoga** offers gentle *asanas*, relaxation, *pranayama*, meditation, *shat kriyas* and hand *mudras*. A **Western herbalist** may suggest improvements to circulation, encouraging better recovery. A **color therapist** may suggest visualizations, with the physical application of colored lights, silks or oils. A **reflexologist** will address the reflexes relating to the head, spine, neck, eye/ear, solar plexus and circulatory systems. A **Chinese herbalist** will offer herbs to regulate the blood condition. In **Ayurvedic medicine** a practitioner offers *panchakarma* therapy for paralysis. **Chiropractic** treatment can be used to ease any neck, shoulder and arm pain that can occur on recovery. **Massage** can help to relax and tone the muscles, but seek advice from a physiotherapist first.

Meningitis

What is it?

Meningitis is the inflammation of the membranes that cover the brain and spinal cord (the meninges). It is usually caused by an infection by a microorganism, normally a virus or bacterium. Viral meningitis is mild in comparison to bacterial meningitis, which can often prove fatal and requires urgent medical attention.

Viral meningitis most commonly occurs in wintertime epidemics. The symptoms of severe headache (made worse by bending forward), fever, nausea and vomiting, dislike of light and stiff neck are only mild and may resemble influenza (see page 322). In cases of meningococcal (bacterial) meningitis the symptoms develop rapidly and are considerably more severe; the patient may become progressively more drowsy and enter a coma within hours. In about 50 percent of cases a red, blotchy skin rash appears. There may be weakness in the muscles, and sometimes speech disturbance or visual problems. In a few cases, loss of hearing, brain abscess or brain damage may result. Meningococcal meningitis sometimes occurs in small epidemics but is more likely to be found in isolated cases, most frequently occurring in young children.

Tuberculous meningitis, which is another form of bacterial meningitis, is less common in the developed countries and is usually found in young children in areas where there is a high occurrence of tuberculosis. The typical symptoms of meningitis may not appear until several weeks after the sufferer first begins to feel ill.

INFANTS WITH MENINGITIS WILL HAVE A HIGH FEVER, VOMITING, PERHAPS CONVULSIONS AND A STRANGE CRY. THE FONTANELLE ON THE TOP OF THE HEAD WILL OFTEN BULGE OUTWARD. IF YOUR BABY SUFFERS FROM ANY OF THESE SYMPTOMS, OR HAS A SUDDEN INEXPLICABLE DARK RED OR PURPLE RASH, CONTACT YOUR DOCTOR IMMEDIATELY.

Causes

The microorganisms that cause meningitis normally reach the meninges via the bloodstream from another part of the body. Causes of viral meningitis include:

- *The herpes zoster virus, which causes chicken pox and shingles.*
- *The poliomyelitis virus.*
- *The mumps virus.*

In these cases, there may be immune deficiencies in the sufferer. Bacterial meningitis can be one of several different strains, one of which is carried in the nose of healthy people who may never catch the disease.

A less common means of transmission is via cavities in the bones from an ear or sinus infection, or via a head injury such as a fractured skull.

Orthodox treatment

Meningitis will be diagnosed by means of a lumbar puncture to remove a sample of cerebrospinal fluid. Viral meningitis which is caused by the herpes zoster virus will be treated with acyclovir. Other forms of viral meningitis are left to run their course and recovery occurs within two to three weeks, with no aftereffects.

Bacterial meningitis is treated with large doses of antibiotics, possibly administered by intravenous drip, for up to two weeks. Exact treatment will depend upon the bacteria causing the meningitis. Tuberculous meningitis is treated with long-term antibiotics. Antibiotics may also be given to people who have come into contact with sufferers from bacterial meningitis.

Alternative Treatment

Homeopathy

While waiting for medical attention, one of the following remedies may be appropriate for use as an emergency treatment where meningitis is suspected:

- Arnica if the symptoms start after a head injury.
- Aconite if the symptoms are accompanied by restlessness, fear, dry skin and great thirst.
- Belladonna if the person is very hot, delirious, with staring eyes.
- Bryonia if severe headache is made worse by the slightest eye movement and the person is becoming steadily more depressed and comatose.

Reflexology

A complete treatment will be offered by a reflexologist, and recovery will be supported by giving special attention to areas according to the specific characteristics of the patient and the symptoms.

Arts therapies

If there are resultant learning difficulties or physical disabilities, one of the arts therapies may be beneficial as they provide an alternative means of communication and the opportunity to express feelings.

Other therapies

Acupressure and **shiatsu** may both be very useful. **Yoga** offers gentle *asanas*, relaxation, *pranayama*, meditation, *shat kriyas* and hand *mudras*. **Chinese herbalists** can treat this disorder with diaphoretics, herbal laxatives and herbal anti-inflammatory agents.

Repetitive Strain Injury (RSI)

What is it?

Repetitive strain injury (RSI) is a blanket term for a range of physical conditions caused by damage to muscles, tendons, joints and ligaments. It affects the hands, arms, neck and shoulders and symptoms include pain, stiffness, pins and needles, swelling, numbness and loss of manual dexterity. Some of the conditions encompassed by RSI include: tenosynvitis (inflammation of the synovial sheaths, usually in the hands and wrists); tendinitis (inflammation and thickening of the tendons); epicondylitis (tennis elbow); and carpal tunnel syndrome (where repeated bending of the wrist causes fluid and tissue to press on the median nerve).

Causes

There are three main causes of RSI: static posture, repetitive movements and stress. Static posture commonly occurs through sitting for long periods at computer workstations, supermarket check-outs and conveyor belts, keeping muscles in a fixed and tensed position so that circulation is decreased and muscle fatigue ensues. Constricted blood vessels, immobile joints and compressed nerves can lead to tension in the neck and shoulders as well as inflammation and nerve pain. Repetitive movements such as those made by computer users can cause local injuries such as tennis elbow; rapid keystroking and hand/wrist stretches put an enormous strain on arms and hands and, combined with poor workstation design and too few breaks, they can cause RSI. Stress exacerbates symptoms, as the body reacts by sending chemical messages from the brain which increase muscle tension, backache and headaches and disrupt the body.

Orthodox treatment

Experts agree that the best form of treatment is prevention. When symptoms occur they should not be ignored because once established RSI is a notoriously difficult condition to treat and can last for years. The first thing that will be recommended is rest from the task that is causing the injury, and some doctors advocate the use of splints or bandages at this stage. Other treatment includes:

- *Analgesic and anti-inflammatory drugs are widely prescribed for pain relief, and sometimes antidepressants to act as a muscle relaxant. Injections of soluble steroid and local anesthetic are also used.*
- *Physiotherapy is probably the most effective form of treatment, and patients should ask for a physiotherapist who is trained in adverse neural tension techniques, which combine gentle stretches with ultrasound, ice, heat and hydrotherapy; manipulation or traction and lifting weights should be avoided.*
- *Surgery is available in extreme cases to patients with carpal tunnel syndrome.*

Alternatve Treatment

Osteopathy

Osteopathy looks for the predisposing factors that relate to injuries in the workplace. The osteopath will manually treat the effects and will also help to prevent the problem recurring.

Alexander Technique

RSI complaints often respond very well to Alexander Technique as it helps to release undue tensions in the cervical spine and generally in the neck and shoulders. The Technique enables the pupil to achieve and maintain freedom and poise while engaging in activities like keyboard operation or playing a musical instrument.

Rolfing

Rolfing alleviates the problem by enabling muscles to move more appropriately and releasing muscles which are causing pain by compressing nerves.

Autogenic training

As the system uses autogenic training to relax and then release the effects of old injuries and tensions, the problem may improve.

Chiropractic

Treatment is aimed at manipulation and mobilization, soft tissue work and occasionally the use of modalities such as ultrasound. Ergonomic advice will be offered.

Other therapies

A **naturopath** may suggest neuromuscular and osteopathic treatment, hydrotherapy, contrast bathing and applied nutrition. **Hellerwork** has reportedly worked wonders with RSI. **Acupuncture, acupressure** and **shiatsu** may be very useful. **Yoga** offers gentle *asanas*, relaxation, *pranayama*, meditation, *shat kriyas* and hand *mudras*. **Western herbalism** will be aimed at local and systemic treatment to reduce inflammation and speed up tissue healing. An **aromatherapy** massage with a blend of essential oils of rosemary, juniper and lavender in a carrier oil of hazelnut will help to alleviate the symptoms. **Kinesiology** offers muscle testing and energy balancing. A **reflexologist** will address the reflexes relating to the cervical spine and elbow. In **Ayurvedic medicine a** practitioner will use Ayurvedic oral formulas, and *panchakarma shirovirechana*. **Massage** can ease muscular tension and maintain good circulation to the resting muscles. Deficiencies of B6 and its cofactors have been linked with RSI, and a **nutritional therapist** may investigate this aspect.

ENDOCRINE SYSTEM

What is it?

The endocrine glands secrete chemical messengers called 'hormones' into the bloodstream. This 'chemical communication' modifies activity of a distant organ or tissue. Hormones help the body to respond to hunger, infection and disease and also prepare the body for stress or physical exertion.

The endocrine glands include: the pituitary, the pineal, the thyroid, four parathyroids, the thymus, the islets of Langerhans in the pancreas, two adrenals and the two gonads (testes or ovaries). The womb's placenta also acts as an endocrine gland to help maintain pregnancy. The pituitary and pineal gland are situated in the brain. The pituitary stimulates and coordinates the other endocrine glands and is called the 'conductor of the endocrine orchestra'. It also produces hormones that influence growth, urine production and uterine contraction. The thyroid gland is located in the neck. It has two connecting lobes and helps control metabolism. The parathyroids, situated at each pole of the gland, maintain correct levels of calcium and phosphorous, which are essential for the healthy working of bones, nerves and muscles. The thymus lies in the thoracic cavity and is thought to help the actions of the immune system. The islets of Langerhans are in the pancreas and secrete insulin and glucogen to maintain the correct levels of glucose in the blood. The pyramid-shaped adrenals lie above the kidneys, and their outer layer produce steroid hormones that regulate salt, sugar and water concentration. They also produce hormones that influence secondary sexual characteristics. The inner layer produces hormones that prepare the body for 'fight, fright or flight' reactions.

What can go wrong?

Problems occur when a hormone level is too high or too low. An underactive *thyroid* gland (hypothyroidism or myxoedema) can cause a sluggish metabolism with weight gain, lethargy or dislike of cold weather. A hyperactive *thyroid* (hyperthyroidism or thyrotoxicosis) speeds up the metabolic rate bringing about weight loss, increased appetite, sweats and dislike of hot weather.

Diabetes is due to lack of insulin and the islets of Langerhans stop working. The cause may be auto-immune or hereditary. Symptoms are weight loss, thirst, and frequent urination.

The glands in the endocrine system release hormones into the bloodstream. These prepare the body for stress. They also help the body react to hunger, infection and disease.

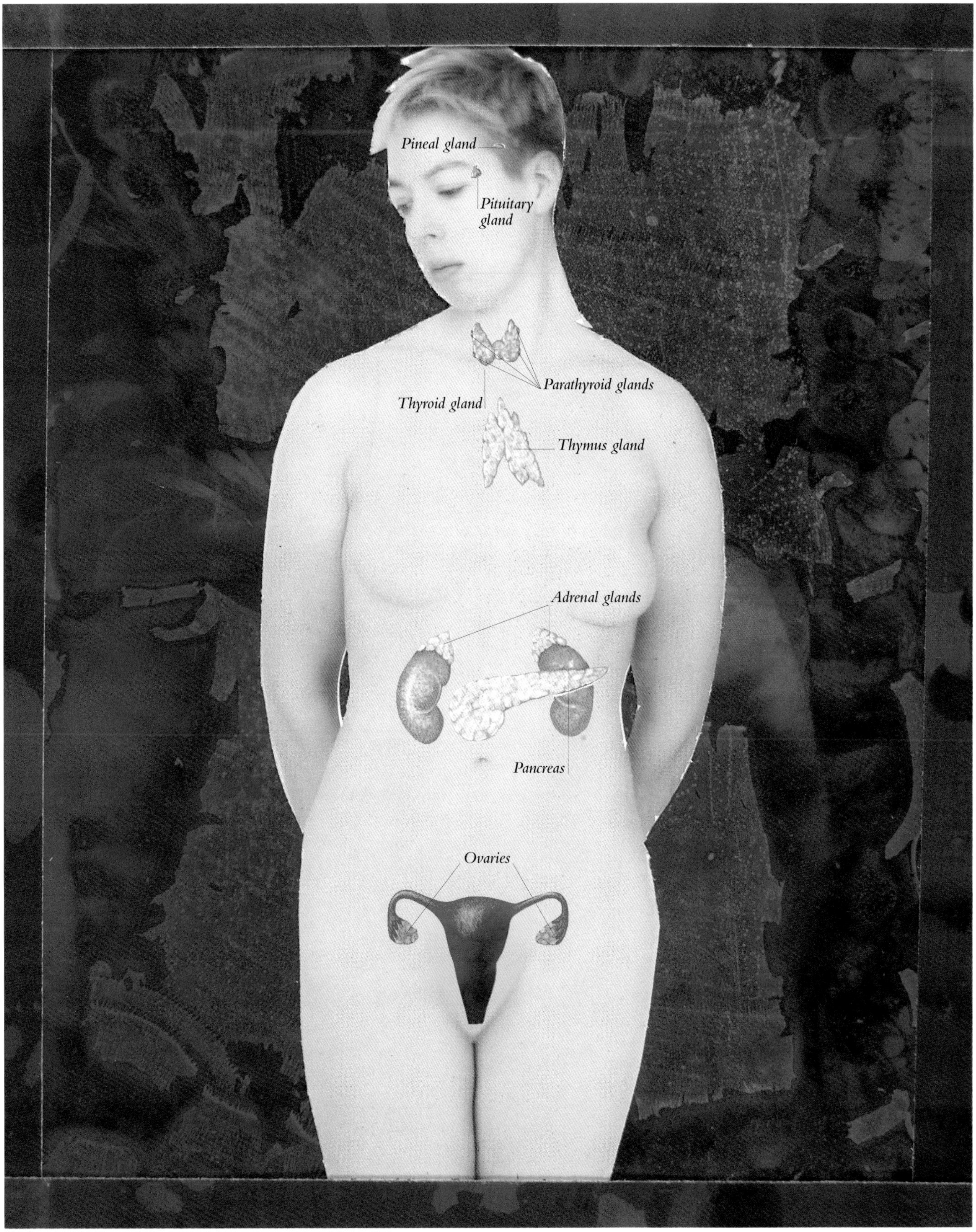
Pineal gland
Pituitary gland
Parathyroid glands
Thyroid gland
Thymus gland
Adrenal glands
Pancreas
Ovaries

DIABETES

What is it?

Diabetes mellitus, the common form of diabetes, is caused by lack of insulin, a hormone manufactured by the pancreas gland. Insulin is responsible for the absorption of glucose into liver and fat cells and muscles which require it for energy, and if there is insufficient supply glucose levels in the blood rise. In Type I (insulin-dependent or juvenile-onset) diabetes insulin levels may be very low (or totally absent), forcing the cells to obtain energy from fat instead, which may lead to diabetic coma and death. It usually first occurs in people under the age of 35 (most often between 10 and 16) and develops rapidly. Type II (non-insulin-dependent or maturity-onset) diabetes is normally found in people over 40, particularly those who are overweight. Onset is gradual and as insulin is not as lacking as in Type I it may go undiagnosed for some time. The symptoms of diabetes include excessive thirst and the passing of large amounts of urine, weight loss, fatigue, hunger, weakness and apathy. Diabetes mellitus is a chronic condition and causes damage to the nerves, premature atheroma (see page 164) and therefore angina and arterial disease in the legs, hypertension, blindness and kidney failure.

Causes

Diabetes mellitus tends to run in families, although not all members who carry the gene will go on to develop the disease; the incidence of those who do is higher in Type II than in Type I. Damage to the pancreas caused by a virus is thought to be the precipitating factor in Type I. Other aggravating factors of diabetes mellitus include:

- *Pregnancy (see pages 220–221).*
- *Certain other illnesses, including hyperthyroidism, pancreatic diseases and thyrotoxicosis.*
- *Treatment with corticosteroids may unmask a tendency to diabetes.*

Orthodox treatment

Type II diabetes mellitus can often be controlled just by weight reduction, dietary restriction and oral medication, with insulin injections where these fail. Type I requires regular self-injections of insulin, together with a diet calculated to avoid fluctuations in glucose levels. Patients need regular check-ups to monitor weight, blood sugar and blood pressure as well as an annual eye test.

ALTERNATIVE TREATMENT

Homeopathy

Homeopathic treatment should be constitutional, and undertaken in addition to orthodox treatment. Apart from advice on diet and lifestyle, treatment may consist of the following specific remedies, which may be taken four times each day for up to two weeks:

- Phosphoric ac. when the symptoms are brought on by nervous exhaustion (grief, working too hard).
- Uranium nit. when symptoms include digestive upsets, weakness, emaciation and bedwetting.
- Silicea when symptoms include cold, sweaty, smelly feet and reduced stamina.
- Argentum nit. when symptoms include swollen ankles.
- Codeinum when symptoms include restlessness, skin irritation and depression.
- Natrum sulph. when symptoms include gout.

Autogenic training

As long as there is some pancreatic function (in other words, the condition is controlled by oral medication) the response can be dramatic. Blood sugar level can be reduced and stabilized. Insulin control may show a slight improvement.

Naturopathy

Dietary advice and applied nutrition may help; in particular, specific nutrients like magnesium and chromium are important in assisting glucose tolerance and can be taken as supplements. Herbal medication may be prescribed. All treatment is complementary to conventional treatment, which must not be neglected.

Nutritional therapy

Recent research has shown that changing to a whole food vegan diet can enable some diabetics to come off insulin and hypoglycemic drugs. Other factors involved in maturity-onset diabetes are nutritional deficiencies, particularly of zinc, chromium, magnesium and B vitamins. Diabetics seem to have a greatly increased requirement for vitamin E. When supplemented, insulin requirements may be reduced.

Other treatments

Acupuncture may dramatically reduce the amount of insulin required. A **Chinese herbalist** may offer herbal hormone tonics and herbal astringents. Diuretic herbs and herbs to regulate the blood condition may be required. In **Ayurvedic medicine** a practitioner may prescribe specific oral formulas to control the blood sugar level. **Macrobiotic** therapists suggest the standard macrobiotic diet, with particular emphasis on good-quality sweeteners in the form of barley or rice malt, raisins and seeds. Fluid restrictions may be necessary. The **metamorphic technique** will focus on a specific area of the foot. **Yoga** therapists may suggest gentle *asanas*, relaxation, *pranayama* and meditation. **Cymatics** may also be useful. **Tai chi** and **polarity therapy** may help to address imbalances causing the condition.

THYROID PROBLEMS

What are they?

The thyroid gland, situated in the front of the neck, produces thyroxine, which controls the body's energy level. An overactive gland with overproduction of thyroxine (hyperthyroidism) causes weight loss, increased appetite, palpitations, anxiety, tremor, irritability, dislike of heat, sweating and infrequent menstruation. Untreated, this condition can lead to heart failure. An underactive gland (hypothyroidism) causes apathy, dislike of cold, hair loss, fatigue, constipation, muscle aches, heavy periods, weight gain, depression and a hoarse voice. If left untreated, hypothyroidism in children may cause growth and mental retardation; in severe cases of hypothyroidism, the sufferer becomes very cold and drowsy and may lose consciousness.

Causes

The most common cause of both hyper- and hypothyroidism is the body developing antibodies against the thyroid gland that cause an increase or reduction respectively in the production of thyroid hormone. Occasionally, hyperthyroidism is caused by enlarged nodules in the thyroid. Other causes of hypothyroidism include iodine deficiency and congenital deficiency (or even total absence of the thyroid gland).

Orthodox treatment

An underactive thyroid is treated by daily tablets of thyroxine. The dose is gradually built up until the condition becomes stable, and then treatment continues for life. Iodine deficiency is now rare, but treatment with thyroid hormones can reverse some of the damage done by the condition. Enlargement of the thyroid (goiter) will be treated according to the cause. An overactive gland is treated with drugs to reduce the levels of thyroxine made by the thyroid gland. If drug treatment fails, surgery to remove part of the thyroid will be undertaken or, in elderly patients, radioactive iodine as a drink to irradiate the gland may be given.

ALTERNATIVE TREATMENT

Homeopathy

Treatment will be constitutional and aimed at controlling acute symptoms. Long-term control of the condition should be undertaken by an orthodox doctor. However, specific remedies which may help hyperthyroidism are:

• Iodum when the sufferer feels hot, cannot stop activity, is obsessive about everything and especially if he or she is dark-haired and dark-eyed.
• Natrum mur. when symptoms are accompanied by constipation, palpitations and an earthy complexion.
• Belladonna if sufferer has flushed face and staring eyes.
• Lycopus if the heart is pounding and racing.

To help hypothyroidism:

• Arsenicum can be taken for up to five days, twice daily, while constitutional treatment is being sought.

Nutritional therapy

Nutritional deficiencies (for example, zinc, vitamin A, selenium and iron) and a toxic overload are thought to be the main factors involved in the onset of hypothyroidism. Researchers have found that exposure to some environmental toxins can cause the body to produce antibodies which attack its own thyroid gland. Nutritional therapists aim to enhance the body's detoxification abilities in treating such patients.

Spiritual healing

Spiritual healing helps to rebalance the entire endocrine system and restore harmony to bodily functions. Other factors also need to be considered with endocrine imbalances and therefore a holistic view of the patient is essential. Hormonal problems may have roots in the emotions – for example, an inability to express anger may affect the thyroid gland. Spiritual healing can help to bring suppressed emotions to the surface. Correct diet is also an important factor in endocrine imbalances. Stress is another common cause, which healing can help relieve.

Autogenic training

Studies have shown that autogenic training has normalizing results: low levels of thyroid production have been increased and high levels reduced. It may also be useful in mild cases of hypo- and hyperthyroidism in order to avoid the use of standard orthodox treatment, which can be long-term.

Other treatments

A **Chinese herbalist** will probably offer herbal products from the sea and in addition heat-clearing herbs for hyperthyroidism. A **Western herbalist** may suggest herbs which are particularly rich in iodine, which acts as a general tonic for the thyroid gland. It may also be possible to provide a thyroid antagonist in mild cases of overactive thyroid. In **Ayurvedic medicine** a practitioner may suggest *panchakarma* for detoxification. The **metamorphic technique** will focus on the conception area. **Kirlian technique** has enabled some patients to understand the energy blocks in the area of the throat, thereby providing some relief from the symptoms. A **reflexologist** will pay particular attention to the pituitary, thyroid and adrenal gland reflexes. A **yoga** therapist may suggest gentle *asanas*, relaxation, *pranayama*, meditation and sound. **Cymatics** may also be useful. **Tai chi** and **polarity therapy** may help to address imbalances causing the condition.

MALE REPRODUCTIVE SYSTEM

What is it?

The male reproductive system consists of the penis, two testes, several glands and the "plumbing" that joins everything together. The penis consists of a head (glans), shaft and erectile tissue. Sexual excitement makes the spongy tissue engorge with blood bringing the penis erect.

The male reproductive cells or sperm are made in the testes. The ideal temperature for sperm manufacture is less than body heat, so the testes lie outside the body in the scrotum. Each sperm resembles a tadpole with a head and a tail. A man produces approximately 20 thousand million sperm each month and can carrying on doing so well into his 60s and 70s, unlike women who stop producing eggs at about 50 during the menopause. The testes also produce the male hormone testosterone, which brings about puberty (between 12–15 years) and the development of secondary sexual characteristics such as male hair growth and genital development. From the testes the sperm travel to the penis, collecting secretions from the seminal vesicles and the prostate gland en route. During sexual intercourse the sperm is ejaculated into the female reproductive tract. With good conditions a sperm will fertilize a female egg (ovum) to produce a "zygote." This will divide to produce an embryo.

What can go wrong?

With each ejaculation some semen containing 60 million sperm is produced for fertilization of one ovum. If there is too little semen, too few sperm, or if too many of the sperm are abnormal then fertilization will not occur.

About one in four men have erection problems. The cause is both psychological and physical, but excessive alcohol, drugs such as beta-blockers or diuretics can also be implicated. Urinary tract infection is less common, but sexually transmitted diseases (STDs) are on the increase. The sufferer can have a penile discharge, painful urination or warts. An enlarged prostate gland occurs in many men over 60. The symptoms are frequency and hesitancy during urination. There is also the possibility of *prostate cancer*, but it is slow growing and often the patient dies of old age before it takes effect. Cancers of the penis and testes are rare, but men should check their testicles regularly for lumps.

Sperm are made in the testes, which along with the penis, several glands and connective plumbing make up the male reproductive system. Men can produce sperm well into old age.

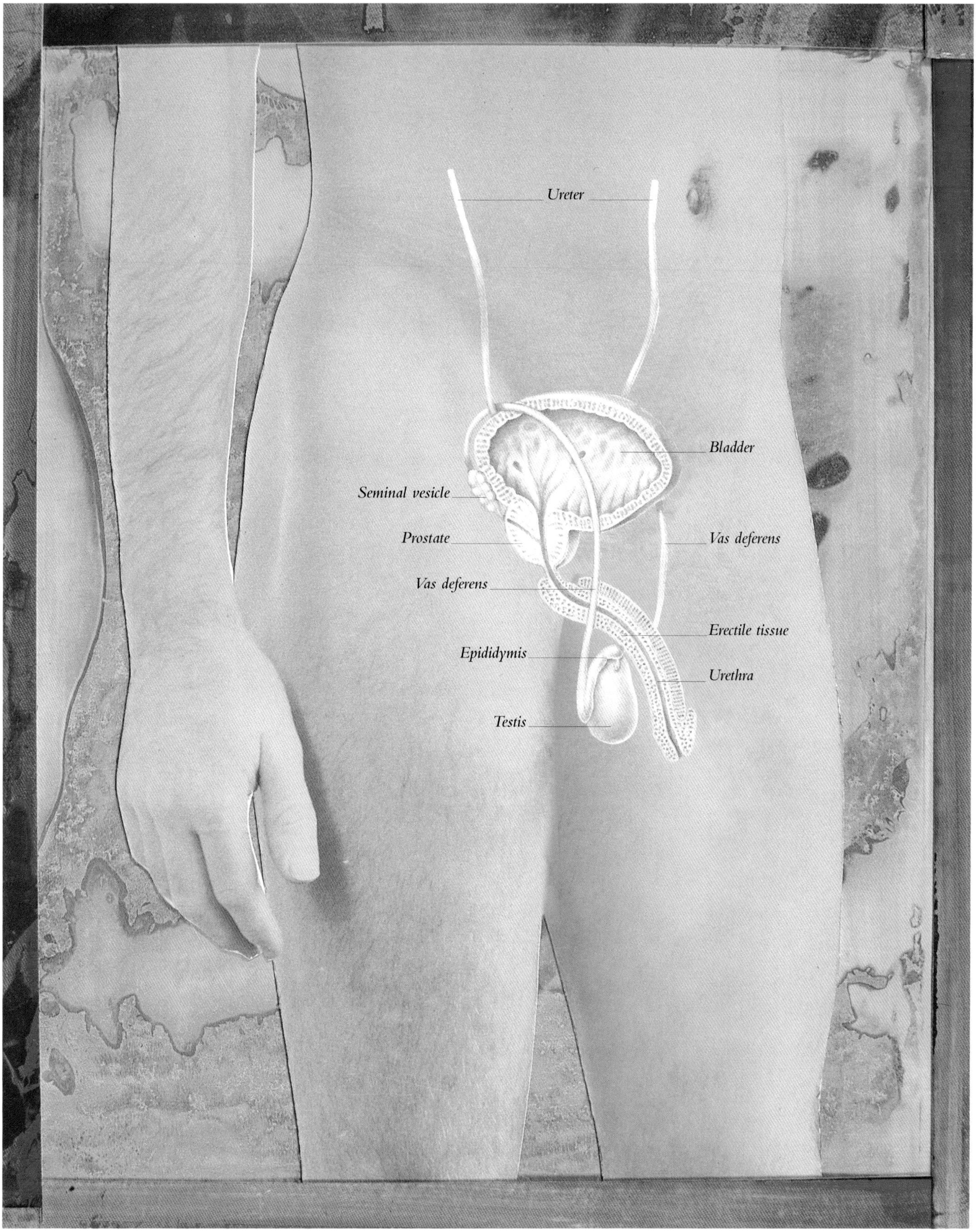
Ureter
Bladder
Seminal vesicle
Prostate
Vas deferens
Vas deferens
Erectile tissue
Epididymis
Urethra
Testis

Prostate Problems

What are they?

The prostate is a small sex gland which lies at the base of the male bladder, surrounding the urethra, the tube which transports urine from the bladder through the penis. The prostate's function is to make the fluid which transports and nourishes the sperm as it is ejaculated.

The most common prostate problem is benign prostatic hyperplasia (BPH). This is a slow, noncancerous enlargement, which progressively constricts the urethra tube, leading to difficulties with urination. Prostatitis, inflammation of the gland itself, is more frequent in younger men, and can be acute (short-term) or chronic (long-term). Its symptoms include the frequent need to urinate, a burning pain when doing so, difficulty in urinating, lower back pain, painful ejaculation and inflamed testes. Prostate cancer (see pages 208-209) is also a potential problem.

Causes

Prostate enlargement occurs naturally in all men as they pass middle age, when an increasing amount of the hormone testosterone is converted to a more powerful form known as DHT (dihydrotestosterone). The balance between men's production of testosterone and estrogen (both of which work together to control prostate growth) also changes as they age. Prostatitis usually results from infection, particularly chlamydia, an infection which is normally transmitted sexually. Stress, and infrequent ejaculation, may also be contributing factors.

Orthodox treatment

For BPH your doctor will probably do a rectal examination. Hospital tests could involve a urodunamic test to check the amount of urine passed, or an ultrasound scan of the prostate. Drug treatment for BPH includes alpha-blockers, traditional hormonal treatment (which can affect libido and potency) or the newer alpha reductase inhibitors which block DHT production.

Surgery to remove part or all of the prostate may be undertaken to allow urine to pass more easily, but may occasionally cause ejaculation problems. Antibiotics will be given for prostatitis, as will alpha-blocker drugs or possibly gentle microwave therapy. Self-help will include avoiding drinks such as coffee, spicy foods and cigarettes, and stress reduction.

Alternative Treatment

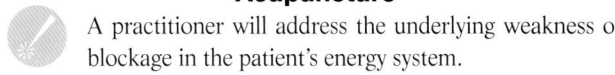

Acupuncture

A practitioner will address the underlying weakness or blockage in the patient's energy system.

- Lifestyle and eating habits will also be examined. Hereditary aspects will be taken into consideration.
- Pressure points on the bladder, conception and governor meridians may be used, and moxibustion may be suitable.

Naturopathy

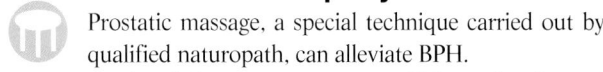

Prostatic massage, a special technique carried out by a qualified naturopath, can alleviate BPH.

- Nutritional and dietary management will be undertaken with herbal medication.
- Hot and cold compresses and sitz baths may be helpful, as may zinc supplements to reduce prostate enlargement, and drinking plenty of fluids (except diuretic drinks).

Homeopathy

Treatment will be according to the cause of the problem, but some very helpful remedies include:

- Sabal for an enlarged prostate and difficult, painful urination.
- Baryta for a frequent urge to urinate although the stream is weak, and the person is thin and perhaps prematurely impotent.

For prostatitis, homeopathic treatment is constitutional but in an acute attack the following remedies may help:

- Sabal, if the prostate is enlarged but the area around it feels cold and intercourse is either impossible or painful.
- Thuja if there is a burning sensation at the neck of the bladder and a frequent urge to pass water.

Western herbalism

Treatment can be very helpful in reducing BPH and also any inflammation or infection that affects the prostate gland. Herbs that have diuretic properties such as couch grass, saw, palmetto and horsetail can be given to help encourage a person to urinate.

Other therapies

Cymatics is extremely useful for the treatment of prostate problems, as it is for most endocrine system function problems. **Kinesiology** and **shiatsu** may be useful for BPH. **Crystal and gemstone therapy** may help to strengthen the immune system and in turn activate the body's natural healing process. **Macrobiotic treatment** may advise a standard macrobiotic diet, in which there is no chicken, egg, meat, salmon or baked foods, and which features a reduced intake of salt. Herbs with hormonal effects and kidney tonics may be suggested by a **Chinese herbalist**. A **yoga** practitioner may recommend gentle *asanas*, relaxation, *pranayama*, meditation and *shat kriyas*. In **Ayurvedic medicine** treatment may consist of Ayurvedic oral preparations and *panchakarma* therapy. **Reflexology** will be aimed at treating points for the endocrine glands and bladder. An **aromatherapist** will incorporate estrogen-like oils such as clary sage and geranium in an all-over body massage.

INFERTILITY

What is it?

Infertility is a symptom that something in the body is not working correctly. Couples are said to have a fertility problem if there is "failure to achieve pregnancy after a year of regular unprotected intercourse." About a third of fertility problems occur solely in women, one third in men and the remaining third are mutual. About one in 12 men have some form of fertility problem.

Causes

The most common cause is a low sperm count. Research has shown that sperm count worldwide has dropped by 50 percent since the 1940s. The reason is probably environmental (food, water and air) pollution involving chemicals such as the non-biodegradable PSB family.

Another common problem is poor sperm quality, and some men's ejaculate contains antibodies to their own sperm. Alternatively, there may be no sperm at all, either because the man is producing none or because other delicate tubes which carry them are blocked. Sometimes sperm cannot penetrate the egg when they reach it; and in a very small number of cases there may be hormonal problems. Risk factors include:

- *Smoking and drinking alcohol.*
- *Raised temperature around the testes (caused by tight trousers and pants, constantly centrally heated environments, varicose veins on the scrotum, or obesity "overhang"). The testes need to be slightly cooler than the rest of the body to make sperm efficiently.*
- *Previous GU infection, or infection with mumps.*
- *Harmful stress.*
- *Certain prescription drugs, such as co-trimoxazole and testerone.*

Orthodox treatment

- *Microsurgery to unblock the sperm ducts or remove varicoceles.*
- *Intra-cytoplasmic sperm injection (injecting the sperm into the egg).*
- *Antibiotics if there is even the smallest subclinical infection.*
- *Cortisone treatment.*
- *Vitamin supplements (usually E) with antibiotics.*
- *Hormonal treatments.*
- *Sperm preselection, in cases of low count or high abnormality rate, the best are skimmed off, activated with a caffeine-like drug and used in any one of several assisted conception processes, including: AID (delivering the sperm with a syringe to the top of the woman's vagina): placing the sperm sample inside the womb itself; IVF, in which sperm and eggs are mixed together in a laboratory and the resulting early embryos are surgically placed in the womb; microassisted techniques such as SUZI (Sub Zonal Insemination) in which the sperm is injected directly into the egg.*

ALTERNATIVE TREATMENT

Naturopathy

A naturopath may suggest the following as treatment for infertility: improving the nutrition of both partners; hot and cold water splashes on the genitals to stimulate circulation locally; avoiding alcohol and smoking for a while, and also getting enough rest.

Bach flower remedies

The following remedies will be helpful for related emotional aspects and will be chosen according to the individual personality and emotional outlook, for instance: willow can be taken for resentment or bitterness over the fertility problem; white chestnut for repetitive, worrying thoughts and pine for feelings of guilt.

Acupuncture

Acupuncture and moxibustion can prove effective, especially when working on the conception meridian. It can improve the number and quality of sperm, address any hormonal difficulties and help to control any stress or anxiety factors.

Homeopathy

Treatment can include sepia if the man has a dragging sensation in the genitals and no desire for sex.

Chinese herbalism

If the condition is acquired and not hereditary, hormone and blood tonics will be prescribed.

Western herbalism

Herbal medicine may focus on general health and vitality, and treat any contributory hormone problems.

Hypnotherapy

A hypnotherapist may use symbolic words and imagery to generate healthy and abundant sperm. Stress reduction techniques and hypno-healing may also be practiced.

Color therapy

Treatment may include wearing red briefs for energy, or blue underwear for excess heat around the genitals.

Other therapies

An **aromatherapist** may give a rose and jasmine massage. In **yoga**, *asanas*, relaxation, *pranayama*, meditation and *shat kriyas* can help. In **Ayurvedic medicine** treatment will include rejuvenation with *panchakarma* and oral preparations for reproductive weakness. The **metamorphic technique** will focus on the prebirth area, and **reflexology** on the testes, prostate and lymph glands.

ERECTILE DYSFUNCTION

What is it?

This condition covers a range of difficulties, from achieving erections which are not quite firm enough for intercourse to one which is very firm but only lasts a moment or two. Actual impotence means that it is not possible to achieve an erection at all.

Causes

Around 40 percent of cases of erectile dysfunction are said to have a purely physical cause, a further 30 percent involve both organic and psychological factors, and the remaining 30 percent are solely psychological in origin. The most common cause of erection difficulties is imperfect blood supply to the penis itself. To become and stay erect, it needs to fill rapidly with blood and to remain filled. Factors that affect this mechanism include:

- *High blood pressure.*
- *Atherosclerosis.*
- *Partial/total venous blockages caused by scar tissue.*
- *"Leaky" blood vessels which allow blood to seep out slowly.*
- *Multiple sclerosis, spinal injury or diabetes.*
- *Ageing.*
- *Depression.*
- *Hormone imbalance (usually related to pituitary gland activity).*

Orthodox treatment

Medical advice will include avoiding cigarettes, alcohol and recreational drugs such as marijuana, and perhaps certain prescription drugs such as antidepressants and tranquilizers. Tests to check for a physical problem will also need to be done, plus a sleep test to see if the man has nocturnal erections. Treatments include:

- *Surgery to tie off the problem blood vessels and prevent leakage.*
- *Vacuum pump devices which fit over the penis, causing it to inflate under negative pressure as air is pumped out of the device.*
- *Penis rings worn around the organ's base to trap blood there.*
- *Sensate focusing (sexual behavioral therapy taught by a urologist or counselor) for psychological "performance anxiety."*
- *Vasoactive drugs such as paparavine injected into the base of the penis to achieve an erection which lasts for one to four hours.*
- *Penile implants (both permanently rigid and inflatable).*
- *Drug therapy, including testosterone and the heart drug glyceryl trinitrate applied to the penis to dilate the blood vessels.*

PREMATURE EJACULATION IS ANOTHER COMMON PROBLEM. SIXTY PERCENT OF MEN CLIMAX WITHIN TWO MINUTES. TREATMENTS RANGE FROM USING THICK CONDOMS, OR AN ANESTHETIC "DELAY" SPRAY TO BEHAVIORAL THERAPY.

ALTERNATIVE TREATMENT

Homeopathy

Specific remedies for this problem include:

- Lycopodium for a man who feels surges of desire but anticipates failure, and whose penis is small and cold.
- Agnus for an erection not firm enough for penetration.
- Conium for an erection which does not last, though great surges of sexual feelings occur after long abstinence.
- Caladium for erections which occur during half-sleep but disappear on waking and for a sexually excited yet flaccid penis.

Chinese herbalism

If appropriate, estrogen herbs and kidney and hormone tonics will be prescribed. Holistic treatment will deal with any overwhelming psychological causes.

Western herbalism

Lowered vitality, or anxiety, and these will be addressed alongside specific remedies for the reproductive system.

Bach flower remedies

The remedies will be helpful for the emotional aspects that are associated with the diagnosis and prognosis, chosen according to personality and emotional outlook, for example: larch for lack of confidence; gentian for a sense of despondency and failure.

Hypnotherapy

The cause can possibly be uncovered using hypnosis. Suggestions, using symbolic words and images, may be used to restore normal penile function. Hypnosis may also be used to increase confidence and self-esteem. Hypnotherapists can teach self-hypnosis for relaxation.

Other therapies

A **macrobiotic** practitioner will suggest a standard macrobiotic diet, avoiding sugar, alcohol, coffee and spices. Salmon head and soy bean stew should be taken twice weekly. The **Alexander Technique** may be appropriate when the cause is stress or anxiety related. A **yoga** practitioner might suggest gentle asanas, relaxation, *pranayama*, meditation and *shat kriyas*. **Autogenic** training may be useful for the general reduction of anxiety, which may be causing problems. In **Ayurvedic medicine** there are special formulas available for impotence, and *panchakarma* therapy may be undertaken. The **metamorphic technique** may be aimed at the birth area. **Reflexology** will be aimed at the reproductive organs. **Spiritual healing** and **polarity therapy** may be useful, as well as **shiatsu. Aromatherapy** will include massage for the lower back (not the front or anywhere near the genitals as these oils are very stimulating) with essential oil of black pepper and ginger. A **color therapist** may suggest wearing red on the lower part of the body next to the skin, such as red briefs.

SEXUALLY TRANSMITTED DISEASES (STDs)

What are they?

Sexually transmitted diseases (STDs) are a group of diseases usually passed on by sexual contact. For men, they include the traditional venereal diseases, syphilis and gonorrhea, and also genital herpes, genital warts, pubic lice, Hepatitis B, nonspecific urethritis and chlamydia. HIV also comes into this category because, although there are many other ways of contacting it (see pages 258–259), it is still most often passed on sexually and the fastest-growing method of transmission is now heterosexual sex.

An STD may be symptomless. For example, chlamydia in men usually has no symptoms which causes problems as it may progress to prostatitis, a painful and often hard-to-treat infection of the prostate gland. The early latent stage of syphilis, which can last a lifetime, is also undetectable without a test. In addition, when symptoms are apparent, they vary greatly depending on the disorder, and may be present in one partner only. An STD may also lie dormant for years and flare up unexpectedly. However, general warning signs include:

- *Burning upon urination.*
- *Discharge from the penis.*
- *Warts, sores or ulcers on or around the penis.*
- *Soreness around the end of the penis during or immediately after*
- *intercourse.*
- *Itchy pubic area.*
- *Pain or itching around the anus.*
- *Trouble conceiving.*
- *Unexplained skin rashes.*
- *General decline in health.*
- *Swollen glands in the groin.*

Causes

STDs are usually caused by sexual contact with an infected person. The best form of protection against most STDs is a condom, and avoiding sharing sex toys. You cannot catch STDs from Jacuzzis, toilet seats, sharing a bath, bath towels or drinking cups. The one exception is pubic lice, which may occasionally be passed on by sharing bedding or a towel with an infected person.

Orthodox treatment

Caught early, nearly all STDs can be effectively treated or, in the case of herpes, contained and kept at bay. Half of all herpes sufferers never experience a second attack anyway, though the virus remains in the body. Treatment varies according to the cause, but the mainstays are:

- *Antibiotics used in cocktails or singly.*
- *Antiviral drugs.*
- *Drugs to boost the immune system.*
- *Caustic treatment to burn off warts.*

Although the symptoms listed can indicate disorders and infections other than STDs, if any are noticed, it is best to visit the local hospital's genito-urinary (GU) clinic, sometimes called a "special clinic" (many are just walk-in affairs needing no appointment). Treatment there remains totally confidential and, if wished, will not even be disclosed to a patient's doctor. The clinics are also properly equipped to carry out the necessary examinations (genital/anal pathogen swabs and blood tests needed to identify the problem and treat it effectively). Left untreated, STDs may cause infertility, and chronic discomfort, for life.

ALTERNATIVE TREATMENT

It is essential that STDs are diagnosed and treated by orthodox medical practitioners in the first instance, because of the dangers of untreated infection or infestation.

Western herbalism

Itchy rashes caused by pubic lice can be treated with tree of life, wild indigo and other parasite-killing herbs; herpes responds well to echinacea, as it does to marigold tea infusions applied locally.

Homeopathy

Treatment must only be undertaken by an experienced homeopath, and usually as a complement to conventional treatment: it can encourage healing following antibiotics, for example. Constitutional treatment can boost resistance to further infection, and there are specific remedies for each of the diseases, for example:

- Herpes may be treated with Natrum mur. (if the genital skin is dry and the lesions hot and puffy) and Capsicum (if the genitals burn and sting with cracked skin and a red itchy rash).
- Penile warts may be treated with Thuja, and if this produces no improvement, if the foreskin is broken, and the warts bleeding, Cinnabar may be suggested.

Other therapies

The **Alexander Technique**, as a stress-management system, can reduce the likelihood of herpes attacks after infection, since the occurrence of herpes can be increased by worry and stress. In **Ayurvedic medicine** treatment will be based around general, immune-enhancing preparations. **Naturopathy** can involve applied nutrition and dietetic management and a naturopath will also recommend detoxification diets. The **metamorphic technique** treatment will be aimed at the birth area. **Crystal** and **gemstone therapy** may be useful, as can **spiritual healing** and **Shiatsu**. **Cymatics** claims to have dealt successfully with some STDs, and enhances the immune system.

CANCER

What is it?

Cancer sounds as if it should be one single disease, but in fact there are more than 200 different types, all with different names, causes and treatments. The cancers which only men can develop, because women do not have the relevant anatomy, are cancer of the prostate gland, testes and penis. The most common cancer for men is actually cancer of the lung, which more than 30,000 men develop each year in Britain compared with 14,000 women. The information here deals specifically with male (andrological) cancers (andrology is the male equivalent of female gynecology.) **Prostate cancer** is the second most common form of cancer affecting men causing 10–12,000 deaths a year in England and Wales. The prostate gland lies between the base of the penis and the anus, circling the urethra, the tube which carries urine from the bladder through the penis. Death from prostate cancer is the second most common cause of death in the Western world (second to lung cancer). The symptoms of the condition mimic benign prostate problems (see page 204) and therefore may take some time to diagnose.

Early prostate cancer produces no symptoms at all. A more developed tumor may produce the sort of urinary problems that are experienced with benign prostatic hyperplasia (BPH, in which the glands grows slowly bigger, partially blocking the exit of urine from the bladder) – a weak urine stream, needing to pass water more often than usual but only in small amounts, needing to pass water frequently at night, and dribbling at the end of urination. Additional symptoms of prostate cancer (NOT BPH), however, include:

- *Blood in the urine (this is always abnormal and should be reported to your doctor immediately).*
- *Pain on passing water.*
- *Bone pain and weight loss in cases of advanced prostate cancer.*

Testicular cancer has a high survival rate (99.5 percent when caught early) and there are only about 1,400 cases a year. However, it is the most common cancer in younger men under 49. Luckily men can feel for any lumps in their own testes (during a warm bath is an ideal time because the skin of the scrotum is relaxed then).

There are two types of testicular cancer, seminoma and teratoma. Symptoms include:

- *Swelling in one of the testes.*
- *Lump seen/felt in the testes.*
- *Change in weight in one testicle, or a feeling of heaviness.*

Penile cancer, or cancer of the penis, is extremely rare, and usually occurs in uncircumcized men in later life. It normally begins with a sore or ulcer on the penis. If it is left untreated this will develop into an invasive form of cancer that can spread first to the prostate and urethra, then to other parts of the body as well. Others signs are a warty growth on the glans or corona (rim of the penis head), and also the lymph nodes in the groin may be swollen if the disease has spread this far.

Causes

The cause of **prostate cancer** is unknown, and it seems to be on the increase. Risk factors include:

- *Family history of this disease.*
- *High-fat diet.*
- *Age – increasingly common in men over 50, peaking between the ages of 60–80.*
- *Higher levels of testosterone. (It is testosterone, or rather its more potent form which adult men produce called dihydrotestosterone (DHT), that encourages prostate growth. Progressively more DHT is produced as men get older. This is why young men do not develop either enlarged prostates or prostate cancer but older ones do.)*
- *Exposure to certain radioactive substances.*
- *Race – Afro-Caribbean men are more prone.*

Testicular cancer is most common in men in their late twenties and early thirties, and in men of a higher social class. Other risk factors include:

- *Testes which descended late (this is on the increase, which may be why testicular cancer is increasing, too) or not at all.*
- *Early puberty.*
- *Family history of the disorder.*
- *Race: white males are six times more likely to develop this.*

As a self-help measure, exercise may have a protective effect against testicular cancer.

Risk factors for **penile cancer** include:

- *Being uncircumcized.*
- *Age: the most common age for developing this form of cancer is 60 to late 70s.*
- *Poor penile hygiene.*
- *Penile warts.*
- *Bowen's Disease (a form of skin cancer).*

Orthodox treatment

Prostate cancer can be very slow-growing, so your specialist may just advise watching and waiting with regular check-ups. Tests for prostate cancer include:

- *Digital rectal examination, which involves your doctor placing a finger into the back passage to see if any lumpiness or a hardened area can be felt that suggests a prostate tumor. This procedure is, unfortunately, not very accurate because only one side of the gland can be felt through the rectal wall.*
- *Blood test to check for levels of a protein called Prostate Specific Antigen (PSA), as PSA levels in prostate cancer are usually high.*
- *Hospital tests include a needle biopsy to take a sample of prostate tissue for cancer analysis, and ultrasound.*

There are several different types of hormonal treatments for prostate cancer, ranging from estrogen therapy to a drug which blocks the "growing" effect of the male hormones on the prostate. All have side effects (at differing levels) ranging from breast development to possible impotence. If such drugs are being used to control prostate cancer, sufferers will need to take them indefinitely or the tumor may return.

For early, or inoperable, **prostate cancer**, radiotherapy is used; chemotherapy only rarely. There is an operation called TURP (trans-urethral resection of the prostate) which can remove cancerous prostate tissue but leave the rest of the gland intact. The other option is removal of the entire gland. Traditionally side effects of the latter often included erection and urinary problems, but with modern surgical techniques such problems are now far less common.

Tests to check for **testicular cancer** include:

- *Physical examination.*
- *Blood tests.*
- *Ultrasound scans.*
- *CT scan or exploratory surgery.*

Most lumps in the testes in fact turn out to be quite harmless, and the most common cause is an ordinary cyst. However, if the lump proves to be cancerous after all, seminomas are usually removed surgically first, then the area is given radiotherapy treatment. Teratomas are treated with surgery, then either, or both, chemotherapy and radiotherapy. If an entire testicle needs to be removed, a false one which feels indistinguishable from the real one can be placed in the empty scrotal sac.

Treatment for **penile cancer** depends on how advanced the condition is. A small number of early cases can be treated just using a laser, but if it has progressed past the skin and outer part of the penis it will be necessary to remove some of the lymph nodes, and also a section of the penis itself. It may be possible to reconstruct part of this later, as well as using a penile implant but this is not usually done in most cases because of the age of the men concerned.

If the cancer is suitable for treatment by radiotherapy, this may sometimes be used instead of surgery, and has the advantage of keeping the penis intact. Chemotherapy is more likely to be used in cases of more advanced cancer.

Alternative Treatment

Alternative therapies should be used alongside orthodox medical treatment for cancer to support the individual physically and emotionally. They must not be used as an alternative to it.

Hypnotherapy

To reinforce treatment while at home or in hospital, hypnotherapy might include:

- Age regression.
- Hypno-healing.
- Cell command therapy.
- Self-hypnosis.

Homeopathy

Treatment for cancer should only be undertaken by an experience homeopath. Most treatment is complementary to orthodox medicine, and will support a system that is battered by conventional treatments such as chemotherapy and radiotherapy. The homeopathic view of all cancer is that it represents a breakdown in health at all levels. Therefore, treatment will always be constitutional, with specific remedies prescribed according to the individual symptom picture.

Aromatherapy

This can be of great help to people with cancer, but early-stage patients should not be massaged as this may encourage the spread of metastasis via the blood/lymphatic systems, so essential oils should be used in the form of room pump dispenser. Oils should also not be used on the skin directly after chemotherapy or radiotherapy. Oils which can help include: uplifting oils such as bergamot, rose, neroli and lavender to give any negative emotions a helpful boost; tea tree oil may be used to help strengthen the immune system.

Massage

Massage communicates care, reduces feelings of isolation and brings comfort by contact with another human being. It may also counteract the feelings of hopelessness and despair which some sufferers experience and help them to deal positively with life. On a physical level, massage can be used to relax muscles and relieve pain, discomfort and tension.

Bach flower remedies

These could play a useful part in promoting a more positive frame of mind in sufferers who are frightened, depressed or affected by other negative attitudes. Remedies should be chosen on an individual basis according to the personality and mood of the person concerned. Possible remedies include olive for draining exhaustion; mimulus for fear; gorse for feelings of hopelessness and defeat; rescue remedy to help deal with the shock of diagnosis.

Other therapies

A standard **macrobiotic** diet may be suggested, liberally interpreted, and the yin version. There have been some excellent success stories through macrobiotic treatment. A **yoga** practitioner may suggest gentle *asanas*, relaxation, *pranayama*, meditation and *shat kriyas*. A **reflexologist** will undertake treatment to support the individual's own healing process. **Cymatics**, **shiatsu**, **spiritual healing** and **crystal and gemstone therapy** claim to treat these conditions successfully.

FEMALE REPRODUCTIVE SYSTEM

The internal female reproductive organs are the ovaries, the Fallopian tubes, the uterus (womb), and the vagina, which connects the uterus to the external genitalia. The clitoris, the labia majora and minora and the pubic hair is in the external genitalia.

The almond-shaped ovaries are on either side of the lower abdomen. When a female baby is born each ovary contains all the eggs (about 400,000) that she will ever have. At puberty the ovaries regularly release the eggs into the Fallopian tubes. They then secrete progesterone and oestrogen hormones which prepare the uterus' lining for a fertilized egg. An egg is fertilized by a male sperm; it divides into a ball of cells (a zygote) which embeds itself in the uterus and develops into an embryo.

If no fertilization occurs, the egg and the lining of the uterus is shed during menstruation, which happens about every 28 days until the female menopause starts at 45 to 55 years.

The Fallopian tubes are about 10cm (4in) long and take the zygote to the uterus. The uterus is a hollow pear-shaped muscular organ in the pelvis. It stretches to accommodate the foetus and its muscular contractions bring about childbirth. The lower uterus is the cervix which protrudes into the 10cm (4in) long vagina. Both stretch enormously (and temporarily) during labour.

What can go wrong?

Menstrual cycle problems and related conditions are common disorders. They are generally caused by disturbances in the circulating sex hormones. Painful, irregular periods are distressing to many women and can badly upset their lives. Suffers of premenstrual syndrome (PMS), caused by fluctuating hormonal levels, complain of mood swings, swollen breasts and bloated stomachs. Hormones, or rather the lack of them, are also the culprits with the menopause. Some women just suffer erratic periods, but others have hot flushes, night sweats or vaginal dryness.

Pelvic pain can be caused by: pelvic inflammatory disease 'PID', fibroids or endometriosis. *Sexually transmitted diseases (STDs)*, such as herpes and warts, can be contracted through sex without a barrier method of contraception. *Thrush* is a common fungal infection which occurs when the acidic balance of the vagina is upset due to hormonal or other changes. Female fertility problems are often due to blocked Fallopian tubes .

The ovaries, Fallopian tubes, the womb and the vagina make up the female reproductive system. Eggs are released by the ovaries; if one is fertilized by a sperm a pregnancy occurs.

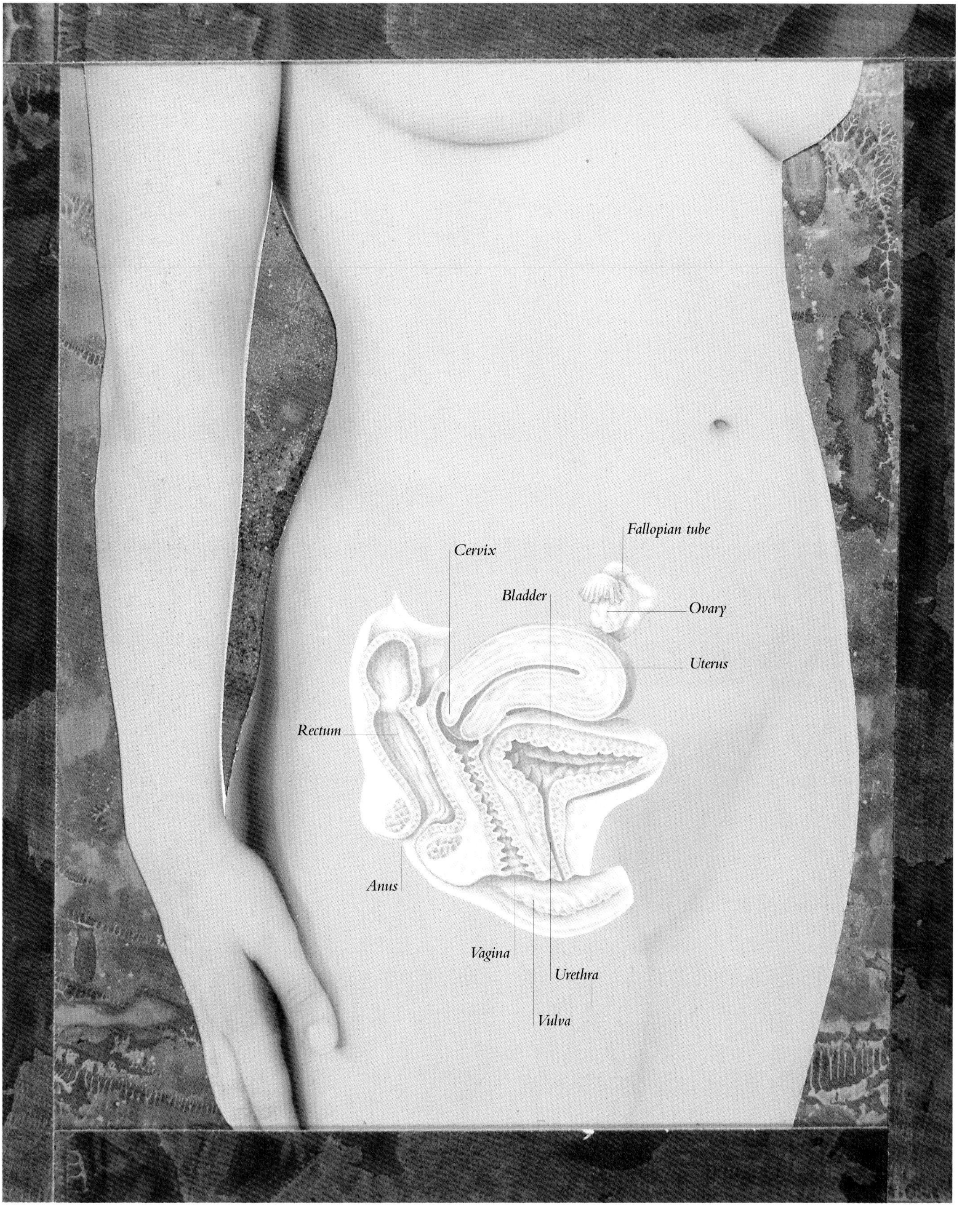
Fallopian tube
Cervix
Bladder
Ovary
Uterus
Rectum
Anus
Vagina
Urethra
Vulva

Premenstrual Syndrome (PMS)

What is it?

Premenstrual syndrome (PMS) is a blanket term for over 150 different symptoms which women may experience, either singly or in combination, every month between ovulation and the start of their period. Some are physical, some are psychological (emotional) and some behavioral.

About 80 percent of women between puberty and menopause experience at least one symptom of PMS regularly every month at some time during the ten to 14 days before their period begins. Different women's experience of PMS varies enormously. Some may find they experience just one minor symptom for a short time, such as mild breast tenderness for a few days before their period begins, while others may suffer several different symptoms at the same time.

Although PMS has a reputation for being an unpleasant condition, some women have found that it produces positive symptoms rather than negative ones. Canadian research carried out at a well-woman clinic in Toronto in 1989 suggested that seven in ten PMS sufferers can name at least one good thing about their premenstrual phase, ranging from additional energy and creativity to increased sexual enjoyment. However, a further one in ten report that the symptoms they experience are so disabling that they cannot carry on with their normal lives.

In a few cases, PMS can be so severe and manifest so suddenly that it has been dubbed the Jekyll and Hyde syndrome, and been used successfully as legal defense in both Britain and America in cases where women have broken the law. These cases have involved uncharacteristic behavior, such as shoplifting, or criminal or physical violence, during their premenstrual phase.

The most common symptoms of PMS fall into three main categories, as follows:

- *Physical symptoms may include breast enlargement/tenderness, abdominal bloating, fluid retention, headaches, pelvic discomfort, constipation/diarrhea, spots, cravings for foods such as chocolate and salty snacks, and tiredness.*
- *Behavioral symptoms may consist of clumsiness, poor concentration or disturbed sleep.*
- *Emotional symptoms may be irritability, anxiety, depression, disturbed sleep, lowered libido or a violent temper or aggressive behavior.*

Some preexisting conditions such as asthma, epilepsy and herpes may worsen during the premenstrual phase too.

Causes

The basic cause of these symptoms is thought to be the hormonal changes which occur from the time a woman ovulates until the time her womb lining begins to shed – the gradual dropping of estrogen levels and rise of progesterone levels. This process affects some women more profoundly than others, possibly due in part to the fact that some women are far more sensitive to these normal hormonal changes. While there are many different factors which can influence the development and severity of premenstrual syndrome, they can generally be divided into two broad categories:

- *Hormonal imbalance can be one of the underlying causes of PMS. This in turn may arise because of a variety of conditions, ranging from gynecological disorders such as endometriosis to recent childbirth. (In fact, in a survey carried out by St. Thomas' Hospital in London in 1985, about four out of ten PMS sufferers said that the problem had developed after the birth of their first or second baby.*
- *Subclinical (small) nutritional deficiencies may also lead to PMS. Such deficiencies can affect the body's production of, and therefore fine balance between, estrogen and progesterone hormones, which in turn can influence the levels of other vital hormones such as insulin. The nutrients especially thought to affect women's hormonal balance include essential fatty acids, zinc, magnesium and vitamin B6.*

Orthodox treatment

There are two approaches to treatment in conventional medicine. One aims to treat PMS hormonally, usually by either suppressing the ovaries' own production of hormones, or adjusting the levels of estrogen and progesterone throughout the menstrual cycle so that these levels remain at a steady level. The drugs used for this form of treatment include the Combined Pill, natural progesterone, synthetic progestogen (Duphaston), estrogen implants, and also Danazol.

The other approach is to treat a person's individual symptoms. This can be helpful in the short term for immediate relief but does not tackle the root cause of the problem. Symptomatic treatments include:

- *Diuretics for water retention and bloated abdomen.*
- *Mild tranquilizers for anxiety.*
- *Bromocriptine for swollen, tender breasts.*
- *Evening primrose oil, available on prescription, for breast pain (though it can help with most other PMS symptoms).*
- *Painkillers for premenstrual headaches.*

Occasionally, women are helped by antidepressant medication, particularly the newer forms such as Prozac.

Well-informed doctors and alternative health practitioners might also suggest that sufferers eat some complex carbohydrate food either as a meal or a snack, every three hours. These are foods such as whole meal bread, baked potatoes, muesli, porridge, pasta or bananas. This is because during the premenstrual phase any imbalance between estrogen/progesterone will affect the body's production of another hormone called insulin, which in its turn regulates the body's sugar levels.

If these levels drop suddenly, then women can start to feel shaky, weak and irritable. However, the sugars in carbohydrate snacks are digested through the body much more slowly (unlike those of sugary foods which women really crave premenstrually) and so provide steadier levels of blood sugar, and help to stabilize a woman's mood.

ALTERNATIVE TREATMENT

Nutritional therapy

Most PMS sufferers treated with nutritional therapy will experience enormous benefit. Deficiencies in magnesium, B vitamins and essential fatty acids are the most common ones that can lead to PMS. The richest sources of essential fatty acids are evening primrose oil, blackcurrant seed oil and borage oil, and these can be useful dietary supplements.

Bach flower remedies

Remedies should be chosen according to a person's symptoms. Aspen can help with anxiety states; gorse can treat sudden depressive feelings and despondency; crab apple can relieve "I'm ugly" feelings, or if menstruation brings on feeling of disgust; cherry plum is good "for the desperate fear of the mind giving way, of insanity and the impulse to do harm to other people," mustard can help with depression that seems to descend for no apparent reason; scleranthus can alleviate disturbing mood swings; olive and hornbeam can help with overwhelming fatigue and tiredness.

Homeopathy

The best course of action is usually constitutional, but there are several remedies which may also help and are worth trying first, including:

- Sepia for PMS with irritability which is worse for stress, wanting to get away from everything, fits of screaming, possible violence, weepiness.
- Natrum mur. for indifference, lack of self-confidence, depression, anxiety, a detached feeling with headaches before periods.
- Kali carb. for irritability, panic attacks, anger, and tension. It may also be used if hair is falling out, and if there is a desire for sweets and sugar, or a reduced sex drive.

Color therapy

For mood swings, anxiety and depression, alternate soft pastels and light blues worn as clothing, underclothing, or silk squares next to skin on the upper part of the body.

For fatigue and lethargy, wear red on upper part of body to increase energy (avoid the throat).

For lifting mood gently, try wearing some coral shades.

Hypnotherapy

Some women develop PMS symptoms because of unconscious, psychological reactions to menstruation, and in such cases hypnotherapy can prove useful. Many who have generations of PMS sufferers in their family are unconsciously recreating the same symptoms they have seen in their female relations.

Some women develop annoying headaches when they first begin menstruating since they link this in their subconscious to a negative view of reaching female maturity, more commonly known as puberty.

Naturopathy

Treatment will consist of dietary modulation, especially to regulate digestion. It may also include: hypoglycemia monitoring and management with eating plans; applied nutrition, especially zinc and magnesium supplements; herbal medicine to regulate any hormonal imbalance.

Spiritual healing

Spiritual healing helps on every level to restore health. It can regulate the menstrual cycle and restore a balanced hormonal picture, thus relieving many PMS symptoms.

Western herbalism

A herbalist may suggest: couch grass as a diuretic for bloating; gentian to improve digestion and control blood sugar; wild oats or skullcap or other nerve restoratives, or a soothing agent such as camomile tea, for mood swings; cleavers, a mild diuretic and lymphatic stimulant, combined with a herbal remedy, to encourage restoration of hormonal balance and so help reduce the irritation of painful breasts; burdock, a valuable cleanser improving cellular nutrition and waste matter disposal, for spotty skin or lank, greasy hair,

Chinese herbalism

Treatment will consist of some detoxifying herbs, blood and hormone tonics, and herbs to promote the flow of blocked energy.

Aromatherapy

Treatment to relieve premenstrual symptoms may consist of: cold lavender compresses and relaxing oil baths for painful breasts; geranium, bergamot and rosemary massage blends if a sufferer has feelings of tiredness and lethargy; lavender oil which can be massaged into the head, neck and shoulders to ease hormonal headaches plus sandalwood and camomile oils to relieve stress and tension and to help relax muscles of the back and the scalp.

Acupuncture

Dr. Mark Yu, London Master of Acupuncture, says that both acupuncture and acupressure can be successfully used to help rebalance the hormonal system.

Reflexology

Treatment will be aimed at the pituitary, thyroid, adrenals, solar plexus and reproductive organs. Massage can relieve symptoms and aid relaxation.

Other treatments

In **Ayurvedic medicine** a practitioner can help to balance the tridoshas according to the individual's specific needs and what problems they are experiencing.

INFERTILITY

What is it?

The medical definition of infertility is failure to become pregnant after a year of regular, unprotected intercourse. Infertility affects one in six British couples (men and women equally) and is not a disease. Rather, it is a symptom that something is preventing the reproductive processes from working properly, and needs treating. Risk factors for women include:

- *Polycystic Ovary Syndrome.*
- *Age (female fertility declines fast after 35).*
- *Abnormal womb shape.*
- *History of pelvic infections or endometriosis.*
- *Being underweight*
- *Fibroids.*

Causes

Common reasons for female infertility include failure to ovulate (including polycystic ovary syndrome), blocked Fallopian tubes (due to endometriosis, for example), and the production of antibodies to a partner's sperm (see also Male infertility page 205).

Orthodox treatment

The simplest and most affordable treatments for appropriate cases are ovulation stimulation and artificial insemination. Microsurgery for blocked tubes is possible, depending on the blockage. In-vitro fertilization ("test tube babies") and other treatments are expensive, and success rates of different clinics are improving but vary.

ALTERNATIVE TREATMENT

Homeopathy

Constitutional treatment for both partners is the best approach but while waiting for one to be found, helpful remedies include:

- Sabina for women who have had miscarriages before 12 weeks.
- Sepia for irregular periods, feeling chilly, weepy, irritable and averse to sex.

Aromatherapy

Aromatherapists may give a clary sage oil massage which acts directly upon the ovarian axis to restore low estrogen levels; rosemary, tea tree, lavender and other anti-infective oils in the abdominal massage to treat pelvic infection leading to inflamed or blocked reproductive tubes.

Hypnotherapy

A hypnotherapist may suggest age regression to uncover a woman's subconscious fears of pregnancy, childbirth and motherhood, of hospitals and medical treatment, or of recreating her own childhood or of a threat to her marriage by the arrival of a new baby.

Western herbalism

False unicorn root may be recommended by the herbalist for restoring hormonal balance and oats, ginseng, and rosemary can help stress.

Nutritional therapy

A nutritional therapist may recommend some dietary changes and to exclude alcohol. He may also suggest giving up smoking and drugs, and increasing the intake of whole foods rich in vitamins and minerals to ensure that the ovaries produce healthy eggs. The intake of essential fatty acids, found in oily fish, fish liver oils, seeds, nuts, pulses, beans and unrefined vegetable oils, may also need to be increased to stimulate the production of sex hormones.

Supplements may include: vitamin E to help regulate the production of cervical mucus; zinc and vitamin A to correct any nutritional deficiencies which may in turn promote some hormonal imbalance; glandulars (extracts from animal adrenal glands) to adjust any hormonal imbalances; pantothenic acid to help relieve stress.

Acupuncture

Acupuncture can help many women by improving their hormonal balance and stimulating certain points in the body which can balance energy, helping to restore their normal biochemical functioning.

Color therapy

Color therapy can include the wearing of oranges if there is a suspected hormonal imbalance at adrenal gland level; reds can be worn to give energy and vitality if the problem is ovarian, and violet is suitable if the pituitary gland is implicated. The colors can be worn as silk squares next to the skin, or as under or outer clothing.

Other treatments

Art therapists who are working in fertility clinics will try to discover if emotional problems are an underlying cause of the problem. **Bach flower remedies** can help to deal with any negative feelings a person may have about infertility, its prognosis and treatment. For example, white chestnut may be recommended if a woman's mind is "tormented by upsetting and repetitive thoughts," willow may be suggested for introspective thoughts and gorse for despondency and pessimism. In **Chinese herbalism** a practitioner may use both blood and hormone tonics to treat any acquired conditions.

PELVIC PAIN (PID)

What is it?

Pain in the pelvic area is a symptom of a range of different disorders. These include endometriosis, womb prolapse (producing a dragging pain or backache), pelvic infection, IUD problems, ovarian abscesses or cysts, sexually transmitted diseases, inflammatory bowel conditions, period problems, bladder infections and pelvic congestion/spasm.

Causes

The two most frequent ones are thought to be:

- **Endometriosis** *which develops when the cells belonging to the womb lining migrate to other places outside the womb, most commonly the ovaries and Fallopian tubes. Here they grow, and continue to bleed each month under the influence of the menstrual cycle's hormones, leading to the formation of blood-filled cysts, scarring that blocks the tubes, and sticky adhesions. Symptoms include painful periods, painful intercourse and infertility.*
- **Pelvic inflammatory disease (PID),** *which is an infection of the female reproductive organs. Causes include sexually transmitted disorders, previous miscarriage or abortion, an IUD. Some women suffer from repeated attacks, and it becomes a chronic long-term condition. Symptoms include abdominal tenderness, high temperature, painful sex, vaginal discharge, bleeding after sex, severe, low stomach pain, back pain, and fatigue. PID can also block the Fallopian tubes with scar tissue, causing infertility.*

Orthodox treatment

Various treatments are available for endometriosis:

- *Hormonal treatments such as Danazol, the combined Pill, synthetic progesterone or LHRH analogues.*
- *Laser or laparoscopic surgery.*
- *Hysterectomy may be carried out as a last resort if pain and bleeding are disabling or if a woman has completed her family.*

For PID, a swab may be taken from the cervix (not the vagina) to see what type of infection is present. Treatment may then consist of:

- *Broad spectrum antibiotics (your sexual partner may also need to be treated).*
- *Painkillers.*
- *Bed rest.*

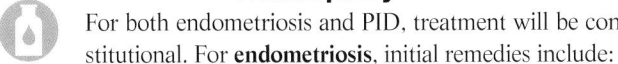

ALTERNATIVE TREATMENT

Homeopathy

For both endometriosis and PID, treatment will be constitutional. For **endometriosis**, initial remedies include:

- Lachesis for pain in left ovary that is worse before periods, or to reduce lower abdominal pain premenstrually.
- Calcarea for a dull aching pain in the lower back, left side of the groin or womb during periods.

For **PID**, initial remedies include:

- Aconite if there is a sudden onset, a mild fever, or if the symptoms are worse.
- Colocynth for cramping pains that are only relieved by doubling over.
- Mercurius for alternate chills and bad-smelling sweats.

Aromatherapy

Endometriosis adhesions may be reduced by oils of rose, camomile, lavender, jasmine and neroli, all of which have a healing and antispasmodic action on muscles and tissues.

For PID, twice-daily massage of the lower abdomen and back with oils like rosewood can strengthen the immune system.

Osteopathy

Some osteopaths are able to perform osteopathic techniques via the vagina to reduce certain types of endometrial adhesion. They may also use osteopathy to encourage venous drainage of the pelvis, reducing uterine congestion and relieving period pain.

Western herbalism

For spasm and inflammation, chaste tree or cramp bark can help with period pain and pain on intercourse.

Other therapies

For **endometriosis**, a standard **macrobiotic** diet may be useful, as will **shiatsu** massage over about eight to 12 months. A **reflexologist** would address all the endocrine glands. **Rolfing** can help by improving circulation, allowing more space around the reproductive organs and promoting relaxation. A **naturopath** will provide nutritional support and dietary detoxification programs. **Self-hypnosis** can be useful to control endometrial pain and induce relaxation. **Chinese herbal** treatment, when combined with acupuncture, can regulate the condition and stagnation of the blood which usually lies at the root of endometriosis.

For **PID**, **Western herbalism** will usually involve echinacea to fight infection. A **reflexologist** will stimulate all the endocrine glands. **Rolfing** can help and **naturopathy** can produce the same results as for endometriosis. Applied nutrition, herbal medication and hydrotherapy may be useful. **Acupuncture** may be useful to stimulate the body's own infection-fighting defenses. **Color therapy** can include the use of indigo lights, or wearing this color. **Chinese herbalism** combined with acupuncture, can regulate the condition of the blood or detoxify the system, depending on the underlying causes. Regular **crystal and gemstone therapy** treatment with a qualified practitioner may help to strengthen the immune system against PID.

Period Problems

What are they?

The three most common menstrual problems are:

- **Dysmenorrhea**, *or painful periods. If no cause for the pain can be found, the condition is called primary dysmenorrhea. If there is a known cause, it is called secondary dysmenorrhea. Symptoms may include sharp, cramping pains or a dull, dragging ache in the lower abdomen or lower back, which may spread down the thighs. There may also be headaches or sweating, nausea, diarrhea, or a frequent need to urinate.*
- **Menorrhagia**, *or heavy periods. Average blood loss is 30ml (1oz), and doctors do not define the loss as a medical problem until it reaches 80ml (2⅔oz) so the best definition of a heavy period is one which interferes with your normal life, or one which is abnormally heavy for you personally.*
- **Amenorrhea**, *or absent periods, of which there are two types – primary amenorrhea, meaning no periods by the time a girl is 16, and secondary amenorrhea if periods have stopped for the past six months..*

Causes

Primary dysmenorrhea may occur because a woman is producing too high a level of prostaglandins, hormone-like substances which stimulate womb contractions, or are especially sensitive to normal levels. For **secondary dysmenorrhea**, causes include:

- *Endometriosis.*
- *Fibroids.*
- *Pelvic infection.*
- *Stress and psychosexual difficulties.*
- *Previous pelvic surgery disrupting the area.*
- *Ovarian cancer (rarely).*
- *Thyroid disorder.*
- *Having an IUD.*
- *Stopping the contraceptive pill.*
- *Giving birth to a first or second baby.*
- *Miscarriage or abortion.*
- *Entering the climacteric, the period before the menopause.*

The causes of **menorrhagia** include:

- *Fibroids.*
- *Chronic pelvic inflammatory disease.*
- *Endometriosis.*
- *Thyroid problems.*
- *Having an IUD.*
- *Injectable contraceptives, such as Depo Provera.*
- *Clotting disorders.*
- *The run up to the menopause.*

Factors contributing to **primary amenorrhea** include:

- *Being underweight.*
- *Heredity – the age at which a woman's mother's periods began and certain rare inherited conditions.*
- *Imperfect hymen.*

Secondary amenorrhea may be caused by:

- *Pregnancy – an obvious cause that is sometimes overlooked.*
- *Low weight.*
- *Excess vitamin A.*
- *Stress, or a severe shock which can stop ovulation.*
- *Anemia.*
- *Thyroid disease.*
- *Starting oral contraception or using injectable contraceptives (Depo Provera).*
- *Polycystic ovaries.*
- *Excess prolactin production.*
- *Endometriosis*

Orthodox treatment

Treatment for **dysmenorrhea** may involve:

- *Painkillers.*
- *Taking the contraceptive Pill or synthetic progestogen, such as Duphaston.*
- *Drugs such as mefanamic acid which counteract the effect of prostaglandins, and antifibrinolytic drugs.*
- *Antibiotics if there is an infection.*
- *Laser surgery to remove the womb lining in women who have completed their families, or to remove any endometriosis adhesions.*
- *Removal of an ovary if there is cancer there.*
- *Hysterectomy (as a very last resort).*

Tests for **menorrhagia** should include testing for anemia and thyroid function, followed by further tests if necessary, such as taking an internal swab for pelvic infection, and perhaps a biopsy of the womb lining. If symptoms are severe or if the doctor cannot find a cause, a woman should be referred to a gynecologist. Appropriate treatments may be:

- *Drugs which work directly on bleeding mechanisms, or which reduce the level of prostaglandins (such as mefanamic acid).*
- *The contraceptive Pill, Danazol, or Duphaston.*
- *Iron and vitamin C supplements if heavy bleeding has caused anemia.*
- *Antibiotics for pelvic inflammatory disease.*
- *Endometrial ablation (removing womb lining by laser).*
- *Hysterectomy (as a very last resort).*

To establish the cause of **amenorrhea**, a pregnancy test and a thorough physical examination will be given, then blood tests will be taken to check the different levels of hormones, and a progestogen challenge test will be done to detect polycystic ovaries (PO). Treatment varies greatly depending on the cause, but can include:

- *Hormonal therapy to encourage ovulation or treat PO.*
- *Iron/folic acid/vitamin C supplements for anemia.*
- *Counseling for stress.*

Alternative Treatment

Nutritional therapy

Painful periods may be caused by nutritional deficiencies, for instance, magnesium and essential fatty acids, calcium and B6.

If caused by fibroids, heavy periods are treated by the therapist as a liver-related problem.

Sometimes heavy periods are caused by weak capillary walls. Nutrients known as flavonoids or bioflavonoids, found in the white pith of oranges, lemons and green peppers, are useful in strengthening capillary walls.

If a thyroid deficiency is causing heavy periods, a clinical nutritionist can help address the problem using kelp or duce.

Nutritional therapists suggest a lengthy absence of periods may be related to hormonal deficiency, caused in turn by shortage of protein, zinc and vitamin A.

Acupuncture

Acupuncture and acupressure can help to promote overall hormonal balance, and may work to reduce any overproduction of prostaglandins causing dysmenorrhea.

Acupuncture can be extremely effective for period pain by treating the local blockage in the flow of energy and blood, as well as the underlying cause of the blockage.

In cases of amenorrhea, a skilled acupuncturist may be able to stimulate the relevant acupuncture points to restore the body's hormonal balance.

Aromatherapy

An aromatherapist can help with painful periods using gentle abdominal massage with antispasmodic oils such as clary sage, cypress, and lavender.

For menorrhagia, an aromatherapist would perhaps suggest estrogen-like essential oils which help to balance the female hormonal interplay or carry out gentle abdominal massage with geranium, rose or cypress to help reduce bleeding.

Amenorrhea might be treated with a daily lower back massage with a mixture of clary sage and fennel until the start of the first period, as these oils can help regulate the general ovarian hormone balance.

Chinese herbalism

For period problems, a Chinese herbalist may recommend herbal hormone and blood tonics, herbs to move stagnation in the flow of energy and blood, and sometimes heat-clearing herbs.

Western herbalism

To relieve dysmenorrhea, a Western herbalist may use cramp bark which acts as a muscle relaxant.

For menorrhagia, the herb ladies' mantle may be suggested as it has an astringent effect and can reduce bleeding, or yarrow which improves blood flow and helps regulate menstruation.

Many herbal medicines act on the hormone balance and control of the period cycle. In cases of amenorrhea, for example, false unicorn root is a uterine tonic which can encourage reestablishment of the menstrual cycle.

Homeopathy

Treatment is often constitutional but for **dysmenorrhea**, helpful homeopathic remedies include:

- Pulsatilla for pains helped by warmth, perhaps also accompanied by nausea.
- Sepia for cramping pains which feel better on bending double.

Menorrhagia may be treated constitutionally, although there are a number of specific remedies which can be used, including:

- Pulsatilla for heavy periods with clots.
- Nux for heavy prolonged periods.
- Belladonna for heavy periods with clotting, or bright red, "gushing" menstrual loss.

There are a number of homeopathic remedies which may be appropriate for **amenorrhea**, for instance, aconite if periods have stopped because of a great emotional shock.

Naturopathy

For painful, heavy or absent periods, a naturopath may suggest dietary management, hydrotherapy, herbal medicine, uterine tonics, antispasmodics and hormone regulation.

Other therapies

For dysmenorrhea, **macrobiotic** treatment will diagnose problems in the yin/yang cycle, and will adjust the diet accordingly. **Shiatsu** can help painful periods by regulating the menstrual cycle, encouraging muscle activity and blood movement. Therapists believe that if you do not "move" this area, waste product, toxins and fatty deposits settle and accumulate "like dirty water sitting in a sink" and unless they are eliminated they will eventually become fibroids, cysts and tumors. If period pain comes in the lower back or is referred down one or both legs, a **chiropractor** can use specific manipulation in the lower back to reduce the severity of the pain and discomfort. **Hypnotherapy** offers hypnohealing and cell command therapy for painful periods. **Rolfing** can help painful, heavy or absent periods by improving the circulation, allowing more space around the reproductive organs and promoting relaxation. **Yoga** treatment for painful or heavy periods may involve gentle *asanas*, relaxation, *pranayama* and meditation. **Color therapy** may calm painful or heavy periods with warm orange then mid-blue tones in the form of lights shone onto bare skin, or colored clothing or underclothes or silk squares worn next to the skin. For heavy or absent periods, **Ayurvedic medicine** may include *panchakarma* and oral preparations. To relieve heavy periods, a **reflexologist** may treat the thyroid, adrenals, solar plexus, uterus, ovaries, Fallopian tubes and the lower spine reflexes. **Osteopathy** may help to relieve any painful spasms of the uterus.

Sexually Transmitted Diseases (STDs)

What are they?

Otherwise known as STDs, the term sexually transmitted diseases groups together all diseases which are usually passed on by sexual contact. They include the venereal diseases syphilis and gonorrhea, genital herpes, genital warts, pubic lice, hepatitis B, nonspecific urethritis (NSU), trichomoniasis and chlamydia. HIV comes into the list but remains a special issue because it is still most often passed on by sexual contact, and the fastest-growing method of transmission is now heterosexual sex although there are many other ways of contracting it (see pages 258–259). The best form of protection against most STDs is a condom.

Symptoms vary greatly depending on the disorder, and some symptoms can be caused by disorders and infections other than STDs. To complicate matters even further, an STD may be symptomless in both partners or produce noticeable symptoms in one partner and not the other. It may also lie dormant following an initial flare-up or initial treatment that was not fully effective, or recur unpredictably when you thought you had been cured.

Causes

STDs are normally caused after sexual contact with a person who has the infection. General warning signs so that you should see your doctor include:

- *Unusual genital discharge or pain when urinating.*
- *Ulcers and warts in the genital or anal area*
- *Soreness or redness in the genital area,*
- *Rashes around the genital area*
- *Pain on intercourse.*

If accompanied by other symptoms, itchiness in the pubic area, abdominal pain, and trouble conceiving could also indicate the presence of an STD (see also Male STDs page 207).

Orthodox treatment

If in any doubt, always seek medical help. Caught early, nearly all the above can be treated effectively or, in the case of herpes, contained and worked around. With a good health program, people with HIV may remain well for many years, and may live for up to five more with AIDS itself. However, any STD will become chronic and increasingly difficult to deal with if untreated, possibly resulting in long-term fertility problems and chronic ill health.

Tests include physical examination, genital/anal pathogen swabs and blood tests. Contact tracing of ex partners is vital.

Treatment for STDs will be according to the cause, but the mainstays are:

- *Antibiotics and antiviral drugs, both singly and in cocktails.*
- *Drugs that boost the immune system.*
- *Caustic treatment to burn off warts.*

Alternative Treatment

It is illegal for anyone other than a registered medical practitioner to treat STDs. However, used alongside orthodox treatment, alternative therapies are useful in boosting the immune system, helping to fight infection and they can also alleviate the diseases' symptoms.

Homeopathy

For herpes, a constitutional treatment can help prevent recurrence but other remedies include:

- Sempervivum for bad ulcers which bleed, with entire genital area tender and painful.
- Natrum mur. if the genital skin is very dry and the lesions hot and puffy.
- Capsicum if the genitals burn, sting, and have cracked skin and a red itchy rash.
- Rhus tox. for genitals that burn and itch and for discomfort that is aggravated by cold or damp.

For vulval warts, constitutional treatment is best, but to begin with both the woman and her partner can be treated with:

- Thuja if the warts are fleshy.
- Medorrhinum if they are itchy.
- Nitric ac. if they are sore.
- Sabina for warts that are intensely itchy and which smart.

Western herbalism

Tree of life, wild indigo and other parasite-killing herbs can help the irritation that is caused by the itchy rashes that are produced by pubic lice.

For herpes, echinacea is valuable, and applying marigold or tea tree infusions locally is often effective.

Other therapies

A **nutritional therapist** will address the immune system, for it is the best protection against the invasion of any infection, apart from condoms. For viral infections such as herpes, vitamin C and Propolis may be suggested. **Ayurvedic medicine** will be aimed at boosting a person's general immunity. **Alexander Technique** practitioners believe certain recurrent infections such as NSU and herpes have a strong stress component, and that regular use of the Alexander Technique can help reduce their incidence and general recurrence.

Miscarriage and Abortion

What is it?

Miscarriage refers to the accidental or spontaneous loss of a growing embryo or fetus before 28 weeks. Around one in every six confirmed pregnancies ends in miscarriage. However, by the time a pregnancy passes the 12-week mark the chances of miscarrying are small. Signs of threatened miscarriage, which you should report immediately to a doctor or midwife, include:

- *Bleeding, clots or a dark-brown discharge from the vagina.*
- *Period-like, cramping abdominal or back pains.*

Sudden, severe abdominal pain between the fifth and tenth weeks may suggest an ectopic pregnancy (one that develops in the Fallopian tube). This can be life-threatening, so report it to a doctor urgently.

If the loss of an embryo or fetus is deliberate, doctors call it a termination of pregnancy or abortion. During the first few weeks, it can be brought about using the "abortion pill" (RU486). Between eight to 14 weeks, it would involve scraping the womb lining and its contents using a D & C (dilatation and curettage) procedure, usually under general anesthetic. After 14 weeks, labor would be artificially induced in hospital.

Causes

In cases of miscarriage, often no explanation can be found. The most frequent one offered is that the embryo or fetus was not developing normally and therefore was shed by the womb.

Orthodox treatment

There is no treatment for a threatened miscarriage, but a woman will later have an ultrasound check to determine if the pregnancy is viable.

After an actual miscarriage, treatment may consist of:

- *A D & C (dilatation and curettage) to avoid infection.*
- *Antibiotics to avoid infection.*

After recurrent miscarriage (at least three in a row), treatment can include:

- *A full physical check-up for both you and your partner, testing especially for dormant infection in the female and male reproductive organs.*
- *Detoxification nutritional programs preconceptually.*
- *Counseling.*

Even when a termination is carried out to end a definitely unwanted pregnancy, whether done early or later in the pregnancy, the process can still be very distressing and traumatic for many women. Caring, post-abortion counseling, emotional support from partner and family and good physical care with adequate rest can all help.

Orthodox medical care will include:

- *Painkillers.*
- *Antibiotics if infection ensues.*
- *Counseling.*
- *A physical check-up after six weeks.*

Alternative Treatment

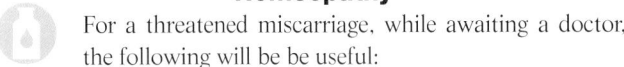

Homeopathy

For a threatened miscarriage, while awaiting a doctor, the following will be be useful:

- Sabina, if the blood is dark, coagulated and has appeared toward the end of the third month.
- Ipecac if the blood is bright red with abdominal cramps.

Post-abortion treatment may involve:

- Ignatia for distress.
- Staphisagria for pain.

Western herbalism

Astringent remedies will be used to discourage bleeding, and others to help a woman cope with emotional distress and to normalize her hormone levels.

Chinese herbalism

Herbal sedatives and carminatives and heat-clearing herbs may be appropriate.

Bach flower remedies

Star of Bethlehem or rescue remedy for shock; gentian for distress; cherry plum for people at breaking point.

Aromatherapy

Helpful oils to get over a miscarriage may include: lavender to help with general relaxation; bergamot to lift or improve a person's mood; clary sage to help normalize a woman's hormonal levels.

Spiritual healing

This treatment helps on every level to restore a woman's health, following miscarriage or abortion.

Other therapies

Massage may help by directly communicating comfort and care, and helping soothe any pelvic/abdominal spasms and pain which is often the temporary result of pelvic surgery, or intense emotional distress. **Kirlian photography** (body logic) can help with relaxation and the release of emotion. A **naturopath** can help with applied nutrition, and exercises to improve pelvic tone. In **Ayurvedic medicine** a practitioner will aim to tone the uterus and improve circulation. For aftercare, **color therapy** will involve healing greens worn over the heart area, and calming and balancing oranges in the form of lights shone on naked skin or worn as clothing or fabric squares next to the skin.

PREGNANCY

What is it?

Pregnancy is when a woman conceives a baby and carries it in the womb for 40 weeks.

There are some women who sail through pregnancy having never felt better in their entire lives; others, unfortunately, seem to be plagued with one discomfort after another for the entire time. The good news is that these problems nearly all disappear as soon as a woman has her baby – and there is always something that can be done to alleviate them.

Fatigue is probably the most common symptom of pregnancy, occurring mainly in the first and last trimesters. During the fourth and seventh months women often report great energy and vitality. Continual extreme tiredness for the entire pregnancy is not usual and should be reported to a doctor.

Nausea and mild vomiting is commonly known as morning sickness, though it can be experienced at any time of the day. It usually occurs in the first 14 weeks. Excessive or continuous vomiting is less common, and requires medical treatment.

Heartburn often occurs after meals, but can happen at any time; it may be triggered by an emotional upset, fatty food, or by eating too quickly. Acidic fluid is regurgitated from the stomach to the esophagus and a burning pain is felt in the chest.

Blood pressure normally falls slightly during pregnancy. Regular blood pressure checks are important throughout pregnancy to detect any rise, however small, which will alert the midwife or doctor to the possibility of hypertension or pre-eclampsia (PE) developing later. The symptoms of PE are raised blood pressure, weight gain, water retention/swelling and protein in the urine (detected by a simple dipstick test). This is a potentially serious condition because it is the forerunner of full-blown eclampsia which, although rare, can produce fits and unconsciousness in the mother and threaten her life and her baby's. Hypertension can cause growth retardation in the baby.

Causes

The very things that help to maintain a pregnancy to full term successfully also cause some discomfort, these are namely:

- *An enormous rise in the levels of estrogen and progesterone; the latter especially is responsible for encouraging the relaxation of all the soft tissues, including muscles and ligaments, which can result in all sorts of unwanted effects from varicose veins to back pain.*
- *Up to twice the amount of blood and fluid in the body, encouraging fluid retention and the need to pass water more often.*
- *The increasing size and weight of the baby, which may lead eventually to breathlessness and the need to pass water often as the lungs and bladder are squashed.*

Fatigue that persists throughout the entire pregnancy can be caused by problems such as pain (for example constant and severe backache), anemia, depression or insomnia. The causes of nausea and vomiting are thought to include low blood sugar, fatigue, low blood pressure, hormonal change and nutritional deficiencies. Heartburn results from the rise in the "softening" pregnancy hormones and the growing size of the baby and the womb. Pre-eclampsia tends to be more common in first pregnancies and also in women who suffer from either diabetes or from kidney disease.

Orthodox treatment

A doctor will try to diagnose the root cause of fatigue and will treat it accordingly, for example, prescribing iron, folic acid and vitamin C supplements if anemia is present. For nausea and vomiting the advice will probably be to take ginger tablets, to eat little and often, and to take more rest; doctors are not usually willing to prescribe anti-sickness drugs (emetics) unless the vomiting is very severe. Gentle exercise may also be suggested. For heartburn, take antacid preparations, eat little and often, avoiding very fatty foods, and do not lie down for two hours following a meal.

The recommendation for mild cases of high blood pressure will be some bed rest, regular gentle exercise and a healthy diet. Moderately severe cases will be treated with anti-hypertensive drugs; very severe cases can only be treated by immediate or early delivery of the baby.

ALTERNATIVE TREATMENT

Homeopathy

If fatigue is caused by anemia, a homeopath will probably suggest taking tissue salts ferr phos. and calc phos. to help absorption of iron supplements. For lower back pain the following remedies may be suggested, to be taken four times daily for up to seven days:

- Kali carb., when the back feels weak and tired, and there are dragging pains in the middle and lower back.
- Belladonna, when there is a hard, tense feeling in the lower abdomen and the head feels hot.
- Pulsatilla when there is a hard, tense feeling in the lower abdomen, the woman feels hot all over and her symptoms worsen in stuffy rooms.
- Nux when there is a hard, tense feeling in the lower abdomen, or a woman feels chilly.

If the backache is due to injury or strain, arnica may be taken twice-hourly for up to ten doses, followed by rhus tox. every six to eight hours for up to seven days if it persists.

For nausea and vomiting a homeopath may recommend the following remedies, taken every two hours for up to three days:

- Nux when the nausea is worse in the morning, vomiting small amounts of food with mucus.
- Ipecac when there is nonstop nausea and both liquids and solids are vomited up.
- Pulsatilla when the nausea occurs in the evening, wearing off at night.
- Ferrum when the nausea occurs a few hours after eating and everything is suddenly vomited.
- Sepia when the vomit is full of milky mucus, particularly if the temperament is melancholy, weepy and irritable.
- Natrum mur. when there is an aversion to bread, fat and slippery food, a craving for salt and feelings of thirst.

For heartburn, one of the following remedies may be recommended, to be taken four times daily for up to seven days:

- Capsicum when there is a burning sensation behind the breastbone, excessive thirst, flatulence and drinking causes shuddering.
- Colchicum when the sight or smell of food causes nausea, cold feeling in the pit of the stomach and craving for fizzy drinks.
- Phosphorus when there is a craving for ice-cold drinks which are vomited up as soon as they become warm in the stomach, and a craving for salt.
- Sulphur when the heartburn is worse around 11am and for drinking milk, and there is a gnawing sensation in the stomach, a craving for sweets, thirst but little appetite.

Western herbalism

A herbalist will probably suggest wild oat, rosemary or vervain for fatigue, and give advice on diet, exercise and rest. For nausea and vomiting, fennel, ginger, peppermint or camomile tea may be advised. Meadowsweet and lemon balm may ease heartburn, and dandelion may cure constipation. A decoction of cramp bark can help to relieve pain experienced in the legs and feet.

Chinese herbalism

An experienced practitioner will be able to prescribe herbs to control nausea; ginger has been used in China for this purpose for many centuries. There are also a number of effective energy tonics to combat fatigue, as well as calming herbs and blood tonics for general support.

Naturopathy

For nausea and vomiting, a naturopath will suggest taking frequent small meals and avoiding any fatty foods. The intake of plenty of fluid will make up for any dehydration resulting from vomiting. Vitamin E supplements will be recommended to reduce any stretch marks. Any brown discoloration of the skin may be alleviated by PABA (para-aminobenzoic acid), which is found in fresh fruit and vegetables, wheat germ, whole grains, liver and mushrooms, and can also be taken in supplement form.

Naturopaths find that fatigue can often be alleviated by improving the diet of the expectant mother and by also giving her supplements of zinc, vitamins B12, B6 and also folic acid.

Acupuncture

Acupuncture can help to relieve fatigue, nausea, heartburn and fluid retention and stabilize blood pressure. Auricular therapy may use ear studs or seeds to reduce nausea and vomiting, and acupressure wrist bands, available from chemists, may also be effective.

Color therapy

A color therapist may use green or warm coral-pink light therapy as these affect the chest and heart area, strengthening the circulatory system as well as enhancing the emotions of nurturing, caring and love.

Hypnotherapy

Techniques taught for pain control during labor itself may also help to combat nausea, fatigue and heartburn during pregnancy.

Bach flower remedies

These remedies will help with the emotional changes and anxieties associated with pregnancy. Crab apple may be suggested for nausea and vomiting; olive for exhaustion.

Chiropractic

If a chiropractor feels that heartburn stems from a spinal problem in the chest area, he or she will use manipulative treatments to reduce irritation of the stomach via changes in the nervous system. Chiropractic may alleviate insomnia, which may be caused by problems at the top of the spine.

Kinesiology

A kinesiologist will offer a range of treatment for problems associated with pregnancy. For fatigue and high blood pressure, the following may be offered: nutritional support for the structure and the endocrine system, including minerals, vitamins B and E, herbs and kelp; checking for food sensitivities and deficiencies.

For heartburn, treatment will consist of: techniques for pain relief; checking for hiatus hernia tendency and lesions and massage of the upper thoracic area.

Yoga

Gentle *asanas*, relaxation, *pranayama* and meditation will keep stress levels low, maintain flexibility and reduce back pain.

Others

Relaxation and visualization will help to ease fatigue, heartburn and high blood pressure. **Autogenic training** will relieve heartburn, fatigue and anxiety. **Reflexology** can help, but should not be used during the first three months of pregnancy. Manipulative therapies such as **rolfing** and **hellerwork** will help to keep the body supple. The **Alexander Technique** can be excellent throughout a pregnancy.

CHILDBIRTH

The process of giving birth to a baby can be exhilarating, exciting, challenging, satisfying – but usually, for at least part of the time, painful too. Every woman manages every labor differently, and although some have said they are conscious only of "a major physical effort" during childbirth, the vast majority of mothers report that their sensations eventually range from considerable discomfort to serious pain. Fortunately, there is plenty of help, both orthodox and alternative, available today to alleviate the more difficult aspects of birth.

Labor itself normally involves several hours of increasingly powerful womb contractions, although some babies can be born in an hour from start to finish. It happens in three stages, the first being generally the longest (averaging seven to nine hours for a first baby, four to six for later births). The second, when the baby is actually pushed out into the world, lasts for anything from a few minutes to two or three hours. The third stage, the expulsion of the placenta, may last from a few minutes to an hour and a half.

The function of the contractions is initially to efface (thin out) and pull back the cervix (the neck of the womb), gradually creating one single passage called the birth canal which consists of the womb, the now open cervix and the vagina (the first stage of labor). The contractions then push the baby down the birth canal and out of the mother. This is the second stage of labor, and the mother will usually now be actively helping by pushing hard herself (bearing down). The contractions continue for the third stage of labor to slough off the placenta from the womb wall and then expel it via the still open birth canal. This part of labor is usually accelerated by an injection of syntometrine, a drug encouraging the contractions.

Some labors progress so slowly that the mother eventually becomes both exhausted and disheartened. This is not uncommon, especially with first babies. The problem is usually that her labor contractions are not managing to thin and pull up the cervix, but sometimes the baby is in a difficult birth position, perhaps bottom first rather than the usual head down.

Orthodox treatment

There are in fact about 20 different types of pain relief available for childbirth, though the majority of hospitals will probably have only four or five available at most. The hospital may also be unwilling to allow a woman in labor to bring a alternative therapist to provide pain relief in the labor ward (independent midwives and home birth attendants tend to be far more relaxed). The most common methods routinely available in hospitals are:

- *Entonox, a mix of oxygen and nitrous oxide. Breathed in, it can help take the edge off pain.*
- *Pethidine by injection (similar to morphine). About a quarter of women find it very helpful.*
- *An epidural delivering strong painkilling drugs into the back via a catheter. Three-quarters of women find it is very effective.*
- *A TENS (transcutaneous electrical nerve stimulation) machine attached to the back delivering low-level electrical impulses to nerve endings to block pain signals. Approximately half of women giving birth find it very useful, though during the first stage only.*
- *The sensation of warm water induces relaxation and helps reduce pain to manageable levels for the majority of women.*

If her amniotic sac (bag of waters) has broken but her contractions are not being effective, the mother may be given prostaglandin pessaries vaginally to encourage contractions, or have an intravenous drip delivering a powerful labor-enhancing drug called oxytocin. If the sac is still intact, the membranes may be broken artificially.

If the problem is the baby's position, there are three clinical options: epidural and assisted delivery; to allow the mother to remain mobile and change position frequently to encourage normal delivery; or to deliver the baby by Caesarean section if the labor has gone on for a very long time and the mother is too tired to push, or the baby is found to be suffering from fetal distress (becoming short of oxygen).

About one in nine births in Britain and one in four births in the United States are by Caesarean section, which involves delivering the baby surgically via two separate incisions in the mother's abdomen and womb. A Caesarean can be done under a general anesthetic or under a heavy epidural, which is safer because the use of general anesthetic is avoided and also means the mother is awake to experience her baby being born. Afterward she remains in bed for one day but is then encouraged to be up and about again.

Full recovery takes about six to 12 weeks. Planned Caesareans are done if a mother has pre-eclampsia (see page 220), if her placenta is low-lying and blocking the baby's exit from the womb, if the pregnancy is a multiple one or the result of sustained IVF treatment, or if the mother's pelvis is too small to permit the baby's head to pass through.

Labor may be artificially induced if the mother has diabetes, pre-eclampsia, considerably raised blood pressure or bleeding late in pregnancy, or is carrying twins. Hypertension causing intrauterine growth retardation in the baby is a further reason.

Methods used are:

- *Cervical sweep, where the midwife inserts a finger into the small passageway in the cervix and moves it around.*
- *Prostaglandin gel or pessaries.*
- *Rupturing the amniotic sac membranes.*
- *An oxytocin drip.*

Self-help methods of inducing labor include taking a long walk, having sexual intercourse, intimate kissing and cuddling husband or partner and getting them to stimulate the nipples for about 20 minutes at a time.

Alternative Treatment

Acupuncture is the only alternative therapy which actually necessitates the presence of the therapist in the labor room. Other therapists can work beforehand, teaching strategies or recommending useful oils, remedies or herbs for the mother, her partner or an open-minded midwife to use (or can keep in phone contact). In labor, it is important not to self-medicate without proper consultation with a professional therapist first.

Homeopathy

Several remedies may be used throughout labor to relieve pain, depending on the emotional and physical state of the mother. They include:

- Coffea when labor is proceeding normally but the contractions are so violent they are almost unbearable, the mother cries out with pain and is nervous and restless between contractions.
- Belladonna for very violent contractions when the mother is in great anguish, talking incoherently, with limbs twitching and eyes staring.
- Nux when the pains are accompanied by frequent urges to pass water or stool and the mother is very irritable and impatient.

To speed a slow labor, a homeopath may suggest the following remedies:

- Secale when the mother is exhausted, the muscles of the uterus are no longer able to push and the death of the baby is suspected.
- Pulsatilla if there is severe backache, the muscles of the uterus are exhausted, the mother is of strong constitution, or if the death of the baby is suspected.
- Opium if the pain stops suddenly due to emotional upset, and the mother's face is red, hot and puffy.
- Hyoscyamus if the mother becomes delirious.
- If there are tears or incisions and stitches to the vulva or vagina, bathing the area three or four times a day with a solution of 10 drops of Arnica mother tincture to 300ml (½pt) of warm water will aid healing.

Western herbalism

For great tension and pain featuring short, sharp, "spiteful" contractions, or a rigid cervix which will not dilate, possibilities include blue cohosh, cramp bark, wild yam, raspberry leaf, taken together or singly as a tea or tincture. To speed up a slow labor, a herbalist may use raspberry leaf tea, with a mix of black or blue cohosh and ginger.

Massage

Massage is effective in between contractions and may help with pain relief during them. About 90 percent of women report that they find it helpful.

Autogenic training

Autogenic Training must be learned in eight to ten sessions prior to childbirth itself. Studies have shown that the first stage of labor is shortened by an average of three hours, and 70 percent of users report notable pain relief too. It can also help with the post-operative pain that follows a Caesarean section.

Hypnotherapy

Self-hypnosis, taught in five to ten group sessions before childbirth, generally reduces pain perception by about a third but can sometimes result in completely pain-free labors. With the aid of hypnosis, Caesareans have been successfully done in Britain under only light epidural. It can also speed up delivery by up to a third.

Acupuncture

Treatment can take place throughout the labor and birth to control pain. Some women claim to have been given almost complete relief through this method. Acupuncture can also speed up labor as well as inducing calm in the mother. Auricular therapy has been reported as having similar beneficial effects.

Reflexology

Reflexology can encourage calm and relaxation, reducing discomfort and hastening the labor; studies suggest that shorter labor times and good level of pain relief can be achieved.

Bach flower remedies

Some mothers who have undergone a Caesarean report feeling a failure for not giving birth naturally; pine may help them. Rescue remedy will be useful if they are shocked; willow is good for feelings of resentment.

Aromatherapy

Aromatherapy can be 60–70 percent successful in giving relief from pain in childbirth, using lavender, clary sage and melissa oils.

Color therapy

Red (the color of energy) may strengthen weak contractions and thus speed up a slow labor. The mother should wear red knickers as the overall stimulating effect of red light may be too much for the baby. The birthing environment should have colors and lights in warm pinks and pale blues, as these are soothing and calming.

Other therapies

Shiatsu treatment may eliminate all need for pain-relieving drugs in labor, and may also be successful in inducing birth. **Chiropractic** treatment throughout the pregnancy can make the birth a good deal easier. A **kinesiologist** will suggest balancing and other techniques for giving pain relief during a woman's labor and the baby's birth.

Post-delivery Problems

What are they?

According to a large, ongoing research project by British midwives called the Avon Longitudinal Study, the commonest physical problems suffered by women after giving birth are:

- *Backache (66 percent of the women studied).*
- *Headaches (58 percent).*
- *Sore stitches (49 percent).*
- *Piles (hemorrhoids) (39 percent).*

Causes

Post-delivery backache and headache often relate back to strain during the birth process. Severe postnatal headache is sometimes associated with an epidural, but should pass within 24 to 48 hours. The stitches needed after an episiotomy may cause initial soreness in the genital area. Piles (hemorrhoids) are swollen varicose veins appearing around the rectum and anus, either as a result of pregnancy, or of pushing the baby out during labor.

Orthodox treatment

General advice for headaches includes avoiding tea and coffee, drinking plenty of plain liquid, and reducing light and movement. For backache and headache, specific remedies include:

- *Analgesics, the mother should check if she is compatible with breastfeeding if she is feeding the baby herself.*
- *Advice on posture when sitting and standing. It may be suggested that the mother feed her baby while both lie down to reduce sitting time, or with a pillow in the small of her back with feet raised slightly (for example, on two telephone directories). A pillow supporting the back in bed while sitting and sleeping may also help.*
- *Gentle stretching exercises (ask the hospital physiotherapist who will usually visit on the wards postnatally.*
- *Warm, relaxing baths if the soreness is muscular.*

For sore stitches, the following may be helpful:

- *An anesthetic gel such as Lignocaine.*
- *An inflatable child's swimming ring to sit on and take pressure off the sore area.*
- *Warm baths with a big handful of salt in them to encourage rapid healing.*
- *Attention to hygiene keeping the vaginal area very clean and dry, to encourage healing.*

Anti-hemorrhoid creams containing shrinking and soothing agents are available. Other treatments for hemorrhoids may include:

- *A mild laxative such as Lactulose to help avoid any constipation, which makes piles worse.*
- *Removal of piles if they contain clotted blood. Some doctors can lance them in their surgeries. However, if they refuse to disappear of their accord within about three to six months, they can be surgically removed.*

Alternative Treatment

Nutritional therapy

Helpful remedies may include taking vitamin B and chromium for stabilizing energy; vitamin E to encourage healing of stitches; dietary advice to prevent constipation which might aggravate the problem of piles.

Homeopathy

Homeopathic remedies to help relieve the condition can include:

- Ignatia for a headache like a tight band.
- Ruta for a bruising headache associated with fatigue.
- Pulsatilla taken every four hours, for three days, for piles.
- Arnica granules to reduce postnatal bruising.
- Tincture of Hyper cal. on a soft sanitary towel worn over stitches to help reduce soreness.

Western herbalism

For sore stitches, a herbalist may suggest external application of herbs such as comfrey and calendula for sore stitches; astringent remedies such as horse chestnut and witch hazel applied to the sore area to constrict the blood vessels; post-birth, anti-infective, healing, herbal bath made from a handful of comfrey, uva ursa and shepherd's purse steeped for 10 minutes, then poured into the bathwater.

For added anti-infective power, boil up a head of garlic with the other herbs.

Aromatherapy

For sore stitches, apply lavender and camomile and helycrismus in apricot or peach kernel oil (made up by an aromatherapist).

Other therapies

For sore stitches, a **Chinese herbalist** may suggest blood tonics and Chinese herbs to discourage blood stasis. Gentle manipulation by an **osteopath** or **chiropractor** can help with both backache and headaches, as can the **Alexander Technique**. Gentle **yoga** stretches, such as the Cat, will alleviate backache. **Hypnotherapy** involving self-hypnosis and hypnohealing, and **acupuncture** can all aid the healing process of sore stitches and reduce pain. A **color therapist** may suggest wearing green, a healing color, in the form of green knickers or sheets or, if there has been physical trauma, orange may be suggested as this helps tissue to bind and heal.

Postnatal Depression

What is it?

Some mothers feel calm and happy from the moment their baby is born, but others (between 50 and 80 percent) feel some very short-term anxiety, fearfulness, irritability and mild depression for a few days afterward, which is known as the Baby Blues. This usually starts about the third or fourth day after the birth, but is normally gone within the week.

If Baby Blues have not disappeared within two weeks, the mothers should see a doctor because there is the possibility that they may deepen into Postnatal Depression (PND). Around one in ten mothers develop PND in the first 4 to 6 weeks after their baby is born, but others may develop symptoms six months later. The symptoms vary and range from sleep problems, obsessive worrying and anxiety, to feeling miserable, inadequate, and exhausted all the time. PND is a physical illness, so if a mother is feeling less able to cope, she should consult a doctor.

Finally there is also a far less common but related condition called postpartum (or postnatal) psychosis. It affects about one in 1,000 new mothers and is far more severe than PND, as sufferers can completely lose touch with reality.

Causes

Baby Blues is thought to be due to the massive drop in pregnancy hormones, aggravated by tiredness, physical discomfort and concern about managing the baby. The specific causes of PND are thought to be similar to those of Baby Blues, except that PND sufferers may react far more strongly to the hormonal changes that occur postnatally.

Orthodox treatment

The Blues need no treatment as such, other than loving support from a partner and family.

With the proper emotional support (from partner and family) and treatment, PND can often be cured within three months. PND can be helped by:

- *Extra help and support at home.*
- *Plenty of sleep.*
- *Counseling.*
- *Antidepressants and/or hormonal therapy.*

Mothers who develop postpartum psychosis will recover fully, but the condition does need hospital treatment, ideally in a mother and baby unit where the baby can remain with the mother all the time.

Treatment may include:

- *Tranquilizers.*
- *Antidepressants.*
- *Counseling and support.*
- *Electro-convulsive therapy (in some cases).*

Alternative Treatment

Acupuncture

Acupuncture can do a great deal to normalize and rebalance a woman's hormonal levels again, and according to London Master Acupuncturist and former Chinese gynecologist Dr. Mark Yu, it can also reduce the risk of depression by helping to release antidepressive substances naturally from within the person's body.

Homeopathy

A homeopath may suggest:

- Pulsatilla for extreme weepiness.
- Natrum mur. to assist feelings of withdrawal, guilt, or possibly irritability.
- Sepia for a lack of interest in things, tiredness and irritability.

Western herbalism

The following treatments can be helpful: chaste tree for restoring hormonal balance; St. John's wort or wild oats to reduce stress.

Nutritional therapy

A clinical nutritionist may suggest that part of the problem is that after pregnancy the mother is lacking minerals and vitamins and may well prescribe:

- Vitamin C, B complex, calcium, iron, magnesium and potassium supplements.
- Amino acid supplements such as phenylalanine, tryptophan and tyrosine to help ease depression.

Bach flower remedies

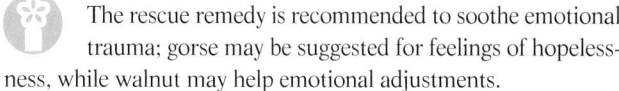

The rescue remedy is recommended to soothe emotional trauma; gorse may be suggested for feelings of hopelessness, while walnut may help emotional adjustments.

Aromatherapy

For relieving stress and fatigue, oils such as clary sage, bergamot and jasmine can be helpful.

Other therapies

Massage can help with relaxation and a positive body image following delivery. **Autogenic training** can help prevent PND, and **reflexology** can speed up the recovery process. In **Chinese herbalism,** tonics can strengthen the spirit and help the body to recover. A **color therapist** will suggest using warm pink/coral tones in lights, bedclothes, underwear and clothes, or worn as small silk squares next to the heart, seat of the emotions.

BREASTFEEDING PROBLEMS

What are they?

According to the World Health Organization, 97 percent of women are physically capable of breastfeeding. However, some women may find that they simply do not like the sensation or, because breastfeeding is a gentle skill mother and baby learn together, they have insoluble problems. The two most common physical problems are pain during breastfeeding, and sore nipples. Less commonly, the nipples may become cracked, or you could suffer from mastitis, inflammation of the milk-producing glands. Practical problems with breastfeeding itself include a slow let-down reflex, the milk-releasing response, so that the milk does not come through immediately the baby starts to suck. Alternatively, it may be let down too forcefully.

Causes

If breastfeeding is painful, it is often because the baby is not quite in the right position and is not latching on to the nipple correctly. Unaccustomed use and dampness can cause nipples to become sore or cracked, and this can lead to infection.

Orthodox treatment

Some breast problems may require treatment with creams or medicines containing drugs, in which case the mother should consult her doctor or health advisor about how to continue breastfeeding in the meantime. Breastfeeding problems can be relieved both by prescribed treatments and by self-help techniques:

- *Painful nipples during breastfeeding can be remedied by altering the baby's position on the nipple very slightly. A midwife or breastfeeding counseler can help here.*
- *Sore nipples can be soothed with ointments containing calendula. Wearing absorbent breast pads, and regular, gentle drying and exposure, when possible, to the air can be preventative and healing.*
- *Cracked nipples should respond to a cream containing anesthetic and anti-infective agents, which a doctor will prescribe.*
- *Mastitis may be treated by antibiotics.*
- *Engorgement (hard, over-full breasts) can be prevented and alleviated by feeding the baby more often, expressing milk by hand, and taking warm, soothing baths.*
- *Thrush from the baby's own mouth affecting the nipple can be treated with ordinary antifungal cream.*
- *Temporary vaginal dryness, caused by breastfeeding, can be remedied with a lubricant gel from a chemist.*
- *Delayed let-down reflex can be helped by relaxing, and making sure that the mother is not distracted while feeding. If the reflex is too fast, express a little milk beforehand.*

ALTERNATIVE TREATMENT

Homeopathy

These treatments may help to alleviate the problem:

- Chamomilla, ignatia, pulsatilla, aconite, sulphur, graphites, silicea for sore or cracked nipples.
- Pulsatilla and calcarea for hard, engorged breasts.
- Pulsatilla, camomile, aconite, hyoscyamus, coffea, and agnus for loss of milk.

Bach flower remedies

rescue® remedy liquid (diluted) and/or cream may be soothing for soreness. (Wash this off before feeding.)

Aromatherapy

Lavender oil can encourage the let-down reflex and heal cracked nipples if applied topically. Caraway, aniseed, and verbena oils massaged on the breasts can encourage milk.

Acupuncture

Acupuncture can to help to increase the milk supply, and prevent engorgement.

Other therapies

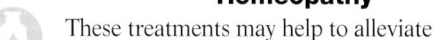

An **osteopath** can help to establish the milk flow by manipulating the thoracic spine to affect the let-down milk-releasing reflex. Breast enlargement may cause some thoracic pain (between the shoulder blades) which can be relieved by a course of **chiropractic** manipulation. **Hypnotherapy** can encourage or reduce milk supply, and soothe any mastitis discomfort. A **Western herbalist** may suggest goat's rue in order to increase the volume of milk. A **Chinese herbalist** may advise some herbal hormone tonics and herbal nutrition for the mother. In **Ayurvedic medicine,** special preparations are available for lack of milk supply. **Reflexology** will be aimed at the endocrine system and breast reflexes. A **macrobiotic** practitioner may use oak milk to increase the milk supply. A **kinesiologist** may suggest techniques to relieve breast congestion, vitamin E for sore nipples, and regular postnatal balancing. **Autogenic training** can help with the milk supply by increasing lactation using affirmations after regular AT practice. **Shiatsu** treatment will be aimed at the stomach meridian. **Self-massage** of the breasts can help to prevent engorgement, and may also give relief in cases of mastitis, as can hot, wet towel compresses. **Color therapists** will use yellow light which is shone onto the breasts, or yellow silk squares which are worn under the bra, to encourage milk supply (this affects the digestive system, hormones and adrenals). Cool blue light, clothing and silks will be used to diffuse the heat in very sore engorged breasts, or alternating warm and cold treatment given with blue and coral pinks.

Breast Problems

What are they?

The most common breast problems are overall pain and general lumpiness, which is likely to be cyclical mastalgia linked to the menstrual cycle. Lumps may also be cysts (noncancerous, fluid-filled capsules). These may appear in groups or singly, and are most common in women in their twenties and thirties. Fibroadenomas, which are also noncancerous lumps, are another common problem. Other, less common forms of breast lumpiness are:

- **Duct ectasia**, *caused by an inflamed blockage in the milk ducts, and a very common reason for breast pain in women in their forties and fifties. This may also cause a small lump, and nipple discharge/retraction.*
- **Fat necrosis**, *in which the fat cells in the breast are broken (often because of a blow to the breast) and scar tissue around the released fat cells forms into a solid lump.*

Even though 95 percent of breast lumps are benign, they should always be reported immediately to a doctor for double-checking. If necessary, he or she can then arrange to for a biopsy (tissue sample) to be taken of it in hospital so if the lump should turn out to be a cancerous one, then effective treatment can be started immediately.

Causes

The most common causes of breast pain and lumpiness are:

- *Hormonal changes if the pain is linked to your menstrual cycle.*
- *Bras which do not offer enough support, or which are too tight and which are underwired.*
- *Breastfeeding problems such as mastitis, or milk engorgement.*

Orthodox treatment

Orthodox remedies for breast problems may involve:

- *Hormonal treatments such as Danazol, bromocriptine and the contraceptive Pill for lumpiness and discomfort.*
- *Evening Primrose Oil for breast tenderness and lumpiness.*
- *Antibiotics for infection and duct ectasis.*
- *Drawing the fluid out of a cyst with a syringe (performed by a doctor) should the cyst not burst on its own.*
- *Danazol for recurrent outbreaks of cysts.*
- *Minor surgery for fibroadenomas, fat necrosis and duct papilloma.*

Alternative Treatment

Homeopathy

Possible homeopathic remedies for PMS-linked breast pain include:

• Natrum mur. when the breasts are full and large because of fluid retention.
• Calcarea when the breast feel heavy and are pendulous.
• Conium when there is some breast enlargement plus some pain and tenderness.
• Carbo an. for breast enlargement which is accompanied by uncomfortable shooting pains.

As a holding measure only, while the right constitutional treatment is being found, helpful remedies for cysts include:

• Pulsatilla if there is sudden, vicious pain coming and going.
• Conium if the area is hard and painful.
• Phytolacca for cysts which feel extra tender before a period and when under emotional strain.

Nutritional therapy

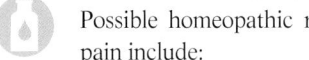

For breast pain, nutritional therapists advise cutting down on salty foods to reduce any water retention in fatty areas such as breast tissue. They may also suggest that you take supplements of evening primrose oil and vitamin B6 which are known to help with the problem.

For breast lumpiness, it will be suggested to reduce or cut out coffee, tea and chocolate as these are all contain high methylxanthines – chemicals which can encourage the formation of cysts and lumps in the breasts.

Naturopathy

A naturopath may suggest dietary modulation, hydrotherapy and herbal medicine for both breast pain and lumpiness. Splashing the aching breasts with cold water each day can also help to relieve the pain.

Western herbalism

For breast pain, a herbalist may recommend using cleavers, which works as a mild diuretic and as a lymphatic stimulant.

Other therapies

An **aromatherapist** may suggest cold lavender oil compresses to alleviate the pain. **Acupuncture** may be useful to help relieve breast pain. For breast lumpiness, **Chinese herbalism** will prescribe some detoxifying herbs and blood tonics. **Autogenic training** teachers say that regular AT training can prevent cysts and even abscesses or, if they are dormant, can make them emerge more quickly so that they can be treated more rapidly and effectively. In **Ayurvedic medicine** practitioners will use herbal preparations such as *panchakarma* for detoxification, and balancing the tridoshas. **Reflexology** treatment can help breast pain by working on the endocrine and breast reflexes. To soothe, cool and heal painful breasts, a **color therapist** may suggest wearing green- or turquoise-colored bras. They may also recommend wearing silk squares that are tucked into the bra, or shining lights onto the bare skin in the same colors.

CANCER

Cancer is a disease of the cells. Of around 500 billion new cells made in the body every day, a few are defective, and are dealt with by the immune system. Occasionally, however, some escape this policing system, and start multiplying fast, developing into a tumor or a cancer and invading healthy tissue. The main cancers that affect women specifically are cancer of the breast, ovaries, cervix and uterus (womb).

Breast cancer is the most common cancer for women. According to the Imperial Cancer Research Fund (the source of all the figures here) there are 32,000 cases each year in Britain alone. Its symptoms can signify other disorders too – nine in every ten breast lumps is benign – but always report them to your doctor immediately. Symptoms can include:

- *Lumps.*
- *Changes in the shape or direction of the nipple.*
- *Bleeding or discharge from the nipple.*
- *"Orange peel" dimpling of the breast skin.*
- *Change in shape, size or weight of one breast.*
- *Small lumps under the armpit.*

Ovarian cancer tends to be detected fairly late because the ovaries are so small – about the size of a pair of kidney beans – and are sheltered deep within the body. Symptoms include:

- *Urinary frequency.*
- *Weight loss.*
- *Persistent bloated feeling in the abdomen, or a swollen abdomen.*

Cervical cancer is cancer of the cervix (neck of the womb). It is more common in women in their forties and fifties, but the proportion of women under 35 developing cervical cancer is growing.

Uterine cancer is very slow-growing and tends to remain within the womb, so survival rates are high. Main symptoms are:

- *Unusual or unexplained bleeding from the vagina.*

Causes

Having children and breastfeeding seem to give some protection against **breast cancer**. However, risk factors include:

- *Family pattern of breast cancer in immediate female relatives.*
- *Early onset of menstruation or late menopause.*
- *Obesity.*
- *A history of benign breast lumps.*
- *Not having any children.*

Having taken the combined contraceptive pill reduces the risk of **ovarian cancer** (by 80 percent if taken for ten years). Risk factors of this form of cancer can include:

- *Family pattern of the disease in immediate female relatives.*

Using barrier methods of contraception (sheath, diaphragm) has a protective effect against cervical cancer. Risk factors for this type of cancer include:

- *Beginning sexual intercourse before the early 20s.*
- *Having many sexual partners (especially if they themselves have also had many).*
- *Smoking.*

Risk factors for uterine cancer include:

- *Age (more common in women over 50).*
- *Obesity.*
- *Early onset of periods or late menopause.*

Orthodox treatment

Early detection of breast cancer increases the chances of recovery, so get into the habit of checking your breasts on the same day each month (two to three days after your period ends, if you are still menstruating). Medical tests include a special breast X-ray called a mammogram, or perhaps a needle biopsy test to check some of the cells from the area.

Treatment for **breast cancer** depends greatly on how developed the cancer is, and may include:

- *Chemotherapy to shrink the tumor (for example, Tamoxifen).*
- *Surgery, usually minimal. (New worldwide research shows that the majority of small cancers removing just the lump is as successful as mastectomy – removing the entire breast – if this is combined with radiotherapy.)*
- *Mastectomy in more advanced cases, in which both the breast and lymph nodes beneath the armpit would be removed.*
- *Radiotherapy and/or chemotherapy, or hormone treatment, for example, Tamoxifen after surgery.*

Tests for ovarian cancer include:

- *Ultrasound scan.*
- *Monoclonal antibodies blood test (injected into the bloodstream, these bond with cancer cells and show up on a scan camera).*

Different levels of surgery may be used to remedy **ovarian cancer**, ranging from the removal of a single ovary to a hysterectomy, plus the removal of both ovaries followed up by chemotherapy, and occasionally radiotherapy, too.

The smear test checks for potentially cancerous abnormalities in and around the cervix, or **cervical cancer** itself. Treatment may involve:

- *Laser surgery to remove the problem cells if the disease is not very advanced, or a minor operation called a cone biopsy which removes just a wedge of tissue.*
- *Removal of the entire cervix in more advanced cases, or even a part or all of the womb, too.*
- *Radiotherapy, and perhaps chemotherapy as well, before and/or after the removal of cervix or womb.*

The range of medical tests that may be used to check for the presence of uterine cancer in a woman include:

- *D and C (dilatation and curettage), an exploratory operation to check the womb lining.*
- *Endoscopic investigation using an hysteroscope to look inside the womb cavity.*

Ultrasound scan.

Treatment for **uterine cancer** will be at least a total abdominal hysterectomy and removal of tubes and ovaries. If the disease is advanced, a more radical type of hysterectomy, known as Wertheim's hysterectomy, is needed, in which all the surrounding lymph nodes are also completely removed, although the ovaries can be left in place.

Radiotherapy always follows surgery. The doses and methods given to each woman will vary depending on the severity of each individual case.

ALTERNATIVE TREATMENT

For cancer, alternative therapies should be used alongside orthodox medicine, not instead of, to help support the person physically and emotionally. The treatments listed can help female cancers generally rather than specifically. The following treatments can be used to help the body fight all the types of cancers that are mentioned.

Nutritional therapy

A well-planned diet can enhance the powers of the immune system and self-healing abilities. Herbs may also be used to improve the liver function so it is more efficient at breaking down any estrogens circulating in the blood stream as they can encourage the development/growth of both benign and cancerous female tumors.

Homeopathy

Homeopaths believe cancer reflects a profound breakdown in health, so will prescribe a constitutional treatment. Certain remedies such as clematis or echinacea may also enhance and stimulate the body's natural defense mechanisms

Acupuncture

Treatment can help the recovery process and aid the body to deal with all the toxic effects of medication, and may also boost a woman's energy levels, help to relieve pain and also reduce depression.

Western herbalism

Treatment may work well alongside the conventional treatments by helping to relieve some of the cancer symptoms, and encouraging the body to fight back against the disease. Useful remedies on both counts include: echinacea to promote healing; sweet violet, cleavers, red clover and burdock for cleansing the system and also boosting the immune defenses; St. John's wort, a mild antidepressant which also acts as a nervous restorative, for helping depression or reducing fear; vervain and rosemary as a gentle tonic to produce a mild stimulating effect on the liver.

Chinese herbalism

Treatment can help support the immune system and also reduce the harmful side-effects felt from both chemotherapy and radiotherapy treatment.

Aromatherapy

This can provide great support and help for people with cancer, but essential oils should not be used immediately before or after chemotherapy, as massage may speed the spread of cancer cells through the body via the lymphatic and circulatory systems. So for those with *early*-stage disease, essential oils should be delivered via warm baths, or room aerosols with an air pump. For people in the *terminal* stages, aromatherapy massage is of great benefit for relaxation and sense of well being, which is why it is widely used in hospices. Oils for specific purposes include: geranium, bergamot and rose for depression; rosemary**,** bergamot**,** sandalwood**,** neroli or melissa for relieving tiredness, and lack of appetite following chemotherapy and/or radiotherapy; camomile and fennel to combat nausea.

Bach flower remedies

These can play a helpful part in promoting a more positive frame of mind in anyone with cancer who feels strong negative emotions, for example: olive for those feeling "drained of energy by long-standing problems"; gorse for any feelings of hopelessness or defeatism; mimulus for fear; willow for resentment; rescue® remedy to cope with the aftereffects of the shock of diagnosis.

Other therapies

Naturopathy will offer supportive and applied nutrition to sustain and promote energy and body defenses. **Autogenic training** will work to strengthen the immune system. **Ayurvedic medicine** will aim to prevent cancer with tridosha balancing and the *panchakarma* method. **Hypno-healing** will provide positive affirmations for well being and change, while self-hypnosis will activate and support the body's own healing process. Cell command therapy will activate healthy cell regeneration and replacement. With certain cancers a **reflexologist** will work every reflex to support the individual. Gentle **yoga** practice, if the person is well enough, may help to reduce overall stress levels and also help to promote relaxation using gentle *asanas*, relaxation, *pranayama* and meditation. To build up and strengthen the immune system, **color therapists** will use indigo and deep blue colored light shone onto the bare skin, or underclothing or silk squares in these colors worn next to skin over the appropriate area. To lift depression and promote self-esteem, clear yellow and fresh green colors will be used.

THRUSH

What is it?

Thrush is not an infection. It is an overgrowth of a tiny yeast organism (a fungus) called *Candida albicans* which lives naturally in all healthy bodies, thriving in warm, damp enclosed areas. Candida is most often found in the vagina but also in the mouth, bowel and even, to a lesser extent, on the skin. Seven out of every ten women get at least one attack of candida overgrowth or thrush in their lives. It is also common for babies to develop this in their diaper area or in their mouths. Men seldom develop it, and when they do they are often symptomless, though they can pass it to their female partner.

In women, the symptoms of vaginal thrush are:

- *Discharge that is thick, white, looks like curd cheese and is not usually offensive smelling.*
- *Sore, dry, red, itchy vulva.*
- *Stinging when urinating.*
- *Soreness in intercourse.*
- *Red rash (occasionally) which extends down the thighs or around the anus.*

Causes

Thrush can be caused by anything that encourages candida growth including:

- *Antibiotics (these kill the other bacteria in the bowel and vagina that usually keep candida in balance).*
- *Immuno-suppressive drugs,*
- *Weakened immune system (during/after periods of illness or severe stress).*
- *Periods of hormonal change which can alter the vaginal acidity and make it easier for candida to flourish, such as pregnancy and the last week of a woman's menstrual cycle.*

Thrush can also be aggravated by anything which abrades or irritates the delicate vaginal or labial tissues – sexual intercourse, tight clothing, poor hygiene, tampons, scented or bubble bath preparations. In addition, a high intake of sugar and refined carbohydrates can raise the glucose level in all the cells of the body including those of the vaginal wall which produces an environment in which thrush may thrive. Some nutritionists also blame an excess of yeast in the diet.

Orthodox treatment

Thrush of any type is normally treated by antifungal drugs such as clotrimazole (Canestan), in the form of ointments, creams or pessaries. There is also a single-dose, oral treatment called fluconazole (Diflucan).

A doctor may also suggest that while suffering from thrush women should avoid tight clothes and wear cotton underwear, rather than nylon, which allows the genitals to "breathe," and that they should also avoid scented bath preparations, soaps and shower gels, and change to washing their underwear in a gentle, soap-free powder.

ALTERNATIVE TREATMENT

Nutritional therapy

Tampons soaked in live yogurt may help the condition. The consumption of sugar tends to encourage the growth of yeasts, so a therapist can help you put together a balanced, anti-Candida diet which is low in refined sugars, fermented foods and yeasts.

Taking lactobacillus acidophilis, a culture of the bacteria normally found in the gut which acts as a balance against candida, may be useful either in dried powder form or as live yogurt.

The allicin found in garlic is also a useful anti-infective and antifungal agent.

Homeopathy

Constitutional treatment is recommended, but specific remedies (for up to five days) include:

- Calcarea if there is marked vaginal itching associated with cervical erosion, yellow or milky discharge, and increased itchiness both before and after periods.
- Lachesis for discharge which burns, plus weariness, bloated abdomen and symptoms worse before and after periods.
- Graphites if the vagina is sore with small ulcers on the labia.

Western herbalism

Western herbal treatment may include applying some live yogurt to the affected area, using a diluted essential oil on the area. Tea tree or garlic is suitable for infection-fighting and calendula is soothing.

Other therapies

An **aromatherapist** may suggest dilute vaginal douches of essential oil of rosemary and tea tree to help ease the irritation. A **macrobiotic** diet can be helpful. A **naturopath** might suggest possible laboratory assessment for internal candidiasis, plus nutritional management and herbal support (perhaps tea tree oil pessaries). **Acupuncture** can restore balance to the system, and help to stimulate the body's own immune system. In **Ayurvedic medicine** a practitioner will use oral medications, and *panchakarma* for cleansing. **Chinese herbal** treatment will involve detoxifying herbs (internal and external) and anti-inflammatory agents. **Color therapy** will employ cool greens and mid-blue colors worn as loose cotton knickers or as light shone onto the bare skin of the affected area, and also used in color visualization to help soothe the irritation and itching.

HYSTERECTOMY

What is it?

Hysterectomy is the surgical removal of the womb and cervix, and usually the Fallopian tubes as well.

Causes

It might be carried out to treat menorrhagia, cancer, or severe endometriosis, fibroids, or for severe prolapse if previous surgical repair has failed. For heavy periods, there is also now an alternative option called endometrial ablation which just removes the womb lining, leaving the uterus itself intact. It is carried out by passing a hysteroscope through the cervix, and so is far less invasive and final than a hysterectomy, but can be less successful.

Orthodox treatment

A full hysterectomy will be done under general anesthetic. It may be done by the more common abdominal route (abdominal hysterectomy) or the technically more difficult vaginal route (vaginal hysterectomy) which leaves no visible scars. Both these operations are followed by a two- to three-month convalescence period. In some women (those without cancer or an enlarged womb) it is now possible to have a key-hole operation which has a less painful and much shorter convalescence. If the ovaries have also been removed, a woman will experience the menopause (unless they have already done so) and may want to discuss treatments such as hormone replacement therapy with a gynecologist. Further, while some women report they are relieved at last to feel "free" of their womb and the problems which led up to the hysterectomy, others experience a powerful emotional reaction to its loss. Talking problems through very fully with a partner, friends, a self-help group, or professional counseling may help greatly.

After the operation a patient will be asked to walk about gently to help the wound heal properly. A drip may be needed to replace lost fluids, and a catheter to drain urine. Stitches will be removed after about five days. Doctors may suggest painkillers and salt baths to help the healing process and bed rest interspersed with gentle movements and exercises to restore mobility. Woman may also need mild laxatives for any constipation, and antibiotics if there is postoperative infection. Counseling will be offered to women who wish or require it.

ALTERNATIVE TREATMENT

Aromatherapy

The aromatherapeutic postoperative treatment conducted by an aromatherapist will help to prevent secondary infection, enhance tissue repair and uplift the psychological and emotional state of the patient. Lavender and geranium oils may be used in gentle, postoperative abdominal massage to help prevent infection and enhance recovery; bergamot and sandalwood oils can help to alleviate any postoperative fatigue.

Homeopathy

Specific remedies for after the operation include:

- Arnica to reduce bleeding and bruising, taken as soon as you wake from the anesthetic. Three doses can be taken hourly initially and then every 12 hours up to five days.
- Staphisagria if there are complications or healing is very slow. Doses of the remedy can be taken every four hours for up to a total of five days.

Western herbalism

Postoperative remedies will include: camomile to relieve any inflammation and pelvic spasm; dandelion to restore normal bowel function (this is always disturbed somewhat by any pelvic surgery); garlic to fight any infection that occurs; ginseng and cola used over a longer term to improve general vitality; false unicorn root and agnus castus to help balance the female hormonal level.

Bach flower remedies

These remedies will be appropriate for the emotional aftercare of a woman who has just had a hysterectomy. The choice of remedies will depend on the individual's outlook, for example: star of Bethlehem can be taken for shock and sense of grief; mustard for nonidentifiable gloom and willow if a woman is suffering from weepy introspection.

Other therapies

Massage may help to lift the spirits by giving a "feel-good" factor to the woman who is receiving the massage. One of the **arts therapies** may be helpful if a woman is experiencing mental difficulties coming to terms with having had a hysterectomy. **Yoga** treatment may involve gentle *asanas*, relaxation, *pranayama* and meditation. An **osteopath** will work on the abdominal muscles to help restore their tone, and alleviate any pain and discomfort. The position which the person lies in during the operation may result in some damage to the lower spine and pelvis, leading to back pain, which can be alleviated with some **chiropractic treatment**. **Hypnotherapy** can be useful, with suggestion therapy and also hypno-healing. A **color therapist** will advise that a deep coral color is worn on the upper part of the body for any post-operative sadness, gold for enhancing feelings of being special and cossetted and cared for, and violet-colored underwear and visualizing violet light around the pelvic area to encourage the body's overall healing process.

Menopause

What is it?

The menopause is not a disorder, but a time of physical change defined medically as the end of menstruation. Coming to terms with the feeling that the childbearing years are now over, and moving on into a new phase in life, can also mean a good deal of emotional adjustment. Some women are delighted to be free at last from menstruation, premenstrual syndrome, pregnancies, worries over contraception and the hard physical work of bringing up young children, yet others are sad to have come to the end of their fertility and youth.

The list of possible menopausal symptoms is long, but a woman may find they are troubled only briefly by one or two of them, and between 25 and 50 percent of all women experience no unpleasant symptoms at all. The symptoms that are experienced can include:

- *Hot flushes.*
- *Dryer vagina.*
- *Dryer facial skin and hair.*
- *Night sweats and insomnia.*
- *Anxiety, irritability, tiredness and depression.*
- *Poor memory and concentration.*
- *Decreased libido and painful intercourse.*
- *Breasts becoming smaller.*
- *Unwanted body hair growth.*
- *Joint pains.*
- *Urinary problems.*
- *Prolapse of the womb.*
- *Onset of osteoporosis: a degenerative, fragile bone disorder.*

Causes

The average age when women reach the menopause is 51. The time period leading up to menopause (the climacteric) lasts for, on average, 10 to 15 years, during which a woman's ovaries gradually cease producing estrogen. It is her slowly dropping estrogen levels which produce most of the physical and some of the psychological symptoms she might experience during this time.

Osteoporosis (see pages 312–313) which affects one in three older women may begin now because of the drop in estrogen levels. Estrogen has a protective effect on the bones and, as levels of the hormone drop, calcium is then lost from the bones. This loss is heaviest during the first five years after the menopause is complete. Estrogen also gives a woman protection against heart disease.

Orthodox treatment

Hormone replacement therapy (HRT) is, say gynecologists, the most effective treatment for the menopause, and involves taking:

- *Small amounts of estrogen on its own. This is called unopposed HRT. It is only suitable for women who no longer have a womb, because the continued regular monthly thickening of the womb lining without the protective effect of added progestogen can encourage the development of cancer in that area.*
- *Estrogen plus progestogen if the womb lining is intact.*

HRT can be taken in the form of skin patches, pills, gels, implants, vaginal rings, suppositories or, for vaginal dryness only, creams. If a woman is taking HRT, she will need to have six monthly blood pressure checks and yearly breast/pelvis checkups, and to examine her own breasts each month. The positive effects of HRT include:

- *Cessation of most menopausal symptoms.*
- *Protection against heart disease.*
- *Increased well being, energy and a higher sex drive than before.*

However, not all menopausal women choose HRT. This is partly because of fears that long-term HRT use may be linked with breast cancer, partly because many women instinctively dislike taking artificial hormones, and partly because many nonspecialist doctors do not know enough about HRT to prescribe it effectively so that the side effects are rarely resolved. There is also the issue of just how long it is safe for a person to take HRT, and whether menopausal symptoms return after a woman ceases to take the medication.

Though there are about 40 different formulations of HRT, usually only the most popular two or three are offered. As with the most popular two or three contraceptive pills, they will not suit every woman and some trial and error is necessary to find the one which has the fewest possible side effects for each particular individual. In addition, many doctors are not sufficiently familiar with the different formulations of HRT available to get around the (sometimes temporary) side-effect problems which can occur, these include:

- *Nausea.*
- *Mood changes.*
- *Weight gain.*
- *Irritability.*
- *Tender, enlarged breasts.*
- *Abdominal cramps.*
- *Return of menstruation and premenstrual syndrome symptoms if a woman is taking progestogen as well.*

Menopausal symptoms are also treated purely symptomatically by orthodox doctors. Such treatments that will be given to women include:

- *Antidepressants for depression.*
- *Mild tranquilizers for anxiety.*
- *Topical estrogen cream for vaginal dryness.*
- *Calcium supplementation.*
- *Dietary and exercise advice to help prevent osteoporosis.*
- *Sleeping pills for insomnia.*
- *Diuretics and dietary advice for weight gain.*
- *Pessaries and/or a course of pelvic exercises with physiotherapy to treat prolapse problems.*

Alternative Treatment

Homeopathy

The homeopathic view is that a woman's menopausal symptoms represent imbalances which have been there for a long time, so treatment needs to be constitutional. There are also some remedies which can even be used as a homeopathic form of HRT, but these should only be used by a very experienced homeopath. Before constitutional treatment begins, some of the following remedies can be very helpful:

- Lachesis for poor memory, difficulty in concentrating, anxiety and depression.
- Pulsatilla for depression, weepiness, changeable moods and headaches.
- Amyl nit. for hot flushes that come on suddenly.
- Graphites for irritability, difficulty in concentrating, depression, weepiness and over-excitability.

Western herbalism

The safety of this form of treatment makes it a sensible choice for menopausal symptoms, as they may continue to affect the woman for many years. As well as specific herbs, a practitioner is likely to offer diet and exercise advice to help maintain general good health and to combat osteoporosis and possible heart disease. Remedies that may be prescribed include: sage which can affect estrogen levels; St. John's wort for mild depression and life root for vein irritability leading to hot flushes.

Aromatherapy

Very gentle self-massage around the breasts with a blend of oils prepared by your aromatherapist may help combat any breast shrinkage that is experienced. Other remedies include: lavender and camomile or other analgesic and calming blends massaged into neck, shoulders and back to remove tension, and clary sage and fennel can help relieve symptoms caused by hormonal imbalance.

Acupuncture

According to Dr. Mark Yu, London Master of Acupuncture, acupuncture can alleviate many menopausal symptoms by rebalancing the hormonal system, especially headaches and migraines, hot flushing, heavy flooding periods, back pain and sagging skin tone. Treatment can also improve the mobilization of chi to the nervous system to aid poor memory and concentration.

Nutritional therapy

Studies suggest that vitamin E supplementation often alleviates menopausal symptoms. A nutritional therapist will also work toward increasing the efficiency of the pituitary and adrenal glands, by ensuring an adequate intake of the right nutrients, and removing foods such as coffee from the diet, which stress the adrenals. The adrenals, located above the kidneys, make a little estrogen even after the start of the menopause, which is often enough to keep women feeling healthy without the need for HRT. The pituitary gland is the master gland which send instructions to all the others. Besides dietary measures, a nutritional therapist may also add the herb agnus castus to a health program, since this herb has direct benefits for the pituitary.

Bach flower remedies

Remedies for menopausal women that will help relieve symptoms are: mustard to alleviate depression which seems to descend for no apparent reason; scleranthus for unexplained mood swings; olive and/or hornbeam for fatigue; mimulus for fear of aging; star of Bethlehem for any sadness experienced at the loss of youth.

Chiropractic

Back pain due to estrogen deficiency or the beginnings of osteoporosis responds well to spinal manipulation and soft tissue work. Chiropractic is also very effective at reducing headaches and migraines caused by tension and stress, and neck problems by restoring normal joint flexibility, and reducing nerve pressure and muscular tension.

Color therapy

This may take the form of light shone on the unclothed body, colored silk squares worn next to the skin or colored clothing/underwear, all in turquoise and magenta to help with balance. Magenta is the link between red (energy) and violet (healing) and may help to calm hot flushes that a woman may be suffering. Poor concentration may be improved by yellows as this is a good stimulator and balancer of the nervous system and mental processes.

Other therapies

The practice of **yoga**, involving relaxation and meditation and promoting muscle tone and flexibility, is useful for reducing stress and anxiety. **Naturopathic** treatment may take the form of dietary modulation, estrogen-rich foods, regulation of blood sugar and applied nutrition. **Chinese herbal** treatment will involve taking hormone, kidney and blood tonics, and is often aimed at strengthening the body's yin, which is its cooling, calming and moistening function. One or more of the **art therapies** may be extremely valuable if a woman is having trouble adjusting emotionally to the menopause, as it may help her to come to terms creatively and powerfully with this new phase of her life. **Hypnotherapy** involving cell command therapy, hypno-healing and self-hypnosis can help with relaxation and stress reduction and also provide positive affirmations for health, energy and well being. **Reflexology** treatment may be aimed at the pituitary, thyroid, and adrenal glands, the solar plexus and reproduction organ reflexes.

URINARY SYSTEM

What is it?

The urinary system filters the blood and expels surplus water and wastes from the body. The system comprises two kidneys, two ureters, the bladder and the urethra. The two kidneys are situated at the back of the abdomen. They are 11cm (4¼in) long and 6cm (2¼in) wide and each weighs about 140g (5oz). The kidneys are connected to the bladder by thin tubes called ureters.

The bladder is a hollow elastic organ that stretches as it fills with urine. When it has collected about 300ml (½pt), nerves within its walls send signals to the brain. If convenient the person will visit a toilet and pass urine out via the urethra. The urethra is only 4cm (1½in) long in females but about 25cm (10in) in males. Each kidney has a million microscopic filtering units called 'nephrons'. Each nephron has a blood supply from the renal artery. The nephron only filters out the smaller molecules, for example, water, glucose or waste products such as urea. The larger substances such as proteins and blood cells remain in the main circulation. As the filtered fluid flows along the nephron, any useful contents are reabsorbed into the bloodstream. The remaining fluid gathers in the kidney and is excreted as urine.

What can go wrong?

Infections are common in the urinary system. Women can suffer particularly from cystitis because of the urethra's proximity to the vagina and anus. The main symptoms are pain on passing urine and frequency of urination. If untreated an infection can spread from the bladder to the kidneys causing high temperatures and groin pain. *Kidney stones* can also form in susceptible individuals. Larger stones will stay in the kidneys but smaller ones may move down the ureter causing intense pain.

Urinary *incontinence* is often a problem in elderly women but it can also occur in women with several children. The pelvic floor muscles weaken and the woman suffers from stress incontinence, leaking urine when laughing or sneezing. The main male problem is an enlarged prostate gland. The prostate surrounds the male urethra and encroaches on it as it enlarges with age. Sufferers complain of a poor urinary flow, and having to pass urine frequently at night.

The urinary system is made up of two kidneys, two ureters, the bladder and the urether. The bladder fills up with waste urine and then sends nerve signals to the brain so that a person knows that they need to go to the toilet.

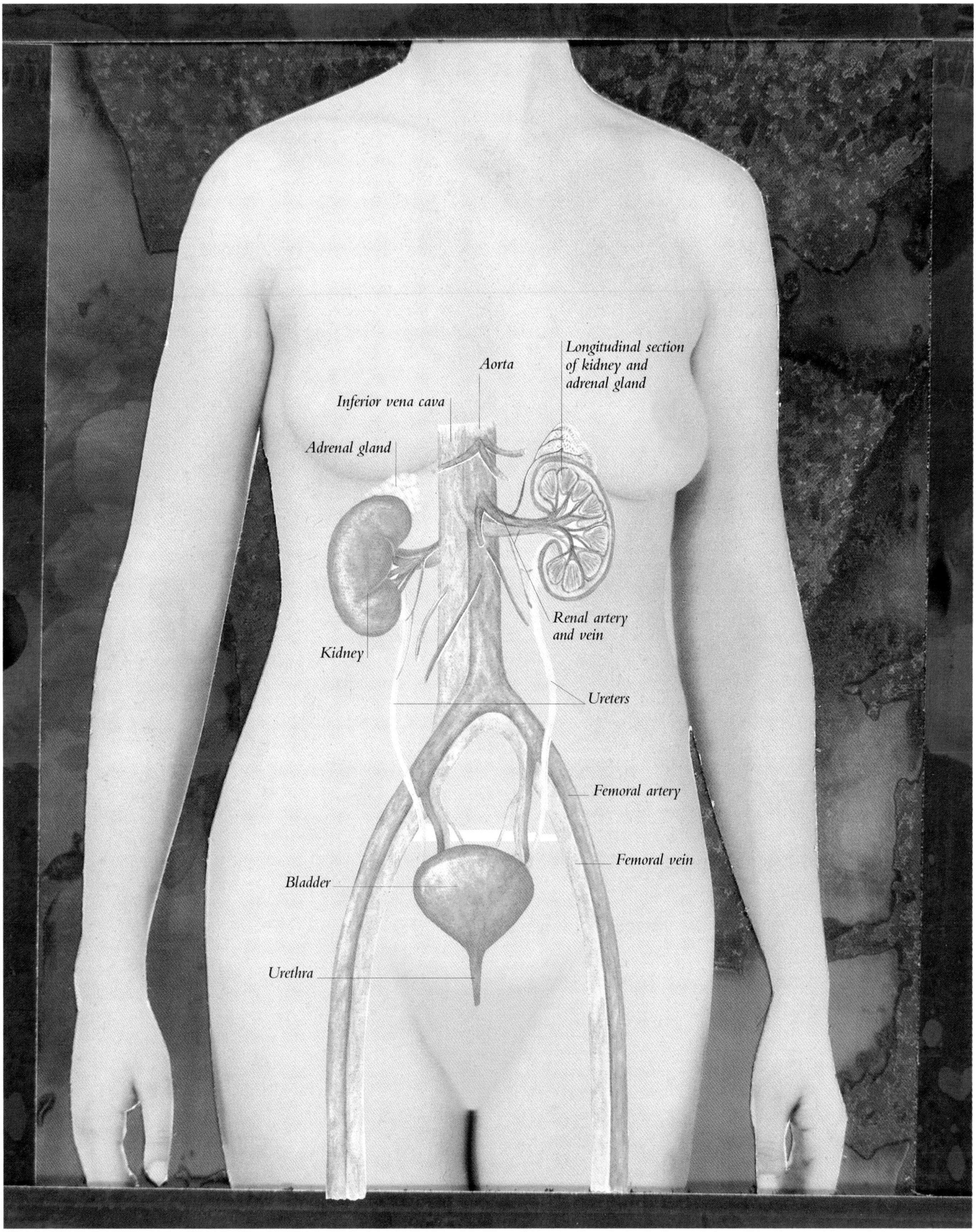
Longitudinal section of kidney and adrenal gland
Aorta
Inferior vena cava
Adrenal gland
Renal artery and vein
Kidney
Ureters
Femoral artery
Femoral vein
Bladder
Urethra

INCONTINENCE

What is it?

Incontinence, or involuntary urination, is very common. The most usual form is stress incontinence, in which a small quantity of urine is leaked when there is increased abdominal pressure, as in coughing, laughing or sneezing. In urge incontinence and total incontinence the bladder is completely emptied.

Causes

Stress incontinence is usually the result of injury or strain to the muscles which form the floor of the pelvis (called the pelvic floor muscles). In women, the overwhelming cause of this condition is pregnancy and childbirth. Other causes of incontinence include injury to or disease of the urethra, bladder stones, mental impairment, damage to the brain or spinal cord, stress, anxiety or anger, and irritable bladder.

Orthodox treatment

Pelvic floor exercises are the best form of treatment for incontinence caused by weak pelvic muscles, particularly during pregnancy and after childbirth. Surgery may occasionally be necessary to remove an obstruction or to tighten or lengthen the urethra. Incontinence, which is the result of infection, will be treated with antibiotics. Irritable bladder may be treated with anticholinergic drugs.

ALTERNATIVE TREATMENT

Western herbalism

Treatment can help to improve the tone of the bladder muscles and encourage better emptying of the bladder.

Chinese herbalism

Treatment works best combined with acupuncture; remedies will include astringents and kidney tonics.

Other therapies

A **naturopath** will suggest pelvic floor exercises, sitz baths, applied nutrition and herbal remedies. A **reflexologist** will address the urinary system, lower spine, pelvis and renals. A **hypnotherapist** may be able to treat incontinence through age regression and NLP. **Relaxation and visualization** can sometimes bring about a total cure. **Acupuncture** can help the elderly.

URETHRITIS

What is it?

Urethritis is inflammation of the urethra, causing a burning sensation and sometimes severe pain on passing urine. There may be blood in the urine, and sometimes a pus-filled yellow discharge. Scarring may result and stricture (narrowing) of the urethra. In nonspecific urethritis (NSU) the symptoms may be milder and the discharge may be clear; in women it is usually symptomless.

Causes

Urethritis may be caused by a number of infectious organisms, including the gonorrhea bacterium. Other causes include damage to the urethra, perhaps from a catheter, and irritant chemicals, including some spermicides. Nearly half of all cases of NSU are caused by chlamydia; a few are caused by other sexually transmitted infections and the remainder have no known cause.

Orthodox treatment

Urethritis is usually treated by antibiotics when there is infection. NSU is also treated by antibiotics, but, as the cause may not be known, the cure rate is only 85 percent. Strict follow-up is required and sexual intercourse must be refrained from until the condition is cleared. A partner must also be treated.

ALTERNATIVE TREATMENT

Homeopathy

Treatment would be much the same as it would be for cystitis (see page 239). Remedies will be prescribed according to the patient's constitution.

Chinese herbalism

Treatment will include detoxifying herbs, antipyretics and anti-inflammatory agents.

Other therapies

Nutritional therapists may suggest cranberry juice extracts. The immune system will also be addressed, and if food allergy exacerbates the condition, dietary changes may be suggested. A **reflexologist** will work on the reflex points relating to the urinary system and the lymph nodes. A **Western herbalist** may prevent recurrence and help damaged tissue to heal. A **hypnotherapist** may suggest hypno-healing and cell command therapy.

KIDNEY STONES

What are they?

Kidney stones are small round stones which form in the kidneys and sometimes other parts of the urinary tract. About 70 percent of stones are made up of calcium oxalate and/or phosphate, and a high level of oxalate in the urine is a predisposing factor for stones. About 20 percent of stones consist of a combination of calcium, magnesium and ammonium phosphate and these are called infective stones. Another 5 percent of stones are composed mainly of uric acid, and other types are very occasionally found.

Stones in the kidney or ureter (the tube from the kidney to the bladder) cause renal colic (severe loin pain). Bladder stones, which are more common in developing countries, are most commonly associated with difficulty in passing urine. Kidneys with stones are susceptible to infection and stones should therefore never be neglected.

Causes

There is no obvious underlying cause for the majority of kidney stones. Mild chronic dehydration may be a factor (there is an increased incidence in the summer) as the urine becomes more concentrated. Other causes include:

- *In the case of calcium stones, hyperparathyroidism (overactivity of the parathyroid glands).*
- *Uric acid stones occur in people with gout.*
- *In developing countries, bladder stones are usually caused by a diet low in phosphate and protein; in Western countries they are normally the result of obstruction to the flow of urine and/or a chronic urinary tract infection.*

Orthodox treatment

Bed rest, analgesic drugs and plenty of fluid to encourage the passing of the stone is often adequate for small stones. Surgery to remove large stones is still recommended on some occasions, but it is more likely that they will be treated by ultrasonic lithotripsy, where an ultrasonic probe is inserted into the body to break up the stone. A newer treatment is the use of an extracorporeal shock wave lithotripter, which shatters any stones present by sending shock waves from outside the body.

ALTERNATIVE TREATMENT

Homeopathy

Kidney stones will be treated constitutionally if they are a recurring problem. When there is extreme, sudden pain, medical attention is urgently required. The following remedies may be appropriate until help arrives:

- Berberis for a stitching pain between the lower ribs and hip when urinating. The pain comes from a central point and is made worse by movement but is relieved by lying on the painful side.
- Nux when the pain is right-sided and stabbing toward the genitals and down the right leg, causing nausea and vomiting, or right-sided pain which shoots into the rectum, causing the urge to defecate. Also weak urine flow which stops altogether on straining, and when the patient is chilly and irritable.
- Lycopodium when the pain is in the right side, stopping at the bladder and not going down the leg, also there may be pain in the back which is relieved by urination. Also for urine with red sediment, and when symptoms are worse between 4pm and 8am.
- Tabacum when pain shoots down the ureter, causing nausea and a cold sweat.
- Cantharis when the pain feels like knives stabbing in all directions, there is a burning sensation in the bladder, and an intolerable urge to urinate. Patient is thirsty but sickened by food.

Chinese herbalism

Where there is infection, a herbalist may suggest anti-inflammatory agents and antipyretics. Herbal diuretics may be useful. Treatment for stones depends on size, but purgatives and herbal evacuants may help if they are not too large.

Western herbalism

Herbal medicine is often extremely good; many remedies have a reputation as a stone-breaker, and will help to soothe damaged tissue and encourage the removal of waste matter. Although many remedies have anti-inflammatory and infection-fighting qualities, it is important not to overlook the need for antibiotics in severe cases of infection.

Nutritional therapy

Kidney stone formation has been linked with deficiencies of vitamin B6 and magnesium. The best protection against an infection is good general health and a healthy immune system (see page 265).

Other therapies

In **Ayurvedic medicine** there are herbal treatments available to help deal with kidney stones, and infection. **Yoga** may help through gentle *asanas*, relaxation, *pranayama* and meditation. **Macrobiotics** may be useful in a preventative sense. In the case of stones, plenty of hot, sweet drinks are recommended, along with **shiatsu** or **acupressure.** A **naturopath** may recommend dietetic management (avoiding calcium-rich foods) to prevent the formation of stones, and herbal remedies. A **hypnotherapist** may suggest creative visualization, which may enable the sufferer to dissolve the kidney stones. A **reflexologist** will work on reflex points relating to the kidneys, ureters, bladder, adrenal and pituitary glands and the lymph nodes. The **metamorphic technique** will be aimed at the prebirth area.

KIDNEY DISEASE

What is it?

There are many conditions which can adversely affect the kidneys, of which the most common are:

- *Infection (pyelonephritis).*
- *Metabolic disorders such as gout or kidney stones.*
- *Tubal damage, such as stricture of the ureter.*
- *An autoimmune disorder (glomerulonephritis).*
- *Congenital abnormalities (for example a missing kidney or*
- *kidneys that are joined together).*
- *Damage to or obstruction of the blood vessels within the kidney.*
- *Polycystic kidneys, where the kidneys are filled with large cysts.*

A SUDDEN TOTAL OBSTRUCTION OF THE KIDNEYS CAN CAUSE KIDNEY FAILURE IN A MATTER OF HOURS, WHICH CAN LEAD TO COMA AND THEN DEATH.

Causes

The causes of kidney disease depend on the nature of the condition. A kidney infection is usually caused by bacteria which most frequently originate in the vagina or intestinal tract; recurrent infections in children are often due to a weakness in the valves between the ureters and bladder, which allow urine to spurt back up the ureters. Cysts are often an inherited condition. Diabetes can cause obstruction in the kidneys and defects in the renal arteries which feed the kidneys. Allergic reactions to some drugs can cause sudden kidney problems, and drugs such as painkillers and strong antibiotics can damage the kidneys.

Orthodox treatment

A kidney infection will be treated with antibiotics which are sometimes administered intravenously. Surgery may be necessary to clear any blockage in the kidneys and ureters. Diuretics may be given to improve the flow of urine and steroids may be prescribed. Dialysis, in which a machine undertakes the function of the kidney, can be used temporarily in the case of acute kidney failure and long-term to keep sufferers alive indefinitely in the case of chronic failure, although a kidney transplant is often the best form of treatment for the latter.

ALTERNATIVE TREATMENT

Homeopathy

For a kidney infection, a homeopathic practitioner may suggest patients take one of the following remedies while waiting to see their doctor:

- Arsenicum where there is scanty urine, a burning sensation when it is passed, and the person is exhausted and restless.
- Aconite where there is sudden onset of disease, the person is fearful, feverish and thirsty, there is painful urination and anxiety on urination, urine is hot, red and scanty, the kidney area is tender and symptoms come on after exposure to cold dry air.
- Uva ursi where there is frequent urge to pass urine, burning or tearing pains in the kidney area, blood and mucus in urine and vomiting.
- Cantharis where there is constant desire to pass urine, or there are cutting, burning pains in the kidney area.

Nutritional therapy

The treatment a nutritional therapist will undertake will depend upon the specific kidney condition as well as the individual characteristics of the sufferer. Nutritional deficiencies may be one cause of kidney disease, and long-term toxic overload leading to gradual loss of kidney efficiency may also be involved.

Naturopathy

Dietetic management and fasting may be suggested, where indicated. Nutritional guidelines may include the reduction of animal protein and avoidance of citrus fruit. Hydrotherapy together with herbal and homeopathic medicine may be recommended.

Macrobiotics

Depending on the type of kidney disease, a practitioner may be able to offer useful advice. Many macrobiotic foods, especially sea vegetables, are high in potassium and are therefore not advised for kidney patients, so if a person is thinking of undertaking the standard diet, they should ensure they have an experienced and registered practitioner. Shiatsu, which is recommended within macrobiotics, is excellent for the kidneys, and a practitioner may also suggest eating warm rather than cold foods, avoiding animal fats and reducing salt.

Yoga

A yoga therapist may recommend gentle *asanas*, relaxation, *pranayama* and meditation.

Other therapies

In **Ayurvedic medicine a** practitioner will recommend herbal preparations. Depending on the cause of disease, a **Chinese herbalist** may recommend kidney and blood tonics alongside **acupuncture**. A **reflexologist** may be able to treat some kidney conditions, paying special attention to the kidneys, ureter tubes and bladder reflexes. **Tai chi** and **shiatsu** are often recommended. A **hypnotherapist** may suggest regression, suggestion, hypno-healing and cell command therapy. **Metamorphic technique** will be aimed at the prebirth area.

CYSTITIS (AND BLADDER INFECTION)

What is it?

Cystitis is inflammation of the bladder, usually caused by a bacterial infection. It is more common in women, because the urethra is shorter and it is therefore easier for bacteria, which are often from the vagina or anus, to pass from the urethral opening to the bladder. Symptoms include an overwhelming and frequent need to pass urine, burning pain when doing so, and occasionally stress incontinence. The amounts of urine passed are small, and it may be foul-smelling or cloudy or contain blood. There may be fever and sometimes a dull ache in the lower abdomen.

Causes

In men, infections and cystitis are less common and are most often the result of an obstruction, perhaps caused by an enlarged prostate gland (see page 204). They should always be investigated. The bacterium which usually causes cystitis is a common one found in the intestinal tract, and it has most often been transferred by sexual intercourse or poor hygiene. Cystitis is common in pregnancy. Diabetics are also more susceptible to urinary tract infections. Cystitis in women at the onset of sexual activity ("honeymoon cystitis") should settle down without treatment, but it is advisable always to empty the bladder after sexual intercourse to avoid aggravating the problem. Other causes of cystitis include:

- *The introduction to the urethra of surgical appliances such as a cystoscope or catheter.*
- *A stone or tumor in the bladder.*
- *The contraceptive diaphragm.*
- *Stricture of the urethra, which may be caused by scarring from previous infections.*
- *Occasionally, vaginal infections.*

AN ATTACK OF CYSTITIS WHICH LASTS FOR LONGER THAN 48 HOURS OR IS ASSOCIATED WITH A HIGH FEVER SHOULD BE BROUGHT TO THE ATTENTION OF YOUR DOCTOR.

Orthodox treatment

Treatment is usually with antibiotics along with plenty of fluids where infection is present. This will also prevent secondary infection of the kidneys. Other causes will be treated accordingly.

ALTERNATIVE TREATMENT

Homeopathy

A homeopath will treat recurrent attacks constitutionally, but one of the following remedies may be prescribed to relieve symptoms during an attack:

- Cantharis for burning, cutting pains in the lower abdomen, a nonstop urge to urinate, or an ache in the small of the back that tends to get worse in the afternoon, a merest trickle of urine with blood in it, or an inability to empty the bladder properly;
- Apis for sharp, stinging pains in lower abdomen, a frequent urge to urinate, scanty urine that is hot and bloody, or if the symptoms seem worse for heat and better for cold;
- Nux for frequent, painful urging with little result;
- Belladonna for a burning sensation along the urethra, a bladder that is sensitive to jarring, bright red urine with clots of blood in it, or an urging that persists even after urine has been passed.
- Tarentula when there is high fever and extreme pain in the bladder area, a swollen and hard bladder, a feeling of extreme restlessness, or a great sense of hurry.

There are many other suitable homeopathic remedies depending on the specific symptoms.

Naturopathy

A naturopath will suggest nutritional management, excluding all irritants. A detoxification diet may be recommended, along with regular intake of fluids. Hydrotherapy, in particular a sitz bath, may be appropriate, and herbal and homeopathic medicines may be recommended.

Nutritional therapy

Nutritional therapists may suggest cranberry juice extracts to help prevent bacteria adhering to the bladder walls. The immune system will be addressed, and if food allergy exacerbates the condition, dietary changes may be suggested.

Western herbalism

There is a wide range of remedies available and they will be prescribed according to individual diagnosis and symptoms. Diuretics and urinary antiseptic remedies will feature strongly, with others to heal urinary tissues as needed.

Other therapies

In **Ayurvedic medicine** a practitioner will suggest *panchakarma* therapy, herbal remedies and oral medications. **Autogenic training** may help relieve chronic cystitis by improving the function of the immune system. **Yoga** may help through gentle *asanas*, relaxation, *pranayama* and meditation. A **Chinese herbalist** may suggest detoxifying and anti-inflammatory herbs. A **hypnotherapist** may suggest pain control and healing hypnosis. **Spiritual healing** soothes inflammation and helps to rebalance the body's internal ecology. An **aromatherapist** may recommend sitz baths with essential oils of sandalwood and juniper, twice daily for five days. A **reflexologist** may work on the reflex points relating to the urinary system, prostate and lower spine. The **metamorphic technique** will be aimed at the prebirth area. **Relaxation and visualization** may be helpful in preventing further attacks.

DIGESTIVE SYSTEM

What is it?

The digestive system starts at the mouth where food enters, is chewed and mixed with saliva which begins to break up the food with enzymes. Other enzymes in the digestive tract's juices break down proteins, fats and carbohydrates for absorption into the small intestine. A "bolus" of food is then swallowed and passed down the gullet or esophagus.

In the stomach the food is mixed with acidic gastric juices which break up the food into a paste called "chyme," that is propelled by contractions into the small intestine. Here bile from the gallbladder and pancreatic juices are added. Most of these juices are then processed in the liver, which is vital in digestion and for storing sugar, fats and proteins. It also neutralizes toxins and drugs and produces bile.

Unabsorbed liquid food passes into the large intestine where most of the water is reabsorbed into the bloodstream. The remaining semisolid fecal matter passes into the rectum for storage until it is expelled from the body.

What can go wrong?

The digestive system helps prevent infections. The gastric juices will kill most viruses and bacteria. Some, however, penetrate and can cause *gastroenteritis* with *diarrhea*, vomiting and abdominal cramps. Travelers' *diarrhea* and food poisoning are common results, so careful food hygiene abroad is essential.

Stress, too much alcohol, or certain drugs may cause excessive stomach acid resulting in indigestion and heartburn. If the cause continues unabated, ulcers can form.

Stomach or esophagus cancer can cause similar symptoms to indigestion or heartburn. Other signs include weight and appetite loss. If caught early, these cancers are treatable.

Constipation is common with our highly refined Western diet. It can also be caused by other diseases, for example, hypothyroidism, and drugs such as codeine. Persistent *constipation* and straining can bring about hemorrhoids, swollen veins in the anal canal. These can be inherited. Blood in the stools can point to *rectal cancer* and should always be investigated. Alternating bouts of *diarrhea*, *constipation* and cramp-like abdominal pain may indicate *irritable bowel syndrome* (*IBS*).

Food is taken into the body through the mouth where it is broken down by saliva. It reaches the stomach via the esophagus where it is broken down further by strong gastric juices.

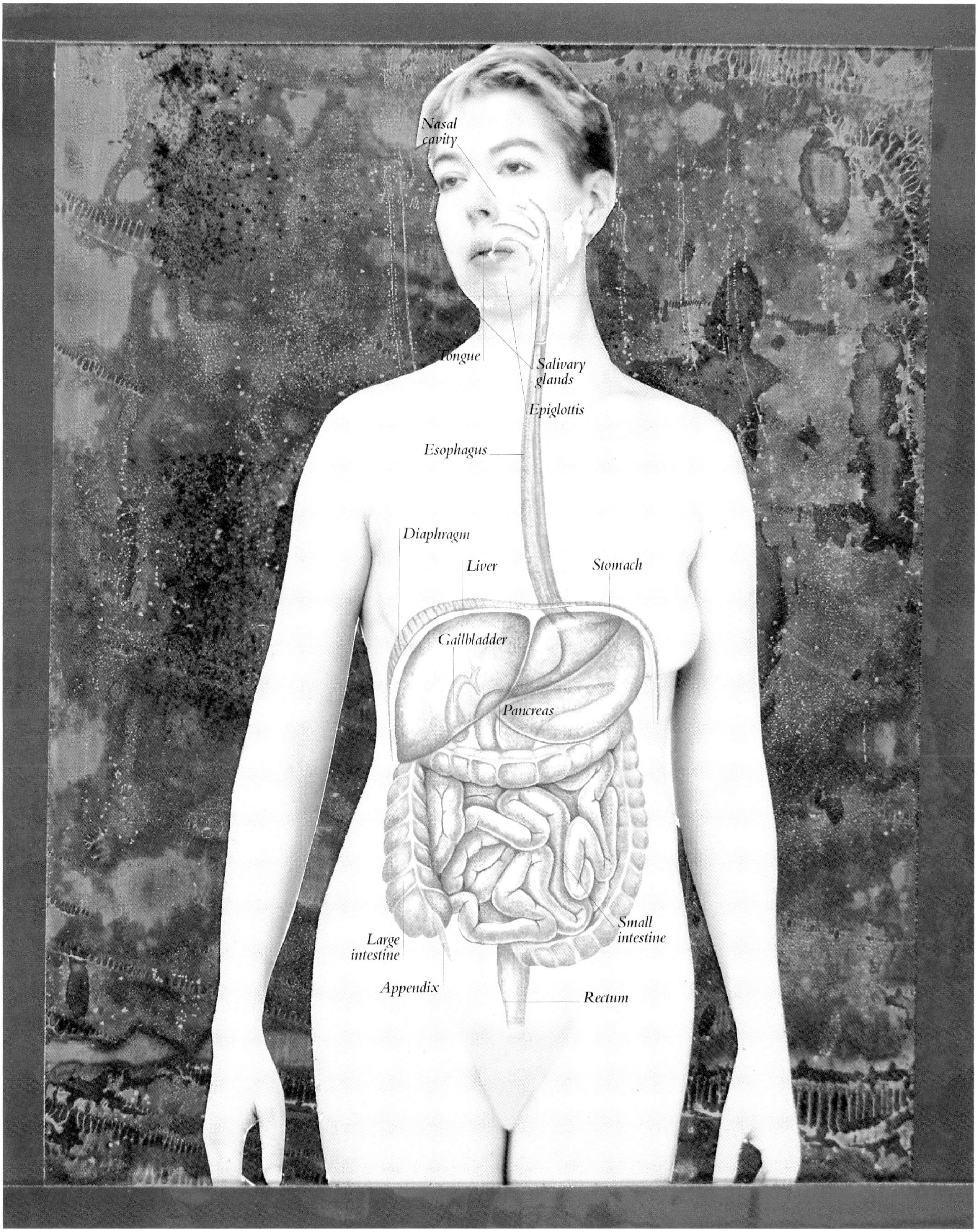
Nasal cavity
Tongue
Salivary glands
Epiglottis
Esophagus
Diaphragm
Liver
Stomach
Gallbladder
Pancreas
Small intestine
Large intestine
Appendix
Rectum

Diarrhea

What is it?

Diarrhea is a symptom rather than an "illness" and is characterized by the passing of frequent runny stools. Associated symptoms may be wind or cramps and vomiting. While diarrhea arising in the small bowel results in large amounts of watery discharge, problems in the large bowel tend to produce bloody stools. Acute diarrhea lasting only a day or two is common and is usually due to eating or drinking contaminated food or water. Chronic (long-term) or often recurring diarrhea may be linked to a serious disorder such as Crohn's disease (see page 255).

Causes

The main causes of diarrhea include:

- *Short-term, acute diarrhea, which is most commonly caused by a bacterial or viral infection taken in with either food or water.*
- *Acute diarrhea may have other causes as well, such as anxiety, food allergies, food intolerances and reactions to drugs.*
- *Chronic, long-term diarrhea (which often takes the form of repeated short attacks) may be caused by such disorders as Crohn's disease, ulcerative colitis, diverticular disease, cancer of the colon and irritable bowel syndrome.*
- *Amoebic dysentery may be the problem if traveling in the tropics.*

IF THE DIARRHEA PERSISTS FOR MORE THAN 48 HOURS, CONSULT A DOCTOR. PEOPLE WITH SEVERE DIARRHEA, FEVER AND VOMITING SHOULD SEEK MEDICAL ATTENTION EARLY ON. BLOOD IN THE STOOLS IS ABNORMAL AND SHOULD BE REPORTED TO A DOCTOR. ALSO CONSULT A DOCTOR FOR CASES OF PERSISTENT DIARRHEA WHICH DEVELOPED ABROAD OR FOR ANY NOTICEABLE CHANGE IN BOWEL HABITS.

Orthodox treatment

Most acute attacks of diarrhea improve naturally. In severe diarrhea, the water and electrolytes (salts) which are lost need to be replaced to prevent dehydration. (This is especially important for infants, children and the elderly – see page 326). Ready-prepared mixtures can be bought to be added to specific amounts of water. Antidiarrheal drugs, such as codeine and loperamide, should not be taken if infection is the cause but may be recommended after 48 hours if there is abdominal pain. Recurring bouts of diarrhea, or diarrhea that persists for over a week or has blood in the bowel movements needs medical investigation. The feces will need to be examined to see if there is an infection present and other tests may follow.

Alternative Treatment

Homeopathy

Chronic diarrhea will be treated constitutionally. Specific remedies for acute attacks include:

- Colocynth if the diarrhea is associated with spasmodic griping pains and with copious amounts of yellowish stools.
- Aloe may be useful if the condition has occurred after eating and if the stools are yellowish-green.

Other useful remedies include aconite, argentum nit., arsenicum, podophyllum, sulphur, veratrum, pulsatilla and china. If antibiotics were a factor, acidophilus capsules can help as they contain the mixed microorganisms normally found in a healthy gut which may be wiped out by antibiotics. Live yogurt is also a good source of these microorganisms.

Hypnotherapy

There is a standard hypnotherapeutic procedure of uncovering and suggestion therapy. Relaxation skills will be taught. Hypno-healing will be used to strengthen and heal the gastrointestinal system. Self-hypnosis can be taught to enable the person to relax more while eating, digest food properly and develop mental and physical powers of assimilation and elimination. At the Wythington Hospital, Manchester, hypnotherapy was used in 1993 to treat irritable bowel syndrome patients. While they had not responded to other treatments, the success rate with hypnotherapy was 80 percent.

Western herbalism

A herbalist will look at the causes. In acute situations, it may be necessary to use herbs with laxative properties to encourage proper cleansing of toxins from the blood. More often, highly astringent and anti-inflammatory herbs will be given. Garlic capsules can be useful for mild infections. An infusion of plantain, geranium or agrimony with pinches of ginger, crushed caraway seeds and cinnamon can also be useful.

Other therapies

Nutritional therapy will look for any food intolerances and allergies. If the digestive system finds a particular food stressful, it may try to expel it as quickly as possible. **Kirlian photography** may enable the patient to understand the body's responses to lifestyle concerns and the pressures causing the diarrhea. **Shiatsu**, **osteopathy**, **crystal and gemstone therapy**, **cymatics** and **kinesiology** may all help. **Acupuncture** combined with **Chinese herbalism** preparations is considered a good treatment for most digestive problems. Astringent, anti-inflammatory agents and herbal detoxicants will be recommended. Regular treatment with **auricular therapy** has a balancing effect on the digestion, especially when the person's problems are stress related. **Macrobiotics** can prove useful. Therapists suggest avoiding fruit. **Aromatherapists** will use thyme linalol rubbed over the lower back and abdominal areas.

CONSTIPATION

What is it?

Bowel habits vary greatly but the difficult and infrequent passing of dry, hard feces is generally described as constipation. This is usually a harmless condition but can signify an underlying disorder, especially if it begins in an adult over the age of 40. Any noticeable change in personal habits should be reported to a doctor for investigation. Generally, regularity and comfort when the bowels are moved are more important factors than the frequency.

Causes

Constipation has many possible causes, including:

- *Insufficient fiber in the diet in more developed countries. Fiber (which is derived mainly from such foods as fresh fruits, vegetables and whole meal bread) supplies bulk which the muscles of the colon require to help move the feces.*
- *In the elderly, immobility and and weakness of the abdominal muscles may be the problem.*
- *Hemorrhoids and anal fissure (see page 244) may inhibit bowel movements.*
- *Irritable bowel syndrome may include constipation, that possibly alternates with diarrhea.*
- *Diverticular disease or cancer (see page 251) may cause a narrowing of part of the colon, leading to constipation.*
- *Some drugs such as narcotic painkillers and iron tablets may bring about constipation.*
- *Hypothyroidism (underactive thyroid gland) because colonic contractions are slowed down.*
- *Hormonal changes, such as pregnancy or the second phase of the menstrual cycle, which can affect many women.*

CONSULT A DOCTOR IF CONSTIPATION OCCURS WITH BLOOD IN THE FECES, PAIN DURING BOWEL MOVEMENTS OR LOSS OF WEIGHT.

Orthodox treatment

Constipation can usually be lessened by increasing fiber in the diet and taking more fluids. If the condition continues over a lengthy period of time, medical advice should be taken. Laxative drugs should be taken only with care as their prolonged use can interfere with the normal functioning of the colon. They should generally only be used if straining to pass feces will exacerbate some other coexisting condition, such as piles.

ALTERNATIVE TREATMENT

Homeopathy

Constipation is considered a constitutional problem. The following remedies are for occasional but not long-term use: nux, for a great urge to pass stools but nothing is passed, or passing stools but feeling there is more to come. It is useful for a patient who is sedentary or elderly. Alumina is used when there is no desire to open the bowels until the rectum is full and even soft movements are difficult to pass and may be mucus-covered.

Hypnotherapy

This can be an effective treatment to help resolve bowel problems. The standard hypnotherapy procedure involves uncovering and suggestion therapy. Relaxation skills can also be taught. Hypno-healing is used to strengthen and heal the gastrointestinal system. Self-hypnosis is taught to enable the person to relax while eating, digest better and develop mental and physical powers of assimilation and elimination.

Western herbalism

The treatment is addressed to the whole person. There will be general advice on improving the diet and relaxation – as well as posture and breathing. Possible laxative remedies include senna pods and also licorice root (taken overnight) and, if they cause any griping pain, a small amount of fennel seeds. Linseeds are useful if sprinkled onto cereal in the mornings or used in stews.

Reflexology

Treatment will be individual, based on characteristics and symptoms, and aimed at the reflex points relating to the small and large intestines, liver, gallbladder, adrenal glands and solar plexus.

Other therapies

Acupuncture, along with herbal preparations, is considered a good approach for most digestive problems. Regular treatment with **auricular therapy** (about three times a week) is said to have a balancing effect on the digestion, especially when the disorders are stress related. An **Ayurvedic medicine** practitioner may suggest *panchakarma* therapy and various medications. **Macrobiotics** will be appropriate, using the standard macrobiotic diet, but adding half a cup of grated daikon and juice, plus one tablespoon of shoy taken daily. Fruit is considered to be acceptable, but the advice will be to reduce salt. A **Chinese herbalist** may recommend standard blood tonics and digestive and evacuant herbs. Therapies like **relaxation and visualization**, **yoga** and **tai chi** may help in cases which are stress related or linked to emotional problems. A **naturopath** will prescribe according to individual characteristics and symptoms, with a high-fiber diet and raw foods being especially important. Regular exercise helps as well. Applied nutrition, relaxation, herbal medicine and **massage** may be incorporated in treatment as well. In some cases, **osteopathic** treatment may be appropriate.

HEMORRHOIDS

What are they?

Hemorrhoids are purple or dark-red fleshy lumps created by swollen veins within the lining of the anus. If they occur near the anal opening, they are described as external hemorrhoids. Some which actually protrude outside the anus are called prolapsing. The condition is common, especially during pregnancy and as a result of giving birth. Bleeding and discomfort or even pain on defecating are the usual symptoms. There may be itching around the anus and mucous discharge from prolapsed hemorrhoids.

Causes

Hemorrhoids are caused by increased pressure in the veins of the anus, because the veins of the anal canal lose their elasticity. This can be a result of chronic constipation. Other causes are the relaxation of the walls of the blood vessels during pregnancy, while some people have a congenital weakness in the anal veins.

Orthodox treatment

Drinking more fluids and eating more fiber are recommended and this is often enough for mild problems. The swelling and pain can be reduced by rectal suppositories and creams. More severe cases may be treated by sclerotherapy (which injects an irritant liquid) or cryosurgery (which applies extreme cold and causes the swollen veins to shrivel). Surgery is usually needed to remove prolapsing hemorrhoids. A doctor should inspect the rectum to exclude the possibility of disorders such as cancer.

ALTERNATIVE TREATMENT

Homeopathy

Constitutional treatment is necessary for chronic piles. In the short term, some of the following remedies may be suggested: paeonia ointment or lint soaked in hamamelis solution, aconite (taken at half-hourly doses), aesculus, aloe, collinsonia, hamamelis, nux and pulsatilla.

Western herbalism

Western herbalists will aim at the general digestive system and improving local blood flood to reduce the swollen veins. Local treatments such as astringent ointments of comfrey, horse chestnut and witch hazel may be given along with internal remedies.

Other therapies

Ayurvedic medicines may be taken orally or via the rectum. **Reflexology** may be aimed at reflex points relating to the lower back and small and large intestines. **Hypnotherapy** can be used to relieve hemorrhoids. **Acupuncture** and **Chinese herbalism** are considered helpful.

ANAL FISSURE

What is it?

An anal fissure is a tear in the sensitive lower anal canal, and this causes the sufferer pain on defecation. While this is generally an isolated problem, it may be linked with other gut diseases. Most fissures are short-lived but they may become chronic (long-term), reach the sphincter muscle and become infected. During bowel movements, the split is irritated, and this can cause minor bleeding and also discomfort.

Causes

Constipation is a common cause and the passage of hard, dry feces tends to tear the lining of the canal.

Orthodox treatment

Laxatives and a local anesthetic may be offered as an ointment or suppository. Lubricants can help to make the passage of feces easier; antibiotics will be prescribed for any infection.

ALTERNATIVE TREATMENT

Homeopathy

Changes in the diet will be suggested. Specific remedies may include:

- Aesculus for sore, burning pain, lower backache and large, dry stools.
- Graphites for sore, sharp pain on passing stools which may be covered in mucus.

Other therapies

Western herbalism may be of help in cleaning up chronic infection or inflammation which can prolong the problem. Local treatment may be appropriate. **Reflexology** is likely to be aimed at the reflex points relating to the colon and the lymph glands. **Naturopathy** will suggest dietary guidelines, such as more high-fiber food and mineral therapy.

HERNIA

What is it?

When part of an organ or tissue protrudes through a weak area in the barrier muscle or tissue around it, this rupture is called a hernia. This usually happens when the intestine pushes through a weakness in the abdominal wall – the first symptoms being a bulge and sometimes discomfort. A hiatus hernia is when the stomach protrudes through the diaphragm into the chest.

Most abdominal hernias are in the groin area and the majority occur in men. These include inguinal hernias, which are the commonest type in males. Femoral hernias are commoner in women and there are also umbilical hernias occurring in the belly-button area of babies. If the supply of blood to a trapped section of intestine is impaired, this is called a strangulated hernia and gangrene, potentially fatal, in the bowel could result.

Causes

Hernias are usually the result of a congenital weakness in the abdominal wall. Other causes are:

- *Weak abdominal and/or lower back muscles.*
- *Substantial weight gain/obesity.*
- *Heavy manual work, including heavy lifting.*
- *Chronic bronchitis and smoking.*

Orthodox treatment

If the discomfort is only slight, a truss may suffice. Surgical repair will be needed if the hernia is causing pain and proving impossible to push back. The aim is to push the protruding intestine back into place and strengthen the weakened muscle wall. Patients may need to avoid lifting heavy objects for some months.

ALTERNATIVE TREATMENT

Western herbalism

Treatment may generally improve the whole digestive function, reducing excess acidity and relieving pressure on the valves. Diet, posture and exercise will be considered.

Alexander Technique

Hiatus hernias can be helped by improved postural balance and a decrease in contractions along the spinal column or points associated with the affected area.

Other therapies

With **reflexology**, treatment will be holistic but specifically aimed at the reflex points associated with the adrenal glands and the affected area. A **homeopath** will prescribe symptomatic relief in the same way as for indigestion. **Acupuncture**, along with herbal preparations, is helpful. Therapies like **relaxation and visualization**, **yoga** and **tai chi** may help in stress-related cases or those linked to emotional problems. **Chinese herbalism** may prescribe digestive herbs, evacuants and aromatic stimulants.

BEER GUTS

What are they?

This is a colloquial term referring to deposits of fat in the male abdominal area and is associated with a sedentary lifestyle and overconsumption of beer. Beer guts are common in men, partly because many are genetically "programmed" for central weight-gain anyway. It may also be because the small bowel loses its elasticity with age and begins to sag, in women dropping down into the roomy pelvis, but in men bulging outward.

Causes

The most common reasons for beer guts are excess alcohol and food, with a lack of regular exercise. Beer/lager is implicated as it is high in calories and is often taken in relatively large amounts.

Orthodox treatment

Advice is likely on reducing or stopping alcoholic consumption, eating less and more healthily, and taking more regular exercise.

ALTERNATIVE TREATMENT

Western herbalism

Treatment can help, plus an effort by the person concerned, to improve the liver and digestive function.

Other therapies

With **auricular therapy**, ear studs can reduce the craving for alcohol and food. **Acupuncture** combined with **Chinese herbalism** is considered a good approach for helping to relieve most digestive problems. **Autogenic training** may help to reduce a person's cravings for beer and alcohol generally. **Nutritional therapy** treatment will focus on following a strict diet and using muscle-toning exercises.The standard **macrobiotic** diet will also be recommended, along with some advice on drinking to reduce the overall intake of alcohol.

Flatulence and Burping

What are they?

Flatulence is a medical term describing an excessive amount of air or gas being expelled. Expulsion via the anus is popularly referred to as "breaking wind" – while "belching" or "burping" is the method by which excess swallowed or gulped air is expelled through the mouth. When a person is standing upright, the flatulence is more likely to be expelled through the mouth – but the air is more likely to pass through the intestine and anus when the person is lying prone. Belching can actually make the problem worse as more air is swallowed in the process of burping – but it is sometimes a help during pregnancy to relieve feelings of nausea and heartburn.

Gas which is passed through the anus is called flatus, containing a mixture of nitrogen and hydrogen sulphide, a bad-smelling gas produced in the colon when bacteria ferments bits of undigested food (often vegetable starches). Some people and foods naturally produce more of this gas than others. It needs to be expelled because the body cannot reabsorb the gas and the abdomen becomes bloated if flatus remains for too long.

The presence of flatus can provoke considerable discomfort in the abdomen if it is present in large amounts – and even normal amounts may be a problem for people who have intestines which are especially sensitive.

Causes

Excessive swallowing of air (aerophagy) may occur when people eat too fast, or in times of stress, and this can be a major cause. Some people swallow too much air as a nervous habit. Flatulence is also a feature of gastrointestinal disorders like dyspepsia, irritable bowel syndrome, and also of colitis and Crohn's disease, while some foods, such as beans and pulses, are likely to produce considerably more flatus than other food.

Flatulence may be worse after a course of antibiotics which destroy the body's natural intestinal flora (healthy bacteria).

Orthodox treatment

Most people with flatulence are not suffering from a serious disorder and advice to reduce certain foods is probably sufficient. Here are other possible treatments:

- *Stress reduction techniques (if stress is the cause).*
- *Milk may need to be excluded from the diet if the flatulence is resulting from a lactose deficiency (a lack of the the enzyme which breaks down the sugar in milk).*

IF THERE IS WEIGHT LOSS, ABDOMINAL PAIN, BLEEDING OR A CHANGE IN BOWEL HABITS, THESE NEED INVESTIGATING.

Alternative Treatment

Hypnotherapy

Hypnotherapy is widely reported as being an effective treatment in resolving bowel problems. There is a standard hypnotherapeutic procedure of uncovering and suggestion therapy. A good hypnotherapist will differentiate between gas which is caused by anxiety and gas caused as a result of food putrefying in the gut. In addition, dietary advice may be given and there will be treatment to strengthen the digestive system as a whole.

Bach flower remedies

If the condition is affected by stress or a negative mental attitude, the Bach remedies will be suggested on an individual basis to help bring a more positive emotional outlook. If the stress if from moving to a new job, walnut may be helpful. Scleranthus is for when the emotional distress is from facing a round of constant dilemmas.

Western herbalism

Herbal medicines are a useful treatment for most digestive problems, having a direct effect as well as a wider systemic approach. Remedies such as sage, thyme, and marjoram or rosemary can be used in cooking. Meadowsweet, camomile or balm tea could be taken between meals.

Alexander Technique

This treatment can benefit the digestive system through improved postural balance and also by encouraging more efficient breathing and relaxation. Many gastrointestinal conditions have a high stress component and are also accompanied by anxiety and postural imbalance. Abdominal discomfort can be connected to a slight sideways displacement of the thorax and sometimes a rotational twist of the dorso-lumbar spine.

Other therapies

Acupuncture together with herbal preparations is considered a good approach for dealing with most digestive problems, including flatulence. Taking regular treatment with **auricular therapy** (about three times a week) is said to have a good balancing effect on the digestion, especially when the disorders are stress related. **Ayurvedic medicine** will suggest various medications along with *panchakarma* therapy. **Macrobiotics** will be useful and **Chinese herbalism** may be successful as well. **Naturopathy** offers a variety of treatments, recommending an initial 24 hours of fasting to clear the system followed by a dietary regime in which carbohydrates and proteins are not eaten at the same meal. For further relief, hot and cold compresses may be put onto the abdominal area to help relieve any discomfort. Eating garlic is also likely to be suggested.

Indigestion and Heartburn

What are they?

Indigestion is a general term for any discomfort in the upper abdomen or chest usually brought on by eating too fast and/or foods which are too fatty, spicy and rich. The medical word is dyspepsia and there may be a variety of symptoms, including hiccups, heartburn, nausea and wind. Very rarely, recurring indigestion could be a sign of gallstones, peptic ulcer or an inflammation of the esophagus (esophagitis) and *Candida albicans* gut infestation.

Possibly the most common symptom of indigestion is heartburn. This causes a burning discomfort in the lower and central part of the chest. It is produced by the stomach's acidic digestive juices backing up past the sphincter flap which usually separates the stomach from the food pipe. A hot, sour taste may appear in the mouth.

Causes

The most common causes of indigestion are:

- *Overeating – especially rich, fatty or spicy food – and excessive alcohol, caffeine and smoking.*
- *Pregnancy.*
- *Eating too fast.*
- *Digestion may be upset by strong, negative emotions such as anxiety distress, anger and fear.*

Orthodox treatment

Those with these problems will find that eating regularly, without rushing, may help symptoms to subside. In addition:

- *Antacid drugs can be taken in the short term but a doctor should be consulted if pain persists for over six hours or if there are other symptoms such as prolonged vomiting or passing very dark feces.*
- *Antiulcer drugs and antibiotics.*
- *Clinical tests may be needed to determine the cause, including an endoscopy (flexible lighted tube investigation), blood count, a barium meal and X-rays.*
- *Propping up the head of the bed and avoiding late meals helps to reduce reflux and heartburn. Advice on stress control and relaxation may be helpful.*

SEE A DOCTOR IF YOU ARE OVER 40 AND DEVELOP INDIGESTION SUDDENLY, IF YOUR BOWEL HABITS ALSO CHANGE NOTICEABLY AND/OR YOU ARE EXPERIENCING FREQUENT PAIN OR WEIGHT LOSS, AS WELL AS INDIGESTION.

Alternative Treatment

Homeopathy

Most minor indigestion can be treated with remedies on a self-help basis. Long-standing or chronic indigestion should be treated constitutionally. If indigestion is accompanied by vomiting, phosphorus may be helpful until medical help is received. Specific remedies which can be prescribed according to specific symptoms include carbo veg. if the stomach is full of wind, even after very plain food; nux for people who experience heartburn half an hour after eating; pulsatilla if the problems seem to be aggravated by rich food about two hours after eating and kali bichrom. for vomiting and/or nausea and if the problem is aggravated by drinking beer.

Western herbalism

Treatment may help to rebalance digestion rather than simply reduce acid levels. In the short term, hot teas such as camomile, cinnamon, fennel, peppermint and lemon balm are useful. Longer-term remedies might include using golden seal, mallow, thyme, meadowsweet or marigold.

Alexander Technique

This treatment can benefit the digestive system through improved postural balance, more efficient breathing and relaxation. Many kinds of gastrointestinal conditions have a high stress component and are accompanied by anxiety and postural imbalance. Abdominal discomfort can often be connected to a slight sideways displacement of the thorax and sometimes a rotational twist of the dorso-lumbar spine.

Reflexology

Treatment will be holistic, aimed at the whole person, and the reflex points relating to the digestive system, solar plexus and adrenal glands may be addressed as well.

Other therapies

Acupuncture, along with herbal preparations, is considered a good approach for most digestive problems. Regular treatment with **auricular therapy** (about three times a week) has a balancing effect on the digestion, especially when disorders are stress-related. An **Ayurvedic medicine** practitioner may suggest tridosha balancing, with medication and detoxification techniques. Using **autogenic training** will reduce hyperacidity, which should help these symptoms. **Macrobiotics** will be useful. **Chinese herbal** practitioners may suggest digestive herbs or those with fragrant odor to remove food retention. Relaxing therapies like **relaxation and visualization**, **yoga** and **tai chi** may be successful in cases which are stress-related or linked to anxiety. **Naturopathic** treatment is recommended. **Color therapists** will use turquoise to help get rid of trapped air in the chest and also yellow which is beneficial for many digestive problems.

Gallstones

What are they?

Gallstones are small, hard pebbles formed from solid elements such as calcium and cholesterol present in bile. The stones may be found either in the gallbladder (a sac under the liver holding concentrated bile) or sometimes in the bile ducts (connecting the gallbladder and liver to the duodenum). Bile is secreted by the liver and stored in the gallbladder from which it passes via the biliary ducts to the duodenum to aid in fat digestion.

Only about a fifth of gallstones cause any complications or symptoms. If a stone becomes stuck in a duct and causes biliary colic, there may be severe pain in the upper abdomen and this can lead to a tenderness under the ribs on the right side. Other kinds of complications include cholecystitis (an inflammation of the gallbladder) and bile duct obstruction.

The symptoms may involve acute, severe upper abdominal pain and also possibly a high fever. With bile duct obstruction, the patient may also become jaundiced, with eyes and skin taking on a yellowish tone.

Causes

Most gallstones arise in people who produce bile which contains too much cholesterol, or too little bile, or by an upset in the chemical composition of the bile. The risk factors include:

- *A high-fat diet. Limiting the consumption of sugar and fat can be a help in avoiding the problem. A high-fiber diet may be helpful as well.*
- *Being female. One in three women and one in five men are affected by gallstones.*
- *Increasing age. Older people are more likely to have gallstones but they are rare in children.*
- *Food intolerance or allergy.*
- *Being overweight.*
- *Taking the contraceptive pill may encourage the gallstones to form at an earlier age.*

GALLSTONES ARE ONLY ONE POSSIBLE CAUSE OF ABDOMINAL PAIN. BE SURE TO CONSULT A DOCTOR IF SUCH PAIN PERSISTS FOR MORE THAN FOUR HOURS.

Orthodox treatment

While most gallstones do not show up on X-rays, they can be seen on ultrasound scans and this is usually the first test to be used. Treatment is only necessary for the minority of gallstones which are causing symptoms:

- *Acute cholecystitis needs treatment with painkillers, intravenous fluids and antibiotics while biliary colic will often settle with painkillers. Surgery may be offered after an attack of acute cholecystitis has resolved or if the attacks of biliary colic are repeated. The gallbladder can be removed by an open operation or by key-hole surgery.*
- *Some hospitals have the technology to break up gallstones without the need for any surgery. In one technique, shock waves are used to shatter the stones. Another technique uses a tube inserted into the gallbladder and a strong solution which dissolves cholesterol is flushed through.*
- *There are also drugs which may dissolve gallstones over a period of several months. In about 50 percent of cases, stones recur after the drug treatment is stopped.*
- *A low-fat diet will be recommended as fatty foods seem to have a strong association with forming gallstones.*

Alternative Treatment

Western herbalism

Bitter herbs can encourage the flow of bile and reduce gall bladder inflammation. A daily cup of centaury tea can aid the digestive process. Herbs which may be used include golden seal, dandelion and gentian. Depending on the size of the stones, treatment may include measures to encourage passing the stones naturally.

Naturopathy

Naturopathy will be aimed at nutritional and dietary management (a low-fat diet, the reduction of carbohydrates, increased intake of polyunsaturated oils plus extra vitamin C). Fresh lemon juice is thought to be especially useful along with bitter salads such as endive, chicory and globe artichoke. There may be gallbladder "flush" and hydrotherapy. Herbal medication may include hepatics and choloagogues. There may be reflex therapy to spinal regions and foot zones.

Other therapies

Reflexology treatment will be holistic, with particular attention being paid to the reflex points which relate to the liver and gallbladder. A **homeopath** may provide treatment such as berberis for stones which do not cause symptoms. China may be used if that does not work and the person is nervy, chilly and somewhat oversensitive. **Acupuncture,** along with herbal preparations, is considered a good approach for most digestive problems. The practitioner will examine to determine the cause and stimulate points on the liver, stomach, bladder, gallbladder, spleen and conception meridians. **Aromatherapy** will use abdominal rubs and also give the person gentle massage with sandalwood or juniper on a regular basis. **Color therapists** will focus on purple as the most powerful healing shade, either in the form of underclothing or as a silk square which could be held in place by fitted clothing. An alternative will be shining a strong violet light over the area onto bare skin.

Irritable Bowel Syndrome (IBS)

What is it?

Irregular bowel habits combined with an intermittent abdominal pain may be signs of irritable bowel syndrome (IBS). There are muscles in the gut wall which propel the partially digested food forward; if there are problems with the coordination of these contractions, the result can be various combinations of pain, diarrhea and constipation. The condition is sometimes also known as irritable colon syndrome and spastic colon.

The symptoms of this tend to subside and even disappear for lengths of time, but the problem is often a recurring one throughout life. While not life-threatening, it can cause considerable discomfort. Younger to middle-aged women are most likely to develop the condition, but it can affect anyone.

The estimate is that about a third of the population has the symptoms at some time in their life and 13 percent will do so regularly; they include cramp-like pain in the abdomen, swelling of the abdomen, general malaise, back pain and feeling full halfway through a meal. There may also be excessive wind. Other symptoms may include feelings of faintness, a reduced appetite, back pain and tiredness.

Causes

Anxiety, food intolerance and stress are thought to be the main causal factors in disturbing the involuntary muscle movement of the large intestine. There is no abnormality of the structure of the abdomen.

Orthodox treatment

The feces may be examined and a sigmoidoscopy may be needed (viewing the colon through an instrument passed up the anus) to eliminate any more serious conditions which have similar symptoms (see Crohn's disease page 255, and cancer of the bowel page 251). There may also be examination of the gut using a barium meal with X-ray. Treatment may include:

- *A high-fiber diet may be recommended, including bulk-forming agents such as bran.*
- *Short courses of antidiarrheal drugs may be given, and also antidepressants.*
- *Antispasmodic drugs may help relieve muscular spasms.*
- *Doctors should test for lactose intolerance, gut infections and any food allergies.*

Alternative Treatment

Bach flower remedies

If the condition is worsened or affected by stress or a negative mental attitude, the Bach remedies will be used to help bring about a more positive emotional outlook. Aspen may help people who are often filled with panic and anxiety. Crab apple may help as it is "the remedy that helps us get rid of anything we do not like, either in our minds or in our bodies." Impatiens is given if the person's temperament is very quick in both thought and action. Gorse is used for depression.

Western herbalism

The holistic approach of herbal medicine is suited to treating conditions like this. Initial remedies may include drinking hot infusions of digestion-enhancing teas such as peppermint and the calming herb camomile. Linseeds can be used in food as a natural gentle bulking agent if constipation is forming part of the problem.

Homeopathy

IBS is best treated with a constitutional remedy but the following remedies may help:

• Argentum nit. for bad flatulence and constantly alternating diarrhea and constipation with mucus in the stools.

• Colocynth can be used for griping abdominal pains only relieved by doubling over, and if the attacks are induced by anger.

• Colchicum can help nausea, pain and some aversion to food. The dose is usually three to four times a day for up to two weeks.

Chinese herbalism

Treatment is best when combined with acupuncture. Digestive evacuants or herbs with fragrant odors used for retention of body fluids in the stomach may be appropriate.

Naturopathy

As the problem may be associated with an unbalanced diet and/or food intolerance, a whole food eating plan will be suggested. Dietary fiber is suggested as a laxative and bowel regulatory instead of medications. If there are food sensitivities, naturopathy will suggest avoiding irritants like coffee, strong spices and alcohol. Advice on relaxation may show patients how to massage their own bowel areas gently.

Other therapies

Color therapists will use tones of orange and green. **Aromatherapists** will use bergamot and, to encourage good digestion, grapefruit oil massaged gently into the lower abdomen and back. **Acupuncture,** along with herbal preparations, is considered a good approach for most digestive problems. A **macrobiotic** practitioner may suggest diet and stress management. Relaxing therapies such as **relaxation and visualization**, **yoga** and **tai chi** may be successful in cases which are stress related. **Reflexology** will be aimed at reflex points relating to the large and small intestines, solar plexus, pituitary and adrenal glands and the digestive system. The **Alexander Technique** can teach a person how to maintain balance under stress.

Liver Problems

What are they?

The liver, which is the largest organ, carries out many functions in the body. Besides eliminating waste products, drugs and poisons from the bloodstream and storing certain vitamins, the liver also aids food digestion and regulates the sugar content of the blood. With such a complex organ, it is not surprising that there are many possible disorders. Three of the most common problems are hepatitis, cirrhosis and jaundice.

Hepatitis is the inflammation of the liver, and the initial symptoms include a general feeling of malaise, nausea, headaches, fever and some abdominal pains. After a couple of weeks, jaundice, which is a symptom of many liver disorders, may appear involving the yellowing of eyes and skin, darkened urine and light-colored bowel movements. (Jaundice results from the accumulation of yellow-brown bile pigment under the skin.)

Cirrhosis results from continuing damage to the liver where there is cell death and hardened scar tissue forms. This prevents normal liver function and cuts off the healthy liver cells from the blood supply they need. Symptoms include weight loss, loss of appetite, continuous indigestion, nausea, vomiting and general malaise. Liver failure (which is potentially fatal) may be the result of poisoning, acute hepatitis or cirrhosis.

Causes

In richer countries, the most common cause of liver disease is excessive consumption of alcohol, whereas in the poorer countries of Africa and Asia, the most serious liver problems are viral cirrhosis and primary liver cancer. Other causes of problems include congenital defects and liver infections caused by bacteria and parasites.

There are many viral causes of hepatitis. These include Type A (infectious hepatitis) which is the most common form and is usually spread through contaminated food and water, and poor hygiene. Type B is spread mainly through blood, semen, saliva, and infected needles, and may be passed from mother to baby during vaginal childbirth.

Orthodox treatment

There are vaccines available for the prevention of hepatitis A and B. General treatment is to recommend rest, a light diet and the avoidance of alcohol. Sometimes steroids may be used and drugs like interferon may be used for chronic carriers. Cirrhosis is treated by slowing the liver cell damage, mainly by abstaining from alcohol. Diuretic or antibiotic drugs may be used and in some cases a liver transplant is the only chance for improvement.

Alternative Treatment

Homeopathy

Treatment of chronic (long-term) hepatitis is constitutional and needs a skilled practitioner. In cases of brief, acute (short-term) hepatitis, the following remedies may be useful:

• Bryonia when symptoms come on after exposure to cold and there is pain and tenderness in the liver region.
• Mercurius when the tongue is yellow and dirty and there is a tender liver.
• Phosphorus when there is a empty feeling in the abdomen and a craving for cold water followed by vomiting.
• Lachesis when the liver feels swollen and tender and there is a distended abdomen which is painful.
• Hydrastis for a swollen, tender liver with yellowish discharge from the nose and throat.

Acupuncture

Treatment will be given at a combination of points which are located on the liver, gallbladder, stomach and spleen meridians.

Reflexology

Massage is used on areas which are connected to the gallbladder, liver, large and small intestine, spleen and also the lymphatic system – as well as to areas which are linked to the solar plexus and adrenal and pituitary glands.

Chinese herbalism

Antipyretic herbs for regulating the blood condition would be prescribed.

Other therapies

According to **hypnotherapists**, cell command therapy can be used. Hypno-healing and the uncovering process may be useful in this context and the immune system will be addressed. **Nutritional therapists** use a number of foods, such as beetroot, which helps to drain toxins from the liver and gallbladder, thus aiding self-repair. A **naturopath** will aim treatment at specific nutritional and dietetic management. Diet is a crucial factor and the liver is considerably stressed by eating inappropriately. Advice will be to avoid alcohol and high-fat foods and also to drink plenty of fresh vegetable juices every day. Hydrotherapy (contrast bathing) and herbal hepatic and cholagogues may be appropriate. Gentle exercises such as **yoga** can help to stimulate the liver as may cold compresses placed over the abdomen. Supplements of lecithin and minerals may also be advised. **Color therapy** will shine yellow light on the lower back over bare skin and use a yellow silk square worn next to the body. **Ayurvedic medicine** treatment will be based on special ayurvedic formulas and detoxification with *panchakarma* therapy. **Western herbalism** will suggest remedies that will help the liver to cleanse and repair itself.

DIGESTIVE CANCERS

What are they?

Cancer involves the unrestrained growth of cells in a body organ or tissue. As the growth develops abnormally, it infiltrates surrounding tissues and may block passageways, affect bone and destroy nerves. The cancer cells may spread to other parts of the body through blood vessels and lymphatic channels. Worldwide, cancers affecting the large intestine (primarily the colon) or rectum are the most common types after lung, female breast and skin cancers. Stomach cancer is less common and cancer of the small intestine is fairly rare. Wherever it is located, successful treatment depends on detecting the cancer early – so symptoms should be heeded.

Early symptoms of colon and rectal cancer include blood or mucus mixed in the stools, a change in bowel habits, abdominal pain and loss of appetite. For esophageal cancer, the warning signs are a difficulty in swallowing, weight loss and some discomfort or burning sensation which may resemble heartburn. Early suggestions of stomach cancer are unexplained and persistent indigestion, weight loss, loss of appetite, vomiting blood, blood in stools, a bloated feeling after eating and gnawing pains in the abdomen.

Causes

Susceptibility to cancer is partly determined by inherited genetic make-up. The cancer occurs when genes controlling cell multiplication are transformed by carcinogens. Various triggers provoke these changes in vulnerable individuals – from viruses to environmental pollutants and smoking. In addition:

- *Cancer of the colon is thought to have mainly dietary causes – with a high-fat, low-fiber diet encouraging the concentration of carcinogens. Ulcerative colitis and polyps may possibly be significant, too.*
- *Cancer of the esophagus is frequently caused by smoking or chewing tobacco, or the excessive consumption of alcohol. There is also a small increased risk in those suffering from hiatus hernia, chronic heartburn, peptic ulcers or other acid diseases. It is more frequent in men than women and has a high incidence in parts of the Far East.*

The likelihood of cancer developing increases with age and detected cancers seem to be increasing as general life expectancies grow longer.

Orthodox treatment

Most patients with esophageal cancer are treated with radiotherapy. Surgery may be offered to remove most of the esophagus. For inoperable cancers, a tube may be inserted through the esophagus to make swallowing easier. The treatment of colon and rectal cancer is almost always surgery, removing the cancerous areas and leaving the rest of the bowel intact. If the disease has spread extensively, the colon may need to be removed. Over half of patients will survive at least five years after colon removal. Cancer of the stomach may be treated with chemotherapy, radiotherapy, surgery, or all three.

ANYONE, AND ESPECIALLY MEN AND WOMEN OVER THE AGE OF 50, WITH MARKED AND UNEXPLAINED CHANGES IN BOWEL HABITS OR THE ABILITY TO SWALLOW SHOULD CONSULT A DOCTOR IMMEDIATELY.

ALTERNATIVE TREATMENT

Alternative therapies can be successfully used to support people suffering from cancer both physically and emotionally, but they must be used alongside orthodox medical treatment, not instead of it.

Bach flower remedies

These could be used on an individual basis as supportive therapy to help bring about a more positive emotional outlook. Sweet chestnut may be helpful for feelings of utter dejection and despair and olive if the person is feeling drained by the problems presented by the illness. Mimulus is recommended for dealing with fear.

Autogenic training

Practitioners believe that any cancer is less likely (and can be prevented) by someone using AT regularly to boost their immune system. AT can help to aid recovery and change attitudes.

Aromatherapy

Someone with an early stage of cancer should not be massaged with oils as this could spread the disease via the circulatory and lymphatic systems, but should use a room pump dispenser. The oils should not be used on the skin following recent chemo- or radiotherapy. If these guidelines are followed, oils, especially bergamot, rose and neroli can help with the emotions – and niaouli can help to strengthen the immune system.

Other therapies

A **nutritional therapist** will use individual dietary programs to improve the body's efficiency in combating illnesses. **Naturopathic** treatment will be aimed at nutritional and dietetic management for support. Psychotherapy and relaxation may be suggested, along with applied nutrition and herbal medicine to support the immune system. **Homeopathy** will offer specific remedies according to symptoms. **Acupuncture** can be used to combat effects of radiotherapy.

OBESITY

What is it?

Obesity is a body state in which a person is 20 percent or more over the maximum desired weight for their height.

The problem is risky in the long term as a variety of medical conditions are either caused by or exacerbated by being so much overweight – including heart attacks, gallstones, arthritis, hiatus hernias, varicose veins, kidney disorders and fertility problems in men. High blood pressure and stroke are twice as likely in obese individuals and adult-onset diabetes mellitus is five times more likely. Excess weight can also aggravate osteoarthritis of the hips and knees. Having so much extra body weight places considerable strain on joints of the back, hips and knees.

For women, the excess weight is linked to added risks of cancers of the uterus and breast.

Causes

The main cause of obesity is taking in more calories than are being used by the body – but overweight people do not necessarily eat more than those who are thin. In addition:

- *Obesity may develop in those who have a low basal metabolic rate (the amount of energy needed to maintain vital body functions at rest) – or those less physically active who need fewer calories.*
- *Genetic factors are present, as children of obese parents are ten times more likely to be obese themselves.*
- *Emotional difficulties, which may run very deep.*
- *Occasionally metabolic disorders such as thyroid problems or drugs like steriods and insulin, which can stimulate appetite.*

Orthodox treatment

An obese person should have a diet with about 500 to 1,000 kilocalories less than his or her energy needs. The deficit is then met by using some of the excess stored fat. Such a diet should lead to a weight loss of up to 1 kg (2 lb) per week until the desired weight level is achieved. The loss of weight is likely to be fastest during the first two weeks of such a diet because of the loss of water which also occurs. Doctors may also recommend:

- *Regular exercise of all kinds from brisk walking to aerobics. This helps by prompting the body to burn extra calories and increasing the metabolic rate.*
- *Drugs that reduce the appetite have been used in the past but these are now rarely suggested by doctors.*
- *Radical surgery can be performed on very obese people but is used only in extreme cases when a person's health is severely affected. These drastic measures can include stapling to temporarily reduce the size of the stomach to make the person feel full after eating a smaller amount of food.*

ALTERNATIVE TREATMENT

Homeopathy

Treatment will be constitutional in additional to the following specific remedies:

- Calcarea for when the person feels chilly, has head sweats, craves eggs and hot foods and suffers from indigestion.
- Graphites for constipation, chilliness and skin problems.
- Capsicum for burning sensations in the stomach or intestines.
- Ferrum for when the sufferer is pale-faced and also experiences cold extremities.

Hypnotherapy

Hypnosis can often help as overeating is often emotionally based. The mind may prefer the overweight condition for safety. After dealing with root causes, the mind may be reprogrammed to lose the desire for the wrong foods and excessive eating. Treatment will include therapy, neurolinguistic programming, hypno-healing and regression.

Arts therapies

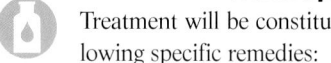

Dance, music or art therapies may be useful and are becoming more widely available for people with eating disorders. Increasing the exercise taken along with dietary changes is important in speeding up the body's metabolism.

Ayurvedic medicine

Treatment may include an ayurvedic diet and weight loss program. *Panchakarma* therapy for tridosha balancing might be undertaken.

Acupuncture

Treatment aims at reducing the appetite by restoring an energy flow along the spleen meridian. Various points located on the stomach, spleen, heart and lung meridians may be stimulated with needles.

Other therapies

Auricular therapy can be useful as ear studs or seeds can be used to reduce appetite. This is effective both for stress-related obesity and that which is hormonally linked. Depending on the cause, **autogenic training** may help the attitude to body image or enhance will-power for improved eating habits. A **Western herbalist** will advise on lifestyle along with treatment to improve digestion. Hormonal issues may be addressed, but it is usually emotional issues which require treatment. **Spiritual healing** can help and **shiatsu** can be useful. **Tai chi** exercises can help to streamline the body over time and the feeling of balance should help to reduce the inclination to overeat.

PEPTIC ULCERS

What are they?

Peptic ulcers are breaks in the skin or mucus lining of the gut that do not heal. Raw areas may appear in the esophagus, stomach or duodenum as acid digests part of the protective lining of the gut and leaves a sore spot or spots. The two types of peptic ulcer are gastric and duodenal and both types are most likely to appear around the time of middle age.

The gastric variety, which are found in the stomach lining, are more common in those over age 40 and both sexes are almost equally affected. Symptoms include a gnawing, burning pain, worse during or just after eating, plus wind, nausea and vomiting. Duodenal ulcers, which are more common than gastric ulcers, are in the gut between the stomach and large intestine. These give an intermittent upper abdominal pain – usually between meals or at night when the stomach is empty. More males than females suffer from these and they appear more than gastric ulcers in younger people.

Occasionally, an ulcer perforates which means that it eats through the wall of the stomach, duodenum or esophagus. The person may collapse with severe pain and shock and needs urgent admission to hospital. More commonly, ulcers bleed slowly and the symptoms include blood in vomit or the person passes tarry black stools; this needs prompt hospital care.

ANY SEVERE ABDOMINAL PAIN THAT IS EXPERIENCED SHOULD BE INVESTIGATED BY A DOCTOR PROMPTLY.

Causes

Peptic ulcers occur in areas exposed to acid and pepsin from the stomach and the main causes are:

- *Anything which increases secretion of acid or impairs the resistance of the gut lining to acid and pepsin makes ulcers more likely. These factors include smoking, stress, excessive alcohol, NSAIDs (nonsteroidal anti-inflammatory drugs, perhaps given for arthritic pain) and genetic background.*
- *Another cause is the bacteria* Helicobacter pylori *which lives in the gut among other places.*

Orthodox treatment

Advice would be to eat a whole food diet, relax more and control stress, take regular exercise, stop smoking, avoid coffee, tea, alcohol and refined sugar. Doctors used to recommend drinking milk; but it is now known this makes things worse. In addition:

- *Antibiotics will be given to eradicate* Helicobacter pylori, *which greatly reduce the chances of ulcers returning.*
- *Other treatments include antacids, histamine H2-blockers and proton pump inhibitors to reduce acid secretion. Drugs can be given to form a coating on the ulcer and prokinetic drugs help speed gastric emptying.*
- *Surgical treatment is used only rarely, for the worst cases.*
- *If a nonsteroidal, anti-inflammatory drug is essential for arthritis, then it may be given with a histamine H-2 blocker to protect the stomach lining.*

ALTERNATIVE TREATMENT

Autogenic training

Treatment will be aimed at reducing hyperacidity and changing the attitude of the sufferer in order to prevent recurrence and speed up recovery.

Western herbalism

The aim will be to heal the ulcers as well as reduce inflammation, improve digestion and reduce stress. Licorice, slippery elm bark and comfrey are useful.

Bach flower remedies

If the condition is caused, worsened or affected by stress or a negative mental attitude, the remedies will be used on an individual basis as supportive therapy to help bring about a more positive mental outlook. Remedies include agrimony if the person is hiding stress and elm if they are feeling stressed by overwhelming pressures and responsibilities.

Chinese herbalism

Ulcers may respond to herbal anodynes, carminatives, antipyretics and herbs to regulate the blood condition.

Acupuncture

Points on the meridians governing the liver, stomach spleen are treated.

Reflexology

Individual symptoms and characteristics of the sufferer are taken into consideration. Emphasis will be on the reflex points relating to the stomach, endocrine glands, solar plexus and colon.

Other therapies

Homeopathic remedies may be appropriate. Regular treatment with **auricular therapy** (about three times a week) is said to have a balancing effect on the digestion, especially when disorders are stress-related. **Macrobiotics** may be useful. Relaxing therapies such as **relaxation and visualization**, **yoga** and **tai chi** may be successful in cases which are stress-related or linked to depression. **Naturopathy** offers treatments which can bring relief. Standard advice is to eat little and often, adding to a plain diet by eating more vegetables and pulses or grains. Smoking, alcohol and sugar should be avoided. Vitamin A is also useful.

GASTROENTERITIS

What is it?

Gastroenteritis is an acute inflammation of the intestines and stomach, which can cause violent upsets. This may take such forms as food poisoning, traveler's diarrhea, cholera, typhoid fever and dysentery — as well as milder upsets.

The symptoms and their severity varies on the type and concentration of the microorganisms or toxic substances which have been responsible for causing the problem. Nausea, diarrhea, vomiting, fever, cramps and abdominal pain are usual – symptoms may last only 24 hours but may persist for several weeks. While symptoms may appear gradually, an attack is often felt fairly suddenly. The effect may cause only slight discomfort and inconvenience – or the attack may be severe enough to cause shock and collapse.

Gastroenteritis tends to be most serious in the very young and very old. The condition is regarded as most dangerous for babies and the elderly because of the risk of dehydration (see page 326). Both vomit and diarrhea contain much water so the sudden fluid loss can be considerable.

Causes

Gastroenteritis can have many causes including:

- *A variety of bacteria, bacterial toxins, viruses and other small organisms which are liable to contaminate water or food. Protection against typhoid fever and cholera is available by vaccination before traveling to countries where there is a risk.*
- *Noninfectious causes include food intolerances, spicy foods, some irritant drugs and excessive alcohol consumption.*
- *In some people, antibiotic drugs may cause similar symptoms to those appearing with gastroenteritis as these drugs can upset the balance of bacteria which occur naturally in the intestines.*

Orthodox treatment

For mild attacks of gastroenteritis, home treatment with bed rest and plenty of fluids should be sufficient. If the case appears serious, a doctor is likely to ask about whether other people have been affected, details of food which has been eaten and recent travel abroad.

The replacement of fluids and electrolytes using an over-the-counter preparation may be needed if a great deal of fluid has been lost through vomiting and diarrhea. If no salt and glucose rehydration mixture is available, the patient may be given a solution of one teaspoon of salt and eight teaspoons of sugar in 1 litre (1¾ pints) of water.

In severe cases, fluids may have to be given by intravenous infusion in hospital. Fluids are then tried orally and, if these are accepted, a bland diet is introduced gradually.

Drugs to control vomiting may be given by injection or as a suppository. While drugs such as kaolin, loperamide and codeine may control the diarrhea, they are not recommended for the first 48 hours.

Most attacks are self-limiting, but antibiotics may be needed if there is fever or a severe illness.

A doctor may give advice about food hygiene and preparation, as better care may be needed to reduce the chances of further attacks of gastroenteritis returning.

ALTERNATIVE TREATMENT

Homeopathy

Specific remedies for gastroenteritis include:

- Arsenicum if there is burning pain in the abdomen, the person feels cold, anxious and needs continual sips of water.
- Podophyllum for severe diarrhea with greenish stools full of mucus, general weakness and cramping abdominal pains.
- Colocynth if the person has a colicky pain relieved by bending over double or pressing the abdomen.
- Phosphorus is suggested when there is diarrhea, vomiting and a craving for ice water which is then vomited.

Auricular therapy

Ear acupuncture has a strong, calming effect on digestion and can be a useful treatment for an acute attack of gastroenteristis.

Nutritional therapy

Nutritional therapists recommend fasting during a brief attack of gastroenteritis. Mildly astringent herbal teas like peppermint and blackberry may be taken, but food is thought to prolong the attack and is best avoided altogether. For mild cases, taking a few garlic capsules a day may help to fight any infection.

Western herbalism

Treatment can be helpful in reducing inflammation, using herbs as gut disinfectants and removing toxins – as well as speeding up the recovery process.

Ayurvedic medicine

Ayurvedic oral medicines, with *panchakarma* therapy, may be appropriate.

Other therapies

Other useful therapies which may be useful for the treatment of gastroenteritis include **crystal and gemstone therapy**, **hypnotherapy**, **kinesiology** and **shiatsu**. **Yoga** and other relaxation therapies may help to improve the immune system and so encourage resistance to infection and also healing.

Crohn's Disease

What is it?

Any part of the gastrointestinal tract may be affected by this chronic inflammatory disease. The symptoms may include pain, diarrhea, fever and a loss of weight. The end of the small intestine at the place where it joins the large intestine is the most frequent site. Some parts may remain only mildly affected.

Crohn's disease most often affects young adults and those over the age of 60. In younger people, there are likely to be spasms of abdominal pain, diarrhea, loss of appetite, weight loss and anemia. The small intestine is less able to absorb food. When the disease affects older people, rectal bleeding is more likely. For all ages, the anus may be affected as well. If the colon is affected, bloody diarrhea may result.

Nearly a third of sufferers may develop a fistula, which is an abnormal passageway. Nearly as many may have abscesses, either around the anus or within the abdomen. Other complications may involve conditions such as eye inflammations, severe arthritis and disorders of the skin.

Causes

While the cause is not certain, it may be an abnormal allergic reaction or response to an infectious agent. There seems to have been a increase in cases over the last few decades. A genetic factor seems present and some racial groups are more susceptible.

Orthodox treatment

This will include the following:

- *An examination may show tender abdominal swellings from a thickening of the intestinal walls. If a sigmoidoscopy (viewing inside the sigmoid colon and rectum) confirms the disease, sulphasalazine and corticosteroid drugs may be given orally.*
- *Severe cases may need admission to a hospital for a blood transfusion and intravenous feeding.*
- *A high-vitamin, low-fiber diet may be advised.*
- *Damaged parts of the intestine may need to be taken out and surgery needed for obstruction, perforation or excessive bleeding. Even after surgery, the problem may well recur.*

Alternative Treatment

Homeopathy

Constitutional treatment may be suggested, plus specific remedies as for diarrhea (see page 242) and also the following remedies:

- Belladonna if pain starts and stops with equal suddenness, as if the abdomen has been gripped by a hand and then released, face red and hot, abdomen tender and sensitive to slightest jarring.
- Bryonia if the pain is like a stitch and the abdomen feels as if it is about to burst, pressure makes the pain worse, pain so severe that person cannot move, think, or talk, breathing shallow.
- Chamomilla if a cutting pain causes the person to double up and cry out and the abdomen is distended with wind. The attack may follow an outburst of anger.
- Colocynth if there is violent, cutting, twisting pain just below the navel, relieved by passing wind, bending forward, or pressing on the abdomen.
- Magnesia phos. if the pain is so violent that the person cries out, and is relieved by warmth, friction, and pressure on the abdomen.

Reflexology

Treatment will be holistic, depending on the symptoms and characteristics of the sufferer. The reflex points corresponding to the small and large intestines will be addressed.

Autogenic training

Autogenic training will have a positive effect, depending on the severity of the condition. It will provide back-up to a flagging system. Any chronic condition such as Crohn's disease can be helped by the patient's awareness that their attitude and state of mind can affect it.

Alexander Technique

Crohn's disease often responds well to a program of Alexander Technique in which the pupil learns to generate a state of psychophysical harmony and relaxation and is then enabled to maintain this balanced state in stressful situations.

Spiritual healing

Digestion involves energy and much of our available energy goes into digesting our food. Healing can raise a person's energy quite substantially, allowing a more effective metabolism of food and elimination of waste products. Too much unfriendly intestinal bacteria is often the cause of digestive problems which spiritual healing can help to rebalance.

Other therapies

Nutritional therapy may be appropriate if there is an allergy to gluten. Scientific studies show that if the permeability of the gut can be reduced, Crohn's disease can be improved. Nutritional therapists use a number of products including comfrey and butyric acid to heal the gut as much as possible and hopefully reduce permeability. A **naturopath** will treat this condition successfully, and prescribe according to an individual's personal characteristics and symptoms. In particular, nutritional management, applied nutrition, relaxation, herbal medicine and massage may be incorporated in treatment. In some cases, **osteopathic** attention may prove appropriate.

IMMUNE (LYMPHATIC) SYSTEM

What is it?

As blood circulates in the body plasma leaks from the capillaries. After the proteins and nutrients have been utilized by the cells this fluid or 'lymph' is collected by the immune (lymphatic) system. The vessels of this secondary circulatory system are blind-ended tubes and are called lymphatics. The lymph is moved by the surrounding muscles contracting and by the valves. Lymphatic glands or 'nodes' appear throughout the system and act as infection filters. By trapping germs the nodes prevent them from travelling to distant organs. They are also important in forming disease-fighting white cells called lymphocytes. The nodes are prominent in the neck, groin and the armpits. The smaller lymphatic vessels converge into two large ducts in the chest which return the lymph back to the veins in the neck.

The spleen contains a concentration of lymph nodes. It helps with blood cell manufacture and storage, destroying old blood cells, and iron metabolism. It is also fights infection by producing white blood cells and antibodies. Lymph tissue is also found in the tonsils, adenoids, thymus and digestive tract.

What can go wrong?

Infections enlarge the lymph nodes. They swell up with millions of lymphocytes as the body mounts an immune response to kill the foreign organism. Particularly noticeable are the neck glands after a sore throat or other upper respiratory tract infection, for instance, *glandular fever*, a viral infection transmitted by saliva. This is common in teenagers, causing painful glands for weeks.

The presence of painless large nodes is more serious. Cancers often spread via the lymphatic system and cause node enlargement. Breast cancer, for example, will cause large nodes to appear in the armpits. Sometimes the cancer will block the lymphatic vessels and a limb will swell up . Cancers of the bone marrow cells (leukaemia) cause lymph node enlargement. *Hodgkin's disease* is a cancer of the lymphoid tissue and patients often complain of neck lumps, fever and weight loss. Human immunodeficiency virus (*HIV*), the *AIDS* virus, affects the lymphocytes, the white blood cells that fight infection. Again the first signs of disease is often enlarged nodes. The sufferer eventually succumbs to infections that the body cannot fight.

The immune system contains lymphatic glands that help to filter out infection. The glands also stop germs from going to infect other body organs.

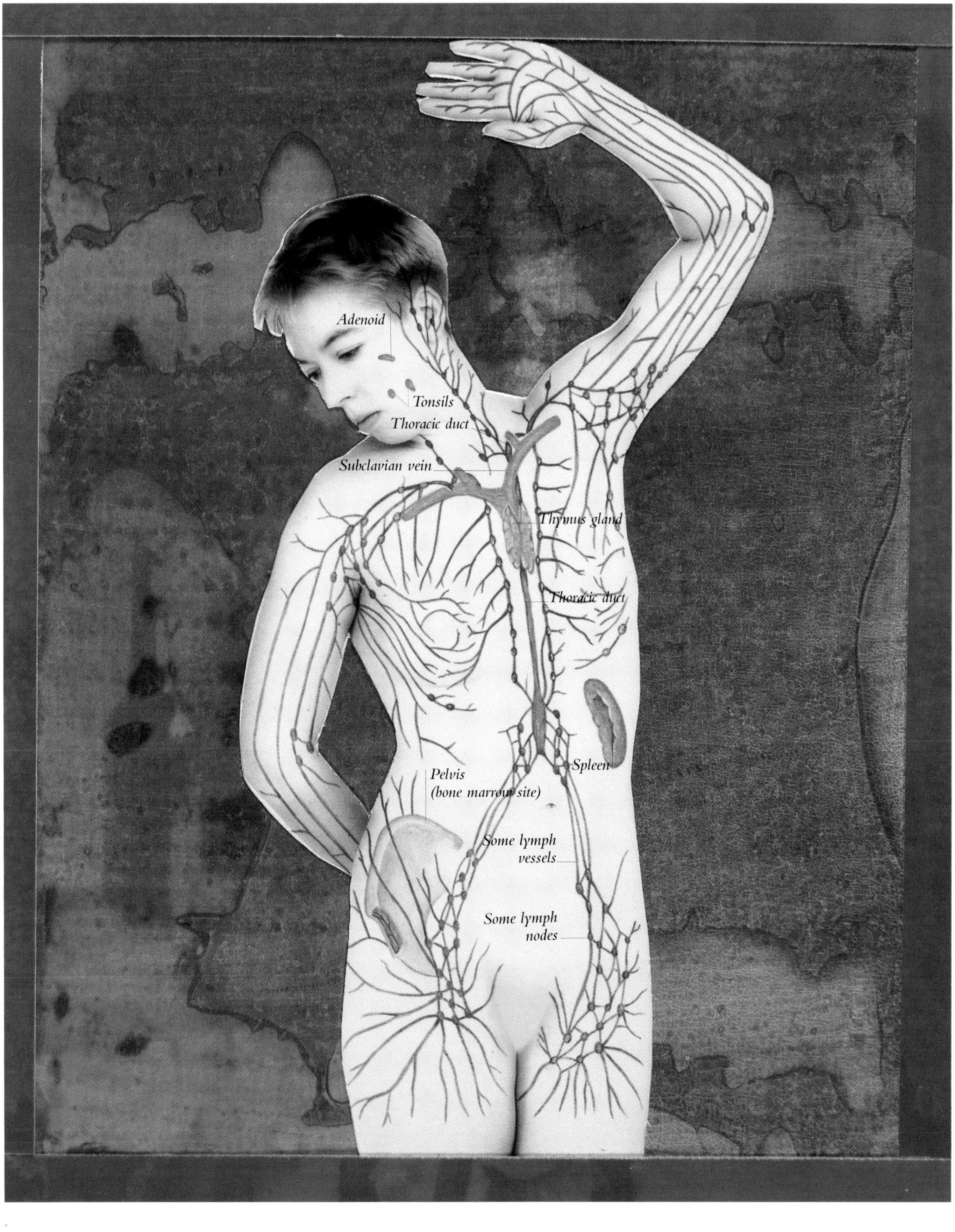
Adenoid
Tonsils
Thoracic duct
Subclavian vein
Thymus gland
Thoracic duct
Spleen
Pelvis
(bone marrow site)
Some lymph
vessels
Some lymph
nodes

HIV AND AIDS

What is it?

HIV is the Human Immunodeficiency Virus. It damages the body's immune system so that it is no longer able to fight off infections. Most clinical experts believe that HIV is responsible for producing Acquired Immune Deficiency Syndrome (AIDS). If someone contracts this virus, doctors say they are HIV-positive. There are other medical terms for it, too, including HIV antibody-positive, body-positive and sero-positive. If someone contracts HIV it will almost certainly remain in their body for the rest of their lives, but they may not notice any ill effects (develop any actual symptoms) for several years.

AIDS itself is still thought to be (eventually) a fatal disease. However it may develop very slowly, especially if the person is doing everything possible to support their health with enough rest, relaxation, good nutrition and alternative therapies. There are some who were infected with HIV 13 years ago who are still well; in other words, they do not seem to have developed any symptoms yet.

About a third of all those who are HIV-positive remember getting some sort of generalized, flu-like illness around the time that their systems were actually making antibodies to the virus. This tends to last between three and 14 days, and is the only symptom likely to be suffered when HIV itself enters the system. After the virus has had the time it needs to deplete the immune system, the symptoms eventually developed include:

- *Heavy night sweats and fevers.*
- *Extreme tiredness.*
- *Weight loss.*
- *Diarrhea, thrush and herpes.*
- *Folliculitis (a red rash caused by infection of the skin's hair follicles).*
- *Mouth ulcers and bleeding gums.*

With AIDS itself, someone might also experience:

- *Neurological problems resulting in dementia and memory loss.*
- *Fits and confusion.*
- *Pneumonia.*
- *Kaposi's Sarcoma, a rare form of skin cancer which produces purple marks on the skin.*
- *Vision problems and eye infections.*

Causes

Fortunately the skin is an efficient barrier against many different types of virus and bacteria, and HIV cannot get past healthy, unbroken skin. It is possible to contract HIV in a medical situation, for instance, from a transfusion of contaminated blood or blood products. In the past, people have been infected via clinical treatment with contaminated people – for instance, about 1,300 British with hemophilia have so far become HIV-positive via clotting factors from infected blood. Now all donors are screened and their blood virally inactivated so there have been no more new cases transmitted in this way. There are only three other ways you can contract the virus:

- *Infected blood passing through the skin barrier, possibly via a deep graze, needle puncture, a cut or a wound.*
- *In the womb or at birth, when a mother who is HIV-positive or who has AIDS passes the infection to her baby. This may take place across the placenta during pregnancy, or during childbirth itself. An HIV-positive mother can also transmit the virus to her baby via breastfeeding.*
- *Having unsafe sex as opposed to "safer" sex. (The term "safe sex" is no longer used.) This is the most common way to contract HIV whether a person is male, female, heterosexual or homosexual. Safer sex is defined as any sexual practice which does not allow the partner's blood or semen inside the body – HIV counselors say the rule is "on, not in."*

The following all come under the heading of safer sex:

- *Intercourse (vaginal or anal sex) using a condom.*
- *Deep kissing. Oral sex using a condom.*
- *Mutual masturbation.*
- *Using sex toys as long as they are not shared.*

Unsafe sex includes:

- *Intercourse of any type without a condom.*
- *Sharing sex toys.*
- *Cunnilingus when a woman is menstruating.*

Even though in the past drug-takers, homosexuals and hemophiliacs were identified as those most likely to contract the virus, it is not helpful to talk about "high-risk groups" because all sexually active people are at risk. People do not need to be promiscuous, male, gay or a drug user. In fact, the fastest-growing route for new HIV-positive cases is through heterosexual sex, and women are more vulnerable to the infection than men. However, a BMJ study in 1989 showed that the chances of catching HIV were less than one percent every time someone had unprotected sex with an infected person.

Orthodox treatment

As well as keeping generally as fit, healthy and well-nourished as possible, additional medical treatment may include:

- *Preempting any related infections. Clinicians can sometimes work out what sort of health problems people are likely to develop depending on how depleted their immune systems are, and so pre-treat certain types of severe infection.*
- *Controlling any opportunistic infections such as thrush.*
- *Using radiotherapy and anticancer drugs to treat KPS (Karposi's Sarcoma).*

The two main treatments that tackle HIV itself as opposed to the problems it causes are the drugs AZT (zidovudine) and ddI (didanosine). Both are fairly toxic and have unpleasant side-effects. AZT can help prolong life for someone who already has AIDS but is of no help to thosc with HIV who are still symptom-free. Its serious side effects include suppression of bone marrow and red blood production. The side effects of ddI are damage to the nerves (arms/legs) and diarrhea. It is often given to sufferers who cannot tolerate the side effects of AZT, or who find, after a year or two, that it no longer has the same effect on their bodies.

There are several new therapies on trial, including Passive Immune Therapy which involves injections of plasma with HIV antibodies. This treatment is suitable for people with AIDS whose immune systems have become completely exhausted.

Alternative Treatment

Alternative therapies can be used successfully to support people with AIDS or who are HIV-positive both emotionally and physically, but must be used alongside orthodox medical treatment, not instead of it.

Alexander Technique

This process promotes a condition of psycho-physical harmony in which both posture and the nervous system are brought into balance. Stress is managed more effectively, and therefore the immune system can gradually be strengthened to become more resilient.

Aromatherapy

Aromatherapeutic treatment may include: bergamot, rose, neroli and lavender and other uplifting oils to help a person's emotional state; tea tree or niaouli oils to strengthen the immune system.

Nutritional therapy

Nutritional therapists aim to use individual dietary programs to improve the body's efficiency in combating illness in general. Success depends on how advanced the illness is, the individual constitution of the sufferer, and other factors such as sleeping patterns and stress. In AIDS patients, the digestive system is often compromised and food can be very poorly absorbed. The nutritional therapist will work closely with patients to improve the assimilation of food.

Bach flower remedies

These may provide emotional support for sufferers who are frightened, depressed, angry or affected by other negative attitudes. Remedies should always be chosen according to the mood of the sufferer, for instance: sweet chestnut if the sufferer is feeling dejection and despair; olive for those who feel drained of energy by old problems and mimulus for fear.

Hypnotherapy

Treatment will be aimed at the immune system and at strengthening the body. Creative visualization combined with hypno-healing may be used to work on the mind and body.

Massage

This therapy is used extensively by people with HIV/AIDS. Massage and the power of touch can help someone strengthen their will to deal positively with all aspects of their life. It may also help with many of the problems associated with this illness, including stress, anxiety, altered body image and the death of friends or a partner from the same illness, by giving physical and psychological comfort and communicating a feeling of caring. Prolonged stress has been clinically proven to suppress the immune system (by, amongst other things, raising the cortisone levels in the blood), and massage can help to relieve the overall stress by releasing muscle tension, calming the mind and thus helping the immune system to function more normally and efficiently.

Color therapy

Treatment is likely to involve indigo, deep violet, or any of the other deeper blue spectrum colors – the resonance of these colors is said to be very healing, and in particular can help to enhance the immune system. A color therapist may use lights in these colors shone on the individual's entire body, preferably unclothed, in a warm room. Alternatively, he or she may suggest wearing underclothes, outer clothing, or small silk squares in these colors next to the skin.

For depression and pessimism associated with the illness, clear yellows and greens may be used to help restore optimism and self-esteem.

Other therapies

Yoga can help to stimulate the immune system through gentle *asanas*, relaxation, meditation, *pranayama*, *shat kriyas* and hand mudras. **Homeopathic** treatment will be constitutional. **Auricular therapy** has been used in HIV centers as an "introduction" to acupuncture, in order to calm and relax sufferers. **Acupuncture** has a very powerful effect on both the immune system and on the sufferer's energy level. A standard **macrobiotic** diet may help to strengthen this, too. **Autogenic training** may be useful as a destressor, and can substantially improve the quality of sleep. **Ayurvedic medicine** has strong immune-enhancing treatments, including *panchakarma* for detoxification and vitality. The **arts therapies** will be very useful in helping people who are living with HIV, or who have AIDS, to cope with the physical and psychological pressures that face them. **Polarity therapy** may be useful, and treatment will be undertaken according to the sufferer's characteristics. **Radionics** has also proved helpful. **Spiritual healing** may also be relaxing, calming to the sufferer and deeply supportive.

ALLERGIES

What are they?

Allergies erupt when the body overreacts to a specific substance, sometimes a harmless one which does not bother other people at all. The term comes from two Greek words, meaning "altered reactivity." In Britain, some doctors suggest that as many as one in six people have some form of allergy.

Any substance or organism that is foreign to the body is dealt with by the immune system, which produces antibodies against it. In this way, any invading virus or bacteria can be attacked and killed before it can cause damage. The body remembers which invader encouraged the production of which antibodies and when that invader appears again, it is quickly recognized and attacked. This efficient system can, however, go wrong, becoming overactive and causing the body to react in an extreme way to normal substances. The body deals with them as though they were harmful invaders, creating an allergic reaction. This is an exaggerated version of the body's normal response to invasion.

Allergies are usually characterized by itching, sneezing, wheezing, a running nose, excess catarrh, bronchial spasm, urticaria and hives, among other things – all of which are known as a histamine reaction. Histamine is a substance produced by the body in response to an attack on it, for example, an injury. It increases the size of the blood vessels, allowing fluids to reach and repair injured tissue.

Causes

There is a hereditary element to allergies; many sufferers of hay fever, asthma and eczema, for example, have other sufferers in the family. Other causes may be:

- *Sensitivity to foods which commonly provoke reactions, such as milk, shellfish and nuts.*
- *Sensitivity to common allergens such as grass pollens, spores, plants, fabrics, drugs and household chemicals.*
- *Extreme stress.*

One theory is that allergies are simply a symptom of an overworked system; another is that the routine childhood immunizations programs of the last 30 years may also be a contributory factor since they have put such a strain on our immature immune systems that they no longer function effectively.

According to top consultant immunologist Jonathan Brostoff of London's University College and Middlesex Hospitals, if a person consults a specialist doctor for treatment there are several different medical terms that may be used to describe different forms and levels of allergic reaction, depending on the cause and nature of the reaction. One is food allergy, which means any adverse reaction to a food when the immune system's involvement can be clearly identified. Another term is false food allergy. This works slightly differently from a real allergy though the end results are exactly the same. Then there is food intolerance, a term which is now becoming far more popular. It generally means "any adverse reaction to a food other than a false food allergy" when the doctors are not sure whether the immune system is involved or not. Food sensitivity is another phrase used: and this is really an umbrella term for food allergy, food intolerance and many other negative reactions to foods when the cause is psychological, rather than physical.

Orthodox treatment

One standard hospital test to check for allergies is a skin prick test, introducing a tiny amount of the suspect substance into the patient's skin, then waiting to see if there is any reaction, such as reddening or swelling over the site. The other is the RAST test which checks a small sample of the patient's blood serum for the level of antibodies it contains against a particular test allergen.

There are also commercial companies that offer to test people for allergies using a sample of hair, sent through the post. These tend to be far less reliable (and more expensive) than being referred by a doctor for tests at an immunology department.

Orthodox treatment for allergies includes:

- *Antihistamine drugs, which relieve the symptoms, but which have side effects of their own such as drowsiness and do not deal with the root cause of the allergy.*
- *Corticosteroids and other similar drugs which are also used to prevent symptoms from developing in the first place. These can be used internally (taken as tablets or suspended in medicine) or externally (applied to the affected area in a cream or gel form).*
- *Desensitization. This involves, over a period of time, injecting the patient with a gradually higher dose of the allergen, for example, grass pollen to treat hay fever, until their body is, in theory, able to produce the normal antibodies against it, meaning that the person will cease to react allergically to the substance. This treatment may be dangerous unless it is being supervised by an expert in this area as it does carry a risk of anaphylactic shock, which can sometimes prove fatal. It may occur within seconds of the injection or some hours afterward, and produces both breathing problems and also vascular collapse.*

There is also a great deal that a person can do in the way of self-help to prevent and ease allergic reactions, for example:

- *Keeping a diary of every single thing eaten and done, every day. This may help provide a link between an allergy reaction and a specific food, drink, or to something like bubble bath, dog hair or dusty carpets.*
- *Small-scale elimination dieting. If it seems that a particular food (such as chocolate or peanuts) is causing the problem, it may be useful to cut it out for a couple of weeks and to see if matters improve, meanwhile, just eat normally. Only one food should be cut at a time except under expert medical supervision, as this can lead to an unbalanced diet that is not sufficiently nourishing for a person, and it will also make it more difficult to pinpoint what is the culprit substance.*

Alternative Treatment

Recently, intolerances, which are a milder form of allergy and do not necessarily produce a histamine reaction (for instance, food allergies or hyperactivity) have been recognized as a fundamental cause of many ailments. The list includes eczema, dermatitis and asthma. The most common symptoms of intolerances are migraine, fatigue, depression, anxiety, hyperactivity in children, attention-deficit disorder, mouth ulcers, aching muscles, water retention, wind, joint pain, rheumatoid arthritis, nausea, vomiting, gastric ulcers, Crohn's disease, abdominal bloating, irritable bowel syndrome and constipation. Alternative therapies can greatly relieve many of these conditions.

Homeopathy

Symptoms produced by an allergy may also be successfully controlled by homeopathic remedies, while the immune system and its efficiency will be addressed by constitutional treatment. These remedies can help relieve the symptoms of the following conditions:

• Natrum mur. for throbbing, blinding migraine headaches, and if the attack is preceded by numbness and tingling in lips, nose and tongue.

• If a hyperactive child reacts violently to a particular food or beverage, try giving them ½tsp bicarbonate of soda in a small glass of water and milk, And then repeat every two hours (but not more than three times).

Kinesiology

An experienced kinesiologist will treat the patient individually, and perhaps undertake some of the following procedures: he will check the endocrine and immune systems for nutritional deficiencies; he will provide adrenal support and give advice on nutrition to help with stress; he will check the dual torque; he will give counseling for stress reduction and check out the ileo-caecal valve; he will examine the atlas and sacrum for lesions and also check for food sensitivities (particularly grain and dairy consumption); he will ask about the intake of water; he will check nutritional hygiene and personal hygiene; he will suggest bowel cleansing or regular kinesiology balancing.

Aromatherapy

An aromatherapist may use the following oils to treat the allergic reactions that a person is suffering: roman camomile and helichism to help relieve the spasms of asthma, and to help soothe the bronchioles and clear any accumulating catarrh; melissa may be used to treat a person who has hay fever, as it is very soothing and can help to reduce the severity of the allergic reaction.

Hypnotherapy

Many allergies can be emotionally based. For this reason, hypnotherapy may involve uncovering techniques to ascertain the origin of the allergy, followed by treatment with suggestion therapy.

Hypno-healing and neurolinguistic programming (NLP) may also be used in the treatment of allergies.

Naturopathy

Naturopathy emphasizes correction of the underlying disturbance of immunity. Reduction or avoidance of exposure to potential allergens is necessary for short-term relief.

Dietetic management and fasting to reduce proinflammatory prostaglandins and leukotrines may be suggested.

Treatment may also include applied nutrition to improve the functioning of the immune system, as well as herbal and homeopathic support for nonspecific resistance and symptomatic relief.

Nutritional therapy

A nutritional therapist can help to identify any problem foods. In people who suffer from multiple allergies, there may be an overall toxic overload which can be eradicated or alleviated.

Work may also need to be done to improve the function of the bowels, the liver and the digestive system.

Color therapy

This may involve the use of blues and greens in the form of light or worn as silk scarves over the throat and neck, and over the chest under the clothes. For hay fever the color orange may be used as this balances the affected area and helps to clear away the mucus.

Autogenic training

This treatment will help to rebalance all the body systems and, in time, all the allergies affecting the sufferer should completely disappear.

Acupuncture

Acupuncture treatment can have a very powerful and positive effect on a person's immune system, and also on the sufferer's energy level.

Ayurvedic medicine

The treatment in this therapy may be aimed at improving the body's overall resistance to allergies by using *panchakarma* and a specialized diet.

Other therapies

Auricular therapy can help to relieve the symptoms of hay fever. A **Western herbalist** may be able to reduce the individual's sensitivity by treatment with specific herbs to make the person's system less allergic and to relieve all the aggravating symptoms. A **Chinese herbalist** may recommend some antipyretics plus treatment with some detoxifying herbs.

Glandular Fever

What is it?

Glandular fever, also called infectious mononucleosis (IM), is a viral infection which is usually transmitted through saliva. It is most common in adolescents and young adults. Early symptoms resemble flu, with fever, a sore throat and headache, but within about two days the lymph glands in the neck, armpits and groin become swollen and painful and a light red rash similar to that of German measles (rubella) may develop. The tonsils are severely swollen, making swallowing difficult and occasionally obstructing breathing, and there is an overwhelming feeling of fatigue and lethargy. Sometimes the spleen becomes enlarged and the liver may be mildly damaged, leading to a brief episode of jaundice. While the symptoms disappear within three to six weeks, full recovery may be slow and energy levels may remain low for several months, with accompanying depression and drowsiness during the day.

Causes

Glandular fever is caused by the Epstein-Barr virus or cytomegalovirus, both of which belong to the herpes family (which is also responsible for shingles, cold sores and chicken-pox). The virus multiplies in the white blood cells and eventually the efficiency of the immune system is reduced. The disease may recur in a milder form within a year or so of the initial infection.

Orthodox treatment

A doctor will do a blood test to confirm the diagnosis, although this is not always reliable as different viruses may be involved and further tests may be required. There is no curative medication, but very occasionally corticosteroid drugs are prescribed to reduce inflammation. Most commonly, bed rest is recommended for about a month in order for the immune system to build up sufficiently to fight off the virus.

Alternative Treatment

Homeopathy

Constitutional homeopathic treatment, combined with bed rest and nutritional supplementation may be suggested. Specific remedies, to be used in the acute stage of the disease, may be:

- Belladonna when there is a sudden high fever, and the person is excited, incoherent and red in the face.
- Cistus when the sufferer feels cold and shivery, and sticking out the tongue out makes glands in the neck feel painful, and cold air and exertion make symptoms worse.
- Ailanthus when there is a headache, weakness, pain in the muscles and ulcers in the throat make swallowing difficult.
- Phytolacca when the tonsils are dark red, swallowing causes shooting pains up toward the ears and food and hot drinks make swallowing more painful.
- Baryta carb. when the glands are distinctly swollen, especially if the sufferer is a child and a late developer.
- Mercurius when the glands feel tender and there is also offensive perspiration.
- Calcarea when there is chilliness, sweating, a sour taste in the mouth and the person's feeling mentally and physically worn out.
- Taking glandular fever nosode may protect other members of the family from contracting the disease.

Alexander Technique

The Alexander Technique has an overall beneficial effect on the immune system. The Technique promotes a condition of psycho-physical harmony in which both posture and the nervous system are brought into balance. Stress is managed more effectively, and the immune system is gradually strengthened to become more resilient to infection.

Western herbalism

Western herbalism will be aimed at boosting the immune system function, and treatment has proved very successful in the past. Infusions of yarrow and elderflower taken three times a day will be suggested for controlling the fever, inducing sweating and keeping the temperature stable. Persistent tiredness after the virus will be alleviated by drinking two or three cups a day of yarrow or rosemary tea and also eating plenty of soup.

Acupuncture

Acupuncture has a very powerful effect on both the immune system and on the sufferer's energy level, helping to speed the slow recovery associated with this illness.

Naturopathy

A naturopath may suggest infusions of yarrow and elderflower to reduce sweating and stabilize the temperature. A light but nourishing diet will be suggested, and perhaps supplements of vitamins B and C to boost the immune system and maintain a healthy nervous system.

Other therapies

Nutritional therapy may help in improving the function of the immune system. A **Chinese herbalist** may recommend antipyretics, detoxifying herbs and evacuants. **Autogenic training** will lessen the severity of the condition, and speed recovery; if a person has been in contact with someone carrying the disease, it will improve the immune system. In **Ayurvedic medicine** a practitioner will suggest cleansing treatment, with *panchakarma* therapy. **Reflexology** and **polarity therapy** may be useful.

MYALGIC ENCEPHALOMYELITIS (ME)

What is it?

There is still considerable debate among the medical profession as to the cause and nature of this condition. ME (myalgic encephalomyelitis, also called postviral fatigue syndrome, chronic fatigue syndrome and Royal Free disease, among others) has been termed "yuppie flu" but in fact affects people from all walks of life, most particularly working mothers. Symptoms usually set in following an ordinary upper respiratory tract or gastrointestinal infection. The prime one is profound fatigue following sometimes even slight physical exertion, typically coupled with a deterioration in mental ability; others include fever, headache, muscle pain, dizziness, nausea, numbness, depression, memory loss, weight loss, slurred speech and sleep problems. These symptoms can sometimes persist for years, and appear to be exacerbated by stress or any real physical effort.

Causes

ME is largely considered to be caused by a viral infection, and among those mooted are herpes, polio, Epstein-Barr (see glandular fever) and enteroviruses. This has not been proved. There is also a theory that the condition may be related to a psychological or neurological disorder, but again, this has not been proved. Other theories include damage to the immune system, longterm use of antibiotics, immunization and candida infestation.

Orthodox treatment

There is no cure for ME. Bed rest is advised for as long as the sufferer feels it necessary. Some people respond to antidepressants. Exclusion diets may be helpful and antifungal drugs may be prescribed if candida appears to be the culprit. A carefully planned exercise program is recommended by some specialists.

ALTERNATIVE TREATMENT

Nutritional therapy

Factors linked with the development of ME include a history of long-term use of antibiotics, vaccinations and exposure to environmental pollutants or other toxins. A study carried out by the charity action for ME revealed that ME patients find nutritional approaches to be the most effective treatment. These need to be individually prescribed, but will include the correction of nutritional deficiencies, improvement of food absorption, identification of food allergies (and removal of the offending foods), and intensive detoxification work, improving liver function with herbs and diet.

Western herbalism

There are a number of herbs which have gentle, long-term effects on the body and on the immune system in particular, making it an important and effective form of therapy for this condition.

Acupuncture

Acupuncture has a very powerful effect on both the immune system and on the sufferer's energy level, which may help to alleviate the fatigue with which this disease syndrome is primarily associated.

Aromatherapy

An aromatherapist will suggest uplifting oils such as bergamot, rose, neroli and lavender for the emotions and tea tree and niaouli to strengthen the immune system.

Alexander Technique

The Alexander Technique can be beneficial by encouraging psycho-physical harmony. The resultant reduction in muscle tension and the improved postural efficiency can help in conserving energy and maximizing recuperation.

Autogenic training

This therapy will help the healing process on both psychological and physiological levels. Autogenic training often provides the patient with opportunities for self-exploration and self-help in coping.

Other therapies

A **hypnotherapist** may use the uncovering process, hypno-healing and cell command therapy, as well as working on strengthening the immune system. **Homeopathic treatment** will be constitutional, and will probably consist of attention to diet and nutrition, anticandida treatment and perhaps identification and treatment of allergies. The specific remedy while waiting for constitutional treatment will be China. A **Chinese herbalist** may recommend herbs to clear disease factors and unclog the system, some herbs to calm or strengthen the spirit, antipyretics, digestives, evacuants, astringents for sweating, or diaphretics if sweating is absent. **Macrobiotics** are very helpful in promoting the function of the digestive system, spleen and kidney, which are connected to the immune system in Chinese medicine. **Massage** may help to relieve muscular aches and pains, providing a feeling of well being. It may also counteract the feelings of helplessness and depression which some sufferers experience, and help them to deal positively with life. A **color therapist** may suggest purples and blues to help boost the immune system, greens to lift depression and yellows for regaining emotional stability and self-esteem. Energy levels may be improved and the immune system strengthened by the use of crystals as guided by a qualified practitioner in **crystal and gemstone therapy**.

HODGKIN'S DISEASE

What is it?

Hodgkin's disease (also called Hodgkin's lymphoma) is a cancer that affects the lymph nodes, or glands. It is an uncommon form of cancer that affects men three times more frequently than women, most usually developing between the ages of 20 and 30 and 55 and 70. The cancer cells multiply in the lymphoid tissue (which is present mainly in the lymph nodes and spleen) and the main symptoms are a large but surprisingly painless enlargement of the lymph nodes, usually those in the neck and armpits, which have a very characteristic rubbery feel to them. The symptoms vary according to the organs affected, but they typically include:

- *Anemia.*
- *Fever.*
- *An enlarged liver or spleen, the latter possibly experienced as a full or dragging sensation in the upper left abdomen.*
- *Loss of appetite and weight loss.*
- *Night sweats.*
- *Itching and breathlessness.*
- *Pain in the enlarged glands after drinking alcohol.*

Lymphoid tissue is an important part of the immune system, and as this becomes increasingly damaged infections which would normally be minor may bring life-threatening complications. Hodgkin's disease can be fatal, depending on the degree to which the immune systems and lymph nodes are affected and which organs have been invaded by the affected lymphoid tissue.

IF YOU HAVE A SWOLLEN GLAND IN THE NECK, GROIN OR ARMPIT THAT PERSISTS FOR MORE THAN TWO WEEKS WITHOUT OBVIOUS CAUSE, CONSULT YOUR DOCTOR.

Causes

The cause of Hodgkin's disease remains unknown. Theories have been advanced that cancer-causing viruses are involved, but this has not been proved.

Orthodox treatment

Hodgkin's disease is diagnosed by means of a biopsy specimen from an enlarged lymph node or other affected organ. Treatment will depend upon the result of further tests such as a CAT scan and a lymphangiogram, and how advanced the disease is when it is first diagnosed. If it is treated early, radiotherapy alone may effect a cure. If the cancer is sufficiently advanced to involve a number of organs anticancer drugs (chemotherapy) will be used, sometimes for several months, and perhaps radiotherapy as well. The prognosis depends upon how far the disease has progressed, but the survival rate is high in patients who are diagnosed and treated early. If there are no further signs of the disease within five years of treatment, it can be considered cured.

ALTERNATIVE TREATMENT

Homeopathy

A homeopath will take the view that cancer represents a profound breakdown in health at all levels. An experienced practitioner may prescribe specific remedies as well as constitutional treatment; sometimes the taking of Bach flower remedies and also vitamin and mineral supplements may be advised.

Nutrition

Nutritional therapists aim to use individual dietary programs in order to improve the body's efficiency in combating illness in general. Many illnesses, including cancers, can benefit from this improved efficiency, but ultimately much will depend upon the stage of the illness and also the patient's constitution.

Spiritual healing

This therapy helps to recharge and restore energy to the immune system, which stimulates the body's own forces of recovery. In this way the immune system is strengthened, so that the sufferer can fight disease. In terms of life-threatening chronic conditions like AIDS or cancer, spiritual healing can help to develop insight and self-awareness, which will help the sufferer cope with illness in a more positive and constructive way. It is of particular value in improving the quality of life in the long term. It can also help to reduce the unpleasant side effects of anticancer drugs (chemotherapy).

Macrobiotics

Most practitioners will advise following conventional treatment, but a liberal standard macrobiotic diet may be very helpful in maintaining optimum health and in effecting convalescence.

Yoga

Yoga can help to stimulate the immune system through gentle *asanas*, relaxation, meditation, *pranayama*, *shat kriyas* and hand *mudras*.

Other therapies

Ayurvedic medicine has immune-enhancing therapies which may prove to be useful in the treatment of this condition. **Polarity therapy** may be useful. **Reflexology** has proved to be successful in some cases.

How to Boost Your Immune System

Our immune system plays an important role in keeping us in good health by providing a network of defenses against damaging microorganisms and other foreign invaders that may try to enter the body. It aims to neutralize and destroy these unwanted interlopers by fighting back. To do this it uses the body's white blood cells. Some lymphocytes make antibodies to neutralize invaders or foreign substances, others attach themselves to the organisms directly. Other white cells contain granules which engulf bacteria coated by the antibodies and release enzymes and chemicals which detoxify them. Some white cells (eosinophils) release histamines and are implicated in hayfever and asthma.

The premise that prevention is better than a cure is fundamental to alternative medicine, and practitioners believe that the immune system is the ideal starting point in the fight to prevent or cure illness, infections or allergies. Most alternative therapies aim to boost a system which may be flagging or impaired by any one of a number of problems, including the following: injuries; surgery; the overuse of antibiotics, which can suppress the immune system and destroy the healthy bacteria of the bowel (flora); some drugs; digestive disorders, like candida, enzyme deficiencies and chronic constipation; poor diet; pollution; stress; genetic problems and inherited weaknesses.

Nutritional therapy

Your nutritional therapist may believe that the immune system is damaged by nutritional deficiencies and to factors which impair the proper absorption of nutrients into the body. A healthy diet will be stressed – including a high intake of vegetables each day, with whole grain cereals like brown rice and whole meal bread, fruit, pulses (beans and lentils) and nuts and seeds for their vital oils. A daily multivitamin and multimineral preparation – especially one containing high amounts of the antioxidant nutrients – acts as an added insurance policy.

Western herbalism

Treatment will always be tailored to the individual, but there are a number of herbs which can be broken into categories according to their use. Herbs to boost immunity include: astralagus, which can be used to increase energy levels and resistance to disease; Chinese angelica, which can restore energy and stimulate white blood cells and antibody formation; licorice, which can enhance recovery, stimulating the formation of white blood cells and antibodies. It is also useful in preventing stress; garlic, which has strong antibiotic properties to help prevent infections, including those which have become immune to antibiotics; echinacea, which is widely used to treat chronic and acute infections, and which cleanses the blood and lymphatic system and stimulates the production of white blood cells and antibodies and ginseng, which can boost immunity and encourage the body to deal efficiently with stress, as well as stimulating white blood cell production, and aiding recovery after illness.

Homeopathy

Homeopathic remedies help the immune system to fight for itself, increasing the white blood cells in the body, and allowing a person to reach a state of mental and emotional balance, which makes the body more responsive. Constitutional treatment is often aimed at the existing ailment, as well as tendencies and symptoms which have not yet become ailments. A homeopath will suggest improved nutrition, fresh air, exercise and rest to build up the immune system. Homeopathic remedies will be prescribed in conjunction with this advice.

Massage

Prolonged stress may suppress the immune system by raising the cortisol levels of the blood. Massage can help to relieve stress by releasing muscle tension and calming the mind. This helps to balance the cortisol levels and encourages better immune function.

Spiritual healing

Many healers suggest that spiritual healing will help to recharge and restore energy to the immune system and stimulate the body's own recovery force. In this way the immune system is reactivated and strengthened, so that it is better able to fight disease. Other factors which may play a part in immune suppression, such as negative emotions and attitudes, can also be overcome by spiritual healing, relieving the overall burden on the immune system. Positive affirmations and visualization also play a valuable role.

Naturopathy

A naturopath will assess a person, and then offer nutritional guidance to ensure gastrointestinal efficiency. Applied nutrition, with vitamin and mineral support, will be appropriate, probably including B-complex vitamins, and vitamins C and E, zinc, selenium, magnesium, potassium. Constitutional hydrotherapy, particularly a sequence of hot and cold packs applied to the front and back, is a proven method of potentiating immunity.

Other therapies

A **hypnotherapist** *may suggest cell command therapy. A* **macrobiotic** *practitioner will give guidelines for healthy living, and a diet to encourage the immune system to function more effectively. An* **Ayurvedic medicine** *practitioner may suggest detoxification with fasting along with advice on diet and lifestyle.*

EYES

What are they?

The eyes are round jelly-filled globes about 2½cm (1in) in diameter. They have three layers. The outer layer, or sclera, is the white of the eye. The front of the sclera is clear and makes up the cornea with its protective membrane – the conjunctiva. The choroid is the central layer and has blood vessels, which supply the eye. The inner layer is the retina with the light-sensitive nerve cells. These cells convert light into nerve impulses, which are relayed to the brain through the optic nerve where they are decoded so that you can see.

The eye's lens lies behind the iris. The latter acts as an aperture to control the size of the pupil which in turn restricts light coming into the eye. As light enters the eye from an object it is bent as it passes through the cornea into the pupil and through the lens. The lens focuses the light onto the retina by changing its shape, aided by the ciliary muscle. The retina has millions of light-sensitive cells or rods and cones. The rods tend to be more sensitive but only "see" black and white; the cones can "see" color but need more light. The eyelids and eyelashes protect the eyes from foreign bodies. Tears released from ducts at the edge of the eyelids drain through a hole ("punctum") inside the lower eyelid into the upper nasal passages.

What can go wrong?

Infections are common. *Styes* are caused by abscesses of eyelash follicles. *Blepharitis*, inflammation of the eyelids, can be due to infection or a form of dermatitis. With *conjunctivitis*, the conjunctiva becomes red and inflamed and itchy because of an infection or an allergic condition. A *cataract* is an increase in the lens' opacity which causes a deterioration in vision. It usually occurs in old age although some people are born with it. The eye has to maintain a certain pressure to prevent it collapsing in on itself. If this is too high, *glaucoma* occurs. If untreated this disease can cause vision loss and blindness. Eyes are also affected by body diseases. Diabetes after many years can cause blindness by bleeding in the eye, *glaucoma*, or retinal detachment.

An eye consists of three layers: the sclera (the white), the conjunctiva and the choroid. The retina converts light into nerve impulses which the brain decodes so that we can see.

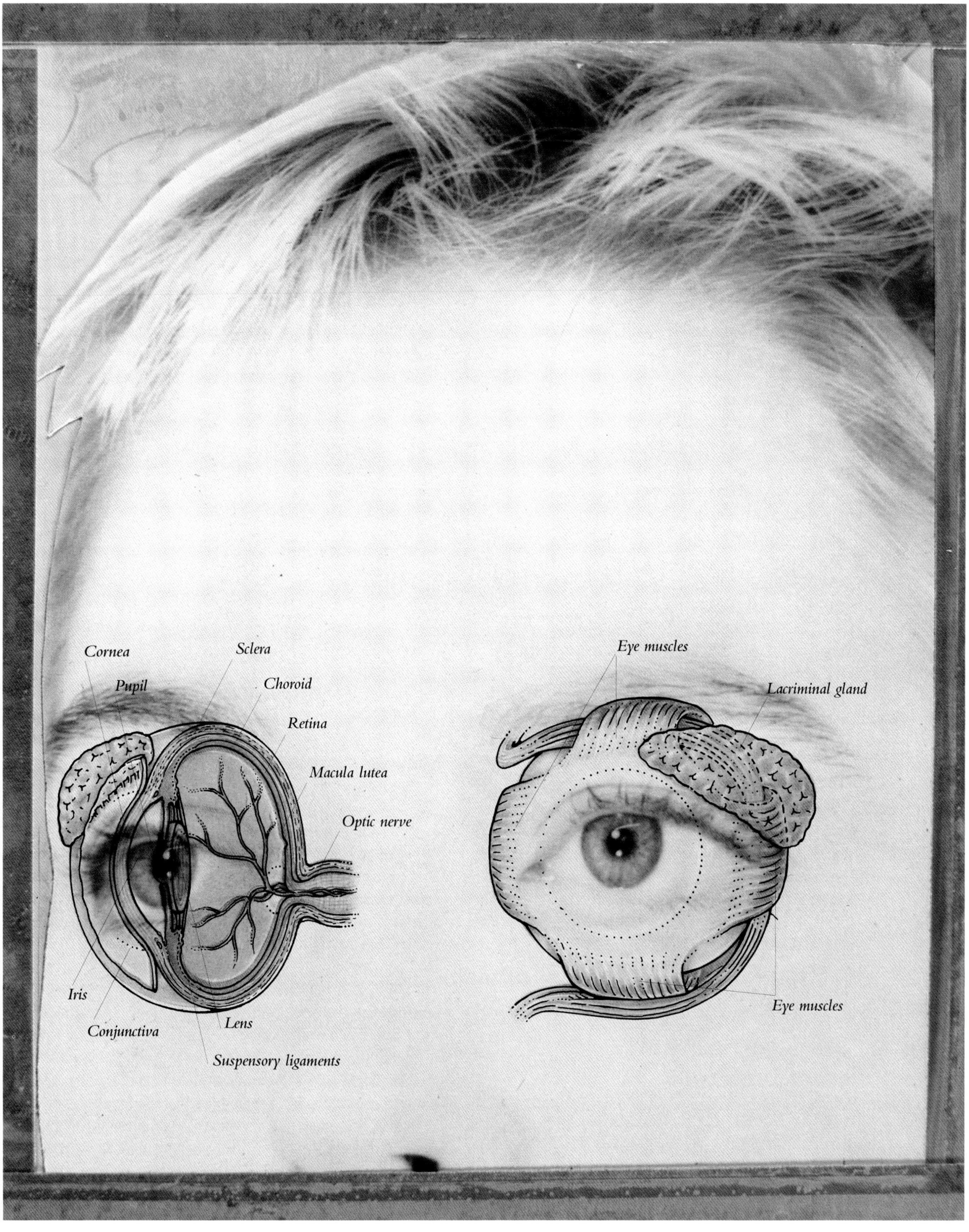
Cornea
Sclera
Pupil
Choroid
Retina
Macula lutea
Optic nerve
Iris
Conjunctiva
Lens
Suspensory ligaments
Eye muscles
Lacriminal gland
Eye muscles

Conjunctivitis

What is it?

Conjunctivitis is the inflammation of the conjunctiva, which is the mucous membrane covering the outer eyeball up to the cornea and lining the eyelids. The affected eye appears red or pink, and may be itchy and sore, with a feeling of grittiness; occasionally the sufferer may experience mild blurring of vision. In bacterial conjunctivitis, there will be a discharge of yellow pus which often hardens on the eyelashes during sleep, causing them to stick together. In viral conjunctivitis the discharge is minimal unless there is secondary bacterial infection. Either type of conjunctivis may affect just one or both eyes. In allergic conjunctivitis there is no discharge, but the conjunctiva and eyelids are swollen and puffy.

Causes

Allergic conjunctivitis arises from allergies to substances such as pollen, cosmetics and contact lens cleansing solution. Infective conjunctivis is caused by bacteria or viruses, spread on the hands or on face cloths and towels. Newborn babies may develop a conjunctivis called ophthalmia neonatorum, which arises from an infection (often chlamydia) transmitted during the birth process. In adults allergic and infective conjunctivitis are not usually sight-threatening, but ophthalmia neonatorum can cause long-term visual disability. Another more significant form of conjunctivis is trachoma, which is caused by a chlamydial infection that is most commonly found in tropical countries.

Other conditions such as acute glaucoma and iritis may give rise to red eyes but there will be other symptoms such as pain and photophobia (sensitivity to light) and vision is often affected.

Orthodox treatment

Bacterial conjunctivitis is treated with antibiotic drops or ointment; viral conjunctivitis is usually self-limiting but may last for several weeks. To avoid spreading infection:

- *Wash your hands before and after touching your eyes.*
- *In allergic conjunctivitis, sodium cromoglycate eyedrops will be given or corticosteroid drops, though these are used only if no infection is present as they could worsen it.*
- *Ophthalmia neonatorum will be treated with antibiotic eyedrops and the mother will also be treated.*

Alternative Treatment

Homeopathy

Each patient should be individually assessed by the homeopathic practitioner, but the following remedies are likely to be prescribed:

- Euphrasia for cases where there is little or no discharge but the eyes are sensitive to bright light.
- Argentum nit where there is copious discharge.
- Aconitum when the eyes are gritty and swollen and water after exposure to wind, cold and light.
- Bathing the eyes with a solution of 10 drops of Euphrasia mother tincture and 1 level teaspoon of salt to 300ml ($\frac{1}{2}$pt) warm water will soothe them. Bathe every four hours (but not more than four times a day), using a disposable eyebath.

Chinese herbalism

The precise cause of the conjunctivitis will first be diagnosed by the practitioner, and then antipyretics, anti-inflammatory agents and also some herbal detoxicants will be prescribed accordingly.

Western herbalism

Local remedies which have anti-inflammatory and astringent effects may be used by the herbalist. If the conjunctivitis is a recurrent problem, internal remedies designed to boost immunity may be appropriate. Soothing compresses of, for instance, cornflower, camomile, echinacea, elderflower, eyebright (euphrasia), goldenseal or marigold infusions may be helpful; always use separate compresses and eyebaths for each eye to avoid spreading infection.

Ayurvedic medicine

An Ayurvedic medical practitioner might suggest *Panchakarma* treatment and *Nasya*, together with inhalations and eyewash.

Naturopathy

A naturopath would address this as an inflammatory catarrhal condition of the eyes, so dietetic management would be considered appropriate (for example, a cleansing diet). Applied nutrition would be useful, as would herbal or homeopathic medication such as euphrasia. Supplements of vitamins A, B2, B3, B6 and C may be advised.

Other therapies

A **nutritional therapist** will probably prescribe treatment to boost the immune system. Zinc supplements in particular may be helpful, but should not be taken for more than a few weeks without professional advice. **Acupuncture** and **crystal and gemstone therapy** may prove to have some benefit. Inflammation generally responds well to the harmonizing action of **auricular therapy;** a course of five to seven treatments one to two days apart can alleviate the condition. A **color therapist** will recommend placing cool, damp, light blue eyepads over the eyes to reduce pain and inflammation.

STYES

What are they?

A stye (also known as a hordeolum) is a small abscess on the eyelid which is most commonly the result of a bacterial infection affecting one of the glands that are responsible for lubricating the eyelashes. The hair follicle is stretched painfully by a pocket of pus, causing redness and swelling; after a few days the stye will come to a head, when a small yellow protrusion will form at the root of the eyelash. The stye will then burst, relieving the pressure and also causing the loss of the eyelash. Styes may develop at the base of any of the eyelashes.

A stye will last for about seven days and sometimes several will afflict the lids at the same time if the bacteria which caused the initial infection have spread. Styes are often recurrent, but while they are irritating, unsightly and sometimes painful, they cause no damage to the eye itself.

A persistent lump on the eyelid may commonly be a Meibomian cyst (orchalazion) rather than a stye, although if it becomes infected it may closely resemble one except in that the pus will be discharged through the inner surface of the eyelid rather than through the rim. Meibomian cysts are never cancerous but they may need to be removed by means of a minor surgical operation.

Causes

The initial infection is generally caused by the staphylococcal group of bacteria, which are a common cause of skin infections. There is no particular reason for the occurrence of styes, except that they can be more common when the body's overall resistance to infection is low. Repeated recurrences of styes may be an indication of diabetes. Never touch your eyes with dirty hands, as this may lead to infection.

Orthodox treatment

A stye will usually clear up without treatment, but steps can be taken to speed the healing process. Applying warm compresses every two or three hours may help; when the pus has been drawn to a head, gently pull out the eyelash to release the pus and then wash the eye until all the pus has been removed. Antibiotic eye ointments can help to prevent reinfection of the adjacent lash follicles. In the case of constant recurrences your doctor will look into your general state of health.

ALTERNATIVE TREATMENT

Homeopathy

The homeopathic practitioner may begin treatment by addressing the overall health of the patient and prescribing constitutional remedies which will boost general resistance to infection. Specific remedies, to be taken every hour for up to ten doses, are pulsatilla or, if that does not effect any improvement, staphisagria. To attempt to disperse the stye and ease the pressure, try wrapping cotton wool around the handle of a wooden spoon then dipping it into very hot water and applying it repeatedly to the stye. Never try to burst the stye by squeezing it.

Naturopathy

A naturopath will probably suggest the application of hot compresses of cotton wool or perhaps grated carrot wrapped in clean muslin or other cloth. In the case of recurrent styes, the naturopath will consider that vitality is lowered and will probably advise the sufferer to exclude refined foods and take supplements such as vitamin C and vitamin B complex. Biochemic natrum sulf may encourage resolution of the stye.

Kinesiology

A kinesiology therapist may suggest the following:

- Checking the upper trapezius muscles.
- Checking liver and kidney energy function.
- Checking nutrition, prescribing perhaps vitamins A and E.
- He may prescribe herbal treatment as a support, including perhaps eyebright (euphrasia).
- Palming.
- Specific exercises in regular applied kinesiology.
- Balancing for the eyes.

Western herbalism

Because recurrent styes are often an indication of the sufferer being run down, a Western herbalist will probably give general treatment such as marigold or poke root taken orally to boost the immune and lymphatic systems. A decoction of camomile or eyebright (euphrasia) applied via an eyebath may help to reduce the swelling and inflammation.

Chinese herbalism

The treatment offered by a Chinese herbalist may include antipyretics, anti-inflammatory agents and herbal detoxicants.

Other therapies

In **Ayurvedic medicine** a practitioner will prescribe much the same treatment as for conjunctivitis. An **acupuncturist** will address treatment at improving the immune system, and a **nutritional therapist** will work toward preventing infections (see Boosting the Immune System, page 265). **Crystal and gemstone therapy** may be useful.

EYESTRAIN

What is it?

Eyestrain is not an accepted medical term, but it is commonly used to describe discomfort or distress related to the prolonged use of the eyes and refers to fatigue of the extra-ocular muscle which keeps the eyes aligned. There may be a feeling of tightness around the eyes, difficulty in focusing on either distant or near objects or recurrent headaches, particularly in a band across the forehead and behind the eyes. Eye specialists believe that eyes cannot actually be damaged by overuse.

Causes

The following are traditionally believed to cause eyestrain:

- *Incorrectly prescribed glasses, or not using glasses at all when they are required.*
- *Intense periods of reading or close work.*
- *Constant use of a VDT screen.*
- *Watching television for long periods in the dark.*
- *Working in extremely bright or dim light.*

Orthodox treatment

The symptoms that are commonly attributed to eyestrain are usually the result of headaches (see page 192), fatigue, tiredness of the muscles around the eye, blepharitis (see opposite), sinusitis (see page 285) and conjunctivitis (see page 268), all of which can be treated individually. For eyestrain itself:

- *When reading, make sure there is good light on the page and take short breaks from time to time.*
- *When using a VDT screen, avoid staring fixedly at the screen and take a 10-minute break every hour, leaving your workstation.*
- *Avoid watching television in the dark.*

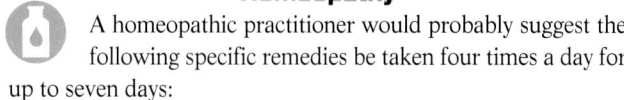

ALTERNATIVE TREATMENT

Homeopathy

A homeopathic practitioner would probably suggest the following specific remedies be taken four times a day for up to seven days:

- Arnica 6c for muscles that are tired from looking into the distance for long periods.
- Natrum mur 6c when the eyes ache upon looking up, down or to the sides.
- Ruta 6c when the eyes burn or feel strained after close work or reading for long periods.
- Phosphorus 6c when the eyes are tired as a result of nervousness, apprehension or sexual overindulgence.

Kinesiology

The treatment offered by a kinesiologist would probably consist of:

- Counseling on the use of the eyes, in particular avoiding stress.
- Corrective pinhole glasses, in some cases.
- Eyesight tests.
- Relaxing eye exercises.
- Work on the upper trapezius muscles.
- Liver and kidney energy function tests.
- Nutritional analysis, with emphasis on vitamins A and E supplementation.
- Herbal remedies, like eyebright (euphrasia).
- Palming.
- Specific exercises in regular kinesiology.
- Balancing for the eyes.

Yoga

A yoga teacher would suggest gentle *asanas*, relaxation, *pranayama*, meditation and hand *mudras*.

Alexander Technique

The Alexander Technique teaches a pupil to unlearn habits of overstraining. This has a particular effect on the neck and facial muscles and can therefore help in recovery from eyestrain.

Western herbalism

A herbalist will suggest cool compresses of herbs such as chickweed, eyebright (euphrasia), marigold or cucumber, made by soaking a piece of clean cloth in an infusion of the herb. Leave the compress in place for about 10 minutes. A simple alternative is to place slices of fresh cucumber on the eyes.

Hypnotherapy

Hypnotherapy would be aimed at relieving the source of the strain. Elements of treatment are likely to be worked around hypno-healing and self-hypnosis conditioning.

Other therapies

Rolfing might help by improving the alignment of the head so that less effort is needed to focus the eyes. Local **massage** of the eye area and head can relax surrounding eye and face muscles. With the **metamorphic technique**, the preconception areas will be addressed. In **relaxation and visualization** therapy, exercises will be taught to ease the tension. A **reflexologist** will address the eyes, neck and kidneys. **Autogenic training** improves eye problems in some people; there is also some evidence that **spiritual healing** may help ease the problem. **Hellerwork** may be effective by relieving chronic muscular tension in the neck and jaw. A **color therapist** will suggest light blue eyepads or looking at cool green. A **naturopath** may advise taking some supplements of vitamin A and vitamin B2.

Blepharitis

What is it?

Blepharitis is an inflammation of the eyelids which can occur in people of all ages and can become chronic. The eyelids become red, irritated and scaly; commonly the eyes themselves may become painful and even red and inflamed. Crusting and painful lids are the most common feature, and if this is left untreated the flakes of skin can fall into the eyes, leading to conjunctivitis (see page 268).

In most cases the condition is not serious, and many people with dandruff and other skin conditions suffer some constant blepharitis. However, in more severe cases the roots of the eyelashes may become infected, causing small ulcers to develop, and the lashes may fall out or grow at abnormal angles so that the eyelashes rub against the eyeball, causing considerable distress and pain; the eyelid margins may be damaged to the extent that the eyelash roots are destroyed altogether. Severe cases of blepharitis can result in corneal ulcers (erosion of the outer layer of the cornea).

Causes

People who suffer from atopy (an allergic complex which exists from birth) often experience regular recurrences of blepharitis and in this case the cause is allergic. Those suffering from skin conditions such as dandruff, seborrheic ezcema, psoriasis and dermatitis are also more likely to be affected. The cause of blepharitis is inflammatory, not infectious, but lids may become secondarily infected as a result of rubbing, in which case styes (see page 269) may result. Recurrent blepharitis of the eyelid margins can be triggered by illness or stress, or by exposure to pollutants such as tobacco smoke.

Orthodox treatment

Mild cases of blepharitis can sometimes be cleared up by simply removing the scaly skin morning and night with cottonballs dipped in warm water. Although cleaning with various agents including diluted baby shampoo or sodium bicarbonate is often recommended it is the physical removal of the crusts which enables healthy skin to grow back normally. If dandruff is present, using an antidandruff shampoo may alleviate the blepharitis. Medical treatment is usually aimed at easing the inflammation, in some cases by the use of steroid ointments which have a powerful anti-inflammatory effect. Eyedrops can ease the irritation but will not prevent the blepharitis from recurring. Secondary infections can be treated by antibiotic eye ointments.

Alternative Treatment

Homeopathy

Treatment will be constitutional, particularly if the condition is chronic and other deep-seated conditions such as dandruff are present. However, specific remedies for blepharitis may include:

- Hepar sulph 6c when the eyelids are red and gummy.
- Graphites 6c when the eyelids are red and swollen, with discharge in the morning.
- Calcarea 6c for extreme itchiness.
- Sulphur 6c where lids are sore and burning, with tiny ulcers, made worse by bathing the eyes with water.
- The homeopathic practitioner may also suggest bathing the eyes at night with a saline solution of 1 teaspoon salt to a glass of warm water and then gently applying Calendula ointment. Nutritional advice would be that the sufferer should reduce intake of animal fats and take 1 tablespoon of cold-pressed linseed oil daily. Supplements of vitamins B and C and of zinc may also be helpful.

Kinesiology

The treatment offered by a kinesiologist can consist of the following:

- Treatment of specific acupressure points for blepharitis.
- Counseling on use of the eyes.
- Corrective pinhole glasses.
- Relaxing eye exercises.
- Eye tests.
- Checking the upper trapezius muscles.
- Liver function tests.
- Nutrition tests, possibly a recommendation of supplementary vitamins A and E.
- Herbal support, such as eyebright (euphrasia).
- Palming.
- Specific exercises in regular applied kinesiology.
- Balancing.

Nutritional therapy

The treatment offered by a nutrional therapist will be aimed at the immune system in order to prevent infection and recurrent allergy.

Other therapies

A **naturopath** will treat blepharitis in much the same way as conjunctivitis (see page 268), relying on homeopathic treatment and dietetic management. Both **Western** and **Chinese herbalism** will address the condition in the same way as for conjunctivitis. The **Metamorphic technique** will focus on the preconception area. Most alternative therapies will place a strong emphasis on improving immune system function, which will then decrease the risk of infection.

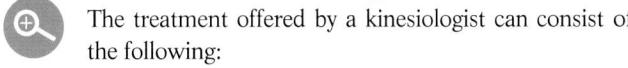

GLAUCOMA

What is it?

Glaucoma occurs when the pressure of fluid within the eyeball becomes too high. Under normal circumstances a minimal level of pressure maintains the shape of the eyeball; if the pressure increases it causes compression and obstruction of the tiny blood vessels which feed the optic nerve. The result is optic nerve fiber damage and loss of vision. The incidence of glaucoma increases with age.

There are two main forms of glaucoma. Acute glaucoma causes a very painful red eye associated with misting of vision. The sufferer may experience nausea and vomiting, and the pupil may be dilated. A warning sign of an acute attack may be subacute glaucoma, which causes symptoms at night or when the pupils are dilated. There is a dull aching pain in the eye, some fogginess of vision and, characteristically, concentric rainbow-colored rings are seen around lights, resulting from light refraction by water droplets forced into the cornea by the raised pressure. These are ocular emergencies, but the commoner form is chronic simple glaucoma in which loss of peripheral vision occurs so slowly it goes unnoticed until damage to the optic nerve is irreversible.

Glaucoma is a major cause of blindness, and loss of vision is irretrievable. However, if it is detected early enough, the damage can be curtailed and patients are now screened for this.

Causes

There is frequently a familial history of glaucoma, so ideally all the first-degree relatives of a sufferer from this condition should have their eye pressure checked annually once they are over the age of 40 years. Other causes of glaucoma include:

- *Congenital causes such as a structural abnormality in the drainage of the eye.*
- *Injury or serious eye disease.*
- *In acute inflammation such as iritis there may be a temporary rise in intraocular pressure.*

SUDDEN PAIN OR A DULL ACHING SENSATION IN THE EYE, WITH FOGGINESS OF VISION AND RAINBOW-COLORED RINGS AROUND LIGHTS, ARE KEY SYMPTOMS OF ACUTE GLAUCOMA WHICH SHOULD NEVER BE IGNORED. SEE YOUR DOCTOR AT ONCE, OR GO TO THE ACCIDENT AND EMERGENCY DEPARTMENT OF YOUR LOCAL HOSPITAL IF THE ATTACK OCCURS OUTSIDE SURGERY HOURS.

Orthodox treatment

For chronic simple glaucoma, treatment usually consists of eyedrops and/or pills which reduce the pressure in the eye. The treatment may have to be continued for life, with repeated checkups by a doctor. If the drugs do not reduce pressure sufficiently, a glaucoma drainage operation may be necessary to open blocked channels or to create a new channel.

Acute glaucoma almost always requires emergency surgery to create a small opening at the edge of the iris so that the fluid can drain more easily (an iridectomy). Medication such as eyedrops and/or pills will be given first to reduce pressure in the eye. If the angle of drainage was damaged by the attack further drug treatment will be necessary and perhaps a drainage operation as in chronic simple glaucoma.

ALTERNATIVE TREATMENT

ACUTE GLAUCOMA IS AN EMERGENCY REQUIRING IMMEDIATE ORTHODOX MEDICAL INTERVENTION AND WILL NEVER BE TREATED BY A REPUTABLE ALTERNATIVE MEDICAL PRACTITIONER. CHRONIC SIMPLE GLAUCOMA CAN, HOWEVER, BE CONTROLLED BY VARIOUS THERAPIES.

Homeopathy

Belladonna can be taken every 15 minutes for up to ten doses when symptoms start. The symptom picture it is most likely to address is blurred vision and pain in one eye, worsened by bright light. It should never be taken for acute glaucoma.

Reflexology

An experienced reflexology practitioner may be able to provide relief from symptoms as well as treatment which rights the fundamental problem that has caused the glaucoma. Treatment would be aimed at the reflexology points for the eyes, kidneys and neck.

Nutritional therapy

According to medical research, some factors which contribute to or aggravate glaucoma are an excessive intake of protein or trans-fatty acids in the diet and a deficiency of vitamin B1, vitamin A, vitamin C, chromium and zinc. A nutritional therapist would therefore aim to correct such imbalances in the diet.

Yoga

Depending on your particular symptoms and the type of glaucoma, your yoga instructor may recommend gentle *asanas*, relaxation, *pranayama* and meditation.

Other therapies

Metamorphic technique, treating the preconception area, may help. **Healing** and **crystal and gemstone therapy** may also be useful, depending on the symptoms present and the overall health and constitution of the sufferer.

Cataracts

What are they?

Cataracts are a gradual clouding of the lens of the eye which is caused by a change in the composition of the protein fibers within the lens. The result is not complete blindness, in the sense that even in advanced cases of cataract there is still some perception of light remaining, but vision becomes cloudy and distorted.

Cataracts usually affect both eyes, although one eye is frequently more severely affected than the other. They are common in old age, when the lens becomes harder, but occasionally are congenital (present at birth). In the elderly the opacification may be confined to the edges of the lens, where it does not affect vision.

There is no pain associated with cataracts, and the loss of vision normally progresses only very slowly. Blurring of vision is the symptom that is most commonly experienced, though increased density in the lens may increase light refraction so that the sufferer temporarily becomes short-sighted. Perception of color is distorted and dimmed. The opacity of the lens may cause scattering of light rays and thus make night driving difficult or dangerous due to glare. Eventually the opacification becomes visible externally, with the pupil appearing whitened.

Causes

Cataracts can be considered to be a "normal" ageing process, but in younger sufferers from this condition there is usually an obvious cause. The causes of cataracts include:

- *Congenital cataracts caused by German measles (rubella) or other infection in pregnancy, and occasionally drugs taken by the mother during the early weeks of pregnancy.*
- *Down's syndrome.*
- *A genetic disorder such as galactosaemia, a condition where an infant is unable to digest galactose into simple sugars, causing its accumulation.*
- *Severe nutritional deficiencies.*
- *Diabetes. Diabetics are more likely to develop cataracts in their forties or fifties than nondiabetics.*
- *Severe skin problems such as eczema.*
- *Long-term use of steroids, or the use of steroid eye drops over several years.*
- *Any injury to the eye, especially a perforating eye injury, may result in accelerated opacification of the lens.*
- *Radiation, such as radiotherapy.*

Orthodox treatment

Eye surgery is the only treatment which will restore sight to an opacified lens, though it is only undertaken when the cataract is advanced enough to impair sight. The operation, which may be done as a day case under local anesthesia, usually consists of removing the opacified lens and replacing it with a plastic lens. If for some reason an intraocular lens is not suitable, contact lenses will give these patients good post-operative vision.

Alternative Treatment

Homeopathy

A homeopath will probably suggest taking supplements of vitamin E, bioflavinoids, potassium and selenium. Specific remedies can be taken up to three times each day for up to a week, then twice a day for up to a month if there is an improvement. If improvement continues, a two-day break can be taken, and then the remedy continued twice a day for another month. Remedies include:

- Phosphorus when there is a sensation of mist before the eyes, or of something being pulled tightly across them.
- Calcarea in the early stages, with circular lines visible in the lens.
- Silicea in the later stages, when the cataract begins to interfere with sight.
- If there is no improvement within two months, consult your homeopathic practitioner.

Nutritional therapy

There is strong evidence that cataracts can be caused by a lack of dietary antioxidants (vitamins A, C and E and the mineral selenium), so a nutritional therapist will suggest boosting the intake of these. Taking supplements of potassium may also be useful.

Naturopathy

A naturopath may take the view that cataracts are partly caused by a deficiency of certain vitamins, minerals and trace elements and suggest ways of remedying this. Some studies suggest that vitamin C plays a protective role and may delay deterioration of the lens.

Reflexology

A registered practitioner may be able to provide relief from symptoms and offer treatment which rights the fundamental problem causing the illness. Treatment would be aimed at the reflexology points for the eyes, kidneys and neck.

Other therapies

Metamorphic technique and **spiritual healing** may have some beneficial effects in cases of cataracts.

EARS, NOSE, THROAT AND MOUTH

What are they?

The ear divides into the external, middle and internal ears. The external ear collects sound waves and transmits them to the ear drum. As this vibrates it sends the sound to three bones in the middle ear. These again vibrate and the sound is carried to the cochlea in the inner ear. Vibrations in the inner ear's fluid-filled cavity are converted to nerve impulses which the brain then translates into sounds.

The ear is vital for balance. Next to the cochlea are the semicircular canals, which maintain equilibrium of the moving body. The Eustachian tube links the middle ear to the back of the throat (pharynx) and helps equalize pressure on either side of the ear drum. The nose has two important functions: it warms the air we breathe and contains smell receptors. When you sniff, a waft of air is sent over these receptors so that we can identify the smell. Taste and smell are intimately linked. The tongue's taste buds distinguish four basic tastes: sweet, sour, salt and bitter. The flavour of food is a combination of the two senses. The tongue and the teeth are also important in digestion. When food enters the mouth it is masticated and mixed with saliva. Stimulation of nerves in the pharynx causes swallowing and the 'bolus' of food passes to the oesophagus. At the same time breathing stops, to prevent choking. The tonsils at the back of the throat are thought to help childhood immunity.

What can go wrong?

Ears get infected easily. Middle *ear infections* are common in children and if left untreated can cause deafness and speech impairment. Occasionally, the condition becomes chronic and is called 'glue ear'. Inner *ear infections* can affect balance, often causing tinnitus and dizzy spells. The air we breathe in contains many organisms, so it is not surprising that the most common infections – pharyngitis and *tonsillitis* – occur in the throat. *Laryngitis* is less common, but causes a hoarse voice. Teeth and gum infections can cause *bad breath* and facial pain. The latter is also caused by sinus infection. *Mouth ulcers*, *oral thrush* and *cold sores* commonly occur with other illnesses or at times of physical and psychological stress.

The ears are vital for balance as they maintain the body's equilibrium; the nose takes in air and lets us smell; the throat and mouth help us ingest and swallow food.

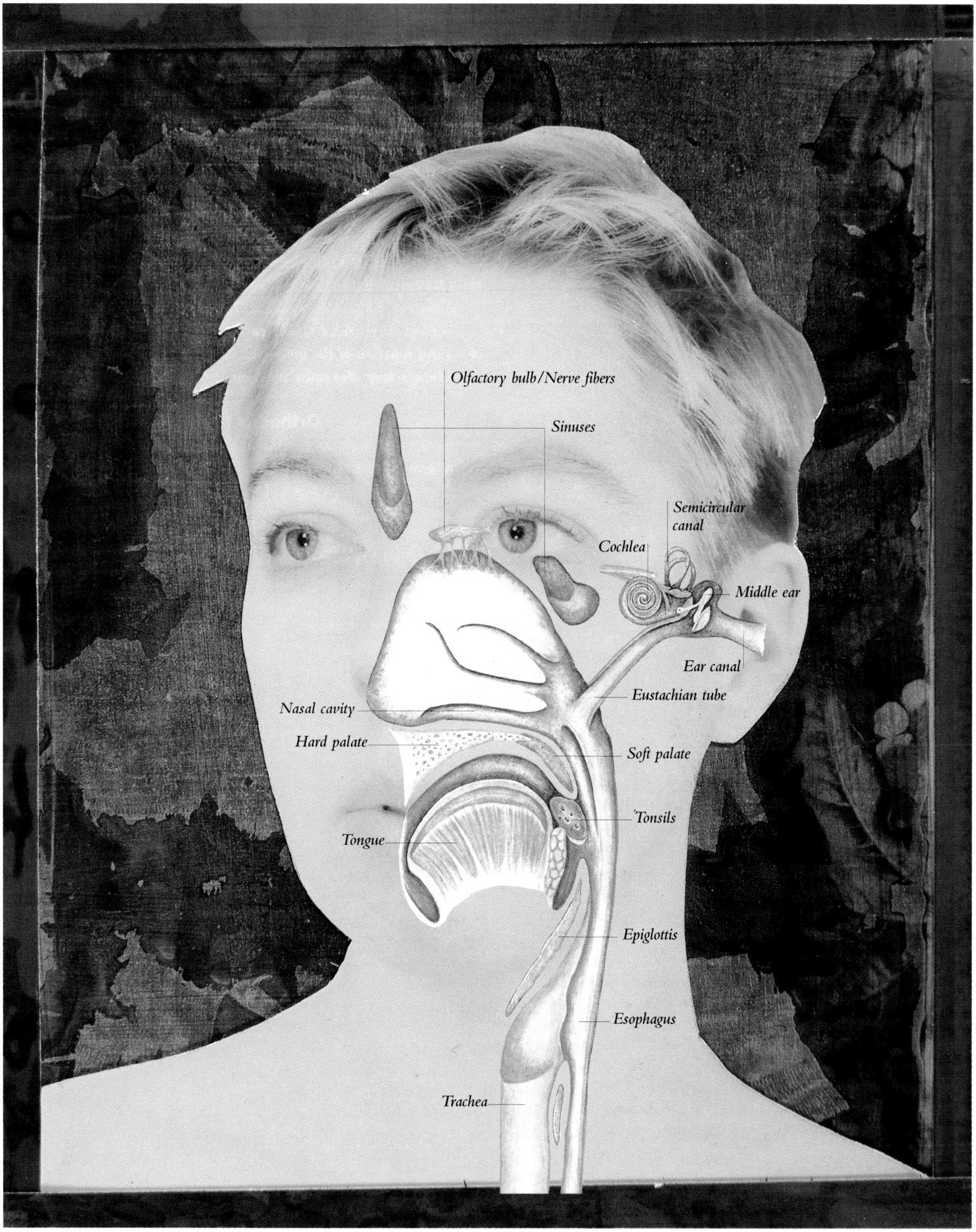
Olfactory bulb/Nerve fibers
Sinuses
Semicircular canal
Cochlea
Middle ear
Ear canal
Eustachian tube
Nasal cavity
Hard palate
Soft palate
Tonsils
Tongue
Epiglottis
Esophagus
Trachea

EAR INFECTIONS

What are they?

The ear comprises three areas – the outer ear, middle ear and inner ear. Each of these areas are prone to infection, leading to a range of symptoms.

Causes

The outer ear can become inflamed or infected, causing pain which is often quite severe. There may be a discharge and hearing is often affected. Causes of outer ear infection include:

- *Otitis externa (ear inflammation) is often caused by infection.*
- *Boils or abscesses The build-up of pus can cause acute pain in the ear, which usually disappears once the boil or abscess bursts and the pus is discharged.*
- *Swimmer's ear, which is an infection brought on by bacteria entering the ear from polluted water. It can become chronic, particularly if the sufferer continues to swim.*
- *Fungal infection causing inflammation. It can be recurrent.*
- *Damage caused by probing with an external object.*

The middle ear is the most common place for ear infection, particularly in children (see Ear infections page 324). It is usually spread from the nose or throat through the Eustachian tube. When the Eustachian tube becomes blocked, infection can also occur. There may be intense pain, and often fever associated with middle ear infection. When the pressure builds within the middle ear, the eardrum may perforate to allow the discharge to be released. This can lead to external ear infection and temporary or longer-term deafness. Other problems include:

- *Glue ear which is a persistent inflammation of the middle ear which usually affects children (see page 324).*
- *Cholesteatoma which is an overgrowth of skin in the middle ear which becomes infected. As it expands, it destroys the architecture of the ear. If left untreated, it can cause deafness and may invade the inner ear.*

Inner ear infections are usually caused by viruses. Other causes of inner ear infections include:

- *Osteomyelitis, an infection of the bony capsule surrounding the inner ear. Organisms penetrate into the inner ear, often caused by inadequately treated middle ear infections.*
- *Viral infection of the inner ear, usually from a cold or flu.*
- *Mumps may also cause infection of the ear (see page 320).*

Orthodox treatment

Analgesics such as aspirin and paracetamol will be given to relieve pain, and when there is bacterial infection in the middle or outer ear, antibiotics will be appropriate.

Viral infections will usually clear in a few days but antihistamine drugs may be given. If a discharge is present in the outer ear, it may need to be sucked out.

When there is "effusion" in the middle ear, causing it to swell and bulge outward, an operation to make a small hole in the eardrum may be necessary to drain the fluid. Grommets (small tubes) are inserted to do this.

External infection may be treated by antifungal or antibacterial drops. For cholesteatoma surgery will be required.

ALTERNATIVE TREATMENT

Homeopathy

Depending on the cause of the infection, there are various homeopathic remedies which may be used by practitioners. Earache is a common symptom of ear infections and the following remedies may be prescribed to treat it:

- Hepar sulph. for earache with sharp pain.
- Belladonna for throbbing earache with redness.

Aromatherapy

Ear infections may be eased by massaging a blend of anti-infectious essential oils below the ear and along the neck. One drop of German camomile oil wiped carefully around the ear will help cool the area and aim at reducing the infection.

Western herbalism

External and internal treatments can reduce inflammation and fight infection. Where the conditions are recurrent a longer-term program of treatment can reduce problems. Glue ear can be reduced in children.

Other therapies

A **naturopath** may suggest fasting and dietetics to reduce catarrhal congestion. Hydrotherapy, lymphatic function stimulus, salt packs for earache, and herbal/homeopathic medicine may be appropriate. **Acupressure** and **shiatsu** may be very useful. **Reflexology** will be aimed at the reflexes related to pituitary, pineal, adrenal, thymus, ear and spleen. **Massage** helps with the elimination of toxins, making the usual routes for the removal of toxins clearer, and so relieving the ears of this job. **Spiritual healing** can reduce inflammation. A **Chinese herbalist** will use antipyretics, anti-inflammatory agents and aromatic stimulants. **Ayurvedic medicine** offers *panchakarma*. **Crystal and gemstone therapists** will select an appropriate crystal to stimulate the body's self-healing mechanism to be worn until the infection subsides. **Color therapists** may recommend wearing deep blues and indigo around the head area but they will also recommend taking antibiotics as well for a bacterial infection. **Auricular therapy** will help greatly in controlling any pain or earache and will treat the specific point on the ear related to the condition.

Ear Wax

What is it?

Ear wax is produced by glands in the outer ear canal to protect the eardrum, preventing the skin from drying and dust and other objects entering. Wax is naturally disposed of from the ear.

Causes

Excessive wax can obstruct the ear canal and cause a blockage, generating a sensation of fullness in the ear and sometimes affecting hearing. Also, as ear wax absorbs water, the blockage can be made worse following swimming or bathing. Cleaning the ear constantly can lead to a build-up of wax. If the blockage is not cleared, inflammation of the ear canal may occur and cause irritation or partial deafness.

Orthodox treatment

For minor ear wax problems, softening the wax with warmed olive oil or almond oil may help. Excess or hardened ear wax can be syringed out by the doctor. Other ways of removing wax are by instruments, or by suction. A warm oil may be syringed into the ear to soften the wax, which then may disperse naturally.

Alternative Treatment

Homeopathy

Remedies which may be of help include:

- Hepar sulph. for earache accompanied by sharp pain.
- Belladonna for throbbing earache with redness.

Aromatherapy

A drop of warm German camomile oil in five drops of olive oil, into the ear, will help to dissolve the wax.

Other therapies

A **naturopath** may suggest that wax is associated with a tendency to catarrh and will treat accordingly. **Acupressure** and **shiatsu** may be useful. A **nutritional therapist** may suggest that excessive ear wax is due to an essential fatty acid deficiency. A **macrobiotic** practitioner may suggest warm, strained sesame or olive oil in the ear. A **Western herbalist** may syringe the ears if the wax is excessive and also look internally to prevent build-up.

Tinnitus

What is it?

Tinnitus is a constant, unpleasant sound in one or both ears that is not caused by any external noise. The sound is usually a ringing noise, but it may also be a buzzing, whistling, hissing or roaring sound. Persistent tinnitus is usually associated with hearing loss, either partial or complete. Occasionally tinnitus is temporary.

Causes

The cause of tinnitus is usually damage to the ear, an ear disorder or a symptom of another condition. Minor causes of tinnitus include colds (see page 174) and flu (see page 175), excessive ear wax or ear infections, while more serious causes include brain or head injuries, heart disease, Ménière's disease or, rarely, anemia. Excessive exposure to noise can also bring on tinnitus.

Orthodox treatment

Treatment depends on the cause of the tinnitus. There are some drugs, including local anesthetics, which can help and a drug (carbamezepine) has been very useful. Persistent tinnitus, which cannot be treated, can be alleviated by providing alternative noise, such as a radio, to mask the symptoms and give the sufferer something else to listen to.

Alternative Treatment

Homeopathy

There are a number of remedies which may be useful but these will depend on the cause. Putting two drops of almond oil in each ear once a week may help mild tinnitus.

Auricular therapy

With regular treatment, this therapy can relieve the problem. However, in some cases tinnitus has recurred once treatment has stopped.

Other therapies

Autogenic training, depending on the cause, may be useful and will help the attitude of the sufferer in coping with the symptoms. A **kinesiologist** will look for cranial faults and correct neck lesions and offer specific exercises for balancing. **Reflexology** will be aimed at the reflexes related to the ear/eye, neck, shoulder and adrenal glands. A **chiropractor** may suggest that tinnitus is associated with problems in the neck and the sufferer may benefit from treatment to that area.

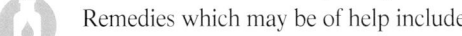

Periodontal Disease

What is it?

Periodontal disease includes any disorder of the tissues surrounding and supporting the teeth including the gums, the periodontal membrane (which holds the teeth in their sockets) and the sockets themselves. Periodontal disease includes inflammation of the gums (*gingivitis*) and the periodontal membrane (*periodontitis*). There can be abscesses on the gums, often called gum boils, resulting from tooth decay and infection. The gums become swollen and red, and in the area of the abscess, there is a pocket of pus, which may burst and leak into the gums around the teeth.

Symptoms of periodontal disease include pain on chewing, bleeding gums, swelling, redness, halitosis, and occasionally earache from referred pain. In chronic periodontal disease there may be damage to the base of the teeth, and the periodontal tissues become inflamed and detached from the teeth. The bacteria also erodes the bones surrounding the teeth.

Causes

Periodontal disease is usually the result of inadequate brushing, which can cause plaque to form, leading to dental caries, damage to the tooth enamel and eventually the loss of the tooth or teeth. Chronic periodontitis is the result of untreated gingivitis.

Gingivitis is sometimes due to infection, but mainly is the result of a build-up of plaque, food particles and bacteria around and under the gums. The gums swell around them, fostering bacterial infection.

Gingivitis is common in pregnant women, when the gums become inflamed and may bleed easily. Gum boils are often caused by poor oral hygiene, but may occasionally be caused by injury to the area.

BRUSHING SHOULD NEVER BE PAINFUL. SEE YOUR DENTIST REGULARLY TO ENSURE HEALTHY TEETH AND GUMS.

In chronic periodontitis, the gums recede to expose the dentine at the roots of the teeth. Dentine, a layer underneath the outer tooth enamel, is very sensitive, and there can be enormous pain when it comes in contact with hot, cold, sweet or sour foods.

Orthodox treatment

Prevention is always better than the cure. Regularly brushing and flossing, and cutting down on sweet and acidic drinks and snacks, may be all that is required for healthy teeth and gums, backed up by regular check-ups and visits to the dental hygienist. However, if disease is present, treatment is essential.

Periodontitis is treated by draining the pus, and then filling the tooth, or by removing the tooth altogether. Root canal work may be necessary when there are dental cysts. It may be necessary to remove the lining from the pocket of the tooth so that the healthy tissue beneath can become attached to the tooth. Gingivitis may be treated by using an antibacterial mouthwash, improved oral hygiene and regular visits to the dentist. For chronic gingivitis the gums may have to be surgically trimmed.

Alternative Treatment

Western herbalism

You will be recommended to have any decaying teeth filled by a dentist. Dietary changes may be advised to promote general health and reduce sugar intake. Tinctures of marigold, myrrh and wild indigo may be prescribed to use as mouth disinfectants and to strengthen gums.

Nutritional therapy

Apart from a visit to a dental hygienist followed by daily brushing and flossing, a healthy diet will promote healthy gums. Vitamin C is important for the production of collagen. Most tissues in the body are made from this. Co enzyme Q10 supplements have been found beneficial in some cases of gum disease.

Homeopathy

Periodontal pain can be relieved by homeopathic treatment. Remedies which may be prescribed to treat gingivitis include:

- Mercurius for bleeding gums with bad breath.
- Natrum mur. for swollen, bleeding gums with ulcers.

Remedies which may be prescribed for toothache include:

- Coffea for toothache with severe shooting pain.
- Chamomilla for toothache with unbearable pain.
- Belladonna for toothache with throbbing pain.

For discomfort after dental treatment, remedies may include:

- Arnica for treating the immediate discomfort.
- Hypericum for persistent pain.

Other therapies

Aromatherapists may recommend using camomile for its calming properties. It should be diluted and then rubbed gently onto the cheeks. An aromatherapy mouthwash made with cinnamon, lemon and lavender may also help. A **Chinese herbalist** will use antipyretics, herbal detoxicants and aromatic stimulants. **Color therapists** may choose yellow to calm the nerve in the tooth cavity if it is causing toothache. **Naturopathic** treatment may consist of nutritional and dietetic support, applied nutrition treatment, herbal medicine (local and systemic). **Acupressure** and **shiatsu** may both be found extremely useful.

Bad Breath (Halitosis)

What is it?

Bad breath, or halitosis, is a symptom of various disorders, ranging from the mild and temporary to the more severe. Often bad breath goes undetected by the sufferer until somebody mentions it to them.

Causes

Bad breath can be caused by various conditions. At its least harmful it is the result of eating certain foods with strong flavors, such as curries, garlic and onions, or drinking alcohol. Food particles which decay in the mouth, possibly because they are trapped in the teeth, can cause temporary bad breath. Smokers may suffer also from bad breath.

Other causes of bad breath include:

- *Tooth decay is a common cause of bad breath, caused by rotting teeth and dental cavities.*
- *Periodontal disease (severe gum disease) (see page 278) may cause pus to form on the gums, causing bad breath.*
- *Tonsillitis (see page 283) When the tonsils become inflamed due to infection there is often accompanying bad breath.*
- *Oral thrush (see page 281) This infection caused by the* Candida albicans *fungus manifests itself with sore, cream-colored raised patches in the mouth. It can also cause bad breath.*
- *Diabetes (see page 200) is accompanied by bad breath and can indicate hypoglycemia or ketosis.*
- *Acute bronchitis (see page 177) – the coughing brings up foul-smelling phlegm.*
- *Liver problems Chronic inflammation of the liver (cirrhosis) (see page 250) can cause bad breath, as can hepatitis.*
- *Cancer of the throat, larynx, tongue, mouth, lungs, esophagus or, rarely, stomach cancer have bad breath as a symptom.*
- *Sinusitis (see page 285) infected sinuses cause an unpleasant-smelling discharge to drip into the back of the throat.*
- *Inflammation of the stomach (chronic gastritis) causes a bad taste in the mouth and sour-smelling breath.*
- *Under-production of saliva can cause bad breath. This explains why breath is often unpleasant first thing in the morning when the mouth is dry.*
- *Constipation (see page 243) As waste matter is not leaving the body it can cause gases to produce foul-smelling breath.*

Orthodox treatment

Treatment of bad breath is according to its cause. Very often improving oral hygiene and rectifying any dental problems will overcome problems of bad breath. Visiting the dentist and dental hygienist regularly will help keep the mouth in order. Brushing the teeth and flossing regularly after meals will get rid of food trapped in the mouth and between the teeth.

Antiseptic mouthwashes and antibiotic lozenges provide only temporary relief from bad breath and using them may upset the natural bacteria (flora) in the body, causing oral thrush.

If any other cause is responsible for the bad breath, this must first be identified and then followed up with appropriate treatment before the symptom can disappear.

Alternative Treatment

Western herbalism

Bad breath is often linked to sinus infection, mild chronic tonsillitis or digestive dysfunction, all of which can be treated by a Western herbalist. Occasional bad breath caused by eating strongly flavored foods or drinking alcohol can be masked or neutralized by chewing parsley or masked by drinking peppermint tea.

Nutritional therapy

Bad breath may be due to poor dental hygiene, but also to constipation. If the bowels do not move regularly, bowel toxins can accumulate and be absorbed into the bloodstream. When they reach the lungs, malodorous molecules may emerge through the breath.

Kinesiology

This treatment will involve checking kidney and digestive energy function, checking the ileo-caecal valve, checking the atlas and scrum for lesions, checking for food sensitivities, checking grain consumption, avoiding roughage, and adding vitamins B, C, betaine hydrochloride, food enzymes and capsicum to the diet. Water consumption, nutritional hygiene, personal hygiene, bowel cleansing and toilet habits counseling will be accompanied by balancing.

Homeopathy

Specific remedies may be useful, according to symptoms. Mercurius will be advised for bad breath associated with tooth decay, gingivitis and tonsillitis.

Other therapies

A **naturopath** will direct attention to catarrhal or gastrointestinal causes such as constipation or sinus problems. **Acupressure** and **shiatsu** may be useful for treating the underlying cause. An **aromatherapist** will prescribe an antiseptic mouthwash. **Autogenic training** can prevent persistent mouth ulcers and speed up their healing. A **Chinese herbalist** will use antipyretics, digestives and evacuants. A **macrobiotic** practitioner may suggest a standard macrobiotic diet to make stomach energy less efficient, cutting out sugar and adding kudzu tea.

COLD SORES

What are they?

A cold sore is a blister which appears on the face, usually around the lips and nose and often in clusters. The raised blister is filled with a pale yellow fluid which crusts over when the blister bursts. The sore is itchy and painful.

Causes

Cold sores are not harmful but they are unsightly and highly contagious. They are caused by the *herpes simplex* virus type 1. They are passed on from someone else who has the virus and are often contracted by kissing. Many succeed in developing a natural immunity to the virus, but for those who do not, the virus remains in the body, lying dormant in the nerve cells until it is triggered off by illness, stress or being run-down. Weather, such as strong sunlight and cold winds can also reactivate the virus.

Orthodox treatment

Cold sores usually disappear after a week, with or without treatment. However, an outbreak can be shortened by using an antiviral cream (acyclovir) as soon as the first warning signs of tingling appear. Avoid getting stressed or run down, if possible, as this can bring on an attack.

ALTERNATIVE TREATMENT

Naturopathy

Naturopaths will recommend vitamins A, B3, B5 and B complex and vitamin C. The amino acid Lysine may also be given. The astringent properties of lemon juice, mixed with water and applied to the sore, may help dry it out.

Nutritional therapy

Herpes-simplex infections are often recurrent, particularly when the immune system is impaired. Vitamin A, E and zinc supplements are all helpful in this condition. Vitamin E oil may be applied topically. Garlic oil may also help.

Other therapies

A **homeopath** may suggest natrum mur. if the cold sores are brought on by infection, emotional stress or grief. An **aromatherapist** may suggest dabbing a drop of essential oil of tea tree or bergamot on the cold sore. A **Chinese herbalist** may give heat-clearing herbs, anti-inflammatories and detoxifying herbs.

MOUTH ULCERS

What are they?

Mouth ulcers are open sores of round and shallow white, grey or yellow spots with an inflamed red edge, that occur anywhere on the lining of the mouth, including the cheeks and the inside of the lips. The ulcers sting and may making eating difficult.

Causes

Mouth ulcers are common and often appear for no reason. Some women get mouth ulcers around their menstrual cycle and they are common in those with compromised immune systems. Stress, being run down, aggressive tooth brushing or ill-fitting dentures can all cause ulcers. Ulcers are also symptoms of other conditions such as ulcerative colitis, gingivitis, anemia, allergies and coeliac disease. In rare cases, they may be a symptom of mouth cancer.

Orthodox treatment

Treatment will depend on the underlying cause. Hydrocortisone ointments or washes can be swilled around the mouth and may help avoid infection. In rare cases where they are caused by bacteria, antibiotic treatment may be appropriate.

ALTERNATIVE TREATMENT

Western herbalism

A tincture of myrrh applied to the ulcers should clear them in 48 hours. As mouth ulcers are often a sign of lowered immunity, dietary advice or tonics will be advised.

Other therapies

A **homeopath** may recommend arsenicum for mouth ulcers that cause a burning sensation. **Nutritional therapists** believe food intolerance may be linked with mouth ulcers, with citrus fruit being a common offender. **Naturopathic** treatment will be through nutrition and dietetics, applied nutrition, herbal mouthwashes and immune support; vitamin supplements of C, E and B2, together with with zinc, may be advised. A **kinesiologist** may suggest vitamin E. A **macrobiotic** practitioner may recommend making the condition more alkaline, or yang, as well as a mouthwash with salty bunchakea.

Oral Thrush

What is it?

Oral thrush is a fungal infection which appears as raised, creamy spots on the mucus membranes lining the mouth, lips and throat. When rubbed, the spots are sore and red underneath.

Causes

Thrush is an infection, caused by the fungus *Candida albicans*, which flourishes in the moist, warm areas of the body. The fungus is naturally present in the mucous membranes of the mouth, as well as in the skin, the intestinal tract and the vagina. Its role is to maintain a balance of flora in the body but, when there is an excessive growth of fungus, it can cause symptoms.

In cases of serious immune deficiency, such as AIDS, thrush can spread to the lungs, where it can be life-threatening.

The long-term use of antibiotics, anticancer drugs or steroids may cause the flora to be destroyed. Oral thrush is common in children, who have immature immune systems, and in adults whose immune systems are impaired by illness or immune-suppressing drugs.

Orthodox treatment

Oral thrush should receive medical attention as the longer the thrush is able to overgrow, the harder it is to eradicate. Oral thrush is usually treated by antifungal drugs, such as clotrimazole or nystatin, taken orally and swilled round the mouth. If oral thrush is an indication of thrush in other areas of the body, these areas will also be treated. Vaginal thrush, for example, is usually treated with antifungal pessaries and/or cream (clotrimazole), once only available on prescription but now available over the counter. One treatment usually clears the condition. When it has been transmitted sexually, both partners may be treated to try to prevent further cross infection. Oral sex should be avoided until the condition clears.

If oral thrush occurs in breastfeeding babies, it is sometimes necessary to treat the mother as well.

Diabetics who contract thrush should always see their doctor for treatment and should also maintain strict control over their blood sugar levels.

Oral thrush usually responds well to treatment. However, thrush in other areas of the body may be harder to control. See a doctor for advice.

Alternative Treatment

Aromatherapy

Tea tree oil with oil of myrrh diluted in water and sluiced around the mouth three times a day can be effective. A gargle of lavender, melissa and thyme may help.

Naturopathy

Oral thrush responds well to treatment and various herbal mouthwashes may be advised. A naturopath may aim to prevent a more widespread fungal attack in the body by suggesting nutrition and dietetics, applied nutrition and immune support. Sufferers may be advised to avoid sugars and refined starches, alcohol, tea and coffee and increase their intake of fruits, vegetables, pulses (beans and lentils) and whole grains. Garlic and acidophilus supplements may also be recommended.

Kinesiology

A kinesiologist might suggest an anticandidal diet, a tea-tree oil gargle and mouthwash, and aim treatment at the endocrine and immune systems, among other things. Support for systems will be offered, as well as balancing.

Western herbalism

There are many useful antifungal remedies for mouthwashes and gargles. Tinctures of myrrh or marigold are recommended as mouthwashes. Oral thrush may be a sign of general fungal problems or of lowered immunity, so systemic treatment is often useful. As antibiotics are thought to upset the balance of microorganisms in the gut and allow the *Candida albicans* to thrive, three or four garlic capsules should be taken daily after a course of antibiotics for seven days. If the thrush does not clear or if it recurs shortly afterward, patients will be recommended to see an orthodox doctor as the underlying cause could be more serious.

Nutritional therapy

Oral thrush is a sign that the immune system is underfunctioning. There are a number of treatments that may be recommended to boost it. In addition, a nutritional therapist may also prescribe natural antifungal substances that can be used as a mouthwash.

Others

Acupressure and **shiatsu** may be useful. Regular **crystal and gemstone therapy** may help strengthen the immune system and encourage more rapid self-healing. An appropriate crystal can be worn during the day or held during daily visualization exercises. **Homeopaths** may recommend constitutional treatment aimed at boosting overall well being and enhancing the immune system. Depending on the diagnosis, various homeopathic remedies may be used to treat oral thrush with good results.

DENTAL PAIN AND PHOBIA

What is it?

A phobia is an intense, irrational fear which gives the sufferer an overwhelming desire to avoid the cause of their fear. The symptoms may cause a raised heartbeat, sweating and a very strong desire to flee from the cause at any cost.

Many people dislike visiting the dentist, associating it with pain, extreme discomfort and facial disfigurement through tooth loss. Until this century, a fear of the dentist was a fear probably well founded as, until anesthetics came into general use, teeth would be extracted, drilled and filled without the benefit of any pain relief. However, dental technology and medical knowledge has improved greatly in the past 20 years and today it is possible for many treatments to be carried out with little or no pain. Despite these developments, some people remain extremely afraid of the dentist, so much so that they develop a phobia about going.

Dental phobias are not at all uncommon, affecting both children and adults alike. Today, however, there are a number of methods of pain relief, both orthodox and alternative, and follow-up treatment which will ease any post-dental discomfort.

Orthodox treatment

Many dentists, now they are allowed to advertise, make a feature of emphasizing how caring they are of those who suffer great distress at the thought of a dental visit. For dental treatment, local anesthetics and gas and air may be used to prevent discomfort. Teeth may be extracted under general anesthetic, especially wisdom teeth.

The drills used to removed decayed parts of the teeth are now much more sophisticated and make much less noise – a feature many patients previously found upsetting. In addition, the wide range of cosmetic techniques available also make disfigurement a thing of the past; in fact, many people elect to have cosmetic dentistry to improve badly positioned teeth and enhance their smile.

For those with dental phobia, a doctor or dentist may suggest behavioral therapy or psychotherapy. It may take a while to overcome the fear, so interim treatment may be with drugs to calm the patient prior to visiting the dentist and afterwards if trauma has been experienced.

Ask your doctor to recommend a dentist who specializes in treating patients with a fear of the dentist.

ALTERNATIVE TREATMENT

Autogenic training

Pain can be reduced by relaxation and attitude. Phobias can be addressed because autogenic training generally reduces anxiety. Special formulas can be used in the exercise to help relaxation during treatment. Some exercises can be used in the dental chair, which increase tolerance to the treatment.

Auricular therapy

Rubbing specific points on the ear with a matchstick can relieve pain temporarily.

Kinesiology

Specific techniques will be applied to relieve any specific pain and phobias. Regular balancing will also be undertaken.

Bach flower remedies

The rescue remedy may be very useful for general fear. If the fear can be accurately identified, any of the following remedies can prove useful: for fear rock rose, mumulus, cherry plum, aspen or red chestnut; for uncertainty cerato, scleranthus, gentian, gorse or hornbeam; for oversensitivity agrimony, centaury or walnut may well help alleviate the feelings.

Homeopathy

Homeopaths may recommend arnica for treating the immediate discomfort and hypericum for treating persistent pain.

Other therapies

Hellerwork *may help with relaxation, including nitre-oral treatment to reduce the accumulated tensions.* **Acupressure** *and* **shiatsu** *may be very useful for pain.* **Reflexology** *will be aimed at the reflexes related to the teeth, and the solar plexus, to calm.* **Spiritual healing** *will help to calm and soothe, and at the same time bring to the surface the real cause of the fear so that it can be dealt with and overcome. A* **Chinese herbalist** *may offer herbal aromatic stimulants and also herbal anodynes.* **Hypnotherapy** *may prove to be helpful.*

TONSILLITIS

What is it?

Tonsillitis is the inflammation of the tonsils located at the back of the throat, which causes them to swell and become red. They may be covered in white or yellow spots of pus. There may also be acute swelling of the lymph nodes in the neck, which can make the entire neck area very tender.

Symptoms include a sore throat, pain when swallowing, headache, fever, a general feeling of malaise, earache, bad breath, pain in the ears and dry cough. In older children and adults with severe tonsillitis, abscesses may form under the tonsils, a condition known as quinsy. Tonsillitis is common in childhood, although it can occur at any age.

THERE ARE A NUMBER OF COMPLICATIONS WHICH CAN RESULT FROM TONSILLITIS, INCLUDING INNER EAR INFECTIONS, RHEUMATIC FEVER AND SEPTICEMIA (A BLOOD INFECTION), BUT THESE ARE RARE.

Most cases of tonsillitis are not actually dangerous. However, in severe cases of bacterial infection (strep throat), the sufferer can actually feel extremely ill.

Causes

Tonsillitis is usually caused by either a viral and bacterial infection, usually the streptococcal bacteria, hence the term "strep" throat. The tonsils' function is to protect the body from infection, but when they become overworked or when the sufferer is run down, they can become infected with the organisms they should be protecting the body against. Rarely, complications may develop such as kidney inflammation or rheumatic fever.

Orthodox treatment

Diagnosis is partly on the basis of the appearance of the tonsils. A throat swab may be taken to identify the exact cause. Analgesic drugs such as aspirin or paracetamol will be given to reduce the fever and pain, and there are several preparations which act as a local anesthetic to the tonsils, so that eating and drinking is possible. Penicillin antibiotics are usually prescribed to treat bacterial tonsillitis.

Chronic tonsillitis may require a tonsillectomy (an operation to remove them) if they no longer fulfill their function of protecting the body. For quinsy, antibiotic injections will be given and a surgical incision to drain the abscess may be necessary.

ALTERNATIVE TREATMENT

Homeopathy

Depending on symptoms, specific remedies will be given for tonsillitis. A homeopath will also recommend resting in bed for several days and taking iron, vitamins C and B complex and zinc. Remedies may include:

- Belladonna for tonsillitis where the throat is very sore and with burning pain that shoots into the head.
- Hepar sulph. for tonsillitis with a stabbing pain in the throat that feels as if a fish bone is stuck in it. Bad breath may accompany hoarseness or voice loss.
- Mercurius for tonsillitis that is accompanied by bad breath and where the throat is dark red, sore and swollen and there is pain on swallowing.

Naturopathy

Treatment may consist of fasting and dietetics, hydrotherapy (including throat and trunk packs), herbal and homeopathic remedies for drainage and gargling, applied nutrition and osteopathy for lymphatic drainage.

Nutritional therapy

Healthy eating, with a good intake of vitamin C, zinc and other nutrients is needed for a healthy immune system, and this can help to prevent recurrent tonsillitis. Once it has started, vitamin C supplements can help to shorten its duration, and the recovery time.

Western herbalism

If there are recurrent bouts of tonsillitis, herbalists believe that they are a key factor contributing to illness in later life. Treatment will therefore be aimed at boosting the immune system as well as relieving the symptoms. Throat gargles of myrrh, sage, thyme or wild indigo may be recommended to reduce inflammation and extra vitamin C will be advised to help improve the immune system.

Reflexology

Treatment will be overall and also specifically aimed at the reflexes related to the neck, lymph, adrenal glands and also the solar plexus.

Other therapies

Acupressure and **shiatsu** may be very useful in relieving symptoms. **Massage** with anti-infectious essential oils may help. **Kinesiology** offers a well-rounded treatment aimed at all parts of the body. A **Chinese herbalist** will use antipyretics, anti-inflammatory agents and detoxifying herbs. In **Ayurvedic medicine** a practitioner will provide a course of antibacterial and antiviral therapy. **Crystal and gemstone therapy** will aim to stimulate the immune system generally and a therapist will also select an appropriate crystal to be worn near the neck in order to help reduce symptoms. **Aromatherapists** may use tea tree oil, massaged onto the throat and neck area.

LARYNGITIS

What is it?

Laryngitis is the inflammation of the voice box (larynx). Although speech is produced by air getting between the vocal cords, an important role of the larynx is to prevent choking. Laryngitis often occurs as a symptom of a cold or a sinus or chest infection. There is often hoarseness, pain, dry coughing, a sore throat and an inability to speak above a whisper. Sometimes there may also be a fever and general feeling of being unwell. Chronic laryngitis may be the result of smoking or using the voice incorrectly.

Causes

Acute laryngitis appears quite suddenly but usually lasts only for a few days. It is usually the result of either a viral infection, such as the common cold (see page 174), flu (see page 175), or an allergy to inhaled pollen or some other substance. If a serious cough is present it may irritate the voice box and cause it to become inflamed.

Chronic laryngitis appears more slowly and lasts for a much longer time. It may be caused by excessive coughing, irritation caused by smoking or overuse of the voice. On rare occasions it may be caused by breathing in toxic fumes.

With laryngitis the larynx and vocal cords become inflamed, swollen and sore, distorting the vocal apparatus and resulting in a characteristic hoarse or croaking voice.

IF HOARSENESS LASTS FOR MORE THAN TWO WEEKS, SEEK MEDICAL ATTENTION TO EXCLUDE THE POSSIBILITY OF CANCER OF THE LARYNX.

Orthodox treatment

People with acute laryngitis should rest their voices as much as possible and avoid smoking or drinking alcohol. A humidifier or vaporizer will help moisten the air for those who suffer from dryness. Menthol chest rubs applied at night may make breathing easier. Painkillers such as aspirin and paracetamol will help an inflamed throat and reduce any fever or discomfort. Most attacks will pass after three or four days.

Chronic attacks may need investigation. A laryngoscopy may be carried out to investigate the larynx. If polyps (benign nodules) are found they will be removed. If necessary, a sample of the tissue may be taken for analysis to rule out cancer. Cancer of the larynx, which accounts for approximately two percent of all cancers, can be cured when treated in its early stages.

ALTERNATIVE TREATMENT

Acupressure

Acupressure may help relieve symptoms. The points are on the thumb and between the base of the thumb and the first finger.

Homeopathy

Chronic laryngitis should be treated constitutionally. In acute cases, where there is infection, one of the following remedies might be useful:

- Aconite for laryngitis with a high fever.
- Phos. for laryngitis with a dry, tickly cough.
- Causticum for laryngitis which features a dry, raw throat and violent coughing.
- Argent nit. for laryngitis which involves loss of the voice caused by too much singing or shouting.

Naturopathy

Treatment may consist of fasting and dietetics, hydrotherapy (including throat and trunk packs), herbal and homeopathic remedies for drainage and gargling, applied nutrition and osteopathy for lymphatic drainage.

Western herbalism

As well as treating the immediate problem, both internally, and perhaps with gargles, herbalism looks at the background causes of stress and exhaustion and will seek to address those if they are contributing to the laryngitis. Throat gargles of marigold, myrrh, raspberry leaf, sage or thyme may all help and are most effective in tincture form. To help fight infection, echinacea or wild indigo may be advised, together with extra vitamin C. To boost resistance to infection, garlic tablets may be recommended.

Reflexology

Reflexology treatment will be aimed at the reflexes related to the throat, neck, endocrine glands, shoulder, solar plexus and lymph gland areas.

Other therapies

Shiatsu may be very useful in relieving the symptoms of laryngitis. The **Alexander Technique** can help the sufferer to avoid unnecessary strain on the vocal cords. **Kinesiology** can be very useful, addressing nutrition and providing support for both the endocrine and immune systems. A **Chinese herbalist** will use herbal antipyretics, anti-inflammatory agents and detoxifying herbs. Blue will be advised by a **color therapist** as it is "cooling" and helps to calm down any inflammation. **Aromatherapists** will recommend using tea tree gargles to relieve any soreness in the throat. **Crystal and gemstone therapists** will select an appropriate crystal, to be worn near the throat or held during daily visualization exercises.

SINUS PROBLEMS

What are they?

The sinuses are air-filled cavities lined with mucous membrane and located within the bone of the face. Mucus flows though the tiny air ducts from the spaces to the nose. The most common problem affecting sinuses is sinusitis, the inflammation of the lining of the sinuses. This inflammation can be caused by various conditions (see below).

When inflammation occurs, the lining swells and this may cause the channel that drains them to become blocked. The mucus discharge cannot escape, and this causes a build-up, leading to pressure in the sinuses which can feel quite painful. In severe cases of sinusitis, there is may be fever, blurred vision or swelling of the face.

Congested sinuses can cause a variety of symptoms. Typically there is nasal congestion with a greenish-yellow discharge, or in the case of allergy or hay fever, a very runny nose and streaming, puffy eyes. Often there is a loss of the sense of smell and a headache. A sensation of pressure in and around the head may be present and there may be pain around the eyes. Sometimes there may be a complete nasal blockage which prevents drainage of the nasal passage.

CONSULT A DOCTOR IF SINUS SYMPTOMS ARE PAINFUL AND PERSISTENT AND DO NOT RESPOND TO SELF-TREATMENT.

Causes

Sinusitis is almost always a secondary infection, usually due to a bacterial infection that develops as a complication of a viral infection, for example with the common cold (see page 174). Other typical secondary infections occur due to:

- *Hay fever.*
- *Allergy.*
- *Abscess infection of an upper tooth.*
- *Nasal polyps.*
- *Upper respiratory infection.*

Orthodox treatment

Most cases of sinusitis last little more than a week and over-the-counter medicines such as decongestant nasal sprays, aspirin or paracetamol are all that is required to ease symptoms. Other self-treatment includes using vaporizers or steam inhalation to help thin the nasal secretions so that they drain more easily. Menthol can be added to the water. Antihistamines can be used for hay fever or allergy. In the case of bacterial infections, treatment is almost always with antibiotics. Occasionally it is necessary to wash out the sinuses, where there is a build-up which refuses to drain. This may be done under general or local anesthetic. It may be necessary to X-ray the sinuses to determine what is causing the blockage.

ALTERNATIVE TREATMENT

Homeopathy

Recurrent sinusitis requires constitutional treatment. Attacks can also be treated homeopathically, and one of the following remedies may be suitable, depending on symptoms:

- Kali bichrom. for sinusitis with stringy, stretchy mucus that is greenish-yellow in color.
- Pulsatilla for sinusitis accompanied by weepiness and where there is pain above the eyes or on the cheekbone.
- Hepar sulph. for sinusitis with facial tenderness.

Nutritional therapy

Nutritional therapists find that the great majority of sinusitis cases are caused by food allergy. Allergies are best identified by consulting a nutritional therapist. who will then devise a balanced diet excluding allergy-inducing foods.

Western herbalism

Treatment will be aimed at reducing mucus, fighting infection and draining the sinuses. Inhalations with essential oils, such as eucalyptus, peppermint, lavender, bergamot, cinnamon, camomile or lemon, can give great relief in the short term, alongside general treatment. Garlic is recommended as a preventative against sinus problems.

Naturopathy

Treatment will be based around a diet low in mucus-forming foods. Fasting and dietetic programs for detoxification will be offered, herbal support, garlic tablets for sinus problems and chronic catarrh, hydrotherapy for friction rubs for general skin elimination and immune boosting, and osteopathic treatment to promote lymphatic function and improve sinus drainage.

Other therapies

In **Ayurvedic medicine,** treatment will involve the elimination of *kapha* with nasya (inhalation of oils). The **Alexander Technique** induces efficient and smooth breathing, allowing the muscles of the face to relax and improving the condition of the sinus passages. **Auricular therapy** can be useful by strengthening the spleen and lungs to resolve phlegm. Steam inhalations of **aromatherapy** essential oils, like lavender, eucalyptus, tea tree and bergamot may be useful. **Reflexology** will be aimed at the reflexes related to the sinus, head, nose, neck, lymph glands, ileocoecal valve, adrenals and pituitary. A **Chinese herbalist** will use antipyretics, anti-inflammatory agents and aromatic stimulants. A **chiropractor** may perform massage over the sinuses in order to relieve pressure.

SKIN AND HAIR

What is it?

The skin, hair and nails make up the largest body organ. The skin has two layers: the epidermis, the outer layer and the dermis, the inner layer. The superficial cells of the epidermis are continually being rubbed off and replaced by newer cells from below. The epidermis contains no bloods vessels or lymphatic vessels (see Immune (Lymphatic) System (pages 256–265), and it obtains nutrients by absorption from the lower dermis.

The dermis is a thicker layer made up of blood vessels, lymphatics, sweat glands, hair follicles, sebaceous glands and nerve endings. It contains connective tissue with tough elastic fibers that give skin its strength and elasticity. With age this is lost and the skin becomes looser and wrinkled. Hairs grow from the hair papilla cells in the dermis. Sebaceous glands protect both the hair and skin with a waterproof layer of sebum.

The skin has five main functions: to control temperature, to protect the body, to feel sensations and warn against harmful stimuli, to absorb substances (such as ultraviolet light, which is converted into vitamin D) and storage. On a hot day, temperature is controlled by sweating and dilatation of blood vessels in the skin to lose heat. In cold weather the hair follicles stand on end, trapping air to warm the body. The skin also protects the body from injury and acts as a barrier to viruses and bacteria.

What can go wrong?

Dermatitis and *eczema* which make the skin dry, inflamed and itchy are common problems. They are often caused by allergies to washing powder, metals (especially nickel) and perfumes. They can occur with asthma and hay fever. Acute allergic conditions can cause an intensely itchy rash or "hives."

Psoriasis is a disease where the cell reproduction rate greatly accelerates. Red scaly patches or "plaques" occur which are often itchy. It can go into remission for several months. The skin also protects us from infection and when the defense mechanism breaks down *boils*, *spots*, *abscesses*, *impetigo* (bacterial) or *ringworm* (fungal) can appear. *Acne* often starts at puberty when a surge in sex hormones causes extra activity of the sebaceous glands. Blockage of the ducts and bacterial infection of the glands causes *acne*.

The skin and hair organ help to protect and insulate the body. Skin has two main layers: the epidermis and dermis. Hair follicles originate in the dermis and hair grows right through to the epidermis.

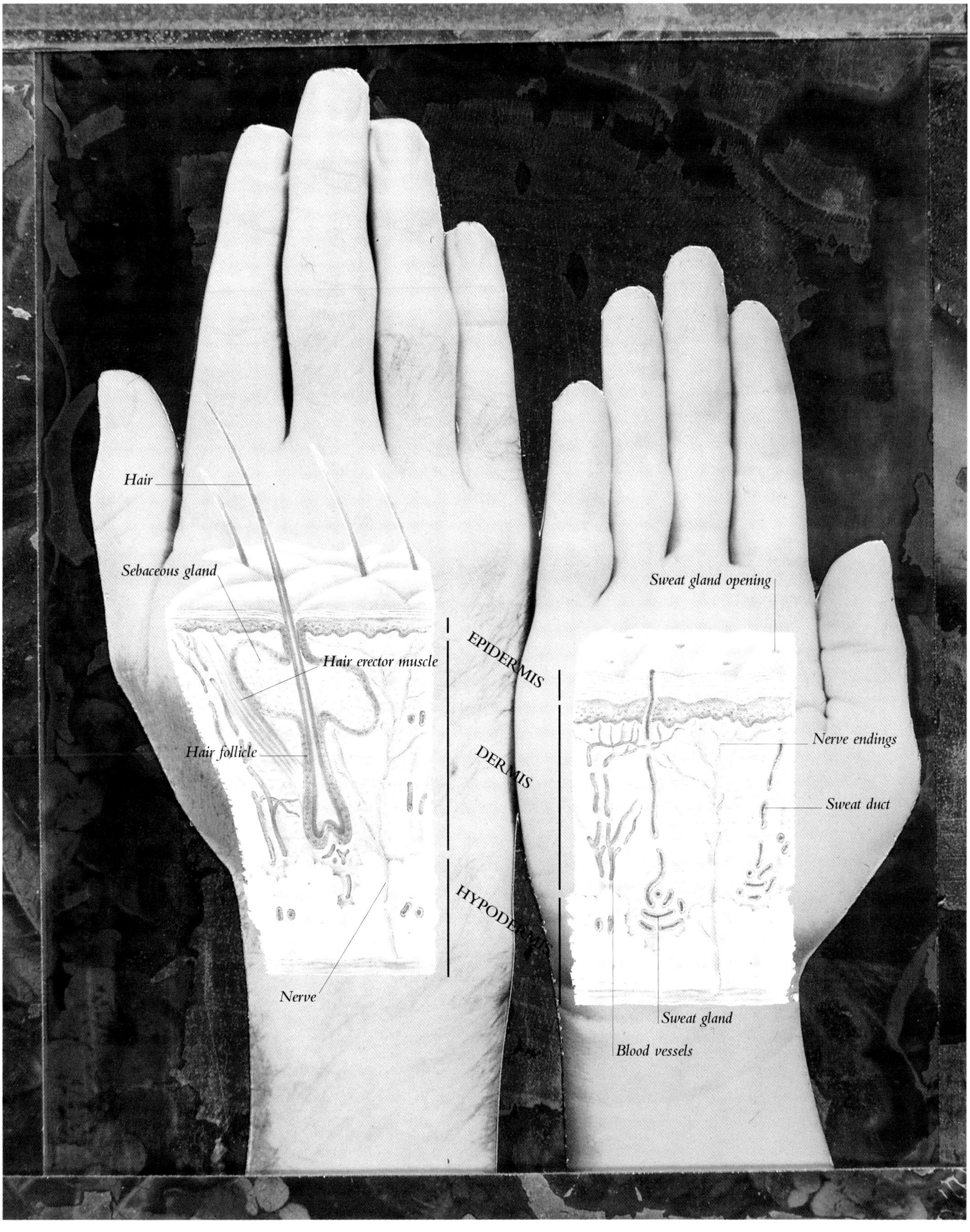
Hair
Sebaceous gland
Hair erector muscle
Hair follicle
Nerve
EPIDERMIS
DERMIS
HYPODERMIS
Sweat gland opening
Nerve endings
Sweat duct
Sweat gland
Blood vessels

ECZEMA

What is it?

Eczema is an inflammation of the skin, causing itching and often enormous discomfort. Eczema is not contagious but, like asthma (see page 178), it is often an hereditary condition and in recent years its incidence has increased and it is now a common complaint, affecting approximately one in 12 people. Eczema is extremely itchy and the subsequent persistent scratching can lead to infection, particularly in young children. It can be very painful, causing dry, red, flaking skin which, in more severe cases, is accompanied by blisters that burst open to form sores. Eczema is often referred to as dermatitis (see page 290). There are many forms of eczema but the most common are:

- **Contact eczema** *which occurs when an allergen comes into contact with the skin. This can be caused by anything from the metal used in jewelry to chemicals contained in cleaning products.*
- **Atopic eczema** *is a form of infantile eczema that occurs in those with an inherited tendency to asthma, eczema or hay fever (see page 179). There is often generalized dryness of the skin with dry, scaly or weepy patches appearing on the face and scalp between the ages of 2–18 months. In time, the rest of the body may be affected. Eventually, in older children, the rash tends to localize on the skin creases behind the knee or in the elbow. The rash is very itchy and often contracts secondary infection. Symptoms improve in childhood but 20 percent of children with eczema may get irritant hand eczema as adults. The skin can be aggravated by fabrics such as wool, heat and cold, sweating, feverish illness and infections.*
- **Pomphylox eczema** *commonly affects the hands and feet, particularly the areas of "emotional" sweating, such as the palms, sides of the fingers, toes and soles of the feet. At first small, itchy blisters form under the skin. The blisters may rupture and secondary infection is quite common. Attacks are more frequent in hot weather and stress may play a role by causing increased sweating on the palms and soles.*
- **Nummular eczema** *predominantly occurs in adults but the cause remains unknown. It forms circular, scaling patches on the skin which itch and look very similar to ringworm (see page 294).*
- **Varicose (stasis) eczema** *occurs in those who have severe varicose veins, often following a deep vein thrombosis many years previously. The lower leg above the ankle is often swollen with tense, shiny skin which can develop greasy scaling and pigmentation. After minor trauma, the area may break down and form a venous ulcer which can be extremely persistent. Although the rash is itchy, it simply reflects poor tissue circulation.*

Causes

The exact cause of atopic eczema is unclear and infantile eczema often improves spontaneously. Contributory factors include:

- *Genetic inheritance. There may be an inherited predisposition of eczema, asthma and hay fever.*
- *Dry skin. Approximately one-third of atopic children have this.*
- *Food intolerance may cause an eczema rash on the face. Sometimes an intolerance to foods such as milk or eggs may aggravate the condition.*
- *Nonspecific stimuli such as extremes of temperature, changes in humidity, sweating, wearing woolen clothing and dry skin may all make the condition worse.*
- *Feverish illness often brings on eczema.*
- *Bacterial infection particularly by the* staphylococcus aureus *bacterium is common. The organism sticks more readily to atopic skin and may cause impetigo (see page 292) or acute weeping outbreaks of eczema.*

Orthodox treatment

A doctor will try to determine the cause of the eczema and will prescribe and advise accordingly. Irritation and discomfort can be alleviated, preventing the scratching which can cause infection, but it will not cure the condition. Treatment may include:

- *Antihistamines, such as phenergan to help reduce itching.*
- *Steroid creams are often prescribed for active areas of eczema, with redness or scaling. A 1% hydrocortisone ointment is safe and effective, even when used on the face. Severe cases may require stronger steroid creams.*
- *Steroid/antibiotic creams supplemented with steroids by mouth will be prescribed if there is a bacterial infection present.*
- *Emollient creams reduce irritation caused by atopic eczema.*

There are several self-help measures which can be taken to avoid an outbreak of eczema. These include:

- *Avoiding soaps, detergents and bubble bath preparations.*
- *Wearing cotton clothing and using a nonbiological washing powder for clothes and bed linen.*
- *Avoiding irritant substances known to cause allergic reactions.*

ALTERNATIVE TREATMENT

Nutritional therapy

Nutritional therapists believe that eczema is a reaction to allergy and will recommend:

- Dietary changes that eliminate additives and refined and processed foods. Dairy products, citrus fruit, wheat and eggs may be excluded from the diet.
- Supplements of B-complex vitamins and vitamin C. For families with a history of eczema and allergic disorders, an approved and prescribed zinc supplement may be taken throughout pregnancy to help prevent the condition in the baby.
- Evening primrose oil rubbed into the affected areas will help reduce the itching and promote healing.

Aromatherapy

Aromatherapists may use a combination of roman camomile, as it is very calming to the skin and helps rid it of soreness and redness, and lavender, which encourages skin healing and helps reduce any burning sensations.

Therapists may also advise on diet and the use of soothing preparations such as creams and lotions. Any lotions containing lanolin should be avoided as this is often a cause of allergy.

Western herbalism

Treatment will be individual to the patient, addressing food intolerances, stress factors and any external environmental irritants. The following may be advised:

- Calendula creams to soothe and moisturize the skin and camomile to ease the pain and itching.
- Infusions of either camomile, burdock, marigold and red clover, drunk several time a day for their curative and anti-inflammatory properties.
- Herbs that improve the action of the immune system, such as echinacea, nettles and yarrow, and preparations of skullcap, vervain and wild oats if the eczema is exacerbated by stress.
- Compresses of burdock, chickweed, marigold, witch hazel or yellow dock to reduce inflammation and heal blisters.

Acupuncture

Acupuncture theory is that eczema is usually associated with exposure to damp, heat and wind and a practitioner will concentrate on balancing these effects. They will also correct any blood and energy deficiencies that may be present.

Homeopathy

The immune system, kidney function and the skin itself will be treated. Remedies for itching include:

- Graphites for moist eczema that has a yellowish discharge and where the skin is dry, cracked or rough and caused either by allergy or through an inherited tendency. This form of eczema appears particularly behind the ears and on the hands.
- Petroleum for moist eczema where the skin is rough and broken and an outbreak is brought on by stress or allergy.
- Sulphur for dry eczema which is rough, red and itchy and brought on by allergy or through an inherited tendency.

Chinese herbalism

Traditional Chinese medicine claims considerable success in curing eczema. Treatment is by redressing the balance of heat and damp in the body and repairing the stomach, lung and kidney functions using acupuncture and/or herbs.

Two clinical trials at London hospitals demonstrated substantial benefit from the use of Chinese herbs for both adults and children with eczema. However, a rare allergy-like reaction to the herbs is possible and can be dangerous. For this reason, always use a traditional Chinese medical practitioner who has been properly trained and has practiced for several years, and discuss the likelihood of having an adverse reaction to treatment.

Bach flower remedies

The rescue® remedy cream may help relieve soreness and irritation and promote healing. If there are severe, widespread outbreaks of the condition the sufferers may become acutely aware of their physical appearance and feel embarrassment about the way they look. If this is the case, crab apple may be advised as it is said to decrease feelings of embarrassment. Both mimulus and clematis may also be advised to help combat feelings of oversensitivity.

Color therapy

Color therapists may recommend exposure to green and pale pink light. They may also advise wearing these colors during an outbreak, as they believe that this will help reduce the symptoms and clear the condition.

Reflexology

Reflexologists will massage the reflex areas related to the parts of the body troubled by the eczema outbreak. They will also massage the areas related to the solar plexus, liver, pituitary glands, digestive areas and reproductive glands.

Chiropractic

Chiropractors may be able to treat the condition by easing muscular tension in the body, which they believe may be inhibiting its normal movement and function, and by easing spinal restriction, which they claim can discourage the healing process.

Naturopathy

Naturopaths believe eczema to be caused by allergy. They will recommend trying to identify the allergen and will give dietary advice to minimize or stop the effects. A diet of raw fruit and vegetables, taken with mineral water, may be advised. Various herbal teas and fresh fruit drinks may be recommended. You may be advised to fast for a couple of days after following this diet, but this decision should be taken only if you have gained your orthodox doctor's approval first. This diet will not be recommended to anyone who is recovering from illness, has a weakened immune system or who is generally run down or suffering from malaise.

Kinesiology

Kinesiology practitioners believe that muscle power is affected by allergy and so will measure muscular responses to suspected substances in order to attempt to identify the allergen causing eczema.

Other therapies

Shiatsu can be effective. **Tai chi** might be useful, particularly for stress-related attacks. **Polarity therapy** may help for the same reason. **Hypnotherapy**, in a suitable candidate, may be able to control the condition by reconditioning the patient's reactions to adverse trigger factors.

DERMATITIS

What is it?

Dermatitis is a very general term meaning inflammation of the skin. It is often used interchangeably with eczema (see page 288) and tends to imply a reaction to a chemical. The appearance of the various forms of dermatitis is similar and may range in severity, but all are characterized by redness, blistering, swelling, weeping and crusting of the skin. There is itching and burning and a strong impulse to scratch, which can lead to infection, prolonging the condition.

Causes

There is a wide variety of causes of dermatitis, the most common of which are included below, with their effects:

- **Primary irritant dermatitis** *results from degreasing of the skin by chemicals such as industrial solvents used at work or from repeated exposure to detergents such as washing-up liquid or shampoo. Household chemicals can also cause a reaction. Those who frequently get their hands wet, such as housewives, cleaners or hairdressers, are often affected. The skin becomes dry, fissured and cracked. Those suffering from eczema are more likely to contract primary irritant dermatitis.*
- **Allergic contact dermatitis** *is an immune reaction by the skin to a chemical to which the body has become sensitized. Once developed, the sensitivity is life-long. Those with eczema are more likely to develop this reaction and an irritant dermatitis also makes sensitization more likely. The hands are particularly affected. Common sensitizers include nickel found in jewelry (this may cause a rash on the earlobes of people who have pierced ears), dyes (including hair dyes), cosmetics, rubber, elastic, leathers or preservatives in some skin creams. Irritation, redness, scaling or sometimes blistering occurs at the site of contact. The rash may become generalized and affect most of the body.*
- **Asteotic dermatitis,** *or eczema cracquele, occurs in the elderly and causes dry skin and irritation which is worse if they wash too frequently with soap. The skin improves when soap is avoided and emollients are used regularly.*
- **Photodermatitis** *is caused by a sensitivity to sunlight. A cluster of blisters or spots appears on the areas exposed to the sun. This may occur on its own, but there are chemicals that can trigger a photosensitive rash including perfumes and some antibiotics and plant extracts, for example, wild parsley and giant hogweed.*

Orthodox treatment

Treatment is similar to eczema. Avoidance of known allergens, protecting the hands with barrier creams and gloves, using soap substitutes such as aqueous creams, using nonbiological washing powders and avoiding perfumed cosmetics and toiletries are all helpful. Emollient creams ease the symptoms and steroid creams help settle the inflammation. Patch testing may be carried out by a dermatologist to identify a specific allergen.

ALTERNATIVE TREATMENT

Diagnostic therapies

A kinesiology therapist will check the endocrine and immune systems for nutritional deficiencies and check for food sensitivities, particularly to wheat and dairy products. Advice may be given to avoid eating irritating roughage for a period, substituting psyllium hulls, vitamin B and C, betain hydrochloride, food enzymes and capsicum. An increase in water intake may be advised. Counseling may be given to combat stress. Nutritional hygiene, personal and bowel hygiene will be assessed; some balancing treatment may be required.

Western herbalism

There may be a detoxification program and food intolerances, stress factors and external irritants will be addressed. Most treatment is internal, as skin problems often reflect inner imbalances, but creams and ointments may be given to ease the external symptoms.

Homeopathy

There are a number of homeopathic remedies which may be used while help is being sought, or while itching is very bad, but overall treatment will be constitutional and dietary advice will be offered. In the meantime, according to your symptoms, one of the following may be appropriate: graphites, petroleum, sulphur, rhus tox., alumina, hepar sulph., arsenicum or psorinum.

Spiritual healing

Skin problems often have a basis in emotional problems or nervous stress, which healing helps to bring to the surface. Spiritual healing can penetrate to the root cause of the disease, and, once that is addressed, the resulting physical symptoms disappear quite naturally.

Other therapies

In **Ayurvedic medicine** a practitioner may prescribe individual medications to balance the tridoshas, as well as *panchakarma* for detoxification. **Bach flower remedies**' rescue remedy cream helps relieve any soreness and irritation and also promotes healing. **Color therapy**, depending on the cause, may use light blue to calm the inflammation. **Alexander Technique** and **relaxation** and **visualization** may help by reducing and controlling stress, a common trigger factor. **Reflexology** will treat both the endocrine gland and kidney areas.

Psoriasis

What is it?

Psoriasis is a common skin condition characterized by patches of well-defined salmon pink plaques covered by silvery scaling. Common sites include the knees, elbows, trunk, scalp and hairline. It does not affect the face. It is often an inherited condition but it is not contagious. Severe cases of psoriasis may be accompanied by a form of arthritis which affects the fingers, knees and ankles and sometimes locates itself in the spine.

The condition does not usually itch but it can occasionally hurt when cracks appear in the dry patches on the hands or the soles of the feet. The worst aspect of psoriasis is that it can be very unsightly and therefore embarrassing for sufferers. Psoriasis usually appears in the late teens and early twenties, although it can also occur in the elderly and children.

Causes

The cause of psoriasis is still unclear but what is known is that the control of cell division in the epidermal layer of the skin is disturbed, causing the cells to divide more frequently and have a faster turnover. Normally, cell division is confined to the lowest level of the epidermis, but with psoriasis the plaque's cell division extends over several layers. Psoriasis recurs in attacks of varying degree and may be triggered by emotional stresses, illness and skin damage. Types of psoriasis include:

- **Guttate psoriasis** *most commonly appears in children, often following a throat infection. It is usually self-limiting. Many small patches develop over a wide area of the body.*
- **Plaque psoriasis** *is the most common form. Patches of inflammation appear on the body, especially on the elbows, knees and scalp. The nails may also be affected, with pitting and thickening. Sometimes they become separated from the nail bed.*
- **Pustular psoriasis** *is characterized by small pustules which usually appear on the palms or soles.*
- **Flexural psoriasis** *appears in moist areas of the body such as the groin, under the breast or on the genitalia. The plaques are well-defined and have a red, glazed appearance but are not scaly.*

OUTBREAKS OF PSORIASIS OFTEN AFFECT BOTH SIDES OF THE BODY IN A SYMMETRICAL MANNER.

Orthodox treatment

Psoriasis cannot be cured but there are many treatments available to help clear the skin. Mild attacks may only require the application of an emollient cream. Moderate attacks are treated with dithranol and coal tar extracts. Steroid creams may be used for flexural psoriasis, and there are specific scalp lotions. Calcipotriol (vitamin D in the form of a cream) is used to treat plaque psoriasis. Psoriasis is often helped by sunlight (sunburn can make the condition worse) and this is achieved through UVA therapy, sometimes combined with a skin photosensitizer taken as a tablet. Rarely, severe attacks may require immuno-suppressant drugs. If the psoriasis is accompanied by arthritis this, too, will be treated, usually with nonsteroidal anti-inflammatory drugs (NSAIDs) or antirheumatic drugs.

Alternative Treatment

Nutritional therapy

Nutritional therapists believe deficiencies of zinc and/or essential fatty acids or toxic overload can contribute to psoriasis and would therefore treat accordingly.

Homeopathy

Treatment is specific to the sufferer, but there are several self-help remedies that may help, for example:

- Sulphur for dry, red and itchy patches.
- Graphites if the skin has a sticky, yellowish discharge.
- Petroleum if the skin is sensitive, cracked and bleeding.

Western herbalism

A detoxification program may be recommended and food intolerances, stress factors and eternal irritants will be considered. Most treatment is internal, as skin problems often reflect inner imbalances, but creams and ointments may help ease the external symptoms. Blood-cleansing herbs such as infusions of dandelion root, red clover flowers and burdock may be used. Herbal baths may be advised.

Aromatherapy

Roman camomile is very calming and helps to reduce redness and soreness. Lavender encourages the skin to heal, while sandalwood provides balance and reduces any anti-allergy reactions.

Other therapies

Chinese herbalism is quite effective for some cases of psoriasis. Sometimes the best results are achieved when treatment is combined with **acupuncture**. **Macrobiotics** might be useful, as practitioners believe psoriasis may be associated with deficiencies of the lungs, colon, liver or kidneys. Your practitioner will assess which, then modify the diet accordingly. **Yoga** breathing exercises will help to maintain calm and control stress. **Color therapy** treatment will depend on the cause, but light blue generally calms inflammation. **Reflexology** might address the circulatory system, lymphatic and urinary systems as well as the related area. In **Ayurvedic medicine** a practitioner may prescribe individual medications to balance the tridoshas, as well as *Panchakarma* for detoxification. **Bach flower remedies** may also help.

Impetigo

What is it?

Impetigo is an infection of the skin which affects adults but is most commonly found in children. It usually appears around the mouth and nose but in severe cases the body may also be affected. An impetigo infection begins with reddening skin and the development of small, fluid-filled blisters. The blisters often burst, revealing wet and weeping areas of skin underneath. As the fluid dries out it forms a yellowish crust. Impetigo spreads rapidly if other parts of the body are touched after touching the blister. It is also very infectious to others. Unless treatment is sought, outbreaks can last for several weeks. Outbreaks tend to be more common in warmer weather and in those who have poor standards of personal hygiene.

Patients with impetigo do not feel ill but on rare occasions a kidney inflammation (*Gomerulonephritis*) or blood poisoning (*septicaemia*) may develop.

Causes

Impetigo is caused by bacteria, such as *staphylococci* or *streptococci*, entering the skin, often where there is damage such as a cut, cold sore (see page 280), eczema (see page 288) or scabies (see page 295). Impetigo is very infectious and spreads rapidly around institutions or families, often by direct contact or via flannels and towels. Children are more prone to the condition, and as outbreaks can occur at schools, infected children should not go to school until their skin has cleared up. In the Western world, outbreaks of impetigo are declining due to a general improvement in hygiene standards.

To prevent transmission to others, towels and bed linens should not be shared. Hands should be washed after touching the infected area.

Orthodox treatment

Impetigo can be controlled by careful hygiene and avoiding contact with those experiencing an outbreak. It can be readily treated with antibiotic creams, but extensive infections may require oral antibiotics. Your doctor may consider it worth looking for a predisposing cause, such as scabies, and providing treatment. It is advisable to keep children away from school until the infection has settled.

The doctor may advise that the loose crusts on the skin should be gently washed off with soap and water and the area dried with a towel prior to applying the antibiotic cream. This should be followed by immediate hand washing. Adults and children alike should avoid touching the affected areas.

Alternative Treatment

Western herbalism

Treatment is based upon strong antiseptic remedies. Applications of antiseptic herbs such as infusions or tinctures of thyme, myrrh or marigold may be advised. Internal treatment to fight infection and cleanse the tissues may be in the form of infusions of burdock or echinacea. The immune system may need to be boosted.

Homeopathy

The following remedies should be effective, but if they do not clear up the infection, see your doctor:

- Antimonium when blisters are present around the nostril and mouth area.
- Arsenicum when blisters are accompanied by physical exhaustion and chilliness.

If you take antibiotics to treat the impetigo, constitutional homeopathic treatment can boost general immunity.

Aromatherapy

Thyme and savory help kill the bacteria that causes impetigo and stop it spreading. They should be applied to the affected area three times a day. Tea tree oil should be used for acute cases. Roman camomile will help soothe the skin.

Hypnotherapy

There is a belief that skin renews itself every month and can be conditioned by using hypnosis to renew itself more perfectly. The hypnotherapist will aim to activate the cell communicators so that a damaged cell will replace itself with one purer, more perfect cell.

Nutritional therapy

A nutritional therapist will investigate to see if the immune system is under-functioning. If a zinc deficiency is present, supplements may be advised.

Other therapies

Spiritual healing may be appropriate, because it stimulates the body's own powers of recovery, helping it to get rid of infection. In **Ayurvedic medicine** a practitioner may prescribe individual medications to balance the tridoshas, as well as *Panchakarma* for detoxification. **Naturopathy** may include taking 3–4 cloves of garlic (or garlic capsules) as it has natural antibiotic properties. Extra A, B and C vitamins may be advised to help boost healing and avoid reinfection. **Reflexology** treatment may focus on stimulating the entire body in order to aid the healing process. **Bach flower remedies** can prove very useful.

URTICARIA

What is it?

Urticaria, also known as hives or nettle rash, is an allergic reaction by the skin, causing the body to release histamine (see allergies pages 260–261) into the affected tissues. Urticaria causes raised, white or yellow, itchy wheals surrounded by an area of red inflammation. The size of the wheal varies, with the larger ones sometimes joining together in places to form an irregular rash.

The wheals often cause severe irritation and usually appear on the limbs and trunk, but can also show elsewhere, for example, extensive swelling of the lips and around the eyes may occur. Sometimes there is a swelling of the tongue and larynx which can come on very suddenly and is dangerous, as it may interfere with breathing. Although the condition can last hours or days, the individual spots go after a few hours, leaving the skin completely normal. Acute urticaria develops rapidly and usually lasts for just a few hours. It is characterized by a feverish, faint feeling and occasionally nausea. Chronic urticaria can persist for a long period of time.

Causes

The rash is caused by the release of histamine and other substances. Although often no cause for chronic uticaria is found, common triggers include:

- *Drugs such as aspirin and penicillin.*
- *Food additives such as tartrazine and benzoate.*
- *Food sensitivity, for example, to milk, eggs, shellfish and nuts. It is common in those who suffer asthma (see page 178), eczema (see page 288) or hay fever (see page 179).*
- *Environmental factors, exposure to cold, heat or sunlight.*
- *Stress and anxiety can aggravate or trigger the condition.*
- *Bites and stings.*

Newborn babies occasionally develop a form of urticaria called neonatal urticaria, characterized by a raised rash with white or yellow lumps surrounded by reddened skin. The rash usually occurs on the second day after birth, but is not serious and does not usually require treatment.

URTICARIA IS NOT DANGEROUS, BUT IF THE SWELLING IS AROUND THE MOUTH AND TONGUE, MEDICAL TREATMENT SHOULD BE SOUGHT URGENTLY.

Orthodox treatment

Urticaria can be self-treated with antihistamines which will prevent the release of histamine and thereby reduce the symptoms, but not the cause, of the condition. Ask your pharmacist to advise you. Your doctor may advise taking a stronger, prescription-only antihistamine drug if you suffer regularly from urticaria. Chronic cases may require corticosteroid drugs. However, in the majority of cases, the condition disappears quickly and so does not require treatment.

ALTERNATIVE TREATMENT

Chinese herbalism

Treatment might consist of heat-clearing herbs, anti-inflammatory agents and detoxifying agents. They may be applied externally or taken internally.

Western herbalism

An infusion of chickweed or camomile applied to the skin may help to relieve itching. Western herbal practitioners may seek to improve the functioning of the liver and digestive system by using herbs such as golden seal, yarrow, gentian and camomile. They might also seek to boost the immune system and reduce oversensitivity.

Homeopathy

Treatment will be constitutional and specific to the individual. Certain remedies can have great effect and may be included in your treatment, for example:

- Apis mel. if the skin is red and burning and there is swelling on the lips and eyelids.
- Urtica if the rash is caused by stinging nettles or if there is a hot, burning sensation accompanied by itchy red blotches, especially if the rash is made worse by heat.

Naturopathy

Cool baths and applying vitamin E cream may be recommended to relieve itching and help promote healing. A high level intake of vitamin C may also be advised. A naturopathic practitioner would probably put the patient on a long-term exclusion diet to try to identify and then eliminate any trigger foods from the diet.

Other therapies

A **nutritional therapist** may suggest that as urticaria is frequently linked with food allergy, that time will need to be spent trying to identify problem foods – they are often very successful in treating the condition. **Bach flower remedies** may be appropriate. The rescue remedy cream may relieve soreness and irritation and promote healing. A **hypnotherapist** may suggest hypno-healing, cell command therapy, and creative visualization to boost the immune system. **Polarity therapy** and **tai chi** may also prove to be useful, particularly in stress-related attacks. In **Ayurvedic medicine,** immune-enhancing preparations may be suggested. A **color therapist** would attempt to determine the cause of the condition and may use pale green for its cooling effect on the body and its calming properties.

CELLULITE

What is it?

Cellulite is believed to be fat accumulating in areas under the skin, causing an uneven appearance where the fat cells have thickened with collagen, fluids and toxins. The surface of the skin has a characteristic "orange peel" look. Cellulite may accumulate around the thighs, bottom, hips and the upper arms. Many orthodox doctors doubt the existence of the condition.

Causes

There is a theory that toxins and waste products that cannot be dispersed from the body are stored where they are in the least danger of being reintroduced into the circulation. There is some evidence that it is linked to female hormones, as it often appears at the menopause and rarely occurs in men. Poor circulation may be a factor and a diet high in food additives, alcohol, caffeine and refined sugars may contribute to a buildup of toxins in the body. Lack of exercise and poor elimination of waste products and fluids through the lymphatic system may also cause the condition.

Orthodox treatment

Doctors may suggest weight loss, if appropriate, exercise and a diet low in unrefined foods. Massage may also be suggested. However, as many doctors do not consider cellulite to be a medical condition, they may not have any views on treatment.

ALTERNATIVE TREATMENT

Western herbalism

Herbal extracts and oils may be used in massage over the affected areas, and there will be advice on diet and exercise. Internal treatment may need to look at lymph flow, digestion, hormone balance and various other factors.

Naturopathy

A largely raw food diet of fruit and vegetables with a reduced intake of starch, fat, protein and sugar may be advised. Exercise to improve circulation and overall fitness may also be recommended.

Other therapies

Massage stimulates the circulation which can lead to an improved appearance. Specialized massage called manual lymphatic drainage can also be very effective. A **nutritional therapist** might suggest a cleansing diet combined with massage treatment. **Rolfing** can improve fluid exchange in the body.

RINGWORM

What is it?

Ringworm, also known as *tinea*, is a fungal infection, forming tiny, raised red rings, hence its name. *Tinea pedis* (see Athlete's Foot, see page 301) affects the feet; *tinea cruris* affects the groin area in men; and *tinea capitis* causes ringworm of the scalp.

Causes

The fungi which cause ringworm are contracted from infected pets or farm animals, but most cases are passed on from human to human. This highly contagious condition can spread under the same conditions as athlete's foot, such as in changing rooms, bathrooms or swimming pools. It is very common in children.

Orthodox treatment

Treatment usually consists of antifungal drugs in creams, lotions or ointments. For the hair or nails, or when the infection has spread across the body, oral antifungal drugs may be necessary. Even mild infections will need up to six weeks of treatment. Some more deep-seated infections, particularly those which affect the toenails, may require a longer course of treatment.

ALTERNATIVE TREATMENT

Naturopathy

Therapists will advise excluding yeast and fungi foods like white bread, alcohol, refined sugars and starches.

Aromatherapy

Tea tree oil can be used because of its antifungal properties, but care must be taken avoid spreading ringworm.

Other therapies

Homeopathic remedies may include sulphur when the scalp is infected and then sepia if there is no improvement, and tellurium when the infection is confined to the trunk. A **nutritional therapist** might suggest that the immune system is underfunctioning. A zinc deficiency might be present. A **Western herbalist** may prescribe antifungal agents to be used locally.

WARTS

What are they?

Warts appear on the skin and cause raised brownish or flesh-colored horny areas. There are several different types of wart:

- **Common warts** *are firm, round, horny bumps in the skin about 5mm (¼in) in size. They appear on the knees, hands and face. Nail biters may get them around the nail or on the lips.*
- **Plane warts,** *or flat warts, are flat, flesh-colored or brown and sometimes itchy. They are common on the face around the mouth and chin, or on the backs of the hands.*
- **Filiform warts** *are long, thread-like warts on the face or neck.*
- **Plantar warts** *are also known as veruccas. They are flat warts which appear on the soles of the foot and may cause pain when walking. They need distinguishing from corns* *(see page 297).*
- *Genital warts are pink, soft and cauliflower-like. They are sexually transmitted.*

Causes

Warts are caused by some 30 different strains of the human papilloma virus. All warts are contagious but none are dangerous, although genital warts have been linked to cervical cancer.

Orthodox treatment

Most warts disappear without any treatment and will not leave a scar. Persistent warts are treated with wart-removing liquid or plasters. Cryosurgery (freezing with liquid nitrogen) and electrocautery may also be used if other treatments fail.

ALTERNATIVE TREATMENT

Aromatherapy

Undiluted lemon oil needs to be applied to the wart daily. Tea tree oil may be used for its antifungal properties.

Homeopathy

Remedies include thuja, causticum, nitric ac., calcarea, antimonium, culcamara and natrum carb.

Other therapies

A **hypnotherapist** may suggest hypno-healing. A **Western herbalist** may use local herbal agents which act steadily to kill off the wart-producing virus. **Color therapists** may use violet and indigo. **Western herbalism** may involve the use of local herbal agents to kill off the virus. There are numerous folk remedies, one of which is to rub the wart with seven white stones.

SCABIES

What is it?

Scabies is an infestation of the skin by a parasitic mite which burrows into the skin and lays its eggs. After 4–6 weeks the sufferer develops an itchy allergic reaction, which often worsens at night. A rash develops which may become infected by scratching.

Causes

Transmission is by skin-to-skin contact with an infected person, and often occurs in bed. Sexual transmission is common and infection is also passed readily amongst children.

Orthodox treatment

Treatment is with insecticide lotions, but all members of the family must undergo treatment at the same time to ensure that further cross-infection does not occur. The lotion should be applied to the whole body and and washed off 24 hours later. This treatment will need to be repeated two weeks later as, although the mite is killed by the treatment, its eggs remain in the skin. Crotamiton cream may be helpful in calming the irritation while waiting for the infestation to clear. After treatment begins, bed linen, towels and clothing should be thoroughly washed.

ALTERNATIVE TREATMENT

Aromatherapy

Tea tree oil mixed with lindol and thyme can be applied twice daily until the infestation clears.

Homeopathy

Psorinum, which is derived from the scabies mite, will be used to treat the condition on the homeopathic principle of "like treating like."

Other therapies

Western herbalists will use herbs, or extracts of essential oils, which can act quite powerfully to kill the offending organisms. Scabies occurs in situations where immunity and hygiene standards are lower than usual, so these factors will be addressed. **Naturopathy** treatment may be herbal, homeopathic and dietetic, alternating soothing and cooling medicines with constitutional remedies. Hydrotherapy treatment may prove useful.

BOILS

What are they?

Boils are inflamed, pus-filled areas which appear at the site of infected hair follicles. They usually occur on the back of the neck, groin and armpits but can also appear on other areas of the body. A stye is a boil on the eyelash and a group of coalescing boils is called a carbuncle. The boil begins as a painful red lump which then swells, fills with pus which hardens and forms a yellow head.

Causes

Boils are usually caused by the *staphylococcus* bacteria which may enter intact skin or through a cut. Other factors which can cause boils include other skin diseases including eczema (see page 288), scabies (see page 295), diabetes (see page 200) or an underlying blood disorder. Recurrent infections are common and associated with the carriage of bacteria in the nose, on the hands and on the perineum. Boils can spread within families.

Orthodox treatment

Small boils may be safely left until they discharge. If there is evidence of spread, with redness, fever or enlarged lymph glands, antibiotics may be given. If the boil is large and painful, it may be lanced to drain the pus. For recurrent infections an antibiotic cream for the nose may be prescribed and a course of antiseptic baths may be advised.

ALTERNATIVE TREATMENT

Aromatherapy

Tea tree with thyme, lindol and ravensara, a very strong antifungal oil which is gentle on the skin, will be mixed together and dabbed on the affected area.

Homeopathy

A homeopath will prescribe belladonna for the early stages when the boil is forming and hepar sulph. for the later stages when the pus has formed. Warm compresses applied to the affected area may also help.

Western herbalism

Practitioners believe that boils are caused by internal impurities, so teas of burdock, echinacea, golden seal or yellow dock may be suggested to help purify the blood. Warm poultices of slippery elm can be applied to the affected area.

ABSCESSES

What are they?

Abscesses are pockets of pus formed after the skin has been infected, usually one of the *staphylococci* bacteria. They can occur in any organ or skin area of the body. In order to prevent toxins entering the bloodstream from the infection, the body effectively seals off the infected area which then becomes a pus-filled abscess. The area will be swollen and painful and will feel hot to the touch. The abscess may be accompanied by fever, sweating and malaise and there may also be a sensation of extreme discomfort and pressure.

Causes

An abscess is usually the result of a puncture wound or injury, but it can also be caused by an infection of a follicle, pore or gland. Some fungal infections can cause abscesses.

Orthodox treatment

Some abscesses burst and drain without treatment but a doctor will prescribe antibiotics and may surgically drain off the pus. An abscess detected on an internal organ of the body, such as the liver or brain, will need surgical treatment.

ALTERNATIVE TREATMENT

Aromatherapy

Tea tree with thyme, lindol and ravensara, a very strong antifungal oil which is gentle on the skin, will be mixed together and dabbed on the affected area.

Naturopathy

Treatment would be based on nutrition and dietetics, especially cleansing programs with fasting. Herbal and homeopathic alternatives would be appropriate. Hepar sulph. is the homeopathic cure for abscesses.

Western herbalism

A Western herbalist may offer internal treatment as the main approach, cleansing the body and removing causes of the abscesses. Local poultices or compresses may be used to bring them to a head and discharge the pus.

CORNS AND CALLUSES

What are they?

Both corns and calluses are thickening of the outer layers of the skin (epidermis). They form to protect any area of the body which is subject to repeated pressure, rubbing or irritation. Corns appear on or between the toes or on the soles of the foot, while calluses may also appear on the hands or knees.

A callus is a rough, thick patch of skin, which usually develops over a bony prominence. The skin becomes hard, thick, slightly raised and insensitive. Calluses usually appear on either the feet, hands or knees of those whose occupations involve excessive pressure in these areas.

Corns are small, raised bumps which appear over a toe joint or on the sole of the foot. Corns measure approximately 4–5mm (⅛–¼in)in diameter and are characterized by a a small hard center. When pressure is put on the center of the corn, it places pressure on the nerve endings, causing pain. Soft corns may appear between the toes caused by friction between the bony points of the toes. Corns may sometimes become infected.

Causes

Both corns and calluses are the result of undue pressure on an area of skin. In order to protect the area, the skin cells around the affected part reproduce at an increased rate, forming hardened areas of skin. While corns may be caused by wearing badly fitting shoes which squeeze the foot, most cases of corns and calluses are caused by poor foot biomechanics which result in localized areas of pressure, often exacerbated by ill-fitting footwear. They occur most commonly in those who have high foot arches, as the arch increases the pressure on the tips of the toes when walking. Wearing high-heeled shoes produces the same effect as they force the toes of the foot forward, placing undue pressure on them.

Calluses often affect those involved in heavy manual work, such as builders, appearing on the fingers, palms or knees. They also affect those who occupations involve applying excessive pressure on their fingers, such as violin or guitar players, or the foot, such as joggers or runners. Sometimes a callus is caused by a foot deformity creating undue pressure.

DIABETICS OR THOSE WITH ARTERIAL DISEASE SHOULD NOT USE OVER-THE-COUNTER CORN PADS OR CALLUS-REMOVING LOTIONS AS THEY CAN DAMAGE THEIR SKIN.

Orthodox treatment

Calluses will invariably clear up once the source of pressure or friction is removed. Wearing protective gloves may help those involved in heavy manual work. Corns are harder to clear but may respond when the pressure on the affected area is relieved. This can be achieved by either placing padding at the friction point of the shoe or discarding the shoes altogether. Pare the thickened area of skin away and apply an emollient cream. If the corn gets worse and becomes very thick you should see a state registered chiropodist for more specialist treatment. Any infection should be treated by a doctor. Diabetic patients need extra care as poor blood supply to the foot and damaged peripheral nerves make them more vulnerable to ulceration.

Calluses caused by foot deformities may require regular chiropody to pare them down, and surgery may be necessary to correct the deformity.

ALTERNATIVE TREATMENT

Alexander Technique

Corns may be caused by incorrect posture which places undue pressure on the feet, particularly in those who walk the feet turning inward. Practitioners will analyze posture and walking gait and teach methods for avoiding incorrect movement. There may well be additional problems, such as a bad back or aching legs, which, like the corns, are a symptom of poor posture, and these will also be treated.

Naturopathy

Regularly washing the feet and gently removing any rough skin with a pumice stone will help remove both the corn or callus. The naturopath may also recommend bathing the feet in a bowl of hot water in which a handful of Epsom salts have been dissolved. People who live near the coast, will find that soaking the feet for ten to fifteen minutes in salty sea water will also help. An alternative is to soak the feet in water to which a handful of table salt has been added.

Western herbalism

Corns can be treated by painting them with fresh lemon juice or by soaking the feet for ten minutes in a solution of one-third vinegar to two-thirds water. Compresses of crushed garlic applied to the corn daily may also help.

Homeopathy

For soft corns a solution of calendula and hypericum may be applied to the affected part four times a day for its antiseptic and pain-relieving properties.

Other therapies

Osteopathy can treat underlying joint and posture complaints which may be contributing to the formation of the corns. Similarly, **chiropractic** treatment can help relieve the corns by manipulating any foot joint disorders which may be causing the corns. **Tai chi** and **yoga** may also help by making body movement more fluid and improving posture.

ACNE

What is it?

Acne (*Acne vulgaris*) is a very common skin disorder which mainly affects adolescents and young adults. It occurs in areas that have a high concentration of sebaceous glands, mainly on the chest, back and face. Typically, red, angry-looking spots form on the skin, but acne also manifests itself in the formation of blackheads, whiteheads, pustules and pus-filled cysts. As the spots heal they fade to a pink mark that disappears later, although spots which become cysts on the skin will usually leave a pockmark.

Causes

Acne is caused by an increase in the oily sebum (the oily secretion of the sebaceous glands, which acts as a lubricant for the hair and skin) and the growth rate of the skin cells. When the sebum becomes trapped it attracts bacteria which build up and eventually causes inflammation of the glands, leading to the red, raised spots. It is also linked with increased levels of male sex hormones, but the condition appears to be hereditary to a certain extent. Excessive sweating can encourage acne and some drugs, for example oral contraceptives and corticosteroids, can aggravate the condition, as can face creams and cosmetics. Some women suffer from acne during or just prior to menstruation due to fluctuating hormone levels.

Orthodox treatment

Washing twice a day helps keep the acne from spreading but it will not be enough to prevent the spots forming. Not picking at the spots is essential to prevent them from spreading to other areas or leaving scars. Acne is treated in various ways:

- *Lotions and creams containing benzoyl peroxide, which unblocks the pores of the skin and removes the sebum, may be used. A more powerful treatment is retinoic acid, which does the same thing but must be prescribed. There are also antibiotic lotions which will prevent the spread and combat local infection.*
- *Persistent acne may require antibiotics to control the bacteria which invade the pores. They may need to be taken for several years.*
- *Severe acne can be treated by Isotrentinoin, which is available from dermatologists. However, although it is very effective it also has many side effects.*
- *Ultraviolet light exposure to UVA, preferably in the form of natural sunlight, can be very beneficial.*

Severe acne may leave unsightly scars which can be reduced by dermabrasion (removal of the top layer of the skin). Collagen injections will plump out the pitting to make the skin's surface appear smooth, but top-up treatments are required every six months or so. For females, the contraceptive pill may help regulate hormone levels.

ALTERNATIVE TREATMENT

Naturopathy

Naturopaths will recommend splashing the affected areas with cold water and wiping gently with cotton balls soaked in witch hazel. Eating garlic for its natural antibiotic properties will be suggested. A propolis ointment may be dabbed on the affected areas several times a day.

Homeopathy

Treatment will be constitutional, but there are specific remedies which may be beneficial, including:

- Hepar sulph. for the large painful spots filled with pus that are thought to be brought on by puberty.
- Pulsatilla for spots which are worse at puberty and when menstruation is about to begin.
- Kali brom. for itchy pimples on the face, chest and shoulders brought on by hormonal changes.

Nutritional therapy

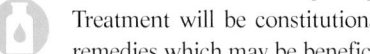

Unlike conventional medical practitioners, nutritional therapists believe that acne *is* linked with excess fat in the diet and also with certain food intolerances, such as cheese or chocolate. Nutritional deficiencies (particularly zinc and vitamin A) will be determined, particularly when associated with liver congestion. It may be brought on by hormonal changes due to menstruation and this will be investigated.

Western herbalism

A detoxification program of herbal treatment may be followed up by hormonal treatments or remedies to reduce stress. An anti-inflammatory skin wash made from calendula, camomile or a mixture of yarrow, elder and lavender will help soothe and reduce the outbreak.

Other therapies

Chinese herbalism will suggest heat-clearing and detoxifying herbs. **Aromatherapists** may use tea tree with thyme and lindol and, for rebalancing, pine or clary sage. Regular treatment with **auricular therapy** can be of some benefit. **Rolfing** may help by improving the fluid exchange in the body, so that toxins can be flushed out. A lotion of diluted **Bach flower remedies**' rescue remedy cream, with crab apple for oversensitivity about appearance, may be helpful. A course of **hypnotherapy** may help. The procedure will include regression, suggestion, hypno-healing, self-hypnosis conditioning and creative visualization. There is a belief that skin renews itself every month and can be conditioned using hypnosis to renew itself more perfectly.

EXCESSIVE PERSPIRATION

What is it?

Excessive sweating, also known as hyperhidrosis, may occur all over the body and is the result of overactivity of the sweat glands. Many people suffer from excessive sweating in one part of their body, for instance the palms of the hands, the armpits or the feet. In very rare but serious conditions, the skin may become damp and damaged. Although sweating is the body's way of naturally cooling itself, excessive sweating, particularly when accompanied by an offensive odor, can be embarrassing as well as uncomfortable.

Causes

The condition is often within the bounds of what is considered to be normal. Sweating in the armpits and groin area, for example, are stimulated by emotional and nervous changes, while general body sweating is stimulated by heat and is the body's way of regulating temperature. Excessive perspiration is a common feature of the menopause and anxiety. Other causes include:

- *An overactive thyroid gland.*
- *An excessive intake of alcohol.*
- *Hypoglycemia – low blood sugar due to too much insulin. The sufferer breaks out in a cold sweat.*
- *Prolonged fever, for example, tuberculosis, chronic infections or some cancers. The patient will feel unwell and lose weight.*

Often a person's general health and diet may affect the amount which they perspire and their body odor. Many cases of excessive perspiration arrive and then disappear without any obvious cause; this phenomenon usually occurs in puberty, although it is common during the menopause or when anxious.

PERSPIRATION IS ODORLESS UNTIL IT COMES IN CONTACT WITH BACTERIA ON THE SKIN, SO SCRUPULOUS HYGIENE MAY HELP TO PREVENT ODOR.

Orthodox treatment

It is not considered healthy to suppress normal perspiration with anti-perspirants, since sweating is necessary to cool the body. However, with excessive sweating the doctor may prescribe preparations of aluminium hydrochloride and aluminium hydroxychloride, which act as powerful anti-perspirants.

A doctor may also suggest wearing natural fabrics, which are more absorbent and allow the body to "breathe," thereby allowing the perspiration to evaporate. Occasionally anti-cholinergic drugs may be prescribed.

In severe cases of excessive perspiration the cause of the condition would have to be diagnosed before any treatment was undertaken. However, for such severe cases it may be necessary to surgically remove the most active glands.

ALTERNATIVE TREATMENT

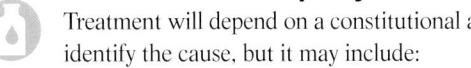

Autogenic training

Anxiety and stress often cause excessive sweating, so the emotionally calming effects of the training may have a large role to play in controlling the condition, particularly if night sweating is a problem.

Aromatherapy

Aromatherapists will seek to balance the action of the sebaceous glands by using the astringent-like properties of cypress and geranium. Rubbing a diluted oil of these ingredients into the affected areas in the morning and at night can help.

Bach flower remedies

If the condition is caused, worsened or affected by stress or a negative mental attitude, the Bach flower remedies can be used as a supportive therapy to help bring about a more positive emotional outlook. Remedies will be chosen according to personality and mood but may include the following in order to treat:

- Fear – rock rose, mimulus, cherry plum, aspen or red chestnut.
- Uncertainty – cerato, scleranthus, gentian, gorse, hornbeam or wild oat.
- Oversensitivity – agrimony, centaury, walnut, holly.

Homeopathy

Treatment will depend on a constitutional assessment to identify the cause, but it may include:

- Sulphur for body odor, particularly if the skin looks unhealthy and if sweaty feet are a problem.
- Hepar sulph. may be given if sweating is profuse and sticky, has a sour smell and the skin is sensitive to touch.
- Sepia may be given for excessive night sweating which occurs on the chest, back and thighs, particularly if these symptoms are associated with the menopause.

Other therapies

Western herbalism will provide remedies that directly reduce excess perspiration, or affect the hormones, which may be the underlying cause of the problem. **Rolfing** may help by improving the fluid exchange in the body, and flushing out any unwanted toxins. A **yoga** therapist might suggest doing *pranayama*. Emotionally based problems may respond to **hypnotherapy**, specifically hypno-healing. Learning **relaxation and visualization** techniques may help if the sweating is made worse by exposure to emotionally disturbing or stressful situations. **Naturopaths** may prescribe some zinc supplements and strongly advise against using anti-perspirants.

BALDNESS

What is it?

Baldness, or alopecia, is excessive hair loss. It predominantly affects men, but women can also suffer. Generally, women tend to lose hair around the crown, whereas men lose it around the crown and also the hairline.

Causes

The chief causes of hair loss are age or disease. Balding can also be hereditary. Other causes of the condition include:

- *Underlying diseases especially iron deficiency, hypothyroidism, systemic lupus eruthematosus (a form of arthritis), and syphilis.*
- *Alopecia areatea – the sudden patches in the beard or scalp.*
- *Pregnancy – during pregnancy the hairs go into a resting phase. The hair is replaced after the birth.*
- *Severe illness when associated with high fever.*
- *Chemotherapy drugs cause hair loss. Excess of vitamin A has a similar effect.*
- *Dermal scarring in conditions such as burns and skin cancers.*

Orthodox treatment

Hair loss is very distressing. Treatment may be recommended with the drug minioxidil, but relapses occur when the drug is withdrawn. *Alopecia areatea* often heals spontaneously but steroids may help. Treatment of iron deficiency or hypothyroidism will cause hair growth. Hair augmentation treatment may be offered.

ALTERNATIVE TREATMENT

Rolfing

Rolfing may stimulate the overall circulation and help to relax muscles so that the scalp is not too tight.

Homeopathy

Premature balding or hair loss through pregnancy would be treated with lycopodium.

Other therapies

Reflexology will treat the head area and the adrenal glands. A **nutritional therapist** may suggest that a zinc deficiency or a toxic overload is the cause. **Chinese herbalism** may consist of blood tonics, hormone tonics and herbal sedatives, although treatment for male pattern baldness will not be recommended. A **hypnotherapist** may use hypno-healing for the hair follicles.

DANDRUFF

What is it?

Dandruff is a disorder of the sebaceous glands in the scalp which causes the excessive production of scales of dry skin. Although dandruff is not dangerous, it is uncomfortable and often unsightly. The scales are most obvious after brushing or combing the hair, which loosens them.

Causes

The outer layer of the skin on the scalp is shed at an increased rate and hair is often oily and lank. Some loss of skin cells on the scalp is normal, as the scalp rejuvenates itself and exfoliates the dead cells. Normal washing and brushing will ensure that they are removed safely. An increase in the normal amount of exfoliation, perhaps because the skin is inflamed or itchy, may also appear as dandruff. Sometimes dandruff is a symptom of eczema (see page 288), psoriasis (see page 291) or seborrheic dermatitis.

Orthodox treatment

Dandruff is usually treated with medicated shampoos, often available over the counter. These contain selenium, zinc and pyrithioneor tar. Seborrheic dermatitis responds well to corticosteroids and, when appropriate, anti-yeast shampoos.

ALTERNATIVE TREATMENT

Homeopathy

There are a number of specific homeopathic remedies available to treat dandruff, and many of them are very effective. Experimentation with the following remedies may provide the solution, or seek a homeopath's advice: Arsenicum, sepia, sulphur, mezereum, fluoric ac., graphites, oleander and natrum mur.

Other therapies

Western herbalists may use local antiseptic remedies to improve circulation to the scalp and hair follicles. A **nutritional therapist** may suggest that dandruff is linked with deficiencies of B vitamins, zinc and essential fatty acids. A **kinesiologist** may suggest tea tree oil, hair and scalp care, selenium shampoo and vitamin A to be taken orally.

Athlete's Foot

What is it?

Athlete's foot is a common term for the fungal infection which occurs between the toes and around the base of the foot. The condition is characterized by itching, followed by painful cracks, peeling skin and occasionally blisters. The rash may be dry and scaly or wet and blistery and the affected foot will have an unpleasant smell. The area between the fourth and fifth toes are usually affected. If the condition persists, the nails may also be infected and may begin to crumble or separate from the nail bed. The condition can be very uncomfortable and, once acquired, it is very difficult to eliminate. Secondary bacterial infection is possible, and it is essential that the fissures that develop are kept clean and dry.

Causes

The *tinea pedis* fungus causes athlete's foot but on very rare occasions it can be caused by bacteria. It is more common in those who do not practice careful personal hygiene, but it is largely contracted by going barefoot in damp environments such as swimming pools, communal showers and changing rooms, hence its name. Athlete's foot is extremely contagious, and it will be necessary to disinfect the floors of showers and gymnasiums to help control the spread. It usually affects those with sweaty feet. Children are rarely affected by the condition.

Orthodox treatment

The fungus cannot penetrate the skin if the surface is dry and unbroken, so your doctor will recommend that you avert further attacks by taking suitable precautions. Initial treatment can be carried out using proprietary medication such as topical antifungal creams for dry outbreaks and powders for wet outbreaks. Most cases respond to antifungal treatment drugs such as clotrimazole, tolnaftate and miconazole.

Washing the feet twice a day and keeping them dry, especially between the toes, will also help make the feet unattractive to fungal invaders. Wearing cotton socks, which allow the feet to breathe, may help to reduce the symptoms. Avoid tight shoes and dust footwear with an antifungal powder.

If the condition does not respond to self-treatment, your doctor may take skin and nail samples to confirm the diagnosis, prior to prescribing a stronger antifungal agent. If the toenails have become affected an oral antifungal treatment course may be prescribed. The drug becomes impregnated into the toenail and kills off the fungus but the tablets will have to be taken for at least three months for them to work effectively. There is also an effective nail lacquer preparation which might be prescribed. You may also be advised to avoid going barefoot in public places.

If these remedies do not work, your doctor may recommend that you see a dermatologist.

Alternative Treatment

Homeopathy

As with many skin conditions, the homeopathic approach is to boost the immune system generally, so treatment is constitutional and often effective.

Naturopathy

Propolis ointment and vitamin C powder applied to the affected area may be prescribed. Wetting a pad with honey or cider vinegar and wrapping it over the affected area at night may also help the condition. A drink to help promote skin healing can be made from the juice of strawberries mixed with the pulp of fresh dates.

Chinese herbalism

A traditional Chinese medical practitioner will assess the condition and prepare herbal powders which should be applied externally, along with anti-inflammatory agents.

Aromatherapy

Treatment may be with undiluted tea tree oil (two to five drops), dabbed directly on the affected area and massaged into the skin three times daily until cleared. A compress of these oils can be made and bandaged around the affected skin. Lavender oil, massaged into the skin on the affected foot, will also help to clear the outbreak.

Western herbalism

Bathing the feet daily in a herbal footbath of golden seal, or a mix of cider vinegar, red clover, sage, calendula and agrimony in water will help. Soak the feet for half an hour, dry well, and powder with arrowroot or golden seal. Dry infections will require applications of calendula cream which will soothe the skin and help fight infection.

Ayurvedic medicine

An Ayurvedic practitioner may suggest stimulating Ayurvedic oils to be applied at home.

Other therapies

A **nutritional therapist** may suggest that a fungal infection is a sign that the immune system is underfunctioning and will devise a diet to combat this. A **kinesiologist** may suggest tea tree oil, counseling on foot care, and selenium. **Spiritual healing** stimulates the body's own powers of recovery, helping it to get rid of unwanted invaders. **Bach flower remedies**' rescue® remedy cream may help to relieve the condition.

MUSCULO - SKELETAL SYSTEM

What is it?

The muscles, bones, ligaments and joints of the body make up the musculo-skeletal system. Its prime functions are movement and protection. The system is built around the body's skeleton, consisting of light and strong bones with a hard outer layer (compact bone) and a light inner honeycombed layer (cancellous bone). Long bones, such as the femur, have a central cavity filled with bone marrow containing tissue that produces the circulating red and white blood cells. The skeleton's bones are connected to each other by different joints. Ball and socket joints (the hip and shoulder) allow the most movement.

The muscles are made up of microscopic cells called muscle fibers. There are two types of body muscle – involuntary and voluntary – which usually work in groups. Involuntary muscles, such as the heart muscle and the digestive tract, are not under our conscious control. They allow movement and transport in the body. The voluntary muscles are under our control and help with activities such as walking and writing. Muscles can contract and relax, and during contraction a muscle can shorten by up to 40 percent. Ligaments surround joints and maintain stability.

What can go wrong?

One of the common problems of the musculo-skeletal system is damage to the joints by injury or wear and tear. Injuries cause swelling and pain. Strained or torn ligaments tend to heal more quickly. A neck fracture of the long thigh bone (femur) is common after a fall in the elderly. This is usually due to thinning of the bones with age (*osteoporosis*).

Wear and tear is often synonymous with osterarthritis and commonly affects the knees, hips and neck in the elderly. Rheumatoid arthritis is an inflammation of the joints causing swelling and stiffness. *Backache* can affect up to 70 percent of people. Usually the problem is brought on by poor posture or heavy lifting which causes muscle and ligament damage. Sometimes *backache* is a trapped nerve (sciatica) resulting in pain at the back of the leg. Occasionally the cause of back pain is a "slipped disc." Genetic illness, such as *muscular dystrophy*, can induce progressive muscle weakness and is often fatal.

Muscle fibers are built around the body's skeleton, which is made up of light and strong bones, joined together by joints. Involuntary and voluntary muscles control body movement.

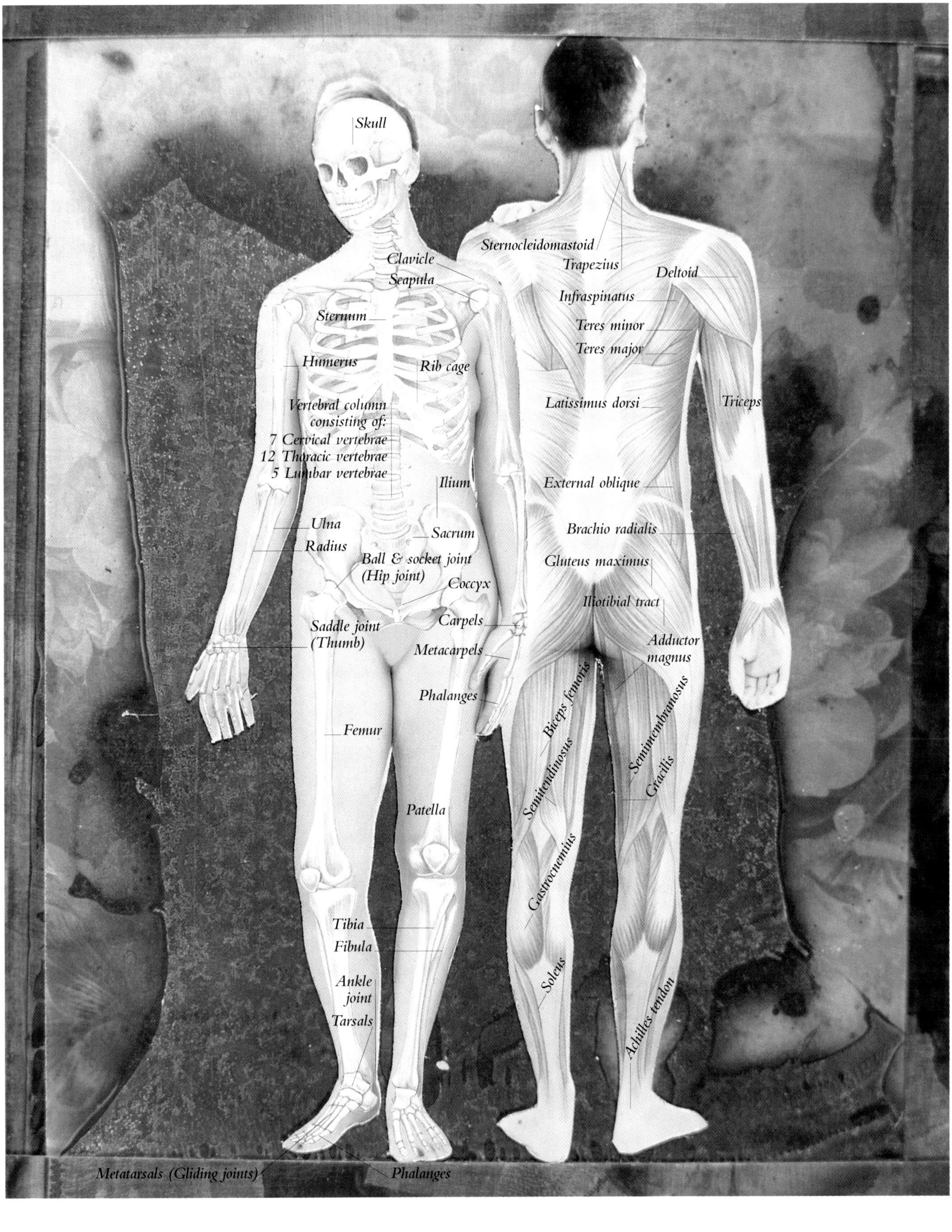
Skull
Clavicle
Scapula
Sternum
Humerus
Rib cage
Vertebral column consisting of:
7 Cervical vertebrae
12 Thoracic vertebrae
5 Lumbar vertebrae
Ilium
Ulna
Sacrum
Radius
Ball & socket joint (Hip joint)
Coccyx
Carpels
Saddle joint (Thumb)
Metacarpels
Phalanges
Femur
Patella
Tibia
Fibula
Ankle joint
Tarsals
Metatarsals (Gliding joints)
Phalanges
Sternocleidomastoid
Trapezius
Deltoid
Infraspinatus
Teres minor
Teres major
Latissimus dorsi
Triceps
External oblique
Brachio radialis
Gluteus maximus
Iliotibial tract
Adductor magnus
Biceps femoris
Semimembranosus
Semitendinosus
Gracilis
Gastrocnemius
Soleus
Achilles tendon

ARTHRITIS

What is it?

Many conditions give rise to arthritis, defined as "inflammation of the tissues of the joints." The two most common are osteoarthritis and rheumatoid arthritis:

Osteoarthritis is a condition in which the cartilage between the joints wears away, normally through ordinary wear and tear. It usually occurs in the areas subject to the greatest stress, such as the knees, hips and neck and spine, although the second joints of the fingers and the joint at the base of the thumb are often affected. Osteoarthritis is so common it could be viewed as part of the ageing process: 85 percent of the elderly have X-ray indications of osteoarthritis, although only a small proportion show symptoms. It is more common in women. Symptoms include:

- *Stiffness and pain in the joints (crepitus) and a creaking sound as the joint is moved, indicating that the cartilage has been worn away and bone is moving against bone without any protection.*
- *Bony swelling of the joint, leading to deformity and accentuated by the wasting of surrounding muscle.*
- *Synovitis, which is acute attacks of pain, swelling and inflammation with warmth and redness, occurs due to inflammation of the membrane lining the joint.*

Initially the symptoms may be intermittent and are often worse in the morning. Generally, osteoarthritis does not seriously impair joint function but, for a small proportion of patients, it is a progressive process, with increasing stiffness, limitation of movement and joint destruction.

Causes

The joints of the body are covered with a layer of smooth cartilage which allows them to move smoothly against each other. It also protects the bone from shocks or jolts which would normally cause it to splinter. With osteoarthritis, the cartilage wears away and as part of the attempt to repair itself, bony outgrowths (osteophytes) form at the margins of the joints. Pain, stiffness and occasionally loss of function result. Inflammation of the synovial membrane can causes swelling from increased fluid in the joint. Osteoarthritis is broken into two categories:

- **Primary generalized osteoarthritis** *which attacks previously normal joints. It runs in families and can be recognized by the bony deformity and swelling on the second joint of the fingers.*
- **Secondary osteoarthritis** *which affects previously damaged joints. It is more common on weight-bearing joints. Those who have had previous joint problems or damage are more likely to experience secondary osteoarthritis. Obesity may accelerate the progress of the condition, especially in the knee.*

Orthodox treatment

Exercise may be recommended to sufferers, although it is important that it does not apply pressure to, or stress, the joints. Mild painkillers will be offered, and anti-inflammatory drugs may be useful. Anti-inflammatory gels can be rubbed into the affected areas. Steroid injections may be given and physiotherapy may be offered. Heat treatment and hydrotherapy may also ease the pain and improve mobility. If the pain and disability are severe, a doctor may refer a patient to a rheumatologist or an orthopedic specialist. Where the degeneration is almost complete, joint replacement surgery (*arthroplasty*) may be necessary. Hip replacements, for example, are now quite common and provide considerable improvement to the quality of life of many sufferers.

Rheumatoid arthritis is a condition in which the joints become inflamed and painful. It affects some two percent of the population and about five percent of women over the age of 55. Unlike osteoarthritis, the patient feels generally unwell, with weight loss, malaise, and pain and stiffness in the hands, feet and knees. It can develop slowly, causing pain and stiffness in the joints, or it can appear quickly, causing a high fever with pain and stiffness in the larger joints. A clue to diagnosis is morning stiffness – it can take over an hour for the joints to loosen up. Ligaments, tendons and muscles may also become inflamed and weakened. Eventually, joints may become deformed, causing pain and disability. The most severe rheumatoid arthritis destroys the joints.

Causes

Although its exact cause is still unknown, rheumatoid arthritis is thought to be an autoimmune disease. Something triggers off an inflammatory process in the synovial membrane lining the joints. The synovium becomes inflamed, swollen and thickened, spreading over the cartilage and eroding it. The condition may occur at any age but it often begins in the thirties, with the incidence rising in the elderly. It affects three times more women than men.

Complications of rheumatoid arthritis are numerous, and include anemia, joint infections, damage to the peripheral nerves, eyes, lungs, heart and ulceration of the lower limbs, as well as side effects brought on by treatment.

Orthodox treatment

Treatment is dependent on the severity of the disease, and ranges from bed rest to surgery. Aspirin is very often prescribed. There are drugs called NSAIDs (nonsteroidal anti-inflammatory drugs) which relieve pain and stiffness. Antirheumatic drugs may slow the progress of the disease. Drugs which suppress the immune system may also slow the course of the disease, but they have side effects. Steroids may be injected into the joints to prevent swelling and provide relief from severe symptoms. In very serious cases, powerful medication may be prescribed.

Some joints may be replaced surgically. Splinting the affected limb may help reduce pain and stiffness. Physiotherapy will help relieve the stiffness and pain and enables sufferers to regain use of the diseased joints. Occupational therapy will help sufferers learn to cope with everyday tasks and therapists will recommend or provide aids for use in the home.

Alternative Treatment

Alexander Technique

The Alexander Technique can be very effective in dealing with osteoarthritis and rheumatoid arthritis. Although symptoms are usually localized in a specific part of the body, the technique takes a holistic view. It promotes a general condition of psychophysical harmony and posture balance and, therefore, specific problems tend to disappear in the process. In particular, it leads to a release of unnecessarily contracted muscles, a freeing up of joints and a lengthening of the spinal column. This improved use reduces mechanical interference and strain, facilitating the efficient use of the body's regenerative and healing powers.

Massage

Massage of the muscles surrounding an arthritic joint may bring relief from pain and stiffness. Caution should be used near those joints where there is active arthritis. General body massage can help to relieve tension and aches in other parts of the body, and help promote a feeling of well being.

Aromatherapy

Geranium oil may be used for its uplifting benefits. Ginger oil will warm and juniper may help remove toxins. Rosemary oil will help encourage the circulation and remove toxins via the blood system.

Western herbalism

Devil's claw is claimed to have positive effects on arthritic conditions. The herb contains several glycosides, powerful anti-inflammatory agents which are thought to help the condition. However, devil's claw should not be taken during pregnancy. An infusion of alfalfa and celery can be taken as a nutritional supplement. Extracts or infusions of aloe vera, bogbean, feverfew, primula and willow will help reduce inflammation. Wild yam and lignum vitae can help attacks of rheumatoid arthritis.

Homeopathy

Homeopaths have found that if sufferers follow an alkaline diet, their symptoms are eased. The following remedies may be prescribed:

• Rhus tox. if there is pain with stiffness, especially when waking in the morning.

• Bryonia if there is severe pain on movement and if the joints are swollen and feel hot.

• Pulsatilla if pain is accompanied by weeping and the pain in the joint moves around.

• Arnica if the pain is aggravated by injury and movement is therefore more difficult.

• Ledum if the pain starts in the feet and moves upward, and if there are stiff, painful joints where the person feels hot inside but the limb is cold to the touch and is relieved by cold compresses.

Acupuncture

Acupuncture can be highly effective and can produce results of lasting benefit. The acupuncturist will aim to warm cold areas or clear areas of excess heat, move stagnant fluids, and promote circulation of energy and the blood. The result is a reduction in inflammation, long-lasting pain relief and improved mobility. Treatment is particularly effective if started in the early stages.

Reflexology

Treatment would be overall, concentrating on areas relating to the affected joints to help relieve pain and inflammation and providing additional treatment to the reflexes relating to the pituitary gland, parathyroid gland, adrenal glands and solar plexus.

Nutritional therapy

Some nutritional factors common to many sufferers are nutritional deficiencies, intolerance to red meat, food allergies and toxic overload due to constipation. Rheumatoid arthritis is often significantly alleviated by identifying food allergies. A number of different nutritional deficiencies have been identified in different rheumatoid arthritis sufferers, including zinc, essential fatty acids, selenium and vitamin A. Supplements of vitamin E, pantothenic acid, copper and boron have been used in various clinical trials and found helpful.

Chiropractic

Chiropractors may be able to treat the condition by easing muscular tension in the body, which they believe may be inhibiting its normal movement and function, and by easing spinal restriction, which they claim can discourage the healing process. The treatment must be done with great care and is more effective the earlier that it is given. Rheumatoid arthritis can respond to mobilization techniques. A chiropractor will be aware of any manipulation dangers concerning spinal rheumatoid arthritis.

Autogenic training

This therapy is suitable for both osteoarthritis and rheumatoid arthritis as it promotes muscular relaxation and improves blood flow to the affected area. It provides pain reduction, a general reduction in stress reaction and therefore lessens the need for drugs.

Other therapies

Acupressure and **shiatsu** may be very useful. **Yoga** offers gentle *asanas*, relaxation, *pranayama* and meditation. **Rolfing** may help by enabling joints to move by working on surrounding soft tissue structures. **Color therapists** will use orange in their treatment as it helps calm inflammation and is very warming. **Ayurvedic medicine** will aim at balancing the tridoshas.

Rheumatism

What is it?

Rheumatism is a general term used to denote any disorder which causes pain and aching in the muscles and bones. The term is used by the layman, rather than the professional, and covers a large number of medical conditions in which sufferers experience pain and stiffness in various parts of the body and, if symptoms are confined to the joints, arthritis (see page 304). It can occur at any age, although it is more common in the elderly. Polymyalgia rheumatica, an uncommon form of rheumatism which tends to affect the elderly, is of sudden onset and causes severe stiffness and pain in the muscles of the neck, shoulders, hips and thighs.

Causes

As the term rheumatism is a catch-all word, the causes of it are diverse. However, conditions which may present with the above symptoms include:

- **Fibrositis or fibromyalgia.** *Symptoms of widespread aches and pain, aggravated by cold and stress, are associated with poor, unrefreshing sleep caused by stress or emotional upset.*
- **Polymyalgia rheumatica and temporal arteritis** *affect those over 50 and are related inflammatory conditions. The former causes pain, stiffness and weakness in the shoulder and pelvic girdle muscles, and the latter headache and tenderness of the temporal artery, with risk of blindness. Rheumatoid arthritis* *(see page 304)* *may show similar symptoms.*
- **Polymyositis,** *which is an inflammation of the muscles that causes pain and weakness. It can be severe, but is uncommon.*
- **Endocrine disorders.** *Hypothyroidism causes aching muscles and stiffness. Hyperthyroidism may cause muscle weakness.*
- **Vitamin D deficiency** *causes bone pain and muscle weakness.*

Orthodox treatment

Most rheumatic conditions will respond to anti-inflammatory painkillers and heat treatment. Anti-rheumatic drugs may slow the progress of rheumatoid arthritis. Steroid injections into inflamed joints or tendons may reduce swelling and provide relief from severe symptoms. Physiotherapy will help relieve stiffness and pain and enable sufferers to regain the use of the joints. Oral steroids are essential for treating polymyalgia rheumatica, and are prescribed immediately for temporal arteritis in order to prevent blindness. An exercise program and a small dose of antidepressants may help treat fibromyalgia.

Alternative Treatment

Acupuncture

Acupuncture can be highly effective and can produce lasting benefit. The acupuncturist will aim to warm cold areas or clear excess heat, move stagnant fluids, and circulate the energy and the blood. The result is a reduction in inflammation, long-lasting pain relief and improved mobility. Treatment is particularly effective if started in the early stages.

Alexander Technique

The Alexander Technique can be very effective in dealing with musculo-skeletal problems. It will aim to release unnecessarily contracted muscles, free up joints and lengthen the spinal column. This reduces mechanical interference and strain, facilitating the efficient use of the body's regenerative and healing powers.

Homeopathy

Homeopaths have found that if sufferers follow an alkaline diet their symptoms are eased. Supplements of vitamin B6, calcium and magnesium may be recommended. The following remedies may be prescribed:

- Bryonia if pain is brought on by movement.
- Pulsatilla if there is pain with weepiness.
- Causticum if there is stiffness due to contracted tendons.
- Rhus tox. if the pain is eased by prolonged gentle movement.
- Ruta grav. if there is pain in the tendons.

Rolfing

Rolfing may help by enabling joints to move by working on surrounding soft tissue structures and by boosting overall circulation.

Reflexology

Treatment would be overall, with special attention paid to the reflexes relating to the pituitary gland, thyroid, adrenal glands, solar plexus, as well as specific areas relating to the affected joints.

Other therapies

Yoga offers gentle *asanas*, relaxation, *pranayama* and meditation. **Western herbalism** may be useful, providing detoxification, anti-inflammatories and analgesic herbs. **Color therapists** would use orange as it is very warming and helps calm inflammation. **Aromatherapy** may include geranium oil for its uplifting properties, while ginger oil will warm and juniper oil may help remove toxins. Rosemary will help encourage the circulation and remove toxins via the blood system. **Ayurvedic medicine** will aim at balancing the tridoshas with medicines and diet. *Panchakarma* will help detoxification. **Radionics** and **polarity therapy** may be useful. Rheumatism can respond to **chiropractic** treatment. A **hypnotherapist** may suggest hypno-healing, cell command therapy, and creative visualization. A **nutritional therapist** may recommend selenium supplements to help muscle pain.

BACKACHE

What is it?

Backache is one of the most common symptoms of ill health. Up to 75 percent of adults suffer from backache or back pain at some time, but only ten percent of that is actually caused by underlying illness. The symptoms vary, but there may be muscle spasm, with pain shooting down the legs. Lower back pain is common, as is knotting in the upper back and shoulders.

Causes

Backache is usually caused by muscles in the back becoming overstrained or injured in some way. Back pain may be caused by a mechanical disorder affecting one of the structures in or around the spine. Pain may be caused by damage to the ligaments, muscles or one of the small vertebral joints or discs. These discs, located between each of the vertebrae in the back, contain a central gelatinous core surrounded by a fibrous ring. With age or injury, the discs can rupture, causing the contents to spill out and press on the nerves that radiate from the spinal cord. This can then lead to referred pain, as in sciatica (see page 314), which is felt in the area of the back that is supplied by the nerve. The most common causes of backache include:

- *Bone structure abnormalities, even minor ones, can place slight but constant stress on the muscles and vertebral joints.*
- *Poor muscle tone and posture, with general lack of fitness, poor seating, unaccustomed lifting or manual work all increase the chances of contracting acute back strain.*
- *Obesity aggravates backache, even if it is not the cause.*
- *Pregnancy. Hormones released in pregnancy may loosen the ligaments. The weight of the baby, carried in front, may cause the spine to arch in order to balance, putting strain on the back muscles.*
- *Stress or depression can make the back muscles tense up, causing aching, pain or interference with sleep (see Stress pages 186–187).*

Orthodox treatment

Most cases of minor backache go in a few days with rest and/or painkillers. Rest will be necessary in the acute stage, although prolonged bed rest is not helpful. Painkillers such as paracetamol may work or NSAIDS (nonsteroidal anti-inflammatory drugs) may be given. Muscle relaxants may be given if the problem is muscular spasm. Physiotherapy may be offered, and manipulation by osteopaths or chiropractors may also be suggested. Weight loss and appropriate exercise may be useful.

ALTERNATIVE TREATMENT

Alexander Technique

The Alexander Technique can be very effective in dealing with musculo-skeletal problems. It will aim to release unnecessarily contracted muscles, free up joints and lengthen the spinal column. This reduces mechanical interference and strain, facilitating the efficient use of the body's regenerative and healing powers.

Chiropractic

Backache or pain is a frequently treated symptom. There are many causes of backache, but most will respond to chiropractic manipulation.

Acupuncture

Treatment is often extremely effective in producing lasting benefit in cases of backache or pain. The treatment aims to reduce spasm and inflammation and promote healing by treating the underlying energy imbalances. A large body of research attests to the value of acupuncture for back pain.

Osteopathy

Osteopaths are skilled in the art of manual therapy, both in diagnosis and treatment, for a wide variety of complaints involving the back. Manipulation involves the use of short-amplitude, high-velocity maneuvers designed to release locked joints and to break down any adhesions in the joints and surrounding soft tissue. Osteopaths use a specific soft tissue massage technique to release tight muscles or to increase tone in loose ones.

Rolfing

Through improved alignment in relation to gravity, the body lengthens and there is less compression, particularly on the lower back. It also helps by improving movement so that the back is not unduly strained.

Massage

It is unwise to have a massage if there is undiagnosed acute back pain, but chronic (long-term) backache may be helped directly by massage if it is of muscular origin. Massage may relieve backache caused by habitually tense muscles by relaxing them and allowing them to regain their former elasticity. Massage is also useful where backache is stress-related.

Other therapies

Hellerwork theory is that backache is often the result of excessive compression in the spine due to poor posture and poor use of the body, which can be reversed by this treatment. **Yoga** offers *asanas*, relaxation, *pranayama* and meditation. **Auricular therapy** can help relieve pain quickly. **Aromatherapy** offers specialist massage treatment with a blend of individually chosen oils. **Reflexology** will treat reflexes corresponding to the spine.

CRAMP

What is it?

Cramp is a painful muscular spasm which usually affects the legs, feet and toes, although it can occur in the hands (writer's cramp) and arms. The pain can be extremely severe and may last for only a few minutes or be prolonged and repeated. It may affect a single muscle or a group of muscles. It is common in athletes and those who use groups of muscles for long periods of time (see RSI page 197). Night cramps are common to many people, particularly the elderly, and usually affect the calf muscles, which spasm painfully for no apparent reason.

Causes

When a muscle contracts it tightens a small part of the fibers of the muscle for a short length of time. However, in cases of cramp a muscle or muscle section experiences continuous contraction without any relaxation of the muscle fibers. This leads to a build-up of muscle waste products, particularly lactic acid, in the area. This causes the pain. Cramp incurred during sports activities can sometimes damage the muscle fibers as the player continues to put pressure on the affected area.

Although the causes of cramp are not always clear, the main symptoms are caused by:

- ♦ *Heavy exercise, which can bring on an attack if the muscles are either overused or not properly warmed up.*
- ♦ *Salt depletion. Excessive sweating, particularly after heavy exertion, may leave the body lacking enough salt.*
- ♦ *Pressure on a spinal nerve caused by a prolapsed disc.*
- ♦ *Neurological disorders such as "writer's cramp."*
- ♦ *Hardening of the arteries in the leg causes pain and cramp in the calf on walking as the blood fails to match the muscles' increased demands when exercising.*
- ♦ *Excessive repetitive movement of a particular limb may cause cramp. This happens in cases of RSI.*

SEE YOUR DOCTOR IMMEDIATELY IF YOU EXPERIENCE CRAMP IN THE CHEST WHICH OCCURS DURING OR AFTER EXERCISE. THIS MAY BE ANGINA (SEE PAGE 165).

Orthodox treatment

Massage or stretching the affected muscles usually helps to relieve pain and calm the affected area. Calf and toe cramp may be eased by putting pressure on the foot and toe and attempting to move around. Persistent night cramps can be eased by taking a dose of quinine at night. Keeping warm in bed will also help.

Salt tablets may help after profuse sweating. Ensuring that you warm up and cool down properly before and after exercise will help avoid attacks. If cramp is brought on by excessive repetitive movements, is particularly severe and painful, or regularly follows exercise, you should see your doctor, who may refer you to a consultant for treatment. An EMG (electromyogram) examination will assess the electrical activity within the muscles and a biopsy of the muscle tissue may be taken.

Athletes or sports enthusiasts may receive specific treatment for their cramp from sports clinics. Physiotherapists will use massage and heat treatment to tone the muscles, either before or after injury, to alleviate or avoid cramp.

ALTERNATIVE TREATMENT

Homeopathy

If cramp occurs frequently for no apparent reason, then constitutional treatment may help. The remedies below may also be useful:

• Cuprum met. for severe cramps mainly in feet or legs, beginning with a twitching of muscles; and if the cause is loss of salt from the body through excessive sweating or from vomiting.

• Arnica for cramps which are the result of muscle fatigue following prolonged exercise.

Chiropractic

Many types of cramp respond to chiropractic treatment. A practitioner will not only treat the affected area but will also address the spine and neck areas.

Massage

Massage is very effective in relieving muscular cramps, particularly those which occur regularly. The whole area of the affected part will be treated and the therapist will aim to warm and relax the muscles by using kneading movements. Other movements will be performed to encourage blood to circulate more freely to the affected area.

Nutritional therapy

Many therapists believe that cramp can be relieved by increasing salt, magnesium or calcium consumption. Salt deficiency is very uncommon and is only likely to occur after lengthy strenuous exercise in a hot climate. Calcium deficiency is less likely to cause cramps than magnesium deficiency.

Other therapies

Acupressure and **shiatsu** may be very useful. **Yoga** offers gentle *asanas*, relaxation, *pranayama* and meditation. **Rolfing** may help by improving the circulation and toning muscles. **Polarity therapy** may be useful. **Macrobiotics** can be very helpful in treating this condition. **Color therapists** may use some red to improve ambulation. **Aromatherapy** may use palmera oil to enhance a person's overall circulation.

Soft Tissue Damage

What is it?

The soft tissues are those which surround the bones and joints in the body. They include ligaments, tendons and muscles. Injury to these soft tissues is very common, and includes strains, sprains, tendonitis and injuries which causes tearing. Soft tissue is present all over the body and serves to protect and allow movement of the bones. Accordingly, damage can be present anywhere in the limbs and torso.

Causes

Any activity which places undue strain on the soft tissues of the body can cause damage. The most common causes are:

- *Impact.*
- *Straining.*
- *Tearing.*
- *Inflammation.*

Sports injuries are common causes of soft tissue damage. Sprains and dislocations are usually the result of torn ligaments. The affected joint will become extremely painful, and possibly unstable if there is a complete tear. Severe sprains may lead to the dislocation of the joint (particularly shoulders), and repeated injury to the same part of the body may cause the ligaments to lose their elasticity and usefulness.

Tendons, which attach the muscles to the bone, may be damaged, and inflamed, and in some cases may become severed or torn, disconnecting the muscle from the bone. Torn tendons will eventually heal, but this may take a great deal of time.

Bursitis affects the bursae, small pouches of fluid which are found around joints, and where the ligaments and tendons cross the bone. They are there to reduce friction at the joints, but inflammation or infection may occur to the bursae, which leads to pain, swelling and tenderness (see Bunions page 311).

Muscle strains may be the result of muscle fatigue. The muscle fibers themselves may be torn, and there will be pain and tenderness upon movement.

Cartilage is often considered a soft tissue, and it too can tear, in the event of injury, causing pain and swelling. Surgery is often necessary to repair damage to cartilage since it does not have the capacity to heal itself.

DAMAGE TO THE BACK IN SPORT AND IN LIFTING HEAVY OBJECTS MAY CAUSE DAMAGE TO THE MUSCLES AND LIGAMENTS. MOST WILL HEAL IN TIME, BUT IF THE VERTEBRAE ARE DAMAGED, THERE MAY BE SERIOUS SPINAL INJURIES.

Orthodox treatment

Any sudden damage or injury must receive immediate medical attention. Examination by sight and touch of the affected part will enable a diagnosis to be made. An X-ray may be required to eliminate bone damage as the cause. Treatment in the first 24 hours includes rest to minimize further damage, cold therapy (ice packs) which reduces bleeding and is analgesic, compression to restrict swelling, and elevation to encourage the fluid to drain.

After a reassessment of the injury, a rehabilitation program based on exercise will begin. Treatments include non-steroidal, anti-inflammatory drugs and local steroid or anesthetic injections. Physiotherapy sessions will also help to speed up the healing of the injured area.

Alternative Treatment

Osteopathy

Osteopaths are skilled in the art of manual therapy, both in the diagnosis and treatment of a wide variety of complaints involving the musculo-skeletal system. Manipulation involves the use of short-amplitude, high-velocity maneuvers designed to release joint locking and to break down adhesions in the joints and surrounding soft tissue. Osteopaths will use specific soft tissue massage techniques to either release tone in tight muscles or to increase tone in loose ones. Most sports injuries and other sprains and strains respond extremely well to this manual therapy.

Rolfing

Rolfing treatment may help after the inflammation and acute pain has subsided by promoting healing. This is done by softening any hardened tissue and encouraging appropriate movement of muscles and joints by inhibiting certain muscles and stimulating others.

Cymatics

Sound wave therapy activates and stimulates the body by using a hand-held applicator, pads or plates which aim high-frequency sounds to the affected parts of the body.

Other therapies

Reflexology treatment will pay particular attention to the adrenals and the areas of the affected part. **Chiropractors** routinely and successfully treat the effects of soft tissue damage. **Homeopathic** treatment with arnica may be appropriate to encourage healing of most conditions. For inflammation and tearing pain, ruta and rhus tox. may help. **Hellerwork** may be useful; whiplash injuries are treated extensively with this therapy in the United States. **Acupressure** and **shiatsu** may be useful. **Western herbalism** can help to speed up recovery with internal remedies and comfrey applied locally. **Kinesiology** will be useful, using magnetic therapy and balancing techniques. **Spiritual healing** will help promote the body's own healing forces.

BREAKS AND FRACTURES

What are they?

The terms "break" and "fracture" are synonymous. A bone breaks (fractures) when excessive force is applied to it. Bones have a slightly elastic fabric, but they will splinter and split under pressure. Symptoms of fracture include swelling and tenderness, and there may be strange deformities and skin discoloration, as well as an inability to move the part affected. There may be a protruding bone, or a grinding feeling when attempting to move it.

There are two main types of fracture:

Simple (or closed) fracture when the soft tissue overlying the damaged bone is intact.

Compound (or open) fracture is much more serious. The skin above the fracture is damaged and the bone is exposed and at risk of infection.

Causes

Most breaks are the result of injury, particularly in sport, but also in accidents such as car crashes and falls. Fractures are most common when the bone has been weakened by disease, as with osteoporosis (see page 312) and some forms of cancer. In these cases, very little force is required for the bone to break.

Causes of fracture may be divided as follows:

- **Stress fractures** *are caused by persistent but small stresses on the bone. They usually occur in the legs more frequently in those who walk or run long distances and those whose profession requires them to place excessive force on their legs, such as sports people and dancers.*
- **Pathological fractures** *are caused when the bone is already weakened by disease, such as osteoporosis, certain sorts of bone cancer and various other conditions. The bones either fracture spontaneously or are caused by a minor injury.*

NEVER MOVE AN ACCIDENT VICTIM – WAIT FOR AN AMBULANCE TO ARRIVE. MOVING THOSE WHO HAVE INJURIES TO THE NECK OR SPINE MAY RESULT IN PARALYSIS.

Orthodox treatment

Once a fracture is suspected a doctor will provide first aid treatment, for example cleaning the wound to prevent infection and immobilizing the limb, and will then refer the patient to hospital. Once at hospital, X-rays will be taken to determine the exact nature and site of the fracture. Treatment will be based at aligning the fracture, so it heals properly. Bone begins healing at once and it is essential that alignment is undertaken at the earliest possible opportunity. A splint or a plaster cast will be used to keep the bone together and properly aligned. At this stage the newly forming bone is very fragile and immobilization ensures that the bones will not become misaligned and form replacement bone in the wrong site. An operation to reposition bone may be necessary, and this will be done under a general anesthetic. In serious fractures, nails, wires, screws or metal plates may be placed across the bone ends to keep them stable. Pins may be inserted thorough the skin and bone, and fixed externally, to keep the bone in position until healing is complete. Painkillers will be offered, and physiotherapy as appropriate for rehabilitation. Gentle exercise will be suggested as soon as it is safe. This will prevent edema and stiffness in the nearby joints and maintain the blood and nerve supply to the area.

ALTERNATIVE TREATMENT

Cymatics

Sound wave therapy activates and stimulates the body. A therapist would use a hand-held applicator, pads or plates which aim high-frequency sounds to parts of the body for healing purposes. The patient may be placed in a warm water treatment pool though which sound waves are passed.

Alexander Technique

Alexander Technique is recommended as a way of maximizing the body's healing process and ensuring that the person avoids developing any compensatory muscular and postural imbalances.

Western herbalism

Herbs can help to speed up the recovery and healing of fractures, particularly comfrey. Also known as knitbone, it is often used to assist in the healing of bones. A practitioner will apply comfrey paste to the affected part and then bind it.

Other therapies

Nutritional therapists will recommend comfrey for aiding the mending of bone breaks and fractures, and zinc and vitamin C supplements. **Rolfing** may help after inflammation and acute pain has subsided, promoting healing by softening hardened tissue and encouraging appropriate movement of muscles and joints. **Reflexology** will be overall, with special attention paid to the areas of the affected part to assist the formation of bone. **Homeopathic** treatment may use symphytum for slow healing fractures. **Acupressure** and **Shiatsu** may be very useful in relieving pain and encouraging healing. **Spiritual healing** is useful for breakages and fractures, as it can reduce pain and swelling and help the body's natural healing forces to come into action. **Massage** may help in the rehabilitation phase of the treatment but it should never be attempted near a recent fracture site. A **hypnotherapist** may use hypno-healing to speed up bone repair and regeneration of healthy bone. **Color therapists** may use indigo as it encourages bone healing.

BUNIONS

What is it?

A bunion is a lay term for the protrusion of the big toe joint known medically as *hallux valgus*. Over this there is a fluid-filled sac (bursa) which gives the joint some protection. When the protruding joint presses against the shoe, hard skin grows over it to form a corn or a callus (see page 297). If the shoe continues to be worn, the prolonged pressure causes the bursa to fill with fluid. The fluid-filled bursa may then become inflamed or infected and develop into a condition known as bursitis.

Sometimes the bunion is so large and pronounced that it can be seen trying to break through the shoe, causing it to become stretched and misshapen. Walking is extremely painful other than in bare feet or wearing soft slippers.

TO PREVENT BURSITIS, ALWAYS WEAR CORRECTLY FITTED SHOES AND USE A PUMICE STONE TO GENTLY RUB AWAY ANY AREAS OF HARD SKIN.

Causes

Some bunions are made worse by wearing ill-fitting shoes, although the underlying toe joint deformity may be hereditary or mechanical. Bunions in children and adolescents are associated with flat feet and wearing narrow footwear. If properly fitted shoes are not supplied frequently enough, their growing feet become constrained. Women suffer from the condition more than men due to wearing unsuitable fashion footwear such as high-heeled or pointed-toe shoes which constrict the toes and push the body's weight forward onto the toes.

THOSE WITH FAMILY MEMBERS WHO SUFFER FROM BUNIONS SHOULD TAKE PARTICULAR CARE OF THEIR FEET AND MAY BENEFIT FROM REGULARLY VISITING A PODIATRIST.

Orthodox treatment

Wearing well-fitting shoes distributes the body's weight evenly and helps avoid bunions. Padding the area where the friction is occurring may help, but getting rid of the shoes aggravating the bunion should be the preferred option.

If corns and calluses on the feet have contributed toward the condition, you may be referred to a podiatrist, who will cut or pare them down. A custom-made insole, known as an orthotic, may be helpful.

A large painful bunion causing extreme difficulty in walking, or which is crowding or causing deformity of the other toes, may require surgery either to remove the protruding part of the bone or to cut and realign the toe. There are a number of procedures available which can be done in hospital as day cases using a local anesthetic. Occasionally, the affected toe may develop osteoarthritis (see pages 312–313).

Bursitis, if present, can be treated by administering anti-inflammatory drugs. If the bursitis has become infected antibiotics will be prescribed.

ALTERNATIVE TREATMENT

Homeopathy

For bunions which are inflamed by bursitis, the following remedies may help:

- Apis for tight, blister-like swellings that are sensitive to the touch and pressure, and when burning, stinging pain is worse for heat and decreases with cold.
- Rhux Tox. when the skin is itchy, red, swollen and burning and joints are stiff but pain decreases with continued movement but worse on starting to move.
- Ruta Grav. for bruised, aching bones and muscles.

Rolfing

Rolfing may help by improving alignment and movement so that pressure is not being exerted inappropriately on the joint concerned, and may be causing bunions.

Western herbalism

Where bursitis is present, treatment may help ease inflammation or swelling with local applications of linseed, marsh mallow, comfrey and slippery elm. Combinations of these remedies can also be made into a poultice and applied to ease the affected joint. Camomile infusions when drunk just before bedtime will help promote sleep if the joint pain is causing disturbed nights.

Naturopathy

Bathing the feet in a bowl of hot water in which a tablespoon of Epsom salts has been dissolved will help ease joint discomfort. Gentle massage will help keep the joint moving. Where bursitis is present, a naturopath will advise resting the affected area as much as possible and providing support by bandaging or splinting the toe. Applying cold compresses three times a day will help reduce any swelling in the area. A whole food diet with additional supplements of vitamins A and C may also be recommended.

Other therapies

Acupressure and **shiatsu** may be very useful in relieving discomfort and encouraging healing. **Alexander Technique** will help readjust incorrect posture and balance. **Acupuncture** treatment is frequently effective in reducing inflammation and promoting the healing of damaged tissues, as in bursitis.

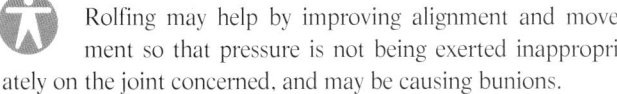

OSTEOPOROSIS

What is it?

Osteoporosis means "porous bones" and is a condition in which the bones progressively lose their density, become thinner and more fragile and brittle. Although bones cannot shrink, they can become porous and less dense, and therefore more likely to fracture. Osteoporosis does not usually cause symptoms until the bones become so brittle and weak that even mild trauma will lead to fractures. Women are more likely to be affected by osteoporosis than men as they have about 30 percent less bone mass.

AFTER THE AGE OF 35, THE BODY CREATES LESS NEW BONE AND BECOMES LESS EFFICIENT AT ABSORBING CALCIUM.

Advanced osteoporosis causes an large number of fractures in the elderly, particularly of the spine. The vertebrae in the back may become so weakened that they collapse on themselves, causing sudden and severe back pain, which settles after a few weeks. This in turn causes the "dowager's hump" present in many osteoporosis sufferers, loss of height, and also reduced rib-cage movements which then causes shortness of breath and pain when the body is exerted.

Little pressure may be required to fracture hips, thighs and wrists, which are the most common sites for osteoporotic fracture. There may be no warning of osteoporosis until a fracture occurs, although loss of height, backache, stooping posture and the appearance of the dowager's hump are all indications.

BY THE AGE OF 75, ALMOST HALF OF ALL WOMEN WILL HAVE EXPERIENCED AT LEAST ONE BONE FRACTURE THAT CAN BE ATTRIBUTED TO OSTEOPOROSIS.

Causes

Although bone provides the structural framework of the body, it is not inert and in adult life there is a continuous process of bone remodeling and reabsorption. In osteoporosis there is an imbalance between these processes leading to a decrease in bone mass. Normal nutrition and growth lead to a peak bone mass by the mid-thirties. After that, both men and women lose bone at a rate of less than one percent a year.

The sex hormones estrogen and testosterone have a direct effect on the bone and reduce the rate of bone reabsorption. Women are particularly vulnerable to osteoporosis as they start out with a lower peak bone mass than men and during the menopause they have an additional bone loss of three to five percent per year for up to ten years. Once the bone mass falls below the "fracture threshold," then fractures become likely. Finely-boned women of Caucasian or Asian extraction are more likely to develop osteoporosis than the more heavily-boned Afro-Carribean women. For unknown reasons, osteoporosis is also associated with chronic bronchitis and emphysema (perhaps due to the link with smoking). Other causes of osteoporosis include:

- *A diet low in calcium, vitamin D and other minerals necessary for health bones.*
- *Lack of exercise.*
- *Prolonged immobility, as with the bedridden or the housebound.*
- *An overactive thyroid.*
- *Heavy consumption of alcohol.*
- *Smoking.*
- *Prolonged lack of estrogen in adult life. Risk factors include premature menopause, delayed onset of puberty and low body weight with scanty or absent periods (as with anorexia nervosa).*
- *Inherited condition, as sometimes osteoporosis runs in families.*
- *Medical conditions associated with osteoporosis include long-term use of corticosteroids, overactive thyroid gland, chronic liver disease and malabsorption syndromes.*

THERE ARE MANY PREVENTATIVE MEASURES THAT CAN BE TAKEN TO AVOID OSTEOPOROSIS. THE EARLIER THESE ARE TAKEN, THE MORE LIKELY IT IS THAT OSTEOPOROSIS CAN BE DELAYED OR MINIMIZED.

Orthodox treatment

Once the mass of the bone has been lost, it cannot be fully restored, although there is evidence that slow rebuilding may be possible. Therefore, prevention is the most important way of avoiding osteoporosis. Measures that can be taken include:

- *Weight-bearing exercise such as walking, weight training and running. This helps promote bone growth and strengthens the surrounding muscles which helps take the strain off the bones. Older people may find less strenuous exercises such as swimming and yoga useful.*
- *A diet rich in calcium. This will help prevent or minimize the development of osteoporosis. Calcium is found in dairy products. Low-fat cheeses and yogurts and skimmed milk will provide calcium without excess fats. Other sources are legumes, cereals and hard water.*
- *Taking vitamin D and calcium supplements.*
- *Giving up smoking and limiting alcohol intake.*

Exercise, if possible, will be recommended and analgesics may be given, particularly if there is back pain. Hormone Replacement Therapy (HRT) prevents further bone loss caused by lack of estrogen in the body, so many will be protected against osteoporosis as a side effect to taking HRT. However, once HRT is stopped, the condition will reappear. Not all women are suitable for the HRT treatment. A bone density measurement test will help select those who are suitable for treatment prior to the onset of osteoporosis.

Etidronate, which is a drug containing phosphorus, may be used in conjunction with calcium supplements to stop the progress of spinal osteoporosis. Men who suffer from osteoporosis should consult a specialist.

Alternative Treatment

Alexander Technique

The Alexander Technique is recommended for osteoporosis sufferers as it can provide a method of maximizing postural balance and mechanical efficiency.

Chiropractic

Chiropractic treatment is commonly used for osteoporosis. It will be done gently and in a varied manner, depending on the severity of the condition.

Rolfing

Rolfing may help by improving fluid exchange and promoting the health of the tissues. In early onset of osteoporosis the practitioner may also concentrate on improving body posture to overcome the hunched shoulders and stooped posture which are characteristic of osteoporosis.

Tai chi

The gentle, rhythmic movements of tai chi will help promote good posture, flexibility and balance to help avoid falls – and therefore potential fractures. The spiritual side of tai chi is said to make the elderly feel young and relaxed.

Yoga

Yoga practitioners would concentrate on breathing exercises to help the body to cope with the changes occurring in the structure of the bones. Emphasis is placed on movement and flexibility to help with posture and balance.

Naturopathy

Naturopaths will look at diet and recommend swimming, as it takes the weight off the body's joints and bones, as well as helping to relax muscles and relieve pain.

Aromatherapy

Aromatherapists will use stimulating herbs in a full body massage and might choose rosemary and juniper.

Western herbalism

Advice on diet and exercise, and reduction of associated symptoms will be included. Hormone balancing will help promote the proper absorption of calcium.

Kinesiology

A kinesiology practitioner may suggest treatment that involves checking for magnesium, HCI and calcium deficiencies and supplying digestive enzymes. It may also involve checking the upper thoracic area for lesions, suggesting various forms of moderate, regular exercise to promote joint and muscle strength, the avoidance of pasteurized milk (which they claim inhibits the uptake of calcium), and suggesting the inclusion of bone marrow in the diet on a regular basis.

Nutritional therapy

Nutritional therapists believe osteoporosis is linked with an excess consumption of protein, which leaves an acid residue in the body, so a diet controlling its consumption would be devised. Other factors they would address include checking for magnesium deficiency and any hormonal imbalance involving the thyroid and parathyroid glands which, between them, control the amount of calcium released from the bones into the bloodstream. Magnesium and zinc supplements are likely to be beneficial, together with the daily consumption of ground sesame seeds and comfrey leaves. Comfrey is said to be an excellent, nutritious herb for repairing damaged bones.

Naturopathy

Naturopaths will advise taking exercise, as they place great emphasis on this to prevent osteoporosis. A diet rich in protein and whole food may be advised. Supplements of calcium and vitamin D will be recommended.

Homeopathy

Homeopathic treatment would be constitutional and would take many different factors into account, including diet. Calcium and magnesium supplements may be advised and their prescriptions may also include:

- Calc. phos. for pain the the bones. This helps promote bone growth. It is often used to treat bone complaints such as painful bones and joints or slow-to-heal fractures.
- Ruta grav. is an important remedy for bruising of the periosteum (the lining of the bones) which is accompanied by deep, aching pain.
- Theridion is a minor remedy which is used to treat bone decay.
- Bryonia may be given for painful joints that hurt if moved, especially after an injury.

Ayurvedic medicine

Ayurvedic medicine places great emphasis on good health and the prevention of ill health. In order to avoid osteoporosis, a practitioner will advise on diet and exercise. For existing osteoporosis sufferers, advice on diet and exercise will be accompanied by massage, oil treatments, yoga, breathing exercises and meditation.

Other therapies

Acupressure and **shiatsu** may be very useful, especially in providing relief from any discomfort caused by the osteoporosis. **Spiritual healing** may help alleviate any pain felt in the bones after a fracture. It can also help the sufferer focus on promoting the formation of healthy bone tissue. A **macrobiotic** diet may prove very helpful in treating this condition. **Chinese herbalists** may provide herbal tonics to treat the condition. **Kirlian photography**, **crystal** and **gemstone healing** and **hypnotherapy** may all have a role to play in treating osteoporosis.

SCIATICA

What is it?

The sciatic nerve is the longest nerve in the body and runs from the lower lumbar and upper sacral vertebrae to the pelvis and down the thigh and back of the leg. Pain experienced along this pathway is called sciatica. This is a type of referred pain where the pain is felt in areas supplied by the nerve, rather than at the site of the damage, and it suggests nerve root irritation.

Pain may be experienced in the lower back, extending down to the leg. The pain can be either mild or more severe, with shooting or burning sensations. There may be muscle weakness or numbness or tingling in the leg, foot or toes, or muscle spasms in the buttock or leg. There may also be loss of nerve reflexes in the knee and ankles.

Causes

The causes of sciatica are varied, but it is often the result of a slipped (prolapsed) disc. The discs in the spine are thick, gel-filled pads enclosed by a wide, fibrous ring. Pressure on, or damage to, the discs can cause them to spill out their center onto the nerve roots at the spinal cord. Depending on the severity of the pressure, there may be minor backache or extreme, debilitating pain which makes walking very difficult. The pain can run right down the foot and there may be a loss of power in the muscle. Sciatica can be associated with pregnancy and childbirth. It may be the after-effect of a strain caused by heavy lifting, stress, injury to the back, and an abnormality or misposition of the sacroiliac joint. Rarely, a tumor may be pressing on the sciatic nerve. Sometimes there is no obvious cause for the condition.

SCIATICA IS NOT DANGEROUS BUT PERSISTENT NUMBNESS OR MUSCLE WASTING, WEAKNESS AND REFLEX LOSS MAY BE DUE TO NERVE ROOT COMPRESSION AND REQUIRES TREATMENT.

Orthodox treatment

Treatment in the acute phase will be rest for a few days and analgesics, sometimes with anti-inflammatory drugs or diazepam for muscle spasm. This may be followed by physiotherapy. Sometimes wearing a corset will help. Most get better on this regime but occasionally an epidural corticosteroid injection is required to reduce pain and speed recovery. Surgery on the back may be offered to the less than one percent of patients who fail to recover. Most cases get better anyway, but sciatica can recur.

ALTERNATIVE TREATMENT

Osteopathy

Osteopaths are skilled in the art of manual therapy, both in diagnosis and treatment, for a wide variety of complaints involving the back. Manipulation involves the use of short-amplitude, high-velocity maneuvers designed to release locked joints and to break down any adhesions in the joints and surrounding soft tissue. Osteopaths use a specific soft tissue massage technique to release tight muscles or to increase tone in loose ones.

Homeopathy

Treatment can be useful, depending on individual symptoms. The following remedies may be appropriate:

- Colocynthis to treat pain that spreads along the sciatic nerve.
- Rhux tox. where joint and muscle stiffness and pain are better for continued movement but worse on first starting to move.
- Gelsemium to work on the spinal cord and muscles.
- Hypericum to help with nerve pain.

Alexander Technique

The Alexander Technique is very effective in dealing with musculo-skeletal problems. Although symptoms are usually located in a specific part of the body, the Technique takes a holistic view. It promotes a general condition of psychophysical harmony and postural balance and therefore specific problems tend to disappear. In particular, it leads to a release of unnecessarily contracted muscles, a freeing up of the joints and a lengthening of the spinal column. As the spine is released from its chronic contraction, the pressure on the discs is reduced and they can reabsorb the spinal fluids, which may have been compressed out. Consequently, the mechanical cause of the sciatic pain is removed.

Other therapies

Acupuncture often produces lasting benefits by reducing inflammation and promoting the healing of damaged tissues. When sciatica is caused by pressure on the nerve from the deep rotator muscles of the hip, **hellerwork** may be useful. Depending on the cause, **yoga** may offer gentle *asanas*, relaxation, *pranayama* and meditation. **Rolfing** may help by improving realignment so that the muscles are not compressing the sciatic nerve. **Auricular therapy** can also prove very effective. There is one point on the ear called the sciatic point which is said to help greatly in relieving symptoms of sciatica. Relief can be quick, but regular treatment may be necessary. **Aromatherapists** will use stimulating oils such as rosemary and juniper combined with massage. **Color therapists** would use yellow, as it greatly helps to fortify the nervous system and diminishes the inflammation of the sciatic nerve. The sound wave therapy used by **cymatics** practitioners activates and stimulates the body. This is achieved using a hand-held applicator, pads or plates which aim high-frequency sounds to the affected parts of the body.

MUSCULAR DYSTROPHY

What is it?

Muscular dystrophy is an umbrella term for a group of inherited disorders which affect the muscles, causing slow degeneration. There are five types of muscular dystrophy, classed according to the age of onset.

- **Duchenne muscular dystrophy** *occurs in about one in 3,000 male infants. Affected boys are normal at birth and early motor milestones such as sitting are reached. However, walking is delayed and half fail to walk by 18 months. About ten percent of boys have a delay in speaking. The first signs are usually apparent before the child is three, and there may be an increase in muscle bulk in the calves, despite the weakness. The leg and back muscles are affected, giving the child a characteristic waddling gait. There may be difficulty in getting up from the floor. By the age of 12, most children can no longer walk and very few survive after their teens. If the mother is a carrier of Duchenne muscular dystrophy, a male child has a 50 percent change of developing it.*
- **Limb girdle muscular dystrophy** *begins in late childhood or early adulthood, affecting the muscles in the hips and shoulders. The progression is slower than Duchenne. The sufferer normally become severely disabled within about 20 years.*
- **Facio-scapulo-humeral muscular dystrophy** *affects the muscles of the face, upper back and upper arm. Its progression is much slower and does not necessarily cause disability.*
- **Becker's muscular dystrophy** *is much the same as Duchenne, which begins later in childhood and is of a much slower progression. Sufferers often survive to 50 years of age or more.*
- **Dystrophia myotonica** *affects the muscles of the hands and feet, and it can develop in childhood. It is associated with cataracts in middle-age, as well as mental disability.*

Causes

A great amount of research has been carried out into the causes of muscular dystrophy, which is hereditary.

- **Duchenne muscular dystrophy** *is caused by a gene on an X chromosome transmitted by the unaffected mother.*
- **Limb girdle muscular dystrophy** *affects both sexes, and is recessively inherited.*
- **Facio-scapulo-humeral muscular dystrophy** *is inherited in an autosomal dominant pattern.*
- **Myotonic muscular dystrophy** *is also inherited in an autosomal dominant pattern.*
- **Becker's muscular dystrophy** *is caused by a gene defect.*

Orthodox treatment

Diagnosis of the condition will involve examining the patient's limbs and observing movement. This may be confirmed by carrying out an EMG (electromyogram) to measure muscle response. Blood tests will confirm if there are levels of a particular enzyme released by the damaged muscles.

There is no cure for this inherited disease but once diagnosis is confirmed, treatment is limited to maintaining muscular movement. Muscles should be exercised regularly to prevent atrophy and a physiotherapist will provide a series of exercises to be carried out. Surgery to the heel tendons may be necessary to aid walking. Avoiding weight gain will be helpful, as it will reduce the strain put on parts of the body weakened by the condition.

Would-be parents who are known carriers of the disease will be offered genetic counseling. There are also various ante-natal tests which can indicate if the fetus is likely to develop muscular dystrophy, such as chorionic villus sampling and amniocentesis.

ALTERNATIVE TREATMENT

Massage

Massage cannot cure this disorder, but will provide a feeling of physical and mental well-being. The aim of massage is to make the condition less severe by toning up and improving the blood supply to the muscles.

Nutritional therapy

According to scientific studies, muscular dystrophy may be linked with deficiencies of vitamin E and selenium. Some cases have also responded to supplementation with co-enzyme Q10. Food allergy can sometimes cause symptoms similar to muscular dystrophy.

Aromatherapy

Aromatherapists may use stimulating oils such as rosemary or juniper which are quite useful when used in a full body massage.

Naturopathy

Treatment will aim to promote and improve the circulation in the affected limbs by combining movement with water jet massage.

Ayurvedic medicine

There is specific Ayurvedic *panchakarma* therapy to help alleviate the symptoms of muscular dystrophy.

Other therapies

Acupressure and **shiatsu** may be very useful in dealing with symptoms and any discomfort caused by the condition. **Polarity therapy** and **radionics** may also be useful. **Western herbalists** believe that herbal therapy can improve the overall health of the sufferer and help promote the body's ability to resist infection. **Spiritual healing** may help relieve some of the symptoms and keep the condition under control.

INFANTS AND CHILDREN

Children can get ill (or better) in a very short space of time. In addition there is what some doctors call the "veterinary" factor: a baby cannot tell you if he or she feels slightly unwell or tell you where it hurts. Sometimes the signs and symptoms of illness are obvious, for example, the child has a cough, diarrhea and vomiting, rashes, a runny nose or a temperature. But often the only clues are that the child starts to behave differently from normal. The otherwise active child becomes drowsy and irritable or the normally hungry baby shows no interest in his feeding. It is not always easy for a parent to know when her child is truly ill. However, most doctors still feel that the best judge of a child's health is the parent.

Parents should always trust their own instincts and commonsense. If they feel it is necessary, they should seek medical advice by phone or by taking their child down to the doctor's office. Most of the common ailments such as coughs and colds, *chicken pox* and *mumps* do not need any active medical intervention. Often all that is needed is some advice and reassurance for the parents. The doctor may also tell the parents what the natural progress of the illness may be – indeed sometimes a child will get worse before she improves. Allowance should also be made for age, as some illnesses show themselves in a different way as a child gets older.

Fortunately, there are very few truly dangerous illnesses in childhood and all of these can normally be satisfactorily treated in general practice or hospital.

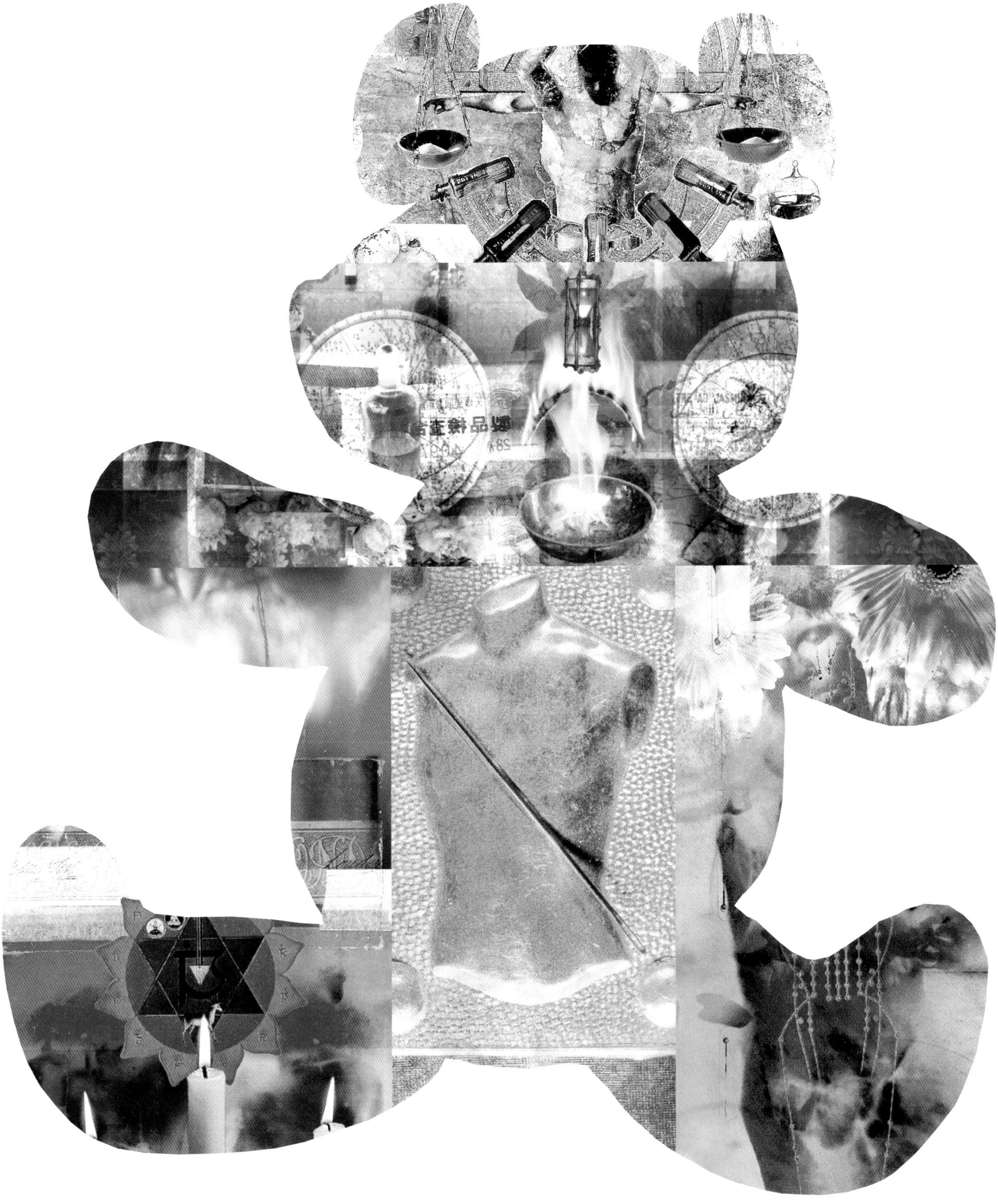

Chicken pox

What is it?

Chicken pox is an extremely contagious viral infection with an incubation period of 14–16 days. The symptoms include headaches and generally feeling unwell, with a raised temperature for about 24 hours. Then the spots begin to develop, usually noticed first on the body and gradually spreading outward from there to the limbs.

The spots can develop anywhere – including in the mouth, on the scalp, around the anus and penis, and even in the vagina and ears. While small and red at the start, the spots enlarge and fill with fluid to become little blisters. These rapidly burst and crust over, eventually drying up altogether to form a scab. The spots are very itchy, and it is important that the child is helped not to scratch them, for scarring and bacterial infection can result.

While chicken pox in childhood is almost always mild, there are other potentially serious complications, such as pneumonia and encephalitis (inflammation of the brain), which adults who catch the disease are much more vulnerable to than children.

Chicken pox in pregnancy may be very serious for the mother, who may contract a life-threatening lung infection. Birth defects are extremely rare, but the greatest risk of infecting the fetus is in the few days before delivery.

It is sensible to allow a child to contract the disease during childhood, when it carries less serious risks and an attack then carries life-long immunity. The chicken pox virus (vericella-zoster) may stay dormant after a bout and appear years later as shingles (herpes zoster). Rarely, a child may even catch chicken pox from an adult with shingles.

Causes

The chicken pox virus may be contracted either via droplet infection in the air or from touching the blister fluid itself. Patients are most infectious from two days before the appearance of the rash until about a week later. The patient remains infectious until all of the spots have crusted over.

Orthodox treatment

Treatment of chicken pox involves making the child comfortable and using calamine lotion for the spots and paracetamol to relieve the slightly higher temperature. In most cases, children can recover within about ten days; adults can take longer.

IF A HIGH FEVER REMAINS AFTER TWO OR THREE DAYS, OR IF THERE IS AN OBVIOUS INFECTION OF THE CHEST, EXCESSIVE COUGHING OR VOMITING, OR ANY INDICATION OF CHICKEN POX PNEUMONIA, CONSULT A DOCTOR IMMEDIATELY. CHICKEN POX PNEUMONIA NEEDS TREATMENT IN HOSPITAL, AND POSSIBLY INTENSIVE CARE.

Alternative Treatment

Homeopathy

Homeopaths may recommend a variety of treatments including:

- Aconite or belladonna for the low fever and general discomfort during the first stages of the disease. A daily dose of ferrum phos. may also help.
- Antimonium tart if the child is whining and not wanting to be left alone with their large blisters.
- Rhus tox. may be used if the child is particularly feverish and is feeling restless.
- Sulphur for a rash or fever.

Western herbalism

There are a number of herbs which can be very useful. An infusion of elderflowers, tincture of comfrey or essential oil of lavender can be dabbed on the spots. Drinking infusions of herbs can also help to bring down a fever and fight the infectious illness.

Reflexology

A reflexologist will provide a series of short and gentle treatments to help strengthen the immune system following debilitating infections.

Bach flower remedies

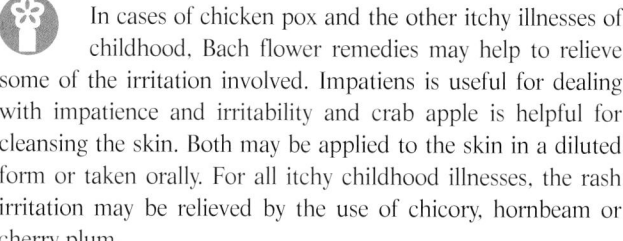

In cases of chicken pox and the other itchy illnesses of childhood, Bach flower remedies may help to relieve some of the irritation involved. Impatiens is useful for dealing with impatience and irritability and crab apple is helpful for cleansing the skin. Both may be applied to the skin in a diluted form or taken orally. For all itchy childhood illnesses, the rash irritation may be relieved by the use of chicory, hornbeam or cherry plum.

Aromatherapy

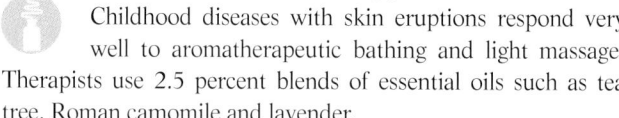

Childhood diseases with skin eruptions respond very well to aromatherapeutic bathing and light massage. Therapists use 2.5 percent blends of essential oils such as tea tree, Roman camomile and lavender.

Other therapies

Spiritual healing may be used to help a child throw off common childhood diseases more quickly than usual, allowing the toxins to be eliminated from the body rather than suppressed. It can also be used to reduce fever and inflammation. **Naturopaths** may suggest plenty of fruit and vegetables and juices followed by a whole food diet during convalescence.

MEASLES

What is it?

Measles is a highly infectious disease affecting mainly children, but it can appear in adults as well. The infectious period lasts from the time of contact with another sufferer until seven to ten days after the rash begins. The disorder itself tends to run its course within seven to ten days. One bout of measles usually gives the patient further immunity.

The disease begins like a cold, with a runny nose and sneezing, watering eyes and a cough. A fever then develops and characteristic little grey-white dots called Koplik's spots appear inside the cheeks, followed rapidly by a fever. (A doctor may be able to identify measles from these spots even before the main rash appears.) The fever tends to become higher as flat, pinkish-brown or red spots emerge, usually behind the ears and on the face. The spots may combine into red, blotchy areas. While measles spots are not especially itchy, the child may feel profoundly unwell. After about three days, the rash begins to fade and the symptoms become less pronounced.

Other symptoms include the swelling of the lymph nodes of the neck, and the child may also show little or no appetite. They may also experience a certain amount of abdominal pain, vomiting and diarrhea.

Potential complications of measles include mainly ear and chest infections (middle ear infections, conjunctivitis, croup, diarrhea and bronchitis). There are also more serious complications which can arise, such as pneumonia and, rarely, encephalitis (inflammation of the brain).

Measles is a serious disease and may even be fatal in those children who have impaired immunity, including those who are being treated for leukemia and those infected with the virus leading to HIV.

Febrile convulsions (a twitching or jerking of the limbs) commonly occur with childhood measles but are not usually worrying. They are the result of the brain's temperature-lowering mechanism being immature.

Causes

Measles is caused by a virus which is:

- *Spread through the air in droplets of nasal secretions as an infected person coughs or sneezes.*
- *The incubation period is about eight to 14 days before the symptoms show.*
- *Children with the infection can pass on the virus from soon after incubation starts until a week after the symptoms appear.*
- *A baby is protected from measles for up to the first eight months of its life as antibodies from the mother are still present within the infant's system.*

Orthodox treatment

Fever is generally controlled with paracetamol, and plenty of liquids should be taken.

Antibiotics are not given for the measles itself but may be necessary if any additional complications develop. In the unlikely event of encephalitis, strong antiviral drugs may be used – but always in a hospital environment.

Children are routinely offered the combined MMR (Measles, Mumps, Rubella) vaccine between the ages of 12 to 18 months. The vaccine should not be given to infants under a year old and it should be delayed if the child shows any signs of fever or infection. The side effects of the vaccine are usually mild. A slight fever, cold and rash may appear about a week after the vaccine is given.

ALTERNATIVE TREATMENT

Homeopathy

A homeopath may recommend:

• Aconite or belladonna for cold symptoms as the fever as the illness begins.
• Euphrasia for cold symptoms, fever or watering eyes.
• Pulsatilla if the child is chilly, feverish and miserable, producing thick green catarrh and complaining that the bright light really hurts his eyes.
• Bryonia or sulphur may be useful when the rash comes out.

If there is persistent fever, or if the child is still ill after the rash has begun to fade, consult a doctor immediately.

Aromatherapy

Itchy skin eruptions will respond to aromatherapeutic bathing and light massage, using 2.5 percent blends of essential oils such as tea tree and Roman camomile.

Western herbalism

Treatments to relieve fever include drinking infusions of yarrow, elderflower or boneset several times a day. For restlessness, aching limbs and muscles, add some camomile to the infusion.

Reflexology

A reflexologist will be likely to provide short and gentle treatments, including complete treatment for prevention and selective treatments to strengthen the immune system following infections.

Naturopathy

Naturopaths will advise lots of fruit and vegetable juices, if the child will accept them. They may suggest the child not be given dairy products during the illness.

MUMPS

What is it?

Symptoms include a general malaise, earache and then a fever with a headache and pains around the neck, a sore throat, dry mouth, and pain on eating or drinking. In post-pubescent males, mumps may also cause orchitis (inflammation of the testes) – leading to infertility in a small minority of cases.

Mumps is infectious for a day before the glands begin to swell until about a week after they have gone down. Many children are not uncomfortable and their swollen glands should subside within ten days. A bout of mumps gives life-long immunity against a further attack.

Causes

Mumps are a caused by a viral infection spread in airborne droplets which produces fever and swelling of the main salivary glands (the parotids) just inside the jaw. This creates the characteristic "chipmunk" appearance. Mumps rarely occurs in children under two or three years of age, and takes about two or three weeks to incubate.

Orthodox treatment

Treatment is usually paracetamol to reduce the fever and relieve pain. (See Measles on page 319 for details of the MMR vaccine.)

ALTERNATIVE TREATMENT

Homeopathy

Specific remedies include aconite at the onset of any fever. Belladonna for high fever and when the child is red in the face. Phytolacca is used if the neck glands feel rock hard and the child's ears hurt.

Western herbalism

A number of herbs will help bring down fever, including infusions of yarrow and elderflower. Some marigold infusion may be added to this mixture every few hours to help to relieve the swollen glands. See a herbalist for individual treatment as there are also stronger remedies – but these need to be used with care.

Other therapies

A **reflexologist** will provide short and gentle treatments, including those to strengthen the immune system following infections. A **naturopath** may recommend cold compresses to help reduce the swelling in the neck, and possibly supplements of vitamins and minerals to boost the immune system.

WHOOPING COUGH (PERTUSSIS)

What is it?

Whooping cough is a highly infectious disease mainly affecting infants and young children. It leads to inflammation of the whole respiratory tract and can be serious.

Whooping cough begins as a normal cold, which develops into a cough. Thick mucus irritates the airways. Gradually, the coughing becomes severe and long bouts begin with a spasm and end with a "whoop" as the child fights for breath. The child may vomit, burst small blood vessels of the eyes (which heal) with the effort of coughing. Extremities may be blue, as the child is temporarily short of oxygen. The illness may last ten weeks.

Causes

Whooping cough is caused by a bacterium which is spread in coughed-out airborne droplets.

Orthodox treatment

Antibiotics can be used in the first stage of the disease but these are of little use once the coughing begins. The child should be kept warm and given plenty to drink. The DTP (Diphtheria, Tetanus, Pertussis) vaccine is routinely offered to babies at two, three and four months. There is a rare chance of an adverse reaction – but a greater danger from the disease itself.

ALTERNATIVE TREATMENT

Homeopathy

Homeopathic remedies which can be taken include drosera if the throat is very ticklish and kali carb. for a hard, dry hacking cough. Use cuprum if coughing leaves the child exhausted and out of breath, if their lips turn blue, their toes/fingers cramp and drinks of cold water appear to help.

Western herbalism

There are a number of herbs which are suitable for children. See your herbalist for individual treatment. Possible helpful remedies include a range of expectorants such as white horehound, mullein flowers and thyme – and relaxants such as lavender and hyssop, if necessary.

GERMAN MEASLES (RUBELLA)

What is it?

This is a very infectious viral disease with an incubation period of two to three weeks. It is usually mild. It begins with symptoms of a cold and loss of appetite, sometimes with a sore throat and swelling of lymph nodes in the neck and mild fever. An itchy rash appears a day later, usually first on the face. Other viral illnesses are identical so women should not assume they are immune because they have had symptoms similar to German measles.

The disease generally runs its course within the week – but if a woman who is not immune comes into contact with it during the first four months of pregnancy, there is a serious risk of miscarriage and birth defects. Children should be kept at home when suffering from rubella, even if they appear quite well.

Causes

The virus, spread in airborne droplets, may be passed from a few days before symptoms appear until a day after they are gone.

Orthodox treatment

Normal treatment for this disease consists of:

- *Paracetamol to bring down any fever and reduce discomfort.*
- *Creams and ointments can be prescribed if the rash is very itchy, including calamine and mild steroid preparations.*

To minimize the risk of rubella in pregnancy, a doctor may do a blood test on teenage girls to ensure they have immunity. A homeopathic doctor could do this using the Rubella nosode. (See Measles on page 319 for details of the MMR vaccine).

ALTERNATIVE TREATMENT

Aromatherapy

Any childhood diseases with itchy skin eruptions respond well to aromatherapy. Try bathing and light massage with 2.5 percent blends of essential oils such as tea tree, Roman camomile and lavender. Tea tree and lavender are especially useful for any viral infections and can be used in very small doses in a warm bath with young children.

Other therapies

A **homeopath** may recommend either phytolacca (for swollen glands, painful ears and if the symptoms are alleviated by cold drinks) or pulsatilla (at the onset of the rash if the child is red-eyed and has yellow catarrh). **Western herbalists** use a variety of herbs to help bring down fever and fight infection, and may suggest rubbing the skin with a cool infusion of lavender.

FEVER

What is it?

Any body temperature above normal – 98.6°F or 37°C – is classed as a fever and is the body's way of helping to eliminate invading pathogens causing infection. Any temperature above 102°F (39°C) in children can be serious, so call a doctor.

Sponge the child's body with lukewarm water and cover with only a cotton sheet. Never put the child into a cold bath. Parents may worry that a high temperature prompts febrile convulsions. These are benign if lasting less than 10 minutes and are only linked with epilepsy in between 2–4 percent of cases.

Causes

Fever is usually caused by a bacterial or viral infection (such as the common childhood diseases: measles, mumps, chicken pox and whooping cough) and upper respiratory tract infections.

Orthodox treatment

Paracetamol may be given to reduce a fever due to infections. Antibiotics will be prescribed for bacterial infections. Rectal diazepan (tranquilizer) may also be used to prevent a fit in very vulnerable children.

ALTERNATIVE TREATMENT

IF A CHILD'S FEVER STAYS ABOVE 102°F (39°C) FOR MORE THAN SIX HOURS, CALL IMMEDIATELY FOR EMERGENCY MEDICAL TREATMENT.

Homeopathy

Remedies include apis if the child feels chilly and complains of stinging pains, arsenicum if the child is exhausted and chilly, and aconite and belladonna for high fever.

Other therapies

Traditional **Chinese** and **Western herbs** may assist and soothe. Western herbal treatments include infusions of borage, German camomile, marigold, eucalyptus, cayenne pepper (perhaps in a warm drink), willow bark and boneset. An **aromatherapist** may suggest lukewarm sponging with essential oils of petitgrain and Roman camomile. **Reflexology** will be aimed at the hypothalamus, endocrine glands and lymphatic system.

COLDS AND INFLUENZA (FLU)

What are they?

Nearly everyone has colds occasionally – but the occurrence is highest among children and tends to decline with age. Adults gradually build up some immunity against existing viruses.

Colds are most common in babies and young children because of their immature immune systems. Older children contract them mainly when their defenses are down, following other illnesses, or when they are stressed or overtired. Schoolchildren are exposed to many different viruses and may develop a spate of infections in their early school years.

Most colds are very contagious and last for between three and seven days, though the aftermath of a still running nose exuding thick mucus can continue for weeks. Colds may appear with or without coughs.

Colds generally begin with a sore throat, sneezing, a minor temperature and a running nose. The inflammation produced irritates the mucous membrane of the upper respiratory tract and catarrh is produced as the body attempts to discharge invaders from the body. The adenoids may also swell, blocking the Eustachian tubes – which may cause "popping," and a secondary infection of the ear. Recurrent colds, especially if they move to the chest areas, can develop into bronchitis or tonsillitis. Some colds are actually symptoms of an allergy, so if a child seems to develop one cold after another, consider the possibility of allergy testing with a specialist immunologist or perhaps a practitioner of kinesiology.

The three main types of influenza virus are labeled A, B and C – with the type B infections in children sometimes causing symptoms which are very similar to appendicitis. The more general malaise of fever, headache, muscle ache and weakness is very typical. The type A virus may cause febrile convulsions (seizures) in babies and is more debilitating than type B.

New strains of influenza appear spontaneously from time to time, sometimes causing serious widespread epidemics, and these may quickly overcome any previous immunity that has been built up to earlier strains.

Causes

Nearly 200 different viruses are known to provoke what we call colds – and the most common are classed as either rhinoviruses or coronaviruses. These are caught when:

- *People breathe in a virus by airborne droplets that have been sneezed or coughed into the air.*
- *The virus can also be contracted by handling contaminated objects (such as towels) and then rubbing the nose or eyes.*
- *Viral infections of the respiratory tract described as influenza cause fever, headache, muscle ache and weakness.*

Orthodox treatment

Most colds clear within a week and a doctor is usually needed only if the infection spreads beyond the nose and throat – or if a chronic chest infection or ear disorder is being aggravated. Here are the standard treatments offered by orthodox medicine:

- *A doctor is likely to suggest giving a child plenty of fluids and rest, and perhaps paracetamol to relieve the discomfort and bring down the fever.*
- *Taking more vitamin C may be advised.*
- *Antibiotics may be given only if there is any appearance of a secondary bacterial infection.*
- *Rest, painkillers and plenty of warm fluids are suggested for children as well as adults suffering from flu.*
- *Flu vaccines are only partially effective to prevent transmission and they must be repeated yearly in order to offer any protection. The vaccines are not generally recommended for children.*

ALTERNATIVE TREATMENT

Homeopathy

There are many different possible homeopathic remedies that may be used, such as aconite (for the first stage), pulsatilla if a child is clinging and tearful and the catarrh is thick and greenish, mercurius when a cold began as sore throat and the child has earache and the neck glands are swollen and tender, bryonia when a child is irritable, extremely thirsty and wants to be left alone, and nux. Chronic colds should be treated with constitutional treatment.

Naturopathy

A naturopath may emphasize dietary action and advise avoiding mucus-forming foods such as dairy products, sugar, eggs and starches; taking an Epsom salts bath; and having plenty of onions, leeks and garlic in the diet for a few days.

Aromatherapy

Eucalyptus smithii is a decongestant and can be used with lavender and tea tree oil in a warm bath. For a baby, use one drop of lavender, one drop of eucalyptus and one drop of tea tree oil in the bath or place two drops of each in a humidifier in the child's room.

Other therapies

Kinesiology can be useful with manipulative techniques. A **nutritional therapist** may suggest a daily vitamin C supplement in addition to emphasizing key foods which are important to maintaining a healthy diet generally. **Chinese herbalism** treatments are offered to ease symptoms and also to help the body fight off infection. **Reflexology** treatments for colds and flu will be aimed primarily at the body's respiratory points.

Coughs

What are they?

Coughs are the body's attempt to rid itself of any blockage or irritation in the airways or a response to irritation of the throat. There are different types of coughs – dry and irritating, or loose.

Causes

A dry cough may be caused by mucus from infections or colds, chemicals in the atmosphere, a foreign object or nervousness which constricts the throat. A loose, wetter cough is caused by inflammation of the bronchial tubes produced by an infection or allergy. A constant night-time cough or one which recurs with each cold and is hard to get rid of may indicate asthma.

Orthodox treatment

Some doctors may prescribe a cough suppressant, but this is not advised unless the cough is nonproductive (not bringing up mucus or sputum) and exhausting the child. The action of coughing is tiring but cleansing to the body. Paracetamol may bring down any fever and reduce the discomfort or distress. An antibiotic may be given for bacterial infections.

Alternative Treatment

Aromatherapy

A very gentle form of eucalyptus called *Eucalyptus smithii* is used as the usual forms of eucalyptus may be too strong for a young child and actually irritate the airways further. Dispense this via a room humidifier with pump action rather than placing the oil on the child's clothing or pillow.

Homeopathy

Recurrent coughs require constitutional treatment. In an acute attack, however, one of the following might be appropriate: aconite, belladonna, bryonia, ipecac, drosera, spongia, hepar sulph., phosphorus, chamomilla, kali bichrom., nux, pulsatilla, rumex, arsenicum, antimonium tart., causticum, stannum, sticta and kali carb. Speak to your homeopath to choose the most appropriate one that will help relieve the child's particular symptoms.

Other therapies

Western herbalism is appropriate, and herbalists will be likely to offer warm infusions of coltsfoot and vervain steeped in boiling water. **Chinese herbalists** will suggest suitable treatments for coughs. **Kinesiology** may be very useful, and **spiritual healing** may help to calm the child, reduce fever, soothe the cough and also stimulate the immune system.

Croup

What is it?

Croup is characterized by a harsh, strident, barking cough and also difficulty in breathing. It generally affects babies, and the under-fives, and is caused by inflammation producing swelling that partially closes the larynx and trachea airways to the lungs. Most cases are mild and soon over, but in more severe cases there may be a blue tinge to the skin as the child becomes short of oxygen while fighting for breath. As croup involves a narrowing of the main airway, the condition can prove serious.

CALL YOUR DOCTOR IMMEDIATELY IF A CHILD IS STRUGGLING TO BREATHE OR TURNS BLUE.

Causes

Croup may be caused by a viral or bacterial infection affecting the larynx (voice-box), epiglottis or the trachea (windpipe). It may also be caused by an allergy.

Orthodox treatment

Croup may be treated by a room humidifier or providing mist for the child to inhale. If the child needs to go to hospital:

- *They may be given humidified oxygen in a tent.*
- *A tube may be passed into the throat, bypassing the obstruction.*
- *For bacterial infection, antibiotics may be appropriate.*
- *An anti-asthma drug may be given to dilate their airways.*

Alternative Treatment

Homeopathy

Croup in babies is best handled by using some of the remedies also favored for coughs – specifically aconite, hepar sulph. and spongia.

Western herbalism

An infusion of 1 tsp vervain and 1 tsp coltsfoot steeped in a cup of boiling water and cooled will be suggested – give 1 tsp to children under age three and 1 tbsp to those older.

Glue Ear

What is it?

Glue ear is a chronic (long-term) condition in which the middle ear fills up with a thick, discharge resembling glue, which impairs normal hearing. It tends to begin with a sudden inflammation of the middle ear and may be a complication of a nose or throat infection.

Glue ear may also be associated with chronically enlarged tonsils, adenoids and lymph glands in the throat and neck, which can also block the Eustachian tube. As the child's hearing is impaired, this often means that an infant will be slower than usual in learning to talk. He or she may also develop unusual pronunciations and learning at school is slower than average.

Causes

The lining of the middle ear cavity may become inflamed, producing too much sticky fluid. Blockage of the Eustachian tube stops the fluid from draining away.

Orthodox treatment

The orthodox treatment for severe glue ear involves a surgical incision in the eardrum, then inserting fine tubes called grommets. These allow fluid to drain from the middle ear, and can be helpful in the short term. Regular antibiotics may be needed to control infection. This myringotomy may also be combined with removing the tonsils, adenoids or both.

Alternative Treatment

Homeopathy

The following remedies help this condition:

• Calcarea if there is discharge from the ear, the neck glands are swollen and the child is prone to night sweats.

• Kali bichrom., if there is thick, stringy mucus down the back of the throat, pain behind the nose or in the sinus area.

• Graphites for honey-colored discharge from the ear and crackling noises.

Other therapies

Because glue ear may be linked with food allergies, a **nutritional therapist** can offer helpful treatment, as can a **Western herbalist.** Glue ear may also respond to **kinesiology** treatment. Many therapists may suggest removing dairy products from the child's diet temporarily, substituting with foods based on soya or goat's milk. **Chinese herbalism** may recommend treatments that can be very helpful as well.

Ear Infections

What is it?

Ear infections are very common in children during the first four years of life and there is frequently ear inflammation with colds. Usually, the inflamed ear does not become sore enough to cause the child any discomfort – but when it does, it can be very painful indeed.

There are two main types of infection: inflammation or infection of the outer ear canal causing swelling and discharge and, most commonly, middle ear infection (otitis media). Chronic ear infections can lead to impairment of hearing.

The affected part may also become red and swollen, and there may by itching and intense pain. A baby may cry for many hours – especially when lying down. For accurate diagnosis, the doctor should check the ears with a lighted instrument.

Causes

Outer ear infection can have several causes:

- *An object in the ear, a boil in the canal of the ear or a scratch.*
- *The middle ear infection is usually carried from the nose or throat by the Eustachian tube.*
- *Catarrh and swollen tonsils can block the opening, causing a build-up of fluid in the middle ear, which becomes infected.*

The child may have fever, be in pain, and have a sticky discharge if the eardrum is perforated.

Orthodox treatment

Middle ear infections are generally treated with antibiotics, which are not helpful if the infection is viral. Analgesic drugs may be prescribed to relieve pain, along with local gentle heat.

Alternative Treatment

Homeopathy

Treatments for acute middle ear infection include hepar sulph. if the pain really throbs and is soothed by warmth, and chamomilla if a child is screaming.

Other therapies

Reflexology will be aimed at points corresponding to the pituitary, pineal and adrenal glands, thymus, ear and spleen. **Acupuncture** from a child specialist can be helpful.

Sticky Eye

What is it?

Sticky eye describes a yellowish discharge from one or both of a baby's eyes, which often develops into crusting. It is common in the first few months, and is most often caused by a blocked tear duct. At birth, the end of these ducts closest to the nose is sometimes covered with a thin membrane which tends to break open within a couple of weeks, allowing the tears to drain through into the corners of the eyes. The eyes of most newborns begin producing tears at around three weeks of age. However, if the covering membrane does not break open fully, the ducts remain wholly or partially plugged and tears may accumulate. If the tear fluid does not drain away, it can become infected and yellow.

Causes

Other causes of sticky eye in babies may include infection contacted during childbirth from sexually transmitted infections, or from contact with childbirth blood or amniotic fluid. In an older child, sticky eye is often a symptom of a common cold – but it may be a sign of conjunctivitis, in which the eyes water, smart and the white becomes pink and inflamed. Conjunctivitis is very contagious, but treatable with antibiotics. In an older child, pink, watering eyes may also be a sign of allergy (such as hay fever) rather than infection.

Orthodox treatment

If there is pus and inflammation of the conjunctiva, it is essential to take swabs and start treatment:

- *In infants, antibiotic eye drops and warm sterile (slightly saline) water can be used to cleanse the eyes regularly.*
- *For older children, conjunctivitis may be treated with antibiotics or, in cases of allergy-related sticky eye, antihistamine drops under the supervision of an ophthalmologist.*

Alternative Treatment

Homeopathy

General remedies for older infants may include pulsatilla for thick, nonirritant discharge, euphrasia (eyebright) if the eyes are watering but become gummed up with sticky mucus. If the eyes are burning, watery and red but improve in warmer air, allium cepa may be appropriate.

Western herbalism

Western herbalists may suggest washing the affected eye with local applications of soothing, cooled herb infusions, which are made from any of the following: marigold, purple loose-strife, American cranesbill, marsh mallow, golden seal or eyebright.

Worms

What are they?

Worms in the digestive system can occur in the cleanest homes and are quite common in young children who usually contract them at school. There are three main types – threadworms, roundworms and tapeworms. Threadworms (pinworms) are by far the most usual in Britain. These tiny worms live in the large intestine. They cause inflammation and extreme itching around the anus for both sexes, and sometimes the vagina for girls.

Causes

Scratching means eggs are transferred to the fingers, and then to objects where other children pick them up. Worms can also be acquired from infected/undercooked meat or contaminated soil.

Orthodox treatment

There are ointments to soothe the anal itching from pinworms, and de-worming drugs are available.

Alternative Treatment

Homeopathy

Threadworms can be treated homeopathically by remedies such as cina, teucrium and santoninum.

Naturopathy

Garlic, carrots and pumpkin seeds can help clear the infection. A therapist will also advise to keep fingernails short and well-scrubbed and to change towels often.

Other therapies

Some **Western herbalism** treatments can paralyze the worms and other treatments will expel them. Treatment will include dietary advice to weaken the worms themselves so they are easier to get rid of (a regular intake of garlic and carrots will have this effect). In **Ayurvedic medicine** oral herbal preparations for worms are available from practitioners. The **metamorphic technique** will address the prebirth area.

VOMITING AND DIARRHEA

What are they?

Involuntary expulsion of stomach contents by mouth (vomiting) and increased frequency and fluidity of bowel movements (diarrhea) are generally not serious unless they are chronic.

The particular worry about these in children is dehydration, which involves not only the loss of water, but also vital body salts called electrolytes. A proper balance between the two is vital for the body's organs to function, and dehydration destroys this balance. Rapid loss of water and salts can become especially dangerous for babies, young children and the elderly and will need prompt medical attention.

Causes

Vomiting and diarrhea are not illnesses in themselves, but can be signs of many different specific disorders, including infection of the intestine (gastroenteritis), colds and food intolerances. They are sometimes the result of antibiotic treatment.

Diarrhea alone may be caused by any of these, plus worms, or inappropriate dietary intake (perhaps just too much fruit juice). Babies who are breast-fed are less likely to contract gastroenteritis.

Ear infections may be a cause of vomiting only, as may disorders affecting the balancing function of the inner ear. Pyloric stenosis, caused by the narrowing of the outlet from the stomach (the pylorus) is characterized by dramatic projectile vomiting in young babies. With gastro-esophagal reflux (a very common cause of vomiting in the early months of a child's life), the cause is similar to adult heartburn in that acidic fluid from the stomach is backing up into the esophagus.

Orthodox treatment

For vomiting, drugs such as metoclopramide may be used, but only in extreme circumstances.

- *Infants with diarrhea should not be given milk initially but rather an electrolyte mixture (which can be bought at chemists) to replace the salts and water being lost.*
- *Milk can be reintroduced gradually if the diarrhea has cleared within 24 hours. Consult a doctor if it continues for more than 48 hours. Avoid dehydration. Formulas low in lactose may be useful for bottle-fed babies.*

The treatment of infants with pyloric stenosis involves rehydration, then corrective surgery is usually required to rectify the problem.

CALL A DOCTOR URGENTLY IF AN INFANT SHOWS SYMPTOMS OF DEHYDRATION, INCLUDING A SUNKEN FONTANELLE (A SOFT SPOT ON THE TOP FRONT AND TOP BACK OF THE SKULL), UNRESPONSIVENESS, DROWSINESS, PROLONGED CRYING, GLAZED EYES, LOOSE SKIN – AS WELL AS A DRY, STICKY MOUTH AND TONGUE.

ALTERNATIVE TREATMENT

Aromatherapy

Inhalations of peppermint, lemon, lavender or bergamot oil might help to alleviate nausea and vomiting, but first check with an aromatherapist on what may be suitable for a young baby.

Naturopathy

A naturopath may introduce a controlled diet and applied nutrition.

Nutritional therapy

A therapist may recommend resting the digestive system, taking only liquid and no food for a while. For children, but not babies, astringent herbal teas such as peppermint and blackberry may help to shorten the recovery time.

Homeopathy

Your homeopath will diagnose the cause of the vomiting or diarrhea, and treat according to the symptoms. Long-term diarrhea should always be treated constitutionally. There are also several remedies available for acute conditions, including podophyllum for copious, bad-smelling stools, pale-green in color, with wind and colic, especially urgent in early morning; china for stools like chopped egg with lots of wind, person very irritable; colocynth if the diarrhea is accompanied by gripping, spasmodic pains, with copious frothy, thin and yellowish stools.

Other therapies

Reflexology treatment will be aimed at the digestive reflexes. Vomiting and diarrhea may respond to **auricular therapy** (massaging the acupuncture points on the ear). Research in China has shown **acupuncture** to be valuable even in cases of severe diarrhea, and the experience of practitioners suggests that acupuncture can be helpful for a whole range of problems of the digestive system. Research in Belfast cites the value of acupuncture for nausea and vomiting after operations, during pregnancy and as a result of chemotherapy. Depending on the cause, **Western herbalism** may be appropriate and can help by cleansing the system, supporting and strengthening the digestive system and reducing inflammation. **Chinese herbalism** treatment is also suggested for relieving all the discomfort that is associated with vomiting and diarrhea.

HYPERACTIVITY

What is it?

Hyperactivity describes a whole group of symptoms which add up to a recognizable pattern. Either it is becoming more common or it is being diagnosed more often. An older, hyperactive child has an excessively high energy level, is restless, demanding, and fidgety. Such a child has a short attention span, is frequently inattentive, excitable and unpredictable. As toddlers, such children are easily frustrated and quick to break into tantrums. Problems with speech, hearing and balance are not uncommon. While just as intelligent as other children, they tend not to do well at school as often they cannot concentrate.

In babies, signs of hyperactivity include colic, prolonged screaming, head-banging and general restlessness. They are often labeled difficult or high need. Hyperactive children of any age are very exhausting and often frustrating for parents. Estimates vary but it is thought that between two and five percent of children may be hyperactive, with up to ten times as many boys as girls.

Causes

Many causes have been suggested, including:

- *Slight brain damage which happened at birth, perhaps because of a prolonged or especially difficult delivery.*
- *Allergies. A wide variety of possible allergens exists including dairy products, wheat products, vinegar, artificial food additives (especially dyes in sweets and sweet drinks) and substances with large amounts of salicylates in them. This includes most fruit (apples, oranges, grapes) as well as peas, vinegar and almonds.*
- *Environmental pollutants – including cadium from cigarette smoke, aluminum, copper, mercury (including amalgam tooth fillings), fluoride, exhaust fumes and chlorinated water.*
- *Candida infection of the bowel.*
- *Marginal deficiencies of important nutrients such as magnesium, zinc, vitamin B6 and certain fatty acids.*

Orthodox treatment

Strangely enough, stimulant drugs such as amphetamines seem to be an effective treatment. (These work by stimulating the midbrain to suppress extra activity.) Help from a child psychologist or family counselor may also be suggested. Tests should check for food allergies, toxic metals and hypoglycemia. Hyperactivity often will disappear at puberty but the problem is sometimes carried on into adult life.

ALTERNATIVE TREATMENT

Naturopathy

Naturopathy can be a very successful treatment. Most practitioners regard food intolerance as the major cause and will give priority to changing a child's diet – taking into account possible non-food factors as well. Simply eliminating high-additive foods and substituting those made from natural ingredients has been known to be helpful.

Arts therapies

Music and dance are helpful in focusing a child on social interactions which they may otherwise be unable to maintain. Through dance, they can express themselves freely and without any criticisms, using both music and dance to explore feelings and emotional problems.

Bach flower remedies

Several may be helpful, including vervain for the over-enthusiastic child; impatiens for a talkative, over-eager, impatient child; cherry plum if there is loss of control; and rescue remedy in emergencies.

Massage

Massage may calm hyperactivity in children. If the child can be persuaded to lie quietly for a few minutes, both mother and child may benefit from the feeling of peace and calm present during the massage.

Other therapies

Nutritional therapists believe that this condition is linked with deficiencies, allergies and exposure to environmental pollutants – among them additives in foods. A revised diet would be suggested, with an emphasis on eating more natural products. The **Alexander Technique** can help a child to recover calmness and also achieve a greater stillness of body and mind, alleviating the problems associated with hyperactivity. An **auricular therapist** may have success in calming a hyperactive child for at least several days.

A **kinesiologist** might check lymphatic draining, and raise the foot of the bed, among other things. There will be counseling and balancing. In **Ayurvedic medicine,** treatment will be aimed at balancing the tridoshas. **Chiropractic** treatment can be used as part of the overall treatment of hyperactivity and is reported to increase coordination and concentration. The full spine is usually treated. Hyperactivity may also respond well to treatment by **cranial osteopathy** and **osteopathy**. Some **acupuncturists** specialize in the treatment of children and achieve good results with cases of hyperactivity.

Kirlian photography and body logic will indicate if an allergy is involved or a chemical imbalance. The **metamorphic technique** will address the post-conception area. Hyperactivity can be addressed by expert constitutional **homeopathic** treatment, and also by using remedies such as tarentula hisp, veratrum and nux vomica.

NIGHT TERRORS

What are they?

Night terrors are when a child awakes abruptly, screaming. He or she is normally in a semiconscious condition and cannot be comforted. Gradually falling asleep again, the child does not remember the fright the next day.

Causes

Night terrors usually begin between the ages of four and seven years and do not suggest any physical or mental problems. Unlike nightmares, they do not seem linked with scary stories and are thought to be a temporary disturbance in the nervous system during sleep. They seem to run in families, and almost all children grow out of them within a few years.

Orthodox treatment

If the terrors are frequent, parents may keep a diary to see what time of night they usually occur. Waking the child up about ten minutes before they usually happen can stop the problem.

ALTERNATIVE TREATMENT

Color therapy

Night terrors may be addressed environmentally by choosing the color of the bedroom and bedclothes in soothing pastel pink, pale warm yellow or a gentle blue shade. Avoid bright red as this is frequently linked with sleep problems.

Aromatherapy

An aromatherapist will suggest rose or neroli essential oil used in a room pump dispenser in the child's room at night to soothe. (Use rosewood oil if these are too expensive.)

Others

Suitable **homeopathic** remedies for night terrors include calcarea, antimonium tart and kali chrom. The **Alexander Technique** can help a child recover a calmness of mind. **Auricular therapy** works on calming the spirit. **Western herbalism** can help in giving more restful sleep. **Shiatsu** treatment for night terrors is said to help. **Autogenic training** is recommended for older children. **Bach flower remedies** may help, including rock rose, aspen and rescue remedy. Night terrors also respond well to **cranial osteopathy** and **acupuncture**.

BED WETTING

What is it?

Most children learn to be dry at night by the age of three – but for those who do not, this is not considered a possible medical problem until they are five (when about 10 percent of children, mostly boys, are still bed wetting). If a child sleeps heavily, it may take longer for night dryness. Often, it is just immaturity on the part of the nervous system controlling the bladder and children grow out of it. Other medical causes include diabetes, urinary infection, or structural abnormality of the urethra/bladder. Bed wetting in children who have already established dry nights is usually caused by emotional or social stress.

Causes

If the child is over the age of five, a doctor should do a careful physical examination so that any structural abnormalities, infections or underlying physical causes can be treated.

Orthodox treatment

Possible treatments include:

- *Waking the child to sit them on the toilet late at night, bed wetting alarms, and restricting evening fluid intake.*
- *Drugs such as imipramine (by mouth) or desmopressin (via nasal spray). Counseling may be suggested.*

ALTERNATIVE TREATMENT

Homeopathy

Constitutional treatment is needed but specific remedies include equisetum, when the wetting occurs during dreams and belladonna when it occurs early in the night.

Other therapies

Western herbalism may work by treating the urinary system and by reducing tension and anxiety factors. **Reflexology** treatment can be addressed at the solar plexus and bladder. In **Ayurvedic medicine** treatment will be aimed at balancing the tridoshas. If the problem is thought to be due to psychological stress, the **art therapies** may be useful. **Hypnotherapy** can be used for programming the child's desire to wake and go to the toilet when the bladder feels full. **Acupuncturists** also treat bed wetting. The **Alexander Technique** may help children by facilitating the child's ability to let go of tension patterns.

CHRONIC SLEEP DISTURBANCE

What is it?

In general, babies sleep about 16 hours a day when newborn, dropping to about 14 hours when a year old. Five- to ten-year-olds sleep for about 11–12 hours per night. Sleep disturbance is so common in infants that surveys of parents with children under three report that a third were woken by their child the night before, dropping to about a fifth for parents with five-year-olds.

Sleep problems tend not to cause the children themselves any developmental problems, so parents are often simply reassured and offered no further guidance. However, prolonged sleep disturbance is an important issue because it can put such severe strain on adults, and therefore on the entire family.

Causes

Repeated sleep disturbance/waking at night may be caused by:

- *Physical factors – including hyperactivity, allergies, food intolerances, conditions such as asthma, eczema or urinary tract infection and a tendency to repeated colds. Children should be checked for allergic problems and for asthma.*
- *Psychological possibilities, including family disturbances such as marital problems, the arrival of a new baby, moving to a new house or school, night terrors, sleep walking (quite common between the ages of five and ten) and school anxiety.*
- *Social factors may include overstimulation from television programs or computer games close to bedtime, irregular bedtimes, disruption of familiar routine and overtiredness.*
- *Environmental factors such as too warm or too cool a room or the air too dry (a common fault in centrally heated houses), too many (or too few) bed coverings or excessive noise.*

Orthodox treatment

A doctor should try to pinpoint the cause of the sleep problems, looking not just at the individual child but also at the family as a whole. Here are just some of the most likely treatments that will be offered:

- *Behavioral therapy, to help teach children to sleep through the night, for babies over six months and infants under five years is said to produce substantial improvement for nine out of ten older babies and toddlers within a week.*
- *If the problem is really severe, referral should be to a specialist pediatric sleep clinic. Clinicians will also approach the issue as one for the entire family rather than just the child alone.*
- *Sedatives for the child may be offered in the short term – these are primarily just to give the parents a breathing space. They are not a long-term solution and do not address the underlying causes of the problem.*

ALTERNATIVE TREATMENT

Aromatherapy

Aromatherapists might well suggest giving the child a hot bath at bedtime containing a relaxing blend of essential oils such as melissa and rosewood, and Roman camomile, or putting these oils into a room pump dispenser in the child's bedroom at night. Lavender is another excellent and traditional sleep-promoter which can be used instead, and it is also less expensive. Do not put any of these oils on the child's pillow or clothing, as they may prove too strong for a very sensitive or jumpy infant.

Homeopathy

Homeopathic treatment will be constitutional, but there are also specific remedies which can be given at bedtime, including: nux if the child is irritable, won't be pacified and regularly wakes in the early morning; coffea for a young baby who is too wound-up or overexcited to sleep or for an older infant who tends to wake in an excited state and start playing with toys in the middle of the night. If a baby is irritable, crying constantly and only stopping when he or she is picked up and carried around, chamomilla may be suggested. Calcarea can be used if a child cries out in anxiety during sleep and experiences head sweats, and cocculus if one disturbed night leads on to a poor sleep pattern for the child.

Other therapies

Bach flower remedies may be appropriate, depending on the cause. Nightmares may respond to rock rose or aspen. Sometimes neck problems can cause tension and anxiety which interrupts sleep. Releasing the tension through **chiropractic** treatment can help normal sleep patterns to return. **Naturopathy** may also be appropriate. The **Alexander Technique** can help to alleviate any fears and anxieties causing sleep disturbance in older children. **Auricular therapy** is effective in calming and relaxing. **Western herbalism** may help, particularly if the condition is related to stress or digestion. If the parents' own sleep has been so disrupted that they cannot sleep properly themselves, valerian may help them regain their proper sleep patterns. A **kinesiologist** may have to balance the kidney meridian, check for vitamin B, magnesium and calcium deficiencies, and use techniques for breaking habits and stress release. **Autogenic training** can help an older child with this chronic problem quite quickly. In children over four, **hypnotherapy** can be used to uncover the cause of the disturbance. In **Ayurvedic medicine,** treatment will be aimed at balancing the tridoshas. Where emotional factors are concerned, the four **arts therapies** may be helpful. Therapists may recommend that parents are involved. Chronic sleep problems may also be successfully addressed by **cranial osteopathy** (even for young babies) and **osteopathy**.

Teething

What is it?

Teething is the process by which the first teeth push their way through the surface of the gums, causing them to become red and swollen. The first set of 20 primary teeth begin to show between the ages of four months and three years. (Replacement permanent teeth start to appear from about the age of six.)

For many babies, teething symptoms include dribbling, fist-chewing, a red patch on one or both cheeks, irritability and sometimes slight diarrhea, which may result in a diaper rash. Other babies develop few, or even no, symptoms.

Causes

The average baby has about six teeth by the time they are a year old, after which there is usually a break for a few months and then half a dozen more tend to appear rapidly, one after the other.

Orthodox treatment

Anesthetic teething gels or creams can be rubbed on the gums or the infant given paracetamol to reduce any pain and fever. It is helpful to offer your baby something hard and cold to chew – such as a sterile teething ring that has been cooled in the fridge.

Alternative Treatment

Homeopathy

Possible remedies including chamomilla (if the child is irritable), mercurius (for dribbling, sore gums and diarrhea) and aconite (for acute pain and a high temperature).

Other therapies

Western herbalism can reduce local inflammation and discomfort. Camomile tea may be suggested, which the baby can drink from a bottle or an infant feeding cup, or it can be made into a cool compress to lay on the cheek. **Shiatsu** is also extremely helpful for alleviating the pains of teething. An **aromatherapist** may suggest using an essential oil of Roman camomile in a two percent blend in sweet almond oil, which can be rubbed into the cheeks. **Reflexology** may be aimed at the reflexes governing the teeth and **auricular therapy** may also be used to help ease the pain of teething.

Constant Crying

What is it?

All babies cry, as it is one way they have of communicating. However, about one in ten do so excessively and this can be distressing and exhausting for the parents. Possible causes include hunger, thirst, feeling lonely, bored, too warm, too cold, wet or soiled, diaper rash, colic, a problem with formula milk, something in the breast-feeding mother's diet disagreeing with the baby, teething (see above) or even hyperactivity (see page 327).

Causes

Crying, plus any signs that the baby is unwell; these include vomiting, fever, diarrhea, floppiness, pallor and very slow weight gain. If any of these symptoms are in evidence, consult a doctor. A very high-pitched cry, with vomiting and persistently bulging fontanelles (two spots of soft membranes, one at the top front and one at the top back of the skull) may suggest a brain infection. Call a doctor immediately. (Some bulging of the fontanelles is normal when babies cry.)

Orthodox treatment

Probably no treatment will be offered unless the baby is physically unwell. A doctor may suggest:

- *Contacting the support group CRY-SIS.*
- *Speaking to a health visitor for practical advice.*

Alternative Treatment

Homeopathy

Depending on the cause, homeopathic remedies such as colocynth, bryonia, veratrum may resolve the crying.

Bach flower remedies

These are gentle enough for babies. For example, chicory can help children and babies who need constant attention and mimulus those who are distressed and fearful.

Other therapies

The **Alexander Technique** can ease tension, anxieties, fear and agitation which may be causing the crying. **Western herbal** treatment such as camomile tea may be appropriate if the causes are digestive or emotional. **Chinese herbs** can work well. **Shiatsu** is extremely good for calming and **reflexology** offers treatment as well. Chronic crying often responds to **cranial osteopathy**, which is gentle and subtle.

COLIC

What is it?

Colic affects up to one in five of all babies, and is characterized by daily bouts of inconsolable crying, usually at around the same time (commonly early evening). If the attacks occur later in the evening, they may wake a peacefully sleeping child.

The baby's legs are drawn up to the abdomen, they appear to be in severe pain, their stomach may rumble loudly and they might also pass considerable amounts of wind. This usually begins within three weeks of the baby's birth and the attacks last on average for between two and four hours at a time. Research suggests that about half of affected babies have grown out of colic by the time they are two months old, 85 percent by three months and the remaining 15 percent have no further episodes after four months.

Causes

There is still disagreement amongst the medical profession as to whether colic exists in its own right as a real disorder. Some pediatricians suggest the problem is caused because tired babies naturally have crying fits in the evenings, and that it is the quantity of air they may gulp as they cry which is responsible for any ensuing discomfort from a bloated abdomen and wind. Others suggest that colic is produced by uncoordinated contractions of the young baby's intestines which may be too immature to contract smoothly and efficiently.

Anything that affects digestion contributes to this, such as intolerance to a particular type of formula milk – or, if the baby is breast-fed, to upsetting foods in the mother's diet. Californian pediatrician Professor William Sears (University of Southern California School of Medicine) suggests that several different types of foods can find their way from a mother's own digestive system into her breast milk – and thus into the digestive system of her baby. These include foods containing caffeine, strong spices and gas-producing vegetables such as broccoli, cabbage and cauliflower. Sears also cites research that the potential allergen beta lactoglobin in cow's milk is definitely transferred to babies via breast milk. Studies eliminating all dairy products from the diets of breast-feeding women with colicky babies have had mixed results – but it may be worth trying for a trial of two weeks to see if there is any improvement.

Sometimes, colic is caused by acid reflux, in which irritating stomach acids pass back up the baby's esophagus after feeding, causing discomfort similar to heartburn for adults. A third of all infants have some degree of this, and it may be suspected if the baby feels far better when upright after a meal and worse when lying down.

Orthodox treatment

Antispasmodic drugs were the traditional course of action but, since there is no definite evidence that intestinal spasm is the cause, they are usually no longer prescribed – particularly for babies under the age of six months. Over-the-counter products can provide some symptomatic relief. Parents may also try carrying the baby upright or cradling the baby facing forward if this seems to help.

Other suggestions include:

- *A hold which supports the baby's abdomen gently, or using a warm (not hot) hot-water bottle as a relaxant for the baby's gut.*
- *Massaging the abdomen gently, following the upside down "c" curve of the colon.*

ALTERNATIVE TREATMENT

Western herbalism

A practitioner may suggest a variety of herbs which can help to ease the symptoms and also to restore digestive balance. A teaspoonful of warm herbal tea (camomile, dill or fennel seeds) after feeding for the baby may help. If the mother is breast-feeding, she should try drinking a cupful 30 to 45 minutes before each feeding or a cupful four times a day at regularly spaced intervals.

Massage

Gentle massage with therapeutic oils may be helpful both to soothe the pain and calm the baby. Massage can help to ease the distress of both infant and parent. The act of massage also gives the parents greater confidence in their own ability to look after their child and also helps to strengthen the relationship. This in itself is often extremely helpful with settling restless babies.

Homeopathy

A homeopath may suggest one of the following specific remedies: colocynth (if the baby seems better with firm pressure on its abdomen), magnesia phos. (if warmth and gentle abdominal pressure help), bryonia (if the baby is very irritable, and screams at the slightest movement), chamomilla (if they are better when carried around, but otherwise seem to be almost impossible to please).

Other therapies

A **metamorphic technique** practitioner may address the quickening area (corresponding to age four to five months in the womb). A **Chinese herbalist** may suggest herbal anti-inflammatories, detoxifying herbs, digestives and evacuants. An **osteopath** would address any strain caused by the birth process. Colic often responds well to gentle **cranial osteopathy**. Frequently **chiropractic** treatment can also be used successfully.

Diaper Rash

What is it?

Diaper rash is a sore, red irritation on the skin, generally around the genital and anal areas. If not treated, it may extend down the inside thighs and over the lower abdomen.

Causes

The rash is caused by the skin being in contact with the urine or feces in a soiled diaper or excess moisture on the skin. Too much moisture takes away the skin's natural oils, and makes skin more prone to mechanical damage from friction. Diaper rash tends to develop in the skin folds around the groin as these provide both constant dampness and rubbing.

ANY RASH WHICH IS SEVERE OR LASTS FOR LONGER THAN SEVEN TO TEN DAYS SHOULD BE SEEN BY A DOCTOR.

Orthodox treatment

The obvious treatment involves changing diapers often and ensuring that all traces of urine and feces are washed from the skin. Use a water-repellent cream after each change. Disposable diapers or diaper liners may help since the newer varieties tend to draw moisture away from skin. (A rash may be exacerbated by the detergent which is used to wash cloth diapers.) A mild corticosteroid drug may be prescribed for keeping inflammation under control. Try leaving the diaper off when practical.

Alternative Treatment

Western herbalism

Local herbal applications can ease inflammation and heal skin, such as marigold (calendula) or chickweed ointment. Cleavers and buchu may be suggested.

Homeopathy

Diaper rash can be treated at home but if it does not resolve within five days, consult a homeopath or doctor. Helpful remedies include sulphur if the skin is dry, red and scaly. Rhus tox can also be used if the rash is an itchy one with small blisters.

Aromatherapy

There is an oil for cleaning diaper areas which can be formulated with a 1 percent blend of high-altitude lavender in apricot kernel oil. Or, add one drop of rosewood oil in apricot carrier oil and use this as a barrier oil.

Other therapies

A **kinesiologist** might suggest the child drinks more water and may check for vitamin A and zinc deficiency. The rash may be soothed by **Bach flower remedies'** rescue® remedy cream applied to the area.

Cradle Cap

What is it?

Cradle cap is a common condition in babies, with thick, yellow scales appearing in patches on the scalp. It is a form of seborrheic dermatitis, and may also occur in the region of the diaper, as well as on the face, neck and behind the ears. While the skin looks unpleasant, it is a not serious so long as the scalp skin remains uninfected.

Causes

The cause is not clear but it may be fungal infection and not the result of bad hygiene. Cradle cap often appears during the first three to nine months of the baby's life and is usually gone by the age of one year, although some cases may last up to three years.

Orthodox treatment

The scalp should be washed daily in a mild shampoo such as cetrimide solution. Warm olive oil or arachis oil can be gently rubbed into the baby's scalp and this will help to soften the scales overnight. The loosened scales may then be removed by the next day's gentle washing. Brush the baby's hair with a very soft brush. Consult a doctor if the skin looks inflamed as an antibiotic or corticosteroid drug may be needed.

Alternative Treatment

Aromatherapy

A blend of strong lavender oil in apricot kernel oil may help. Or use a drop of rosewood oil in apricot carrier oil instead of one of the usual skin barrier creams.

Homeopathy

Calendula ointment may be suggested first. If this does not help, and the skin is scaly and dry but not infected, lycopodium may be appropriate.

THRUSH (CANDIDIASIS)

What is it?

Thrush is not an infection as such, but an overgrowth of the yeast-like fungus Candida albicans which lives naturally on the skin and gut of every healthy body. It also thrives in moist, warm areas such as enclosed folds of the skin, mouth and vagina.

In infants, candidiasis may occur along with diaper rash (see page 332). In the diaper region, it often takes the appearance of an itchy red rash and there are flaky white patches. This may be sore, or itchy, or cause the baby little discomfort.

Babies may also develop an overgrowth of the fungus in their mouths – the symptoms including white patches on the mouth and white curd-like discharges which look like partially digested milk but on closer inspection cannot be wiped away. From here the infection can be transferred to the mother's nipples, if she is breast-feeding. The symptoms of nipple thrush include redness, soreness, swelling and cracking which is not soothed by the usual nipple emollient creams.

If babies develop thrush vaginally, as is common in adult women, the symptoms include redness, itching, and small amounts of a white, curdy discharge.

Causes

The basic cause of thrush in the diaper region is:

- *Ordinary diaper rash, which is a result of skin irritation caused by contact with urine and feces contained in the diaper. The rash is sometimes followed by a bout of thrush because once the skin has become inflamed, it is not such an efficient barrier to infection, and is therefore more vulnerable to attack by other organisms, including the fungus Candida albicans.*

Orthodox treatment

Treatment may include giving the child:

- *Antifungal drugs. This drug treatment will be in cream or ointment form for thrush affecting the diaper area and skin folds, with perhaps oral drops given as well to help treat the condition internally too.*
- *Mouth thrush is generally treated with some oral drops. If the mother is breast-feeding the baby and the baby develops a case of oral thrush, antifungal ointment will also be prescribed for treating the mother's nipples.*

ALTERNATIVE TREATMENT

Western herbalism

A therapist may use local treatments with antifungal properties, such as aloe vera mouthwash (which is also available in an own-brand form from selected chemists). The herbalist will also look internally, as thrush may be a sign of a weakness in the immune response – and treatments will be used to boost the immune system as well.

Other therapies

Aromatherapists may treat oral thrush by preparing a mouthwash solution with lavender, lemon or peppermint in spring water. Rinse the baby's mouth, or dab a few drops on the affected areas. For thrush in the diaper area, a drop of antifungal tea tree oil in apricot carrier oil can be smoothed on. **Reflexology** and **Chinese herbalism** can be helpful as well.

IMPETIGO

What is it?

Impetigo is a very contagious infection of the skin which appears commonly in children. It most often emerges around the mouth and nose as fluid-filled blisters, which burst and crust over.

Causes

Impetigo is the result of bacteria entering the skin through some broken area, such as a cut.

Orthodox treatment

This is what will be suggested by an orthodox doctor:

- *Antibiotic drugs will be prescribed in tablet or ointment form for the infection.*
- *He will advise that the problem usually clears in about five days and that loose crusts of skin can be gently washed away. Use separate towels and flannels and boil after use.*
- *He will advise keeping children at home until the infection clears.*

ALTERNATIVE TREATMENT

Western herbalism

Western herbalists will try to boost the immune system and use tinctures such as marigold and myrrh.

Aromatherapy

Aromatherapists may rub a mixture of essential oils such as savory or tea tree on the skin to kill the bacteria.

Childhood Leukemia

What is it?

Cancer is very rare in children – but when it does occur, the most common form, called leukemia, affects the infection-fighting, white blood cells. The normal control mechanisms of the white blood cells break down and large numbers of abnormal white cells, called blast cells, are produced. These take over the bone marrow and then invade the blood system and vital organs.

Leukemia occurs most often between the ages of two to five years. The disease is slightly more common in boys.

There are two main types: myeloid leukemia (AML) affects the bone marrow production sites making two types of white blood cells – the monocytes and granulocytes. Lymphoblastic leukemia affects the other important type of white blood cell called the lymphocyte, originating in the lymph glands. (Lymphobasts are immature forms of lymphocytes.)

Both types are subdivided into whether the disease is acute (having a rapid onset and being usually short-lived) or chronic (developing slowly and persisting). Most children (85 percent) with leukemia have the acute lymphoblastic (ALL) type.

The symptoms of all acute forms of childhood leukemia are those of bone marrow failure. The list may include lack of energy and pallor from anemia, persistent infections such as tonsillitis and ear infections (due to a weakened immune system), blood spots on the skin, unexplained bleeding and bruising, swollen lymph glands in the neck and groin, pain in the bones and joints (often the first sign may be a limp or a very young child who refuses to stand/walk) and a swollen abdomen due to enlargement of the spleen.

Causes

Possible causes include exposure to certain chemicals and to radioactive leaks. One type of ALL may be caused by a virus similar to the one responsible for AIDS. Inherited factors and chromosomal abnormalities may also bear some responsibility.

Orthodox treatment

Most modern treatment programs last two to three years. For both types of leukemia, the treatment is in two phases:

- *For ALL, this first phase lasts three to four weeks and is in hospital, where high doses of chemotherapy are given intravenously until the abnormal white "blast" cells are destroyed. A combination of radiotherapy and chemotherapy is then used to clear these from the central nervous system.*
- *The second phase for ALL is a long one of oral treatment involving steroids, chemotherapy and sometimes preventative antibiotics to avoid possible infections attacking the child's weakened immune system. It is carried out at home, while the child continues to lead as normal a life as possible. When the treatment has destroyed all the abnormal white cells (checked with a blood test), the child is said to have gone into remission.*

It is harder to achieve remission with AML, so its chemotherapy and radiotherapy treatment regimes are more aggressive. Children may also have a bone marrow transplant afterward. Marrow transplants may also be used for children with ALL. After initial treatment, 90 to 95 percent of ALL cases will go into remission, and up to 70 percent of ALL cases will be cured completely. The survival rates for AML are not yet as high, but are improving steadily.

Alternative Treatment

Alternative therapies are being increasingly used alongside orthodox medicine in major pioneering NHS oncology centers, but always in conjunction with orthodox cancer therapy.

Aromatherapy

Aromatherapy can be supportive for both children and adults with cancer. However, the essential oils should be delivered by a humidifier which can pump them into the air of the environment. Massage should not be used with any cancer in its early stages – particularly leukemia – as this may encourage the spread of the disease via the blood circulatory and lymphatic systems. Bergamot is uplifting and niaouli helps to boost the immune system.

Homeopathy

A homeopath will probably prescribe specific remedies as well as constitutional treatment, to be taken alongside conventional medical treatment.

Bach flower remedies

These can be helpful as an emotional support during physical illness. The remedies may also be useful for the child's parents. Possibilities include agrimony for those hiding their true feelings of distress behind a cheerful face, crab apple (the cleansing remedy) is helpful for those who feel distaste for their illness, elm for those finding the pressures of their responsibilities overwhelming (again, perhaps helpful for parents), red chestnut for those afraid of something happening to their loved ones, mimulus for fear of the reality of a diagnosed cancer and rescue remedy for the shock of diagnosis.

Other therapies

Infants and children respond well to **spiritual healing** and diseases often clear more quickly. This may help a child when the immune system is weakened by cancer. A **nutritional therapist** may use dietary programs, which may include vitamin C therapy and having the acidity cleaned out of the body.

The Immunization Debate

Alternative views

Immunization has long been the focus of debate between alternative and orthodox medical practitioners. The orthodox view is that mass immunization is necessary and that without it former childhood killers such as smallpox, diphtheria and polio would still be rampant. Immunization has all but eradicated these illnesses in richer countries, along with a dramatic decline in whooping cough (pertussis), tuberculosis, measles, mumps and rubella (German measles).

Immunization may be either passive (injecting antibodies to provide short-lived protection) or active (injecting a modified microorganism – vaccine – to prime the body to make its own antibodies and give longer-lasting immunity).

Many alternative practitioners would prefer to avoid conventional immunizations as they believe these weaken the immune system. However, as orthodox vaccines for diphtheria, polio, tetanus, rubella and measles appear to have minimal side effects, many therapists suggest that they be given. Children who are in any category with special risk factors (see right) are an exception.

While there can be very rare reactions to conventional vaccination for whooping cough (including seizures and brain damage), the orthodox view is still that the risks of vaccination are far less than the dangers caused by contracting the disease itself.

Weighing up the arguments

Orthodox immunizations are not obligatory but are strongly recommended. Any small reaction is usually only an indication that a child is fighting the infection and developing an immunity. Alternative practitioners fear there may be additional subtle long-term side effects and argue that developing a natural immunity is better than one that is artificially acquired.

There is a moral decision involved for anyone opting against conventional vaccinations. Many parents frown upon those who decide against vaccinating their children, believing that they are creating a weak link in the community's immunity. No child should be denied conventional immunizations without very careful regard for what can be serious consequences.

If a child is strong and healthy, he or she is unlikely to be affected by the usually minor side effects of conventional immunizations. Orthodox practitioners will argue that the risks of vaccinations are usually considerably smaller than the risks involved with the diseases themselves.

Many alternative practitioners believe there is a fundamental imbalance caused by immunizations, leaving behind echoes of the original infection. Various alternative therapies offer post-immunization treatment for side- and "echo effects." Alternative therapists also offer a variety of treatments to generally help build up the immune system. These can be used along with accepting routine immunizations (see next column).

Typical schedule for orthodox vaccinations:

2 months	*Diphtheria, tetanus, pertussis (DTP injection). Oral poliomyelitis*
3 months	*Diphtheria, tetanus, pertussis (DTP injection). Oral poliomyelitis*
4 months	*Diphtheria, tetanus, pertussis (DTP injection). Oral poliomyelitis*
12–18 months	*Measles, mumps, rubella (MMR injection).*
4–5 years	*Booster injection against diphtheria and tetanus. Oral poliomyelitis booster*
10–14 years	*BCG injection against TB*
15–18 years	*Booster injection against tetanus and poliomyelitis*

Some children should not be immunized:

- *Live vaccines (including MMR, BCG and polio) should not be given to children on any immune-suppressive treatment, those with an immune deficiency disease or those who have certain cancers.*
- *Children showing a violent reaction to eggs should not receive routine vaccinations for measles and mumps.*
- *Children who show a serious reaction to a dose of vaccine should not automatically continue with a further dose.*
- *Whooping cough vaccine should not be given automatically to children with brain damage until the condition is stabilized.*
- *Vaccinations should be delayed if the child has an infection or fever.*

Homeopathic immunization

Many homeopaths believe that it is better to boost general resistance to disease rather than expose a child unnecessarily to the influence of powerful disease organisms. Homeopathic immunization does not work in the same way as orthodox immunization. Instead of introducing live or dead viruses or antibodies into the body, remedies are prepared from diseased tissue or secretions using the traditional dilution and succession method. They contain, in a very potent form, the essence of the disease organism and its toxins. The body reacts to such remedies, known as nosodes, by improving its immune response.

Homeopathic prevention of childhood illnesses:

Illness	Homeopathic Remedy
Chicken pox	*Varicella or Rhus tox. (if your child has been in contact with it)*
Measles	*Morbillinum*
Mumps	*Parotidinum, or Rhus tox. (during incubation period)*
Rubella	*Rubella*
Whooping Cough	*Pertussin*
Diphtheria	*Corynebacterium diphtheriae (based on the diphtheria bacteria)*

HOME AND EMERGENCY FIRST AID

The emphasis in this section is on basic orthodox first aid treatment for conditions such as simple cuts and abrasions, bruises or sprains. The treatment for more severe conditions such as broken bones, burns and scalds should be handled in a hospital environment and the medical procedure that will be followed is discussed. The alternative health treatment that is detailed is for minor injuries or for long-term help.

Ideally, everyone should be a trained first aider, but even if you have no training, when someone you know suffers a bee sting, a sprained ankle, a nosebleed or a road traffic accident, the general rules are virtually the same. The first aider needs to be cool, calm and in control of the situation. He or she needs to speak to the casualty with confidence and reassure the person and their relatives.

When you examine the casualty be gentle, but firm, and speak to them as you do so. Children in particular may well be very upset and will need constant reassurance. Assess the situation and if it is a minor injury follow the treatments suggested in the following pages. If it is more serious, call a doctor or an ambulance immediately while keeping the patient warm.

Practicing first aid can seem daunting, and it is well worth doing an approved first aid course which will cover the theory and practice of first aid with useful demonstrations and "mock" casualties. Going on a course, such as those run by the Red Cross, will go a long way to improving your confidence and ability.

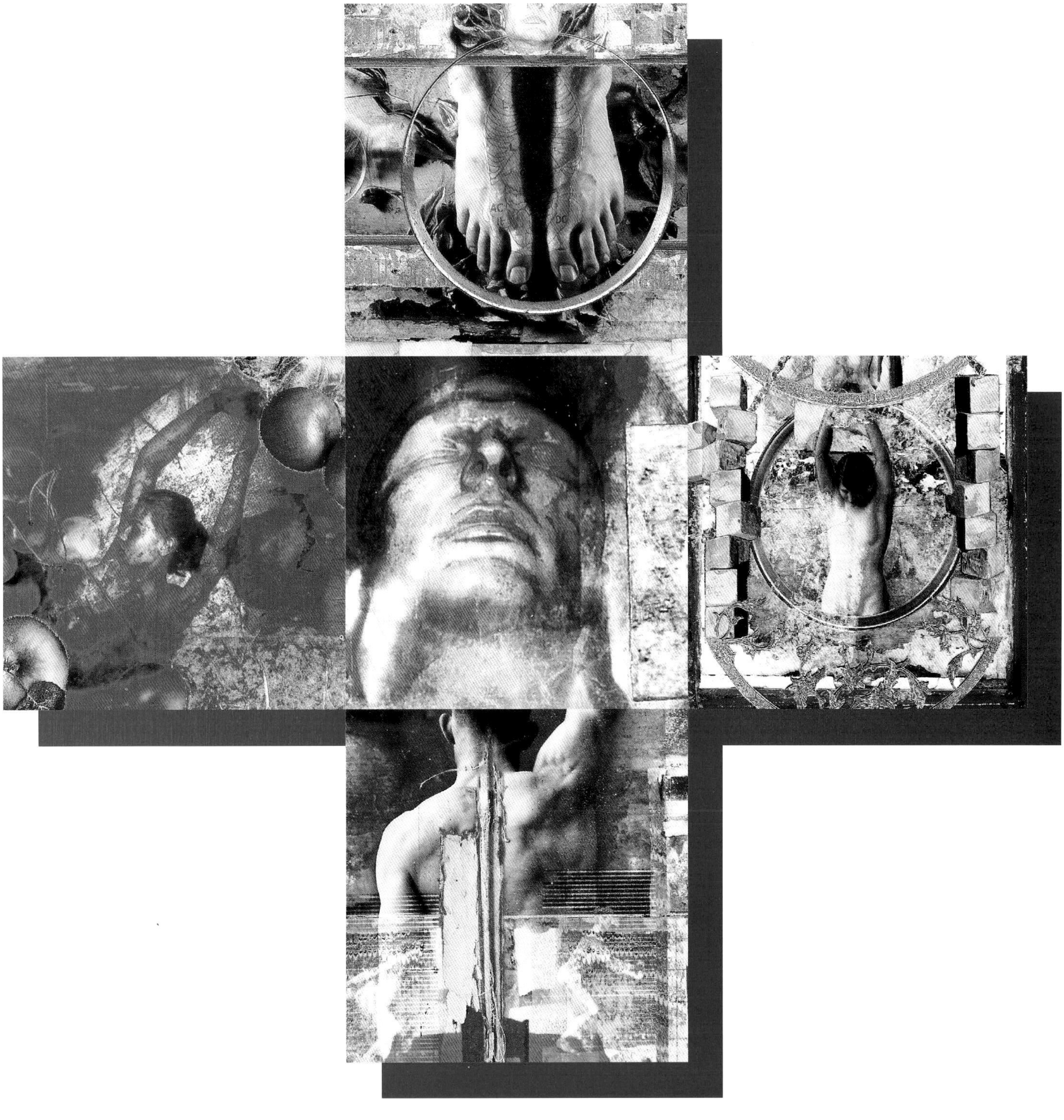

BITES AND STINGS

What are they?

Both bites and stings pierce the protective layer of skin and can cause local swelling, redness or infection. Those sensitive to stings, for example from bees or wasps, can have an allergic reaction, which may be serious.

IF PAIN AND SWELLING DO NOT RESPOND TO TREATMENT OR IF SUFFERER FEELS FAINT AND UNWELL, SEEK MEDICAL HELP

Causes

Insects such as bees, wasps and horseflies and other creatures such as spiders, snakes and jellyfish, as well as many plants including stinging nettles, produce poisons as a defense mechanism. These can be painful and may cause a reaction in humans.

Orthodox treatment

For animal bites, wash the area in warm water with soap or a mild antiseptic fluid and cover with a sterile dressing. If infection develops, a doctor may prescribe antibiotics and advise a tetanus injection. Paracetamol or aspirin will help ease pain and anti-inflammatory (antihistamine or hydrocortisone) creams or tablets will reduce swelling. The sting of the insect should be removed carefully with tweezers. Bees stings can be neutralized by an alkaline substance such as bicarbonate of soda. Wasp stings can be neutralized by lemon juice or vinegar. With allergy to stings, there is a danger of anaphylactic shock. Emergency treatment with an injection of adrenaline and antihistamine may need to be administered. If you are at all worried about a bite or a sting, do not hesitate to seek medical treatment.

ALTERNATIVE TREATMENT

Homeopathy

Bite wounds can be cleaned with pure tincture of hypericum. Stings should be removed with tweezers and pyrethrum tincture should be dabbed on the area. A practitioner may also advise taking aconite for shock and arnica to help control bruising from animal bites. Other homeopathic remedies for stings include ledum, if the area is swollen, bruised and painful, or apis if the skin is hot, red and swollen.

Other therapies

The **Bach flower remedies**' rescue remedy can be diluted in water and applied to the sting or bite. **Western herbalists** recommend plunging the affected area in iced water with a teaspoon of baking soda; marigold ointment may help to reduce swelling. **Naturopaths** will also recommend iced water with bicarbonate of soda, and calendula cream. **Aromatherapists** recommend lavender, as it reduces stinging and burning sensations.

BRUISES

Causes

Bruises occur when the body receives an impact blow. Blood is released from the capillaries which have been broken open and it enters into the tissues under the skin, causing the characteristic blue/purple color. Occasionally bruises may also occur without mechanical damage: certain conditions feature spontaneous bruising but they are usually benign; occasionally they may suggest a serious condition such as hemophilia.

Orthodox treatment

If bruising is minor and not associated with other more serious injuries, a cold compress should be placed with moderate pressure over the affected area straightaway. A badly bruised limb may need to be rested for 24 to 48 hours, preferably raised up on pillows to reduce blood flow to the injured area. Unless bruising appears for no apparent cause, or has not cleared up within two weeks, no medical help is required.

ALTERNATIVE TREATMENT

Homeopathy

A homeopath is likely to suggest arnica, taken internally to reduce bruising and relieve symptoms. Applied gently as an ointment or cream, it will help disperse bruising.

Other therapies

A **macrobiotic practitioner** may suggest soaked wakame (kelp), bandaged in place and left overnight. A **Western herbalist** may suggest compresses of herbs to reduce swelling and bruising. Rosemary can be applied as a compress to encourage the circulation and healing process. An **acupuncturist** may suggest applying a moxa stick to the affected area to stimulate the circulation and restore the flow of Chi. There are several **Ayurvedic medicine** ointments for bruising. An **aromatherapist** may recommend a natural beeswax cream, rose water and sweet almond oil with lavender oil to ease inflammation and encourage healing.

Blisters

What are they?

Blisters are small swellings formed by capsules of the watery part of blood (serum) collecting under the skin to protect the soft tissue below. They look like raised, fluid-filled bubbles.

Causes

Blisters are usually the result of friction. However they may also develop because of heat damage such as sunburn, a scald or a dry heat burn to the skin, or as part of the body's reaction to an insect bite. Certain infectious diseases also produce blisters.

Orthodox treatment

Unbroken blisters should be covered with a dressing to prevent damage. As the blister heals new skin grows underneath the blister, causing the serum to be reabsorbed and the old skin to flake off. If a blister is punctured, the flesh beneath it becomes liable to infection so it is essential that the blister is kept clean and dry. Usually only the top layers of skin are affected and it heals within the week. If infection does occur, oral or topical antibiotics may be suggested. If there is no obvious reason for the blisters, a doctor may carry out tests to determine the cause.

Alternative Treatment

Homeopathy

Cantharis will be advised if the blister is itchy or rhus tox. if it is itchy, swollen and red. A calendula and hypericum solution can be dabbed onto burst blisters.

Other therapies

An **aromatherapist** may advise dabbing the blister with a tea tree oil solution or dabbing the area with neat lavender oil. There are specific **Ayurvedic medicine** ointments designed to facilitate healing and discourage infection. The **Bach flower remedies**' rescue remedy may be applied directly to the blistered skin in either tincture form or as a cream. A **Western herbalist** may advise simmering cabbage leaves in milk, allowing them to cool and then applying them to the blister with a poultice. A **macrobiotic** practitioner may recommend cold, salty water to discourage infection and help the blister to dry out.

Shock

Causes

Shock causes a sudden loss of blood flow as the body diverts blood to the vital organs, such as the heart, lungs and brain. Mild shock may be brought on by dehydration due to diarrhea, vomiting, emotional factors and allergic reaction. Symptoms include clammy, pale skin, shallow and rapid breathing, dizziness, anxiety, nausea, restlessness, thirst and vomiting. With severe shock, this can lead to unconsciousness. Severe shock may be caused by heart attack, blood loss or an electric shock.

Orthodox treatment

Treatment for mild shock, for example emotional shock or fainting, is to get the supply of blood to the brain and heart. This can be done by lying the person down and covering them up to keep them warm. In the case of fainting, the person is already lying down. For emotional shock, give comfort and reassurance.

FOR SEVERE SHOCK AFTER AN ACCIDENT SEEK EMERGENCY MEDICAL ATTENTION. OTHER TREATMENT MAY BE REQUIRED.

Do not move the patient unless you are sure there are no bone, neck or spinal injuries. If these injuries are absent, raise the legs to get the blood moving to the brain and vital organs. For electric shock, disconnect the power or stand on a dry object, using a wooden broom handle to lever the person away from the electrical source. Give no food or drink to people in severe shock.

Alternative Treatment

Bach flower remedies

The rescue® remedy can be applied to the temples and pulse points, to reduce symptoms and ease panic.

Homeopathy

A homeopath may recommend aconite or ignatia, taken every five minutes until the shock has eased.

Other therapies

An **aromatherapist** may suggest essential oils of lavender, melissa or peppermint dropped on a handkerchief and held under the nose until help arrives, or the condition stabilizes. **Ayurvedic medicine** offers several treatments for emotional shock, and emergency remedies can be provided while awaiting help. **Western herbalists** can offer calming herbal drinks.

Acute Toothache

Causes

Toothaches may be a pain emanating from a tooth or from several teeth. Occasionally they hurt below gum level. Most toothache is the result of tooth decay, gingivitis, sensitive teeth, inflammation of the pulp of the tooth, neuralgia, an abscess, or sinusitis (in which case the pain is referred). The pain can be a continuous throbbing or intermittent. Sometimes it is brought on by eating something that irritates the exposed nerve of the tooth. After a tooth has been treated there may be some pain but this should ease as the area around the tooth calms down.

Toothache should always be investigated as soon as possible by a dentist but, while waiting for an appointment, there are many treatments which provide temporary symptomatic relief.

Orthodox treatment

Aspirin or paracetamol will help relieve inflammation and ease pain while waiting to see a dentist. At the surgery, the dentist will thoroughly examine the mouth to identity the cause of the pain and provide treatment. Antibiotics may be prescribed for infections, for example, on the root of the nerve, in the pulp of the tooth, or where bleeding gums present the risk of one. Toothaches combined with a temperature may mean an abscess and speedy treatment is needed. An abscess may be lanced, treated by antibiotics and/or given a pain-killing injection.

Emergency treatment is needed for severe toothache that keeps the person awake at night, if the gums swell or if the side of the face where the pain is experienced becomes swollen.

Alternative Treatment

Homeopathy

As toothache is usually a sign of tooth decay it will require a visit to the dentist. Meanwhile, homeopathic treatment may include:

- Coffea for toothache with severe shooting pain.
- Chamomilla for toothache with unbearable pain.
- Belladonna for toothache with throbbing pain, particularly if the gums and cheeks are swollen.

Other therapies

A **Western herbalist** may recommend tinctures of echinacea or myrrh to encourage healing and reduce the risk of infection. Cayenne can act as a local anesthetic to relieve pain. A **reflexologist** may stimulate the points on the hands and feet corresponding to the teeth. An **auricular therapist** can provide pain-relieving emergency treatment. **Bach flower remedies**' rescue® remedy may be applied directly to the tooth.

Cuts and Abrasions

Causes

Most cuts and abrasions are minor and only the capillaries are damaged, causing a small amount of blood to be released into the surrounding tissues, or to escape from the wound. This blood will soon clot and requires little treatment.

For severe cuts, particularly to a vein, blood loss must be stopped urgently and medical help sought.

Orthodox treatment

Abrasions need to be cleaned and a loose dressing applied to keep them clean. Cuts should be cleaned and direct pressure should be applied to the bleeding area until the blood flow ceases. Holding the area upright helps achieve this. Loose dressings may be needed to keep the cut clean, although exposure to air will help the healing process. More severe cuts may require stitches or tissue glue to help the skin join up during healing.

Alternative Treatment

Homeopathy

A homeopath is likely to suggest cleaning the wound or graze with a cotton ball soaked in a calendula and hypericum solution to stop infection. A practitioner may also suggest:

- Arnica if the cut or abrasion is accompanied by moderate to severe bruising.
- Ledum if the wound feels numb and cold. A cold compress will help soothe the pain.
- Hypericum if there is a shooting nerve pain with the wound.

Other therapies

Western herbalists may suggest using calendula ointment after washing the cut with running water to remove dirt. They may also recommend soaking a cotton ball in a calendula and water mix and holding it over the site of the wound. A **macrobiotic** practitioner may suggest cleaning the area and then applying a miso paste dressing over the area. An **aromatherapist** may recommend lavender on the wound. **Bach flower remedies**' rescue remedy diluted in water and applied to the area may help.

SPRAINS

Causes

Sprains are ligament injuries which happen when a joint is abruptly stretched beyond its normal range of movement. The fibers of the ligament (whose function is to help hold the joint together) tear, causing pain and then weakness in the joint itself. In severe cases the ligament may rip completely, leaving the joint vulnerable and unstable. A sprain can also be caused by bleeding into the joint.

Symptoms include swelling, stiffness, pain and bruising. It is difficult in some cases – especially with a child who has broken a very small bone in their foot or hand – to distinguish between a bone fracture and a sprain. If in doubt, seek medical attention but as a general rule, if you can still use the joint it is not broken.

Orthodox treatment

Self-treatment for a strain requires applying a cold compress to the site of the injury to reduce swelling and any possible internal bleeding. Bind the affected part securely, but not too tightly, with an elastic or crêpe bandage. Raising the affected limb also helps to reduce inflammation.

While a sprain is healing, do not lift heavy objects or put a strain on the area, to avoid damaging the ligament.

Severe strains may require medical treatment. The joint may need to be immobilized, for example, a strained arm would be put in a sling. Generally, gently moving the limb is the preferred option, as this speeds up the recovery process and avoids the likelihood of muscle wasting or joint stiffness setting in.

ALTERNATIVE TREATMENT

Osteopathy

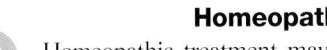

An osteopath may manipulate the joint to prevent locking and to break down any adhesions. Soft tissue massage will release tone in tight muscles or increase it in loose ones.

Homeopathy

Homeopathic treatment may include arnica for pulled tendons and ligaments with pain and stiffness, followed by ruta. A cold compress of diluted arnica tincture can be applied to reduce swelling.

Other therapies

Aromatherapists may suggest lavender massaged into the affected area. A **macrobiotic** practitioner will recommend hot and cold compresses and a tofu plaster if there is swelling. **Bach flower remedies**' rescue® remedy cream may help discomfort.

BONE BREAKS

Causes

There are several different types of fracture (see Breaks and Fractures page 310) and the symptoms include swelling, pain, misalignment of the injured area, immobility and protrusion of bone through the skin.

IF YOU SUSPECT A NECK OR SPINE FRACTURE DO NOT MOVE THE VICTIM. GET MEDICAL HELP URGENTLY.

Orthodox treatment

Breaks and fractures are usually caused by injury and should be treated by a doctor. Watch out for shock (see page 339) and cover any bleeding with a clean cloth. Immobilize the affected joint with a sling or splint. Do not give any food or drink.

DO NOT TRY TO FORCE BACK A DISLOCATED JOINT INTO POSITION YOURSELF AS THIS COULD CAUSE MORE DAMAGE.

ALTERNATIVE TREATMENT

Western herbalism

There is no first aid treatment for breaks but herbs can help to speed up the recovery and healing process, particularly comfrey, which is also known as knitbone.

Other therapies

The **Bach flower remedies'** rescue remedy can be applied to the temples and pulse points of the casualty to reduce panic symptoms. An **aromatherapist** may suggest essential oils of lavender, melissa or peppermint dropped on a handkerchief and held under the nose until help arrives or the condition stabilizes. **Ayurvedic medicine** offers several treatments for emotional shock, and emergency remedies can be provided while awaiting help. After treatment for the fracture **nutritional therapists** will recommend comfrey, for aiding the mending of bone breaks and fractures, and zinc and vitamin C supplements. **Reflexology** will be overall; special attention will be paid to the areas of the affected part to assist the formation of bone.

Splinters

Causes

Splinters, usually small pieces of wood or thorns becoming embedded in the skin, are common injuries and are usually very minor, requiring little treatment. However, they should be removed as infection may occur.

Orthodox treatment

Self-treatment is by sterilizing a pair of tweezers either by boiling them for ten minutes or by passing them through the flame of a lighter. Meanwhile, the skin around the site of the injury should be carefully cleaned using soapy water or an antiseptic wipe. Wipe away from the wound to prevent any dirt being wiped over the area. Dab the skin dry very carefully with a piece of cotton or a tissue. Using the tweezers, pull the splinter out very carefully, to ensure that it does not break. Once the splinter has been removed, clean the area again and cover with a plaster. If the splinter is deeply imbedded or the wound becomes infected or swells, consult a doctor. The doctor will treat the wound and may advise having a tetanus injection or booster.

Alternative Treatment

Homeopathy

A warm compress helps draw the splinter to the surface. Silicea should be taken for a stinging, burning pain.

Other therapies

After removing the splinter as described above, an **aromatherapist** may advise dabbing the area with a tea tree oil solution or applying neat lavender oil to take away the stinging sensation. There are specific **Ayurvedic medicine** ointments designed to facilitate healing and discourage infection. The **Bach flower remedies**' rescue® remedy may be applied directly to the skin in either tincture form or as a cream. A **macrobiotic** practitioner may recommend cold, salty water to discourage infection and help the wound to dry out.

Travel Sickness

Causes

Travel sickness, also known as motion sickness, effects certain individuals who are sensitive to a repetitive movement of the whole body. Traveling in cars, boats, planes and buses are the usual causes, but the effect may also be brought on by fair rides and sometimes by going up or down in a lift.

The symptoms include nausea, heavy breathing, dizziness, fatigue, vomiting, headache, pallor, sweating and discomfort in the abdominal area.

The cause of travel sickness is thought to be connected to the balancing mechanisms within the ear which help the brain co-ordinate information about space and movement. As well as physical causes, there may also be a psychological cause brought on by fear of movements over which the person has no control.

Orthodox treatment

Travel sickness is rarely suffered by the person driving the car or boat as they feel more in control of the movement. However, it is unwise for passengers who suffer from travel sickness to eat heartily before setting out. There are various drugs available over the counter to counteract the symptoms but people may have to try out several before finding a suitable one. Such drugs usually contain atropine and antihistamines. The tablets should be taken at least one hour before the start of the journey. If taken while traveling there is a risk of vomiting them up. For long journeys a doctor may prescribe a stronger drug.

Avoid alcoholic drinks when traveling as motion sickness drugs can have a sedative effect. Other side effects of such drugs include blurred vision.

Alternative Treatment

Acupressure

Pressing on the wrist with the fingers at a certain point can help alleviate travel sickness. Find the point three fingers' width above the wrist crease on the inner wrist, in line with the middle finger. Press on this point. Wristbands are available which perform the same function by pressing on the acupressure point.

Other therapies

An **aromatherapist** can recommend dabbing essential oils of peppermint and ginger onto a hanky and inhaling from it. The **Bach flower remedies'** rescue remedy can be applied to the temples and pulse points, to ease panic. A **homeopath** may suggest tabacum for nausea, giddiness and faintness or nux for queasiness, headache and sensations of chilliness.

Nosebleeds

Causes

Nosebleeds are very common, often resulting from a direct blow to the area, infection of the mucous membrane which lines the nose, or drying and crusting caused by extreme cold. In addition, nose-picking, sinus problems and high blood pressure can also cause nosebleeds.

Orthodox treatment

Nosebleeds can be controlled by pinching the nostrils together for about five or ten minutes with the head tilted back to lessen the blood flow to the area. A small ice pack on the nasal bridge may also help.

NOSEBLEEDS WHICH DO NOT STOP WITHIN A COUPLE OF HOURS, SHOULD BE CHECKED BY A DOCTOR.

Medical treatment may include numbing the nose with a local anesthetic, packing the bleeding nostril with gauze and checking blood pressure. When the bleeding has stopped the bleeding point may be cauterized to prevent recurrence.

Alternative Treatment

Aromatherapy

An aromatherapist will suggest a drop of lavender on a cotton ball, which should then be gently inserted into the bleeding nostril.

Homeopathy

A homeopath will advise sitting down with the head forward and pinching the lower part of the nostrils for ten minutes. In addition, arnica may be advised for a nosebleed brought on by injury or phosphorus for a nosebleed brought on by blowing the nose violently.

Other therapies

Bach flower remedies' rescue remedy is appropriate if there is any emotional distress. Place a few drops on a damp flannel placed on the nose. A **naturopath** will recommend ice compresses.

Burns and Scalds

Causes

The difference between burns and scalds is that burns are caused by forms of dry heat, such as fire, electricity, strong sunlight or chemicals. Scalds are produced by damp heat from boiling liquids or steam.

The effects of both on the skin and soft tissues are the same, as is the treatment. With mild (first-degree) burns the damage is restricted to the outer layer of skin and symptoms include redness, soreness, heat and sometimes blistering. They can be very painful but are seldom actually dangerous unless they cover a large area. Sunburn produces first-degree burns and may also cause fever and produce some swelling of the affected skin. With more serious (second-degree) burns the damage goes deeper into the skin, damaging its lower layers and producing blisters. Third-degree burns are very serious and affect the soft tissue and nervous system deep beneath the skin. Sometimes second- and third-degree burns may be accompanied by shock (see page 339).

Orthodox treatment

For burns, the area should be bathed in cold water for ten to 15 minutes and then covered lightly with a clean bandage or cloth. Do not put anything else on the burn site, or apply butter or fat, as is traditionally recommended.

LARGE BURNS SHOULD BE TREATED BY A DOCTOR. IF A BURN DOES NOT HEAL MEDICAL TREATMENT SHOULD BE SOUGHT.

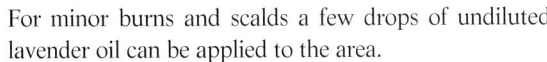

Alternative Treatment

Aromatherapy

For minor burns and scalds a few drops of undiluted lavender oil can be applied to the area.

Homeopathy

A homeopath may recommend arnica when blistering has occurred and where there is searing, smarting pain. This should be followed by cantharis. Urtica should be taken for continuous, stinging pain.

Other therapies

Bach flower remedies' rescue® remedy can help promote healing if there is emotional stress. **Western herbalism** advises aloe vera for unbroken skin, or calendula cream on broken skin.

Sunburn and Sunstroke

Causes

Sunburn is the general term for inflammation and skin damage caused by prolonged exposure to ultraviolet light. It causes the skin to redden, flake and then peel off. There may be soreness and some blistering.

Sunstroke is caused by the body's heat regulating mechanism breaking down and causing the body's temperature to rise dangerously high. It comprises two different conditions: heat stroke and heat exhaustion. Heat stroke occurs when the body cannot control its temperature by sweating. Symptoms include hot, dry skin, headaches, thirst, nausea, dizziness and drowsiness. The temperature rises to above 40°C (104°F). Confusion and unconsciousness may occur. Heat exhaustion is caused by profuse sweating, causing loss of salts from the body. Symptoms include muscle cramps, headaches, vomiting, dizziness and pale, cold and clammy skin. There is a rapid pulse and collapse may occur.

Orthodox treatment

Calamine lotion and an increased intake of fluids will help ease sunburn. Painkillers such as aspirin and paracetamol may help. Severe sunburn may be treated with corticosteroid creams to relieve inflammation. Occasionally, blistering can lead to infection, which is treated with topical antibiotics. Prolonged and excessive exposure causes not only premature wrinkling of the skin but, more seriously, may lead to skin cancer.

For heat stroke, remove the sufferer from the heat, undress and wrap in a sheet soaked in cold water. Once the temperature reaches 38°C (101°F) the sheet can be replaced with a dry one. Check the temperature regularly and repeat cooling treatment if it rises again. For heat exhaustion, remove the sufferer from the heat, check temperature and pulse and remove outer clothing. If unconscious, put the sufferer in the recovery position. If conscious, give salted water every 10 minutes to rehydrate.

Alternative Treatment

Western herbalism

Calendula and comfrey, either as creams or infusions will be given for sunburn to help reduce inflammation. Hypericum ointment or lavender may be used to offer relief from pain and burning sensations.

Other therapies

For sunburn, **homeopathic** treatment may include aloe vera gel or urtica urens ointment. **Aromatherapists** may recommend diluted lavender oil as a soothing aftersun treatment. **Naturopaths** may suggest applying vitamin E moisturizing cream.

Food Poisoning

Causes

Food poisoning is usually caused by eating food or drinking water that has been contaminated with bacteria. Reheating or partially cooking food also encourages the growth of bacteria. Partially cooked chicken (salmonella) and unpasturized cheeses (lysteria) are two examples of food poisoning sources. Symptoms include sharp abdominal pain, vomiting and diarrhea, possibly with dehydration.

Orthodox treatment

Mild cases of food poisoning can be self-treated. Drinking plenty of fluids and avoiding solids until the stomach settles will help. Antidiarrhea medications containing kaolin will help. Sugary drinks or drinks of electrolyte solutions available from chemists will replace lost salts caused by dehydration. Severe cases of food poisoning such as salmonella need to be reported via a doctor to health officials.

Alternative Treatment

Western herbalism

An emetic may be advised if toxic substances have been ingested. Disinfectant remedies may be used with eliminative treatments to remove the poisons. For mild cases of food poisoning, 3–4 garlic capsules taken each day will help fight infection. Camomile tea may help reduce intestinal or stomach inflammation. Hot, spicy ingredients used in Eastern cooking, such as curry powder and cayenne pepper, may have a protective effect against contracting food poisoning.

Other therapies

Homeopathic treatment may involve the use of aloe if there is diarrhea caused by food intolerance. A **nutritional therapist** may suggest fasting until all the symptoms have subsided. Vitamin C and blackberry and peppermint teas can then be taken until the stomach is stronger. **Acupuncture** and **acupressure** will help relieve symptoms of nausea. **Shiatsu** may also be useful. A few drops of **Bach flower remedies'** rescue® remedy on a hanky can be inhaled to help relieve the symptoms of nausea.

Alternative Healthcare Medicine Chest

Most alternative health practitioners acknowledge the importance of conventional medical techniques in treating certain conditions, including emergencies. However, this does not undermine the value of alternative treatments; when a therapist acknowledges that conventional medicine is required, alternative treatment is aimed at supporting and supplementing the orthodox treatments. Indeed, because most alternative medical practitioners view treatment holistically, with particular emphasis on emotional and psychological factors, they aim not only to make those who are unwell get better, but also to make them feel more comfortable during the recovery process. If you are taking alternative medicine, for example homeopathic or herbal remedies, you should tell your doctor when being treated for an injury, as some orthodox treatments may not work well with the alternative medicines prescribed.

FOR SERIOUS ILLNESS, INJURIES OR ACCIDENTS, IT IS ABSOLUTELY ESSENTIAL TO CALL A CONVENTIONAL DOCTOR OR AMBULANCE.

However, for everyday illnesses and ailments, an alternative medicine chest is an invaluable aid to have in the home. Listed below are some of the remedies that you can use safely to treat minor problems.

Bach flower remedies' rescue remedy cream *Use on cuts, grazes, bites and burns. Cases of skin irritation may be eased by applying the cream to the affected area. It can be invaluable in soothing itchy childhood infectious diseases such as chicken pox, for example.*

Bach flower remedies' rescue remedy tincture *Good for nervousness and trembling, worry and panic. It can be given after injury or accident to steady the casualty.*

Lavender essential oil *Excellent for treating burns, reducing inflammation and redness and taking away any stinging sensation. Also good for soothing headaches and relieving the symptoms of coughs.*

Calendula cream and infusions *Good for minor burns and scalds, sunburn, eczema, acne and skin infections. When calendula is made into an infusion or a poultice, it can help relieve minor respiratory problems, colds and indigestion.*

Slippery elm *Good in cases of digestive problems and inflamed skin. Available as tablets and powders and can also be made into a poultice.*

Ginger *Infusions of ginger can help relieve nausea, travel sickness, morning sickness and aid general digestion. Warming drinks of ginger help alleviate symptoms of a cold.*

Arnica cream, tablets or tincture *Emotionally arnica helps steady the nerves after injury. Physically it reduces swelling and heals bruised tissues.*

Camomile *Helps induce relaxation and calm. Good in cases of anxiety, tension, headaches and insomnia.*

Rhus tox. *Used to relieve joint pains, such as arthritis and backache. Can also help relieve restlessness and nervousness.*

Witch hazel *For treating cuts, bruises, sprains and relieving minor burns.*

Tofu plasters *Apply to cuts and grazes.*

Peppermint *To calm an upset stomach and aid digestion.*

Aloe vera gel *For burns, cuts, sunburn and blisters.*

Comfrey cream *To treat fractures, cuts and bruises.*

Vitamin E cream *To treat minor skin complaints and help to relieve sunburn.*

Urtica urens ointment *Useful for burns and to treat allergic skin irritations.*

Garlic capsules *Garlic's strong antiseptic properties are ideal for treating digestive and respiratory tract infections, skin infections, and boosting the immune system to protect against winter colds and flu.*

Other useful remedies
Miso paste, hypericum ointment, arsenicum, comfrey cream, marigold cream, petroleum, tabacum and cayenne pepper.

DIRECTORY

The directory contains useful addresses and telephone numbers (where possible) for the 30 therapies detailed in this book. Information is also given on how to find a practitioner, what a treatment might cost, and the complaints procedure to follow if you are unhappy with a therapy treatment. Further addresses in connection with some ailments are also detailed. International addresses are also given where possible.

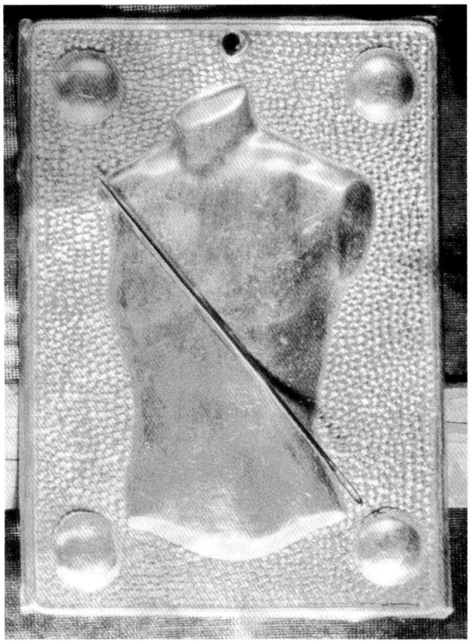

ACUPUNCTURE

How to find a qualified practitioner

The practice of TCM (Traditional Chinese Medicine) in Britain is still in its early stages and unlike other forms of complementary treatment, there are still no generally accepted governing bodies or associations. The British Acupuncture Accreditation Board (BAAB) has set up its own system of self-regulation, and it is linked closely with the Council for Acupuncture, the Council for Complementary and Alternative Medicine, and the Register of Traditional Chinese Medicine (RTCM). Your practitioner should be affiliated with one of these bodies, and have undergone four years of training.

Acupuncture is not generally available on the National Health Service (NHS) although it is becoming increasingly popular with doctors, a few of whom are also qualified acupuncturists, other fund holding GPs may refer you to an acupuncturist. Some medical professionals working in hospitals are also using acupuncture for pain relief.

Contact:

Acupuncture Research Resource Centre
Centre for Complementary Health Studies
University of Exeter
Exeter EX4 4RJ
Tel: 01392 264 459

British Acupuncture Council
63 Jeddo Road
London W12 9HQ
Tel: 020 8735 0400

British Medical Acupuncture Society
Newton House
Newton Lane
Whitley,
Warrington
Cheshire WA4 4JA
Tel: 01925 730 727

The Council for Acupuncture
10 Panther House
38 Mount Pleasant
London WC1X 0AN

How much does it cost?

Treatment varies depending on where you live and the experience of your practitioner, but you can expect to pay between £30–£60 for an initial consultation, and about half that per treatment session thereafter.

Many acupuncture schools also run clinics where supervised students will treat you for a nominal fee.

Complaints procedure

All members registered with the BAC must adhere to a strict code of conduct and are insured to practise acupuncture. If you have a complaint to make about a BAC-registered therapist, call the Council where someone will put you in touch with the Registrar of the ethics committee. Your complaint will be listened to and recorded, and both sides will be interviewed. If the problem cannot be resolved amicably, the practitioner may eventually be struck off. Members of the BAC are insured to practise acupuncture only. If your acupuncturist uses another therapy (perhaps herbs) with which you were unhappy, you must contact the organization with which he is registered to practise that therapy.

AURICULAR THERAPY

How to find a qualified practitioner
TCM acupuncturists who have also trained in auricular therapy use the initials Dip AK Aur. All registered traditional acupuncturists in Britain belong to the British Acupuncture Council (BAC). Standards are currently being revised for Modern auricular therapists. For a register of Modern practitioners affiliated to the Institute of Complementary Medicine (ICM), but not to the BAC, send a sae to: John Lewis, Secretary of the European Federation of Modern Acupuncture, 11 Level Lane, Buxton, Derbyshire SK17 6TU. Qualified practitioners follow a code of ethics and have been assessed to a standard approved by the European Federation of Modern Acupuncture (EFMA).

Contact:

British Acupuncture Council
63 Jeddo Road
London W12 9HQ
Tel: 020 8735 0400

How much does it cost?
The costs for Auricular acupuncture are similar to the costs for acupuncture (see opposite).

Complaints procedure
If you have a complaint about treatment, first discuss the problem with your practitioner. If you can't resolve it, approach the organization with which he is registered.

Acupuncture for animals
Because of the successful treatment of animals with acupuncture there is now a British Association of Veterinary Acupuncture with a register of vets who use the therapy. Contact The British Medical Accupuncture Society for a list of vets (see previous page for address).

ALEXANDER TECHNIQUE

How to find a qualified teacher
A qualified Alexander teacher will have completed a three-year training course and hold a certificate issued by the Society of Teachers of the Alexander Technique (STAT). The initials MSTAT will also appear after their name.

Contact:

The Society of Teachers of the Alexander Technique
20 London House
266 Fulham Road
London SW10 9EL
Tel: 020 7351 0828

How much does it cost?
Prices will vary according to the location of the classes and the experience of the teacher. You can expect to pay between £15–£30.

Complaints procedure
Teachers registered with the Society of Alexander Teachers must abide by the society's strict code of conduct and be insured to practice. Any proof of misconduct or malpractice means the teacher is liable to disciplinary procedures by the Society. If you have a complaint about a teacher registered with the society contact them at the address detailed.

AROMATHERAPY

How to find a qualified practitioner
A qualified aromatherapist should have trained to the minimum standard defined by the Aromatherapy Organisations Council (AOC). She should be a member of a professional association with a code of conduct and ethics and be insured to practise. The AOC is the umbrella group for the aromatherapy profession in the UK. It represents associations rather than individuals, but is indirectly responsible for almost 6,000 therapists.

Contact:

Aromatherapy Organisations Council
PO Box 19834
London SE25 6WF
Tel: 020 8251 7912

For a list of practitioners:
International Federation of Aromatherapists
Stamford House
2–4 Chiswick High Road
London W4 1TH
Tel: 020 7935 2143
(Send an A5 sae and a cheque for £2)

How much does it cost?
The cost will depend on where you live, and the experience of your therapist. Most sessions last between 60–90 minutes, costing £20–£45.

Complaints procedure
Contact the association to which your therapist belongs. All registered practitioners are bound by their association's codes of practice, ethics and disciplinary procedures.

Other organizations

International Society of Professional Aromatherapists
ISPA House
82 Ashby Road
Hinckley
Leicester LE10 1N
Tel: 01455 637 987

ARTS THERAPIES

How to find a qualified practitioner
All qualified therapists should have a degree in their field, and at least a year's experience in clinical training. Your therapist will also have a post-graduate certificate which is recognized by the Department of Health.

Specifically, art therapy takes about two years' of full-time education, and the others about a year. It is a prerequisite for many therapists to have undergone some therapy themselves.

There is no overall body for the registration of Arts therapies, but each has a professional association which holds a register of approved therapists. Many therapists can be referred through your doctor or hospital, and many work within these institutions.

Contact:

Association for Dance Movement Therapy UK
c/o Quaker Meeting Rooms
Wedmore Vale
Bedminster
Bristol BS3 5HX
(*Written enquiries only*)

British Association of Art Therapists
11A Richmond Road
Brighton
Sussex BN2 3RL

How much does it cost?
Treatment may be on the NHS, depending on where you live. Private treatment is also dependent on where you live, but most therapists charge about £20–£30 per hour.

Complaints procedure
Therapists registered with all of the above associations must abide by their codes of practice. If you have a complaint against a therapist, write to the relevant organization at the addresses above.

AUTOGENIC TRAINING

How to find a qualified practitioner
All Autogenic Training teachers have two year's training (often part time), and are trained in medicine or psychotherapy. A list of qualified teachers can be obtained by sending an A5 stamped addressed envelope to the British Association for Autogenic Training and Therapy (BAFATT) (see below).

Contact:

British Association for Autogenic Training and Therapy (BAFATT)
c/o Royal London Homoeopathic Hospital
Great Ormond Street
London WC1N 3HR

How much does it cost?
Costs will depend on where you live. A course of ten lessons may cost between £150–£300, depending on whether you are taught in a group, or individually. This figure includes assessment and follow-up. It is also possible to get some training on the NHS at the Royal London Homoeopathic Hospital.

Complaints procedure
All practitioners are covered by professional public liability insurance as individual complementary therapists. The British Association for Autogenic Training and Therapy requires therapists to abide by a code of ethics; failure to do so can result in disciplinary procedures. Address complaints to: The Secretary at BAFATT (see above).

AYURVEDIC MEDICINE

How to find a qualified practitioner
Practitioners who qualified in India and Sri Lanka will have completed a five-year degree course and one-year internship in an Ayurvedic hospital. There are few qualified practitioners in Britain, but a list can be obtained from the Ayurvedic Medical Association (see below).

Contact:

Ayurvedic Medical Association UK
17 Bromham Mill
Giffard Park
Milton Keynes MK14 5QP
Tel: 01908 617 089

How much does it cost?
Your consultation will be at least an hour in length, and cost roughly £40–£60, depending on where you live and the experience of your practitioner. Subsequent treatments will cost from £20–£40 per session.

Complaints procedure
All practitioners registered with the Ayurvedic Medical Association UK are governed by a code of conduct, must have insurance to practise, and are liable to disciplinary procedures. If you have a complaint against any of its members, contact the Association at the above address.

BACH FLOWER REMEDIES

How to find a qualified practitioner

There is no professional qualification for Bach Flower therapists, and as it is complementary to many other therapies, it is often used in other disciplines. However the Bach Centre does offer practitioner training with certification and registration for those who successfully complete the course.

Contact:

The Dr Edward Bach Centre
Mount Vernon
Sotwell
Wallingford
Oxon OX10 0PZ
Tel: 01491 834678

How much does it cost?

Costs will vary according to where you live, and whether or not it is incorporated in another therapeutic treatment. The average fee is £10–£20.

Individual remedies cost from £2.40 for 10ml bottles and £4.25 for a 20ml bottle of rescue® remedy. All remedies keep for at least five years.

Complaints procedure

If you have a complaint about any of the remedies or a practitioner, write first to the Dr Edward Bach Centre. Staff there will either deal with the complaint themselves or pass it on to the relevant body.

BODYWORK

ROLFING

How to find a qualified practitioner

A qualified practitioner will hold a diploma from the Rolf Institute in Boulder, Colorado, United States.

Contact:

Jennie Crewdson
Tel: 020 7834 1493

European Rolfing Association
Kapuziner Str 25
80337 Munich
Germany

The Rolf Institute Headquarters
205 Canyon Boulevard
Boulder
Colorado 80302
United States
Tel: 001 303 449 5903

Loan Tran
Neal's Yard Therapy Rooms
2 Neal's Yard, Covent Garden
London WC2 H9DP
Tel: 020 7379 7662

How much does it cost?

Prices vary according to where you live, and the experience of your practitioner, but you can expect to pay in the region of £30–£50 per session.

Complaints procedure

Practitioners must abide by the code of ethics of the Rolf Institute of Structural Integration. Practitioners who fail to do so are liable to disciplinary procedures by the Institute. If you have a complaint to make about a British practitioner contact the European Rolfing Association at the above address.

HELLERWORK

Members of the European Hellerwork Association (see below) must adhere to a strict code of conduct, and have the appropriate insurance to practise.

Contact:

The European Hellerwork Association
c/o Roger Golten
The Ability Centre
29 Crawford Street
London W1H 1PL
Tel: 020 7723 5676

How much does it cost?

The first session may be slightly more, at about £60, and subsequent treatments will be £30–£50.

Complaints procedure
Members of the European Hellerwork Association must abide by a code of conduct, have insurance to practise and are liable to disciplinary procedures from the Association. If you have a complaint against a member, contact the European Association at the above address.

BIODYNAMIC THERAPY

How to find a qualified practitioner
In Britain, your practitioner will have graduated from the Gerda Boyesen Centre, and can practise with supervision after three years of training, and unsupervised after five. Some practitioners have qualified to register with the UK Council for Psychotherapy (UKCP).

Contact:

The Gerda Boyesen Centre
Acacia House
Centre Avenue
London W3 7JX
Tel: 020 8743 2437/ 8746 0499

How much does it cost?
Treatment ranges from between £20–£35 per hour, depending on where you live and the experience of your therapist. However, most therapists give concessions for people on low incomes.

Complaints procedure
The Gerda Boyesen Centre has an ethics committee, which you should approach if you wish to make a complaint against one of its therapists. In the unlikely event that the problem should not be resolved by the Centre it will be passed on to the UKCP.

Chinese herbalism

How to find a qualified practitioner
In Britain there is no recognized qualification required for practice, so it is essential that you find a registered practitioner.

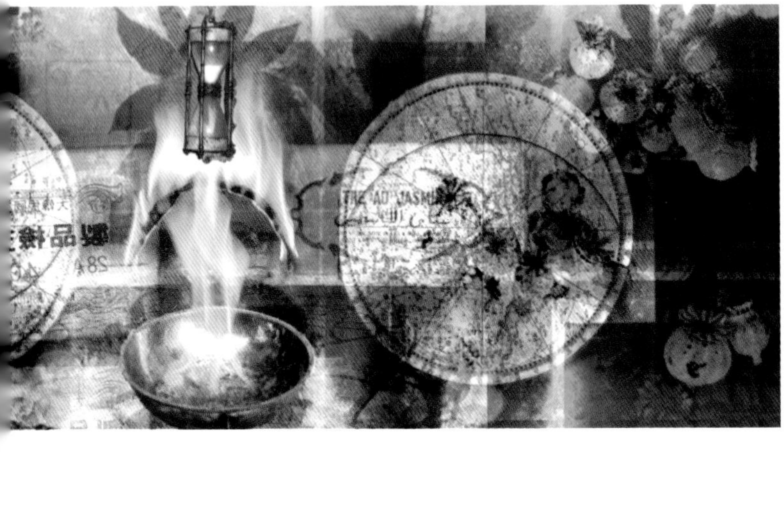

Contact:

The Register of Chinese Herbal Medicine
PO Box 400
Wembley
Middlesex HA9 9NE
Tel: 020 7470 8740
(Send an sae, and £1.50 for the register)

How much does it cost?
Prices will vary according to where you live, and the experience of your practitioner. Treatment may be offered alongside other Chinese disciplines, such as acupuncture. The first consultation is usually about £25–30, and subsequently £10–£15. Herbs may be purchased separately.

Complaints procedure
If you have a complaint about a practitioner who is registered with Register of Chinese Herbal Medicine, contact:

John Gavin
PO Box 400
Wembley
Middlesex HA 9 9NZ
07000 790 332

Chiropractic

How to find a qualified practitioner
A qualified practitioner should have a BSc in chiropractic, which is awarded after a five-year, full-time course at a recognized college. Members use the initials DC, BSc or BAppSc, or a mixture depending on where they are qualified.

Contact:

The British Chiropractic Association
Blagrave House
17 Blagrave Street
Reading RG1 1QB
Tel: 0118 950 5950

How much does it cost?
Prices are dependent on where you live, but you can expect to pay about £30–£40 on your first visit (all X-rays are extra, and can cost up to £50 per time). Subsequent visits are shorter and cost about £10–£30.

Complaints procedure
If you have a complaint you should take it to the chiropractor concerned. If that proves fruitless you should put your complaint in writing and send it to the Executive Director of the British Chiropractic Association, Blagrave Street, 17 Blagrave Street, Reading. This is the standard procedure for complaints against chiropractors registered with the BCA, which has an established disciplinary procedure, a strict code of ethics, and requires all practitioners to be insured to practise. A leaflet outlining the full details of the procedure is available from the BCA.

McTIMONEY CHIROPRACTIC

How to find a qualified practitioner

Practitioners qualified in McTimoney are registered with the McTimoney Chiropractic Association, and licensed to practise through that regulatory board. There is a strict code of practice. The initials MC will follow their name, and if they are licensed to treat animals, the initials AMC will follow their name.

Contact:

The McTimoney Chiropractic Association
21 Hight Street
Eynsham
Oxford OX18 1HE
Tel: 01865 880 974

How much does it cost?

A treatment costs about £25–£40 for a first hour-long consultation, £15–£35 for subsequent treatments.

Complaints procedure

Contact the McTimoney Chiropractic Association (see above) with any complaints, for there is a very strict code of professional behaviour to which all members must conform.

COLOUR THERAPY

How to find a qualified practitioner

There are two organizations in Britain which can provide details of qualified practitioners. Qualifications differ between them, but both have high standards of control of their members.

Contact:

The International Association for Colour Therapy (IACT)
PO Box 3688
London SW13 0XA

How much does it cost?

The first consultation is normally about £45 for an hour or 90 minutes; after that, expect to pay between £20–£30.

Complaints procedure

All qualified therapists registered with the above associations are covered by indemnity insurance and work to a code of ethics. If you wish to make a complaint against a therapist first contact the therapist and if you are still not satisfied, contact the association to which she belongs.

CRYSTAL AND GEMSTONE THERAPY

How to find a qualified practitioner

All qualified crystal healers should have successfully completed a two-year diploma course, although licentiate members may have completed their first year only. The initials they use depend on the school from which they qualified. The ACHO (see below) represents a total of eight member organizations.

Contact:

The Affiliation of Crystal Healing Organisations (ACHO)
46 Lower Green Road
Esher
Surrey KT10 8HD
Tel: 020 8398 7252.
(Send a large sae for a register of practitioners)

How much does it cost?

Some therapists just operate on a donation basis. Those who make a charge can ask anything between £10–£35 for a session lasting up to one and a half hours. Individual crystals vary in price from as little as 50p up to thousands of pounds.

Complaints procedure

Find a therapist who is registered with the Affiliation of Crystal Healing Organisations. That way, if you do have a complaint you can contact the governing body, which requires all its members to abide by a strict code of conduct.

CYMATICS

How to find a qualified practitioner

Many cymatics practitioners are doctors or nurses, and there are only about 125 trained practitioners in Britain. Practitioners must prove that they have a thorough understanding of anatomy and physiology in order to be taken on for training.

Contact:

Dr Sir Peter Guy Manners
Bretforton Medical and Scientific Academy
Bretforton Hall
Bretforton
Vale of Evesham
Worcestershire WR11 5JH
Tel: 01386 830537

How much does it cost?

Treatment costs will vary according to the area in which you live, and also the experience of your practitioner. The initial consultation may cost about £30, but the following treatment sessions are usually cheaper, at £15–£20.

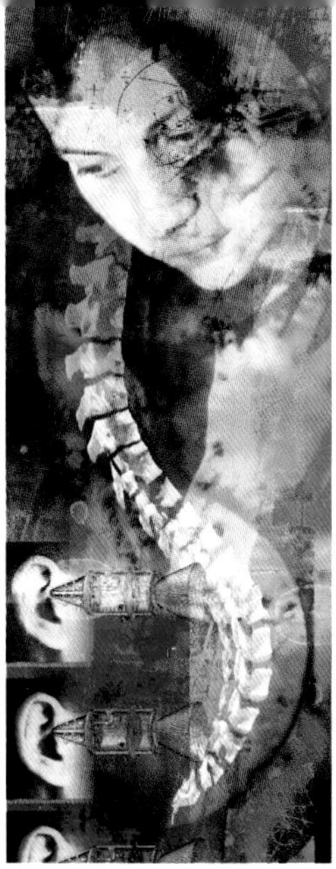

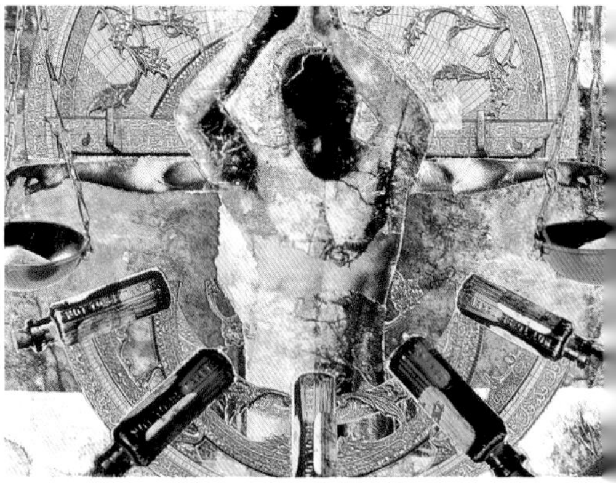

Complaints procedure
Practitioners are governed by a strict code of conduct, covered by insurance and are all liable to disciplinary procedures. Complaints about a practitioner should be addressed to the Bretforton Trust at the address given above.

DIAGNOSTIC THERAPIES

KINESIOLOGY

How to find a qualified practitioner
Qualified practitioners will hold a diploma from The Association of Systematic Kinesiology (dipASK), and will have completed a minimum of two years training. They must also be insured and comply with the Association's code of ethics and practice.

Contact:

Association of Systematic Kinesiology
39 Browns Road
Surbiton
Surrey KT5 8ST
Tel: 020 8399 3215

How much does it cost?
Treatments usually take between 15–40 minutes and cost on average between £25–£35.

Complaints procedure
All practising members of the Association of Systematic Kinesiology must be thoroughly trained and professionally competent. If you are dissatisfied with any treatment that you have had from a member of this organization, you can write to the trustees of the Association at the address given above.

IRIDOLOGY

How to find a qualified practitioner
All trained and qualified iridologists use the initials RIr and RCIrA and MGNI after their names.

Contact:

Guild of Naturopathic Iridologists
94 Grosvenor Road
London SW1V 3LF
Tel: 020 7834 3579

International Association of Clinical Iridologists
853 Finchley Road
London NW11 8LX

How much does it cost?
The cost is usually dependent upon where you live, and the experience of your iridologist. The first consultation will range between £25–£60 per hour, and thereafter about £15–£30.

Complaints procedure
Members of the above associations must abide by a strict code of ethics and be insured to practise. Should they fail to do so they are liable to disciplinary measures imposed by their association. If you have a complaint contact the body to which your practitioner belongs.

KIRLIAN PHOTOGRAPHY

How to find a qualified practitioner
The Body Logic method of Kirlian Photography is still quite rare in Britain, although there are some acupuncturists who use it with traditional treatment.

Contact:

Institute for Complementary Medicine (ICM)
PO Box 194
London SE16 7QZ
Tel: 020 7237 5165
(For a list of practitioners send an sae and letter of what you require)

How much does it cost?
The cost of treatment varies enormously between practitioners, some of whom may charge you nothing but just ask for a donation. Most people pay in the region of £35–£45 for a first session, and then £5 for each subsequent picture. At exhibitions such as Mind, Body and Spirit exhibition you can have your picture taken and explained for about £15.

Complaints procedure
There is no central register and so no recognized complaints procedure. Any complaints must be made against the individual therapist in the usual legal manner.

HOMOEOPATHY

How to find a qualified practitioner
Doctors who have been trained in homeopathy are registered as either a member or a fellow of the Faculty of Homoeopathy and use the letters MFHom and FFHom, respectively.

Contact:

The British Homoeopathic Association
27a Devonshire Street
London W1N 1RJ
Tel: 020 7935 2163
(For a list of homoeopathic doctors and veterinary surgeons send a sae with 60p worth of stamps)

The Faculty of Homoeopathy
The Royal London Homoeopathic Hospital
Great Ormond Street
London WC1N 3HR
Tel: 020 7837 8833

If you want to find a qualified homoeopath who is not a doctor it is best to find one who is registered with the Society of Homoeopaths (see below) and uses the letters RSHom or FSHom.

Contact:

The Society of Homoeopaths
4 Artizan Road
Northampton NN1 4HU
Tel: 01604 621 400
(Send a large sae for a list of practitioners)

How much does it cost?

Although some homoeopathic treatment is available free in Britain, by referral through the NHS, most homoeopaths work privately. Homoeopathic doctors working within the NHS can also refer you to one of the five homoeopathic hospitals in Britain. These are based in London, Glasgow, Liverpool, Bristol and Tunbridge Wells. The initial consultation, which lasts from 45 minutes to an hour, usually costs in the region of £30–£60, although that will be dependent upon where you live. Subsequent treatment tends to be shorter (about 20 minutes) and usually costs about £15–£30. Most homoeopaths include the price of the remedies in treatment.

Complaints procedure

If you are dissatisfied with the homoeopathic treatment you received from a homoeopathic doctor you should contact the Faculty of Homoeopathy. If your complaint concerns the general medical care you received at the hands of a homoeopathic doctor contact the General Medical Council (GMC) 178, Great Portland Street, London, W1N 6JE. If your homoeopath is not medically trained but is registered with the Society for Homoeopaths, take your complaint to the Society.

HYPNOTHERAPY

How to find a qualified practitioner

Hypnosis can be dangerous in the hands of someone untrained, so it is essential that you get someone who you can trust. It is suggested that you meet the practitioner before committing yourself to treatment.

Contact:

British Council of Hypnotist Examiners
Blinking Sike
Caxton Way
Eastfield Business Park
Scarborough
North Yorkshire
YO11 3Y2
Tel: 01723 585960

British Hypnosis Research
St Matthew's House
1 Brick Row
Darley Abbey
Derbyshire DE22 1DQ
Tel: 01332 541030
(Send an sae for a register of practitioners)

Central Register of Advanced Hypnotherapists
28 Finsbury Park Road
London N4 2JX
Tel: 0207 7354 9938
(Send an sae for a register of practitioners)

National Council of Psychotherapists (and Hypnotherapy Register**)**
46 Oxhey Road
Oxhey
Watford
Hertfordshire WD1 4QQ

The National Register of Hypnotherapists and Psychotherapists
12 Cross Street
Nelson
Lancashire BB9 7EN
Tel: 01282 699378
(Send an sae for a register of practitioners)

How much does it cost?

Treatment is dependent upon the level of experience of your practitioner, and often varies between locations. You can expect to pay anything from £25–£100 for the first sessions, and anything from £25–£50 thereafter.

Complaints procedure

Practitioners registered with all of the above organizations are qualified to a standard that is acceptable to the registering body, are covered by indemnity insurance and are obliged to abide by a code of ethics. If you have a complaint to make about a registered practitioner contact the association to which they belong.

MASSAGE

How to find a qualified practitioner

The British Massage Therapy Council represents several massage associations, and provides a list of registered practitioners.

Contact:

Massage Therapy Institute of Great Britain
PO Box 27/26
London NW2 4NR
Tel: 020 8208 1607
(Send an sae for register of practitioners)

The British Massage Therapy Council
78 Meadow Street
Preston PR1 ITS

How much does it cost?
Treatment varies according to the area in which you live, and the experience of your practitioner. Aromatherapy massages may be more expensive. Expect to pay between £25–£50 for a 1–1½ hour session.

Complaints procedure
If you have a complaint about treatment, discuss it first with your therapist and if it cannot be resolved address your complaints to the British Massage Therapy Council (see above), or The International Therapy Examination Council, 10–11 Heathfield Terrace, Chiswick, London W4 4JE (Tel: 020 8994 4141).

Other organizations

Aromatherapy Organisations Council
PO Box 19834
London SE25 6WF
Tel: 020 8251 7912

London College of Massage
5 Newman Passage
London W1P 3F
Tel: 020 7323 3574

METAMORPHIC TECHNIQUE

How to find a qualified practitioner
There is no formal training or qualification required for practitioners.

Contact:

The Metamorphic Association
67 Ritherdon Road
London SW17 8QE
Tel: 020 8672 5951

How much does it cost?
One session costs between £15–£25.

Complaints procedure
The Association runs short courses, but there is no recognized qualification, code of ethics, or any recognized complaints procedure.

NATUROPATHY

How to find a qualified practitioner
A qualified naturopath has studied for four years, full-time, and will have a naturopathic diploma (ND). Members of the Register of Naturopaths will have the initials MRN after their name.

Contact:

The General Council and Register of Naturopathy
Goswell House
2 Goswell Road
Street
Somerset BA16 OJG
Tel: 01458 840 072

How much does it cost?
Depending on where you live, treatment can cost anything from £25–£70 for the first visit, and about half that for subsequent visits. You will have to pay extra for any herbal remedies or food supplements.

Complaints procedure
If your practitioner is registered with the General Council and Register of Naturopaths (see opposite). Members are insured to practise, must abide by a strict code of conduct and are liable to disciplinary procedures in cases of misconduct.

Other organizations

Institute of Optimum Nutrition
13 Blades Court
Deodar Road
Putney SW15 2NU
Tel: 020 8877 9993

NUTRITIONAL THERAPY

How to find a qualified practitioner

Many nutritional therapists are doctors who have trained in nutrition; others receive training on specialist courses. Many are naturopaths, acupuncturists, herbalists and other disciplines which require a specialized knowledge of nutrition. The Society for the Promotion of Nutritional Therapy is the leading nutritional therapy body in Britain, administering a professional register of qualified nutritional therapists.

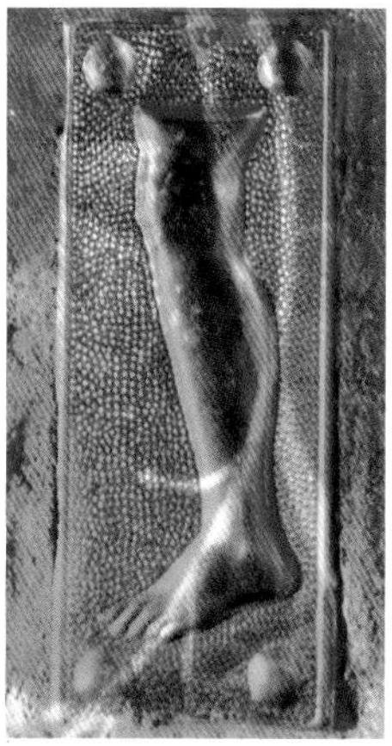

Contact:

Dietary Therapy Society
33 Priory Gardens
London N6 5QU
Tel: 020 8348 8242

Society for the Promotion of Nutritional Therapy
PO Box 85
St Albans
Hertfordshire AL3 7ZQ

How much does it cost?

Treatment ranges from £20–£50 per session, plus the cost of any supplements necessary for treatment. Follow-up treatment may be considerably less (about half).

Complaints procedure

For complaints regarding nutritional therapists or dieticians trained in conventional nutrition (state-regulated), contact The British Nutrition Foundation, 15 Belgrave Square, London SW1. For guidance on other nutritional matters, get in touch with the Society for the Promotion of Nutritional Therapy.

Other organizations

Institute of Optimum Nutrition
13 Blades Court
Deodar Road
Putney SW15 2NU
Tel: 020 8877 9993

MACROBIOTICS

How to find a qualified practitioner

Macrobiotic practitioners will have studied at the Kushi Institute, for a two-year period. Qualified practitioners will be registered with the Kushi Institute.

In Britain, contact:

The Macrobiotics Association of Great Britain
377 Edgware Road
London W2 1BT
Tel: 07050 138 419

Jon Sandifer
PO Box 69
Teddington
Middlesex TW11 9SH
Tel: 020 8977 8988

Worldwide, contact:

The Kushi Institute
PO Box 7
Becket
MA 01233
United States
413 623 5741

How much does it cost?

Treatment generally costs between £35–£50 for your initial consultation, and £25–£40 for each session thereafter.

Complaints Procedure

Contact the Kushi Institute (see above) with any complaints about a practitioner, or in Britain, there is a governing body for most disciplines connected with nutrition, called CNEAT, 34 Wadham Road, London SW15 2LR. They have guidelines and codes of ethics for anyone practising nutrition, and will deal with your complaint.

OSTEOPATHY

How to find a qualified practitioner

Osteopathy is fast becoming an all-graduate profession. Qualified osteopaths use the letters DO (diploma in osteopathy) or BSc(Ost) after their name. Medical doctors who have trained at the London College of Osteopathic Medicine use the initials MLCOM. Other letters usually indicate the professional body to which the practitioner belongs – there are five in all.

General Osteopathic Council
Osteopathy House
176 Tower Bridge Road
London SE 1 3LU
Tel: 020 7357 6655

How much does it cost?
The cost of treatment varies a great deal, according to where you live. A first consultation may cost up to £70, but subsequent visits are usually between £20–£40.

Complaints procedure
Your osteopath should be a member of a professional body, in which case he will have professional indemnity insurance, work to a code of ethics, and be liable to disciplinary procedures. If you have a complaint to make about a registered practitioner, contact the General Osteopathy Council (see above).

CRANIAL OSTEOPATHY

How to find a qualified practitioner?
All cranial osteopaths should be trained and qualified osteopaths, with special training in cranial osteopathy. Not all osteopaths are trained in cranial techniques, and it is important that you do not undergo treatment without that qualification.

Contact:

General Osteopathic Council
Osteopathy House
176 Tower Bridge Road
London SE 1 3LU
Tel: 020 7357 6655

How much does it cost?
The cost of treatment may be dependent upon where you live. The initial consultation is usually between £30–£60, with subsequent visits costing from about £20–£30 thereafter.

Complaints procedure
Osteopaths who use cranial technique are governed by the same regulations as any other osteopath. If you have a complaint about a registered practitioner contact the association to which he belongs or the **General Osteopathic Council** (see above).

POLARITY THERAPY

How to find a qualified practitioner
Registered polarity therapists must have a minimum of two years training and use the initials RPT (Registered Polarity Therapist), ISPT (International Society of Polarity Therapists) and PEA (Polarity Energetics Association).

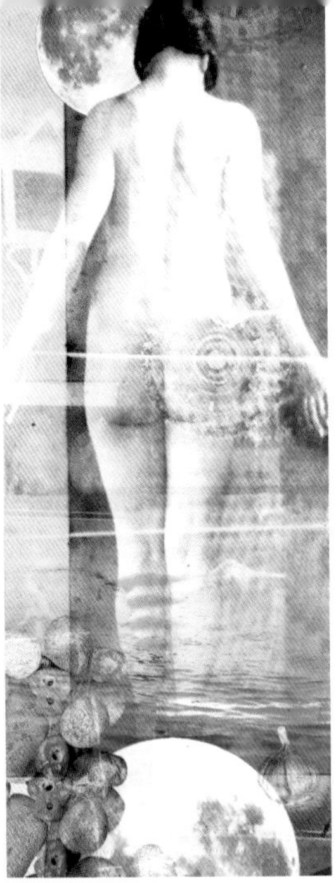

Contact:

The Polarity Therapy Association (UK)
Monomark House
27 Old Gloucester Street
London WC1N 3XX
Tel: 01483 417714

How much does it cost?
Treatment for a one hour session is between £15–£40, depending on where you live.

Complaints procedure
There is currently a new register being set up, which will incorporate all existing associations. Complaints will be made through this body.

RADIONICS

How to find a qualified practitioner
A qualified practitioner should have the initials M.DSRad; Lic. DSRad; M.Rad. A; Lic.Rad.A; M.PSR; or Lic PSR.M.D after their name. A radionic practitioner studies for four to five years, and, as a part of their code, are not allowed to advertise for business. All new business is on a referral basis.

Contact:

The Confederation of Radionic and Radiesthesic Organisations
c/o The Radiesthesia Trust
Wincanton
Somerset BA9 8EH
Tel: 01963 32651

How much does it cost?
The first analysis costs about £40–£50, but daily treatment thereafter can be as little as £30–£40 per month.

Complaints procedure
Practitioners are governed by a code of ethics, are insured to practise, and are liable to disciplinary procedures. If you have a complaint against a registered practitioner contact The Confederation of Radionic and Radiesthesic Organisations, at the above address.

REFLEXOLOGY

How to find a qualified practitioner
There are a number of regulatory boards, and any one of the following should be able to provide you with a list of registered practitioners

Contact:

International Institute of Reflexology UK
255 Turleigh
Bradford on Avon
Wiltshire BA15 2HG
Tel: 01225 865 899

The Association of Reflexologists
27 Old Gloucester Street
London WC1N 3XX

The British Reflexology Association
Monks Orchard
Whitbourne
Worcester WR6 5RB
Tel: 01886 821207

The Holistic Association of Reflexologists
The Holistic Healing Centre
92 Sheering Road
Old Harlow
Essex CM17 OJW
Tel: 01279 429 060

The International Federation of Reflexologists
78 Edridge Road
Croydon
Surrey CR0 1EF
Tel: 020 8667 9458

The Reflexologists Society
39 Prestbury Road
Cheltenham
Gloucester GL52 2PT

How much does it cost?
The cost varies, depending on where you live, but you can expect to pay between £15–£40. Occasionally the first session is free.

Complaints procedure
Contact the relevant professional organizations which must ensure that their practitioners are fully qualified, insured to practise, and abide by their organization's code of conduct.

RELAXATION AND VISUALIZATION

How to find a qualified practitioner
There is no statutory qualification in relaxation therapy and no central register. Most occupational therapists learn it as part of their training, but they rarely offer private lessons. Many other orthodox health professionals are learning and teaching relaxation skills. Many alternative practitioners use relaxation techniques along with other therapies. Therapists often advertise in suitable places such as your doctor's surgery or someone may personally recommend a therapist. In both cases, check the therapist's qualifications. For a list of non-medically trained complementary therapists contact: British Register of Complementary Practitioners through the Institute of Complementary Medicine PO Box 194, London SE16 1QZ

How much does it cost?
Costs vary, depending on where you live, and you can expect to pay anything from £10–£70 per session. Occasionally treatment may be offered on the NHS in Britain.

Complaints procedure
Complaints can only be brought against a member of one of the conventional healthcare professions such as the United Kingdom Central register of Nursing (UKCCN), if the therapist is a registered qualified nurse or British Medical Association (BMA), if she is a registered qualified doctor, or any other recognized professional healthcare organization to which the therapist belongs. Alternative practitioners registered with the British Register of Complementary Practitioners are liable to disciplinary procedures imposed by the Register.

SHIATSU & ACUPRESSURE

How to find a qualified practitioner
All registered practitioners must have a minimum of three years part-time training, with at least 500 hours of tuition. Qualified practitioners will have the initials MRSS following their name, and will be registered with the Shiatsu Society of Great Britain.

Contact:

British Medical Acupuncture Society
Newton House
Newton Lane
Lower Whitley
Warrington
Cheshire WA4 4JA
Tel: 01925 730727

International College of Oriental Medicine
Green Hedges House
Green Hedges Avenue
East Grinstead
West Sussex RH19 1DZ
Tel: 01342 313106

How much does it cost?
The cost of a one hour treatment varies depending on where you live and the practitioner's experience. Most practitioners, however, charge between £15–£50 depending on where you live.

Complaints procedure
If you have a complaint against a practitioner registered with the Shiatsu Society of Great Britain, contact the Society at the above address. All registered practitioners are obliged to have indemnity insurance, must abide by a code of ethics, and are liable to various disciplinary procedures enforced by the Society.

SPIRITUAL HEALING

How to find a qualified practitioner
Contact the National Federation of Spiritual Healers (NFSH) (see below), which runs a National Healing Referral Service to help you find a healer in your part of the country.

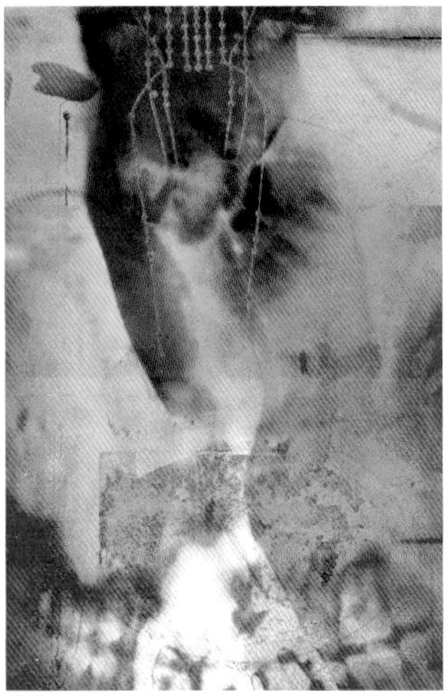

Contact:

The National Federation of Spiritual Healers (NFSH)
Old Manor Farm Studio
Church Street
Sunbury-on-Thames
Middlesex TW16 6RG
Tel: 01932 783164

How much does it cost?
Some healers are free of charge, and others will ask you to pay what you can. The NFSH advises not to pay more than £25 an hour.

Complaints procedure
You are advised to find a healer who is registered with the NFSH, who will be insured to practise and must abide by a strict code of conduct. Unregistered healers can offer you no safeguards.

TAI CHI

How to find a qualified instructor
There is no main register of instructors, nor is there one central body responsible for the promotion of Tai chi and the maintenance of standards. Many classes are run by local education authorities. Qualified instructors will have obtained a diploma from a master, and should have at least ten years' experience.

Contact:

67 Kilpatrick Gardens
Clarkston
Glasgow G76 7RF
Tel: 0141 638 2946

How much does it cost?
Prices range from as little as £2–£5 per session for authority-run classes, and £30–£50 per hour for a lesson from a master.

Complaints procedure
Because there is no central register of practitioners, tai chi instructors need abide by no established code of practice, nor are they liable to disciplinary procedures. If you have a complaint against a teacher you must take it up with him personally or take the individual to court.

WESTERN HERBALISM

How to find a qualified practitioner
A member or fellow the National Institute of Medical Herbalists (see below) will have the initials MNIMH or FNIMH after their name, and they will be trained and recognized by their official body.

Contact:

The National Institute of Medical Herbalists
56 Longbrook Street
Exeter EX4 6AH
Tel: 01392 426022

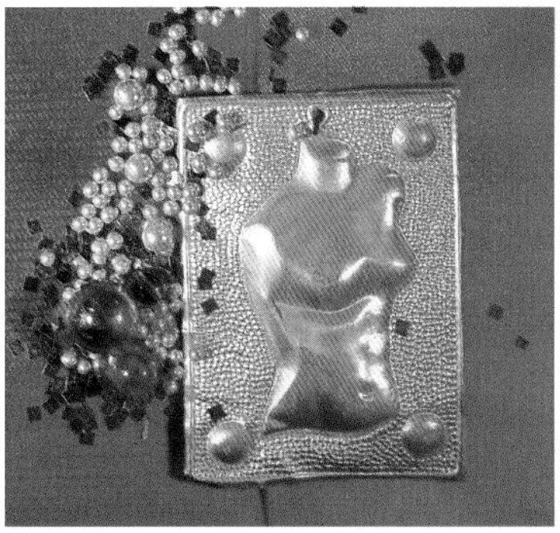

How much does it cost?
Fees vary, but an initial hour-long consultation will cost on average £25–£30. Fees in central London can cost as much as £50. Subsequent visits tend to be shorter (about half an hour) and are priced accordingly. In addition to the consultation you may have to pay for the herbs which cost about £3 a week.

Complaints procedure
Herbalists who belong to professional organizations such as those mentioned must be abide by a strict code of conduct and be insured to practise. If you have a complaint to make about a registered herbalist, contact the relevant organization, which will have a recognized disciplinary procedure to follow.

YOGA

How to find a qualified teacher
Yoga can be undertaken on many different levels, all dependent on the focus and training of the teacher.

Contact:

British Wheel of Yoga
1 Hamilton Place
Boston Road
Sleaford
Lincolnshire NG34 7ES
Tel: 01529 306 851

Life Foundation School of Therapeutics
Maristowe House
Dover Street
Bilston
West Midlands WV14 6AL
Tel: 01902 409164

The Iyengar Yoga Institute
233A Randolph Avenue
London W9 1NL
Tel: 020 7624 3080

The Yoga for Health Foundation
Ickwell Bury
Ickwell
Biggleswade
Bedfordshire SG18 9EF
Tel: 01767 627 271

The Yoga Therapy Centre
Royal London Homeopathic Hospital
60 Great Ormond Street,
London WC1N 3HR
Tel: 020 7419 7195
(For details of therapists who can treat people with specific medical problems such as back pain and asthma)

How much does it cost?
Private classes cost about £2.50 per class. One-to-one tuition will run to between £20–£50 per session.

Complaints procedure
Yoga is not a therapy in the same way that herbalism or massage is and there is no requirement for teachers to have insurance to practise or to abide by any code of conduct, neither is there a central body to which you can complain. If you believe that your teacher has been negligent or you sustained an injury in the class that was not your fault, then you would either take the teacher to court or contact the body with which she trained. Organizations such as the British Wheel of Yoga issue their teachers with diplomas, which are recognized and accepted by local education authorities.

General advice Britain

British Complementary Medicine Association
Kensington House
33 Imperial Square
Cheltenham
Gloucestershire
GL50 IQZ
Tel: 0116 282 5511

British Holistic Medical Association
179 Gloucester Place
London NW1 6DX

Council for Complementary and Alternative Medicine
63 Jeddo Road
London W12 6HQ
(For information send a sae and cheque/postal order for £2.50)

Institute for Complementary Medicine (ICM)
PO Box 194
London SE16 7QZ
Tel: 020 7237 5165
(For information send a sae and two loose stamps)

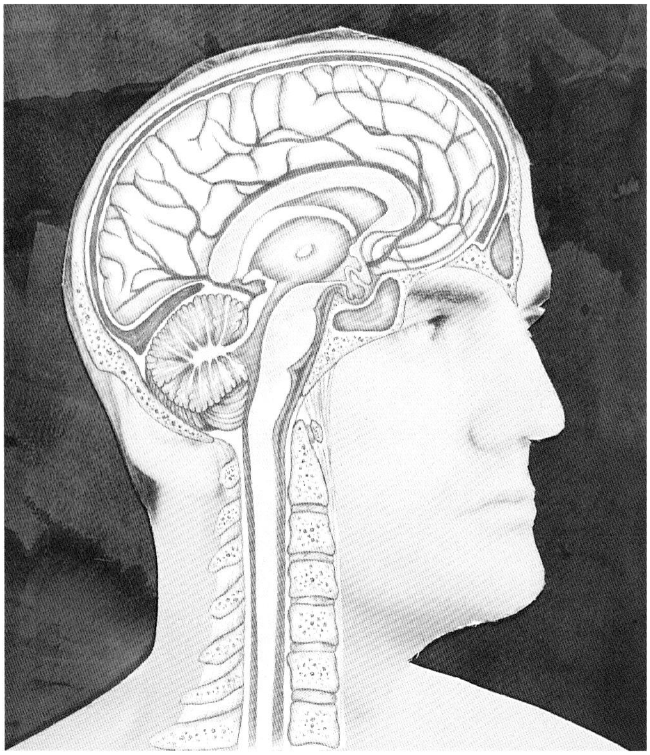

Useful addresses Britain

CIRCULATORY SYSTEM

British Heart Foundation
14 Fitzhardinge Street
London W1H 4DH
Tel: 020 7935 0185

Leukaemia Care Society
14 Kingfisher Court
Venny Bridge
Pinhoe
Exeter EX4 8JN
Tel: 01392 464 848

The Leukaemia Research Fund
43 Great Ormond Street
London WC1N 3JJ
Tel: 020 7405 0101

RESPIRATORY SYSTEM

National Asthma Campaign
Providence House
Providence Place
London N1 0NT
Tel: 020 7226 2260

MIND AND NERVOUS SYSTEM

Be Not Anxious
33 Broadway Avenue
Rainham
Kent ME8 9DB

British Epilepsy Foundation
New Anstey House
Gateway Drive
Leeds LS19 7XY
Tel: 0113 210 8800; Helpline: 0808 800 5050

British Migraine Association
178a High Road
Byfleet
Surrey KT14 7ED
Tel: 01932 352468

Depressives Anonymous
PO Box FDA
Ormiston House
32–36 Pelham Street
Nottingham NG1 2EG
Tel: 01702 433 838

Depressives Associated
PO Box 5
Castletown
Portland
Dorset DT5 1BQ

Disabled Living Foundation
380–384 Harrow Road
London W9 2HU
Tel: 020 7289 6111

International Stress and Tension Control Society
The Priory Hospital
Priory Lane
London SW15 5JJ

Mental Health Foundation
20–21 Cornwall Terrace
London NW1 4QL
Tel: 020 7535 7400

MIND (National Association for Mental Health)
Granta House
15–19 Broadway
Stratford
London
E15 4BQ
Tel: 020 8519 2122

National Society for Epilepsy
Chesham Lane
Chalfont St Peter
Gerrard's Cross
Bucks SL9 0RJ
Tel: 01494 601 300; Helpline: 01494 601 400

Parkinson's Disease Society
215 Vauxhall Bridge Road
London SW1 1EJ
Tel: 020 7931 8080

PAX (Panic Attacks and Anxiety)
4 Manorbrook
Blackheath
London SE3 9AW
Tel: 020 8318 5026

RADAR (Royal Association for Disability and Rehabilitation)
Unit 12 City Forum
250 City Road
London EC1V 8AF
Tel: 020 7250 3222

Stress Management Training Institute
Foxhills
30 Victoria Avenue
Shanklin
Isle of White
PO37 6LS
Tel: 01983 868 166

The Stroke Association
Stroke House
123–127 Whitecross Street
London EC1Y 8JJ
Tel: 020 7490 7999

ENDOCRINE SYSTEM

British Diabetic Association
10 Queen Anne Street
London W1M 0BD
Tel: 020 7323 1531

Diabetes Foundation
177A Tennison Road
London SE25 5NF
Tel: 020 8656 5467

Eating Disorders Association
1ST Floor
Wensum House
103 Prince of Wales Road
Norwich
Norfolk NR1 1DW
Tel: 01603 621 414

Hypothyroidism Self-Help
47 Crawford Avenue
Tyldersley
Manchester M29 8ET

Juvenile Diabetes Foundation
25 Gosfield Street
London W1P 8EB
Tel: 020 7436 3112

Overeaters Anonymous
PO Box 19
Stretford
Manchester M32 9EB
Tel: 01426 984 674

MALE REPRODUCTIVE SYSTEM

British Association for Betterment of Infertility and Education (BABIE)
PO Box 4TS
London W1A 4TS

Group B Hepatitis
Basement Flat
7A Fielding Road
London W14 0LL

Herpes Association
41 North Road
London N7 9DP
Tel: 020 7609 9061

ISSUE: The National Fertility Association
114 Lichfield Street
Walsall WF1 1FZ
Tel: 01922 722 888

FEMALE REPRODUCTIVE SYSTEM

Active Birth Centre
25 Bickerton Road
London N19 5JT
Tel: 020 7561 9006

Association for Post Natal Illness
25 Jerdan Place
London SW6 1BE
Tel: 020 7386 0868

Association of Breastfeeding Mothers
Sydenham Green Health Centre
Holmshaw Close
London SE26 4TH

BACUP (British Association of Cancer United Patients)
3 Bath Place
Rivington Street
London EC2A 3DR
Tel: 0808 800 1234

Breast Care and Mastectomy Association
Kilm House
210 New Kings Road
London SW6 4NZ
Helpline: 020 7384 2365

British Association for Betterment of Infertility and Education (BABIE)
PO Box 4TS
London W1A 4TS

Caesarean Support Group
81 Elizabeth Way
Cambridge
CB4 1BQ

Cancer Winners
Omega House
New Street
Margate
Kent CT9 lEG

Endometriosis Society
Unit F8A, Shakespeare Business Centre
Herne Hill
245a Cold Harbour Lane
London SW9 8RR
Tel: 020 7222 2776

Foresight (Pre-Conceptual Care)
28 The Paddock
Godalming
Surrey
GU7 1XB
Tel: 01483 427839

Group B Hepatitis
Basement Flat
7A Fielding Road
London W14 0LL

Herpes Association
41 North Road
London N7 9DP
Tel: 020 7607 9661

ISSUE: The National Fertility Association
114 Lichfield Street
Walsall WF1 1FZ
Tel: 01922 722 888

La Lèche League of Great Britain (Breastfeeding)
Box BM3424
London WC1 6XX

Miscarriage Association
c/o Clayton Hospital
Northgate
Wakefield WS1 3JS
Tel: 01924 200799

National Association for Pre-menstrual Syndrome
25 Market Street
Guildford
Surrey GU1 4LB

National Childbirth Trust
Alexandra House
Oldham Terrace
London W3 6NH
Tel: 020 8992 8637

Pelvic Inflammatory Disease Support Network
WHRRIC
52 Featherstone Street
London EC1Y 8RT

Pre-Eclamptic Toxaemia Society
Ty Lago
High Street
Llanberis
Caernarfon
Gwynnedd
LL55 4HB

Pre-menstrual Society
PO Box 102
London SE1 7ES

Self-Help in Pain
33 Kingdown Park
Tankerton Kent
CT5 2DT

Stillbirth and Neonatal Death Society
28 Portland Place
London W1N 4DE
Tel: 020 7436 7940

The Amarant Trust
Grant House
56–60 St John Street
London EC1M 4DT
Tel: 202 7490 1644

Women's Health Concern (WMC)
93–99 Upper Richmond Road
London SW15 2TG
Helpline: 020 8780 3007

URINARY SYSTEM

Cystitis and Candida
75 Mortimer Road
London N1 5AR

National Kidney Federation
6 Stanley Street
Worksop
Nottinghamshire SH1 7HX
Tel: 01909 487795

DIGESTIVE SYSTEM

British Digestive Foundation
PO Box 251
Edgeware
London HA8 6MG
Tel: 020 7486 0341

Coeliac Society of the United Kingdom
PO Box 220
High Wycombe
Bucks
HP11 2HY
Tel: 01494 437278

National Association for Colitis and Crohn's Disease
4 Beaumont House
Sutton Road
St. Albans
Hertfordshire AL1 5HH
Tel: 01727 844296

IMMUNE SYSTEM

Action Against Allergy
23–4 High Street
Hampton Hill
Middlesex TW12 1PD

Body Positive (AIDS)
14 Greek Street
Soho
London W1V 5LE
Tel: 020 7287 8010

Breakspear Hospital (Allergy and Environmental Medicine)
Lord Alexander House
Waterhouse Street
Hemel Hemstead
Hertfordshire HP1 1DL
Tel: 01442 261 333

Food and Chemical Allergy Association
27 Ferringham Lane
Ferring by Sea
West Sussex BN12 5NB

London Lighthouse
111–117 Lancaster Road
London W11 1QT
Tel: 020 7792 1200

ME Action Campaign
PO Box 1126
London W3 0RY

Myalgic Encephalomyelitis (ME) Association
4 Corringham Road
Standford-Le-Hope
Essex SS17 OAM
Tel: 01375 642466

Terrence Higgins Trust
52–4 Gray's Inn Road
London WC1X 8JU
Tel: 0171 831 0330

EARS, NOSE, THROAT AND MOUTH

British Tinnitus Association
4th Floor
White Building
Fitzallen Square
Sheffield S1 2AZ
Tel: 0114 279 6600

National Association of Deafened People
103 Heath Road
Widnes
Cheshire WA8 7NU

Royal National Institute for the Deaf (RNID)
Pelham Court
Pelham Road
Nottingham NG5 1AP
Tel: 0345 090210

SKIN AND HAIR

Acne Support Group
1st Floor
Howard House
The Runway
South Ruislip
Middlesex HA4 6SE

Hairline International
The Alopecia Patients Society
Lions Court
1668 High Street
Knowle
West Midlands B93 OLY
Tel: 01564 775 281

National Eczema Society
163 Eversholt Street
London NW1
Tel: 020 7388 4097

The Psoriasis Association
7 Milton Street
Northampton NN2 7JG
Tel: 01604 711129

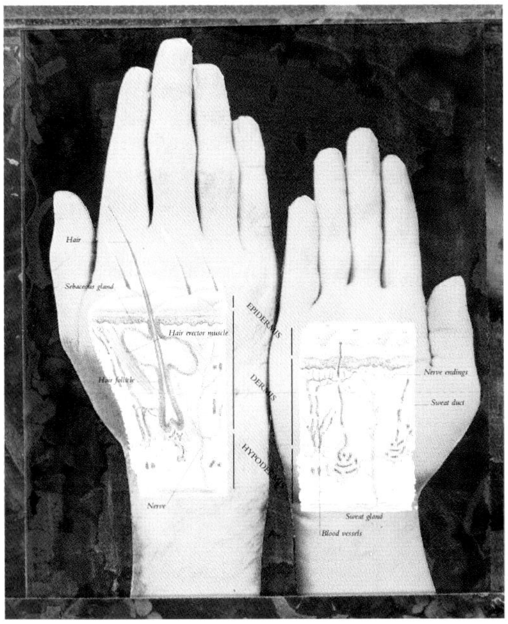

MUSCULO-SKELETAL SYSTEM

Arthritic Association
Hill House
1 Little New Street
London EC4A 3TR
Tel: 020 7491 0233

Arthritis and Rheumatism Council for Research
PO Box 177
Chesterfield
S41 7TQ
Tel: 01246 558033

Arthritis Care
18 Stephenson Way
London NW1 2HD
Tel: 020 7961 1500

Muscular Dystrophy Group of Great Britain and Northern Ireland
7–11 Prescott Place
London
SW4 6BS
Tel: 020 7720 8055

National Back Pain Association
16 Elmtree Road
Teddington
Middlesex TW11 8ST
Tel: 020 8977 5474

National Osteoporosis Society
PO Box 10
Radstock
Bath BA3 3YB
Tel: 01761 471771

Spinal Injuries Association
76 St James Lane
London N10 3DF
Tel: 020 8444 2121

INFANTS AND CHILDREN

Association for Child Psychology and Psychiatry
39-41 Union Street
London SE1 1SD
Tel: 020 7403 7458

Association of Parents of Vaccine Damaged Children
2 Church Street
Shipton-on-Stour
Warwickshire
CV36 4AP

Children's Cancer Help Centre
14 Kingsway
Petts Wood
Orpington
Kent BR5 1PR

CRY-SIS Support Group
BM Cry-sis
London WC1N 3XX
Tel: 020 7404 5011

Hyperactive Children's Support Group
71 Whyke Lane
Chichester
West Sussex PO19 2LD
Tel: 01903 725182

HOME AND EMERGENCY FIRST AID

Helpline for Burns
22 Westwood Gardens
Chandlers Ford
Eastleigh
Hants S05 1FN

AUSTRALIA

ACUPUNCTURE

Accepuncture Association of Victoria
1 Central Avenue
Morrabbin
VIC 3189, Australia

Australian Acupuncture & Chinese Medicine Association
PO Box 5142
Westend
Queensland 4101
Australia
Tel: (07) 384 652 276

The Australian Medical Acupuncture Society
1/77 Albert Avenue
Chatswood
NSW 2067, Australia
Tel: (02) 415 3880

ALEXANDER TECHNIQUE

Australian Society of the Teachers of the Alexander Technique
PO Box 716
Darlinghurst
NSW 2010
Australia
Freephone in Australia (1800) 677 037

AROMATHERAPY

International Federation of Aromatherapists
1/390 Burwood Road
Hawthorn
VIC 3122, Australia

AYURVEDIC MEDICINE

Maharishi Ayurveda
579 Punt Road
South Yarra
VIC 3141, Australia
Tel: (03) 9866 1999

BODYWORK

Rolfing

Australian Rolfing Office
131 Hargrave Street
Paddington
NSW 2021
Australia

Rolfing Australia
28 Davies Street
Brunswick
VIC 3056, Australia

CHIROPRACTIC

Chiropractors' Association of Australia
PO Box 748
Wagga Wagga
NSW 2650, Australia

Chiropractors' Association of Australia (National) Ltd
459 Great Western Highway
Faulconbridge
NSW 2776, Australia

DIAGNOSTIC THERAPIES

Kinesiology
Kinesiology Association of Victoria
PO Box 155
Ormond
VIC 3204, Australia

HOMOEOPATHY

Australia Federation Of Homoeopaths
238 Ballarat Road
Footscray
VIC 3011, Australia
Tel: (03) 9318 3057

Australian Federation of Homoeopaths
21 Bulah Close
Berowra Heights
NSW 2082, Australia

Australian Institute of Homeopathy
7 Hampden Road
Artarmon 2064
Sydney
NSW, Australia

HYPNOTHERAPY

The Australian Society Of Clinical Hypnotherapists
200 Alexandra Parade
Fitzroy
VIC 3065, Australia

MASSAGE THERAPY

Association of Massage Therapists
250 High Street
Prahran
VIC 3181, Australia
Tel: (03) 9610 3930

Massage Association of Australia
PO Box 1187
Camberwell
VIC 3124, Australia

NATUROPATHY

Australian Naturopathic Practitioners & Chiropractors Association
1st Floor, 609 Camberwell Road
Camberwell
VIC 3124, Australia
Tel: (03) 9889 0488

Naturopathic Physicians Association Of Australia Inc.
2 Beaumont Road
Canterbury
VIC 3126, Australia

NUTRITIONAL THERAPY

Australian College of Nutritional & Environmental Medicine
13 Hilton Road
Beamaris
VIC 3193, Australia
Tel: (03) 9589 6088

Macrobiotics

The Australian School of Macrobiotics
1 Arundel Street
Glebe
NSW 2037, Australia
Tel: (02) 9365 7872

OSTEOPATHY

Australian Osteopathic Association
PO Box 424
Thornleigh
NSW 2120, Australia
Tel: (02) 9980 8511

REFLEXOLOGY

Reflexology Association of Australia
44 Florence Road
Sunny Hills
VIC 3127, Australia

SHIATSU

Shiatsu Therapy Association of Australia
332 Carlisle Street
Balaclava
VIC 3183, Australia
Tel: (03) 9530 0067

YOGA

BKS Iyengar Yoga Association of Australia Inc.
Mosman, NSW, Australia
(Freephone in Australia 1800 677 037)

OTHER USEFUL ADDRESSES

GENERAL ADVICE

AFONTA
8 Thorp Road
2232 Woronara, Australia

AIDS Pastoral Care
PO Box 73
Borswood
WA 6100
Tel: (08) 9470 4931

Agoraphobic Support
Livingtone Foundation
2 Thorogood Street
Victoria Park
WA 6100, Australia

Allergy and Environmental Sensitivity Support and Research Association
PO Box 298
Ringwood
VIC 3134, Australia

Arthritis Foundation of Australia
PO Box 121
Sydney
NSW 2000, Australia
Tel: (02) 9221 2436

Association of Remedial Masseurs
22 Stuart Street
Ryde
NSW 2112, Australia
Tel: (02) 9807 4769

Australian Crohn's and Colitis Association
PO Box 201
Mooroolbark
VIC 3138, Australia
Tel: (03) 9726 9008

Australian Natural Therapists Association
7 Highview Grove
Burwood East
VIC 3151, Australia

Australian Traditional Medicine Society
120 Blaxland Road
Ryde
NSW 2112, Australia

Breast Cancer Support Service
Cancer Foundation of Western Australia
334 Rokeby Road
Busiaco
WA 6008, Australia

Cancer Support Association
80 Railway Street
Cottesloe
WA 6011, Australia
Tel: (08) 9384 3544

Chronic Pain Support Group
16 Ashworth Street
Cloverdale
WA 6105, Australia

Concern for Infertile Couples
PO Box 412
Subiaco
WA 6008, Australia

Depression Anonymous
PO Box 271
Wembley
WA 6014, Australia

Endometriosis Association
GPO Box 1954
Hobart 7001
Tasmania, Australia

Herpes Support
WISH
80 Railway Street
Cottesloe
WA 6011, Australia

Midlife and Menopause Support Group
PO Box 1112
Subiaco
WA 6008, Australia

National Herbalists Association of Australia
PO Box 61
Broadway
NSW 2007, Australia

National Herbalists Association of Australia
Suite 305, 3 Smail Street
Broadway
NSW 2007, Australia

Nursing Mothers Association of Australia
16 Dinsdale Place
Hamersley
WA 6022, Australia
Tel: (08) 9340 1200

Pregnancy Problem House
114 Great Eastern Highway
Belmont
WA 6104, Australia

Self-Realization Healing Centre (Spiritual Healing)
53 Regent Street
Paddington
NSW 2021, Australia

The Society of Clinical Masseurs Inc.
GPO Box 278
Kew
VIC 3101, Australia

True Grit Stroke Club
9 Burges Street
Geraldton
WA 6530, Australia

West Australian Epilepsy Association
14 Bagot Road
Subiaco
WA 6608, Australia

NEW ZEALAND

New Zealand AIDS Foundation
PO Box 663
Wellesley Street
Auckland 1
New Zealand
Tel: (09) 303 3124

New Zealand Homeopathic Society
Box 2929
Auckland
New Zealand
Tel: (09) 630 5458

Self-Realization Healing Centre
2 Harbour View Road
PO Box 129
Leigh, New Zealand

Spiritual Healing
100 Highstead Road
Bishopdale
Christchurch, New Zealand

The Health Alternatives For Women Inc (THAW)
PO Box 884
Christchurch, New Zealand
Tel: (03) 379 6970

USA

ACUPUNCTURE

American Association of Acupuncture and Oriental Medicine
4101 Lake Boone Trail Ste 201
Raleigh, NC 27607, United States

National Commission for the Certification of Acupuncturists
1424 16th St. NW Ste 601
Washington DC 20036, United States
(202) 232 1404

Traditional Acupuncture Institute
American City Building
Suite 108
Columbia, MD 21044
United States
(410) 997 3770

ALEXANDER TECHNIQUE

The American Society the Alexander Technique
PO Box 517
Urbana, Ill 61801 0517, United States
(800) 473 0620
www.alexandertech.org

AROMATHERAPY

The Pacific Institute of Aromatherapy
PO Box 6842
San Raphael, CA 94903, United States
(415) 479 9129

Nature's Apothecary
1558 Cherry Street
Louisville, Colo. 80027, United States
(303) 664 1600

ARTS THERAPIES

American Art Therapy Association
1202 Allanson Road
Mundelein, Ill 60060, United States

AUTOGENIC TRAINING

Mind Body Health Sciences
393 Dixon Road
Boulder, Colo 80302, United States
(303) 440 8460

AYURVEDIC MEDICINE

The Ayurveda Institute
PO Box 23445
Albuquerque, New Mexico 87192-1445

BACH FLOWER REMEDIES

Nelson Bach USA Ltd
Wilmington Technology Park
100 Research Drive
Wilmington, MA 01887-4406
United States

BODYWORK

Rolfing

The Rolf Institute
205 Canyon Blvd
Boulder, Colo 80302, United States
(303) 449 5903

Hellerwork

Hellerwork International
406 Berry Street
Mount Sh, CA 96067, United States
(530) 926 2500

Biodynamic therapy

Bay Area Biofeedback Association
3468 Mt Diablo Blvd Sre B203
Lafayette, CA 945 49 3917, United States

Tools for Exploration
9755 Independence Avenue
Chatsworth
CA 91311, United States
(818) 885 9090

CHINESE HERBALISM

The American Herbalist Guild
PO Box 1683
Sequel, CA 95073, United States

CHIROPRACTIC

American Chiropractic Association
1701 Clarendon Blvd
Arlington, Virginia 22209, United States
(703) 276 8800

World Chiropractic Alliance
2950 N Dobson Road Ste 1
Chandler, AR 85224, United States
(800) 347 1011

COLOUR THERAPY

College of Sytonic Optometry
1200 Robeson Street
Fall River, Mass 02720 5508, United States

Dinshaw Health Society
PO Box 707
Malaga, NJ 08328, United States
(856) 692 4686

CYMATICS

Electro Medical Inc
18433 Armistad
Fountain Valley, CA 92708, United States
(800) 422 8726
(714) 964 6776

Tools For Exploration
4460 Redwood Hwy Ste 2
San Raphael, CA 94903, United States
(800) 456 9887

DIAGNOSTIC THERAPIES

Kinesiology

International College of Applied Kinesiology
6405 Metcalf Avenue
Suite 503
Shawnee Mission, KS 66 202 United States
(913) 384 5336

Iridology

Rayid International
408 Dixon Road
SASR
Boulder, Colo 80302, United States

HOMOEOPATHY

Homeopathic Educational Services
2124 Kittredge Street
Berkeley, CA 94704, United States
(510) 649 0294

International Foundation for Homeopathy
2366 East Lake Avenue
East Suite 301
Seattle, WA , United States

National Center for Homeopathy
801 North Fairfax Street
Alexandria, VA 22314, United States
(703) 548 7790

HYPNOTHERAPY

American Council of Hypnotist Examiners
Hypnotism Training Institute of Los Angeles
700 South Central Avenue
Glendale, CA 91204, United States

American Institute of Hypnotherapy
16842 Von Karmen Ave, Ste 475, Irvine, CA
92606 United States
(949) 261 6400

American Society of Clinical Hypnosis
2200 E Devon Ave, Ste 301
Des Plains, Ill 60018, United States

MASSAGE THERAPY

American Massage Therapy Association
820 Davis Street Ste 100
Evanston, Ill 60201, United States
(847) 864 0123

NATUROPATHY

American Association of Naturopathic Physicians
2366 Eastlake Ave E Ste 322
Seattle, WA 98102, United States
(206) 323 7610

NUTRITIONAL THERAPY

American College of Advancement in Medicine
PO Box 3427
Laguna Hills, CA 92654, United States
(949) 583 7666

Macrobiotics

Kushi Foundation
Brookline, Mass, United States

OSTEOPATHY

American Academy of Osteopathy
3500 Depauw Blvd Ste 1080
Indianapolis, Ind 46268, United States
(317) 879 1881

American Osteopathic Association
142E Ontario Street
Chicago Ill 60611, United States
(312) 202 8000

POLARITY THERAPY

American Polarity Therapy Association
PO Box 44–154
West Sommerville, MA 02144, United States

American Polarity Therapy Association
PO Box 19858, Boulder, Colo. 80308,
United States
(303) 545 2080

REFLEXOLOGY

International Institute of Reflexology
PO Box 12642
St Petersburg, Florida 33733, United States
(727) 343 4811

RELAXATION AND VISUALIZATION

Mind/Body Health Sciences Inc
393 Dixon Road
Boulder, Colo 80302, United States
(303) 440 8460

SHIATSU

American Shiatsu Association
PO Box 718
Jamaica Plain, MA 01230, United States

SPIRITUAL HEALING

Spirtual Healing Common Boundary Inc
7005 Florida Street
Chevy Chase
MD 20815, United States

WESTERN HERBALISM

The American Herbalists Guild
PO Box 1683
Sequel, CA 95073, United States

YOGA

Dean Ornish Programme
Pacific Presbyterian Medical Centre
University of California School of Medicine
San Francisco, United States
(415) 666 6886

OTHER USEFUL ADDRESSES

La Lèche League International
9616 Minneapolis Avenue
PO Box 1209
Franklin Park, Ill 60131-8209, United States

National Resource Centre on Women and AIDS
2000 P Street NW, Suite 508
Washington DC 20036, United States

Touch for Health Foundation
1174 North Lake Avenue
Pasadena, CA 91104-3797, United States

CANADA

Acupuncture Foundation of Canada
7321 Victoria Park Avenue
Unit 18
Markham
Ontario L3R 2ZB, Canada

Canadian AIDS Society
130 Albert Street, Suite 90, Ottawa, Ontario K1P 5G4
(613) 230-3580

Canadian Cancer Society
10 Alcorn Ave, Suite 200, Toronto, M4V 3B1, Canada
(416) 961-7223

Canadian Chiropractic Association
1396 Eglinton Avenue West
Toronto, Ontario M6C 2E4, Canada
(416) 781-5656

Canadian College of Naturopathic Medicine
1255 Sheppard Ave East, Toronto, Ontario M2K 1E2, Canada
(416) 498 1255

Canadian Holistic Medical Association
42 Redpath Avenue
Toronto, Ontario M4S 2J6, Canada

Canadian Institute of Stress
1235 Bay Street
Toronto, Ontario M5R 3K4, Canada
(416) 236-4218

Canadian Natural Health Association
439 Wellington Street
Toronto, Ontario, M5V 2H7, Canada
(416) 280-6025

Canadian Society of Homeopathy
87 Meadowlands Drive West
Nepean
Ontario K2G 2R9, Canada

College of Massage Therapists
1867 Yonge Street
Toronto, Ontario
M4S 1Y5, Canada
(416) 489-2626

Migraine Foundation
365 Bloor Street East, Toronto, Ontario M4W 3L4, Canada
(416) 920-4916

National Institute of Nutrition
265 Carling Ave, Ste 302,
Ottawa, Ontario K1S 2E1, Canada
(613) 235-3355

Ontario Herbalists Association
7 Alpine Avenue
Toronto, Ontario M6P 3R6, Canada
(416) 536-1509

Pre-Menstrual Syndrome Centre
1077 North Service Road
Applewood Plaza
Mississauga
Ontario K0A 3G0, Canada

Toronto Vegetarian Association
2300 Yonge Street, Suite 1101, PO Box 2307, Toronto, Ontario M4P 1E4, Canada
(416) 544 9800

SOUTH AFRICA

ACUPUNCTURE

ALEXANDER TECHNIQUE

AROMATHERAPY

Association of Aromatherapists South Africa
PO Box 23924
Claremont
7735, South Africa
Contact Person: Moyra Metcalf

AYURVEDIC MEDICINE

South African Ayurvedic Medicine Association
c/o Dr S. Parvathi
85 Harvey Road
Morningside
Durban
4001, South Africa
Contact Person: Dr Swami Parvathi
Tel: (012) 346 1230

COLOUR THERAPY

DIAGNOSTIC THERAPIES

Kinesiology

Association of Specialized Kinesiology Southern Africa
14 Osborne Road
Claremont
7700, South Africa
Contact Person: Kevin Campbell
Tel: (021) 61 8021

HYPNOTHERAPY

Hypnotherapy Contact
59 Strawberry Lane
Constantia
Cape Town, South Africa
Contact Person: Christa Hal Stanford Ph.D
Tel: (021) 794 2767

MASSAGE THERAPY

Holistic Massage Therapy (South Africa)
PO Box 37
659 Valyland 7978, South Africa
Contact Person: Briony
Tel: (021) 782 5909

Massage Institute
PO Box 3443
Edenvale
1610, South Africa

NATUROPATHY

South African Naturopathic Association
PO Box 5035
Waterfront
8002, South Africa
Contact Person: Dr. Chase Webber
Tel: (021) 426 2218

NUTRITIONAL THERAPY

Nutritional Institute
Contact Person: Prof Len Evans

POLARITY THERAPY

Polarity Therapy Association South Africa
PO Box 441
Constantia
7848, South Africa
Contact Person: Doug Harrrow-Smith
Tel/Fax: (21) 794 7838

REFLEXOLOGY

Centre of Creative Consciousness
PO Box 915, Kloos, Natal 3650, South Africa
Tel: (031) 764 5471

Holistic Reflexology Association
50 Windemere Road
Muizenberg
7945, South Africa
Contact Person: Gail Hansen
Tel: (021) 788 8347

Reflexology Academy of Southern Africa
PO Box 1280
Rivonia
2128, South Africa
Contact Person: Chris Stormer or Liz

The Cape Reflexology College
50 Windemere Road
Muizenburg
7945, South Africa
Tel: (021) 788 8347

The South Africa Reflexology Society
PO Box 201858
Durban North
4016, South Africa
Contact Person: Meryl Daykin
Tel/Fax: (031) 702 8531

YOGA

BKS Iyengar Yoga Institute of South Africa
Johannesburg Region
Contact Person: Carole
Tel: (011) 616 2525

South African Remedial Yoga Teachers Association
24 Sprigg Road
Rondebosch East 7780, South Africa
Contact Person: Swami Parvathi
Tel: (021) 696 2078/ 696 1821

OTHER USEFUL ADDRESSES

COCHASA: The Confederation of Complementary Health Associations of South Africa
Contact Person: Annie Allan
Tel: (021) 58 8709
Or write to:
PO Box 2471
Clareinch, 7740, South Africa

Body Stress Release Association
PO Box 569, Wilderness, 6560, South Africa
Contact Person: Gail Meggersee
Tel: (021) 61 3475

Kushido Academy of Health
42 Kasteel Street
Bothasig
7441, South Africa
Contact Person: Annie Allan
Tel/Fax: (021) 58 8709

Life Force Association
PO Box 26106
Hout Bay
7872, South Africa
Contact Person: Christo Trautmann
Tel/Fax (021) 790 3772

The Herb Society of South Africa
PO Box 37721
Overport, South Africa
Contact Person: Joan Symmons

All addresses were checked before publication, but the publishers cannot accept responsibility for associations who have changed their address or phone number in recent months.

INDEX

Page numbers in italic refer to the illustrations

A

B

C

D

E

F

G

O

P

Q

R

S

T

ACKNOWLEDGMENTS

The publishers would like to thank Dr. Marion Newman and Dr. Melita Brownrigg for all their help in checking the authenticity of all the ailment copy detailed. We would also like to thank Dr. Tanvir Jamil for writing the body system introductions and the Index of Symptoms.

THE THERAPISTS

The following therapists have greatly contributed to this book by supplying helpful information on how their therapy can help cure or relieve the ailments detailed in the second section. They have also given useful advice to our writers and editors.

ACUPUNCTURE AND ACUPRESSURE

Stuart Lightbody MAc., MTAc.S

Stuart Lightbody has been the Director of the Halifax Clinic of Natural Medicine in West Yorkshire since 1979. He qualified as a Master of Acupuncture in 1985 and is a member of the Traditional Acupuncture Society and the British Acupuncture Council. He studied at the College of Traditional Chinese Medicine in Chengdu, China in 1984 and also in San Francisco in 1986. He has also made some appearences on television.

ALEXANDER TECHNIQUE

Anthony P. Kingsley B Sc Hons, MA

Anthony P. Kingsley has a private practice in central London, which he also manages. He works as a trainer in the Alexander Technique on the North London Teachers' Training Course and has given lectures and seminars in industry on the Alexander Technique in connection with RSI prevention and stress management. He also works closely with other health professionals as he believes that teamwork are often beneficial to the pupil or client.

AROMATHERAPY AND COLOR THERAPY

Dr. Vivian N. Lunny MIFA reg., MRQA, MGCP, MIACT

Dr. Lunny is the founder and managing director of REAL (Real Essences and Leisure) and a Fellow and Executive Director of the English Société de l'Institut des Sciences Biomedicales, France. She is a member of the British Register of Complementary Practitioners, the International Federation of Aromatherapists and the Register of Qualified Aromatherapists. She qualified in medicine, specializing in pathology, and then trained in holistic and scientific aromatherapy in England and France and in color therapy in Britain and Eastern Europe.

ARTS THERAPIES

Alison Barnes

After teaching art and textiles in a secondary school for several years, Alison Barnes trained as an art therapist at Goldsmith's College, University of London in 1982 and has since worked in several large psychiatric hospitals. She is now head of the Arts Therapies department based at Springfield Hospital (now Pathfinder Mental Health Services NHS Trust) in south London and also gives clinical supervision to dance movement therapists and music therapists as well as other art therapists. She is now training to be a psychoanalytic psychotherapist.

AURICULAR THERAPY

Oran Kivity B Ac.

Oran Kivity graduated from the International College of Oriental Medicine in 1987 and in1992 spent four months studying at a teaching hospital in China. He was the first acupuncturist to work at the London Lighthouse, an HIV and AIDS resource center, and now works with drug and alcohol abusers in two centers in London. A member of the International Register of Oriental Medicine and the British Acupuncture Council, he teaches at the London School of Acupuncture.

With thanks also to **Ken Andrews** for his help on this subject.

AUTOGENIC TRAINING

Jane Bird RGN, Member BAFATT, Member BASF

Jane Bird teaches autogenic training at her private practice in Watford and also at centers for complementary medicine and some industrial settings. A founder member of the British Association for Autogenic Training and Therapy (BAFATT), she acts as their Training Organizer as well as one of the lecturers. She first learned autogenic training for her own use in managing stress, the effect of which sparked her interest in the mind-body link in the causes and response to illness and trained as a autogenic therapist with the late Dr. Wolfgang Luthe, author of much research.

AYURVEDIC MEDICINE

Dr. Shantha Godagama DAMS, MBAcA, MF(Hom), MAcF

The founder/president of the Ayurvedic Medical Association UK, Dr. Shantha Godagama studied Ayurvedic medicine at Colombo University in Sri Lanka, and then took a postgraduate course in *panchakarma* therapy. In 1972 he set up in private practice in Sri Lanka, combining conventional and traditional medicine, later studying acupuncture and homeopathy. He came to Britain in 1979 to become a consultant at the Tyringham Clinic, a complementary medicine clinic, and in 1986 became its Director of Therapies. He is now a visiting consultant at London's Hale Clinic.

BACH FLOWER REMEDIES

Judy Howard SRN, SCM, HV

The Bach flower remedies have been part of Judy Howard's life since she was a child, and from 1985 she has been working at the Bach Center, running the teaching and training program of the Dr. Edward Bach Foundation as well as preparing the Mother Tinctures with her colleagues in the summer. She qualified as a nurse at the Queen Elizabeth Hospital in Norfolk in 1980 and as a midwife at the Whittington Hospital in London in 1982. In 1983 she qualified as a Health Visitor in Nottingham. Judy has written several books on the Bach flower remedies.

CHINESE HERBALISM

Richard Blackwell

Richard is the Deputy Principal of the Northern College of Acupuncture in York, where he also practices acupuncture and Chinese herbal medicine. He obtained a first-class honors degree in Medical Science before studying acupuncture and Chinese herbal medicine with highly respected teachers in both China and Britain. He is also the past president of the Register of Chinese Herbal Medicine. Richard has written extensively in professional journals on the treatment of specific diseases with Chinese herbal medicine. He has also written on research into the subject and most recently on issues of safety and good practice for how Chinese herbal medicine in used in the Western world.

CHIROPRACTIC

Susan L. Steward DC

A chiropractor in private practice, a council member of the British Chiropractic Association and a former president (1987–1990), Susan Steward received the Diploma Doctor Chiropractic from the Anglo-European College of Chiropractic in 1976 and also holds the Diploma and the Advanced Diploma in Eriksonian Clinical Hypnosis, Cognitive Psychotherapy and Neurolinguistic Programming. She has written books on chiropractic and has appeared on radio and television.

With thanks also to **Lynn Waters** for supplying the McTimoney Chiropractic information.

CRYSTAL AND GEMSTONE THERAPY

Stephanie Harrison FGS

The founder and principal of the International College of Crystal Healing, Stephanie Harrison began working in the field of crystal and gemstone therapy in the early 1980s when she developed her gift of healing. Her fascination with stones and crystals led her to evolve her own way of healing. She travels extensively giving workshops and seminars on various aspects of crystal healing and teaches the second year of the ICCH training course in Austria and Norway as well as Britain. She has appeared on television, radio and has also written a book on the crystal healing.

CYMATICS

Dr. (Sir) Peter Manners MD, MA

Dr. Peter Manners has worked for more than 30 years on the use of cymatics and bio-magnetics for medical diagnosis and treatment, and on the healing effects of certain sound vibrations and harmonics on the structure and chemistry of the body. He qualified in osteopathy and natural and electro-magnetic medicine in England and Germany and has worked with many scientists in England, Europe and the USA. He has lectured at the World Health Organization in Europe and holds the Dag Hammarskjold Merit of Excellence Award for Benefits to Humanity.

HELLERWORK *(Bodywork)*

Roger Golten BA (Hons)

A former shipbroker in the City of London, Roger Golten trained in the United States with Joseph Heller in 1983 and has been a full-time Hellerwork practitioner ever since. He regularly returns to the United States for conferences on Hellerwork and for additional training and gained his advanced certificate in 1987. He now has practices in central London and Hertfordshire and visits in central and northwest London, Hertfordshire and Buckinghamshire and worldwide by arrangement. He has been featured in articles in the *Sunday Times* and the *Daily Express*.

HOMEOPATHY

Dr. Andrew H. Lockie, MB, ChB, MF Hom., 1974, Dip. Obst. RCOG 1976, Family Planning Certificate MRCGP 1976.

Andrew Lockie is a homeopathic physician in private practice in Guildford, Surrey and an Information Officer for the Faculty of Homeopathy. He qualified in medicine at Aberdeen University in 1972 before studying at the Royal London Homeopathic Hospital in 1973–1974. He then took house officer posts in obstetrics and gynecology and pediatrics in various hospitals before training as a general practitioner in Southampton. He is the author of several books including *The Family Guide to Homeopathy*, published by Hamish Hamilton.

HYPNOTHERAPY

Marisa Peer DP. PSYCH., C.HYP., CMH, CAH, CA HYP., D HYP., MHEC (USA & UK)

A psychotherapist as well as a hypnotherapist, Marisa Peer is particularly interested in cell regeneration therapy and is studying how to reverse the ageing process and is writing a book on the subject. She trained at Gil Boyne Institute and UCLA in the USA and at the Atkinson Ball College of Hypnotherapy and Hypno-healing and at the Proudfoot School of Psychotherapy and Neuro-Linguistic Program. She has appeared on British TV discussion programs and has made programs on hypnotherapy and psychology for other TV stations.

IRIDOLOGY *(Diagnostic therapies)*

Adam J. Jackson LL B (HONS), LCSP (PHYS)

A practicing clinical iridologist, Adam Jackson is President of the International Association of Clinical Iridologists, Principal of the UK College of Iris Analysis, Principal of the Canadian Institute of Iridology and President of the Iridologists' Association of Canada. He is editorial advisor to the *Journal of Alternative & Complementary Medicine*, editor of *Alternatives in Health TM*, and a member of the London & Counties Society of Physiologists. He is the author of seven books including *Iridology*, published by Vermilion and *Eye Signs*, published by Thorsons.

KINESIOLOGY *(Diagnostic therapies)*

Brian H. Butler BA

Brian Butler is President of the Association & Academy of Systematic Kinesiology. In 1975 he became the first English person to train in Applied Kinesiology in the USA. He has pioneered AK training in Britain and Europe and has run the Kinesiology for Health and Wellbeing Clinic in Surbiton since 1975 and has formulated a lay program for anyone wishing to take responsibility for their health. He has also written books on kinesiology including: *An Introduction to Kinesiology and Kinesiology for Health and Wellbeing* published by Task Books.

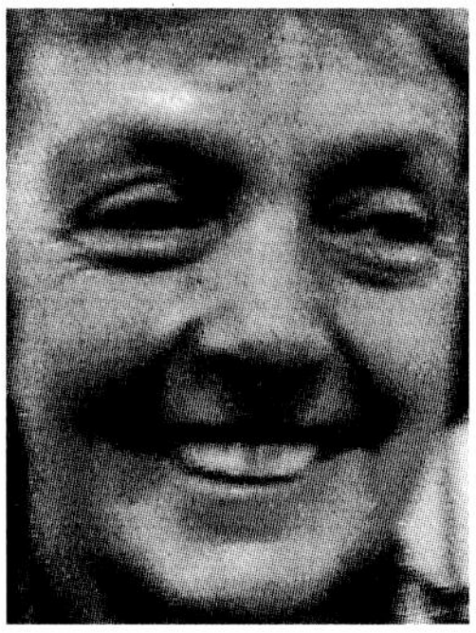

KIRLIAN PHOTOGRAPHY
(Diagnostic therapies)

Rosemary (Ro) Steel

For nearly 20 years Ro Steel has been working as a bodywork therapist counselor and an Adult Education lecturer – the last 14 years of which included kirlian photography. As a major part of her degree Ro spent four years on the photographic parameters of kirlian photography and ran the Second International Conference. She has also developed Bodylogic, a process by which she integrates her bodywork and her counseling experience with the kirlian photographic image. Ro has also lectured on kirlian photography in many countries.

MACROBIOTICS

Jon Sandifer

A freelance teacher of oriental medicine, diagnosis, macrobiotics, oriental astrology, shiatsu and yin/yang philosophy, Jon Sandifer studied with Michio Kushi between 1977 and 1980 and trained in oriental diagnosis and shiatsu massage. From 1983–1990 he directed the Kushi Institute in London, developing the curriculum with Michio Kushi and the directors. He was a dietary counselor with the Community Health Foundation and is now (1996) chairman of the British Macrobiotic Association. He has written for many magazines and newspapers.

MASSAGE

Clare Maxwell-Hudson

Clare is the director of the Institute of Health Sciences in London and principal of The Clare Maxwell-Hudson School of Massage. A registered massage therapist, she teaches doctors at the British Post Graduate Medical Association and runs courses for nurses at two major London teaching hospitals. She is also a trained beauty therapist, contributes to radio and television, and has written for newspapers and journals. Her books include *The Complete Book of Massage* and *The Aromatherapy Massage Book*, published by Dorling Kindersley in 1988 and1994.

METAMORPHIC TECHNIQUE

Clare Harvey

Clare Harvey studied the metamorphic technique with Robert St. John, the founder of the method, in 1978 and since the beginning of the 1980s has practiced at the Middle Piccadilly Natural Healing Center in Dorset, of which she is a founder member. She has used the technique to initiate a releasing of deeply held birth and prebirth trauma, and worked with ingrained psychological patterns that predispose people to illness and disease. She has also made several appearances on television and radio in both Britain and the United States.

NATUROPATHY

Roger Newman Turner B AC., ND, DO, MRO, MRN, FBACA

Roger Newman Turner is a second generation practitioner of naturopathy, osteopathy and acupuncture, with practices in north Hertfordshire and London. He graduated from the British College of Naturopathy and Osteopathy in 1963. He is the author of a number of books on natural health and diet and has contributed to several encyclopedias and handbooks. He has lectured and broadcast on naturopathic medicine in many parts of the world. He is also Trustee of the Research Council for Complementary Medicine and was its chairman from 1993–1996.

NUTRITIONAL THERAPY

Linda Lazarides

Linda Lazarides is a nutritional therapist with several years' experience of working with a general practitioner. She is also a writer and campaigner, the director of the Society for the Promotion of Nutritional Therapy and editor of the society's magazine, *Nutritional Therapy Today*. She is on the advisory panel of *Here's Health* magazine and is the former nutrition editor of the *Journal of Alternative and Complementary Medicine*. Linda is an advisor to the Institute for Complementary Medicine and to BACUP (British Association of Cancer United Patients).

OSTEOPATHY (AND CRANIAL OSTEOPATHY)

Stephen E. Sandler DO, MRO, FE CERT.

Stephen Sandler is in private practice as a consultant osteopath at the Portland Hospital for Women and Children in London and has his own general practice in Chingford, northeast London. He is the Founder and Director of the Expectant Mother's Clinic, and a senior lecturer in Obstetrics and Gynecology and is in the Gastrointestinal System at the British School of Osteopathy. He has also been a guest lecturer at the London College of Osteopathic Medicine. He is the author of *A Guide to Osteopathy*, published by Hamlyn in 1989.

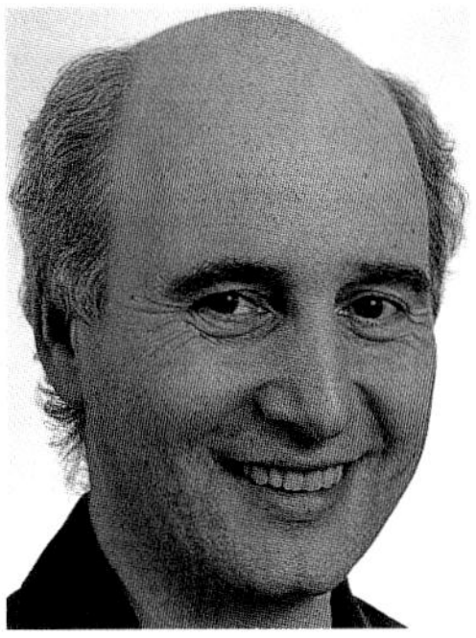

POLARITY THERAPY

David Haas RPT, RCST

A chartered engineer, David Haas became a therapist after years of trying various therapies for himself. He became aware of polarity therapy energy medicine and after receiving treatment was impressed by its healing possibilities. He has since become a Registered Polarity Therapist with the Polarity Therapy Association, of which he is now a council member, and practices in London and the home counties. He has also completed a diploma course in craniosacral therapy with Franklyn Sills, and is a registered Craniosacral Therapist with the Craniosacral Therapy Association.

POLARITY THERAPY

Dianne Vanness

Dianne Vanness has been practicing and training students in polarity therapy for 13 years. She maintains that it is her clients and students who show her the next step in her learning process. Dianne got interested in complementary health 15 years ago when she met the founder of polarity therapy, Dr. Randolph Stone, at an ashram in India. She was a founder member of the British Complementary Medical Association (BMCA) and helped form the Polarity Therapy Educational Trust, of which she is the Educational Director. Dianne has also given TV interviews on the subject.

RADIONICS

Gordon Smith

The founder of the Radionic & Radiesthesia Trust, Gordon Smith is a member of the Management Committee of the National Consultative Council for Alternative and Complementary Medicine and of the Management Committee of the British Complementary Medicine Association. He is also the founder of the Maperton Trust, which is an educational charity whose main aims are to see that the best in orthodox medicine is then combined with the best in complementary medicine to provide an enhanced healthcare system for everybody.

REFLEXOLOGY

Mo Usher MAR, MGCP

The former Chairman of the Association of Reflexologists, Mo Usher is now an Honorary Life Member and President of the Association. She is on the Advisory Board of the *Journal of Alternative and Complementary Medicine*, is a former member of the Executive Board of the British Complementary Medicine Association and a member of the Royal Society of Medicine. She was President of the International Council of Reflexologists and is on the executive committee of Reflexology in Europe. She has broadcast on reflexology on radio and television.

RELAXATION AND VISUALIZATION

Carol Horrigan M Sc., SRN, RCNT, Dip N, PGCEA, RNT

Carol Horrigan began training in complementary therapies in 1963, and added nursing qualifications from 1977. She has studied and now uses in her practice, relaxation and visualization therapies, massage, reflex therapy, therapeutic touch, chakra balancing, reiki, Bach flower remedies and yoga. From 1988, she developed the posts of Lecturer in Complementary Therapies at Bloomsbury College of Nursing and at the Institute of Advanced Nurse Education at the Royal College of Nursing. She has also contributed to several books.

RELAXATION AND VISUALIZATION (*for children*)

Janet Balaskas

Janet Balaskas is the Director of the Active Birth Center in London, and is the founder of the Active Birth Teacher Training Course and the Active Birth Teachers Association. With her husband Keith Brainin she is co-Director of Active Birth Pools – the leading birth resource center in Britain. In the 1970s she introduced an innovative approach to birth preparation using relaxation and visualization techniques and yoga-based exercises focusing on body awareness. She has written several books including *New Life* published by Sidgwick and Jackson.

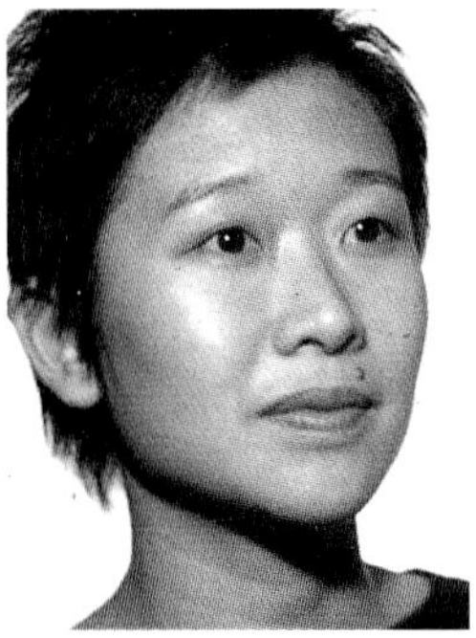

ROLFING *(Bodywork)*

Loan Tran BA HONS, DIPLOMA IN ROLFING

Loan Tran began rolfing at Neal's Yard Therapy Rooms in Covent Garden, London in 1993 where she still practices. She first started rolfing in Paris after receiving her diploma in rolfing in 1989 in Munich. She served on the executive board of the European Rolfing Association from 1991–1993 and helped in the creation of a European branch of the Rolf Institute. In 1992 she co-established Access Point Center in Paris. She has written a section on rolfing for the *A–Z Guide of Natural Therapies* published by Thorsons in 1994.

SHIATSU

Ray Ridolfi

Ray Ridolfi is the founder of the British School of Shiatsu-Do and has been involved in the bodywork field for 20 years traveling extensively where he experienced many traditional therapies. He became interested in bodywork, oriental culture and eventually shiatsu-do through his university studies, sports and martial art activities. His main teachers have been Saul Goodman and Ohasi Sensei who have greatly influenced his development of shiatsu-do. He teaches in Europe and the Middle East and is co-writing a book called *Shiatsu for Women*.

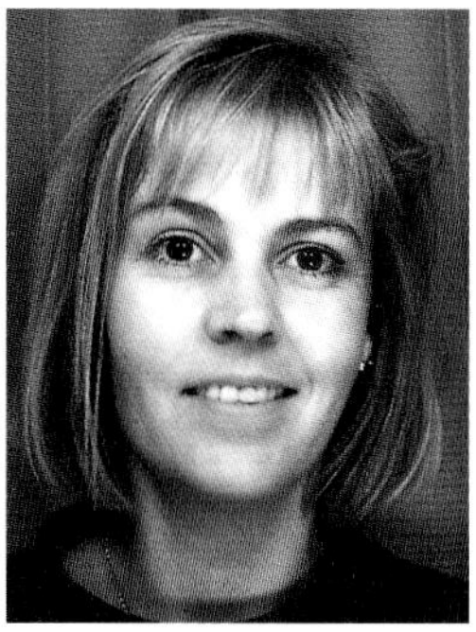

SPIRITUAL HEALING

Midi Fairgrieve

A healer and counselor, Midi Fairgrieve has a practice in Edinburgh which also caters for all kinds of animals in need of healing. She trained in healing and counseling over several years with the Self-Realization Healing Center in Somerset and is a member of the International Self-Realization Healing Association. She also studied nutrition in London where she gained a diploma in nutritional medicine. Before becoming a complementary medical practitioner, she worked in radio broadcasting and was a producer for BBC Radio 4.

SPIRITUAL HEALING

Don Copland

Formerly a partner and director of a structural engineering company, Don Copland became a Healer Member of the National Federation of Spiritual Healers in 1976 and held the position of Regional Chairman for several years. In 1982 he was made President and became responsible for national publicity and public relations, organizing the national training program. He has appeared on television and has produced four books on spiritual healing including *So You Want to be a Healer*. He is now the Administrator of the National Federation of Spiritual Healers.

TAI CHI

Master Lam Kam Chuen

At present Master Lam Kam Chuen teaches tai chi and practices Chinese herbalism at the Lam Clinic in London's Chinatown. He is trained in martial arts, and he also studied Chi Kung, a system for the cultivation on the body's internal energy. Using his medical knowledge of Chi Kung, Master Lam developed a new form of tai chi known as Lam Style Tai Chi. He came to the West in 1976 and became the first tai chi instructor to teach for the Inner London Education Authority. He has written *The Way of Energy*, which is published by Gaia Books.

WESTERN HERBALISM

Mark Evans B. PHIL.

The Director of the Bath Natural Health Clinic, a multidisciplinary center for complementary medicine, and Principal of the Bath School of Massage, Mark Evans runs practices in Bath and Bristol offering herbal medicine, massage, aromatherapy and reflexology. He is a Fellow of the National Institute of Medical Herbalists and a former President and council member. He holds a B. Phil. in Complementary Health Studies from Exeter University and has had research papers published in the European Journal of Herbal Medicine and the British Journal of Phytotherapy.

CONSULTANT EDITOR

Nikki Bradford

Nikki is an experienced freelance health writer. She was formerly Health Correspondent for *Good Housekeeping* and Associate editor on *Health & Fitness* magazine. She has written *The Well Woman's Self-Help Directory* for Sidgwick and Jackson and *Men's Health Matters* for Random House (Vermilion). She is also Honorary Secretary of the Guild of Health Writers and initiated the first men's counseling helpline run by the Medical Advisory Service (MAS) which operated from the House of Commons. Nikki is also a probationary healer with The National Federation of Spiritual Healers.

WRITER: THERAPY ESSAYS

Sheila Lavery

Sheila is a health writer who contributes to *Here's Health*, *Top Santé*, *Daily Mail*, *The Sunday Times* and *XL Magazine*. She is in the process of writing a book on sleep and is a member of the Guild of Health Writers.

CLINICAL RESEARCH

Fara Begum-Baig

Fara is the youngest fellow of the Institute of Biomedical Sciences, and worked in clinical research at Cambridge University. She has a post-graduate degree in biochemistry and pioneered complementary medicine within NHS hospitals such as Addenbrookes, Cambridge. As principal lecturer of Cambridge Holistic Health, she researches, teaches and practices reflexology and stress management. Fara also contributes to radio and television.

CLINICAL REFERENCES

All the references detailed refer to the clinical study information contained at the end of many of the therapies. The page number for the relevant therapy is detailed and the number of the study is given to help with cross-referencing.

ACUPRESSURE page 23
(5) Lumbar pain
Jiaying W, Guangzhoa L, Shuhua M, Guicheng P, Journal of Traditional Chinese Medicine 1986; 6 (3): 168–170.
(6) Morning sickness – Double-blind trial: Dundee J W, Souri F B R, Ghaly R G, Bell P F, Journal of Royal Society of Medicine 1988; 81: 456–7.
ACUPUNCTURE page 19
(1) Chronic alcoholic – Controlled placebo trial: Bullock M, Cilliton P, Olander, R, Lancet 1989, 1435–1439.
(2) Drug addiction – Single blind placebo trial: Lipton D, Brewington V, Smith M, Journal of Substance abuse 1994, vol 11 no 3 205-215.
(3) Nicotine addiction
Clavel F; Benhamou S; British Medical Journal 1985: 291; 1538-9.
ALEXANDER TECHNIQUE page 121
(40) Posture and performance – Barlow.
(41) Performance stress reduction – Valentine E.
AROMATHERAPY page 73
Chronic bronchitis – Double blind trial: 'Gouttes aux Essences' (Essence Drops) Phytotherapy Research Vol 3 no 3 1989. J P Ferley, N Poutignat, Zmirou, Y Azzopardi and F Balducci 106.
(23) Vaginal thrush (*Candida albicans*)
Dr Paul Belaiche, September 1985, Phytotherapy no 15 13–15 191.
(24) Cardiac surgery
C J Stevensen, Complementary Therapies in Medicine 1994, 2 27–35 Middlesex Hospital Intensive Care Unit, London 283.
(25) Post-cardiotomy patients – Randomized double blind trial research: with support of Bristol cardiac team led by surgeon Mr Wishaert. Jane Buckle, Nursing Times, May 19, vol 89, no 20 1993.
ARTS THERAPIES page 151
Music therapy
(36) Heart surgery
Barnson S, Zimmerman L, Nievan J, Heart and Lung 1995; 24(2): 124–32.
(57) Anxiety
Stroudenmire J, Journal of Clinical Psychology 1975; 31(3): 490–2.
(58) Depression
Hanser S B, Thompson L W, Journal of Gerontology 1994 Nov; 49 (6): 265–9.
AUTOGENIC TRAINING page 133
(49) Hypertension
Aivazyan T A, Zaitsev V P,Yurenev A P, Health Psychology 1988; 7 (Suppl): 201-8.
(50) Anxiety
Stetter F, Walter G, Zimmermann A, Zahres S, Straube E R Psychotherapie, Pschosomatik, Medizinische Psychologie 1994; 44 (7): 226-34.
AYURVEDIC MEDICINE page 35
(9) Diabetes mellitus
Baskartan K, et al Journal of Ethnopharmachology 30 1990, pp 295–305.
(10) Parkinson's disease
Manyam B V, et al. The Journal of Alternative and Complementary Medicine Vol 1, No 3, 1995, pp 249–255.
CHINESE HERBALISM page 29
(7) Endometriosis
Wang D Z, Wang Z Q, Zhang Z F, Chung Hsi I Chieh Ho Tsa Chih, Sept 1991, 11.9 pp 524–6, 515.
(8) AIDS
Weibo L, Journal of Traditional Chinese Medicine 15 (1) 3–9, 1995.
CHIROPRACTIC page 53
(13) Low back pain
Meade T W, Dyer S, Browne W, Townsend J, Frank A O, British Medical Journal 1990, vol 300 pp 1431–1437 and BMJ 1995 vol 311, 349–51 and Dr Alan Breen, British Chiropractic Association.
(14) Leg or low back pain – Controlled placebo trial: Rupert R L, Wagnon R, Thompson P, Ezzeldin M T, International. Review of Chiropractic 1985, Winter 58-60.
COLOR THERAPY page 137
(54) Arthritis – Controlled trial: McDonald S F, International Journal of Biosocial Research 3, No 2, 1982 pp 49–54.
(55) Migraine
Anderson J, Brain/Mind Bulletin 15, No 4, Jan 1990 p 4.
DIAGNOSTIC THERAPIES page 153
Iridology
(59) and (60) Studies on *Arcus senilis* marking in iridology
November 1987, the Los Angeles Herald Examiner and the January 1990 edition of the Journal of the American Optimetric Association.
HOMEOPATHY page 79
(26) Asthma/House dust mite allergy
Reilly D, Taylor M, Beattie N, Campbell J, McSharry C, Aitchison T C, Carter R, Stevenson R D, The Lancet Vol 344 1601–1606, 1994.
(27) Dermatological Complaints – Double blind trial: Dr Schawb Alenavia. Proceedings of the 45th congress of the LMHI, p 166–168.
(28) Migraines – Double-blind trial: Brigo B, Serpelloni G, The Berlin Journal on Research in Homeopathy, Vol 1 No.2 March 1991, pp98–105.
HYPNOTHERAPY page 127
(42) Pain relief for burns
Wakeman R J, Kaplan J Z, American Journal Clin Hypn, 1978: 21: 3–12.
(43) Tinnitus – Cross-over control trial with blind evaluation
Marks N J, Karl H, Onisiphorou C, Clinical Otolaryngol 1985; 10; 43–46.
(44) Smoking
Stanton H E; International Journal of Clinical and Experimental Hypnosis 1978; XXVI; 1: 22–29.
(45) Tension headaches
Carasso R; Kleinhauz M; Peded; O Yehuda S American Journal of Clinical Hpynosis 1985; 27; 4: 216–218.
(46) Warts
Ewin D, American Journal of Clinical Hypnosis July 1992, 35; 1:1–9.
MASSAGE page 59
(15) Anxiety – Controlled trial: Field, Morrow, Valdeon, Larson, Kuhn and Scanberg, Journal of the American Academy of Childhood and Adolescent Psychiatry 1992, 31; 1: 125–131
(16) Pain relief and insomnia
Farrow J, Nursing Standard, 1990; 4 (17): 26–28.
(17) Breast cancer
Sims S, Nursing Times 1986; 82 (13): 47–50.
(18) Premature baby growth
Scarfidi F S, Field T M, Schanberg S M Bauer, Tucci, Roberts, Morrow and Kuhn, Infant Behaviour and Development 1990; 13: 167–88.
NATUROPATHY page 103
(35) Rheumatoid arthritis – Single-blind controlled: Kjeldsen-Kragh J, Haugen M, Borchgrevink C F, Laerum E, Eek M, Mowinkel P, Hovi K, Forre O, Lancet 1991; 338 (8772): 899–902.
(36) Rheumatic disease and diet
Haugen M, Kjeldsen-Kragh J, Nordvag B Y, Forre O, Clinical Rheumatology 1991; 10(4): 410–7.
NUTRITIONAL THERAPY page 91
(29) Nutritional therapy
Lazarides L, Society for Promotion of Nutritional Therapy, June 1993.
(30) Esophagitis/pellagra
Segal I, et al. Nutritional Cancer 1990; 14 (3–4): 233–8.
(31) Coronary heart disease
Stampfer M J, Willet W C, et al, New England Journal of Medicine, May 20 1993 328 (20):1487–9.
(32) PMS
Nicholas A, First International Symposium on Magnesium Deficit in Human Pathology, Paris, Springer, Verlag, 1973: 261–3.
OSTEOPATHY page 45
(11) Low-back pain during menstrual cramping
Boesler D, et al Journal of American Osteopathic Association 1993, 93, 2, 203–8 and 213–4.
(12) Non specific low-back pain – Controlled trial: MacDonald R S, Bell C M J, Spine, May 1990, 15, 5, 364–70.

REFLEXOLOGY page 65
(19) Sickness at work
Madsen S, Andersen J, Forenede Danske Zoneterapeuter, Nov 1993.
(20) Childbirth
Dr Gowri Motha and Dr Jane McGrath, Bradford N, Chamberlain G, Pain Relief in Childbirth, Pub. Harper Collins 1995, pp 201–2.
(21) PMS
Oleson T, Flocco W, Obstetrics and Gynaecology 1993; 82; (6) 906–11.
RELAXATION AND VISUALIZATION
(37) Inflammatory bowel disease – Single-blind controlled: Milne B, Joachim G, Niedhardt J, Journal of Advanced Nursing 1986; 11 (65) 561–7.
(3) Tension headaches
Van Dyke R, Zitman F G, Linssen A C, Spinhoven P, Int J Clin Exp Hypn 1991 Jan; 39 (1): 6–23.
(39) Raynaud's disease
Keefe F J, Surwit R S, Pilon R N, Journal of Applied Behaviour analysis 1980; 13 (1) 3–11.
SPIRITUAL HEALING page 135
(51) Wound healing – Double-blind trial: Wirth D P, Subtle Energies 1990; (1): 1, 1-20.
(52) Tension headache – Placebo trial: Leller E, Bzdek V M, Nursing Research, 1986; 35: 2,101–105.
(53) Heart disease
Byrd R C, Southern Medical Journal 1988; 81, 7: 826–29 .
WESTERN HERBALISM page 97
(33) Valerian extract and insomnia – Controlled study: Schults I I, Stoltz C, Muller J, Pharmacopsychiatry, 1994 July, Vol: 27 (4), P 147–51, ISSN: 0176–3679.
(34) High cholesterol – Randomized, double-blind trial: Jain A K, Vargas R, Gotzkowsky S, McMahon F G, Clin-Investig 1993, May, Vol 71 (5), P:383-6, ISSN: 0941-0198.
YOGA page 131
(47) Osteoarthritis
Garfinkle M S et al, Journal of Rheumatology 21(12):2341-3, Dec 1994.
(48) Bronchial asthma
Nagarathna R, Nagendra HR, British Medical Journal vol 291, 19 Oct 1985 pp 172.

BIBLIOGRAPHY

Sheila Lavery used the following books for reference while writing the therapy essays in this book:
The Complete Guide to Homeopathy by Dr Andrew Lockie and Barbara Geddes (Dorling Kindersley); *The Dictionary of Acupuncture and Moxibustion* by Nguyen Duc Hiep (Thorsons); *New Ways to Health: A Guide to Acupuncture* by Peter Firebrace and Sandra Hill (Hamlyn); *Your Health, Your Choice* by Simon Mills (Papermac); *Dynamic Chiropractic Today* by Michael Copland Griffiths (Thorsons); *Optima Alternative Health Guides – Chiropractic* by Susan Moore; *Massage Therapy* by Adam Jackson; *Reflexology* by Anya Gore; *Osteopathy* by Stephen Sandler; *Shiatsu* by Ray Ridolfi (these are now all published by Vermilion); *Chinese Herbal Medicine* by Stephen Tang and Richard Craze (Piatkus); *Chinese Medicine the Web That Has No Weaver* by Ted J. Kaptchuk (Rider); *Competences Required by Osteopathic Practice* (General Council and Register of Osteopaths); *The Fragrant Mind* by Valerie Ann Worwood (Doubleday); *The Reflexology Handbook – A Complete Guide* by Laura Norman (Piatkus); *The Complete Book of Massage* by Clare Maxwell-Hudson (Dorling Kindersley); *Your Guide to the Alexander Technique* by John Gray (Gollancz); *The Metamorphic Technique – Principles and Practice* by Gaston St. Pierre and Debbie Shapiro (Element); *Naturopathic Medicine* by Roger Newman Turner (Thorsons); *The Handbook of Complementary Medicine* by Stephen Fulder (Oxford); *Self-Hypnosis and Other Mind Expanding Techniques* by Charles Tebbetts (Westwood publishing company); *Better Health through Natural Healing* by Ross Trattler (Thorsons); *The Art of Tai Chi* by Paul Crompton (Element); *Radionic Healing – Is It for You?* by David Tansley (Element); *Ayurveda the Science of Self-Healing* by Vasant Lad; *The Book of Ayurveda* by Judith Morrison (Gaia)

PICTURE CREDITS

Academy of Systematic Kinesiology, 39 Browns Road, Surbiton, Surrey KT5 8ST. Tel: 0181 399 3215 153 left
Ancient Art and Architecture Collection/Ronald Sheridan 12 left
The Dr. Edward Bach Center, Mount Vernon, Sotwell, Wallingford, Oxon OX10 0PZ. Tel: (01491) 834678 106 center, 106 top left, 106 top right
Deni Bown Associates/Deni Bown 73 top left, 73 top right
Bridgeman Art Library/British Library, London 94 top left
British School of Shiatsu-Do, 6 Erskine Road, London NW3 3AJ. Tel: 0171 483 3776 23
Collections/Sandra Lousada 59 top right, 59 bottom right, 59 bottom left, 59 top left, 115 bottom left, 115 top right, 118 center right, 118 far right, /Anthea Sieveking 41 top left, 73 bottom
Dee Conway 150 right
E.T. Archive /National Palace Museum, Taiwan 12 right
Mary Evans Picture Library 26 top right, 70 top left
Format Partners /Mo Wilson 135 top left
John Glover 97 bottom left, 108, 109
Robert Harding Picture Library 86 top left, 97 bottom right, /BBC Enterprises/RedwoodPublishing 70 bottom left, /Cole Group 86 top center, /Robert McLeod 150 top right
Hutchison Library/Beddon 112 middle left, /Pierrette Collomb 32 top left, /R. Ian Lloyd 28 left, /Liba Taylor 65 bottom right
Image Bank/Marc Romanelli 35 right
Images 15, 19 bottom left, 26 bottom left, 26 bottom center, 32 bottom, 32 top center, 82 top right, 82 bottom right, 85 bottom left, 86 bottom center, 112 top left, 112 bottom left, 112 right, 137 top left
Stuart T. Lightbody 13
Marshall Cavendish Picture Library 42 right, 50 top left, 103 left, /Bill Petch 76 right, /Ray Duns 106 bottom
McOnegal Botanical/Rowan McOnegal 97 top
Osteopathic Information Service, PO Box 2074, Reading, Berkshire RG1 4YR. Tel: (01734) 512051 42 left, 44 bottom right
Reed International Books Ltd 46 right, 50 top right, 149 left, /Peter Chadwick 76 bottom left, 76 top left, 79 bottom left, 79 top, /Melvin Grey 88 bottom right, 94 center right
Rolf Institute/R.A Thompson, 205 Canyon Boulevard, Boulder, Colorado 80302, USA. Tel: 001 (303) 449 5903 145 left
Science Photo Library 40 center, /Argentum 154 top left, /Ricardo Arias 85 top left, /John Bavos 41 bottom left, /John Bavosi 154 bottom left, /BSIP/LBL 19 top left, /BSIP, Roux 40 center, /BSIP Taulin 62 top left, /BSIP/Krassovsky 124 left, /Oscar Burriel/Latin Stock 124 bottom right, /Simon Fraser 26 top center, /John Greim 100 top right, /Adrienne Hart-Davis 82 left, /Seth Joel 85 bottom right, /Bill Longcore 46 left, /Damien Lovegrove 70 right, /Tim Malyon & Paul Biddle 16 bottom, 16 top, /Andrew McClenaghan 19 bottom right, /Will & Dent McIntyre 28 right, /Richard Megna/ Fundamental 141 top right, /Paul Biddle 94 bottom left, /Philippe Plailly 124 top left, /Francoise Sauze 52 left, 53 left, 62 right, 127 bottom left, 154 right, /Jane Shemilt 62 bottom left, /Hattie Young 44 top right
Shift Productions/Mel Herdon 32 top right
Society of Teachers of the Alexander Technique, 20 London House, 266 Fulham Road, London SW10 9EL. Tel: 0171 352 1556 121 bottom left, 121 top left
Still Pictures/Claude Sauvageot 131 left **Tony Stone Images** 85 top right, 118 bottom left, 118 top left, /Bruce Ayres 127 top left, /Erika Craddock 88 top, /Zigy Kaluzny 19 top right, /Ian O'Leary 102, /Alan Levenson 139 top left, /Andre Perlstein 56 right, 129 left, /Christel Rosenfeld 86 top right, /Ralf Schultheiss 100 bottom, /Ken Scott 35 left, 56 left, /Charles Thatcher 127 top left, /Nick Vedros, Vedros & Associates 20, /Paul Webster 88 bottom left, /Rosemary Weller 100 top left **U.K. Polarity Therapy Association/Tony Hutchings, Monomark House, 27 Old Gloucester Street, London WC1N 3XX. Tel: 01483 417714** 37 **John Walmsley Photo-Library** 50 bottom left, 50 bottom right, 65 top right, 67 left, 103 right, 133 left, 143 top left, 146 middle right, 146 top right, 150 left **Weleda U.K. Ltd, Heanor Road, Ilkeston, Derbyshire DE7 8DR. Tel: 0115 944 8200** 79 bottom right

ENCYCLOPEDIA OF COMPLEMENTARY HEALTH

Commissioning Editors: Sian Facer, Jane McIntosh
Art Director: Keith Martin
Art Editor: Les Needham
Project Manager: Mary Lambert
Editors/writers: Clare Hill, Diana Vowles, Diana Craig
and Nance Fyson
Assistant Editor: Humaira Husain
Proofreader: Anne Crane
Consultant Editor: Nikki Bradford
Illustrators: Jo Agis, Birgit Eggers, Steve Rawlings,
Philip Wilson
Picture Research: Liz Fowler
Production Controller: Nick Thompson

First published in Great Britain in 1996 by Hamlyn
an imprint of Octopus Publishing Group Limited

This 2001 edition published by Chancellor Press,
an imprint of Bounty Books,
a division of Octopus Publishing Group Limited
2-4 Heron Quays, London E14 4JP

ISBN 0 7537 0472 2

A CIP catalogue record for this book is available from
the British Library

Produced by Toppan Printing Co Ltd

Printed in China

Note

This book is not intended as an alternative to personal medical advice. The reader should consult a physician in all matters relating to health and particularly in respect of any symptoms which may require diagnosis or medical attention. While the advice and information are believed to be accurate and true at the time of going to press, neither the authors nor the publisher can accept any legal responsibility or liability for any errors or omissions that may be made.

ENCYCLOPEDIA OF COMPLEMENTARY HEALTH

CONSULTANT EDITOR: NIKKI BRADFORD
WRITERS: SHEILA LAVERY KAREN SULLIVAN
WITH CLARE HILL, DIANA VOWLES AND NANCE FYSON
CLINICAL RESEARCH: FARA BEGUM-BAIG

CHANCELLOR PRESS

CONTENTS

Introduction

In the fast pace of today's world where everybody is under constant pressure, people are now taking more interest in maintaining good health and well-being. There is general concern about disease and the environment: in particular how pollutants are affecting our health, and the way in which pesticides or contaminated animal feeds are affecting the vegetables and meat that we eat in our daily diet. Adults and children also seem to be developing more allergic reactions to food and general pollutants in the environment, and diseases such as asthma are now particularly affecting children. One theory is that childhood asthma is on the increase because of increased traffic fumes, and also dust mites that are present in everybody's homes.

People are also developing an increasing resistance to antibiotics given to treat different infections and are investigating alternative healthcare treatments that will help to build up their immune systems. There are also new diseases, such as Myalgic Encephalomyelitis (ME), which can start after a viral infection, that have arisen over the last 10–15 years. There is no cure at present for ME, however, alternative healthcare treatments such as aromatherapy, Western herbalism and nutritional therapy have been found to help sufferers by improving and balancing their general diet and boosting their immune systems, which are often at a very low ebb.

There has also been an overall rejection of the materialistic values of the hedonistic Eighties. In the more caring Nineties, people are having to work harder, often juggling work and children, and are suffering more stress because of it. But today they are more willing to undertake holistic therapies such as yoga, tai chi and massage to help them cope with tension and overwork by relaxing both their bodies and minds.

Alternative therapies are definitely becoming more popular. In fact, in recent research it was discovered that eight out of ten people had tried a treatment and three-quarters of them reported that it had either helped or cured them. Doctors are also becoming more aware of the benefits of alternative health therapies when orthodox treatment alone does not seem to work. In fact, they will now often refer a patient to an osteopath or chiropractor, for example, for manipulation of a back problem that is proving difficult to resolve. Some doctors are also trained in an alternative therapy, such as homeopathy, and this treatment is now becoming more widely available.

Alternative health treatments can do so much to improve a person's mental attitude and to help or cure various ailments, but in cases of serious or terminal illness only certain therapies will be suitable and should never be undertaken instead of orthodox treatment, but rather alongside it. Acupuncture, for example, can greatly boost the immune systems of cancer or HIV patients while also improving their overall mental attitude and their general perspective of their disease.

HOW TO USE THIS BOOK

The One Spirit Encyclopedia of Complementary Health is a comprehensive reference book which is divided into two major sections: the first section discusses in detail 30 major and minor therapies; the second section covers the illnesses that can affect everyone, what is the orthodox medical treatment, and which alternative treatments can help relieve or cure the condition. An Index of Symptoms and a useful Directory of resources is also included.

THE THERAPIES

The first section of the book contains 30 major and minor therapies. Each one is clearly explained under headings such as how it works, what happens in a consultation, what problems can it treat and is it safe for everyone. All the therapies are addressed in the same way, whether it is a well-known treatment such as Aromatherapy or a lesser known one such as Cymatics.

To make it easier to find specific therapies, helpful colored symbol icons are used to identify them so that you can easily locate where they are in this section and elsewhere in the book.

Therapists tailor their treatments very much to the individual: the precise nature of the treatment that people receive will vary, depending on their medical history, symptoms, lifestyle and other relevant details. The information contained in this book indicates the type of things a therapist is most likely to do or recommend. Do not be surprised if because of your symptoms they feel you need something slightly different. The information on alternative healthcare is meant purely as an indication of likely treatments; it is not meant as a self-help guide to the medical uses of the different therapies.

The results from clinical studies that have been carried out in recent years have been included at the end of the therapies, where they have been available. The bibliographical references for these studies can be found in the acknowledgments section on page 378.

Some of the clinical studies in the book have been termed:
Single-blind trial – this means that the patient is unaware of the type of treatment they are being given.
Double-blind trial – this means that the patient and observer are unaware of the type of treatment being given.
Controlled trial – This means that the groups of people involved in the trial either have specific treatment in connection with the therapy or do not receive any medical treatment at all.

The term **placebo** has also been used. This is when the patients in the trial are given a treatment that in acupuncture, for example, uses dummy points, or a medication is given that has no active ingredients.

THE AILMENTS

The second section of the book contains the ailments which appear in either two-page, one-page or half-page entries. These sections are color-coded according to body system. There are 13 body systems in all and two further sections on Infants and Children and Home and Emergency First Aid. If you were looking for an entry on Anemia, for example, you would find it under the Circulatory system, which is color coded dark red. If you then wanted to find Angina, which is in the same section, you could use the index or contents or just look through the dark-red section until you found the right entry.

The orthodox medical treatment that is recommended to a patient is covered first in each ailment entry followed by the most suitable alternative treatments, which are again highlighted by colored icons to make them instantly recognizable and simple to find.

INDEX OF SYMPTOMS

This section has been compiled as a ready reference section so that people can look up a person's symptoms and be referred to the possible ailment (one or more) and the relevant page number.

THE DIRECTORY

The Directory of resources includes an overview of the alternative therapy; general information, when practical, about treatment and costs; and information about how to find a qualified practitioner.

NOTE

This book is not intended as an alternative to personal, professional medical advice. The reader should always consult a physician in all matters relating to health, particularly with respect to any symptoms that may require diagnosis or medical attention. While the advice and information are believed to be accurate and true at the time of publication, neither the authors nor the publisher can accept any legal responsibility or liability for any errors or omissions that may be made.

ACUPUNCTURE

ACUPUNCTURE is now enjoying renewed popularity as a highly sophisticated and effective form of alternative treatment. Indeed, many of us tend to think of stimulating the body's healing energy as a peculiarly 1990s phenomenon, but acupuncture as a holistic treatment appears to have existed long before anyone chose to record it. Stone acupuncture needles dating from the Neolithic period (2500 BC) have been found in tombs in inner Mongolia. The earliest written account of acupuncture appears in the *Nei Jing* (*The Yellow Emperor's Classic of Internal Medicine*), which dates from around 200 BC and is the oldest comprehensive medical text book. Pien Chueh, a famous physician of his time, used stone acupuncture needles, moxibustion and herbs to bring a prince out of a coma. So important was his work that even though the incident took place in the fourth century BC, the Chinese still celebrate his birthday every year on April 28th.

ACUPUNCTURE is a traditional Chinese health treatment, which involves the use of needles to stimulate energy points in the body. It can help many conditions including stress, back pain, menstrual problems and addictions.

In China, acupuncture has been a major part of primary healthcare for the last 5,000 years. Its uses range from preventing and treating disease, to relieving pain and even anesthetizing patients for surgery. However, the emphasis has always been on prevention. In traditional Chinese medicine, the highest form of acupuncture was given to enable you to live a long, healthy life. To the Chinese, a sick man visiting an acupuncturist is comparable to a thirsty man starting to dig a well.

What is acupuncture?

Acupuncture literally means "needle piercing," a rather painful-sounding term for the practice of inserting very fine needles into the skin to stimulate specific points called acupoints. The acupoints are stimulated to balance the movement of energy in the body and the process can cause slight discomfort rather than the pain that its name suggests. Acupuncture is a major part of traditional Chinese medicine (TCM), a sophisticated and complex system of healthcare that also includes the use of moxibustion, herbalism (see Chinese herbalism pages 24–29), massage (see pages 54–59), dietary therapy and also exercise such as tai chi (see pages 130–131).

Acupuncture has become very popular in recent years among conventional doctors in the West, some of whom now use it to treat symptoms of disease as if it were just another part of Western medicine. But it has been shown to work best when it is kept within the context of the Chinese tradition in which it is so firmly entrenched.

To really understand how acupuncture works, you need to make yourself familiar with the basics of Chinese philosophy. The philosophies of the Dao or Tao, yin and yang, the eight principles, the three treasures and the five elements are all fundamental to traditional Chinese acupuncture and its specific role in helping to maintain good health and a person's wellbeing.

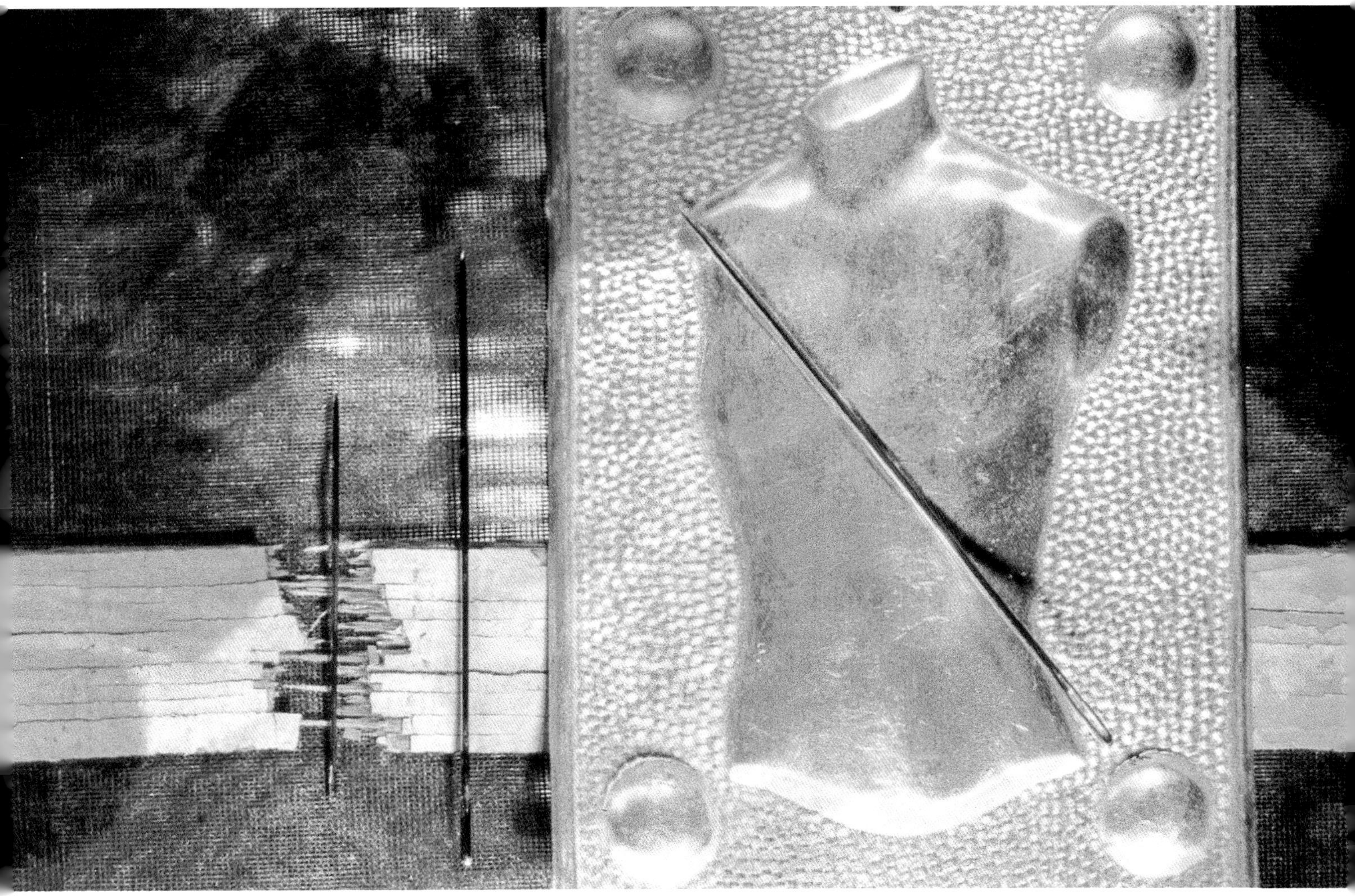

The philosophy of the Dao

There is no accurate translation of the Dao, but it can be described as "the path" or "the way of life." The laws of the Dao advocate moderation, living in harmony with nature and striving for balance. Moderation applies to all areas of life, and the ancient Chinese believed that it was essential to a long and fruitful life. Their reasoning was perfectly logical. They claimed we are "fueled" by three treasures: Qi or Chi (pronounced chee), Shen, and Jing. Chi is energy and will be discussed in detail later on. Shen is the spirit, the treasure that gives brightness to life and is responsible for consciousness and mental abilities, and Jing is your Jing, as does excessive emotional reactions. Working too hard also depletes it as does inappropriate sexual behavior. The ancient Chinese had some very balanced views about sex. In the West we worry about not getting enough sex, but the Chinese have always been concerned about getting too much. Too many ejaculations, they claimed could deplete a man's Jing because he loses his essence and, not surprisingly, giving birth too many times could deplete a woman's. So seriously did the Chinese take this subject that they laid down guidelines for the minimum and

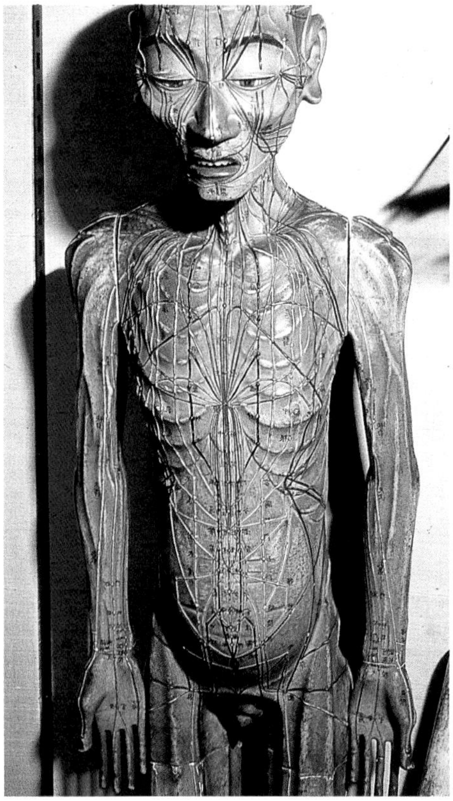

ABOVE: This ancient acupuncture study figure was used for reference by the Chinese therapists of the Ming Dynasty in the 17th century.

ABOVE: Here in this ancient Sung Dynasty painting a country doctor is burning the herb moxa on a man's back to stimulate the relevant acupuncture point.

our essence. Jing is responsible for growth, development and reproduction. We are born with our full quota of Jing and it is lost little by little as we go through life. The important thing to remember about Jing is that once you lose it, you cannot get it back. It is depleted by wrong or careless living, but preserved by moderation, and its loss can be slowed down to some degree by acupuncture. The role of the acupuncturist therefore is to restore your health and enable you to live a little closer to the Dao. By doing so, you can preserve your Jing and consequently live to a ripe old age. By overdoing it and living a life of excess you squander your Jing and get burned out. Drinking too much depletes

maximum number of ejaculations a man should have at any given age. *The Classic of the Simple Girl* (Sui Dynasty AD581–681) contains the guidelines which cover the age groups 15–70. For example, a 20-year-old man in good health should not ejaculate more than twice a day; if he is in average health it should be no more than once a day. On the other hand, a healthy 60-year-old man should leave a space of ten days between each performance and 20 days if he is only moderately healthy. The guidelines seem strict, but the message of the Dao was intended to be more moderate. The emphasis was not on cooling sexual relations, but on sharing intimacy. By shifting the emphasis from the male orgasm, the man could concentrate on giving pleasure to his partner in other ways, so that there was a balance of sexual power and balance in all things was considered the key to good health and long life.

In order to increase their understanding of the Dao, the Chinese developed two concepts that together form the basis of Chinese thought: yin and yang and the more detailed system of the five elements.

Yin and Yang

The idea of harmony and balance are also the basis of yin and yang. The belief that each person is governed by the opposing, but complementary forces of yin and yang, is central to all Chinese thought because it is believed to affect everything in the universe, including ourselves.

ABOVE: The tai chi symbol shows how yin and yang are opposites, but inseparable.

Traditionally, yin is dark, passive, feminine, cold and negative; yang is light, active, male, warm and positive. Modern therapists would simply say that there are two sides to everything – happy and sad, tired and energetic, cold and hot.

Yin and yang are the opposites that make the whole, they cannot exist without each other and nothing is ever completely one or the other; there are varying degrees of each within everything and everybody. The tai chi symbol illustrates how they flow into each other with a little yin always within yang and a little yang always within yin. The same happens within the body as after exercise (yang) the body wants to rest (yin), after a fever breaks (yang), you get chills (yin) and within the head (yang) the mind is yin. The body, mind and emotions are all subject to the influences of yin and yang. When the two opposing forces are in balance we feel good, but if one force dominates the other, it brings about an imbalance that can result in ill health.

One of the main aims of the acupuncturist is to maintain a balance of yin and yang within the whole person to prevent illness occurring and to restore existing health.

Yin and yang are also part of the eight principles of traditional Chinese medicine. The other six are: cold and heat, internal and external, deficiency and excess. These principles allow the practitioner to use yin and yang more precisely in order to bring more detail into his diagnosis.

The five elements

The yin and yang philosophy was further refined into the system of the five elements to gain a deeper understanding of how the body, mind and spirit work.

The five elements have numerous associations. Among other things each one is related to a season, an organ, a taste, a color, a smell, an emotion, a body part and even a grain. The system is a complex one, based on the belief that life is an ever-changing process. It is probably most simply explained in terms of seasonal change and the smooth cyclical process of nature. The five elements of wood, fire, earth, metal and water relate to the seasons in the following way: wood to spring, fire to summer, earth to late summer, metal to autumn and water to winter, and each element then flows into the next in the same way that one season slowly gives way to another.

THE QUALITIES OF THE FIVE ELEMENTS:

	Wood	Fire	Earth	Metal	Water
Color	green	red	yellow	white	blue/black
Emotion	anger	joy	sympathy	grief/sadness	fear
Voice	shouts	laughs	sings	weeps	groans
Smell	rancid	scorched	fragrant	rotten	putrid
Taste	sour	bitter	sweet	pungent	salty
Season	spring	summer	late summer	autumn	winter
Climate	windy	hot	humid/damp	dry	cold
Body part	soft tissue	heart/blood	flesh	skin/hair	bones/marrow
Officials	liver gall bladder	heart small intestine pericardium three heater*	spleen stomach	lungs large intestine	bladder kidneys

In the same way, a seed planted in spring blooms in summer, seeds itself in late summer to autumn, dies in winter, and a new seed grows again in spring. It is part of a never-ending cycle and each phase has its role to play in maintaining the balance of nature. The same process of change occurs within the body. Cells grow and die to make way for new cells, and body systems depend upon each other in a similar way to the seasons, working together to ensure the balanced functioning of the body, mind and spirit and the healthy flow of life through the whole person.

Within the person, the five phases relate to organs and the emotions associated with those organs. For example, summer is connected to the fire element which contains the heart, the small intestines, the heart protector (pericardium) and the three heater* (the body's physical and emotional thermostat). The pericardium is often associated with physical heart problems such as palpitations or angina, while the heart itself is related to more spiritual, mental and emotional concerns. Most importantly, the heart is the home of Shen. Shen is the spirit, the driving force of the mind and the personality, and ruler of all the organs. It is forever changing and developing and is as vital to the mind and emotions as the heart is to the body.

It is worth mentioning that the Chinese compared the body to their own kingdom and gave the organs names to signify their position and function within the kingdom. Not surprisingly, the heart is the emperor presiding over his kingdom, in charge of various ministers who have specific functions within the body, mind and spirit. The gall bladder minister is responsible for making decisions, the liver is likened to a general who uses his planning, judgment and organizational abilities to keep the kingdom running smoothly. The small intestine has the job of separating the good from the bad, both physically and mentally. The spleen is the transport minister, responsible for the smooth conveyance of thought, energy, blood and so on. There are 12 officials within the kingdom, which lie within the five elements and keep the body, mind and emotions running smoothly.

The aim of the treatment is not only to cure health problems but to balance the body and prevent illness occurring.

Like the kingdom, each one of us possesses all five elements. When we are functioning well, all the elements are in balance. But ill health arises from a weakness or excess of one of the elements, which throws the rest of the body out of balance. The imbalance is demonstrated by a specific color, tone of voice, smell, taste, season, inappropriate emotional behavior and ultimately physical illness. For example, someone with an imbalance in their earth element may love the color yellow, can have a yellow tinge to the skin on their face, has a sing-song voice and loves to sing, has a fragrant smell, craves sweet things, loves or hates late summer, needs lots of sympathy or is sympathetic by nature, worries too much and may have digestive problems, eating disorders, menstrual problems, or a bad memory.

The thrust of five element diagnosis is to isolate and treat the imbalanced element, because an imbalanced element is like a weak link in your energetic chain that can undermine the strength of your mind, body and spirit.

How does it work?

There are a variety of scientific theories about how acupuncture works. These range from the belief that acupuncture works on the nervous system to the fact that it helps release endorphins – the body's natural pain relievers. But, although scientific theories can in part explain the immediate pain-relieving effects of acupuncture, they cannot explain acupuncture's ability to relieve chronic health problems, conditions which are not pain-related and the effect of the therapy on the whole person.

The Chinese explanation is more philosophical than scientific, but it does explain the holistic benefits of acupuncture. The Chinese believe that disease affects us on every level – a physical illness upsets the mind and emotions and mental anxiety registers in a related organ. So a worrier could have a stomach ulcer, because excessive mental activity affects the functioning of the stomach, while an imbalance in the liver can express itself as inappropriate anger. For this reason illness is never treated as a set of isolated symptoms or diseased organs, but as an expression of disharmony within the mind, body and spirit. To arrive at a diagnosis, the acupuncturist usually aims to do two things: identify a weak link in your energetic chain through the system of the five elements and weave all the symptoms of your disease together to make up "a pattern of disharmony."

The concept of Chi

Inner harmony relies on a healthy, balanced and unobstructed flow of Chi. Chi could be described as the vital energy or life force which drives every cell of the body. It supports, nourishes and defends the whole person against mental, physical and emotional disease. It is an invisible, intangible flow of energy which modern researchers have described in terms of electromagnetic energy. Chi flows around the body in invisible channels known as meridians. There are 12 main meridians, six of which are yin and six are yang and numerous minor ones, which form a network of energy channels throughout the body.

Each meridian is related to, and named after, an organ or function, the main ones are: the lung, kidney, gallbladder, stomach, spleen, heart, small intestine, large intestine, gall bladder, urinary bladder, san jiao (three heater) and pericardium (heart protector/ or circulation sex meridian).

Dotted along these meridians are 365 main acupuncture points. These are listed by name, number and the meridian to which they belong. The names are very descriptive and often beautiful, but the numbers are possibly more useful. For example, "Leg three miles" is the name for stomach 36 (St 36), "Happy calm" is Liver 3 (Liv 3) and "Bright and Clear" is gall bladder 37 (GB37). One point has 17 different names.

When Chi flows freely through the meridians, the body is balanced and healthy, but if the energy becomes blocked, stagnated or weakened, it can result in physical, mental or emotional ill health. An imbalance in a person's body can result from inappropriate emotional responses such as: excess anger, over-excitement, self-pity, deep grief and fear.

Other factors, which are what the Chinese call the "pernicious external influences" are: cold, damp/humidity, wind, dryness, and heat. Any one or more of the internal and external factors can upset the balance of Chi by making it too hot, too cold, excessive, deficient, too fast, stagnant or causing it to

CLINICAL REFERENCES

All the references detailed refer to the clinical study information contained at the end of many of the therapies. The page number for the relevant therapy is detailed and the number of the study is given to help with cross-referencing.

ACUPRESSURE page 23
(5) Lumbar pain
Jiaying W, Guangzhoa L, Shuhua M, Guicheng P, Journal of Traditional Chinese Medicine 1986; 6 (3): 168–170.
(6) Morning sickness – Double-blind trial: Dundee J W, Souri F B R, Ghaly R G, Bell P F, Journal of Royal Society of Medicine 1988; 81: 456–7.
ACUPUNCTURE page 19
(1) Chronic alcoholic – Controlled placebo trial: Bullock M, Cilliton P, Olander, R, Lancet 1989, 1435–1439.
(2) Drug addiction – Single blind placebo trial: Lipton D, Brewington V, Smith M, Journal of Substance abuse 1994, vol 11 no 3 205-215.
(3) Nicotine addiction
Clavel F; Benhamou S; British Medical Journal 1985: 291; 1538-9.
ALEXANDER TECHNIQUE page 121
(40) Posture and performance – Barlow.
(41) Performance stress reduction – Valentine E.
AROMATHERAPY page 73
Chronic bronchitis – Double blind trial: 'Gouttes aux Essences' (Essence Drops) Phytotherapy Research Vol 3 no 3 1989. J P Ferley, N Poutignat, Zmirou, Y Azzopardi and F Balducci 106.
(23) Vaginal thrush (*Candida albicans*)
Dr Paul Belaiche, September 1985, Phytotherapy no 15 13–15 191.
(24) Cardiac surgery
C J Stevensen, Complementary Therapies in Medicine 1994, 2 27–35 Middlesex Hospital Intensive Care Unit, London 283.
(25) Post-cardiotomy patients – Randomized double blind trial research: with support of Bristol cardiac team led by surgeon Mr Wishaert. Jane Buckle, Nursing Times, May 19, vol 89, no 20 1993.
ARTS THERAPIES page 151
Music therapy
(36) Heart surgery
Barnson S, Zimmerman L, Nievan J, Heart and Lung 1995; 24(2): 124–32.
(57) Anxiety
Stroudenmire J, Journal of Clinical Psychology 1975; 31(3): 490–2.
(58) Depression
Hanser S B, Thompson L W, Journal of Gerontology 1994 Nov; 49 (6): 265–9.
AUTOGENIC TRAINING page 133
(49) Hypertension
Aivazyan T A, Zaitsev V P,Yurenev A P, Health Psychology 1988; 7 (Suppl): 201-8.
(50) Anxiety
Stetter F, Walter G, Zimmermann A, Zahres S, Straube E R Psychotherapie, Pschosomatik, Medizinische Psychologie 1994; 44 (7): 226-34.
AYURVEDIC MEDICINE page 35
(9) Diabetes mellitus
Baskartan K, et al Journal of Ethnopharmachology 30 1990, pp 295–305.
(10) Parkinson's disease
Manyam B V, et al. The Journal of Alternative and Complementary Medicine Vol 1, No 3, 1995, pp 249–255.
CHINESE HERBALISM page 29
(7) Endometriosis
Wang D Z, Wang Z Q, Zhang Z F, Chung Hsi I Chieh Ho Tsa Chih, Sept 1991, 11.9 pp 524–6, 515.
(8) AIDS
Weibo L, Journal of Traditional Chinese Medicine 15 (1) 3–9, 1995.
CHIROPRACTIC page 53
(13) Low back pain
Meade T W, Dyer S, Browne W, Townsend J, Frank A O, British Medical Journal 1990, vol 300 pp 1431–1437 and BMJ 1995 vol 311, 349–51 and Dr Alan Breen, British Chiropractic Association.
(14) Leg or low back pain – Controlled placebo trial: Rupert R L, Wagnon R, Thompson P, Ezzeldin M T, International. Review of Chiropractic 1985, Winter 58-60.
COLOR THERAPY page 137
(54) Arthritis – Controlled trial: McDonald S F, International Journal of Biosocial Research 3, No 2, 1982 pp 49–54.
(55) Migraine
Anderson J, Brain/Mind Bulletin 15, No 4, Jan 1990 p 4.
DIAGNOSTIC THERAPIES page 153
Iridology
(59) and (60) Studies on *Arcus senilis* marking in iridology
November 1987, the Los Angeles Herald Examiner and the January 1990 edition of the Journal of the American Optimetric Association.
HOMEOPATHY page 79
(26) Asthma/House dust mite allergy
Reilly D, Taylor M, Beattie N, Campbell J, McSharry C, Aitchison T C, Carter R, Stevenson R D, The Lancet Vol 344 1601–1606, 1994.
(27) Dermatological Complaints – Double blind trial: Dr Schawb Alenavia. Proceedings of the 45th congress of the LMHI, p 166–168.
(28) Migraines – Double-blind trial: Brigo B, Serpelloni G, The Berlin Journal on Research in Homeopathy, Vol 1 No.2 March 1991, pp98–105.
HYPNOTHERAPY page 127
(42) Pain relief for burns
Wakeman R J, Kaplan J Z, American Journal Clin Hypn, 1978: 21: 3–12.
(43) Tinnitus – Cross-over control trial with blind evaluation
Marks N J, Karl H, Onisiphorou C, Clinical Otolaryngol 1985; 10; 43–46.
(44) Smoking
Stanton H E; International Journal of Clinical and Experimental Hypnosis 1978; XXVI; 1: 22–29.
(45) Tension headaches
Carasso R; Kleinhauz M; Peded; O Yehuda S American Journal of Clinical Hpynosis 1985; 27; 4: 216–218.
(46) Warts
Ewin D, American Journal of Clinical Hypnosis July 1992, 35; 1:1–9.
MASSAGE page 59
(15) Anxiety – Controlled trial: Field, Morrow, Valdeon, Larson, Kuhn and Scanberg, Journal of the American Academy of Childhood and Adolescent Psychiatry 1992, 31; 1: 125–131
(16) Pain relief and insomnia
Farrow J, Nursing Standard, 1990; 4 (17): 26–28.
(17) Breast cancer
Sims S, Nursing Times 1986; 82 (13): 47–50.
(18) Premature baby growth
Scarfidi F S, Field T M, Schanberg S M Bauer, Tucci, Roberts, Morrow and Kuhn, Infant Behaviour and Development 1990; 13: 167–88.
NATUROPATHY page 103
(35) Rheumatoid arthritis – Single-blind controlled: Kjeldsen-Kragh J, Haugen M, Borchgrevink C F, Laerum E, Eek M, Mowinkel P, Hovi K, Forre O, Lancet 1991; 338 (8772): 899–902.
(36) Rheumatic disease and diet
Haugen M, Kjeldsen-Kragh J, Nordvag B Y, Forre O, Clinical Rheumatology 1991; 10(4): 410–7.
NUTRITIONAL THERAPY page 91
(29) Nutritional therapy
Lazarides L, Society for Promotion of Nutritional Therapy, June 1993.
(30) Esophagitis/pellagra
Segal I, et al. Nutritional Cancer 1990; 14 (3–4): 233–8.
(31) Coronary heart disease
Stampfer M J, Willet W C, et al, New England Journal of Medicine, May 20 1993 328 (20):1487–9.
(32) PMS
Nicholas A, First International Symposium on Magnesium Deficit in Human Pathology, Paris, Springer, Verlag, 1973: 261–3.
OSTEOPATHY page 45
(11) Low-back pain during menstrual cramping
Boesler D, et al Journal of American Osteopathic Association 1993, 93, 2, 203–8 and 213–4.
(12) Non specific low-back pain – Controlled trial: MacDonald R S, Bell C M J, Spine, May 1990, 15, 5, 364–70.

REFLEXOLOGY page 65
(19) Sickness at work
Madsen S, Andersen J, Forenede Danske Zoneterapeuter, Nov 1993.
(20) Childbirth
Dr Gowri Motha and Dr Jane McGrath, Bradford N, Chamberlain G, Pain Relief in Childbirth, Pub. Harper Collins 1995, pp 201–2.
(21) PMS
Oleson T, Flocco W, Obstetrics and Gynaecology 1993; 82; (6) 906–11.
RELAXATION AND VISUALIZATION
(37) Inflammatory bowel disease – Single-blind controlled: Milne B, Joachim G, Niedhardt J, Journal of Advanced Nursing 1986; 11 (65) 561–7.
(3) Tension headaches
Van Dyke R, Zitman F G, Linssen A C, Spinhoven P, Int J Clin Exp Hypn 1991 Jan; 39 (1): 6–23.
(39) Raynaud's disease
Keefe F J, Surwit R S, Pilon R N, Journal of Applied Behaviour analysis 1980; 13 (1) 3–11.
SPIRITUAL HEALING page 135
(51) Wound healing – Double-blind trial: Wirth D P, Subtle Energies 1990; (1): 1, 1-20.
(52) Tension headache – Placebo trial: Leller E, Bzdek V M, Nursing Research, 1986; 35: 2,101–105.
(53) Heart disease
Byrd R C, Southern Medical Journal 1988; 81, 7: 826–29 .
WESTERN HERBALISM page 97
(33) Valerian extract and insomnia – Controlled study: Schults I I, Stoltz C, Muller J, Pharmacopsychiatry, 1994 July, Vol: 27 (4), P 147–51, ISSN: 0176–3679.
(34) High cholesterol – Randomized, double-blind trial: Jain A K, Vargas R, Gotzkowsky S, McMahon F G, Clin-Investig 1993, May, Vol 71 (5), P:383-6, ISSN: 0941-0198.
YOGA page 131
(47) Osteoarthritis
Garfinkle M S et al, Journal of Rheumatology 21(12):2341-3, Dec 1994.
(48) Bronchial asthma
Nagarathna R, Nagendra HR, British Medical Journal vol 291, 19 Oct 1985 pp 172.

BIBLIOGRAPHY

Sheila Lavery used the following books for reference while writing the therapy essays in this book:
The Complete Guide to Homeopathy by Dr Andrew Lockie and Barbara Geddes (Dorling Kindersley); *The Dictionary of Acupuncture and Moxibustion* by Nguyen Duc Hiep (Thorsons); *New Ways to Health: A Guide to Acupuncture* by Peter Firebrace and Sandra Hill (Hamlyn); *Your Health, Your Choice* by Simon Mills (Papermac); *Dynamic Chiropractic Today* by Michael Copland Griffiths (Thorsons); *Optima Alternative Health Guides – Chiropractic* by Susan Moore; *Massage Therapy* by Adam Jackson; *Reflexology* by Anya Gore; *Osteopathy* by Stephen Sandler; *Shiatsu* by Ray Ridolfi (these are now all published by Vermilion); *Chinese Herbal Medicine* by Stephen Tang and Richard Craze (Piatkus); *Chinese Medicine the Web That Has No Weaver* by Ted J. Kaptchuk (Rider); *Competences Required by Osteopathic Practice* (General Council and Register of Osteopaths); *The Fragrant Mind* by Valerie Ann Worwood (Doubleday); *The Reflexology Handbook – A Complete Guide* by Laura Norman (Piatkus); *The Complete Book of Massage* by Clare Maxwell-Hudson (Dorling Kindersley); *Your Guide to the Alexander Technique* by John Gray (Gollancz); *The Metamorphic Technique – Principles and Practice* by Gaston St. Pierre and Debbie Shapiro (Element); *Naturopathic Medicine* by Roger Newman Turner (Thorsons); *The Handbook of Complementary Medicine* by Stephen Fulder (Oxford); *Self-Hypnosis and Other Mind Expanding Techniques* by Charles Tebbetts (Westwood publishing company); *Better Health through Natural Healing* by Ross Trattler (Thorsons); *The Art of Tai Chi* by Paul Crompton (Element); *Radionic Healing – Is It for You?* by David Tansley (Element); *Ayurveda the Science of Self-Healing* by Vasant Lad; *The Book of Ayurveda* by Judith Morrison (Gaia)

PICTURE CREDITS

Academy of Systematic Kinesiology, 39 Browns Road, Surbiton, Surrey KT5 8ST. Tel: 0181 399 3215 153 left
Ancient Art and Architecture Collection/Ronald Sheridan 12 left
The Dr. Edward Bach Center, Mount Vernon, Sotwell, Wallingford, Oxon OX10 0PZ. Tel: (01491) 834678 106 center, 106 top left, 106 top right
Deni Bown Associates/Deni Bown 73 top left, 73 top right
Bridgeman Art Library/British Library, London 94 top left
British School of Shiatsu-Do, 6 Erskine Road, London NW3 3AJ. Tel: 0171 483 3776 23
Collections/Sandra Lousada 59 top right, 59 bottom right, 59 bottom left, 59 top left, 115 bottom left, 115 top right, 118 center right, 118 far right, /Anthea Sieveking 41 top left, 73 bottom
Dee Conway 150 right
E.T. Archive /National Palace Museum, Taiwan 12 right
Mary Evans Picture Library 26 top right, 70 top left
Format Partners /Mo Wilson 135 top left
John Glover 97 bottom left, 108, 109
Robert Harding Picture Library 86 top left, 97 bottom right, /BBC Enterprises/RedwoodPublishing 70 bottom left, /Cole Group 86 top center, /Robert McLeod 150 top right
Hutchison Library/Beddon 112 middle left, /Pierrette Collomb 32 top left, /R. Ian Lloyd 28 left, /Liba Taylor 65 bottom right
Image Bank/Marc Romanelli 35 right
Images 15, 19 bottom left, 26 bottom left, 26 bottom center, 32 bottom, 32 top center, 82 top right, 82 bottom right, 85 bottom left, 86 bottom center, 112 top left, 112 bottom left, 112 right, 137 top left
Stuart T. Lightbody 13
Marshall Cavendish Picture Library 42 right, 50 top left, 103 left, /Bill Petch 76 right, /Ray Duns 106 bottom
McOnegal Botanical/Rowan McOnegal 97 top
Osteopathic Information Service, PO Box 2074, Reading, Berkshire RG1 4YR. Tel: (01734) 512051 42 left, 44 bottom right
Reed International Books Ltd 46 right, 50 top right, 149 left, /Peter Chadwick 76 bottom left, 76 top left, 79 bottom left, 79 top, /Melvin Grey 88 bottom right, 94 center right
Rolf Institute/R.A Thompson, 205 Canyon Boulevard, Boulder, Colorado 80302, USA. Tel: 001 (303) 449 5903 145 left
Science Photo Library 40 center, /Argentum 154 top left, /Ricardo Arias 85 top left, /John Bavos 41 bottom left, /John Bavosi 154 bottom left, /BSIP/LBL 19 top left, /BSIP, Roux 40 center, /BSIP Taulin 62 top left, /BSIP/Krassovsky 124 left, /Oscar Burriel/Latin Stock 124 bottom right, /Simon Fraser 26 top center, /John Greim 100 top right, /Adrienne Hart-Davis 82 left, /Seth Joel 85 bottom right, /Bill Longcore 46 left, /Damien Lovegrove 70 right, /Tim Malyon & Paul Biddle 16 bottom, 16 top, /Andrew McClenaghan 19 bottom right, /Will & Dent McIntyre 28 right, /Richard Megna/ Fundamental 141 top right, /Paul Biddle 94 bottom left, /Philippe Plailly 124 top left, /Francoise Sauze 52 left, 53 left, 62 right, 127 bottom left, 154 right, /Jane Shemilt 62 bottom left, /Hattie Young 44 top right
Shift Productions/Mel Herdon 32 top right
Society of Teachers of the Alexander Technique, 20 London House, 266 Fulham Road, London SW10 9EL. Tel: 0171 352 1556 121 bottom left, 121 top left
Still Pictures/Claude Sauvageot 131 left **Tony Stone Images** 85 top right, 118 bottom left, 118 top left, /Bruce Ayres 127 top left, /Erika Craddock 88 top, /Zigy Kaluzny 19 top right, /Ian O'Leary 102, /Alan Levenson 139 top left, /Andre Perlstein 56 right, 129 left, /Christel Rosenfeld 86 top right, /Ralf Schultheiss 100 bottom, /Ken Scott 35 left, 56 left, /Charles Thatcher 127 top left, /Nick Vedros, Vedros & Associates 20, /Paul Webster 88 bottom left, /Rosemary Weller 100 top left **U.K. Polarity Therapy Association/Tony Hutchings, Monomark House, 27 Old Gloucester Street, London WC1N 3XX. Tel: 01483 417714** 37 **John Walmsley Photo-Library** 50 bottom left, 50 bottom right, 65 top right, 67 left, 103 right, 133 left, 143 top left, 146 middle right, 146 top right, 150 left **Weleda U.K. Ltd, Heanor Road, Ilkeston, Derbyshire DE7 8DR. Tel: 0115 944 8200** 79 bottom right

40–744